BRIEF CONTENTS

W9-AYN-477

Choices

A Writing Guide with Readings

[SIXTH EDITION]

Choices
A Writing Guide with Readings

Kate Mangelsdorf | **Evelyn Posey**
The University of Texas at El Paso

Bedford/St. Martin's
A Macmillan Education Imprint

Boston • New York

For Bedford/St. Martin's

Vice President, Editorial, Macmillan Higher Education Humanities: Edwin Hill
Editorial Director, English and Music: Karen S. Henry
Senior Publisher for Composition, Business and Technical Writing, Developmental Writing: Leasa Burton
Executive Editor: Vivian Garcia
Developmental Editor: Leah Rang
Senior Production Editor: Harold Chester
Production Manager: Joe Ford
Executive Marketing Manager: Joy Fisher Williams
Copy Editor: Virginia Perrin
Director of Rights and Permissions: Hilary Newman
Senior Art Director: Anna Palchik
Text Design: Castle Design
Cover Design: William Boardman
Cover Image: © Cheekylorns/Getty Images
Composition: Jouve
Printing and Binding: RR Donnelley and Sons

Manufactured in the United States of America.

0 9 8 7 6
f e d c b

For information, write: Bedford/St. Martin's, 75 Arlington Street, Boston, MA 02116
(617-399-4000)

ISBN 978-1-4576-9817-0 (Student Edition)

Acknowledgments

Text acknowledgments and copyrights appear at the back of the book on pages 541–42, which constitute an extension of the copyright page. Art acknowledgments and copyrights appear on the same page as the art selections they cover. It is a violation of the law to reproduce these selections by any means whatsoever without the written permission of the copyright holder.

For the past twenty-five years, we have had the good fortune to work with talented students, instructors, reviewers, and editors who have helped shape our thinking about teaching reading and writing. In this sixth edition of *Choices: A Writing Guide with Readings*, we draw from this considerable experience to share the approach and strategies we know work best to ensure that students will be successful college readers and writers.

Choices is based on sound classroom practices that encourage students to discover their own ideas and their own voices. It is comprehensive, offering a rhetoric, readings, and a Handbook to give students sufficient structure to read and write a complete college-level essay. From the beginning, activities in the text ask students to write on personally meaningful topics that are also appropriate for academic and workplace contexts. *Choices* offers engaging readings to model the writing process; teach critical thinking; provide collaborative learning activities; and help students apply what they learn in class to their other courses, the workplace, and the community. Above all, *Choices* respects the wealth of knowledge and experience that students bring with them to the writing classroom.

Choices works by providing student writers with comprehensive yet user-friendly, step-by-step instruction for writing essays. Each assignment chapter in Part Two follows a student writer through choosing a topic, brainstorming and prewriting, drafting, revising, editing, and sharing an essay—demonstrating to students that writing is a skill that is conceived, developed, and consumed socially. *Choices* offers a variety of engaging assignments and strengthens students' reading, thinking, and writing skills.

We made the sixth edition of *Choices* even more engaging and helpful to students by adding a new emphasis on reading to improve writing. To strengthen students' active and critical reading, thinking, and writing, we updated many of the professional and student models; added a brand-new chapter, "Reading to Improve Writing," to better emphasize the connection; and added a fourth reading to each assignment chapter. To help students become better academic writers, we updated and streamlined coverage of source-based writing in Part Three, which follows one student through brainstorming and managing a research project to a final, source-based essay. Rather than simply talking about how to write, *Choices* gets students actively involved in the writing process.

Most important, *Choices* builds students' confidence by encouraging them to think of themselves as writers with important ideas to communicate. We continue to invest in the diverse ways our students already communicate and to consider how we can help them build on existing strengths. They text their friends and family, sometimes using multiple languages;

they celebrate special events by creating videos; and they post updates on Facebook and Twitter. To build on these interests and skills, *Choices* features tips for writing using digital technologies—and reading topics related to important areas of composition like social media—to encourage students to use the knowledge and skills they already have in their everyday writing as they learn to become competent, confident academic writers.

❨ How *Choices* Works

Choices is divided into four parts. Part One, "Composing Ourselves, Writing for Others," has four introductory chapters that present writing as purposeful and creative:

- **Chapter 1, "The Writing Process,"** introduces the stages of the writing process and follows one student through each stage.
- **Chapter 2, "Reading to Improve Writing,"** shows how reading can improve writing and explains active reading strategies and summary writing.
- **Chapter 3, "Crafting Paragraphs,"** focuses on the elements of good paragraphs, showing the development of a sample student paragraph.
- **Chapter 4, "The Patterns of Development,"** describes nine common patterns of development and follows one student through the process of using some of these patterns to develop an essay.

Part Two, "Writing to Share Ideas," consists of six chapters organized by purpose and theme—for example, "Explaining: Cultural Symbols, Traditions, and Heroes" (Chapter 6). Every chapter includes four professional readings and a step-by-step guide for writing essays, complete with student models. Each chapter also highlights patterns of development, includes dedicated group and peer review activities, and gives helpful sentence editing and grammar tips. A Chapter Checklist and the opportunity for students to reflect on their own writing appear at the end of each chapter.

Part Three, "Writing with Sources," focuses on basic research strategies and leads students through the process of writing a brief researched essay. The first chapter in this section helps students conduct primary and secondary research, while the second chapter concentrates on evaluating and using sources, both print and online. A complete, formatted student essay—featuring research, source integration, and proper citation—concludes the section.

Part Four, "Handbook with Exercises," is a practical, concise resource that shows students how to identify and correct errors, rather than explaining grammatical concepts and terms at length. The last chapter provides guidelines and grammar tips that are particularly helpful to multilingual students.

❨ Core Features of *Choices*

Complete, Accessible Instruction for Writing at an Affordable Price

Choices contains everything students need to become effective writers:

- a clear, step-by-step explanation of the writing process
- six assignment chapters covering expressive, informative, argument, and source-based writing
- student writing samples at all stages, from prewriting and paragraphs to fully developed essays
- excellent model essays that generate ideas for writing
- in-depth information on conducting research projects
- a comprehensive Handbook

Step-by-Step, "Show-and-Tell"-style Guidance through the Writing Process

At the heart of *Choices* are the six writing assignment chapters in Part Two, "Writing to Share Ideas," which guide students through the steps of the writing process:

1. **exploring** choices
2. **drafting**
3. **revising**
4. **editing**
5. **sharing** work with others

Student models in every chapter illustrate each of these steps, so students follow a student writer's journey through the writing process and share in the experience as they simultaneously make their own writing choices. In addition, each chapter's abundant writing activities and helpful How To boxes are designed to give students the support they need.

The focus on sharing work as the last step in the writing process is part of the book's overall emphasis on helping students communicate effectively to a specific audience and for a specific purpose rather than simply practicing a particular mode of writing. Newly designed Peer Review boxes further underscore the social nature of composition.

Unique Guidance on Choosing Topics That Matter

Every assignment chapter in Part Two offers three engaging topic suggestions, each illustrated with professional readings. Students are invited to use different invention strategies to explore the topic—each with a student writer's demonstration of the strategy. Students then make an informed decision about the topic that is most meaningful to them. This unique approach—and inspiration for the title of the book, *Choices*—makes writing relevant for students and provides flexibility for instructors.

Help with Writing Paragraphs and Using the Patterns of Development

Chapter 3, "Crafting Paragraphs," provides a base for student writing by helping students develop and organize paragraphs and teaching them about topic sentences, introductions, and conclusions. The chapter is designed for use in the beginning of the course or as accompaniment to any of the assignment chapters in Part Two.

Chapter 4, "The Patterns of Development," illustrates the rhetorical patterns using example paragraphs. Additional coverage of the patterns can also be found in each assignment chapter.

Advice on Special Writing Strategies

Choices integrates writing instruction for specific assignments with important writing strategies that help prepare students for a variety of writing situations they will encounter in other college courses or on the job:

- A focus on **keeping journals** for brainstorming or tracking ideas and research is part of Chapter 2, "Reading to Improve Writing."
- Guidance on **writing summaries** for reading comprehension is also part of Chapter 2, "Reading to Improve Writing."
- Advice and tools for **conducting research projects** are the focus of Chapter 11, "Conducting Research," and Chapter 12, "Evaluating and Using Sources," in Part Three.
- **Tips about digital writing** throughout the book help students use digital and social media to improve their writing. Topics include blogging to test out ideas, using social networking sites to share ideas and write drafts, and using word-processing programs to help organize thoughts.

Additional advice for instructors on guiding student writing through essay exams or writing résumés and cover letters is available in the comprehensive *Instructor's Manual for Choices*, Sixth Edition.

Comprehensive Handbook with Exercises

The Handbook in Part Four covers sentence grammar, word choice, spelling, punctuation, mechanics, and style with more than 150 exercises for practice correcting sentences, editing paragraphs, and combining sentences.

The Handbook concludes with an extensive "Guide for Multilingual Writers" chapter, which covers topics of particular importance to ESL students.

New to This Edition

A New Chapter Emphasizes Active and Critical Reading to Improve Writing

A new Part One chapter, **Chapter 2, "Reading to Improve Writing,"** expands coverage on the reading-writing connection to build students' critical reading and thinking skills, leading to better writing. With a focus on active reading strategies, the chapter illustrates techniques such as keeping a journal, taking notes, and annotating readings effectively. The chapter includes its own writing assignment to demonstrate the interconnectedness of good reading and writing, features a sample annotated essay, and concludes with a sample student summary.

Stronger Integration of Writing Instruction and Student Models to Illustrate the Writing Process

A revised **Chapter 1, "The Writing Process,"** weaves together instructional material—on exploring topics and rhetorical choices, drafting, revising, and sharing—with models from a student writer so students can begin the composition course by seeing the writing process in action. In addition, **more highlighting** puts the spotlight on **thesis statements** in student discovery drafts in the Part Two assignment chapters, allowing students to identify an essay's main idea more easily and track its evolution through drafting, revision, and editing.

More Readings and New Student Models to Spark Ideas for Writing

For the sixth edition, we have added **an extra reading** to each Part Two chapter (for a total of four professional readings) and replaced approximately 40 percent of the readings with **new, timely, and engaging pieces**, such as

- **Mike Rose** on whether college is the right choice for everyone;
- **Jessica Winter** on "selfie culture" and the narcissism of social media; and
- **Louise Aronson** on robot caregivers as the solution to our national neglect of the elderly.

We have also added **eleven new student models**, allowing students to see peer writing examples, which in turn helps them make smarter writing choices. New topics include a personal reflection on a gift that raised the writer's cultural awareness and pride, an argument essay on the acceptance of women in the gaming community, and a researched essay on mental health among Asian Americans. These new student models are a direct response to instructors such as Amy Camp from the College of DuPage, who says, "Probably the number one feature that I like about *Choices* is the examples of student writing that mirror the writing process from prewriting through editing."

An Updated and Restructured Focus on Research and Academic Writing

A newly revised **Part Three, "Writing with Sources,"** gives students the foundation for research and source use first introduced in Chapter 7, "Analyzing." **Chapter 11, "Conducting Research,"** helps students make the right choices for locating sources and includes increased coverage on researching online and with databases—complete with new student examples and activities. **Chapter 12, "Evaluating and Using Sources,"** guides students on how to use the sources they've researched, including how to

- evaluate sources for reliability and relevance;
- take notes on sources to determine usefulness to a student's own argument;
- integrate summaries, paraphrases, and quotations effectively and responsibly; and
- format a researched essay and citations in MLA style.

Both chapters respond to a writing assignment and follow one student writer as she makes choices for conducting and managing a research project, evaluating her sources, and incorporating them into her essay to support her argument. The chapters are designed to be flexible for instructors and can be assigned concurrently with a Part Two chapter or on their own.

Reimagined Getting Started Activities to Increase Visual Literacy

Each Part Two chapter kicks off with Getting Started activities that use the full-page chapter-opening photographs to engage students and introduce the chapter's writing purpose—such as remembering, explaining, or arguing a position—and theme. Students are asked to work with their peers to consider and evaluate the image and its rhetorical impact: Why might the photographer have framed the photo in a particular way? How does the subject of the photo express an emotion? How well does the image reflect a particular idea? The connection to the chapter's student writing model—thematically and with a quote from the student essay—demonstrates to students how ideas can be expressed, analyzed, and understood in more than one medium.

❰ Features of *Choices* Correlated to the Writing Program Administrators (WPA) Outcomes Statement (2014)

WPA Outcomes	Relevant Features of *Choices*
Rhetorical Knowledge	
Learn and use key rhetorical concepts through analyzing and composing a variety of texts.	▪ Chapter 1, "The Writing Process," introduces students to the writing choices they will make by giving them the tools to understand the writer's **audience** and **purpose**. ▪ Chapter 2, "Reading to Improve Writing," teaches students active and critical reading skills designed to **analyze** a variety of readings in a particular genre. ▪ In Part Two, "Writing to Share Ideas," each chapter (Chs. 5–10) includes a section on Analyzing Your Audience and Purpose and begins with a chapter-opening image to build **visual analysis** skills. ▪ Each Part Two chapter includes four professional model essays (the first one annotated to point out **key rhetorical concepts**) and one student essay to demonstrate the writing genres.
Gain experience reading and composing in several genres to understand how genre conventions shape and are shaped by readers' and writers' practices and purposes.	▪ See above. The **composing practice** in Part Two is built around six genre assignments: remembering, explaining, analyzing, evaluating, arguing a position, and proposing a solution. ▪ With four professional essays and one student essay as models and a step-by-step writing guide to completing each assignment, these chapters emphasize the connection between **reading and composing in a particular genre**.
Develop facility in responding to a variety of situations and contexts, calling for purposeful shifts in voice, tone, level of formality, design, medium, and/or structure.	▪ Chapter 1 features A Writer's Audience and A Writer's Purpose sections, which explain the differences in voice, tone, and formality in expressive, informative, and persuasive writing. ▪ In Part Two, students **practice responding** to a variety of rhetorical situations and contexts through reading, group, and writing activities. A distinct Revising section points out what makes a text structurally sound by focusing on ways to support and organize ideas to best suit the genre and the rhetorical situation. ▪ Chapter 12, "Evaluating and Using Sources," shows a formatted academic paper, with a figure, to show students an example of appropriate document **design**.
Understand and use a variety of technologies to address a range of audiences.	**Tips for digital writing** throughout the text advise students on how to use different digital resources—ranging from word-processing programs to websites—to compose, and how to interact with their **social media audiences** to generate, develop, and share ideas.
Match the capacities of different environments (e.g., print and electronic) to varying rhetorical situations.	In addition to the tips for digital writing (see above), Part Three, "Writing with Sources," demonstrates ways to conduct a research project using both **print and electronic resources and tools**.

WPA Outcomes	Relevant Features of *Choices*
Critical Thinking, Reading, and Composing	
Use composing and reading for inquiry, learning, thinking, and communicating in various rhetorical contexts.	■ The *Choices* approach is **inquiry**-based. Each Part Two chapter features a Step 1: Explore Your Choices section that asks students to use a variety of idea-generation strategies; chapters conclude with a prompt for students to share their compositions, providing a specific **rhetorical context** for each assignment.
	■ A section titled Write Research Questions (Ch. 11) demonstrates how to guide a research project through inquiry.
	■ Headnotes and questions following the selections prompt students to examine and understand each reading, then apply the **genre features** to their own writing.
Read a diverse range of texts, attending especially to relationships between assertion and evidence, to patterns of organization, to interplay between verbal and nonverbal elements, and how these features function for different audiences and situations.	■ See the Rhetorical Knowledge section above, especially the first two sections that discuss **texts**, **genres**, and **rhetorical situations**.
	■ Chapter 3, "Crafting Paragraphs," attends especially **to patterns of organization**: general-to-specific, topic-illustration-explanation, progressive, directional, question-and-answer, and specific-to-general order.
	■ Getting Started activities ask students to evaluate how well the chapter-opening **image** reflects the student essay featured in the chapter.
	■ Developing Your Ideas sections focus on ways to **support assertions** with evidence and with the patterns of development most appropriate to the writing genre and **rhetorical situation**.
Locate and evaluate primary and secondary research materials, including journal articles, essays, books, databases, and informal Internet sources.	■ Part Three, "Writing with Sources," offers extensive coverage of **finding**, **evaluating**, and **using** print and electronic resources, with guidance for responsibly using the Internet, e-mail, and online communities for research. Chapter 11, "Conducting Research," addresses **primary** and **secondary research**.
Use strategies—such as interpretation, synthesis, response, critique, and design/redesign—to compose texts that integrate the writer's ideas with those from appropriate sources.	■ Chapter 12, "Evaluating and Using Sources," offers detailed **strategies** for **integrating research into a composition**, including advice on how to integrate and introduce quotations, how to cite paraphrases and summaries so as to distinguish them from the writer's own ideas, and how to avoid plagiarism.
	■ In Chapters 9–10, which cover argument, there is also discussion of the need to **anticipate opposing positions** and readers' objections to the writer's thesis (called "pro and con points").
Processes	
Develop a writing project through multiple drafts.	■ Chapters 1, 3, and every Part Two chapter feature an accessible but thorough **Step-by-Step**, "show-and-tell"-style process to guide students through the steps of the writing process: Explore Your Choices, Write Your Discovery Draft, Revise Your Draft, Edit Your Sentences, and Share Your Essay.
	■ These steps emphasize a **recursive writing process** that builds an essay from brainstorming and preliminary **drafting** through **revision** that moves from higher to lower-order concerns.

WPA Outcomes	Relevant Features of *Choices*
Develop flexible strategies for reading, drafting, reviewing, collaboration, revising, rewriting, rereading, and editing.	Within each step explained below, students are given a number of strategies and encouraged to choose what works best for them (inspiring the text's title *Choices*): ■ Step 1: Explore Your Choices offers activities for **generating ideas** about different themes. Strategies include brainstorming, freewriting, clustering, asking questions, researching, consulting with others, and relating aloud. ■ Step 2: Write Your Discovery Draft advises students to be flexible in their writing by providing strategies for choosing a topic and by stressing **the importance of anticipating multiple drafts.** ■ Step 3: Revise Your Draft offers a variety of patterns of development and organization to strengthen a first draft. Students choose which strategy best fits their essay, and a dedicated **Peer Review** activity box encourages **collaborative revision**. ■ Step 4: Edit Your Sentences provides instruction on sentence-level **editing**, complete with exercises.
Use composing processes and tools as a means to discover and reconsider ideas.	■ Central to Chapters 1 and 5–10 is the idea of using **composing to discover ideas**. Students are offered specific steps for inventing, researching, planning, composing—and for evaluating and improving their work over the course of multiple drafts. ■ Steps in Part Two (Chs. 5–10) break writing assignments down into doable, focused thinking and writing activities that engage students in the **recursive process of invention** to find, analyze, question, and synthesize ideas. ■ Checklists and Reflecting on Your Writing questions at the end of each chapter ask students to **reflect** on their progress and their knowledge of key concepts learned in each chapter.
Experience the collaborative and social aspects of writing processes.	■ *Choices* features several **collaborative activities**: Getting Started visual activities at the beginning of the chapter, group activities following the readings and in the revision steps, and Peer Review boxes that provide question guides for evaluating fellow writers' drafts. ■ In addition, Step 5: Share Your Essay emphasizes the social context of and opportunities for writing.
Learn to give and act on productive feedback to works in progress.	■ Step 4: Revise Your Draft allows students to analyze the sample student draft in each Part Two chapter. ■ Once students are comfortable with peer evaluation using the model essay, they move to the newly designed Peer Review box, which offers a guided question set aimed at giving **specific advice and constructive feedback** on the work of their classmates.
Adapt composing processes for a variety of technologies and modalities.	Integrated tips for digital writing include online **how-tos for using technology** to generate ideas and share compositions.
Reflect on the development of composing practices and how those practices influence students' work.	■ A Chapter Checklist asks students to actively review what they accomplished and learned while composing for a particular assignment. ■ A set of Reflecting on Your Writing questions asks students to **reflect** on how they responded to the chapter's assignment, what strategies worked best for them, and what they might have done differently.

WPA Outcomes	Relevant Features of *Choices*
Knowledge of Conventions	
Develop knowledge of linguistic structures, including grammar, punctuation, and spelling, through practice in composing and revising.	■ Genre-specific **editing** and **proofreading** advice and activities appear in Step 4: Edit Your Sentences in Part Two chapters. ■ A comprehensive Handbook in Part Four offers extensive instruction and practice with topics of grammar, punctuation, and mechanics. ■ Additional practice activities of sentence-level skills are featured in *LaunchPad Solo for Readers and Writers*, available free when packaged with *Choices*.
Understand why genre conventions for structure, paragraphing, tone, and mechanics vary.	Analyze Your Audience and Purpose sections present several basic **characteristics of a specific genre**, including **genre-specific issues of structure**, paragraphing, tone, and mechanics, which are addressed in the Edit Your Sentences sections of Chapters 5–10.
Gain experience negotiating variations in genre conventions.	■ Students **read**, **analyze**, and **compose a variety of texts** in Part Two, "Writing to Share Ideas" (Chs. 5–10). In each of these chapters, a Read to Write section asks students to analyze model selections in terms of **purpose**, **audience**, and **genre conventions**. ■ Each chapter's Developing Your Ideas section supports student composers with detailed help for responding to different rhetorical purposes: to remember, to explain, to analyze, to evaluate, to argue a position, and to propose a solution.
Learn common formats and/or design features for different kinds of texts.	Each example of a student's final, shared draft is presented in proper MLA format, as is the sample paper that concludes Part Three. Examples of a photograph (Ch. 1) and of a figure (Ch. 12) embedded in student papers also appear.
Explore the concepts of intellectual property (such as fair use and copyright) that motivate documentation conventions.	■ The book's research coverage (Part Three, Chs. 11–12) teaches specific strategies of evaluating and integrating source material—and **citing the work of others**. ■ Chapter 12, "Evaluating and Using Sources," offers a dedicated section on Avoiding Plagiarism to define and explain the need to research and write responsibly.
Practice applying citation conventions systematically in students' own work.	Chapter 12, "**Evaluating and Using Sources,**" offers ■ detailed coverage of evaluating, using, and acknowledging primary and secondary sources; and ■ coverage of **MLA documentation** in addition to an annotated sample student research paper.

❮ Get the Most out of Your Course with *Choices*, Sixth Edition

Bedford/St. Martin's offers resources and format choices that help you and your students get even more out of your book and your course. To learn more about or to order any of the following products, contact your Macmillan sales representative, e-mail sales support (**sales_support @bfwpub.com**), or visit the website at **macmillanhighered.com /choices/catalog**.

Choose from Alternative Formats of *Choices*

Bedford/St. Martin's offers a range of affordable formats, allowing students to choose the one that works best for them. For details, visit **macmillanhighered.com/choices/catalog**.

- *Paperback* To order the paperback edition, use **ISBN 978-1-4576-9817-0**.

- *Popular e-book formats* *Choices* is available as a value-priced e-book in a variety of formats for use with computers, tablets, and e-readers. For details, visit **macmillanhighered.com/ebooks**.

Select Value Packages

Add value to your text by packaging one of the following resources with *Choices*. To learn more about package options for any of the following products, contact your Macmillan sales representative or visit **macmillanhighered.com/choices/catalog**.

- *LaunchPad Solo for Readers and Writers* includes multimedia content and assessments, including diagnostics on grammar and reading and LearningCurve adaptive quizzing, organized into prebuilt, curated units for easy assigning and monitoring of student progress. Get all our great resources and activities in one fully customizable space online; then assign and mix our resources with yours. To order *LaunchPad Solo for Readers and Writers* packaged with the print book, contact your sales representative for a package ISBN. For details, visit **macmillanhighered.com/readwrite**.

- *LearningCurve for Readers and Writers*, Bedford/St. Martin's adaptive quizzing program, quickly learns what students already know and helps them practice what they don't yet understand. Game-like quizzing motivates students to engage with their course, and reporting tools help teachers discern their students' needs. *LearningCurve for Readers and Writers* can be packaged with *Choices* at a significant discount. An activation code is required. To order *LearningCurve* packaged with the print book, contact your sales representative for a package ISBN. For details, visit **learningcurveworks.com**.

- *The Bedford/St. Martin's ESL Workbook* includes a broad range of exercises covering grammar issues for multilingual students of varying language skills and backgrounds. Answers are at the back. To order the *ESL Workbook* packaged with the print book, contact your sales representative for a package ISBN.

- **The Bedford/St. Martin's Planner** includes everything that students need to plan and use their time effectively, with advice on preparing schedules and to-do lists plus blank schedules and calendars (monthly and weekly). The planner fits easily into a backpack or purse, so students can take it anywhere. To order the *Planner* packaged with the print book, contact your sales representative for a package ISBN.

- **The Bedford/St. Martin's Textbook Reader, Second Edition**, by Ellen Kuhl Repetto, gives students practice in reading college textbooks across the curriculum. This brief collection of chapters from market-leading introductory college textbooks can be packaged inexpensively with *Choices*. Beginning with a chapter on college success, *The Bedford/St. Martin's Textbook Reader* also includes chapters from current texts on composition, mass communication, history, psychology, and environmental science. Comprehension questions and tips for reading success guide students in reading college-level materials efficiently and effectively. To order the *Textbook Reader* packaged with the print book, contact your sales representative for a package ISBN.

Make Learning Fun with *Re:Writing 3*

macmillanhighered.com/rewriting
New, open online resources with videos and interactive elements engage students in new ways of writing. You'll find tutorials about using common digital writing tools, an interactive peer review game, *Extreme Paragraph Makeover*, and more—all for free and for fun.

Instructor Resources

macmillanhighered.com/choices/catalog
You have a lot to do in your course. Bedford/St. Martin's wants to make it easy for you to find the support you need—and to get to it quickly.

- **The Instructor's Annotated Edition of Choices** provides practical page-by-page advice on teaching with *Choices*, as well as answers to exercises. It includes discussion prompts, strategies for teaching ESL students, ideas for additional classroom activities, suggestions for using other print and media resources, and cross-references useful to teachers at all levels of experience. To order the *Instructor's Annotated Edition*, contact your Macmillan sales representative or use **ISBN 978-1-4576-9832-3**.

- **The Instructor's Manual for Choices, Sixth Edition**, is available as a PDF that can be downloaded from the Bedford/St. Martin's online catalog at the URL above. It provides new and seasoned instructors alike with the support they need for teaching writing. The free manual includes information and advice for structuring your course, introducing students to the writing center, facilitating collaborative learning, teaching multilingual writers, and assessing student writing and progress. New material includes using *Choices* in an ALP-style course and chapter-specific FAQs and rubrics for each writing assignment chapter. Available for download; see **macmillanhighered.com/choices /catalog**.

- *Additional Resources for Instructors Using Choices* is a collection of grammar diagnostics, mastery, and exit tests that can easily supplement the editing and Handbook sections of *Choices*. Available for download; see **macmillanhighered.com/choices/catalog**.

- **TeachingCentral** offers the entire list of Bedford/St. Martin's print and online professional resources in one place. You will find landmark reference works, sourcebooks on pedagogical issues, award-winning collections, and practical advice for the classroom—all free for instructors. Recent titles include *The Bedford Bibliography for Teachers of Basic Writing*, Fourth Edition, by Chitralekha Duttagupta and Robert Miller; *Teaching Developmental Reading: Historical, Theoretical, and Practical Background Readings*, Second Edition, by Sonya Armstrong, Norman A. Stahl, and Hunter Boylan; and *The Bedford Bibliography for Teachers of Adult Learners* by Barbara Gleason and Kimme Nuckles. Visit **macmillanhighered.com/teachingcentral**.

☾ Acknowledgments

We are grateful to the many people whose inspiration and hard work helped us improve this sixth edition. We are especially indebted to students Andrea Benitez, Moushumi Biswas, Javier Esparza, Susannah Goya-Pack, Autumn Harrison, Angelica Hopkins, Paul LaPrade, Charles Lujan, and Carlos Montijo, who allowed us to use their essays in this book.

We especially want to thank Traci Garner, Virginia Tech, who suggested many of the digital tips, and the following reviewers for their many helpful suggestions: Mohammed Alam, Georgia Gwinnett College; Amy Camp, College of DuPage; Simona Chitescu, Georgia Gwinnett College; Latasha Goodwyn, Tyler Junior College; Elizabeth Jones, Georgia Gwinnett College; Dawn Lattin, Idaho State University; John Knight, University of San Francisco; Thomas Lugo, University of San Francisco; Christopher Morelock, Walters State Community College; Patricia Moseley, Central Carolina Technical College; Heather Moulton, Central Arizona College; Lara Nosser, Richmond Community College; Jamie Sadler, Richmond Community College; Desha Stewart, Tyler Junior College; Nina Thompson, St. Louis Community College–Forest Park; Raymond Watkins, Central Carolina Technical College; and others who wished to remain anonymous but whose feedback is no less valued.

For the extraordinarily fine improvements to this edition, we thank our editors Leah Rang and Karrin Varucene who provided guidance, attention to detail, and an insistence on excellence that has ensured that this is our best edition yet. We thank Harold Chester for ably guiding the text through production, Virginia Perrin for her copyediting expertise, and Kathleen Karcher and Connie Gardner for their assistance in securing permissions. We also thank Edwin Hill, Vivian Garcia, Angela Beckett, Jonathan Douglas, Christina Shea, William Boardman, Tracy Keuhn, and Elise Kaiser for their dedication to and hard work in all aspects of development, marketing, cover design, and production.

We have had the pleasure of working with Bedford/St. Martin's co-founder Joan Feinberg and Editor-in-Chief Karen Henry for over twenty years and thank them and other truly dedicated professionals at Bedford/St. Martin's for building a talented team that offers the mutual respect and collaborative work environment that we have come to appreciate so much.

CONTENTS

8 **Evaluating:** Products, Performances, and Places 225

9   Arguing a Position:
Media, Censorship, and
Stereotypes   269

12 Evaluating and Using Sources   375

PART FOUR
Handbook with Exercises   401

13 Writing Sentences   403

14 Expanding Sentences   424

Choices
A Writing Guide with Readings

Composing Ourselves, Writing for Others

Writing is an important way to communicate—in class, in the workplace, and for personal enjoyment. Many of us are writing more than ever, whether it be sending texts to friends, e-mailing coworkers, or updating our Facebook pages. No matter what the writing task, good writing skills are a must.

In Part One, you'll explore why writers write, how reading helps improve writing, and how writers go about getting their ideas down on paper. You'll discover your own writing process and begin to use it to communicate the important ideas you have to share. You will learn how to write effective paragraphs, an important step when putting your ideas in writing. And you'll learn about patterns you can use to develop your writing.

The Writing Process

What comes to mind when you think of a writer? You might picture a writer whose works you like to read, such as J. K. Rowling, Malcolm Gladwell, or Stephen King. Or you might think of the stereotypes we have of writers, such as the newspaper reporter who submits a late-breaking story minutes before a deadline, or the tortured poet who wears a beret, lives in a cold attic, composes brilliant sonnets on scraps of paper, and dies before receiving any recognition.

Writers are more common than you might imagine. A consumer who writes a letter to the electric company is a writer, as is a student who completes a report for a course, a child who writes her name for the first time, a father who records the birth of his baby in a journal, and an engineer who writes a proposal to build a bridge. A lover who sends a valentine is a writer, and so is an angry voter who composes a letter to the city council. A writer is anyone who uses written language to communicate a feeling, a fact, or an opinion.

If the idea of writing frightens you, you are not alone. Even the most experienced writers get anxious when faced with a new project. But understanding how writers find ideas, organize them, and complete a piece of writing can help relieve any fears you might have about writing. How do writers transform their ideas into a polished piece of

In this chapter, you will write a brief essay about your attitude toward writing. As you work on your essay, you will

- Learn how to analyze your audience.
- Examine different purposes for writing.
- Learn the importance of keeping a journal.
- Explore the steps of the writing process.
- Discover several strategies for gathering ideas.
- Follow one student through the writing process.

writing to be shared with readers or turned in for a grade? What do they do first, next, and last? As you'll learn in this chapter, writing is best completed in distinct steps over a period of time.

In each chapter of this textbook, a student writer will complete the steps of the writing process for a college project. For example, in this chapter, you will follow Charles Lujan, a student writer, as he writes a short essay about his experience with writing. You'll see that although good writing takes effort, it's not nearly as frightening or mysterious as it may seem.   ■

Writing Assignment

Your first assignment is to "compose yourself" as a writer. Think back over your life to consider when and to whom you have written. Consider all types of writing, such as sending texts, posting to websites and social media, writing complaint letters, responding to essay exams, and filling out forms. How frequently do you write? Who reads your writing? What are your purposes for writing? In addition, make a note of your feelings about writing. Do certain types of writing interest you more than others? Does writing excite you or make you anxious? Does writing come easily to you, or do you struggle to find the right words? Get your ideas flowing by writing for a few minutes nonstop in response to the following questions:

- What have been some of the most important writing events in your life? Consider not only formal writing assignments for school or work but also e-mails, texts, and posts on social media sites such as Facebook and Twitter.

- What are the most common types of writing that you do? What are your purposes for writing, and who reads your writing? What happens as a result of your writing?

- What languages have you used for writing? Do you enjoy writing in one language more than another, or do you prefer to go back and forth between two languages? Why?

- Who was most influential in your development as a writer? How did this person influence you?

- Can you recall any time when you felt inadequate as a writer? What was the event? Why did you feel this way? What changes did you make as a result?

- What are three words that best describe you as a writer? Discuss these three words.

Use your best ideas to write a brief essay for your classmates and instructor explaining how you feel about yourself as a writer. Follow the steps of the writing process described in this chapter.

A Writer's Composing Process

Although it's easy to think of writing as simply putting words on paper, most writers use a particular *writing process*, or method, to turn ideas into finished essays. Here is a typical process that many writers follow:

Step 1   Explore your choices.
Step 2   Write a draft to discover your ideas.
Step 3   Revise the draft to make your ideas clearer for readers.
Step 4   Edit the draft for grammar, spelling, and punctuation.
Step 5   Share the final draft of your essay with an audience.

You'll probably find that your writing process does not exactly follow the steps in the order outlined here but that you prefer to move back and forth among the various steps. For example, while revising an essay, you may discover you need more information. To get that information, you have to return to exploring your choices. You may discover, too, that you prefer to revise for quite a while, producing perhaps three or four revised drafts. Figure 1.1 illustrates the recursive nature of the writing process.

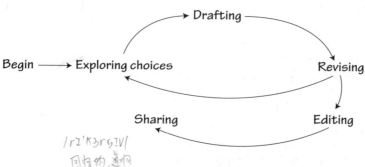

Figure 1.1: The Recursive Nature of the Writing Process

To discover your own writing process, experiment with the various ways of exploring choices, drafting, revising, editing, and sharing explained in this chapter and throughout Part Two of this book. The methods that work best for you will lead you to discover your preferred writing process. Let's get started.

(Step 1 Explore Your Choices

The first step of the writing process, often called *prewriting*, includes all that you do before you actually begin to write a draft. This step involves activities such as writing, talking, reading, and thinking. But first, you must think about who will read your essay and why you're writing it.

Analyzing Your Audience and Purpose

As you begin to work on an assignment, you want to keep your readers in mind. After all, you're writing to communicate something of interest, so you want to be sure readers get your message. It's also important to understand why you are writing and the kind of message you want to communicate.

A Writer's Audience

No matter what you're writing about, your *audience* influences how you write. A writer's audience consists of those who will read the writing—yourself, family members, friends, classmates, instructors, colleagues at work, political leaders. The possibilities are limitless.

Writing to an audience is not the same as speaking to an audience. In fact, writing has some advantages. Have you ever said something you wished you could take back? This is less likely to happen when you write because you can revise your words before your audience sees them.

Writing is also different from speaking because your audience isn't actually in front of you. When you speak, your audience can smile, frown, or ask questions. When you write, however, you must envision, or picture in your mind, how your readers will respond to your words. To envision your audience, ask yourself these questions:

- *Who are my readers?* Sometimes your audience is someone specific, such as the sociology professor who will read your term paper. At other times, your readers will be the general public, such as subscribers to the local print or online newspaper who read your letter to the editor.

- *What do my readers know about my topic?* Your readers' knowledge of the topic is important because you don't want to bore people by telling them what they already know. Instead, you want to tell them something new—for example, where they might go for career counseling or how to speed up their wireless connection.

- *What do my readers need to know about my topic?* Answering this question can help you decide how much information you need to give your readers. For instance, if you're explaining how to change a tire, will your readers know what a tire jack is? Or must you describe it and explain how to use it?

- *How do my readers feel about my topic?* If your readers know nothing about your topic or might even find it dull, you'll want to find a way to capture their interest. Alternatively, your readers might be opposed to your message. If you're writing an e-mail asking your supervisor for a raise, don't assume that he or she will automatically agree to it. Instead, try to anticipate your supervisor's reasons for not giving you a raise and take them into account when you make your case.

A Writer's Purpose

Whenever you write, whether for yourself or others, you have a *purpose*. Most writing is primarily expressive, informative, or persuasive.

Expressive Writing   In *expressive writing*, writers communicate their thoughts, feelings, and personal history. When you write about the day's events, describe your vacation on Facebook, or blog about your children, you're writing expressively.

For information about journaling, see p. 10 or p. 38.

In the following example of expressive writing, student Scott Weckerly describes the morning he left home for college:

> The impact of saying good-bye and actually leaving did not hit me until the day of my departure. Its strength woke me an hour before my alarm clock would, as for the last time Missy, my golden retriever, greeted me with a big, sloppy lick. I hated it when she did that, but that day I welcomed her with open arms. I petted her with long, slow strokes, and her sad eyes gazed into mine. Her coat felt more silky than usual. Of course, I did not notice any of these qualities until that day, which made me all the sadder about leaving her.

This sample paragraph is expressive because it describes Weckerly's thoughts and feelings at an important time in his life. When he tells us that the reality of his departure didn't sink in until that morning, we understand what he was thinking. By describing his reactions to his dog, we know he was sad about leaving home. In re-creating an important incident in his life, Weckerly's writing is expressive.

Informative Writing   Sometimes we write not to express ourselves but to convey information. *Informative writing* explains: it tells how something works, how you can do something, what something looks like, how two things are alike or different, or what the cause or outcome of an event is. Informative writing typically uses facts, examples, or statistics. Most writing we encounter is informative. Nutritional labels on food containers are informative, as are directions for going through airport scanners or for administering CPR. Textbooks, including the one you're reading now, are also in this category. Most sections of the newspaper are informative.

The following is an example of informative writing:

> Studies based on 2010 census data show that a college student's future income may be directly related to his or her choice of major. Over a lifetime, individuals with a college degree will make 84 percent more than those with only a high school diploma. Among college graduates, however, average incomes differ greatly. Math, engineering, and computer science majors make

between $98,000 and $120,000 annually, whereas counseling psychology
majors and early childhood education majors make roughly $30,000 to
$35,000 annually.

This piece of writing is informative because the author uses facts and statistics to compare the amount of money that college graduates who major in
different fields make in the workforce.

Persuasive Writing *Persuasive writing* differs from expressive and informative writing because it attempts to change readers' opinions or convince
readers to take a particular action. Newspaper editorials and advertisements are
two types of persuasive writing: the *Times-Picayune* wants you to support the
school bond issue, and Ben & Jerry's wants you to buy its brand of ice cream.
Some of the world's most memorable writing is persuasive, such as these words
from President John F. Kennedy's 1961 inaugural address: "Ask not what your
country can do for you; ask what you can do for your country."

Martin Luther King Jr.'s famous "I Have a Dream" speech is another
example of persuasive writing. His purpose was to motivate civil rights workers to continue striving for racial equality. Here's an excerpt:

> Go back to Mississippi, go back to Alabama, go back to South Carolina,
> go back to Georgia, go back to Louisiana, go back to the slums and ghettos
> of our northern cities, knowing that somehow this situation can and will be
> changed. Let us not wallow in the valley of despair.

As with many persuasive pieces, King's audience is urged to believe something—in this case, that the battle for civil rights will be won. At the same
time, the audience is told to do something: King wants the marchers to
return home to continue the fight.

While most writing is primarily expressive, informative, or persuasive,
rarely is a piece of writing entirely one type. Much of the time, all three types
occur in a single piece. The *primary purpose* is the one that you consider the
most important reason for writing your piece.

HOW TO Know Your Purpose for Writing

- *Expressive:* You write to communicate your thoughts, feelings, and personal history.
- *Informative:* You write to explain something you know about— how it works, what it looks like, what caused it, or what outcome it had.
- *Persuasive:* You write to convince others to accept your opinion.

GROUP ACTIVITY 1 Identify Purposes

Working in groups of two or three, identify the following paragraphs as primarily expressive, informative, or persuasive.

1. From the Leukemia & Lymphoma Society website:

   Whether you chose The Leukemia & Lymphoma Society's traditional Team In Training program, or TNT Flex, a flexible, customized, online training option developed by TNT's renowned coaches, you get all the support you need to cross the finish line at the marathon, half marathon, triathlon, century ride, and hike adventure of your choice. Both offer a choice of world class events, travel arrangements to your exciting destination, and a fabulous, activity-filled weekend once you're there.

   Purpose: _____ Persuasive. _____

2. From *In a Sunburned Country* by Bill Bryson:

   And so, because we know so little about it, perhaps a few facts would be in order: Australia is the world's sixth largest country, and its largest island. It is the only island that is also a continent, and the only continent that is also a country. It was the first continent conquered from the sea, and the last. It is the only nation that began as a prison.

   Purpose: _____ Informative _____

3. From Frommer's *Australia* by Elizabeth Hansen:

   Is Paul Hogan in *Crocodile Dundee* a typical Aussie? Some Australians might like you to think so, but facts show that less than 15% of the population lives in rural areas. Instead, the average Australian lives in one of eight capital cities and has never seen native fauna anywhere but in a zoo or wildlife park.

   Purpose: _____ Informative _____

4. From the *AARP Bulletin*:

   We must create a more positive and accurate image of aging and help people recognize that people are living longer, more productive lives. As a nation, we must let go of our obsession with the number of years in life and focus instead on the life in those years.

   Purpose: _____ Persuasive _____

5. From *One Writer's Beginnings* by Eudora Welty:

   Of course it's easy to see why they both overprotected me, why my father, before I could wear a new pair of shoes for the first time, made me wait while he took out his thin silver pocket knife and with the point of the blade scored the polished soles all over, carefully, in a diamond pattern, to prevent me from sliding on the polished floor when I ran.

   Purpose: _____ Expressive _____

Journaling

If you want to write well, you must practice, just as a musician practices for a concert or a basketball player practices slam dunks for the big game. Your tool—the equivalent to the musician's instrument or the athlete's equipment—is a journal. This could be a notebook, an electronic file, or an online space for jotting down your ideas, opinions, feelings, and memories. The more time you spend writing in your journal, the more practice you'll get as a writer.

Use your journal as a place to plant seeds of ideas, experiment with different ways of writing, or write without the pressure of being evaluated. Journal writing can help you find topics for writing. It can also help you clarify and organize your ideas, and reflect on how your writing turned out. But most important, writing in a journal helps you become an active thinker, rather than being a passive reader or listener. This, in turn, will help you write better papers in college and get that promotion at work.

As you follow student writers in each chapter of this textbook, you'll discover that some use a journal to record their ideas. For example, in this chapter, Charles Lujan records much of his writing process in his journal. As you read his journal entries, think about your own writing process and how it resembles or differs from his. We'll begin with Charles's thoughts about his audience and purpose.

Charles's Audience and Purpose

After receiving the assignment, Charles thought first about his audience: his classmates and instructor. Although he planned to show his final draft to several classmates and a good friend from high school, he knew his primary audience was his English instructor. In his journal, Charles explained how he felt about this audience:

> Jan. 18
>
> The first thing I thought about when my instructor gave this assignment on the first day of the semester was fear. This is because the last time I had to write for school I was taking an essay exam that I needed to pass in order to graduate. I did well on that exam, but the thought of writing a school assignment, especially for an English instructor, still bugs me even though I've been out of school for a few years. But I'm determined to get rid of that fear and do well on any writing assignment that I have to complete in college.

Charles also thought about his purpose. He knew that it was expressive because the assignment asked him to communicate his own thoughts, feelings, and personal history. He wrote the following about his purpose in his journal:

Although I'm afraid to write for my classmates and instructor, I feel pretty good about writing to express my ideas. It's easy to write about my own thoughts and feelings. It's not like I have to do any research or anything. If I can get over the idea that I'm writing for my instructor, I think I'm going to like writing about myself.

Gathering Ideas

Once you know your audience and purpose, you can begin to gather ideas for any topic you might want to write about.

Imagine, for example, that you are taking a course in criminal justice and your instructor gives you the following essay assignment: "Write a two- to three-page essay in which you explain a problem in the criminal justice system. Suggest a solution for the problem." Any of the following methods could help you explore possibilities for your essay.

Brainstorming

When you brainstorm, you list all the thoughts that come into your head on a topic. You don't consider whether your ideas are good or bad; you just write them down. For the criminal justice assignment, you could brainstorm a list of problems in the criminal justice system, such as prisons that are overcrowded or innocent people who are jailed.

Here is student writer Jerry's list of problems in the criminal justice system:

Some problems
kids being tried as adults
does it make them more responsible?

Another problem
racial profiling
can it be prevented?
prisoners being released and doing more crimes
no schools in prison
you just get out of prison and do more crimes
how to stop this?

In addition to brainstorming by yourself, you can brainstorm in a group. In this case, you would name a topic and then ask each group member to call out ideas on it. Asking others to brainstorm with you greatly increases the number of ideas you have to choose from for your essay.

Freewriting

Freewriting means writing for a specific period of time without pausing or until reaching a certain page limit. You don't stop, go back, or correct freewriting. You can focus on one topic or go on to new ones as they pop into your mind. Freewriting helps you develop fluency as a writer.

Here is student writer Crystal's freewriting about the use of DNA evidence in the court system:

> Heard on the news that they released another prisoner because DNA evidence showed he was innocent. He'd been in jail for eleven years! How sad. DNA evidence is so much better than any other way of seeing if someone is guilty. They gather DNA evidence from a tiny piece of skin. It's like fingerprints. Everyone has their own DNA. I hope more innocent prisoners can be released. They should be given money for the time they had to spend in jail.

Clustering

Clustering is similar to brainstorming, but instead of listing your ideas, you draw a cluster of those ideas. To begin clustering, you write your subject in the center of a blank page and draw a small circle around those words. Then, as ideas about the topic come to mind, you write them down, put circles around them, and draw lines from them to the center circle. As you think of additional details, you circle and join them to their main ideas. Clustering can thus help you organize your ideas as well as generate ideas.

Figure 1.2 on page 13 shows how student writer Lee used clustering to gather ideas about problems in the criminal justice system.

 Do your clustering online

Online mind-mapping tools can help make clustering easy and productive. Try using free versions of mind-mapping tools, programs, and software such as Connected Mind, Stormboard, and MindMeister online.

Asking Questions

The six questions that journalists use to gather details about the news can also help you discover ideas about your topic:

- Who?
- What?
- When?
- Where?
- How?
- Why?

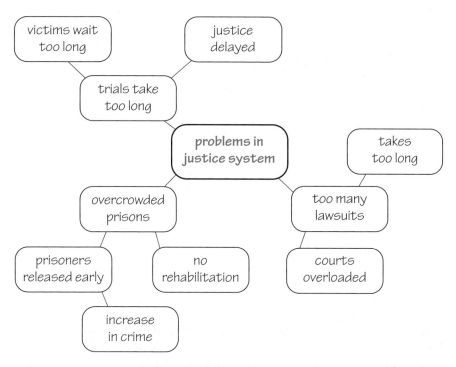

Figure 1.2 Lee's Clustering

Researching

As you gather ideas for an essay, you may discover that you need to learn more about your topic. The more you learn about your topic, the more supporting details you'll find. Research can also spark your own ideas for writing.

You can do firsthand, or primary, research by interviewing, surveying, or observing people. Alternatively, you can conduct secondary research by reading articles, books, or websites on your topic. When you conduct secondary research, keep in mind that some sources are better than others. To find reliable information, examine the writer's credentials, point of view, and purpose. Knowing these things will help you decide whether the information is something you should use. When conducting research, be sure to avoid just cutting and pasting information into your paper. Instead, integrate your research by paraphrasing and quoting your sources. Cite your research both in the essay itself and at the end. For more help in conducting and using research, see Chapters 11 and 12.

Consulting with Others

Consulting with people who know about your topic is an excellent way to gather information and interesting details for your paper. Also, you can enliven your writing by using quotations from the discussion.

For more information on conducting interviews, see pp. 364–65.

The first step is finding someone to consult with. For the criminal justice assignment, for instance, you could talk to a family member or friend involved in the criminal justice system, such as a police officer or an attorney. You could also consult with someone who has been a victim of a crime or has been accused of committing a crime.

HOW TO Consult with Others

- Prepare questions to ask. You might begin with the journalists' questions: Who? What? When? Where? How? Why? Avoid yes-no questions.
- Listen carefully and take notes.
- Ask questions when you don't understand something.
- Go over your notes with the person to fill in any gaps in your understanding.

Relating Aloud

Relating aloud simply means talking about your topic with others. Tell friends or classmates about what you plan to write, and get their feedback. Do they ask questions that indicate you need to supply more details or background information? Talking through what you plan to write is also a good way to realize that you have more to say than you think.

HOW TO Gather Ideas

Use one or more of these strategies:

- *Brainstorming:* List all thoughts that come to mind about a topic.
- *Freewriting:* Write without stopping for a certain period of time (five to ten minutes) or until you reach a certain page length.
- *Clustering:* Write down your topic in the middle of a page, and circle it. Write down more specific ideas, circle them, and draw lines to connect them to the larger idea.
- *Asking questions:* Ask a series of questions about the topic, such as Who? What? When? Where? Why? How?
- *Researching:* Read and take notes on your topic.
- *Consulting with others:* Ask a knowledgeable person about your topic.
- *Relating aloud:* Talk about your topic with others.

After you have tried some of these ways to gather ideas, be sure to reflect on your topic possibilities for a few hours or days, letting your ideas develop before you begin to write.

⏻ **Record your thoughts on your topic**

If you are feeling reluctant to share your thoughts, you might consider using a digital recorder, computer, or smartphone to talk about your topic, and then share this with others later.

Charles's Brainstorming

In order to gather ideas on his topic, student writer Charles brainstormed about his previous experiences writing. He decided to use a chart to help him recall these experiences and organize his thoughts.

Writing for . . .	Kinds of writing	Thoughts
High school	Essay exam to graduate	Nervous about passing, even though I did well. I want to do better when I write in college.
Work	Forms and e-mails to my supervisor and other firefighters on my team	Just the facts. I use spell-check so I don't make stupid mistakes.
Family	Texts, notes	Let people know where I am, when I'll pick them up. No one cares how well I write.
Friends	Texts	Quick messages. Just the facts. Jim — loved to write short stories!

Figure 1.3 Charles's Brainstorming Chart

◖ Step 2 Write Your Discovery Draft

A *discovery draft* is a first attempt at getting your ideas down on paper. When you write a discovery draft, concentrate on writing down your ideas without being too concerned about things like sentence structure, word choice, grammar, spelling, or punctuation.

Drafting styles vary widely. Some writers draft quickly and spend considerable time revising; others draft more slowly and write fewer drafts. The more you practice and experiment with writing, the better you'll know what works for you.

⏻ **Turn off your word-processing tools**

Before beginning your discovery draft, consider turning off the grammar- and spell-check features on your word-processing program so that you won't be distracted by the squiggly lines that appear under words as you type. You can turn them back on when you revise and edit your draft. (Keep in mind that these tools will not spot all of your errors.)

Choosing a Topic

Sometimes a topic will be given to you. For instance, your psychology instructor might ask you to write a definition of *psychosis*, or your supervisor at work might ask for a brief report on your visit to a local manufacturing plant. In such cases, you'll know what to write about, although you may not always be interested in the topic.

Often you'll have more of a choice. All of the writing assignments in Part Two of this book, for instance, ask you to gather ideas on three broad topics before you select one to write about. In such cases, your job is to select a topic that will interest you and your readers. In the criminal justice assignment, for example, you would need to first select a problem in the criminal justice system to write about and then think of a solution to that problem.

HOW TO Select a Topic

Make a list of possible topics. Then answer the following questions:

- How much does this topic interest me?
- How much do I know about this topic?
- If I select this topic, how much, if any, research will I have to do? Is this research available to me? Can I complete the research in time to write the paper?
- Is the topic narrow enough to be explained in detail, given the word or page limit?
- How well does this topic satisfy the audience? For instance, if readers want an informative essay, will this topic lead to an informative essay?

Use your responses to these questions to decide on a good topic.

Once you have identified a general topic, you need to make sure that it is narrow enough to be sufficiently developed in the space you have. For instance, suppose you want to write about how advertising on television has changed. As you start to write, you realize you could probably write a book on that topic. To narrow the topic, ask yourself questions such as the following: What kind of advertising? What time period should I cover? What particular change do I want to focus on? Questions like these help you narrow a broad topic so that you can go into more depth.

HOW TO Narrow a Topic

Break the topic into parts by asking questions like these:

- What particular thing happened?
- Who is involved?
- What is the time period?
- What type is it?
- Where does it happen?
- Why does it happen?
- How does it happen?
- What is the result of it?

GROUP ACTIVITY 2 Narrow Topics

Working with two or three other students in your writing class, assume that a sociology instructor has asked you to write a three-page essay about how technology has changed American life. Using the questions in the How to Narrow a Topic box above, rewrite the following topics to make them narrow enough for a three-page essay.

EXAMPLE: BROAD TOPIC How transportation has changed American life

NARROWED TOPIC   *The influence of cars on the creation of the suburbs in the*

1950s

1. How computers have changed our lives
2. Recent changes in telephone technology
3. How technology has changed the home
4. Negative effects of technology
5. How travel has changed in recent years

Sharing Your Ideas

Once you have selected and narrowed your topic, the next step is to write a discovery draft that puts your ideas together. Most of the time, this first draft will be very rough. Paragraphs might be skimpy; the organization might not make any sense; sentences will probably have mistakes in them. That's fine. The purpose of a discovery draft is to see what you have to say. Nobody writes a perfect, finished essay in one try.

Write a Preliminary Thesis Statement

As you begin a draft, first think about your *thesis statement*, the sentence (or sentences) that explains the main point of the essay. This thesis statement will probably change as you refine your ideas when revising, but it's a good place to start.

From your readers' point of view, a good thesis statement makes an essay easier to understand. From your point of view, an effective thesis statement gives you a solid place to work from. It also helps you keep track of your ideas as you write.

A good thesis statement does three things:

- It announces the topic of your essay.
- It shows, explains, or argues a particular point about the topic.
- It gives readers a sense of what the essay will be about.

Compare the following ineffective and effective thesis statements.

INEFFECTIVE   My daughter was arrested last week for shoplifting.
EFFECTIVE   After my daughter was arrested for shoplifting, I made several important changes in how I raise my children.

INEFFECTIVE   Some people think that having more female police officers is good.
EFFECTIVE   Increasing the number of female police officers has helped the police department handle domestic violence and child abuse cases more effectively.

In the first example, we learn the topic, but a particular point isn't being made. In the second example, the point being made is too vague for readers to predict what the essay will be about.

Where should your thesis statement appear in your essay? Usually, the thesis is given in the first or second paragraph. Knowing the main idea from the start gives your readers a road map for reading the whole essay.

HOW TO Write a Thesis Statement

Ask yourself these questions about your topic:

- What point do I want to make about my topic?
- How can I show, explain, or argue this point?
- How can I break this point down so that I can develop one idea about it in each section of my essay?

Working in small groups, identify the following thesis statements as either effective or ineffective. Then rewrite the thesis statements that need improvement.

1. Reality shows are some of the best shows on television. *✗ why. just opinion*
2. A successful marriage requires patience, good communication, and a sense of humor. *✓*
3. There have been too many budget cuts at this university.
4. If you have time on your hands, do community volunteer work.
5. Even though I didn't make the Olympic ski team, my years of training taught me important skills, such as discipline, time management, focus, and persistence.

Get Organized

Once you have a topic and a preliminary thesis statement in hand, look back at the ideas you gathered. Decide which ones appear most promising, and use the techniques you have learned to gather as many additional ideas as you think you might need. Some writers prefer to organize their ideas before they begin to write. Others prefer to discover what they have to say while writing the discovery draft. Try to write your discovery draft in one sitting.

As you draft, use your thesis statement as a guide. Keep in mind that you are free to change your thesis statement later. After all, your discovery draft is for exploring your ideas. The most important thing is to write. If you reach a place where you need more information, write "add information here" in bold or colored type to remind yourself to add more to this part of your essay.

Charles's Drafting

Using the brainstorming that he did on the topic (Figure 1.3, p. 15), Charles wrote the following discovery draft. (Note that the draft includes the types of errors that typically appear in a first draft.)

Thinking about Writing

I write a lot more than I thought I did before I had to do this assignment. At first all I thought of was school writing. All I remember from high school was preparing for the tests that you had to take in order to graduate. You were given a topic and then you had about 30 minutes to write. This made me incredibly nervous. I'm determined that in college I'll get the help I need from the Writing Center so I'll do well. Also, I write texts and notes to my family, such as when I have to tell them where I am or when I'll get home. I'm not worried about how well I write these because my family just cares about the message. At the fire department I have to write e-mails, mostly to my supervisor. I have to be sure to get my facts straight. I wish I could have the incredibly positive attitude about writing that my friend from high school Jim did. He wrote short stories and even won a contest. So I'm an anxious writer, but I'm also hopeful that I can be like Jim and start to really enjoy writing.

Step 3 Revise Your Draft

Revising is an important part of the writing process. When you revise your discovery draft, you focus on developing and organizing your ideas while keeping your readers' expectations in mind. Usually, the more you revise, the better your essay will be.

Developing Your Ideas

The more you read, the more you'll notice that writers make their essays more interesting and convincing by developing them in detail. Supporting details increase interest, help readers understand the writer's thoughts, and support the writer's main ideas.

Writers use specific methods, or patterns, to develop the details in their paragraphs and essays. The most common of these patterns are description, narration, examples, process explanation, classification, definition, comparison and contrast, cause and effect, and argument. Chapter 4 explains in detail how each of these patterns works, and the Developing Your Ideas section in each chapter in Part Two shows you how to use them in your own writing.

Building Your Essay

When you build your essay, you look for ways to clarify your ideas for your readers, such as adding topic sentences to your paragraphs, giving more supporting details, or rearranging your points. The questions in the How to

---

HOW TO Revise an Essay

Ask yourself these questions as you revise:

- Have I followed all the instructions for this assignment?
- Do I begin the essay in a way that encourages readers to continue reading?
- Do I need to revise my thesis statement?
- Do I include enough main ideas to support my thesis statement?
- Do I support each main idea with details?
- Do I vary my sentences and use the appropriate words?
- Do I end the essay clearly and effectively?

HOW TO Give and Receive Feedback on Your Writing

When you're giving someone suggestions for revision, follow these guidelines:

- Always say something positive about the piece.
- Be specific. Don't say, "You need to improve the organization." Say, "Why don't you combine your second and third paragraphs?"
- Don't make the feedback personal. Focus on the writing, not the writer. Don't say, "I can't believe you really believe that!" Say, "I was confused by your claim. Do you mean to say that the death penalty should be used for all convicted drug felons?"

When you're receiving feedback, follow these guidelines:

- Write down the suggestions you receive.
- Ask questions to clarify what the readers are suggesting.
- Don't take the suggestions personally. Remind yourself that your classmates are discussing your writing, not you. Consider all feedback you get. The more suggestions you receive, the better your essay will be.

Revise an Essay box on page 20 will help you find ways to improve the content and organization of your draft.

One way to revise is to set your essay aside for a day or two, reread it, and then rewrite it as you see fit. A better way to revise is to enlist the help of others, a strategy that is often called *peer review*. Ask a friend or classmate to read your essay and suggest ways it could be improved.

Charles's Revising

After finishing his discovery draft, Charles reflected again on his audience and purpose. He decided that his instructor would want an essay that would be easier to follow; after all, she had over a hundred students who would be turning in essays. This meant that his essay had to be better organized and more fully developed, with a good thesis statement. Charles asked several classmates in his class to read his discovery draft and give him suggestions for revision.

In his journal, Charles explained how he revised his essay:

Jan. 20

Before I revised my essay, I wrote an introduction with a thesis statement: "I write for many different reasons and occasions, and I have a different attitude toward each type of writing." I based the rest of the essay on this thesis statement. When I wrote the revised draft, I used a standard essay format—introduction, body paragraphs, and a conclusion. I decided to use a lot of examples to support my points, such as the phrase "catch a hydrant." I also wrote a conclusion that expressed my hope that I would write well in college. Then I went to the Writing Center for help with putting the sources into the essay and correctly using documentation.

Here is Charles's revised draft. (You may spot errors that Charles will correct when he edits his draft.)

Thinking about Writing

When I first began to think about writing, the first thing I remembered was the standardized essay exam I had to take in high school in order to graduate. But then I realized that I actually do a lot of writing, such as texts, e-mails, and forms. I write for many different reasons and occasions, and I have a different attitude toward each type of writing.

Some of the most important writing that I've done is related to my family. The overall conventions of our family are good honest values with the purpose of supporting and loving each other unconditionally. I and members of my family will use different types of writing. From short letters to family members of simple hellos and updates on our family, to notes being left to let someone know where we are. We often use texting for quick messages about personal family news or simple conversations. Different kinds of words are used depending on the situation, for example, when I text with my parents I try to use correct spelling, but when I text my brother I use shortcuts and slang. When I write something for my family, I'm usually in a good mood and don't worry about what the reader will think about how I write.

As a firefighter for the El Paso Fire Department, I know that the purpose of all my writing is to make sure everyone stays safe. I have written professional e-mails to my supervisor and fellow firefighters on subjects from training activity to actual live fire and medical calls that we have dealt with. Sometimes we use special jargon in e-mails or reports about fire events; this jargon lets us simplifie and deliver a clear message. For example, writing "catch a hydrant" means a firefighter pulled a five foot fire hose from the back of the fire truck, wrapped it around a fire hydrant, and then connected the hose to the fire hydrant. When I write for my job, I focus on getting the facts correct. As long as I dont have to rush, I don't feel stressed about how good the writing is because my readers are just interested in the message.

When I write for school, I can get anxious, mostly because of the standardizied writing tests I had to take in high school. Even though I'm no

---

The thesis statement tells readers what the essay will be about.

The topic sentence states the main point of the paragraph. All of the paragraphs in the body of this essay begin with clear topic sentences.

Examples support the topic of the paragraph.

This example gives readers a better understanding of the writing that Charles does on the job.

By talking about his attitude, Charles responds directly to the writing assignment.

longer in high school, the anxiety remains. Because I've just started college, I haven't had to write much, but I know that I might get worried and not know what to say. I also don't have a lot of practice with using computers to write essays. During orientation I was told about the Writing Center, where tutors can help you make your writing better. Going to the Writing Center will help me improve my mood and make me feel more confident.

The person who most helped me develop as a writer was my friend Jim from high school. He loved creative writing and even won a state writing contest for a short story. Jim used to talk to me about how much he loved to write. I had never met anyone who loved to write before, so he showed me that writing can be much more than just taking essay exams to graduate from high school. Because of Jim, one of the ways that I would describe myself as a writer is hopeful. I'm hopeful that my writing will continue to improve and that I will come to enjoy writing as much as he does.

This topic sentence addresses another part of the writing assignment—the effects that previous writing experiences had on Charles.

By explaining how he plans to relieve his writing anxiety, Charles gives readers more information about the type of writer that he is.

In his conclusion, Charles looks to the future in an optimistic way.

▌ GROUP ACTIVITY 4 Analyze Charles's Essay

Discuss the following questions with your classmates:

1. Charles was not satisfied with his essay's title. What title would you suggest?
2. Does Charles's introduction make you want to read more? Why or why not?
3. How effective is Charles's thesis statement?
4. What details did Charles include in the revised draft to improve on his discovery draft?
5. How effective is Charles's conclusion? What more would you suggest he add?
6. What else could Charles do to improve his essay?

◖Step 4 Edit Your Sentences

When you edit, you revise your sentences and words so that they communicate clearly. Since you have already devoted a great deal of time and effort to communicating your ideas, you don't want to spoil the essay with awkward sentences or distracting errors. Therefore, edit your essay carefully before sharing it with your readers.

Using Standard Written English

You may identify yourself as an English-speaking person, but actually you speak a dialect of English. A *dialect* is a variety of a language, and every language has many dialects. Dialects are characterized by pronunciation, word choice, and sentence structure. People speak different dialects based on where they live and their ethnic backgrounds. Here are some examples of dialects:

1. From *The Quilters: Women and Domestic Art.* Rosie Fischer is talking in 1974 about her life on a farm in Rowlett, Texas:

   > Well, anyway, I was dreaming on havin' all kinds of pretty things in my home after I married. Well, I found out right quick that livin' out on a farm, what with all the chores that had to be done, a person didn't have a whole lot of time for makin' pretty things.

2. From Robert Kimmel Smith's *Sadie Shapiro's Knitting Book*, a novel about a Jewish widow from Queens, New York:

   > "Listen, darling," Sadie said patiently, "we all have our ways and that's it. . . . I lived with my son Stuart and his wife for three years after my Reuben died, he should find eternal peace. And what happened? My daughter-in-law and I drove each other crazy. I'm a neat person, I think you can tell that, but she . . . Well, I wouldn't exactly call her a slob, but the best housekeeper in the world she isn't. Not that I want to talk badly about her, mind you. But by me you don't wash a floor with a mop. That's not what I call clean."

3. From "Black Children, Black Speech," an essay by Dorothy Z. Seymour:

   > "C'mon, man, les git goin'!" called the boy to his companion. "Dat bell ringin'. It say, 'Git in rat now!'" He dashed into the school yard.
   >
   > "Aw, f'get you," replied the other. "Whe' Richuh? Whe' da muvvuh? He be goin' to schoo'."
   >
   > "He in de' now, man!" was the answer as they went through the door.

Northern, southern, and midwestern dialects have developed from the languages spoken by European immigrants. The structure of some African American spoken English is similar to several West African languages. In areas where people have emigrated from Latin America or Spanish-speaking parts of the Caribbean, dialects such as Spanglish have developed.

All these dialects are different from standard English, which is taught in American schools and used in business, government, and the media. The written version of standard English is known as standard written English.

Because standard written English is generally considered the appropriate language to use in school and business, every chapter in Part Two of this book shows you how to use it in your writing. However, no language is better than another; languages are just different. Standard written English is a tool that will help you advance in college and in your workplace. It doesn't replace the other regional or ethnic dialects you might speak; it adds to them.

Correcting Errors

Before you can consider an essay finished, you must check your revised draft for any errors in grammar, spelling, and punctuation. It's perfectly acceptable to make mistakes when you're drafting and revising; most writers do. But if your readers are distracted by errors in your writing, they'll pay less attention to what you have to say. You'll have several opportunities throughout this book to learn what the most common errors are and how you can fix them. You should also refer to the Handbook in Part Four whenever you have a question about the correct way to structure a sentence. Remember: Editing is not a punishment; it is your final chance to make a good impression on your readers.

⏻ **Use spell-check and grammar-check to edit**

Be careful when you use the spell-check and grammar-check features of your word-processing program. While spell-check helps you spot typos and words that you have misspelled, it won't spot all errors. For instance, it won't notice if you use *their* when you're supposed to use *there* or *to* when you meant *too*. It also won't recognize "textese" in your essay, such as *going 2 school* or *B4*. Grammar-check also has limitations. For example, it tends to label all long sentences as incorrect, when the length of a sentence has nothing to do with its grammatical correctness.

Charles's Editing

Charles described editing his essay in his journal:

Jan. 22

I used my spell-checker to catch some misspelled words. I also took my draft to the Writing Center, where a tutor showed me how to correct some errors. Finally, I proofread my essay by reading it from the end to the beginning.

Here is Charles's edited essay. (The brackets and underlining indicate where he corrected errors during the editing stage.)

Charles Lujan
Professor Evelyn Posey
English 1311
25 Jan. 2011

Thinking about Writing

When I first began to think about writing, the first thing I
remembered was the standardized essay exam I had to take in high
school in order to graduate. But then I realized that I actually do a lot
of writing, such as texts, e-mails, and forms. I write for many different

1

reasons and occasions, and I have a different attitude toward each type of writing.

2

Some of the most important writing that I've done is related to my family. The overall conventions of our family are good honest values with the purpose of supporting and loving each other unconditionally. I and members of my family will use different types of writing, from short letters to family members of simple hellos and updates on our family, to notes being left to let someone know where we are. We often use texting for quick messages about personal family news or simple conversations. Different kinds of words are used depending on the situation; for example, when I text with my parents I try to use correct spelling, but when I text my brother I use shortcuts and slang. When I write something for my family, I'm usually in a good mood and don't worry about what the reader will think about how I write.

Sentence fragment corrected.

Comma splice corrected.

3

As a firefighter for the El Paso Fire Department, I know that the purpose of all my writing is to make sure everyone stays safe. I have written professional e-mails to my supervisor and fellow firefighters on subjects from training activity to actual live fire and medical calls that we have dealt with. Sometimes we use special jargon in e-mails or reports about fire events; this jargon lets us simplify and deliver a clear message. For example, writing "catch a hydrant" means a firefighter pulled a five foot fire hose from the back of the fire truck, wrapped it around a fire hydrant, and then connected the hose to the fire hydrant. When I write for my job, I focus on getting the facts correct. As long as I don't have to rush, I don't feel stressed about how good the writing is because my readers are just interested in the message.

Spelling error corrected.

Apostrophe added.

4

When I write for school, I can get anxious, mostly because of the standardized writing tests I had to take in high school. Even though I'm no longer in high school, the anxiety remains. Because I've just started college, I haven't had to write much, but I know that I might get worried and not know what to say. I also don't have a lot of practice with using computers to write essays. During orientation I was told about the Writing Center, where tutors can help you make your writing better. Going to the Writing Center will help me improve my mood and make me feel more confident.

Spelling error corrected.

5

The person who most helped me develop as a writer was my friend Jim from high school. He loved creative writing and even won a state writing contest for a short story. Jim used to talk to me about how much he loved to write. I had never met anyone who loved to write before, so he showed me that writing can be much more than just taking essay exams to graduate from high school. Because of Jim, one of the ways that I would describe myself as a writer is hopeful. I'm hopeful that my writing will continue to improve and that I will come to enjoy writing as much as Jim does.

Unclear pronoun reference corrected.

(Step 5 Share Your Essay

In the final step of the writing process, you share your revised and edited essay with your audience. You may just submit your essay to your instructor for a grade, but if you're proud of what you have written, you may wish to share it with your classmates as well.

At times, you may share your writing in a more public way. You may submit it to your local or campus newspaper for possible publication. Some magazines will share essays and articles submitted by their readers. If your essay proposes a change of some kind, you might want to use it as the basis of a letter that you send to a public official who can take action.

HOW TO Use the Writing Process

Exploring Your Choices
- Analyze your audience.
- Discover a purpose for writing.
- Brainstorm, freewrite, cluster, ask questions, research, consult with others, or relate aloud.

Drafting
- Select and narrow a topic.
- Write a tentative thesis statement.
- Get your ideas down on paper.
- Don't be concerned about sentence structure, word choice, grammar, spelling, or punctuation.

(continued on next page)

Revising
- Focus on helping your audience understand your essay.
- Improve your organization and supporting details.
- Strengthen the introduction, thesis statement, and conclusion.
- Polish sentence structure and word choice.
- Receive and consider feedback from peer review.

Editing
- Correct errors in grammar, spelling, and punctuation.
- Use a dictionary and the Handbook in Part Four.
- Don't rely on spell-check and grammar-check to catch all errors.

Sharing
- Share the final draft of your essay with your audience.

Charles's Sharing

Writing in his journal, Charles summed up his feelings about the final draft of his assignment:

> Jan. 25
> I was really worried about the grade I would get for this essay because it was one of the first I've written in college. I was hoping for a B but was surprised when I received an A! All that revising paid off, and because I understand the writing process, I feel more confident about writing for my professors. The next time I have to write an essay, I'll have a plan for what to do.

In this chapter, you've followed Charles Lujan's work through each step of the writing process. For the rest of the book, look for each student's process near the end of each chapter to see how student writers apply the ideas they learned.

CHAPTER CHECKLIST

- ❏ There are five steps in the writing process: exploring choices, drafting, revising, editing, and sharing.
- ❏ The writing process is recursive; that is, you often need to go back and forth among the steps.

❏ Your audience affects what you write. Identify your audience—your readers—and take into account what they know about your topic, what they don't know about your topic, and how they feel toward your topic.

❏ You may have three purposes for writing:

    ❏ Expressive writing communicates thoughts, feelings, or personal history.

    ❏ Informative writing conveys information.

    ❏ Persuasive writing seeks to change readers' opinions or to convince readers to take a particular action.

❏ Keeping a journal can give you a place to practice your writing before you share it with others.

❏ The techniques for gathering ideas include brainstorming, freewriting, clustering, asking questions, researching, consulting with others, and relating aloud.

❏ When you draft, focus on getting your ideas down on paper. Use a tentative thesis statement as a guide.

❏ When you revise, aim to improve your writing and to communicate your ideas effectively and clearly.

❏ Skilled writers usually revise a draft several times.

❏ Standard written English (SWE) is taught in American schools and used in business, government, and the media. It is important to learn SWE for writing in college and in the workplace.

❏ When you edit your writing, eliminate errors in grammar, spelling, and punctuation, which, if left uncorrected, may prevent your readers from focusing on your message.

❏ Share your finished writing with others.

REFLECTING ON YOUR WRITING

To help you reflect on the writing you did in this chapter, answer the following questions:

1. What did you learn from writing this essay?

2. How will your audience benefit from reading your essay?

3. If you had more time, what more would you do to improve your essay before sharing it with your readers?

4. How will learning about the writing process help you?

Once you answer these questions, freewrite about what you learned about the writing process and about yourself as a writer.

Visit **LaunchPad Solo for Readers and Writers > Writing Process** for additional tutorials, videos, and practice with **Purpose, Audience, and Topic; Prewriting; Thesis Statements;** and more.

Reading to Improve Writing

As a college student, you read and interpret a variety of texts all the time. You read textbooks to learn about a subject and to pass your classes. You go to Twitter or a newspaper to keep up with current events, and you might enjoy reading a novel and comparing it with the movie version of the same story. Maybe you read social media posts and texts, celebrity websites, and statistics about sporting events. Texts such as these add value to your life and help you make sense of your world.

In this chapter, you will write a paragraph in which you summarize a reading. As you work on your paragraph, you will
- Learn about different purposes for reading.
- Practice active reading strategies.
- Learn how to keep a reading journal.
- Write a summary of a reading.

The advantages of reading multiply when you read as writers read, by paying attention to different writing strategies so you can use these strategies in your own writing. When you examine a piece of writing to learn how the author communicates a certain idea, you're like an athlete who improves by watching other athletes perform. Just as a soccer player studies examples of different kicking techniques to find what works best at a particular angle to the goal, you can study the different strategies that authors use to capture their readers' attention. As a result of reading like a writer, you learn more about how to express your ideas for different audiences and purposes. ■

Writing Assignment

Write a summary of an article, an essay, or a selection from a textbook for your classmates and instructor. The piece that you summarize should be about two to three pages long and on a topic that interests you.

Use active reading strategies to read the selection, and then follow the steps in this chapter that explain how to write a summary. The first sentence of the summary should include the title, the author's name, and the main point of the text. Explain the important supporting points and in the last sentence rephrase the main point and the significance of the piece. Throughout the summary, use your own words rather than simply copying down the author's ideas. Use the steps in the writing process that you learned in Chapter 1—exploring ideas, drafting, revising, editing, and sharing.

Purposes for Reading

Probably one of the most frequent reasons that people read is for specific information. You might download the bus schedule to find out when you need to leave the house in the morning, go to your college's website to see your final exam time, or check out your friends' statuses on Facebook to keep up with their lives. But people also read for other reasons:

- To understand concepts, ideas, and principles, such as the process of photosynthesis or the symptoms of autism.
- To evaluate the quality of something, such as reviews of a video game's graphics or a proposal for a new homeless shelter.
- For pleasure, such as your favorite author's newest book or a humorous article posted and shared online by friends in your social network.

Reading for Pleasure

While you might think reading for pleasure is just a way to pass the time, it can be useful in other ways.

Improve your vocabulary   Suppose that one of your favorite authors is the suspense novelist Mary Higgins Clark. Here is an excerpt from Clark's *While My Pretty One Sleeps*, a book about a fashion designer named Neeve:

> To Neeve's dismay, as she crossed Thirty-Seventh Street she came face to face with Gordon Steuber. Meticulously dressed in a tan cashmere jacket over a brown-and-beige Scottish pullover, dark-brown slacks and Gucci loafers, with

his blaze of curly brown hair, slender, even-featured face, powerful shoulders and narrow waist, Gordon Steuber could easily have had a successful career as a model. Instead, in his early forties, he was a shrewd businessman with an uncanny knack of hiring unknown young designers and exploiting them until they could afford to leave him.

The word *meticulously* might not be familiar to you, but from the context of this passage you can guess that it means "carefully" or "precisely." From this passage, you can also guess that *uncanny* means "unusual" or "remarkable" and that *exploit* means "to use." Verify your guesses by looking up unfamiliar words in a dictionary, and keep a list of new words and their meanings so that you can refer to them when you read and write.

Learn writing strategies   Suppose you can't decide how to begin a paper on whales for your biology course. Around the same time, you read an article on hallucinogenic drugs in *Outside* magazine called "One Toad over the Line," written by Kevin Krajick. Here is its beginning:

> It's big, it looks like a cowpie with eyes, and many people believe it can bring them face to face with God. It's the Colorado River toad, a once obscure amphibian whose fame has spread in recent years thanks to the venom secreted by its skin. When dried and smoked, the venom releases bufotenine, a substance that one California drug agent calls "the most potent, instantaneously acting hallucinogen we know."

From this paragraph, you learn two strategies for beginning an essay. First, a startling comparison ("a cowpie with eyes") can get your audience's attention. Second, stating the topic of an essay (in this case, the hallucinogen bufotenine) at the beginning helps your audience understand right away what your piece is about.

For more information about introductory paragraphs, see pp. 59–61.

HOW TO Expand Your Vocabulary

- Pay attention to unfamiliar words when you read for pleasure. Guess the meanings using context clues and verify your guesses by using an online or print dictionary.
- Keep lists of new words with examples of how to pronounce and use them.
- Connect new words to your own experiences. The word *meticulous*, for example, might remind you of a relative who tends to be precise and careful.
- Use online resources such as dictionaries, "Word of the Day" sites and apps, and word games.
- Read, read, read!

For more practice on improving your vocabulary, see pp. 469–73.

> **GROUP ACTIVITY 1 Purposes for Reading**
>
> With several other students, make a list of things you read, from the short and very informal (social media posts, text messages) to longer texts (novels and textbooks). What are your purposes for reading these materials? Which of these purposes are your favorites?

Myths about Reading

No matter what your purpose for reading, you want to use a process that is based on tried-and-true strategies rather than on myths or false assumptions about reading.

Myth #1: *Look up every word you don't understand in a dictionary.* While a dictionary is a valuable way to learn new vocabulary, looking up every word you don't understand can do more harm than good. Why doesn't this work? For one thing, it will be hard to finish the assignment. When studying, use a dictionary to focus on the most important words and concepts, which will be the ideas that your instructor stresses and that are emphasized in the textbook.

Myth #2: *Reading all of the assigned material just once will prepare you for the exam.* Most of the time, reading the material just once isn't enough because you're likely to forget important points. To master the material, you'll need to reread important sections in order to understand and remember them. Taking notes as you read or using other active reading strategies (such as those described on pp. 35–38) will help.

Myth #3: *Never skip any part of a reading.* Actually, you can skip certain sections of the reading such as sidebars and illustrations if they do not include important content. Sometimes authors add these elements as a way to keep readers' attention rather than to impart vital information. Your instructor or a tutor can help you decide if there are parts that you can skip.

Myth #4: *Slow readers are bad readers.* How fast you read is not related to how well you understand the text. While the instruction in this chapter might help you read more quickly, faster isn't necessarily better. In fact, sometimes when you read something fast you miss understanding key ideas. Read at a pace that allows you to understand the important concepts in the text.

☾ Active Reading

When you read a text sent from a friend, consult driving directions from an online source, or relax by reading a novel, you can read quickly to get just the information that you need. However, reading in college is different: it requires time, critical thinking, and good reading strategies.

Becoming an Active Reader

An active reader is one who reads a text in order to understand it, evaluate it, and use it. Active reading involves *activity:* note-taking, consulting reference sources, summarizing, and discussing. The tools and strategies you use to actively read will help you understand, remember, and respond to the material.

Before You Read

Skim the text to learn the general topic of the material before you dig in to the reading. Read the introduction and conclusion, headings and subheadings, italicized words, charts, and lists. What does the title mean to you? Do you recognize the author's name? Is there a headnote that gives you information about the author? Write a sentence that explains the general topic.

Divide the material into manageable sections. Instead of trying to read an entire chapter in one sitting, read just one section at a time and take short breaks. This will allow you to keep mentally fresh as you proceed through the material.

Ask questions about the material that you can answer as you read. For instance, if the general topic of the material is Martin Luther King Jr.'s 1955 bus boycott in Montgomery, Alabama, jot down questions such as these: Who was involved?, How long did it last?, Who started it?, and What effect did it have? These questions will help you focus on the material.

Prepare to make connections between the material, what your instructor has told you about the topic, and what you might have previously read. Review your class notes and other materials from the course, such as presentation slides or study material on the course website. Keep these materials handy so you can easily refer to them.

While You Read

Take notes on the thesis, topic sentences, and supporting points in the text. The thesis is the main idea of the whole text; the topic sentences give the main idea of each paragraph. Supporting points in each paragraph can include examples, facts, and reasons. Pay attention to the supporting points,

For more on topic sentences, see pages 50–53.

but focus more on the thesis and topic sentences using strategies such as highlighting or underlining.

For more on journaling, see pp. 10 and 38.

Write the key ideas in your own words to help you remember and understand them. You can write these ideas in the margins (these notes are called "annotations"), on post-it notes, or in a reading journal. While you might be tempted to just highlight important points, writing them in your own words gets you to think more deeply.

Ask specific questions. The questions you ask before you start to read are more general and intended to help you focus on main ideas; now that you are reading the material, ask questions in response to what you learn. For example, as you read about the Montgomery bus boycott, you learn that King and his followers were subjected to violent attacks and jail terms. You could ask "How did King maintain nonviolent civil disobedience under such circumstances?" or "Why did King and his followers voluntarily go to jail?" These more focused questions will help keep you curious and engaged.

Pay attention to concepts that appear multiple times throughout the material. Usually, important points will be emphasized through repetition. For instance, an important term will be given in a heading, a topic sentence, and in a summary paragraph at the end of a passage or chapter. Look for transitions such as "most importantly," "significantly," "in conclusion," and "in sum," which indicate when the author is emphasizing key ideas. Focus in particular on the introduction and conclusion because the main idea of the reading is usually announced in the introduction and repeated in the conclusion for emphasis.

Look up unfamiliar words and phrases that are key to the topic. These key words or phrases will be those that are repeated throughout the material. For the reading on the Montgomery bus boycott, you might circle and then consult a dictionary or encyclopedia about *civil disobedience*. Reference websites and apps such as dictionary.com and merriam-webster.com make these consultations easy.

Reread passages that are confusing or seem especially important so you can make sure you understand them. To help focus on these passages, read them aloud or write parts of them out. If you're still confused, ask a classmate, your instructor, or a tutor for assistance.

Relate the text to class lectures and other materials. As you read, refer to the course materials that you have handy that show what your instructor has emphasized in lectures and presentation slides. Highlight and take notes on terms and concepts that appear in both the reading and the class.

 Download study apps

To help you take and organize notes as you read, use your smartphone or Internet browser to download study apps that feature digital flashcards or page organizers.

After You Read

Review the notes you took as you were reading. Take time to discover the answers to your questions, look up the important words you didn't know, and remind yourself of the main points and the ideas that were repeated throughout the text.

Connect key ideas to deepen your understanding. One technique is to create a concept cluster. Take a key concept in the text, write it in the middle of a page, and circle it. Then create a cluster (or map or web) by drawing lines to supporting ideas. This cluster helps you identify the main and supporting ideas, as well as see how the ideas relate together. For instance, a concept cluster about the Montgomery bus boycott could relate the boycott to King's principle of nonviolent civil disobedience.

For more on clustering, see pp. 12–13.

Respond to the text by writing about your personal experience of the text. How does it connect to your own concerns and experiences? What are your feelings about what you read? Share notes and ideas about the reading with fellow students or others who have read the material. If you are studying for a test, review the terms and concepts that were emphasized by your instructor and that also appear in the material.

HOW TO Become an Active Reader

Before you read

- Skim the material to get a sense of the main idea.
- Divide the material into manageable sections.
- Ask general questions that you can answer while reading.
- Prepare to make connections by examining your class notes.

As you read

- Identify the thesis, topic sentences, and supporting points.
- Write the key ideas in your own words.
- Ask specific questions about and in response to the content.
- Pay attention to the repetition of concepts and terms.
- Look up unfamiliar words that are key to the topic.
- Reread passages that are confusing or especially important.

After you read

- Review your reading notes to answer your questions, look up important words, and remind yourself of main points.
- Connect key ideas with a concept cluster.
- Write your personal response to the text.
- Discuss the material with others.
- Relate the material to class lectures and materials.

> **⏻ Use digital notes and annotations**
>
> If you're using a tablet or other device, use the Help menu to learn how to take notes in the margin and highlight key points. If reading online, create a document or mind map for your notes.

READING ACTIVITY 1 Practice Active Reading

Select a chapter from a textbook and practice using at least one active reading strategy, such as taking notes or creating a concept cluster. What was it like to use this strategy? How helpful do you think it will be when reading textbooks for your other classes?

Keeping a Reading Journal

Keeping a reading journal (sometimes called a reading log or notebook) is yet another way to become an active reader. Writing in a reading journal helps you explore your ideas more extensively than if you just think or talk about a text, and it helps you formulate questions and clarify ideas. Your journal is a place to collect and arrange your thoughts, draw conclusions, and evaluate what you have learned.

One of the most effective types of reading journals is the two-column reading journal. You write down the main points of the reading selection in one column and your thoughts about it in the other column. The advantage of this style of journal is that the two columns make it easier both to summarize and to think about the reading. If you decide to keep your reading journal on your computer, just use the word-processing feature that sets up columns.

Here's an entry from the two-column reading log that student writer Kevin kept for his psychology textbook:

Notes	Thoughts
Memory—	I never realized there were three
Where information is held.	kinds of memory. I'm not surprised
3 types:	that we forget so much sensory info:
sensory	there's so much of it. Short-term
short-term	memory is what I am thinking now,
long-term	drawing on what is happening
sensory—all info that enters the	around me. I think of long-term
senses	memory kind of like a book in the
short-term—where all conscious	library. If I want to retrieve it, I
thought takes place	hope that it is there.
long-term—representation of all	
that is known	

Writing Summaries

A *summary* is a condensed description of a longer work, such as an article, film, or performance. Many of us have summarized the plot of a favorite television series for a friend, and some of us have written summaries on the job and in college classes. Instructors may ask you to summarize books, articles, essays, plays, television shows, movies, or speeches. These summaries help you practice active reading strategies as you condense important source information, reflect on what you have learned, and demonstrate your knowledge to others. You may also choose to write summaries of a reading assignment, a lecture, or other classroom materials for yourself as a way to learn and recall information for class discussions, reports, or exams.

A summary is written in your own words but does not include your judgment or opinion. To summarize well, you must be able to analyze and evaluate the source information and then condense it, using your own words. Doing this can help you develop your writing, reading, listening, and thinking skills. Summaries test your understanding of the original information as well as your ability to effectively communicate what you have learned.

As with other skills, writing a good summary takes practice. If you are writing a text message to a friend or family member in which you describe the movie you saw last night, you would draft quickly and hit the Send button. Other times—especially if you are summarizing a document for an employer or a textbook reading assignment for an instructor—you may need to use the writing process to gather ideas, write and revise several drafts, and edit your final summary to eliminate errors. A number of strategies will help you consistently write better summaries.

> Visit **LaunchPad Solo for Readers and Writers > Writing Process > Integrated Reading and Writing** for videos and practice on writing summaries.

Reread the Original Text

Whether you are assigned a summary or decide to write one for yourself, go back and reread the original material using active reading strategies. You can write a good summary only if you fully understand the original text. A sure way for you and your readers to test whether you know a certain piece of material is to see whether you can summarize it accurately.

Include the Elements of a Summary

A summary includes the main ideas and important supporting points from the original, and it leaves out overly specific details and examples. Your summary will include the following parts:

Main Idea

In the first sentence, identify the title, the author's name, and the main idea of the original source in your own words. This is the sentence that tells your readers the source of the original text and its main topic. Remember, even when you use your own words, you must let readers know that you borrowed the information from another source.

> In "Black Men and Public Space" (p. 104) Brent Staples describes how he is perceived as a threat because he is a young black man.

Important Supporting Points

Learning to summarize helps you streamline the process of reading and recording information. Because you can't quote everything you read, you select and include only the most important points. Summaries also provide you with a version that you can reread later as you prepare for a class discussion, a report, or an exam.

For more on using direct quotations, see pp. 384–85.

Decide which pieces of information you need to include to get the main idea across quickly. Write these down in your own words. Try to stay true to the meaning the original author intended. Use direct quotes sparingly— no more than one or two.

> Even though he has never been violent, Staples often encounters people who assume he is dangerous, especially when he is walking alone at night. He writes that he has become used to people crossing the street or locking their car doors when they see him. Most significantly, the author has realized that "being perceived as dangerous is a hazard in itself." Staples has developed ways to make himself less threatening to others, such as not coming close to people and humming classical music when he walks at night.

Conclusion

Write a conclusion that restates the main idea or that restates the author's opinion or recommendations. The conclusion helps bring the summary to a close and helps your readers understand what you consider to be important.

> Staples's essay demonstrates the damaging effects that prejudice can have on innocent people.

READING ACTIVITY 2 Organize a Summary

The sentences in this summary of "A Doctor's Dilemma" by James Dillard (pp. 101–3) have been rearranged. Number each sentence in the order in which it should appear, keeping in mind the parts of a summary: the main idea, supporting ideas, and conclusion.

_____ Dillard hesitates at first because a lawsuit would have destroyed his career, but then he begins to treat the man and saves his life.

_____ After he graduates from medical school, Dillard realized that he did a foolish thing when he stopped to help.

_____ In "A Doctor's Dilemma," James Dillard writes about the difficulties doctors experience when they have to decide between saving a patient and saving their careers.

_____ Dillard needed to move the man to save him, but this action could have resulted in the man being a quadriplegic.

_____ Dillard's essay illustrates the tough choices that doctors must make to balance the obligation to help the sick and the need to protect their careers.

_____ The man, who was a drunk driver, survives and ends up walking out of the hospital that was treating him.

_____ While he was a doctor in training, Dillard witnessed a serious car accident in which a man nearly died from a crushed windpipe.

HOW TO Write a Summary

- Reread the material, underlining the important points.
- Write a sentence that states the title, the author's name, and the main point of the original text.
- In your own words, write the important supporting points.
- Leave out overly specific details and examples.
- Write a conclusion that restates the main point and talks about why the topic is important.

(A Student's Reading and Writing Process

On the following pages, you'll follow the writing process of a student, Ofelia Johnson, as she responds to the writing assignment at the beginning of this chapter. As you recall, this assignment asked you to write a summary of an article, an essay, or a selection from a textbook for your classmates and instructor. Ofelia uses active reading strategies in order to summarize the following essay, "Beauty Is More Than Skin Deep: The Different Types of Attractiveness," which was part of a reading assignment in her psychology class. Some of these strategies are indicated in the margins of the essay.

On the next page, you'll see how Ofelia annotates the reading by asking questions in the margin, taking notes to identify key points, circling and underlining important or confusing words, and highlighting the main idea. Ofelia's notes are in italics.

Ronald E. Riggio
Beauty Is More Than Skin Deep: The Different Types of Attractiveness

Ronald E. Riggio, PhD, is a professor at Claremont McKenna College in Clare-mont, California. He has written many books and articles on the topic of leader-ship and social psychology, and he founded a column in the *Los Angeles Times* that deals with workplace problems and issues. Riggio is a regular blogger for the magazine *Psychology Today*, where this article first appeared in 2011.

There is more to being physically attractive than just good looks. Many   1
believe that people are born beautiful or handsome—that (static) qualities, such
as a pretty face, nice hair, or a shapely body, are inherited. You either have it or
you don't. Our research, however, suggests there is another type of attractiveness: what we call dynamic physical attractiveness.

What is dynamic attractiveness? Perhaps the Beatles song says it best . . .   2
"Something in the way she [or he] moves attracts me like no other lover . . ." In
this research we focused on how the expression of a person's personality, physical
grace, and body language impacted perceptions of who was attractive and who
was not.

The idea that people have an (expressive) style goes back to the 1930s when   3
early social/personality psychologist, Gordon Allport, claimed that people have a
consistency in how they express elements of themselves in how they walk, talk,
and even in their handwriting. We also knew from our research that people who
were emotionally expressive—people who spontaneously express emotions (particularly positive emotions) were more attractive to others. So, we set out to
examine how expressive style contributed to impressions that someone is physically attractive.

In order to look at different types of attractiveness we brought college stu-   4
dents into a lab where they were photographed and videotaped while meeting
people or while giving a short speech. We then took the photos and videos, and
by masking them, we showed only the faces, or only the bodies, and had different groups of judges rate attractiveness from only still photos of faces, bodies,
and another group focused only on the attractiveness of how they were dressed.
Other groups of judges rated different degrees of attractiveness, including how
much they liked each individual, would want to be friends with them, and how
attractive they were as a dating partner.

We were then able to statistically control for the different types of attractive-   5
ness. What we found was that in the videotaped interactions, dynamic expressive
style (measured by the person's emotional expressiveness and social skills) predicted who was rated as physically attractive over and beyond the effects of
static qualities of beauty (face, body, and dress attractiveness). We have found
that dynamic expressive style is a major component of what makes a person
(charismatic).

Marginal notes:

Before she began to read, Ofelia noted the title, author, and information about the author given in the headnote. This helped prepare her for the summary assignment.

What kind of research was done on this topic? What are the different types of attractiveness?

"Not moving"

This seems to be the main point.

So "dynamic attractiveness" means how someone talks, walks, moves, etc.?

This word is repeated. It means "conveying or giving a meaning, feeling, or thought."

The topic of this essay makes me think of all the plastic surgery that celebrities get to improve their faces when that's not really what makes people like them.

The experiment: People described how attractive others were, based on photos and videos.

So attractiveness means how much people like someone as a friend and as a romantic partner?

Repeated, so important point!

Definition: to be charming so people want to follow you.

So, what are the implications of this research?

First, personality, and the expression of personality, matters. As we all know, a person can be beautiful on the outside, but not so nice on the inside, and vice versa. Moreover, our research suggests that dynamic expressive style might compensate for lack of static physical attractiveness. In other words, there are plenty of people who are not classically beautiful or handsome, but are still very attractive to others.

Second, attractiveness can be "manipulated" to some extent. Dress, use of makeup, and keeping physically fit can affect perceptions of attractiveness. In one of our "charisma training" studies, we found that women who were trained to be better at expressing emotions and (positive) affect started to give greater concern to how they dressed and when they wore makeup, even though our training had not focused on that.

As they say, beauty is in the eye of the beholder, but attractiveness is complex, made up of both static and dynamic qualities, and both affect perceptions of attractiveness.

6 *"What's the point?!"*

7 *You don't have to be beautiful; a good personality matters.*

8 *To be more attractive: Being positive and upbeat helps. You can dress better, use makeup, exercise, etc.*

Is this related to body language?

9 *Concluding point: Beauty can be just physical appearance, but it can also be how you present yourself and your attitude toward life.*

References

Allport, G.W. & Vernon, P.E. (1933). *Studies in expressive movement*. New York: Macmillan.

Riggio, R.E., Widaman, K.F., Tucker, J.S., & Salinas, C. (1991). Beauty is more than skin deep: Components of attractiveness. *Basic and Applied Social Psychology*, 12(4), 423–439.

After she finished reading, Ofelia reviewed her annotations and discussed the essay with several classmates to make sure she understood it.

Ofelia's Choices

Ofelia freewrote about this essay and the assignment in her journal.

I think this study is interesting because everyone can learn something from it. I like that you don't have to have a beautiful face in order for someone to think you're nice looking. I can't help thinking of the cliché "you can't tell a book by its cover." I know I'll have to keep my personal thoughts out of the summary.

Ofelia's Drafting

After she freewrote about the article she needed to summarize, Ofelia wrote the following discovery draft. (Note that her draft includes the types of errors that typically appear in a first draft.)

What Makes People Attractive?

In this essay the author lets people know that there is more to beauty than your face or body. He writes about a study that he did in which they photographed and videotaped college students as they gave a short speech or met people. They then asked other people to rate the attractiveness of the college students, the results showed that people's social skills and the way they expressed themselves determined who was physically attractive. This study shows that beauty is based more on personality and personal style than on physical things.

Ofelia's Revising

Before revising her discovery draft, Ofelia reviewed the information about writing summaries contained in this chapter. She also asked her classmates to suggest how to improve the summary. She realized that she had omitted some necessary information and needed to improve the organization. (You will notice a few errors in this revised draft that Ofelia will correct when she edits her summary later on.)

What Makes People Attractive?

Ofelia gives the title, the author's name, and the main idea in the first sentence.

In Beauty Is More Than Skin Deep: The Different Types of Attractiveness, Ronald Riggio's main point is that beauty is more than just a person's face or body, beauty is more about people's personalities, physical movements, and body language. As a result, people can make themselves more attractive even if they can't change their face or their bodies.

Ofelia explains how the study was conducted, which is one of the most important supporting points.

Ofelia uses her own words to describe the study.

The main evidence for this point comes from a study that the author and his colleagues conducted in which they photographed and videotaped college students as they gave a short speech or met people. They then asked other people to rate the attractiveness of the college students, sometimes by just focusing on faces or bodies, and sometimes by looking at how they were dressed. Other people were asked to decide if they liked the college students or wanted to be friends with them or even date them. The results of the study showed that the peoples social skills and the way they expressed themselves determined who was judged as physically attractive, more than the appearance of a person's face, body, or clothing.

The results are another of the most important supporting points

In her conclusion, Ofelia restates the main idea and helps readers understand why this idea is important.

This study shows that beauty is based more on personality and personal style than on physical characteristics it also shows that people can make themselves more attractive, even if they can't change their physical looks, by focusing on how they express themselves. This is an important point because our society is so obsessed with appearances.

Ofelia's Editing

Using the Handbook in Part Four, Ofelia corrected the errors in her summary. Her corrections are noted in the margin.

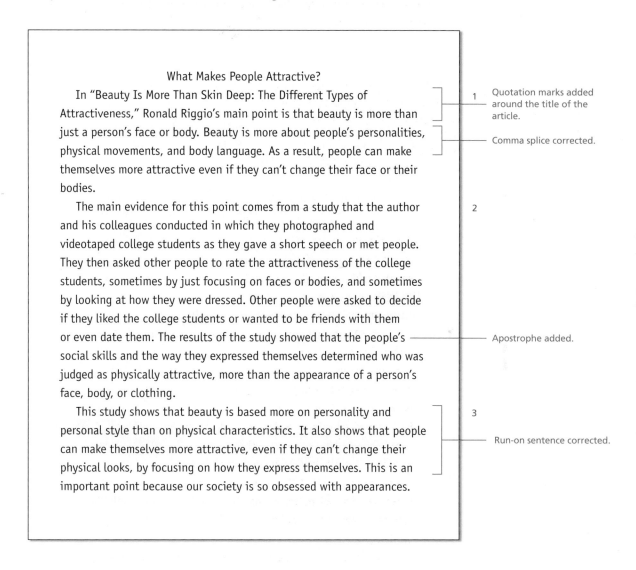

What Makes People Attractive?

In "Beauty Is More Than Skin Deep: The Different Types of Attractiveness," Ronald Riggio's main point is that beauty is more than just a person's face or body. Beauty is more about people's personalities, physical movements, and body language. As a result, people can make themselves more attractive even if they can't change their face or their bodies.

1 Quotation marks added around the title of the article.

Comma splice corrected.

The main evidence for this point comes from a study that the author and his colleagues conducted in which they photographed and videotaped college students as they gave a short speech or met people. They then asked other people to rate the attractiveness of the college students, sometimes by just focusing on faces or bodies, and sometimes by looking at how they were dressed. Other people were asked to decide if they liked the college students or wanted to be friends with them or even date them. The results of the study showed that the people's social skills and the way they expressed themselves determined who was judged as physically attractive, more than the appearance of a person's face, body, or clothing.

2

Apostrophe added.

This study shows that beauty is based more on personality and personal style than on physical characteristics. It also shows that people can make themselves more attractive, even if they can't change their physical looks, by focusing on how they express themselves. This is an important point because our society is so obsessed with appearances.

3

Run-on sentence corrected.

Ofelia's Sharing

Ofelia shared her completed summary with several classmates, and as a result they began to talk about how society's obsession with appearances can lead to unhealthy behavior.

CHAPTER CHECKLIST

❏ By reading like a writer, you can learn new techniques and express yourself more easily.

❏ Purposes for reading include gathering specific information, learning concepts, evaluating texts, and entertaining yourself.

❏ Reading for pleasure can help expand your vocabulary and show you effective writing strategies.

❏ Active reading strategies help improve your comprehension and response to the text.

  ❏ Before you read, skim the title, author, headings, subheadings, charts, lists, and illustrations. Ask general questions that you think the reading will answer.

  ❏ As you read, identify main and supporting ideas, put these ideas into your own words, ask questions, pay attention to ideas that are repeated, and look up unfamiliar words that are important.

  ❏ After you read, review your reading notes, create a concept cluster, discuss the material with others, relate it to class lectures and materials, and write a personal response to the text.

❏ A reading journal can help you read actively.

❏ A summary includes the main point, supporting points, and a conclusion.

REFLECTING ON YOUR WRITING

To help you read to improve writing, answer the following questions about the chapter:

Visit **LaunchPad Solo for Readers and Writers** > **Reading** for additional tutorials, videos, and practice with active reading—as well as sample readings with quizzes.

1. List the times when you read for information, for understanding, for evaluating, and for pleasure. How can these kinds of reading help to improve your writing?

2. What are some of the most effective strategies for reading actively?

3. What are some of the challenges of summarizing a piece of writing?

4. In your perspective, what are some of the challenges of reading? How might you overcome these challenges?

Once you answer these questions, freewrite about what you learned about the writing process and about yourself as a writer.

Crafting Paragraphs

Just as a football game is divided into quarters, an essay is divided into paragraphs. The quarters of a football game divide the game into shorter time periods so that athletes won't get overtired and spectators won't get bored or confused. Similarly, paragraphs divide information into chunks so that readers can more easily follow your ideas. Paragraphs separate the main ideas of an essay into easily understood sections. They tell your readers where one main idea ends and another begins. They also help your readers make connections between these ideas. This chapter focuses on important elements of good paragraphs: topic sentences, unity, and organization. You'll learn to write special types of paragraphs, such as introductions and conclusions. You'll also follow a student, Javier Esparza, as he uses the writing process to write a descriptive paragraph. ■

In this chapter, you will write a paragraph in which you describe an experience and explain its significance. As you work through this chapter, you will

- Compose topic sentences.
- Learn about paragraph unity and organization.
- Practice writing special kinds of paragraphs.

Writing Assignment

Imagine you are applying for an internship. You are required to submit an application form and letters of recommendation. Because your potential employer is interested in knowing something about you personally, you also have to submit a writing sample in which you describe an experience that is meaningful to you and that reveals your character.

The experience can be formal—such as an important family occasion, wedding, or birthday—or it can be a memory of a special place or a gathering of friends. Alternatively, you can select either a current or historical event that captures your attention; the point is to depict an experience that is meaningful to you. To gain inspiration, you could look through photographs that you have saved or that you find on a website or in an archive.

Write a paragraph in which you describe your chosen experience and explain what it reveals about your character. (If you choose to describe a photograph, assume that your readers do not have a copy of the photograph.) Use the writing process when you compose your paragraph. As you learned in Chapter 1, the steps in the writing process are

- exploring your choices
- drafting
- revising
- editing
- sharing

❰ Topic Sentences

When it comes to paragraphs, the phrase "one thing at a time" is useful to remember. The "one thing" you explain in a paragraph is stated in a topic sentence. To write an effective topic sentence for each paragraph in your essay, follow these guidelines:

- Break up your thesis statement into several specific supporting ideas.
- Write a complete thought for each of these specific ideas.

A topic sentence functions as a mini-thesis for each paragraph. Here are some examples of thesis statements and the topic sentences that might follow from them:

To review the characteristics of a strong thesis statement, turn to pp. 18–19.

THESIS STATEMENT   Hiking is excellent exercise because it strengthens muscles, offers a chance to enjoy nature, and relieves stress.

Topic Sentences

- Hiking provides a strenuous workout for many parts of the body, especially leg and back muscles.
- Whether in the desert or in the woods, hikers enjoy beautiful scenery and clear air.
- A hike in a beautiful area takes people completely away from the daily grind of school, family, and work.

These are effective topic sentences because they support the thesis statement that hiking is excellent exercise.

⏻ **Think of a topic sentence as a status update**

Writing a topic sentence is similar to posting a status update on Facebook or Twitter. Your update has to express your main idea in a sentence or phrase that is short, direct, and informative.

Here is another set of topic sentences that supports the thesis statement:

THESIS STATEMENT If this university continues to increase tuition year after year, it will no longer be an asset to our community.

Topic Sentences

- As a result of tuition increases, families on limited incomes will not be able to send their children to college.
- Students who have already spent several years in college—and who have invested thousands of dollars in their education—will be forced to drop out.
- High school students will lack the motivation to study because they'll feel that college costs too much.
- Companies will decide not to locate here because they won't be able to find well-educated workers.

These topic sentences are effective because they explain the negative effect that tuition increases will have on the community. Consider one more set of examples:

THESIS STATEMENT Before I moved to the United States, I lived in Japan, a very different country and culture.

Topic Sentences

- Housing is much more spacious in the United States than it is in Japan. Even small apartments in this country are large by Japanese standards.

- Americans are informal, and even strangers use first names, whereas people in Japan are reserved and formal.
- People in the United States emphasize individuality, whereas people in Japan emphasize conformity to a group.

HOW TO Write a Topic Sentence

- Write several complete thoughts that make a point about your thesis statement. These are your topic sentences.
- Check that these topic sentences tell something informative and interesting about your thesis statement.
- Check that you can add details to show or explain these topic sentences.
- Check that you are writing on the topic assigned.

GROUP ACTIVITY 1 Write Topic Sentences

With your classmates, write several topic sentences for each of the following thesis statements.

1. No two people could be more different than Matt and Jerry, but they are my two closest friends.
2. Living with your parents when you're an adult has its disadvantages, but so does living on your own.
3. Time management skills are important for students holding a full-time job while working toward a college degree.
4. Today's communications technology—from smartphones to Facebook—makes life more stressful, not more efficient.
5. Because anyone can use it, the Internet can be a dangerous place for children and adults alike.

Should your topic sentence appear at the beginning, middle, or end of the paragraph? A topic sentence can fall anywhere in the paragraph. Most often, however, it comes first. Just as placing the thesis statement at the beginning of an essay helps guide readers through the paper, putting the topic sentence at the beginning of the paragraph helps guide readers through the paragraph. To put it another way, giving the main idea at the beginning is like giving readers a hook on which to hang the details that follow.

In the following paragraph, the topic sentence (highlighted) comes first. The author, Garrison Keillor, states in the topic sentence that when he was a child, denim pants represented freedom to him. In the rest of the paragraph, he gives facts and examples to support this idea:

Thus denim came to symbolize freedom to me. My first suit was a dark brown wool pinstripe bought on the occasion of my Aunt Ruby's funeral, and I wore it to church every Sunday. It felt solemn and mournful to me. You couldn't run in a suit, you could only lumber like an old man. When church was over, and you put on denim trousers, you walked out the door into the wide green world and your cousin threw you the ball and suddenly your body was restored, you could make moves.

—**GARRISON KEILLOR**, *"Blue Magic"*

Sometimes, however, you may need to provide background information or explain the connection between two paragraphs before the topic sentence can be presented. In either case, the topic sentence may fall in the middle of the paragraph. In the following paragraph, the topic sentence (highlighted) is given after the first sentence, which explains the connection between this paragraph and the previous one:

I don't mean that some people are born clearheaded and are therefore natural writers, whereas others are naturally fuzzy and will never write well. Thinking clearly is a conscious act that writers must force upon themselves, as if they were working on any other project that requires logic: adding up a laundry list or doing an algebra problem. Good writing doesn't come naturally, though most people obviously think it does. Professional writers are constantly being bearded by strangers who say that they'd like to "try a little writing sometime"—meaning when they retire from their real profession, which is difficult, like insurance or real estate. Or they say, "I could write a book about that." I doubt it.

—**WILLIAM ZINSSER**, *"Simplicity"*

Occasionally, placing a topic sentence at the end of a paragraph can dramatize the main idea. In the following example, the topic sentence (highlighted) appears at the end. By giving several specific examples before stating the generalization, the writer emphasizes the main point of the paragraph:

Most black Americans are not poor. Most black teenagers are not crack addicts. Most black mothers are not on welfare. Indeed, in sheer numbers, more white Americans are poor and on welfare than are black. Yet one never would deduce that by watching television or reading American newspapers and magazines.

—**PATRICIA RAYBORN**, *"A Case of 'Severe Bias'"*

GROUP ACTIVITY 2 Write Topic Sentences

With your classmates, brainstorm for several minutes about a photograph. In addition to describing the photograph, jot down ideas about what the photograph means to you. Then, as a group, write topic sentences that summarize each group member's thoughts about the photograph.

(Unity 統一性

Once you have an effective topic sentence, you need to make sure that all other sentences within the paragraph relate to that topic sentence. This is called *paragraph unity*. Paragraphs that lack unity contain sentences that distract and confuse readers because they aren't on the topic. These are called *irrelevant sentences*. In the following paragraph, several irrelevant sentences have been added (in italics); notice how these irrelevancies distract you from the topic of the paragraph.

> I went to high school in the Fifties, when blue denim had gained unsavory cultural associations—it was biker and beatnik clothing, outlaw garb, a cousin to the ducktail, a symbol of Elvis, and as such, it was banned at our school. *Elvis Presley was my favorite singer at the time.* Every September, we were read the dress code by our homeroom teacher: you could wear brown denim, or grey, or green, but not blue. *Blue is my favorite color.* Why? "Because," she explained. *She lived a block away from me.* There have to be rules, and blue denim was a statement of rebellion, and we were in school to learn and not to flaunt our individuality. So there.
>
> —GARRISON KEILLOR, *"Blue Magic"*

During the drafting stage, you may include irrelevant sentences as you focus on getting your thoughts on paper. When you revise, however, you need to eliminate them to achieve paragraph unity. Reread your paragraphs and topic sentences, and delete any statements that are off the topic.

GROUP ACTIVITY 3 Improve Paragraph Unity

With your classmates, read the following sentences. Place a checkmark next to the sentences that do not relate to this topic sentence: *I had defied a direct order, but I didn't expect my dad to do anything about it.*

_____ My dad looked as if he were trying to recover from a gunshot wound.

___✗___ Gun control is a topic I would like to write about some day.

_____ His eyes fluttered and his mouth gaped. "You're saying no to me?" was all he could say.

_____ "Yeah, I'm saying no to you."

_____ I felt like a newborn colt, prancing around, kicking, testing my limits.

___✗___ Riding horses is one of my favorite hobbies.

_____ "Well, pack your bags and leave," he shouted.

_____ Uh-oh, I hadn't expected that.

___✗___ My Samsonite bag is stored on the top shelf of my closet.

_____ "Okay, I will."

◖ Organization

You must organize the ideas in your paragraphs. If you don't, your readers won't be able to follow what you're saying, they'll become frustrated, and they'll stop reading. You can use general-to-specific order, topic-illustration-explanation order, progressive order, directional order, question-and-answer order, or specific-to-general order to organize your ideas.

General-to-Specific Order

General-to-specific order is one way to organize ideas in a paragraph. Whereas general statements are broad, specific statements are more focused. For example, the statement "I love dogs" is general because it refers to all dogs. But the statement "I love my dog Rupert because he's smart, funny, and affectionate" is specific because it cites a particular dog and several details.

In general-to-specific order, the most general idea is given at the beginning of the paragraph in the topic sentence. The more specific ideas that follow help support and explain the general statement. The following paragraph illustrates this order:

> The *quinceañera*, or coming-out party, is a tradition for many young Latinas. In this ritual, parents proudly present their fifteen-year-old daughter to their community. The ceremony consists of a Mass followed by a dinner and dance. Fourteen young couples serve as the girl's court. Long formal dresses, tuxedos, live music, and video cameras are all part of the spectacle.

Topic-Illustration-Explanation Order

Topic-illustration-explanation (TIE) order is used to organize paragraphs that contain examples such as facts and expert testimony. As in general-to-specific order, the paragraph starts with a topic sentence. You can organize the paragraph in this way:

- State the topic.
- Give an illustration (such as a fact or expert testimony).
- Explain the significance of the illustration.

The topic-illustration-explanation method of organization is used in the following paragraph about an American cultural symbol—the T-shirt. Notice that the writer states the topic, gives an illustration, and then explains why the illustration is important.

> T-shirts with political or controversial statements can require the viewer to think about the message. A few years ago the slogan "A woman's place is in the House" was seen on many T-shirts. To understand this slogan, the viewer had to know the original saying, "A woman's place is in the home," and then

realize that the word *House* on the shirt referred to the House of Representatives. The House of Representatives, a part of Congress, has always had fewer female than male members. A person wearing this T-shirt, then, advocated electing more women to political office.

In this paragraph, the topic is stated in the first sentence: T-shirts with political statements may require some thought. To illustrate, the writer uses a slogan—"A woman's place is in the House"—and then explains the significance of the slogan.

Progressive Order

Another way of organizing the ideas in your paragraphs is to use *progressive order*, in which ideas are arranged from least to most important. Since the final idea in a paragraph (or in an essay, for that matter) is the one that readers tend to remember most readily, ending with the most important idea is usually very effective. Thus, rather than presenting your examples randomly, you can arrange them progressively to emphasize the most important one.

Here's another paragraph from the essay about the American T-shirt. Notice that the writer uses progressive order to illustrate the various functions that the T-shirt serves in our culture.

> The common, ordinary T-shirt tells us much about the American culture. The T-shirt is a product of our casual lifestyle. People have been known to wear T-shirts under blazers at work and under evening dresses at the Academy Awards. The T-shirt is also associated with people of all ages, from the elderly to newborn babies. Most important, the T-shirt gives us a way to express ourselves. It tells others about our favorite schools, sports teams, or cartoon figures. It can also let others know our political views—whether or not they care to know.

In this paragraph, the most important function of T-shirts is stated at the end. The writer emphasizes this function with the introductory words *most important*.

Directional Order

When you use *directional order*, you describe something from one location to another, such as left to right, down to up, or near to far.

For example, suppose you want to describe a photograph of your brother taken while he was in the army. To organize your description, you might use top-to-bottom directional order, as in the following example:

> This is my brother Antonio in his army uniform. His face is clean shaven, and his haircut is regulation style. He's smiling his big lopsided smile. He has an athletic build, like a body builder's. He wears his uniform proudly. It is perfectly pressed, and every brass button is perfectly shined. The crease in his pants is as sharp as a blade. His shoes are like black mirrors.

Question-and-Answer Order

Question-and-answer order is another method for organizing ideas in a paragraph. It involves asking a question at the beginning of the paragraph and then answering that question in the rest of the paragraph. In the following paragraph, the writer uses the question-and-answer method when discussing the causes of homelessness:

> What's the root of the homeless problem? Everyone seems to have a scapegoat: Advocates of the homeless blame government policy; politicians blame the legal system; the courts blame the bureaucratic infrastructure; the Democrats blame the Republicans; the Republicans, the Democrats. The public blames the economy, drugs, the "poverty cycle," and the "breakdown of society." With all this finger-pointing, the group most responsible for the homeless being the way they are receives the least blame. That group is the homeless themselves.
>
> —L. CHRISTOPHER AWALT, *"Brother, Don't Spare a Dime"*

Specific-to-General Order

In *specific-to-general order*, the most specific ideas are stated first, and the general idea appears at the end of the paragraph. Use this type of organization when you want to position a topic sentence at the end of a paragraph.

In the example that follows, the writer organizes ideas from the most specific to the most general:

> The audience gasps as colors explode in the night sky—red, blue, yellow, green. The explosions grow bigger and bigger until they cover the night sky, and then they slowly disintegrate like silvery rain. Although everyone enjoys

HOW TO Organize a Paragraph

- Write a **topic sentence** that states the main point of the paragraph.
- Include **supporting sentences** with details that support your topic sentence, arranged using one of these orders: general-to-specific, topic-illustration-explanation, progressive, directional, question-and-answer, or specific-to-general.
- Write a **concluding sentence** that restates the main point of the paragraph.
- Indent the first line of each paragraph by pressing the Tab key one time.
- Check that each sentence is a complete thought and ends with a period (.), question mark (?), or exclamation mark (!).

a fireworks spectacle on the Fourth of July, few understand the origin of this ritual celebration. The Fourth of July commemorates America's fight for independence, and the fireworks are to remind us of the historic battles that ended the Revolutionary War.

GROUP ACTIVITY 4 Identify Types of Organization

With your classmates, identify the type of organization in each of the following paragraphs as general-to-specific, topic-illustration-explanation (TIE), progressive, directional, question-and-answer, or specific-to-general. Some types of organization may overlap.

1. With about a half-billion passengers a year boarding scheduled U.S. flights, air travel has become so routine that it's easy for people to forget what's outside their cabin cocoon. The atmosphere at 35,000 feet won't sustain human life. It's about 60 degrees below zero, and so thin that an inactive person breathing it would become confused and lethargic in less than a minute.

   —**CONSUMER REPORTS**, *"Breathing on a Jet Plane"*

   Organization: _____

2. When you need a new car, do you go to the nearest auto dealer and buy the first car you see? Most of us don't. We shop and compare features, quality, and price. We look for the best value for our money.

   —**O. M. NICELY**, *"Using Technology to Serve You Better"*

   Organization: _____

3. When you go on a hike in the desert, the least of your worries is snakes and scorpions. If you stay away from them, they'll stay away from you. Instead of worrying about reptiles and bugs, worry about the sun. To avoid a serious burn, apply sunscreen to exposed skin and wear a hat. Most important, bring plenty of water—at least a gallon per person.

   Organization: _____

4. When many dogs hear the words "Let's go on a hike!" they can't contain their excitement. They wag their tails, jump up and down, and even bring their leashes to their owners. Most dogs love to hike, and their owners love to take them. Just as with humans, though, dogs need to be prepared for a rigorous day on the trail.

   Organization: _____

5. Almost everyone knows that smoking is bad for one's health, yet young people continue to start smoking every day. According to the National Cancer Institute, 20 percent of U.S. high school students are tobacco smokers. Experts believe that many young people take up smoking because they think it will make them look cool.

   Organization: _____

☾ Special Kinds of Paragraphs

In addition to focusing on topic sentences and paragraph unity and organization, you need to keep in mind the special requirements of two different
but important types of paragraphs: introductions and conclusions.

Introductions

First impressions are important. In a job interview, employers prefer someone who is well spoken and neatly dressed over someone who mutters and is
dressed to go to the gym. Similarly, the introduction to an essay provides
readers with a good first impression of your ideas.

In a short essay (two to three pages), the introduction usually consists of
only the first paragraph; longer essays often have introductions that are several paragraphs in length. A good introduction has three characteristics: it
gets readers' attention, narrows the topic, and states the thesis.

Get Your Readers' Attention

The technique of getting your readers' attention is often called the *hook*.
You want your introduction to grab your readers and pull them into your
essay, just as a hook lures a fish to bite on the line. In addition to getting
readers' attention, the hook contains information relevant to the topic of
your essay. A hook can consist of a question, an interesting fact, a brief story,
or a vivid image, or it can be a definition or classification of key terms to help
readers begin to understand the topic.

Pose a Question   Posing one or more *questions* at the start of an essay
can arouse readers' curiosity about your topic, making them want to read on
to find the answers. In the following introduction, the author uses a question to begin her essay about her father's heroism during World War II.

> "Who is your hero and why do you admire him?" is the question my son,
> Andy, had to answer on his application to a private school. The school's head-
> master made an eloquent speech linking the growing incidence of drug abuse,
> suicide, and violence among teenagers to the absence of heroes in contempo-
> rary life.
>
> —IRINA HREMIA BRAGIN, *"What Heroes Teach Us"*

Provide an Interesting or Surprising Fact   Introducing a topic with
facts—statements that can be verified as true—has two important effects on
readers. It signals them that you know your topic well, and it encourages
them to read further to see what you have to say. An interesting or surprising
fact can also get readers' attention, as in this essay on how to drive safely:

> The first automobile crash in the United States occurred in New York City
> in 1896, when a car collided with a bicyclist. We've had [over] 100 years since

then to learn how to share the road, but with increasingly crowded and complex traffic conditions, we're still making mistakes, mostly because we assume that other drivers—and their vehicles—will behave the way we do.

—CAROLYN GRIFFITH, *"Sharing the Road"*

Most readers would be intrigued by the date of the first car accident and would want to read more about this topic.

Tell a Story   Beginning with a *brief story* or an *anecdote* related to a topic can help draw readers into your essay because most readers like to read about other people's lives:

The Hollywood blockbuster had been playing for about 20 minutes when one of the characters took a gunshot in the face, the camera lingering on the gory close-up. Fifteen rows from the big screen, a little girl—no more than six years old—began shrieking. Her mother hissed, "Shut up," and gave her a stinging slap.

—ALVIN POUSSAINT, *"Let's Enforce Our Movie Ratings"*

In addition to getting readers' attention, this story illustrates the writer's point in his title that movie ratings need to be enforced.

Describe a Vivid Image   An introduction that contains vivid *description* sets the scene and draws readers into your essay. Because readers like to imagine scenes, a vivid image is another effective way to hook readers:

Joe Flom is the last living "named" partner of the law firm Skadden, Arps, Slate, Meagher and Flom. He has a corner office high atop the Condé Nast tower in Manhattan. He is short and slightly hunched. His head is large, framed by long prominent ears, and his narrow blue eyes are hidden by oversize aviator-style glasses. He is slender now, but during his heyday, Flom was extremely overweight. He waddles when he walks. He doodles when he thinks. He mumbles when he talks, and when he makes his way down the halls of Skadden, Arps, conversations drop to a hush.

—MALCOLM GLADWELL, *Outliers: The Story of Success*

This colorful description introduces an important character in the book.

Define a Term   Defining the meaning of a word works well in an introduction when you need to explain an unfamiliar topic for your readers.

As a lifelong crabber (that is, one who catches crabs, not a chronic complainer), I can tell you that anyone who has the patience and a great love for the river is qualified to join the ranks of crabbers. However, if you want your first crabbing experience to be a successful one, you must come prepared.

—MARY ZEIGLER, *"How to Catch Crabs"*

The writer uses definition to ensure her readers' understanding of her topic and thesis statement. Notice also that she uses humor in the definition to further engage her readers. Her thesis sentence is the last one in the paragraph.

Break the Topic into Categories   You may wish to use *classification* in an introduction when categorizing by types can help narrow your topic and focus your readers' attention on the one type discussed in your essay.

> Quick—what do you call a person who plays a trumpet? A trumpeter, of course. A person who plays the flute is referred to as a flutist, or flautist, if you prefer. Someone who plays a piano is usually known as a pianist, unless of course he plays the player piano, in which case he is known as a player piano player rather than a player piano pianist. Got the hang of this yet? Okay, then, what do you call someone who plays that set of instruments belonging to the percussion family? Why, you call him a percussionist, don't you? Wrong! It's not quite as easy as all that. There are two types of musicians who play percussion instruments, "drummers" and "percussionists," and they are as different as the Sex Pistols and the New York Philharmonic.
>
> —KAREN KRAMER, *"The Little Drummer Boys"*

The writer classifies various types of musicians before focusing attention on the essay's topic: the two types of musicians who play percussion instruments, drummers and percussionists. The writer's thesis statement comes last in the introduction.

Narrow the Topic

An introduction announces the general topic of the essay and then narrows the subject to the more specific point stated in the thesis. Just as a photographer focuses the lens on a specific object for greater clarity, a writer narrows the scope of the essay.

In the following example, the writer introduces the general topic of the earth and its environment in the first paragraph before focusing on her main point—that human beings have been endangering the earth's environment—at the end of the first paragraph and into the beginning of the second paragraph:

> The history of life on earth has been a history of interaction between living things and their surroundings. To a large extent, the physical form and the habits of the earth's vegetation and its animal life have been molded by the environment. Considering the whole span of earthly time, the opposite effect, in which life actually modifies its surroundings, has been relatively slight. Only within the moment of time represented by the present century has one species—man—acquired significant power to alter the nature of his world.
>
> During the past quarter century this power has not only increased to one of disturbing magnitude but it has changed in character. The most alarming of all man's assaults upon the environment is the contamination of air, earth, rivers, and sea with dangerous and even lethal materials.
>
> —RACHEL CARSON, *"The Obligation to Endure"*

By gradually narrowing her topic, Carson prepares her readers for her thesis statement (highlighted) that human contamination is damaging the environment.

State the Thesis

For more information about thesis statements, turn to pp. 18–19.

After getting your readers' attention and narrowing the topic, you're ready to state your thesis. Generally, the thesis appears at the end of the introduction; depending on the length and complexity of the essay, it can range from one sentence to several sentences long. As you read in Chapter 1, the thesis of an essay states the topic; shows, explains, or argues a particular point about the topic; and gives readers a sense of what the essay will be about.

In the following introduction, notice how the writer attracts readers' attention, narrows her topic, and then states her thesis (highlighted):

> People love to ask kids the question, "What do you want to be when you grow up?" . . . When we are grown up and the question comes, we are expected to know where we are going to be or at least have a plan in place to get us where we want to go. But what if we don't? What if we are stable, successful and happy, but don't know exactly where we are going or how we are going to get there? Is that OK? The truth is that the answer, no matter how old you are, is still, at best, a guess.
>
> —**WHITNEY CAUDILL**, *"The Best Careers Are Not Planned"*

HOW TO Write an Introduction

- Use a hook—such as a question, an interesting fact, a brief story, a vivid image or description, a definition, or a classification—to get readers' attention.
- Narrow the topic to one main point.
- Write a thesis statement.

GROUP ACTIVITY 5 Unscramble an Introduction

The following sentences are from the introduction of an essay about a young college student's reaction to the birth of his child. The sentences are out of order. With several other classmates, put the paragraph into the best order.

_____ I thought I would have to give up my dream of graduating from college in four years.

_____ When I discovered I was going to be a father at age nineteen, I thought my life was over.

_____ Now, however, I can't imagine my life without my daughter.

_____ Instead, I would need to find a full-time job to support my new family.

_____ She has taught me that despite the responsibilities of parenthood, the joy and love make it worthwhile.

_____ In fact, I thought I would have to give up going to college altogether.

Conclusions

Often the last thing people read is what they remember the most. Therefore, your conclusion needs to be well written and memorable. The standard way to end an essay is to restate your thesis, summarize your major points, or broaden your focus.

Restate the Thesis

By restating your thesis, you ensure that your readers remember your main point. However, don't use the same words you used in your introduction. Instead, vary your word choice so that your main point isn't unnecessarily repetitive. The restated thesis can appear at either the beginning or the end of the conclusion.

STATEMENT OF THESIS IN INTRODUCTION	If we make it a point to be considerate of all the occupants of our roadways, from cars and trucks to motorcycles and pedestrians, we can make our streets much safer places to be.
RESTATEMENT OF THESIS (ITALICIZED) IN CONCLUSION	But no matter how much time elapses, the basic principles of sharing the road safely won't change much. Just watch out for *the big guys, cut the little guys some slack, pay attention to "vehicular diversity,"* and above all, enjoy the ride.

—CAROLYN GRIFFITH, *"Sharing the Road"*

By varying her word choice, Griffith restates her thesis in an interesting way.

Often, an *effective quotation* can restate your thesis in an interesting, attention-getting way that emphasizes your main point. In the conclusion to an essay on increased life expectancy, Gregg Easterbrook ends with a startling quotation that reinforces his main point that we can't be sure what will happen with longer life spans.

Regardless of where increasing life expectancy leads, the direction will be into the unknown—for society and for the natural world. Felipe Sierra, the researcher at the National Institute on Aging, puts it this way: "The human ethical belief that death should be postponed as long as possible does not exist in nature—from which we are now, in any case, diverging."

—GREGG EASTERBROOK, *"What Happens When We All Live to 100?"*

Summarize Your Points

For a lengthy and complex essay, a *summary* can pull ideas together and reinforce main points in the conclusion. The author of an essay on the New England clambake summarizes her important points about the clambake in her conclusion:

A clambake may remind you of Boston and Paul Revere's ride, but to ensure a successful meal, remember these important points: start early, dig a pit that is at least two feet deep, feed the charcoal fire with hardwood, and use seaweed-soaked canvas. While your clams are cooking, get out the iced tea and beer and enjoy playing volleyball or strolling along the beach while taking part in this cherished New England tradition.

Broaden the Focus

In your introduction, you state the general topic and then narrow your focus until you give the thesis statement. In the conclusion, however, you want to broaden your focus—widen the lens of the camera—to tell your readers how your main point connects to other important ideas.

In the conclusion to her essay on illegal immigrants, Linda Chavez broadens the focus of her argument by pointing out that the immigration question is about more than whether or not to grant amnesty—it's about supporting values that are important to all of us:

> The fact that so many illegal immigrants are intertwined with American citizens or legal residents, either as spouses or parents, should give pause to those who'd like to see all illegal immigrants rounded up and deported or their lives made so miserable they leave on their own. A better approach would allow those who have made their lives here, established families, bought homes, worked continuously and paid taxes to remain after paying fines, demonstrating English fluency and proving they have no criminal record. Such an approach is as much about supporting family values as it is granting amnesty.
>
> —LINDA CHAVEZ, *"Supporting Family Values"*

Chavez's final sentence invites readers to think about the immigration question in a deeper way.

In the following example from an article about the popularity of collecting baseball cards, the writer concludes with a call for action by asking readers to consider joining a baseball card club:

> After collecting baseball cards for several years, our greatest desire is to start a baseball card club in Los Angeles. If you would be interested in joining such a club, write to the above address with a note, "Count me in!"

HOW TO Write a Conclusion

- Restate the thesis to remind readers of your main point.
- Sum up what has been said in the essay.
- Broaden the focus or make an additional observation about your main point.

GROUP ACTIVITY 6 Unscramble a Conclusion

The following sentences are from the essay about a young college student's reaction to the birth of his child. The sentences are out of order. With a group of your classmates, put the sentences in the best order.

_____ Because of her, I get angry when I hear people talk about how bad it is when young people have children.

_____ In fact, for some people, it's the best thing that can ever happen to them.

_____ It's not always bad.

_____ My daughter has improved my life in many ways, from making me more responsible to teaching me what love really means.

From a Paragraph to an Essay

Have you noticed that most writers don't write just one paragraph, but instead combine these various types of paragraphs into a longer piece of writing such as an essay? An essay is a short piece of prose, composed of multiple paragraphs, that focuses on and develops one point or thesis. The parts of an essay are similar to the parts of a paragraph:

Paragraph	**Essay**
• Topic sentence	▪ Thesis statement
• Supporting sentences	▪ Supporting paragraphs
• Concluding sentence	▪ Concluding paragraph

As you learned earlier in this chapter, the first paragraph of an essay, or *introduction*, grabs readers' attention and reveals the topic of the essay. The main idea of the essay is included in a *thesis statement*, which usually appears near the end of the introduction. Supporting paragraphs explain ideas related to the main idea. The last paragraph, or *conclusion*, summarizes or restates the main idea. The number of paragraphs in the essay varies, depending on the topic, purpose, and audience. Some essays will be short, with just three

HOW TO Organize an Essay

- *Introduction:* Hook readers, give background information, and state the thesis.
- *Body Paragraphs:* Give the main point of each paragraph in a topic sentence. Use details, facts, and examples to support each topic sentence.
- *Conclusion:* Refer back to the thesis. Explain the importance of the subject.

to five paragraphs, while others that must explain more complex topics will have many more. You will have the opportunity to write essays, using all of the types of paragraphs, in Part Two of this textbook.

◖ A Student's Paragraph

As you recall, the writing assignment for this chapter is to write a paragraph for part of an internship application in which you describe an experience and explain what it reveals about your character. On the following pages, you'll follow Javier Esparza, a student writer, as he writes his paragraph for this assignment. Use Javier's writing process as a guide to writing your own paragraph.

Javier's Choices

In his journal, Javier freewrote about the assignment:

> I thought it would be easy to pick an experience to write about. I guess I didn't realize a big part of this application is finding an experience that really demonstrates my character. Should I write about my trip to Mexico? How my family celebrates Christmas? My younger sister? Then I saw it. On the floor was a stack of newspapers, and on the front page of one of them, there was a picture of a Ft. Bliss soldier getting ready to leave for Afghanistan. He looked so fearless, and I knew then that I had to write about when I left for the Air Force, since it was such an emotional time. It definitely brought out my character traits.

Javier's Drafting

After referring to his freewriting, Javier wrote the following discovery draft. (Note that the example includes the types of errors that typically appear in a first draft.)

> As the escalator slowly lifted me up towards the chaos of the airport, I looked back at my family and smiled. I probably looked silly, as I waved down to my family. I had struggled internally with my decision to join the Air Force since the day I walked into the recruiters office. Being young and impressionable and desiring to travel and to aleviate some of the financial burden that college tuition puts on a lower-middle class family, had made my choice quite easy. Yet, I could not help but feel guilty over me for leaving my loved ones behind, I was determined to finish what I had begun and to represent my family proudly, no matter what challenges lay ahead for me.

Javier's Revising

Javier read his paragraph aloud to several classmates so that they could give him suggestions for revision. Because his classmates were confused about what this experience revealed about his character, Javier decided to begin his paragraph with a topic sentence that would make it clear how the experience revealed his character; the topic sentence would then be supported by the rest of the paragraph. His classmates also suggested that Javier restate the importance of this experience in his concluding sentence.

Here is Javier's revised draft. (Because he focused on getting down his ideas, you may spot editing errors he will still need to correct.)

Leaving

The day I left for the Air Force demonstrates that I am a self-reflective person who is in tune with his surroundings. As the escalator slowly lifted me up towards the familiar chaos of airport security, the annoying metal detectors, and crowded airplane seats, I looked back at my family and mustered the most courageous smile that I could. I probably looked silly, as I waved down to my mother, father, sister, brother, and even a few of my cousins who had come to see me off. I had struggled internally with my decision to join the Air Force since the day I walked into the recruiters office. Being young and impressionable and desiring to travel and to aleviate some of the financial burden that college tuition puts on a lower-middle class family had made my choice quite easy. Yet, as I boarded the plane, I could not help but feel a shadow of guilt looming over me for leaving my loved ones behind, I was determined to finish what I had begun and represent my family proudly, no matter what challenges lay ahead for me. The various feelings I had on this day show how much I value family, challenges, and hard work, and how these are the driving forces behind all of my actions.

Javier added a title.

Javier added a topic sentence.

Added details help readers visualize the scene.

Repetition of topic sentence emphasizes Javier's point.

Javier's Editing

To help him edit his paragraph, Javier went to his college's writing center. He also used the spell-check on his word-processing program.

Here is Javier's edited paragraph. (The underlining indicates where he corrected errors during the editing stage.)

Leaving

The day I left for the Air Force clearly demonstrates that I am a self-reflective person who is constantly assessing his surroundings. As the escalator slowly lifted me up towards the familiar chaos of airport

Apostrophe added. ——

Spelling error corrected. ——

Comma splice fixed. ——

security, the annoying metal detectors, and crowded airplane seats, I looked back at my family and mustered the most courageous smile that I could. I probably looked silly, as I waved down to my mother, father, sister, brother, and even a few of my cousins who had come to see me off. I had struggled internally with my decision to join the Air Force since the day I walked into the recruiter's office. Being young and impressionable and desiring to travel and to alleviate some of the financial burden that college tuition puts on a lower-middle class family had made my choice quite easy. Yet, as I boarded the plane, I could not help but feel a shadow of guilt looming over me for leaving my loved ones behind, but I was determined to finish what I had begun and represent my family proudly, no matter what challenges lay ahead for me. The various feelings I had on this day show how much I value family, challenges, and hard work, and how these are the driving forces behind all of my actions.

Javier's Sharing

In a journal entry, Javier explained how he shared his paragraph:

> When I revised my paragraph, I made it more interesting to read. I read my revised paragraph aloud to my group. They told me that I really captured the details and emotion of leaving my family. They too could see how this experience demonstrated my character traits. Then I turned the paragraph in to my teacher for a grade.

CHAPTER CHECKLIST

❑ Remember the phrase "one thing at a time" when you write paragraphs. The "one thing" you explain in each paragraph is stated in the topic sentence.

❑ Write effective topic sentences by breaking down your thesis statement into several specific supporting ideas. Then write a complete thought for each specific idea.

❑ Maintain paragraph unity by sticking to the topic introduced in your topic sentence.

❑ Organize the ideas in your paragraphs by using

   ❑ general-to-specific order.

   ❑ topic-illustration-explanation (TIE) order.

   ❑ progressive order.

   ❑ directional order.

   ❑ question-and-answer order.

   ❑ specific-to-general order.

❑ In your introduction, get the readers' attention, narrow the topic, and state the thesis.

❑ In your conclusion, restate the thesis, summarize your points, and broaden the focus.

REFLECTING ON YOUR WRITING

To help you reflect on the writing you did in this chapter, answer the following questions.

1. In your description of an experience that reveals your character, which step of the writing process (exploring choices, drafting, revising, editing, and sharing) did you find the easiest to do? Which was most difficult? Why?

2. What pleases you most about your paragraph?

3. If you had more time, what parts of your paragraph would you continue to revise?

Once you answer these questions, freewrite about what you learned about the writing process and about yourself as a writer.

Visit **LaunchPad Solo for Readers and Writers** > Reading > **Topic Sentences and Supporting Details** for more tutorials, videos, and practice with crafting paragraphs.

The Patterns of Development

Suppose you visit one of your favorite websites and find words scattered randomly over the screen. Photos and artwork are upside down or obscured by blotches of color. Incomprehensible music blares out from your speakers. The website has no order. You don't know what to look at first, and you can't understand what message is being conveyed. Similarly, an essay that lacks order will confuse and frustrate readers, who won't be able to understand the connection between your ideas or the main point you're trying to make.

As you learned in Chapter 1, when you write an essay, you write a thesis statement that focuses on your main point, and you organize, in a logical order, the paragraphs that support that thesis statement. And, as you learned in Chapter 3, each of these paragraphs contains a topic sentence that focuses on the main point of the paragraph. In this chapter, you will learn how to use different patterns of development to expand and structure your thoughts within those paragraphs and across the essay as a whole. Essays usually contain several patterns, but one pattern may be dominant. Using different patterns of development enables you to

- increase interest in your topic.
- communicate your thoughts clearly to your readers.
- support your main ideas.

> **In this chapter, you will write a brief essay on a topic of your choice. As you work on your essay, you will**
>
> - Learn about the patterns of development: description, narration, examples, process explanation, classification, definition, comparison and contrast, cause and effect, and argument.
> - Practice using each of these patterns of development.
> - Follow one student through the process of using the patterns to develop an essay.

In this chapter, you'll practice using each of the patterns of development and then follow a student writer, Carlos Montijo, as he uses some of them to develop an essay. ■

Writing Assignment

Write a practice essay for your classmates in which you take a position on a topic of importance to you. You may choose the topic and the audience, but it should be a topic that everyone is talking about, on which people have differing opinions, and on which you would like to present your views. To find such a topic, read through some online newspapers, magazines, or blogs to find current issues, such as the effects of a toxic oil spill or the need for college students to vote in a local election.

Use the steps of the writing process that you learned in Chapter 1— exploring your choices, drafting, revising, editing, and sharing—when composing your essay. Support your points by using some of the patterns of development described in the pages that follow.

◖ Description

When you use description in your writing, you allow your readers to become more involved. The key is to go beyond describing experiences in general ways ("We had a great time; that day really changed me.") to describing them in enough detail that your readers relive those moments with you.

Notice how one writer, Benjamin Alire Sáenz, improves the following sentences from his short story "Cebolleros" by adding description in the revised version:

Original

He was getting good grades in everything except chemistry. And the teacher hated him. His brother wrote to him and told him to calm down, told him everything would be all right.

Revised

He was getting good grades in everything except chemistry. If he didn't pass, he'd have to go to summer school because it was a required course. All those good grades, and it had come down to this. He was a borderline student in that class and he knew it, but there wasn't any time. There wasn't any time.

And the teacher hated him. He could feel the teacher's hatred, the blue-eyed wrestling coach who favored athletes and nice-looking girls.

His brother wrote to him and told him to calm down, told him everything would be all right. "Just graduate and go to college. Do whatever it takes, just don't join the Army."

To use description, start with a general statement and then add details to make it more specific. Use these questions:

- Who is involved?
- What happens?
- When and where does it happen?
- Why does it happen?
- How does it happen?

Here's an example of a general statement to which detailed observations have been added:

Original

My cousin's wedding was really beautiful.

Revised

My cousin Veronica's wedding took place in the flower garden of Haven Park on a sunny June day. Veronica and Samuel took their vows surrounded by red, pink, and yellow roses. In addition to the three bridesmaids and the best man, there was a ring bearer—my four-year-old son, Jason. I've never seen Jason smile so much. Other family members were both smiling and crying. My aunt Liz had tears streaming down her face as she watched Veronica and Sam walk through the garden arm in arm. Even my uncle Albert, usually so stern, had tears in his eyes.

GROUP ACTIVITY 1 Use Description

With several classmates, add description to make the following paragraphs more interesting and vivid. Use the journalist's questions: Who? What? When? Where? Why? How?

1. The first time I baby-sat for my brother's children was a disaster. One of them kept throwing things around. The other one wouldn't stop crying. I was relieved when my brother and his wife returned home.

2. I was so happy when the Little League team I coach won the city tournament. The final play was very suspenseful. The score was tied. The parents were probably more nervous than the players. But no one could have been happier than the kids when they won.

3. One of my favorite pastimes is backpacking in the mountains. I love the fresh air and the scenery. At night, my friends and I lie awake and look up at the stars. One night, we even saw a shooting star.

Narration

Narration is writing that tells a story that is based on either fact or fiction. You use narration when you want to develop ideas by relating a series of events. In most cases, you will organize events in chronological order. Occasionally, however, you might use a flashback. You might also use dialogue to make a narrative more immediate and real.

Chronological Order

Generally, stories are told in the order in which they actually happened, called *chronological order*. Imagine that you want to narrate a story about your family's tradition of taking a family photograph at the start of every new year. Here's how you might organize a narrative paragraph in chronological order:

> On picture-taking day, we all rush around trying to get ourselves to look as good as possible for the camera. In the bathroom, my mother puts makeup on my stepfather's nose to hide the redness caused by a cold. When they emerge from the bathroom, my stepsister announces that she refuses to be in the picture because her hair is too puffy. Then my brother rushes into the kitchen to clean up the grape juice he spilled on his shirt, while I look through the cupboards in the utility room for shoelaces. Finally, we're ready to make our trip to the photographer's studio.

Notice how the sentences in the paragraph are arranged in the order in which the events of the story occurred. This gives readers a sense of the flow of the events in the story.

Flashback

An alternative way to organize a narrative is to use a *flashback*: you begin the story in the middle, flash back to the beginning, and then resume telling the story in the middle again. You often see this technique used in movies: the picture becomes fuzzy, and a scene from an earlier time appears. The flashback technique is useful when you want to contrast then and now or highlight a key scene. Here's how the paragraph about the picture-taking ritual might be organized using the flashback technique:

> In the photograph, my family appears calm and relaxed. Our hair is perfectly combed, and our clothes are neatly pressed. The expressions on our faces seem calm and happy. But as I stare at the photograph, I recall the chaos that preceded the snap of the camera. My stepfather had such a terrible cold that my mother had to put makeup on his nose to cover the redness. My stepsister didn't want to be in the picture because her hair was too puffy. My brother had spilled grape juice on his shirt, and I had broken my shoelace. To

make matters worse, we had a flat tire going to the studio. But when I look at this photograph, I know it was all worthwhile.

Dialogue

In a narration, *dialogue* consists of the actual words that people say, indicated by quotation marks. Use dialogue when you want to highlight an important scene or portray a certain person through his or her own words.

Dialogue can make a narration more interesting and fast paced. Consider this narrative paragraph:

> I couldn't have survived my first semester in college without my roommate, Lisa. She encouraged me to study harder, helped me find a job, and introduced me to new friends. One night, while I was studying for my calculus exam, I became so frustrated I yelled and threw the calculus book across the room. Lisa comforted me. That's the kind of roommate she was.

Here's the same paragraph, expanded to five paragraphs to include dialogue. Notice that the dialogue makes the scene more vivid.

> I couldn't have survived my first semester in college without my roommate, Lisa. She encouraged me to study harder, helped me find a job, and introduced me to new friends. One night, while I was studying for my calculus exam, I became so frustrated that I yelled as loud as I could, "I can't take it anymore!" and threw the calculus book across the room.
>
> Lisa, who was studying for her psychology exam, looked up at me from across the room. "What's wrong with you?"
>
> "I can't do this! I know I'm going to flunk!"
>
> "Calm down," she said, putting her book down. "Let me see if I can help." She spent the next hour explaining the problems to me.
>
> That's the kind of roommate she was.

WRITING ACTIVITY 1 Practice Narration

Write a paragraph in which you use narration to describe a scene that took place in one of your favorite movies or television shows. Relate the events in chronological order. If there was a flashback within the scene, describe that as well. Wherever possible, include some of the actual dialogue spoken by the actors. Read your paragraph aloud to your classmates, and listen to their paragraphs to develop your ear for narration.

Examples

In writing, examples are used to clarify, explain, and support ideas. Two of the most common types of examples are facts and expert testimony.

Facts

Facts provide support for your ideas. Unlike opinions or guesses, facts are statements that can be objectively verified as true. For example, the statement "Golden retrievers are beautiful" represents the opinion of the writer. In contrast, the statement "A golden retriever is a breed of dog" is a fact that can be verified in an encyclopedia or some other reliable source. Facts may include names, dates, numbers, statistics, and other data relevant to your topic or idea. Notice in the following paragraph that facts are used to support the idea that Asian Americans are very diverse:

> Asian Americans are an especially diverse group, composed of Chinese, Filipino, Japanese, Vietnamese, Cambodians, Hmong, and other groups. The largest Asian American groups are Chinese Americans (24 percent), Filipino Americans (20 percent), and Japanese Americans (12 percent). Other groups, such as Vietnamese, Cambodians, Laotians, and Hmong, are more recent arrivals, first coming to this country in the 1970s as refugees from the upheavals resulting from the Vietnam War. In the 1980s, Koreans and Filipinos began immigrating in larger numbers. The majority of Asian Americans live in the West.
>
> —BRYAN STRONG AND CHRISTINE DEVAULT,
> *The Marriage and Family Experience*

 Research facts on Wikipedia

Google the search term "researching with Wikipedia." What does the Wikipedia site say about using its entries for academic research? Is it a good idea? Why or why not? How will you use Wikipedia?

Expert Testimony

Statements made by knowledgeable people are considered *expert testimony*. Examples supported by expert testimony make your writing more convincing. For example, citing the surgeon general's warning that cigarette smoking greatly increases your risk of lung cancer is more convincing than offering the statement without support or citing someone with no medical background or authority to advise American citizens on health matters.

In the following paragraph, an author writing an article about how cooking has become an expensive hobby uses expert testimony to develop her point that the amount of time people spend cooking and preparing meals has dropped dramatically during the past century:

> When my grandmother was growing up in the 1920s, the average woman spent about 30 hours a week preparing food and cleaning up. By the 1950s, when she was raising her family, that number had fallen to about 20 hours a week. Now, according to the U.S. Department of Agriculture, women average

just 5.5 hours—and those who are employed, like me, spend less than 4.4 hours a week. And that's not because men are picking up the slack; they log a paltry 15 minutes a day doing kitchen work. One market-research firm, the NPD Group, says that even in the 1980s, 72 percent of meals eaten at home involved an entrée cooked from scratch; now just 59 percent of them do, and the average number of food items used per meal has decreased from 4.4 to 3.5. That's when we're home at all: by 1995, we consumed more than a quarter of all meals and snacks outside the home, up from 16 percent two decades earlier.

—**MEGAN McARDLE**, *"The Joy of Not Cooking"*

WRITING ACTIVITY 2 Find Examples

Using the practice essay topic you chose for this chapter's writing assignment, find several facts and at least one piece of expert testimony to support your opinion. To do this, you may need to do some research: interview people with experience on your topic or read what others have written about it. Read your facts and expert testimony to your classmates, asking them what more they would like to know about your topic.

Process Explanation

Writers use a technique called *process explanation* to explain how something works or how to do something. Cookbooks and repair manuals come to mind when we think of process explanation writing, but booksellers' websites are filled with all sorts of other "how to" books explaining processes— from how to microbrew beer to how to arrange your closet.

In a paragraph about your favorite hiking trail, for instance, you might explain the process of preparing to hike the trail and locating the trailhead, as Laurence Parent does in the following paragraphs about hiking to Wheeler Peak in New Mexico:

Be sure to get a very early start on this hike. To minimize problems with storms, you ideally want to be on the summit before noon. Snow flurries are possible even in mid-summer. Be sure to take rain gear and extra-warm clothing. Lightning and hypothermia are real threats on Wheeler Peak and the exposed summit ridge.

At just short of one mile you will pass marked Trail 63, the Long Canyon Trail to Gold Hill, coming in from the left. Ignore it and continue climbing up the northeast valley. Just past the trail junction, the trail hits an old road. Turn left onto the road and follow it the rest of the way up the valley.

—**LAURENCE PARENT**, *The Hiker's Guide to New Mexico*

In process writing, it is important to use transitions and to present each step in the process clearly so that your readers can follow along with you.

Classification 分类 区/分

Writers use *classification* to organize their ideas and thus to aid their readers' understanding of those ideas. When you classify, you categorize something into types on some particular basis. For example, you might classify cars on the basis of their type or size (sports car, SUV, compact, midsize, and full size) or on the basis of their country of origin (Volvos and Saabs from Sweden, Hyundais and Kias from Korea). You might also classify cars on the basis of their resale value, safety record, popularity as indicated by sales, or some other basis you deem important.

In the following paragraph about her job as a store clerk in the women's clothing department at Walmart, Barbara Ehrenreich classifies women's clothing first by style and then by type of item:

> Moving clockwise, we encounter the determinedly sexless Russ and Bobbie Brooks lines, seemingly aimed at pudgy fourth-grade teachers with important barbecues to attend. Then, after the sturdy White Stag, come the breezy, revealing Faded Glory, No Boundaries and Jordache collections, designed for the younger and thinner crowd. Tucked throughout are nests of the lesser brands, such as Athletic Works, Basic Equipment, and the whimsical Looney Tunes, Pooh, and Mickey lines, generally decorated with images of their eponymous characters. Within each brand-name area, there are of course dozens of items, even dozens of each kind of item. This summer, for example, pants may be capri, classic, carpenter, clam-digger, boot, or flood, depending on their length and cut, and I'm probably leaving a few categories out.
>
> —**BARBARA EHRENREICH**, *Nickel and Dimed: On (Not) Getting By in America*

 Electronic file classification

Think about the classification systems you have created when arranging your music files on iTunes or sorting your photo boards on Pinterest. What are some of the different classifications you have used? Why did you choose to classify this way?

 GROUP ACTIVITY 2 Use the Patterns

Following are several topic sentences. For each one, decide with your group whether you will use narration, examples, process explanation, or classification as the primary method of development. Then use that method to develop the topic sentence into a brief paragraph.

1. With the right tools, it's easy to change a flat tire.

    Primary method of development: _____

2. Rock music can be divided into various categories.

   Primary method of development: _____

3. I'll never forget the first time I tried to drive a car.

   Primary method of development: _____

4. The music on my iPod illustrates the different parts of my personality.

   Primary method of development: _____

◖ Definition

Writers use *definition* to explain and clarify. Thus, when you define something, you tell your readers what it means. A good definition has two parts: first the term being defined is placed in a general category, and then an explanation of how it fits within that category (a discussion of its distinguishing features) follows. For example, to define the term *skydiving*, you might first define it generally as a risky sport and then explain what distinguishes skydiving from other risky sports, such as rock climbing and hang gliding.

In the following paragraph, the writer defines the Khan Academy, the online learning tool that has changed the way students learn math and science in schools. He begins by defining the topic generally as an education website, before pointing out its distinguishing feature: it focuses on math, science, and economics education.

> Khan Academy is an education website that, as its tagline puts it, aims to let anyone "learn almost anything—for free." Students, or anyone interested enough to surf by, can watch some 2,400 videos in which the site's founder, Salman Khan, chattily discusses principles of math, science, and economics (with a smattering of social science topics thrown in).
>
> —**CLIVE THOMPSON**, *"The New Way to Be a Fifth Grader:*
> *How Khan Academy Is Changing the Rules of Education"*

▍ WRITING ACTIVITY 3 Practice Definition ▍

Using the essay topic you chose for this chapter's writing assignment, define one key word that will help your readers understand your topic. For example, if you chose to write on a toxic oil spill, you might define the word *dispersant*, explaining how the word is used to describe the action taken to remedy the effects of the oil spill. Read your definition aloud to your classmates, and listen to their definitions. Create a vocabulary list of the words that are new to you.

For more information and practice on building your vocabulary, see pp. 469–73.

❰ Comparison and Contrast

When you *compare*, you identify the similarities between two or more things; when you *contrast*, you identify the differences between things. Sometimes the focus is on one or the other, but at other times both similarities and differences are included.

Writers use comparison and contrast to clarify relationships. How are people, places, or ideas alike? How are they different? For example, in the following paragraph, the author writes about the voluntary separation between black and white students at his high school. He contrasts the distance he now feels from his black friend with the closeness he felt when they were younger:

> Ten years ago, we played catch in our backyards, went bike riding, and slept over at one another's houses. By the fifth grade, we went to movies and amusement parks, and bunked together at the same summer camps. We met while playing on the same Little League team, though we attended different grade schools. We're both juniors now at the same high school. We usually don't say anything when we see each other, except maybe a polite "Hi" or "Hey." I can't remember the last time we talked on the phone, much less got together outside of school.
>
> —**BRIAN JARVIS**, *"Against the Great Divide"*

When you write a comparison, you can order your ideas point by point or subject by subject. Point-by-point organization means that you explain two topics according to points of comparison. For instance, you can compare two coworkers by examining their work habits, personalities, and professionalism. Each section in the body of the essay focuses on one of the points.

First section: work habits
    Explain work habits of coworker 1
    Explain work habits of coworker 2 (how they are similar to or different
        from those of coworker 1)
Second section: personalities
    Explain personality of coworker 1
    Explain personality of coworker 2 (how it is similar to or different from
        that of coworker 1)
Third section: professionalism
    Explain professionalism of coworker 1
    Explain professionalism of coworker 2 (how it is similar to or different
        from that of coworker 1)

Alternatively, you can organize your ideas subject by subject; each coworker is discussed only once in the body of the essay.

First section: coworker 1
    Work habits, personality, professionalism
Second section: coworker 2
    Work habits, personality, professionalism

> ◖ **GROUP ACTIVITY 3** Find Similar Subjects for Comparison ◗

Work with your classmates on the following list of subjects. For each main subject, identify three similar subjects that could be used to make a comparison.

EXAMPLE: SUBJECT Ford Explorer

SIMILAR SUBJECTS _____ *Cadillac Escalade, Lincoln MKX, Nissan Murano* _____

1. Subject: The movie *X-Men: Days of Future Past*

   Similar subjects: _____

   _____

2. Subject: McDonald's

   Similar subjects: _____

3. Subject: Buffalo wings

   Similar subjects: _____

4. Subject: Walmart

   Similar subjects: _____

◖ Cause and Effect

When you use *cause and effect*, you explain why something happened (the cause) and what the result of it was (the effect). Writers use cause and effect to show a necessary or logical connection between two things. It is not enough to say that two things happened at the same time. For example, if a freeze ruins the orange crop and orange prices go up, that's cause and effect. If there also happens to be a full moon on the night of the freeze, that's a coincidence. It is the freeze, not the full moon, that ruins the crop.

In the following paragraph, the author explains her reactions to her daughter getting her driver's license. She shows a clear and logical connection between the cause (her daughter getting her license) and the effect (feeling fearful and unnecessary).

> In a primitive part of my parental mind, I figured that I would pick her up from school . . . well, if not forever, then at least until graduation. And then suddenly, she got her license. I was obsolete. Just like that! It took my breath away. Our old Volvo, long stationed like a stalwart in front of the house, was now her car. A hundred other things changed then, too, the most terrifying of which has been familiar to parents since the advent of the automobile. . . . My daughter was out driving at night. I had two strategies for coping with that development: text messaging (some evenings) and Ambien (others).
>
> —**ANN PACKER**, *"Life Lessons"*

WRITING ACTIVITY 4 Use Cause and Effect

Using the practice essay topic you chose for this chapter's writing assignment, write a paragraph in which you explain why something happened (the cause) and what the result of it was (the effect). Read your cause-and-effect paragraph to your classmates, asking them if you've demonstrated a logical connection between the cause and the effect.

Argument

For more strategies on developing argument, see pp. 291–99.

When you make an *argument*, you try to persuade readers to change their perspectives or alter their behavior in some way. In an essay that uses argument, the thesis statement contains the *claim*, or your argumentative point. The rest of the paragraphs contain *reasons* and *evidence* that justify the claim.

In the following paragraphs, an advocacy group uses reasons and evidence to support the claim that mining and drilling in public lands need to be reduced.

> Protecting our public lands from mining and drilling will safeguard America's natural heritage, preserve wildlife habitat, help keep our air and water clean, and combat climate disruption. Development currently proposed on our public lands by coal, oil, and gas companies would release more than 100 billion tons of carbon pollution into the atmosphere, worsening climate disruption. We need to keep these dirty fossil fuels in the ground.
>
> The vast majority of America's public lands remains highly vulnerable to threats from mining, drilling, fracking, and other forms of fossil-fuel extraction. Protecting land and water will preserve landscapes and wildlife habitat and keep our air and water clean, it will also stimulate nearby local economies and create jobs. Increasingly, recreation is replacing fossil-fuel extraction as an economic driver on America's public lands. The outdoor recreation economy generates $646 billion each year and supports 6.5 million jobs. These numbers will continue to grow if we keep our public lands and waters unsullied.
>
> —THE SIERRA CLUB, *"Keeping Dirty Fuels in the Ground"*

WRITING ACTIVITY 5 Practice Argument

Using the essay topic you chose for this chapter's writing assignment, write a preliminary thesis statement that contains the argumentative claim that supports your position. List three pieces of evidence that support your argument.

GROUP ACTIVITY 4 Use the Patterns

Following are several topic sentences. For each one, decide with your group whether you will use definition, comparison and contrast, cause and effect, or argument as the primary method of development. Then use that method to develop the topic sentence into a brief paragraph.

1. The meaning of *love* differs from person to person.

   Primary method of development: _____

2. Since the implementation of the TV rating system, violence in children's programming has decreased.

   Primary method of development: _____

3. Cheerleading is a sport in its own right, not just a peppy sideshow for a football game.

   Primary method of development: _____

4. Both my boss and my best friend are total introverts.

   Primary method of development: _____

HOW TO Use the Patterns of Development

- Use **description** when you want to make your writing more interesting and vivid.
- Add **narration** when you want to relate a series of events.
- Use **examples** when you decide to clarify, explain, and support ideas.
- Use **process explanation** in order to tell how something works or how to do something.
- Use **classification** to put ideas into different categories according to a particular basis.
- Use **definition** when you want to explain what something means.
- Use **comparison** to help you identify similarities and **contrast** to help you show differences.
- Use **cause and effect** to explain why something happened and to identify the consequences or results.
- Use **argument** to persuade readers to change their perspectives or alter their behavior.

(A Student's Writing Process

Look back at the writing assignment given at the beginning of the chapter (p. 72), which was to write an essay on a topic of importance to you, using some of the patterns of development to help support your points. On the following pages, you'll follow Carlos Montijo, a student writer, as he writes his essay. Carlos decided to write on the role that television plays in children's lives because this topic was being discussed in one of his education classes. As you follow Carlos through the writing process, you'll notice that he uses some of the patterns of development to strengthen his essay, make it more interesting, and support his ideas. You'll also notice that he conducted research on his topic, cited his sources within his paper, and added a Works Cited page at the end.

Note that some essays are written using one particular pattern of development. A piece about hiking to the top of a mountain, for example, might be written using narration. An essay about how to cook a five-course dinner for eight people in your tiny apartment kitchen might be written using process explanation. An article in a magazine on the different types of cell phones available today might use classification to show the choices on the market. But in most writing you will encounter, writers use a combination of patterns to produce an effective, clear, and compelling essay. This is what Carlos did when writing his essay.

Carlos's Ideas

After receiving the assignment, Carlos thought first about his audience and his purpose. Although he planned to show his final draft to a friend who had just had a child, he knew his primary audience was his writing instructor. He knew that the research he would do on the topic would help make his essay persuasive because it would show that he was knowledgeable about this subject. In his journal, Carlos explained how he chose a topic and started to gather ideas for his essay:

Oct. 15

A couple of weeks ago, I baby-sat my neighbors' two kids, who are four and seven years old. I was shocked when they told me they got to watch as much TV as they wanted. I know that their parents are really busy trying to make a living, but they are using TV as a babysitter. I think the seven-year-old is too aggressive when he plays with his friends, which is probably from watching violent TV shows. He's also kind of chubby because he's spending too much time watching TV. I decided that I wanted to research this topic and maybe show my paper to my neighbors to let them see that too much television watching might be harmful to their kids.

Carlos decided to use clustering, too, to help him think about his topic:

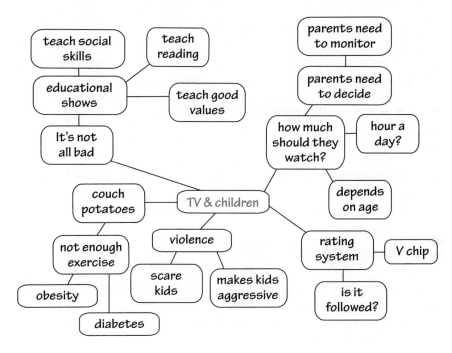

Figure 4.1 Carlos's Clustering

Carlos's Drafting

Using his journal writing and the clustering that he did on the topic (Figure 4.1), Carlos wrote the discovery draft below. (Note that the draft includes the types of errors that typically appear in a first draft.)

Too Much Television

Most children watch too much television. Parents use it like a babysitter, but this isn't good for their kids. Many shows on TV are violent, and young children can be disturbed by this. Everyone is susceptible to the influence of television, but children are especially gullible because they have not fully developed their critical sensibilities. Unfortunately, many television programs contain obscenity, violence, and sex. Which can be harmful to children, especially if they watch a great deal of it. They can become too aggressive and try to imitate what they see on TV. For instance, if they see a fight break out on a TV show, they might think this is a good way to solve a problem instead of trying to talk it out. The actors seem cool, which makes the kids want to be just like them. Plus if children are watching TV all the time, they aren't reading, which can make them bad students. They aren't playing with other children, which might hurt their social skills. They also might not get enough exercise, which can make them overweight and unhealthy. Excessive television viewing can decrease childrens activity levels, resulting in health problem such as obesity and diabetes. It is simply naive to think that viewing a great deal of television will not affect children's behavior or moods.

I know that not all TV is bad. Some children's shows are educational and some are pretty harmless. But the point is that children are watching too much TV, and they're watching shows that have too much violence or sex. The violence can make them scared or upset them. Almost all shows in the evening hours are unsuitable for children. TV violence is so grained in American culture that it is hard to find a dramatic program completely void of it. Critics like Jacob Weisberg argue that the problem is not the amount of violence shown on TV but the kind of violence, children may not be bothered by silly, cartoonish violence (Weisberg). Also, it's true that some children may stay out of trouble because "if you're at home watching TV, you're not out on the streets punching someone's head in" (Mackay 1). But is this how we want to protect children, by having them watch TV?

Children younger than two years however should not even be exposed to television because their minds are still very tender; the younger children are, the more susceptible they are to visual media (American Academy of Pediatrics). Parents need to be very careful about regulating their children's viewing habits. It might be hard for parents to do this because they can't be home all the time, but it's very important that children not be exposed to too much TV at an early age.

Carlos's Revising and Editing

After finishing his discovery draft, Carlos reflected again on his audience and purpose. He decided that his instructor would want an essay that would be easier to follow; after all, she had more than a hundred students who would be turning in essays. This meant that his essay had to be better organized and more fully developed, with a good thesis statement. Carlos asked several students in his education class to read his discovery draft and give him suggestions for revision.

In his journal, Carlos explained how he revised and edited his essay:

Oct. 20

Before I revised and edited my essay, I wrote a new thesis statement: "Parents need to regulate both the amount of time their kids spend watching television and the types of programs they watch." I based the rest of the essay on this thesis statement. I also went to the library and asked a librarian to help me find some good sources. He helped me find sources that were objective and well researched. When I wrote the revised draft, I used a standard essay format—an introduction, body paragraphs, and a conclusion. I decided to use cause and effect to help support my point about TV violence, and I also used comparison and contrast to add information about the positive things about television, such as how it can be educational, so that my audience would know I had considered both sides of the issue. I also worked hard on my introduction because sometimes people form their opinion of the essay based on the introduction. Then I went to the Writing Center for help with putting the sources into the paper and correctly using documentation. Finally, I used my spell-checker to catch spelling errors in my essay and proofread my draft by reading it from beginning to end.

Here is Carlos's revised and edited draft.

Carlos Montijo
Professor Al-Tabaa
English 0311
12 Nov. 2015

Television and Children

During the twentieth century, the invention of the television changed American culture and paved the way for the modern era. Even though people today use many different kinds of media (such as Facebook and video games), television is still very popular. As a result, everyone is susceptible to the influence of television, but children are especially gullible because they have not fully developed their critical sensibilities. Unfortunately, many television programs contain obscenity, violence, and sex, which can be harmful to children, especially if they watch a great deal of it. Research has shown that this kind of exposure can result in overstimulation and sometimes even destructive behavior. Parents need to regulate both the amount of time their kids spend watching television and the types of programs they watch.

Naturally, not all television is bad for children. Some channels, such as PBS, have educational shows that can teach children important skills or show them interesting aspects of the world. One study found that watching certain TV shows may help 3- to 5-year-old children learn how

1

2

Sentence fragment is corrected.

Carlos introduces the cause (too much television) and effect (results).

The thesis shows that argument is the dominant pattern used in this essay.

Carlos uses comparison and contrast to show both sides of the issue.

Comma splice is corrected.

Carlos uses research throughout to explain his points.

Carlos continues to use cause and effect.

Spelling error is corrected.

The source exemplifies the point that children watch too much TV.

When using research, Carlos relies mostly on paraphrasing (putting others' words into your own words) rather than quoting. This gives the essay a better flow.

Examples about the negative effects of TV help support Carlos's point.

Carlos uses definitions to define terms.

This example helps support the main point of the paragraph.

to read (Stanton 1). Other channels, such as Nickelodeon and Disney, have shows that might have a positive message or that are at least harmlessly entertaining. Also, not all violence is always harmful to children. Critics like Jacob Weisberg argue that the problem is not the amount of violence shown on TV but the kind of violence; children may not be bothered by silly, cartoonish violence. Also, it's true that some children may stay out of trouble because "if you're at home watching TV, you're not out on the streets punching someone's head in" (Mackay 1). But is this how we want to protect children, by having them watch TV?

Children who watch a great deal of television are exposed to shows with inappropriate and possibly damaging content. Many experts have been concerned about this. According to Carter and Weaver, "For almost a century now, the apparent ability of the media to negatively affect individual behavior has been one of the foremost concerns around media violence for government officials, pressure groups, media scholars, and citizens" (2). TV violence is so ingrained in American culture that it is hard to find a dramatic program completely void of it. Moreover, the average American child is in a home with a television that is on for about seven hours a day (Gerbner 45). According to the American Academy of Pediatrics, violence in the media can make children aggressive and afraid of being harmed. It can also make children think that violence is a good way of settling arguments or solving problems (American Academy of Pediatrics). Children might start to believe that it is cool because the actors who are being violent on TV seem cool. Also, studies have found that watching television at a young age can lead to attention-deficit problems and disorders (Condon 1). Excessive television viewing can also decrease children's activity levels, resulting in health problems such as obesity and diabetes. It is simply naive to think that viewing a great deal of television will not affect children's behavior or moods.

Television warning labels are not very useful in helping to curb children's television watching. Most prime-time TV shows are labeled TV14, meaning they're not appropriate for children under fourteen, or TVPG, meaning that children should watch these shows only with their parents. However, these warning labels are not easy to spot; on TVGuide.com, for instance, the label for each show appears in a tiny

3

4

black box next to the time and date of the show. Based on these ratings, virtually all shows that are on in the evenings are not appropriate for children. Parents can use the V-chip that comes with their televisions to block certain shows from their sets, or they can adjust the settings on their DVRs or cable and satellite streams. However, many adults might want to watch these shows themselves, and so they don't bother blocking shows or don't understand how to do it.

5

Parents need to become more aware and active in the lives of their kids and regulate what they view at all times. According to the American Academy of Pediatrics, a good plan is to allow a child to view no more than one hour of safe, preferably educational television daily. Children younger than two years, however, should not even be exposed to television because their minds are still very tender; the younger children are, the more susceptible they are to visual media (American Academy of Pediatrics). Excessive exposure to television will hinder a child's potential because it easily distracts them, consumes their time, encourages them to develop bad habits that are difficult to correct, and gives them a false, distorted sense of reality. Parents must seriously consider the consequences of exposing their kids to too much television.

Works Cited

American Academy of Pediatrics. "Media Violence." 124.5 (2009): 1495–1503. Web. 5 Nov. 2015.

Carter, Cynthia, and C. Kay Weaver. *Violence and the Media*. Buckingham, England: Open UP, 2003. Print.

Condon, Deborah. "TV Is Bad for Young Kids." *Irish Health*. Health on the Net Foundation, 4 July 2004. Web. 4 Oct. 2015.

Gerbner, George. "Television Violence at a Time of Turmoil and Terror." *Critical Readings: Violence and the Media*. Ed. C. Kay Weaver and Cynthia Carter. New York: Open UP, 2006. 45–53. Print.

Mackay, Hugh. "Answer to TV Violence: Turn It Off." *Sydney Morning Herald* 5 Mar. 2005. Web. 5 Nov. 2015.

Stanton, Carina. "TV Viewing Good and Bad for Kids, Seattle Study Says." *Seattle Times* 5 July 2005. Web. 14 Oct. 2015.

Weisberg, Jacob. "What Do You Mean by 'Violence'?" *Slate* 15 May 1999. Web. 5 Nov. 2015.

This description of using a V-chip or digital and satellite settings comes from Carlos's own personal experience; no citation is needed.

Missing commas are inserted.

This specific recommendation strengthens Carlos's conclusion.

These final sentences remind readers of the main points of Carlos's essay.

The Works Cited page follows correct MLA format. Information about the sources will help readers find the sources themselves if they want to read more about the topic.

> **GROUP ACTIVITY 5** Analyze Carlos's Revised and Edited Essay

Discuss the following questions with your classmates.

1. What do you think of the title of Carlos's essay? What title would you suggest?
2. Does Carlos's introduction make you want to read the essay? Why or why not?
3. How effective is Carlos's thesis statement?
4. What details did Carlos add to the revised and edited draft to improve his essay?
5. In what ways did Carlos's research help make his essay more persuasive?
6. How effective is Carlos's conclusion? What more would you suggest he add?
7. What else could Carlos do to improve his essay?

Carlos's Sharing

Writing in his journal, Carlos summed up his feelings about the final draft of his essay:

> Dec. 16
>
> Rereading my paper, I see how much I learned about my topic while I was writing it. I'm also glad I took the time to proofread and correct my errors, so my readers will take me seriously. The next time I babysit for my neighbors, I'll tell them about the research I did for this essay and ask if they want to read it. For the sake of their kids, I hope they learn from what I wrote.

CHAPTER CHECKLIST

❑ The patterns of development help readers make sense of your thoughts and can be used to write a more effective paragraph or essay.

❑ Description helps readers picture your ideas.

❑ Narration allows you to tell a story.

❑ Examples let you clarify, explain, and support ideas.

❑ Process explanation helps you explain how something works or how to do something.

❑ Classification leads you to categorize something into types.

❑ Definition allows you to tell readers what something means.

❑ Comparison and contrast lets you explain similarities and differences.

❑ Cause and effect helps you explain why something happened and its result.

❑ Argument lets you persuade readers to change their perspective or perform an action.

REFLECTING ON YOUR WRITING

To help you reflect on the writing you did in this chapter, answer the following questions:

1. Which patterns of development did you use in your practice essay on a topic of importance to you? Why did you choose these patterns to support your position?

2. Which pattern do you think is the easiest to use? The hardest to use? Why?

3. How did learning about the patterns of development help you as a writer?

Once you answer these questions, freewrite about what you learned about the writing process and about yourself as a writer.

Visit **LaunchPad Solo for Readers and Writers > Reading > Patterns of Organization** for more tutorials, videos, and practice with crafting paragraphs.

PART TWO

Writing to Share Ideas

Writing provides a permanent record of our ideas. Writing also allows us to communicate with others and to share what we know in ways that express our thoughts, inform, and persuade.

In Part Two, you'll learn how to improve your writing as you write to share your ideas. You'll read some sample essays to get you thinking about that chapter's writing purpose and topic. You'll experiment with different methods of gathering ideas and practice writing discovery drafts. You'll learn how to revise and how to use the patterns of development to expand and organize your thoughts. You'll improve your sentences and learn how to choose just the right word to communicate what you want to say. You'll edit your writing to ensure that you communicate your ideas clearly. Finally, you'll share your writing with an audience.

At the end of each chapter, you'll check to see that you've completed all the steps of the writing process, and you'll have an opportunity to reflect on your own writing process.

"As I stepped out of my home, I felt like a butterfly breaking out of its cocoon."

MOUSHUMI BISWAS, "THE MOST BEAUTIFUL GIFT"

Remembering
Significant People, Events, and Experiences

We all have memories of important people, events, and experiences in our lives. Some of these memories are happy: a supportive mentor, the birth of a child, a year as a foreign exchange student. Others are less pleasant: a cruel coworker, a serious traffic accident, a long-term illness.

Memories change who we are and how we see ourselves. To a great extent, we are all defined by important people, events, and experiences in our lives. In this chapter, you will learn how to write an essay that shows how someone or something in your past has changed you. You will begin by reading essays by professional writers about an important person or change in their lives. You will also follow a student, Moushumi Biswas, as she writes her essay, "The Most Beautiful Gift," in which she remembers an important event: the first time she wore a sari.

Exploring your own memories in writing will help you better understand who you are and what is meaningful to you. Working through the readings and activities in this chapter will guide you in the process of writing an essay about a person, event, or experience that had an impact on your life. Once you have completed your essay, you can share your written memories with the people who are close to you. This is what good writing is about—communicating something important to readers so that they learn something new. ■

> **In this chapter, you will write about a significant person, event, or experience in your life. As you follow the steps of the writing process, you will**
>
> - Explore the chapter topic by reading essays about a significant person, event, or experience.
> - Gather ideas by brainstorming, relating aloud, and clustering.
> - Develop your ideas using **description** and **narration**.
> - Practice writing effective thesis statements, topic sentences, and focused paragraphs.
> - Combine sentences with coordinating conjunctions.
> - Learn how to correct run-on sentences.
> - Share your essay with your classmates.

📷 **GETTING STARTED** **Think about Personal Changes**
The photograph on page 94 captures a mother helping her daughter with her sari. Consider the facial expressions of the two women, their body language, and other details of the photo. What memories might the mother be having? What might the daughter be thinking? Can you think of a time that you first felt like an adult or like part of something bigger? Share memories and photographs of significant people, events, and experiences with your classmates.

Read to Write — **Reading Essays That Remember a Significant Person, Event, or Experience**

Reading is an excellent way to start thinking about a topic. Learning other people's stories may spark some memories from your own past.

At the same time, examining what others have written will help you discover new strategies for sharing your ideas. Before you start work on your own essay, read the following short essays about how a significant person, a memorable event, or an important experience changed someone. As you read, pay close attention to how the writers use description and narration to explain their thoughts to their readers and to make their stories interesting and compelling. Notice, too, how the writers introduce their topics and how they use paragraphs to develop each main idea. You can use what you learn from reading these essays to get you started writing your own essay.

A Significant Person: An Annotated Reading

JOSHUA BELL
My Maestro

Joshua Bell became interested in music at an early age. His parents, eager to encourage their son's interests, gave him his first violin when he was four years old. Even though he liked to play computer games, basketball, and tennis, by the age of twelve he was committed to playing the violin. When he was fourteen, he made his professional debut with the Philadelphia Orchestra and later toured with major orchestras in the United States, Europe, Australia, and Asia. He has recorded numerous classical works and played with musical legends, such as the cellist Yo-Yo Ma. In this essay, Bell credits Josef Gingold—his maestro, or master teacher—for showing him that music could be "more than a hobby."

As a boy, I played the violin surrounded by ghosts. My teacher, Josef Gingold, plastered his Bloomington, Ind., studio walls with autographed photos of musical greats he admired or had met on his travels. Their faces watched our music-making, and inspired my small fingers to coax songs from the strings.

1 Bell uses the image of ghosts to get his readers' attention and to introduce his thesis statement.

When I became Gingold's pupil at age 12, he was already a legend at Indiana University, a gregarious Old World exile who had played under Arturo Toscanini and George Szell.

2 Bell begins to narrate his story.

We almost didn't meet. The day before my first solo recital—which someone had convinced him to attend—I was tossing a boomerang at my parents' farm. My mother fretted whether this was wise. Sure enough, the boomerang whirled back and sliced my chin open. The ER doctor stitched me up. Two inches to the left and I couldn't have held my violin. But I played, wounded.

3 Bell uses a short, catchy topic sentence and a description to paint a picture of himself as a child.

Gingold liked what he heard. I enrolled in a chamber music program he taught that summer in upstate New York. There, I realized I had never met anyone who found music so fun. He would play two parts of a string quartet at once. He laughed and laughed, and I left those lessons buzzing. My parents saw my excitement, and asked Gingold to continue to teach me back at home. He was wary. Too many children had been pushed on the violin, Gingold thought, and were living others' dreams. But he let me try.

4 In this unified paragraph, every sentence explains why Gingold was significant to Bell.

So I went to his studio with the ghosts on the walls, to enter the long tradition of one musician's hands guiding another's. My teacher taught me that music could be more than a hobby. It could be a life.

5 Bell explains another way Gingold was significant to him.

Born in Russia in 1909, he came to America in 1920 and studied violin with Vladimir Graffman. In 1937 he won a spot in the NBC Symphony Orchestra, and later was the Cleveland Orchestra's concertmaster.

6 Bell helps his readers get to know his teacher through narrating a bit of Gingold's life.

But Gingold found his true calling as a teacher. He was a musical inspiration for kids, who brought him joy. Unlike many maestros, he refused to scold his students, a decision that stemmed from a childhood horror. As a boy, he had once played his violin at a school assembly. His fellow students loved it, and applauded for so long the principal had to order them to stop. Later, Gingold's art teacher pulled him aside. "Let me see your hands," she said. "Are those the hands that made that beautiful music?" He beamed, so proud to be recognized for what he could do. Then she took a wooden pointer, smacking his palm so hard it damaged a nerve. Years later, he still felt pain. The teacher had decided he shouldn't feel so good about himself. That stuck with him. He went the opposite way with his students.

7

Bell uses the actual words of Gingold's art teacher to help his readers envision what happened.

Sometimes I wish he had been more strict. I was a kid, I goofed off. He wanted me to have a normal childhood and was secretly pleased when my mother told him I'd spent all day playing video games instead of music. During my afternoon lessons, we'd take breaks and listen to records. He let me play his Stradivarius. I was amazed by the depth of sound, the colors floating from that instrument. He helped me create a very personal relationship with music, but he did not teach me how to play every note. Many teachers have students copy all their fingerings. Gingold gave me the tools to teach myself—chamber music, solos, anything.

8 Yet another example of Gingold's significance.

Bell uses description to show how Gingold was like a grandfather to him.

I studied with him for nine years, and he became the grandfather I didn't 9 have. In my family, everyone played an instrument. During holidays, we gathered for informal concerts we called musicales. One year, Gingold joined us. He invited some of his international students to come play too. He led our little orchestra most of the night in this multicultural circle of warmth and music, tucked away from the Indiana cold. He couldn't stop smiling. With Toscanini or in a crowded living room, he was happy if he had a violin in hand.

Bell continues to tell the story.

Gingold didn't pull strings to further my career, but I pushed myself. Soon 10 the spotlight found me. I made my professional debut at 14, playing Mozart's Third Violin Concerto with the Philadelphia Orchestra. He flew to see me. At 17, I played at Carnegie Hall, and he saw me there, too, smiling like a proud grandpa.

Bell uses description to paint a picture of his last visit with Gingold.

When I moved to New York at 21, I couldn't see Gingold as much as I'd have 11 liked. His health was failing, and I dreaded the day he would leave me. On New Year's, 1995, I paid him a visit, bringing a photo of him I wanted autographed, to hang on my wall like the ghosts on his. I walked into his house, and in his hand he had one last gift for me—a rare picture of Niccolò Paganini, the crown jewel of his studio collection. He signed his own photo. I played. We talked through that last wonderful afternoon. The next day he had a stroke. He died two weeks later.

Early success can be dangerous for a musician. You hear of prodigies who 12 rise fast and flame out. Sometimes that's because teachers spoon-feed these young people every musical idea. At some point they feel they don't need teaching anymore, so they stop learning. Gingold was always learning. So am I.

Bell concludes by again referring to the ghosts, a good way to bring his essay full circle.

Someday I want to teach too. Gingold's ghost—the autographed photo on 13 my wall hung next to Paganini—will be watching.

READING ACTIVITY 1 Build Your Vocabulary

Determine the meanings of the following words from the context of Joshua Bell's essay. Then check their meanings by looking up the words in a dictionary: *gregarious* (2), *fretted* (3), *wary* (4), *maestros* (7), *Stradivarius* (8), *fingerings* (8), *prodigies* (12).

GROUP ACTIVITY 1 Discuss the Reading

Discuss the following questions about "My Maestro" with your classmates.

1. Why is Josef Gingold a significant person in Bell's life? Where does Bell express this main point?

2. Reread the paragraph about Gingold's childhood experience at a school assembly (7). How does this story help explain why Gingold is special to Bell?

3. What details does Bell use to show how his violin teacher influenced his life?

4. What do you want to know about Josef Gingold that the writer doesn't tell you?

Write a paragraph or two about a person whose personality is exceptional, like Gingold, who was able to bring a sense of joy and happiness to the rigorous world of classical music education. Describe what this person was like and tell a story about him or her. As you write, think about why this person is important to you. Share what you have written with your classmates.

A Significant Person

THOMAS L. FRIEDMAN

My Favorite Teacher

Thomas L. Friedman has been a foreign affairs columnist for the *New York Times* since 1981. He holds a master's degree in modern Middle East studies from Oxford University in England, and he has won three Pulitzer Prizes for journalism. Friedman has written several best-selling books, including *From Beirut to Jerusalem* (1989), which won the National Book Award, and *Hot, Flat, and Crowded: Why We Need a Green Revolution—and How It Can Renew America* (2008). If we're lucky, we find someone in our lives who teaches us what is truly important. In "My Favorite Teacher," which first appeared in the *New York Times* on January 9, 2001, Friedman tells of such a person.

1   Last Sunday's *New York Times Magazine* published its annual review of people who died last year who left a particular mark on the world. I am sure all readers have their own such list. I certainly do. Indeed, someone who made the most important difference in my life died last year—my high school journalism teacher, Hattie M. Steinberg.

2   I grew up in a small suburb of Minneapolis, and Hattie was the legendary journalism teacher at St. Louis Park High School, Room 313. I took her Intro to Journalism course in 10th grade, back in 1969, and have never needed, or taken, another course in journalism since. She was that good.

3   Hattie was a woman who believed that the secret for success in life was getting the fundamentals right. And boy, she pounded the fundamentals of journalism into her students—not simply how to write a lead or accurately transcribe a quote, but, more important, how to comport yourself in a professional way and to always do quality work. To this day, when I forget to wear a tie on assignment, I think of Hattie scolding me. I once interviewed an ad exec for our high school paper who used a four-letter word. We debated whether to run it. Hattie ruled yes. That ad man almost lost his job when it appeared. She wanted to teach us about consequences.

4   Hattie was the toughest teacher I ever had. After you took her journalism course in 10th grade, you tried out for the paper, *The Echo*, which she supervised. Competition was fierce. In 11th grade, I didn't quite come up to her writing standards, so she made me business manager, selling ads to the local pizza

parlors. That year, though, she let me write one story. It was about an Israeli general who had been a hero in the Six-Day War, who was giving a lecture at the University of Minnesota. I covered his lecture and interviewed him briefly. His name was Ariel Sharon. First story I ever got published.

Those of us on the paper, and the yearbook that she also supervised, lived in Hattie's classroom. We hung out there before and after school. Now, you have to understand, Hattie was a single woman, nearing 60 at the time, and this was the 1960's. She was the polar opposite of "cool," but we hung around her classroom like it was a malt shop and she was Wolfman Jack. None of us could have articulated it then, but it was because we enjoyed being harangued by her, disciplined by her and taught by her. She was a woman of clarity in an age of uncertainty.   5

We remained friends for 30 years, and she followed, bragged about and critiqued every twist in my career. After she died, her friends sent me a pile of my stories that she had saved over the years. Indeed, her students were her family— only closer. Judy Harrington, one of Hattie's former students, remarked about other friends who were on Hattie's newspapers and yearbooks: "We all graduated 41 years ago; and yet nearly each day in our lives something comes up— some mental image, some admonition that makes us think of Hattie."   6

Judy also told the story of one of Hattie's last birthday parties, when one man said he had to leave early to take his daughter somewhere. "Sit down," said Hattie. "You're not leaving yet. She can just be a little late."   7

That was my teacher! I sit up straight just thinkin' about her.   8

Among the fundamentals Hattie introduced me to was the *New York Times*. Every morning it was delivered to Room 313. I had never seen it before then. Real journalists, she taught us, start their day by reading the *Times* and columnists like Anthony Lewis and James Reston.   9

I have been thinking about Hattie a lot this year, not just because she died on July 31, but because the lessons she imparted seem so relevant now. We've just gone through this huge dotcom-Internet-globalization bubble—during which a lot of smart people got carried away and forgot the fundamentals of how you build a profitable company, a lasting portfolio, a nation state or a thriving student. It turns out that the real secret of success in the information age is what it always was: fundamentals—reading, writing and arithmetic, church, synagogue and mosque, the rule of law and good governance.   10

The Internet can make you smarter, but it can't make you smart. It can extend your reach, but it will never tell you what to say at a P.T.A. meeting. These fundamentals cannot be downloaded. You can only upload them, the old-fashioned way, one by one, in places like Room 313 at St. Louis Park High. I only regret that I didn't write this column when the woman who taught me all that was still alive.   11

READING ACTIVITY 2 Build Your Vocabulary

Determine the meanings of the following words from the context of Thomas L. Friedman's essay. Then check their meanings by looking up the words in a dictionary: *annual* (1), *lead* (3), *transcribe* (3), *comport* (3), *harangued* (5), *admonition* (6), *imparted* (10), *portfolio* (10).

GROUP ACTIVITY 2 Discuss the Reading

Discuss the following questions about "My Favorite Teacher" with your classmates.

1. Select the one sentence in Friedman's essay that you think best captures the essence of Hattie M. Steinberg. Then explain why this sentence describes her well.

2. Explain the significance of this sentence in your own words: "She [Hattie] was a woman of clarity in an age of uncertainty" (5).

3. Why does the author believe that Hattie's lessons are still important in the information age?

4. Friedman writes at the end of his essay, "I only regret that I didn't write this column when the woman who taught me all that was still alive" (11). If you could write a letter to someone who has influenced you, who would that person be?

WRITING ACTIVITY 2 Share Your Ideas

Write a paragraph or two about a significant teacher or mentor, describing what this person looked like and telling a story about him or her. As you write, think about why this teacher or mentor is important to you. Share what you have written with your classmates.

A Memorable Event

JAMES DILLARD
A Doctor's Dilemma

James Dillard is recognized as one of America's leading authorities on pain and pain management. A frequent lecturer and former clinical director of Columbia's Rosenthal Center for Complementary and Alternative Medicine, Dillard is known for integrating modern medicine and pharmaceutical practices with alternative treatments. He has appeared on national television multiple times and has written two books, *Alternative Medicine for Dummies* (1998) and *The Chronic Pain Solution* (2002). In this essay, Dillard describes how and why—as a doctor in training—he helped an accident victim despite the risks that a potential malpractice lawsuit could have posed to his career in medicine.

It was a bright, clear February afternoon in Gettysburg. A strong sun and layers of down did little to ease the biting cold. Our climb to the crest of Little Roundtop wound past somber monuments, barren trees and polished cannon. From the top, we peered down on the wheat field where men had fallen so close together that one could not see the ground. Rifle balls had whined as thick as   1 bee swarms through the trees, and cannon shots had torn limbs from the young men fighting there. A frozen wind whipped tears from our eyes. My friend Amy huddled close, using me as a wind breaker. Despite the cold, it was hard to leave this place.

Driving east out of Gettysburg on a country blacktop, the gray Bronco ahead   2 of us passed through a rural crossroad just as a small pickup truck tried to take a left turn. The Bronco swerved, but slammed into the pickup on the passenger side. We immediately slowed to a crawl as we passed the scene. The Bronco's driver looked fine, but we couldn't see the driver of the pickup. I pulled over on the shoulder and got out to investigate.

The right side of the truck was smashed in, and the side window was shat-   3 tered. The driver was partly out of the truck. His head hung forward over the edge of the passenger-side window, the front of his neck crushed on the shattered windowsill. He was unconscious and starting to turn a dusky blue. His chest slowly heaved against a blocked windpipe.

A young man ran out of a house at the crossroad. "Get an ambulance out   4 here," I shouted against the wind. "Tell them a man is dying."

I looked down again at the driver hanging from the windowsill. There were   5 six empty beer bottles on the floor of the truck. I could smell the beer through the window. I knew I had to move him, to open his airway. I had no idea what neck injuries he had sustained. He could easily end up a quadriplegic. But I thought: he'll be dead by the time the ambulance gets here if I don't move him and try to do something to help him.

An image flashed before my mind. I could see the courtroom and the driver   6 of the truck sitting in a wheelchair. I could see his attorney pointing at me and thundering at the jury: "This young doctor, with still a year left in his residency training, took it upon himself to play God. He took it upon himself to move this gravely injured man, condemning him forever to this wheelchair. . . ." I imagined the millions of dollars in award money. And all the years of hard work lost. I'd be paying him off for the rest of my life. Amy touched my shoulder. "What are you going to do?"

The automatic response from long hours in the emergency room kicked in. I   7 pulled off my overcoat and rolled up my sleeves. The trick would be to keep enough traction straight up on his head while I moved his torso, so that his probable broken neck and spinal-cord injury wouldn't be made worse. Amy came around the driver's side, climbed half in and grabbed his belt and shirt collar. Together we lifted him off the windowsill.

He was still out cold, limp as a rag doll. His throat was crushed and blood   8 from the jugular vein was running down my arms. He still couldn't breathe. He was deep blue-magenta now, his pulse was rapid and thready. The stench of alcohol turned my stomach, but I positioned his jaw and tried to blow air down into his lungs. It wouldn't go.

Amy had brought some supplies from my car. I opened an oversize intrave-   9 nous needle and groped on the man's neck. My hands were numb, covered with freezing blood and bits of broken glass. Hyoid bone—God, I can't even feel the thyroid cartilage, it's gone. . . . OK, the thyroid gland is about there, cricoid rings are here . . . we'll go in right here. . . .

It was a lucky first shot. Pink air sprayed through the IV needle. I placed a 10 second needle next to the first. The air began whistling through it. Almost immediately, the driver's face turned bright red. After a minute, his pulse slowed down and his eyes moved slightly. I stood up, took a step back and looked down. He was going to make it. He was going to live. A siren wailed in the distance. I turned and saw Amy holding my overcoat. I was shivering and my arms were turning white with cold.

The ambulance captain looked around and bellowed, "What the hell . . . who 11 did this?" as his team scurried over to the man lying in the truck.

"I did," I replied. He took down my name and address for his reports. I had 12 just destroyed my career. I would never be able to finish my residency with a massive lawsuit pending. My life was over.

The truck driver was strapped onto a backboard, his neck in a stiff collar. The 13 ambulance crew had controlled the bleeding and started intravenous fluid. He was slowly waking up. As they loaded him into the ambulance, I saw him move his feet. Maybe my future wasn't lost.

A police sergeant called me from Pennsylvania three weeks later. Six days 14 after successful throat-reconstruction surgery, the driver had signed out, against medical advice, from the hospital because he couldn't get a drink on the ward. He was being arraigned on drunk-driving charges.

A few days later, I went into the office of one of my senior professors, to tell 15 the story. He peered over his half glasses and his eyes narrowed. "Well, you did the right thing medically of course. But, James, do you know what you put at risk by doing that?" he said sternly. "What was I supposed to do?" I asked.

"Drive on," he replied. "There is an army of lawyers out there who would 16 stand in line to get a case like that. If that driver had turned out to be a quadriplegic, you might never have practiced medicine again. You were a very lucky young man."

The day I graduated from medical school, I took an oath to serve the sick and 17 the injured. I remember truly believing I would be able to do just that. But I have found out it isn't so simple. I understand now what a foolish thing I did that day. Despite my oath, I know what I would do on that cold roadside near Gettysburg today. I would drive on.

READING ACTIVITY 3 Build Your Vocabulary

Determine the meanings of the following words from the context of James Dillard's essay. Then check their meanings by looking up the words in a dictionary: *somber* (1), *dusky* (3), *heaved* (3), *sustained* (5), *quadriplegic* (5), *thundering* (6), *gravely* (6), *condemning* (6), *traction* (7), *magenta* (8), *thready* (8), *intravenous* (9), *arraigned* (14).

> **GROUP ACTIVITY 3** Discuss the Reading

Discuss the following questions about "A Doctor's Dilemma" with your classmates.

1. What is Dillard's thesis? Does he regret helping the victim of a car accident? Why or why not?

2. Examine how the author orders the events in his story. Why does he include details about things that happened before and after he helped the truck driver?

3. Compare how Dillard feels about this event now—as a licensed medical doctor—with how he felt about it as a medical student.

4. Reread paragraph 8, in which Dillard describes the truck driver's body. How does the author's use of description help explain why he was willing to risk his medical career?

> **WRITING ACTIVITY 3** Share Your Ideas

Write a paragraph or two about an event that caused you to take a risk such as the one taken by Dr. Dillard. Describe what happened, and let your classmates know if you still think you did the right thing.

An Important Experience

BRENT STAPLES
Black Men and Public Space

Have you ever noticed you were making someone else uncomfortable not because of anything you were doing but because of what you are—male or female, black or white, young or old, skinny or heavy, rich or poor? Perhaps you've even felt such discomfort about someone yourself. Some kinds of prejudice can be relatively harmless (an American who avoids french fries because France was against the war in Iraq). Other kinds can be deeply damaging. In "Black Men and Public Space," African American journalist Brent Staples uses examples from his own life to show how hurtful prejudice can be. This essay originally appeared in *Harper's* magazine.

My first victim was a woman—white, well dressed, probably in her early 1 twenties. I came upon her late one evening on a deserted street in Hyde Park, a relatively affluent neighborhood in an otherwise mean, impoverished section of Chicago. As I swung onto the avenue behind her, there seemed to be a discreet, uninflammatory distance between us. Not so. She cast back a worried glance. To her, the youngish black man—a broad six feet two inches with a beard and billowing hair, both hands shoved into the pockets of a bulky military jacket—

seemed menacingly close. After a few more quick glimpses, she picked up her pace and was soon running in earnest. Within seconds she disappeared into a cross street.

That was more than a decade ago. I was twenty-two years old, a graduate student newly arrived at the University of Chicago. It was in the echo of that terrified woman's footfalls that I first began to know the unwieldy inheritance I'd come into—the ability to alter public space in ugly ways. It was clear that she thought herself the quarry of a mugger, a rapist, or worse. Suffering a bout of insomnia, however, I was stalking sleep, not defenseless wayfarers. As a softy who is scarcely able to take a knife to a raw chicken—let alone hold one to a person's throat—I was surprised, embarrassed, and dismayed all at once. Her flight made me feel like an accomplice in tyranny. It also made it clear that I was indistinguishable from the muggers who occasionally seeped into the area from the surrounding ghetto. That first encounter, and those that followed, signified that a vast, unnerving gulf lay between nighttime pedestrians—particularly women—and me. And I soon gathered that being perceived as dangerous is a hazard in itself. I only needed to turn a corner into a dicey situation, or crowd some frightened, armed person in a foyer somewhere, or make an errant move after being pulled over by a policeman. Where fear and weapons meet—and they often do in urban America—there is always the possibility of death. 2

In that first year, my first away from my hometown, I was to become thoroughly familiar with the language of fear. At dark, shadowy intersections, I could cross in front of a car stopped at a traffic light and elicit the *thunk, thunk, thunk, thunk* of the driver—black, white, male, or female—hammering down the door locks. On less traveled streets after dark, I grew accustomed to but never comfortable with people crossing to the other side of the street rather than pass me. Then there were the standard unpleasantries with policemen, doormen, bouncers, cabdrivers, and others whose business it is to screen out troublesome individuals *before* there is any nastiness. 3

I moved to New York nearly two years ago and I have remained an avid night walker. In central Manhattan, the near-constant crowd cover minimizes tense one-on-one street encounters. Elsewhere—in SoHo, for example, where sidewalks are narrow and tightly spaced buildings shut out the sky—things can get very taut indeed. 4

After dark, on the warrenlike streets of Brooklyn where I live, I often see women who fear the worst from me. They seem to have set their faces on neutral, and with their purse straps strung across their chests bandolier-style, they forge ahead as though bracing themselves against being tackled. I understand, of course, that the danger they perceive is not a hallucination. Women are particularly vulnerable to street violence, and young black males are drastically overrepresented among the perpetrators of that violence. Yet these truths are no solace against the kind of alienation that comes of being ever the suspect, a fearsome entity with whom pedestrians avoid making eye contact. 5

It is not altogether clear to me how I reached the ripe old age of twenty-two without being conscious of the lethality nighttime pedestrians attributed to me. Perhaps it was because in Chester, Pennsylvania, the small, angry industrial town 6 where I came of age in the 1960s, I was scarcely noticeable against a backdrop of gang warfare, street knifings, and murders. I grew up one of the good boys, had perhaps a half-dozen fistfights. In retrospect, my shyness of combat has clear sources.

As a boy, I saw countless tough guys locked away; I have since buried several, too. They were babies, really—a teenage cousin, a brother of twenty-two, a childhood friend in his mid-twenties—all gone down in episodes of bravado played out in the streets. I came to doubt the virtues of intimidation early on. I chose, perhaps unconsciously, to remain a shadow—timid, but a survivor. 7

The fearsomeness mistakenly attributed to me in public places often has a perilous flavor. The most frightening of these confusions occurred in the late 1970s and early 1980s, when I worked as a journalist in Chicago. One day, rushing into the office of a magazine I was writing for with a deadline story in hand, I was mistaken for a burglar. The office manager called security and, with an ad hoc posse, pursued me through the labyrinthine halls, nearly to my editor's door. I had no way of proving who I was. I could only move briskly toward the company of someone who knew me. 8

Another time I was on assignment for a local paper and killing time before an interview. I entered a jewelry store on the city's affluent Near North Side. The proprietor excused herself and returned with an enormous red Doberman pinscher straining at the end of a leash. She stood, the dog extended toward me, silent to my questions, her eyes bulging nearly out of her head. I took a cursory look around, nodded, and bade her good night. 9

Relatively speaking, however, I never fared as badly as another black male journalist. He went to nearby Waukegan, Illinois, a couple of summers ago to work on a story about a murderer who was born there. Mistaking the reporter for the killer, police officers hauled him from his car at gunpoint and but for his press credentials would probably have tried to book him. Such episodes are not uncommon. Black men trade tales like this all the time. 10

Over the years, I learned to smother the rage I felt at so often being taken for a criminal. Not to do so would surely have led to madness. I now take precautions to make myself less threatening. I move about with care, particularly late in the evening. I give a wide berth to nervous people on subway platforms during the wee hours, particularly when I have exchanged business clothes for jeans. If I happen to be entering a building behind some people who appear skittish, I may walk by, letting them clear the lobby before I return, so as not to seem to be following them. I have been calm and extremely congenial on those rare occasions when I've been pulled over by the police. 11

And on late-evening constitutionals I employ what has proved to be an excellent tension-reducing measure: I whistle melodies from Beethoven and Vivaldi and the more popular classical composers. Even steely New Yorkers hunching toward nighttime destinations seem to relax, and occasionally they even join in the tune. Virtually everybody seems to sense that a mugger wouldn't be warbling bright, sunny selections from Vivaldi's *Four Seasons*. It is my equivalent of the cowbell that hikers wear when they know they are in bear country. 12

■ READING ACTIVITY 4 Build Your Vocabulary

Determine the meanings of the following words and phrases from the context of Brent Staples's essay. Then check their meanings by looking up the words in a dictionary: *uninflammatory* (1), *quarry* (2), *wayfarers* (2), *errant* (2), *elicit* (3), *warrenlike* (5), *bandolier* (5), *bravado* (7), *ad hoc* (8), *labyrinthine* (8), *give a wide berth* (11), *constitutionals* (12).

■ GROUP ACTIVITY 4 Discuss the Reading

Discuss the following questions about "Black Men and Public Space" with your classmates.

1. What main point is Staples making about how black men in public spaces are perceived?
2. What examples does the author provide to support his main point?
3. Why do you think Staples ends his essay by describing the precautions he takes to avoid being mistaken for a criminal?
4. Have you ever felt that your presence was causing someone discomfort? Describe one or two of these moments and the feelings they evoked in you.

■ WRITING ACTIVITY 4 Share Your Ideas

Write a paragraph or two about an important period in your life when either you caused someone else to feel uncomfortable or someone made you feel uncomfortable. What made this experience uncomfortable? What helped you get through it? Does the same situation still bring about that same feeling? Why or why not? Compare your experiences with those of your classmates.

Writing Your Essay A Step-by-Step Guide

Now that you've read some essays remembering a significant person, event, or experience in the writer's life, it's time to write your own essay. First, read the writing assignment that follows. Then, use the step-by-step advice that follows to discover ideas, develop them as you draft, and polish your writing into a finished essay that writers will find both interesting and expressive:

Step 1   Explore Your Choices 108
Step 2   Write Your Discovery Draft 113
Step 3   Revise Your Draft 115
Step 4   Edit Your Sentences 125
Step 5   Share Your Essay 131

Writing Assignment

What made you the person you are today? Introduce yourself to your classmates and your instructor by writing a brief essay that explains how someone or something in your past changed your sense of who you are and what's important to you. You (or your instructor) may decide to approach this assignment in one of several ways:

- Write about a person who has had an impact on you.
- Write about an event that was memorable for you.
- Write about an important experience in your life.

Step 1 Explore Your Choices

If you're like most people, choosing something to write about is a challenge. Of all the people you have known and things you have experienced, how can you possibly pick one to help explain who you are? Before you choose a topic to write about, you will first think about who your readers are and what you want them to know about you. Then you will learn some techniques for gathering ideas, and you will use those techniques to explore the three major topic possibilities (people, events, or experiences) presented in this chapter. Experimenting with your options will help you identify the most promising topic to write about and find good details to support your ideas.

Analyzing Your Audience and Purpose

For more on audience and purpose, see pp. 6–8.

You are writing an essay about a significant person, a memorable event, or an important experience in your life because you want the other students in your class to know you better. Your classmates are your readers. Before you write for this audience, consider what you know about them as well as what they already know about you. What do you want your classmates to learn about you?

Consider also how this essay will help you explain something in your life that changed you. You may want to express your thoughts and feelings about someone important, as Joshua Bell does in "My Maestro" and Thomas L. Friedman does in "My Favorite Teacher," or, like James Dillard, you might inform your readers of something you learned. You might even want to persuade your classmates to think differently about something that matters to you, as Brent Staples does in "Black Men and Public Space." Always remember, though, that your primary purpose for this essay is expressive—to share your thoughts and feelings about an important person, event, or experience in your life.

> **WRITING ACTIVITY 5** Analyze Audience and Purpose

Your responses to the following questions will help you decide how to approach this chapter's writing assignment. Be sure to come back to these questions after you have chosen a topic.

1. Does the assignment call for primarily expressive, informative, or persuasive writing?
2. What is the average age of your audience?
3. How many readers are female? How many are male?
4. What parts of the country or world are they from?
5. How many might have had experiences like yours?
6. In what ways are your readers similar to or different from you?
7. How will these similarities and differences with your readers affect the way you write your essay?

Gathering Ideas

When you gather ideas, or *prewrite*, you explore your thoughts about a topic without worrying about where those thoughts will lead you. Many different methods can help you discover ideas before you write. In this chapter, you will review three of these methods (brainstorming, relating aloud, and clustering) and use each method to explore one of the three possible topics: a significant person, a memorable event, or an important experience in your life. As you practice these techniques, you may decide to apply the ones that work best for you to your other topic choices as well.

For more on ways of gathering ideas, see pp. 11–15.

Brainstorming about a Significant Person

One of the most productive techniques for gathering ideas is *brainstorming*. When you brainstorm, you write down everything that comes to mind without judging which ideas are better than others or how they might connect. Instead, you express as many thoughts as possible so that you can go back and select the ones that are most helpful.

Think about the significant people in your life. Who would you name? You might name your parents, a partner, a friend, or a teacher or coach—such as the one you may have written about after reading Joshua Bell's "My Maestro" (p. 96) or Thomas L. Friedman's "My Favorite Teacher" (p. 99).

You might even remember an acquaintance or a stranger you met only once but who nevertheless gave you a new perspective at a critical time in your life. Whomever you choose, the person should be someone who has influenced your sense of who you are and who you strive to be.

If you have trouble thinking of things to write about someone important to you, answering the following questions can help you get started:

- How would you describe this person to someone who has never met him or her?
- How would you describe places you have visited with this person?
- What special objects do you associate with this person? Why?
- What song, book, or movie do you associate with this person? Why?
- What holidays or other special occasions are memorable because of this person? Why?
- How do you feel when you think of this person?

Here's how one student writer, Jesus, brainstormed about his father. He started by answering a few of the preceding questions and wrote down other ideas as they occurred to him.

My father
short (5' 6"), green eyes, brown hair, lots of hair
in good shape
kind
understanding
always tries to be helpful
soft-spoken but firm!
doesn't talk much, but when he does, everyone listens!
we've been so many places together that it's hard to name only a few:
      grandparents' house
      Uncle Jim's
      church
      the mall
      auto-parts store
      Disneyland
      fishing
      baseball games
rents movies for us to watch together
Field of Dreams — Dad loves baseball so much that if he had a cornfield,
    he'd turn it into a baseball field, too
anything about baseball
Cardinals' cap
remote control
favorite chair
newspaper
coffee mug

WRITING ACTIVITY 6 Brainstorm about a Significant Person

Think of someone who has meant a lot to you and write that person's name at the top of a page. Then brainstorm whatever comes to mind. You may use the questions on page 110 to get started, but follow whatever direction your mind takes you.

Relating a Memorable Event

In addition to the people in your life, events have changed you in some way. Whether you did something to make these events happen (such as earning a scholarship or running a marathon) or saw them change your life unexpectedly (such as performing at a talent show or learning you need surgery), such moments have influenced who you are.

One good way to explore ideas about an important event is to *relate* it—to talk about it with other people. By simply sharing a story or a thought orally without the pressure of having to write it down, you will usually discover that you have quite a bit to say about it. At the same time, you have the advantage of an audience who can provide immediate feedback—giving you a sense of what will interest your readers and how you can best explain your ideas. For example, you may want to tell more of the details of the risk you may have written about after reading James Dillard's "A Doctor's Dilemma" (p. 101).

After thinking about some of the important events in her life, student writer Moushumi decided that her classmates might be interested in the significance of the first time she wore a sari in her homeland of Bengal. Moushumi told them about that event as another student took notes. This is her story:

> On the first day of spring around the time of my sixteenth birthday, my mother surprised me by pulling out a sari and asking me to try it on. Girls in Bengal have always worn saris on Saraswati Puja day, so I tried to get one on. After what seemed like forever, I looked in the mirror and said, "Holy cow, I'm becoming a woman!" I felt like a butterfly coming out of a cocoon. My mother looked at my father, her eyes full of joy. My father looked at me, smiling but also concerned. I wasn't the only one who had this experience; girls in India and maybe everywhere share it. Coming of age is an experience filled with a sense of happiness and expectations, but in Bengal, it also comes with the gift of a sari.

Moushumi's story prompted many questions from her peer response group. For example, one student asked, "What did the sari look like?" Others asked, "Can you remember anything else that you or your mother said?" and "How did you feel during all of this?" Finally, someone asked Moushumi why this experience was significant to her and if she still wore saris.

Relating the experience aloud and reading over her classmate's notes from the discussion helped Moushumi focus on the details and understand what the story meant to her. Answering the group's questions also helped Moushumi identify her main idea: wearing the sari for the first time represented her coming of age from youth to adulthood.

GROUP ACTIVITY 5   Relate a Memorable Event

Working with a small group, relate a memorable event out loud. The moment may be happy or sad, but it should have markedly affected who you are. Ask someone to take notes on your story or use a recording device. When you finish relating aloud, respond to the group's questions about your topic. Then read over your classmate's notes from the discussion (or listen to the recording) to gather additional ideas.

Clustering about an Important Experience

Unlike an *event*, which occurs at a specific time or on a particular day, an *experience* can take place over days or months. For example, you could write about the summer you spent away from home, your first six months of marriage, or the year you dedicated to getting in shape. You may already have written about one important experience in your life after reading Brent Staples's "Black Men and Public Space" (p. 104).

Clustering is another useful technique that can help you gather and organize your thoughts. Especially if you're a visual thinker, drawing connections can open your eyes to fresh ways of looking at something.

To begin clustering about an important time in your life, write a word or phrase that describes that time in the center of a blank page and draw a circle around it. As ideas about the topic come to mind, write them down, put circles around them, and draw lines from them to the center circle. As you think of ways to describe your ideas, write down the descriptions, circle them, and join these circles to the ideas they describe.

Student writer Maria clustered her ideas about an important experience in her life—the three years she worked at a job that made her so unhappy she decided to return to college. (See Figure 5.1 on page 113.)

WRITING ACTIVITY 7   Cluster about an Important Experience in Your Life

Spend a few minutes thinking about a time in your life that was very happy or very unhappy and that had a profound effect on who you are today. In the center of a blank page, write a word (or phrase) that describes that time and draw a circle around it. Then write down any words or phrases about the experience that occur to you and draw lines to connect related ideas. For each word or phrase you write, try to think of additional words and phrases related to them.

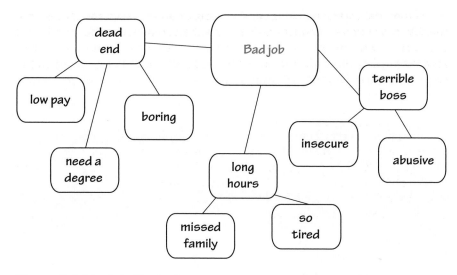

Figure 5.1 Maria's Clustering

☽ Step 2 Write Your Discovery Draft

It's time to move to the stage of the writing process where you put your ideas together so that you can see what you have to work with.

For more on drafting, see pp. 15–20.

When you write a discovery draft, you aim to explore possibilities rather than follow a map that's already been drawn. You might find that your thoughts take you in an unexpected direction; follow the path that seems most interesting to you. You'll have time later on to revise and edit your discovery draft.

Choosing a Topic

You have gathered ideas on three possible topics—a significant person, a memorable event, and an important experience in your life—that changed you in a meaningful way. Before you can begin drafting, you must choose one topic to write about.

Review all of the material you compiled as you gathered ideas and look for a promising topic that you can develop into an essay that explains how something changed you. You might discover that one option—a person, an event, or experience—gave you the best ideas. On the other hand, if you find that one theme emerged as you explored different topics, consider creating a topic that combines two or three ideas. For example, you might connect your significant person with a memorable event or important experience in your life. Whatever you decide to do, be sure to choose a topic that you have many ideas about and that will interest both you and your readers.

Student writer Moushumi decided to write about a significant event—wearing a sari for the first time—but she was also drawn to the importance of the sari to her as she was coming of age from youth to adulthood. This allowed Moushumi to provide supporting details about her growing awareness of the importance of family and tradition and thereby develop her ideas more fully in her discovery draft.

WRITING ACTIVITY 8 Choose Your Topic

Review your brainstorming, notes made by your classmates when you related aloud to other students, and your clustering. Based on the ideas you have gathered, decide which topic will be most interesting for you and your readers (and make sure you have something to say about it). To ensure that you have generated enough details to support a draft, you may want to do more brainstorming, relating aloud, and clustering on the topic of your choice.

Sharing Your Ideas

When you begin drafting, try to write a preliminary thesis statement that indicates the main point of your essay. You can then use this statement as a guide while you write. As you draft, feel free to use ideas that you have already gathered and to add new ones as they come to you. Remember that your main goal at the drafting stage is to get your ideas down on paper. You'll revise and edit your essay later.

A Student's Discovery Draft

Student writer Moushumi Biswas, whose prewriting you saw earlier in the chapter, wrote the following preliminary thesis statement and discovery draft about the experience of wearing a sari for the first time. (Note that Moushumi's draft includes the types of errors that typically appear in a first draft.)

It was the first day of spring in Bengal, a month after my sixteenth birthday, the designated day of the year to offer prayers. My mother asked me to wear a sari for the first time. I remember, too, that my mother gave me a necklace for my sixth birthday and that was a first, too! After half an hour of struggle, l looked in the mirror. I discovered a new me.

Moushumi's preliminary thesis statement

It may have escaped my own eyes but not my mother's. She chose the time and occasion to celebrate my coming of age. My mother loves to cook elaborate family dinners to celebrate special occasions. My mother looked at my father, her eyes laden with joy, pride, and tears. My father looked at me, the smile at the corner of his mouth partly shadowed by a hint of concern in his eyes.

My tale is not unique, it speaks for girls in India, or perhaps everywhere. Coming of age is an experience filled with a sense of fulfillment, happiness, expectations, and apprehension as well. In my homeland, Bengal, it also comes with the gift of a sari.

WRITING ACTIVITY 9 **Write Your Discovery Draft**

First, write a preliminary thesis statement that identifies your topic and explains why the person, event, or experience you are writing about is important to you. Then write a discovery draft that explores your ideas. Don't worry about the details. For now, focus on getting all of your ideas in writing. If you wish, you may write drafts on two or three topics to see which one you prefer to continue working on.

Step 3 Revise Your Draft

When you revise a discovery draft, you focus not only on what you want to communicate to your audience but also on how you communicate it. In this stage, you concentrate on supporting your ideas and making your points easy to follow. Writers often move back and forth among the stages of the writing process. Thus, it's possible that as you revise, you might need to return to gathering ideas. After you've gathered enough ideas, you can go back to revising.

For more on revising, see pp. 20–21.

As you revise, always think about what your readers need to know to understand the significance of that special person, event, or experience in your life.

Developing Your Ideas

When you wrote your discovery draft, you probably wrote the story quickly, as Moushumi did. When you revise, you want to add details that make your piece interesting and memorable. You need to go beyond describing experiences in vague, general ways to describing them with details that help your readers feel as if they were there with you.

For more on description and narration, see pp. 72–75.

For this chapter's writing assignment, you will develop your ideas and support your thesis statement by using description and narration. These strategies serve several important functions in an essay:

- They increase readers' interest in your topic.
- They help readers understand your main ideas.
- They help convince readers to identify with your point of view.

Description

Although you have firsthand experience of the person, event, or experience you're writing about, your readers don't. Consider adding description to make your essay more colorful and interesting. As you learned in Chapter 4, using description creates vivid images that explain how something looks, sounds, smells, tastes, or feels. For example, James Dillard, in "A Doctor's Dilemma," draws on sight, touch, and smell to describe the injured truck driver. This description of the accident victim helps readers feel as if they were at the scene themselves:

> He was still out cold, limp as a rag doll. His throat was crushed and blood from the jugular vein was running down my arms. He still couldn't breathe. He was deep blue-magenta now, his pulse was rapid and thready. The stench of alcohol turned my stomach, but I positioned his jaw and tried to blow air down into his lungs. It wouldn't go.

HOW TO Use Description

- Draw on as many senses—sight, sound, smell, taste, and touch—as you can.
- Be specific. Instead of "The apartment smelled bad," write "The apartment smelled of stale cigarettes and boiled cabbage."
- Make comparisons, such as "The baby's eyes are like gray marbles."
- Avoid common phrases, such as "as pretty as a picture" or "as cute as can be."

WRITING ACTIVITY 10 Use Description to Develop Ideas

Use the following questions to brainstorm for descriptive details about a person, thing, or place: How does it smell? Taste? Sound? What does it feel like? Look like? Review your answers and select details to add interest to your essay.

Narration

Whether you're writing about a person, an event, or an experience in your life, you probably have at least one story to tell. As you learned in Chapter 4, you can use *narration* to describe an event or a series of events as they happened in time. Use words such as *first, now, then, eventually, at last*, and other similar words that help you show placement in time. Good narration also includes specific details, and it often contains dialogue in which people's actual words are quoted.

In the following example from "My Maestro," Joshua Bell explains in narrative form why his violin teacher never punished his students:

> As a boy, he had once played his violin at a school assembly. His fellow students loved it, and applauded for so long the principal had to order them to

stop. Later, Gingold's art teacher pulled him aside. "Let me see your hands," she said. "Are those the hands that made that beautiful music?" He beamed, so proud to be recognized for what he could do. Then she took a wooden pointer, smacking his palm so hard it damaged a nerve. Years later, he still felt pain. The teacher had decided he shouldn't feel so good about himself. That stuck with him. He went the opposite way with his students.

Student writer Moushumi reviewed her discovery draft and decided that she could add some narration that included descriptive details to explain the experience of wearing a sari to a relative's wedding. She drafted this new paragraph for her revision:

> One sari in particular, featuring a traditional floral motif embroidered in gold and silver thread against a rich burgundy background, is a favorite of mine. I recently wore it to the church wedding of a relative from the village of Milan in northwestern New Mexico. The reaction of the guests was as expected my sari was the object of as many camera lenses as the bride and groom. One of the guests even said, "You look like a burrito wrapped in silk!"

HOW TO Use Narration

- To support your thesis, tell a series of experiences in the order in which they occurred.
- Narrate only the most important experiences.
- Use descriptive details and dialogue to illustrate important points.

WRITING ACTIVITY 11 Use Narration to Develop Ideas

Review your discovery draft, looking for ideas that you could expand with a story. Draft at least one narrative paragraph that supports the main idea of your essay (you may or may not decide to use it in your revised draft). Include descriptive details and, if possible, quote some dialogue.

Building Your Essay

Once you have developed your ideas, you want to make sure that your essay communicates those ideas as clearly as possible. In this section, you will focus on organizing your thoughts so that your readers can understand your message.

To organize, first review your thesis statement to ensure that it is effective. Next, make sure that each of your preliminary paragraphs has a topic sentence, so that readers can follow your train of thought. Then check that the details in each paragraph support their topic sentences.

Revise Your Thesis Statement

For more on writing a thesis statement, see p. 18.

When you started your discovery draft, you prepared a preliminary thesis statement to help guide your writing. When you revise, you need to make sure that your thesis statement reflects what you actually wrote and helps prepare readers to understand your ideas.

As you learned in Chapter 1, an effective thesis statement

- announces the topic of the essay.
- shows, explains, or argues a point about your topic.
- gives a sense of what the essay will be about.

A thesis statement may be one or two sentences, and normally it appears at the beginning of an essay. In the introduction to "Black Men and Public Space," for example, Brent Staples provides the following thesis statement about a significant experience in his life:

> It was in the echo of that terrified woman's footfalls that I first began to know the unwieldy inheritance I'd come into—the ability to alter public space in ugly ways.

In addition to indicating the topic of the essay (prejudice), this thesis statement shows a point (that Staples's mere presence can prompt a negative response) and gives a sense of what the essay will be about (how his presence alters public space).

For her discovery draft, student writer Moushumi wrote the following preliminary thesis statement: "I discovered a new me." This early thesis statement was a good start because it announces a topic (a discovery about herself). As she reviewed her draft, however, Moushumi realized that what she wrote didn't really explain the point of her essay (her coming of age). She revised her thesis statement to reflect the focus of her essay: "I discovered a new me, a young girl becoming a woman."

WRITING ACTIVITY 12 Revise Your Thesis Statement

Reread the preliminary thesis statement you wrote for your discovery draft. Does it announce the topic, show a point about the topic, and give a sense of what the essay will be about? Because your discovery draft may have developed differently than you expected, revise your thesis statement as necessary to make it more effective.

Include Topic Sentences

For more on topic sentences, see pp. 50–53.

Once you have a revised thesis statement, you need to show how the different parts of your essay develop your main idea. The best way to guide your readers is to provide topic sentences that explain how the details in each paragraph support the thesis statement. As you revise, make sure that every paragraph includes a topic sentence.

As you learned in Chapter 3, effective topic sentences break up a thesis statement into several supporting ideas and express a complete thought for each of those specific ideas. For example, here is the thesis statement followed by some of the topic sentences Brent Staples provides in "Black Men and Public Space." Notice how each of these topic sentences identifies a specific supporting idea that develops the thesis statement.

Thesis Statement

It was in the echo of that terrified woman's footfalls that I first began to know the unwieldy inheritance I'd come into—the ability to alter public space in ugly ways.

Topic Sentences

In that first year, my first away from my hometown, I was to become thoroughly familiar with the language of fear.

After dark, on the warrenlike streets of Brooklyn where I live, I often see women who fear the worst from me.

It is not altogether clear to me how I reached the ripe old age of twenty-two without being conscious of the lethality nighttime pedestrians attributed to me.

Over the years, I learned to smother the rage I felt at so often being taken for a criminal.

A topic sentence may fall anywhere in the paragraph. Most often, however, it comes first. For example, in the following paragraph from "A Doctor's Dilemma," the topic sentence (italicized) comes first, and the rest of the paragraph tells us what Dillard imagined:

An image flashed before my mind. I could see the courtroom and the driver of the truck sitting in a wheelchair. I could see his attorney pointing at me and thundering at the jury: "This young doctor, with still a year left in his residency training, took it upon himself to play God. He took it upon himself to move this gravely injured man, condemning him forever to this wheelchair. . . ." I imagined the millions of dollars in award money. And all the years of hard work lost. I'd be paying him off for the rest of my life. Amy touched my shoulder. "What are you going to do?"

WRITING ACTIVITY 13 Revise and Add Topic Sentences

Reread your discovery draft and underline your thesis statement and the topic sentence in each paragraph. Where necessary, revise the topic sentences to show how each paragraph supports your thesis statement. If any paragraphs are missing their topic sentences, add them.

Strengthen Your Focus

For more on paragraph unity, see p. 54.

As you learned in Chapter 3, once you have effective topic sentences for each paragraph, you need to make sure that all other sentences within a paragraph relate to its topic sentence. If a paragraph includes any sentences that do not support the topic sentence, you can revise them to make them clearly relate to your point, move them to another paragraph, or remove them from your essay.

The following paragraphs from Moushumi's discovery draft include a couple of irrelevant sentences that don't support the story that she is telling in this essay. Notice how these irrelevant sentences (in italics) detract from the topic sentence (highlighted):

> It was the first day of spring in Bengal, a month after my sixteenth birthday, the designated day of the year to offer prayers. My mother asked me to wear a sari for the first time. *I remember, too, that my mother gave me a necklace for my sixth birthday and that was a first, too!* After half an hour of struggle, l looked at the mirror. I discovered a new me.
>
> It may have escaped my own eyes but not my mother's. She chose the time and occasion to celebrate my coming of age because she knew it was important. *My mother loves to cook elaborate family dinners to celebrate special occasions.* My mother looked at my father, her eyes laden with joy, pride, and tears. My father looked at me, the smile at the corner of his mouth partly shadowed by a hint of concern in his eyes.
>
> My tale is not unique, it speaks for girls in India, or perhaps everywhere. Coming of age is an experience filled with a sense of fulfillment, happiness, expectations, and apprehension as well. In my homeland, Bengal, it also comes with the gift of a sari.

Here are the same paragraphs from Moushumi's draft with the irrelevant sentences removed:

> It was the first day of spring in Bengal, a month after my sixteenth birthday, the designated day of the year to offer prayers. My mother asked me to wear a sari for the first time. After half an hour of struggle, l looked at the mirror. I discovered a new me.
>
> It may have escaped my own eyes but not my mother's. She chose the time and occasion to celebrate my coming of age. My mother looked at my father, her eyes laden with joy, pride, and tears. My father looked at me, the smile at the corner of his mouth partly shadowed by a hint of concern in his eyes.
>
> My tale is not unique, it speaks for girls in India, or perhaps everywhere. Coming of age is an experience filled with a sense of fulfillment, happiness,

expectations, and apprehension as well. In my homeland, Bengal, it also comes with the gift of a sari.

GROUP ACTIVITY 6 Strengthen Focus

With the other members of your peer group, read the following paragraph and underline the topic sentence. Cross out any irrelevant sentences that don't support the topic sentence.

> The results of the election for student body president would be revealed at the meeting that day. My stomach was in knots anticipating the outcome. I knew that being president would be trying, but it was a risk worth taking. Once I took a risk when I rode the Shock Wave roller coaster at Six Flags. "You can breathe," a classmate said, but I didn't want to miss a word of the announcement. I took a CPR course when I was thirteen and learned a lot about how to get someone breathing again. Slowly but surely, the dean of students announced the name of the next president. The dean of students is a really nice woman who just moved here from California. Holding my breath hadn't helped because I still didn't hear what she said. My friends gave a little cheer, and the rest of the group applauded and chanted, "Speech, speech, speech." I was an awful public speaker, but as the newly elected student body president, I gave it my best.

WRITING ACTIVITY 14 Strengthen Your Focus

Examine your current draft, checking each paragraph for sentences that don't support the topic sentence. Make your paragraphs more unified by deleting, relocating, or revising any irrelevant sentences that you find.

A Student's Revised Draft

Before you read Moushumi's revised draft, reread her discovery draft on pages 114–15. Notice how in the revision she has used description and narration to develop her ideas, improved her thesis statement and topic sentences, and strengthened her focus. (You will notice that as Moushumi developed her essay, she also introduced a few punctuation errors into the draft; these will be corrected when she edits her essay later on.)

The Most Beautiful Gift

Moushumi's title draws readers into the essay.

It was the first day of spring in Bengal, the day of the year to offer prayers to Saraswati, goddess of learning. I had just celebrated my sixteenth birthday and was surprised when my mother pulled out an ice-blue chiffon sari from her wardrobe and asked me to try it on. "How about going to the temple wearing this?" she suggested. I struggled to put on five meters of sheer, gleaming fabric that seemed to have a mind of its own. Half an hour later, l finally got it on and looked in the mirror. "Holy cow! Who's that?" I discovered a new me, a young girl becoming a woman.

Moushumi uses vivid details to make the significance of the sari easier to understand.

Dialogue "hooks" readers in the introduction.

I stepped out of my home I felt like a butterfly breaking out of its cocoon. My mother had chosen this time and occasion to celebrate my coming of age. As she looked at my father, her eyes were full of joy, pride, and tears. My father looked at me, the smile at the corner of his mouth partly shadowed by a hint of concern in his eyes. He would have to be more protective of me from now on. His little girl was growing up.

Moushumi uses a comparison to make the point clearer.

My tale is not unique it speaks for girls in India, or perhaps everywhere. Coming of age is an experience filled with a sense of fulfillment, happiness, expectations, and apprehension. In my homeland, Bengal, it also comes with the gift of a sari. When my mother handed me the sari that spring morning, she was initiating me into a "girly" tradition carried down from her generation when the first day of wearing a sari denoted coming of age.

Moushumi adds narration to make the essay more interesting.

Several years ago, when my grandmother discarded her entire collection of the finest silks in the prettiest colors to pick up all-white widow's weeds, she was grieving the loss of her husband by following a cultural practice that had come down to her through several generations. Wearing the white clothing meant that she was faithfully upholding society's demand that she remain loyal to her husband even when he was dead. White, the color of mourning in India, was meant to ensure that she remember, for the rest of her life, her vow to him when they got married. The sari stands for much more than attire it is a cultural statement.

1

2

3

4

Even though I grew up wearing western clothes for the sake of convenience, my wardrobe is also full of saris. One of them in particular, featuring a traditional floral motif embroidered in gold and silver thread against a rich burgundy background, is a favorite of mine. I recently wore it to the church wedding of a relative. The relative was from the hamlet of Milan in northwestern New Mexico. The reaction of the guests was as expected: my sari was the object of as many camera lenses as the bride and groom. One of the guests even said, "You look like a burrito wrapped in silk!" I have made it a point to learn to wear five meters of cloth effortlessly—as my mother and grandmother did—and always to wear saris to special occasions. Even though I moved to a different continent several years ago, today the seemingly endless yards of graceful fabric tie me to my roots in the most beautiful way I could ever imagine.

5 Moushumi added a paragraph to tie the ancient tradition to the present day.

Description helps readers imagine a red sari and emphasizes its beauty and significance to the writer.

Dialogue helps readers see the guests' reaction.

Moushumi revised her conclusion to emphasize the sari's significance in her life.

GROUP ACTIVITY 7 Analyze Moushumi's Revised Draft

Use the following questions to analyze how Moushumi improved her draft through revision.

1. What is Moushumi's thesis statement? How did she improve it from her preliminary thesis statement?

2. How well does Moushumi use topic sentences? After examining all of her topic sentences, focus on one paragraph. Identify the topic sentence, and explain how its idea is developed in the paragraph.

3. What details has Moushumi included to improve her essay?

4. Look back at paragraph 1 of Moushumi's discovery draft (p. 114). She added a description of her sari. Why do you think she decided to do this? Was it a good decision?

5. Does Moushumi convince you—her reader—that the sari was a significant gift? Explain.

6. What other revisions could Moushumi make to improve her draft?

Peer Review for an Essay That Remembers

Now that you have made some revisions to your discovery draft, form a group with two or three other students and exchange copies of your drafts. Read your draft aloud while your classmates follow along. Then ask your group members the following questions about your essay. Write down your classmates' responses. If you don't understand what a classmate is suggesting, ask for clarification before you write it down. You will want to read these notes later for suggestions on how to improve your draft.

1. What do you like best about my essay?

2. What is my thesis statement? Do I need to make the thesis clearer?

3. Examine my topic sentences. How well do they connect to my thesis and indicate the main idea of each paragraph?

4. Where in the draft could I better develop my ideas by using description or narration?

5. Is each paragraph in my draft unified? Or do some paragraphs contain irrelevant sentences that need to be omitted or revised?

6. Where in my draft did my writing confuse you? How can I clarify my ideas?

7. Have I followed all the instructions for this assignment?

▓ **WRITING ACTIVITY 15** Revise Your Essay ▓

You have already developed your ideas, revised your thesis statement, added topic sentences, and strengthened your focus. But your classmates have probably given you additional suggestions for improving your essay. Taking your classmates' peer review responses into consideration, revise your draft as a whole so that readers will understand how a significant person, event, or experience in your life changed you.

◖ Step 4 Edit Your Sentences

When you wrote and revised your discovery draft, you were busy getting your thoughts on paper. Your sentences may not have come out as clearly as you would have liked, and you may have made some surface errors. You're now ready to edit your draft for readability and correctness.

Read your revised essay carefully, looking at each word for errors in grammar, spelling, and punctuation and for awkward sentences. Consult the Handbook in Part Four and a dictionary. As you edit your essay for this chapter's assignment, you will focus on combining sentences with coordinating conjunctions and on eliminating run-on sentences.

Combining Sentences Using Coordinating Conjunctions

One way to ensure that your ideas are well received is to consider sentence variety. Readers get bored easily when they read many sentences that are short and sound alike. You may have noticed, for example, that Moushumi's last paragraph in her revised draft contained a few short sentences. To improve her writing, Moushumi decided to use a technique known as *sentence coordination*.

Like Moushumi, you can combine short, closely related sentences with *coordinating conjunctions*. Here are seven coordinating conjunctions and their meanings:

for	because
and	in addition
nor	neither
but	opposite
or	alternatively
yet	opposite
so	as a result

One way to remember these words is to think of the word *FANBOYS*, which is spelled with the first letter of each of the seven coordinating conjunctions.

For more on sentence combining and coordination, see pp. 438–51.

Use appropriate coordinating conjunctions to combine short, closely related sentences. Put commas before the conjunctions. See the examples below.

Short Sentences

Last Saturday, I went to an outlet store to buy a business suit. I saw a movie with my best friend.

Combined Sentence with *And*

Last Saturday, I went to an outlet store to buy a business suit, and I saw a movie with my best friend.

Short Sentences

The plane was an hour late getting to Denver. I missed my connecting flight.

Combined Sentence with *So*

The plane was an hour late getting to Denver, so I missed my connecting flight.

Short Sentences

I gave my girlfriend another chance to show her commitment to me. She started dating my best friend.

Combined Sentence with *But*

I gave my girlfriend another chance to show her commitment to me, but she started dating my best friend.

HOW TO Combine Sentences Using Coordinating Conjunctions

- Be sure that two closely related sentences are complete by checking that each one has a subject and a verb and that each conveys a complete thought.
- Select an appropriate coordinating conjunction (*for, and, nor, but, or, yet, so*).
- Use a comma before the coordinating conjunction.

EDITING ACTIVITY 1 Use Coordinating Conjunctions

Combine the following sentences with an appropriate coordinating conjunction.

EXAMPLE I played baseball when I was young~~. I~~ , but I lost interest in the sport.

1. Baseball is a multimillion dollar business. It is also one of America's oldest organized sports.

2. Baseball is still popular. Newer sports, such as basketball and football, have become more popular.

3. Hundreds of Major League Baseball players earn more than a million dollars a year. Many athletes are attracted to the sport.

4. Women's softball has increased in popularity. This game is played at many colleges and at the Olympics.

5. At this time, a softball player can't earn a living playing softball. Not many athletes are interested in the sport professionally.

> **WRITING ACTIVITY 16 Combine Your Sentences**

Examine your revised draft for short, closely related sentences. Where it makes sense to do so, combine them with coordinating conjunctions.

Correcting Run-on Sentences

Remember, the more attention your readers pay to errors in your writing, the less attention they pay to what you have to say. Run-on sentences are a common mistake.

For more on run-on sentences, see pp. 456–59.

A *run-on sentence* occurs when two complete sentences, or *independent clauses*, are written together without any punctuation between them, as if they were one sentence. Here are some examples of run-on sentences:

RUN-ON Arizona has some of the hottest spots in the country don't visit it in August.

RUN-ON Going to college while working full time has been hard I never get enough sleep.

RUN-ON Student athletes often experience great pressure to do well they might need extra support from their schools.

RUN-ON I bought a minivan after I had my third child we needed the room.

Correct run-on sentences in one of three ways:

- Use a period.

   CORRECT Arizona has some of the hottest spots in the country. Don't visit it in August.

- Use a semicolon. You may follow the semicolon with a conjunctive adverb (such as *however, in addition, also, therefore,* or *furthermore*) and a comma if you like.

   CORRECT Going to college while working full time has been hard; I never get enough sleep.

CORRECT Student athletes often experience great pressure to do well;
therefore, they might need extra support from their schools.

■ Use a comma and a coordinating conjunction.

CORRECT I bought a minivan after I had my third child, for we needed
the room.

EDITING ACTIVITY 2 Correct Run-on Sentences

Correct each of the following run-on sentences by adding a period, a semicolon, or
a comma and a coordinating conjunction.

EXAMPLE Everybody has at least one wacky relative mine is my uncle.
. Mine

1. My uncle has a plastic spider he likes to take it out of his pocket to frighten
young children.

2. When there's a full moon, our cat gets crazy he climbs the curtains and howls
when we try to get him down.

3. My youngest daughter is only three she can already write her name.

4. My father was treated for cancer he's doing well now.

5. I'm returning to school to enter one of the health-care professions I plan to be
a physical therapist.

WRITING ACTIVITY 17 Edit Your Sentences

Read your essay carefully, looking at each word for errors in grammar, spelling, and
punctuation. Focus on run-on sentences. Use a dictionary and the Handbook in Part
Four of this book to help you find and correct any mistakes.

A Student's Edited Essay

Using the Handbook in Part Four, Moushumi corrected the errors in her
essay. Her corrections are noted in the margins.

Moushumi Biswas
Professor Posey
English 0311
16 Sep. 2015

The Most Beautiful Gift

It was the first day of spring in Bengal, the day of the year
to offer prayers to Saraswati, goddess of learning. I had just
celebrated my sixteenth birthday and was surprised when my
mother pulled out an ice-blue chiffon sari from her wardrobe and
asked me to try it on. "How about going to the temple wearing
this?" she suggested. I struggled to put on five meters of sheer,
gleaming fabric that seemed to have a mind of its own. Half an
hour later, l finally got it on and looked in the mirror. "Holy cow!
Who's that?" I discovered a new me, a young girl becoming a
woman.

As I stepped out of my home, I felt like a butterfly breaking
out of its cocoon. My mother had chosen this time and occasion to
celebrate my coming of age, and as she looked at my father, her
eyes were full of joy, pride, and tears. My father looked at me, the
smile at the corner of his mouth partly shadowed by a hint of
concern in his eyes. He would have to be more protective of me
from now on. His little girl was growing up.

My tale is not unique; it speaks for girls in India, or perhaps
everywhere. Coming of age is an experience filled with a sense of
fulfillment, happiness, expectations, and apprehension. In my
homeland, Bengal, it also comes with the gift of a sari. When my
mother handed me the sari that spring morning, she was initiating
me into a "girly" tradition carried down from her generation when
the first day of wearing a sari denoted coming of age.

Several years ago, when my grandmother discarded her entire
collection of the finest silks in the prettiest colors to pick up all-
white widow's weeds, she was grieving the loss of her husband by
following a cultural practice that had come down to her through
several generations. Wearing the white clothing meant that she
was faithfully upholding society's demand that she remain loyal to

1

2   A run-on sentence is
     corrected.

— Sentences are combined.

3   A run-on sentence is
     corrected.

4

her husband even when he was dead. White, the color of mourning in India, was meant to ensure that she remember, for the rest of her life, her vow to him when they got married. The sari stands for much more than attire; it is a cultural statement.

A run-on sentence is corrected.

Even though I grew up wearing western clothes for the sake of convenience, my wardrobe is also full of saris. One of them in particular, featuring a traditional floral motif embroidered in gold and silver thread against a rich burgundy background, is a favorite of mine. I recently wore it to the church wedding of a relative from the village of Milan in northwestern New Mexico. The reaction of the guests was as expected: my sari was the object of as many camera lenses as the bride and groom. One of the guests even said, "You look like a burrito wrapped in silk!" I have made it a point to learn to wear five meters of cloth effortlessly — as my mother and grandmother did — and always to wear saris to special occasions. Even though I moved to a different continent several years ago, today the seemingly endless yards of graceful fabric tie me to my roots in the most beautiful way I could ever imagine.

Short sentences are combined.

Courtesy of Moushumi Biswas

A photo of me wearing a sari at a wedding.

5

◖ Step 5 Share Your Essay

Share your finished essay with your instructor and classmates, perhaps by e-mail or by posting it to a class website. Ask your peer review group to comment on the improvements you made. Don't be surprised if someone says, "I can't believe this is the same essay. It's so much better!"

CHAPTER CHECKLIST

❑ I read essays about a significant person, event, or experience to explore and learn about the chapter's theme.

❑ I analyzed my audience and purpose.

❑ I gathered ideas on my topic by brainstorming, relating aloud, and clustering.

❑ I wrote a discovery draft.

❑ I revised my draft by

    ❑ using description and narration to develop ideas.

    ❑ revising my thesis statement.

    ❑ adding topic sentences.

    ❑ improving paragraph focus.

❑ I combined short, closely related sentences with coordinating conjunctions.

❑ I edited my draft to correct errors, including run-on sentences.

❑ I shared my draft with my instructor and classmates.

REFLECTING ON YOUR WRITING

To help you continue to improve as a writer, answer the following questions about this assignment:

1. Did you enjoy writing an expressive piece in which you shared your thoughts and feelings?

2. Which method of gathering ideas worked best for you?

3. Which details most improved your essay?

4. If you had more time, what parts of your essay would you want to improve before sharing it with readers? Why?

After answering these questions, freewrite about what you learned in this chapter.

Visit **LaunchPad Solo for Readers and Writers > Writing Process** for more tutorials, videos, and practice developing your essay with each step.

"Dr. Martin Luther King Jr. and Aung San Suu Kyi were activists who felt that civil disobedience could be used to bring about change."

AUTUMN HARRISON, "TWO PEOPLE, ONE IDEA"

6

Explaining
Cultural Symbols, Traditions, and Heroes

When you explain something, you are communicating what you know to others. You might explain a particular concept or idea, demonstrate how something works, or share information with others on a topic you know about. When you write an explanatory essay, your purpose is to teach or tell your readers something—to inform them about a subject. Your goal is to present your subject in a way that is interesting, that includes your own thoughts about the subject, and that teaches your readers something new. In this chapter, you will use this type of informative writing to examine a culture.

Have you ever traveled to another country? Were you surprised by what you saw and heard? Did people drive on the left or right side of the road? How did they entertain themselves? Were shopping practices different from what you are accustomed to? Were you introduced to new foods or styles of dress? Although they can be unsettling at times, such encounters enable us not only to learn about other cultures but also to better understand our own.

The term *culture* refers to the customs, beliefs, values, objects, and languages shared by members of a particular group. Although many people grow up as part of a single culture—Vietnamese, Brazilian, or German, for instance—more and more people are

> **In this chapter, you will write about a cultural symbol, tradition, or hero that is meaningful to you. As you follow the steps of the writing process, you will**
>
> - Explore the chapter topic by reading essays about a cultural symbol, tradition, or hero.
> - Gather ideas by clustering, asking questions, and freewriting.
> - Develop your ideas using **examples** and **process explanation**.
> - Practice writing introduction and conclusion paragraphs and making connections with transitions and keywords.
> - Combine sentences with conjunctive adverbs.
> - Learn how to identify and correct sentence fragments.
> - Share your essay with others.

recognizing themselves as *multicultural*, or as having roots in more than one culture. In addition to identifying ethnic heritage or national origin, *culture* can also refer to the beliefs and customs of any particular group. The hippie culture of the 1960s, for example, favored social and personal rebellion, encouraged a distinctive lifestyle, and came to use the peace sign as its symbol. Although members of a given culture might take its unique characteristics for granted, outsiders are sometimes fascinated, puzzled, or even frightened by things about that culture that they don't understand.

In this chapter, you will learn how to write an essay that explains a cultural symbol, tradition, or hero. You will begin by reading essays by professional writers about an aspect of culture. You will also follow a student, Autumn Harrison, as she writes about cultural heroes Dr. Martin Luther King Jr. and Aung San Suu Kyi in "Two People, One Idea."

By examining a specific aspect of a culture, you will gain a stronger understanding of your own beliefs and values and will probably want to share your knowledge with others. The readings and activities in this chapter will help you explain your ideas about a particular culture to your readers. As you work through the readings and activities in this chapter, you will practice transforming your knowledge of and experience with a culture into an essay that teaches your readers about something important to you. ■

[📷] **GETTING STARTED** Think about Cultures

The photos on page 132 show Dr. Martin Luther King Jr., who fought for civil rights in the United States, and Aung San Suu Kyi, who has fought for democracy in the Asian country of Burma (also called Myanmar). Does pairing these two photos together make the subjects—King and Suu Kyi—seem similar? Why? With several classmates, discuss the role that cultural heroes can play in improving society. What characteristics do cultural heroes need in order to serve as leaders for positive change? What can happen when cultural heroes fail to live up to these standards?

Read to Write Reading Essays That Explain a Cultural Symbol, Tradition, or Hero

Most of us are fascinated by how other people live, think, and behave. In fact, learning about unfamiliar cultures is one of the major reasons that people travel. But familiar cultures can also be fascinating. By examining what we value and whom we admire in our own culture, we can better understand the way we lead our lives. Cultural experiences, whether familiar or unfamiliar, make for interesting reading and can lead to important insights.

Before you start considering possibilities for your own writing, read the following professional essays about cultural symbols (the Korean delicacy kim chee and the Indian rice dish pulao), a cultural tradition (the quinceañera in Latino/a cultures), and a cultural hero (Captain Chesley Sullenberger). As you read, notice how the writers provide examples and explain processes to help readers understand what their subjects mean to them. Notice, too, how the writers use effective introductions to get their readers' attention and powerful conclusions to leave a lasting impression about their subjects.

A Cultural Symbol: An Annotated Reading

NORA OKJA KELLER
My Mother's Food

Nora Okja Keller is a freelance writer and journalist who often writes about the intersection of Korean and American cultures. Her articles have appeared in *Newsweek*, *Time*, and the *New York Times*. She has also written several books, including the novels *Comfort Woman* (1998), which won the American Book Award, and *Fox Girl* (2002).

Keller was born in Seoul, Korea, but her family immigrated to the United States and settled in Hawaii when she was a young child. As a teenager, she rebelled against her mother's Korean culture in an effort to be seen as "American." In "My Mother's Food," Keller writes about the role food played in her rebellion.

1   I was weaned on kim chee. A good baby, I was "able to eat anything," my mother told me. But what I especially loved was the fermenting, garlicky Chinese cabbage my mother pickled in our kitchen. Not waiting for her to lick the red peppers off the won bok, I would grab and gobble the bits of leaves as soon as she tore them into baby-size pieces. She said that even if my eyes watered, I would still ask for more.

2   Propping me in a baby carrier next to the sink, my mother would rinse the cabbage she had soaked in salted water the night before. After patting the leaves dry, she would slather on the thick red-pepper sauce, rubbing the cloves of garlic and green onion into the underarms of the cabbage, bathing it as she would one of her own children. Then, grabbing them by their dangling leafy legs, she would push the wilting heads into five-gallon jars. She had to rise up on tiptoe, submerging her arm up to the elbow, to punch the kim chee to the bottom of the jar, squishing them into their own juices.

3   Throughout elementary school, our next-door neighbor Frankie, whose mother was the only other Korean in our neighborhood, would come over to eat kim chee with my sisters and me every day after school. We would gather in our garage, sitting cross-legged around a kim-chee jar as though at a campfire.

Keller captures her readers' attention by beginning her essay with a memorable image of a baby being "weaned" on kim chee.

Keller explains the process of making kim chee using descriptive examples.

Daring each other on, we would pull out long strips that we would eat straight, without rice or water to dilute the taste. Our eyes would tear and our noses start to run because it was so hot, but we could not stop. "It burns, it burns, but it tastes so good!" we would cry.

This dialogue helps readers imagine this scene.

Afterward when we went to play the jukebox in Frankie's garage, we had to 4 be careful not to touch our eyes with our wrinkled, pepperstained hands. It seemed as if the hot, red juice soaked through our skin and into our bones; even after we bathed, we could still feel our fingers tingling, still taste the kim chee on them when we licked them. And as my sisters and I curled into our bed at night, nestling together like sleeping doves, I remember the smell lingered on our hands, the faint whiff of kim chee scenting our dreams.

This description of the children in bed creates a vivid image.

We went crazy for the smell of kim chee—a perfume that lured us to the 5 kitchen table. When my mother hefted the jar of kim chee out of the refrigerator and opened the lid to extract the almost fluorescent strips of cabbage, she didn't have to call out to us, although she always did. "Girls, come join me," she would sing; even if we weren't hungry we couldn't resist. We all lingered over snacks that lasted two or three hours.

But I didn't realize that I smelled like kim chee, that the smell followed me to 6 school. One day, walking across Middle Field toward the girls' locker room, a girl I recognized from the gym class before mine stepped in front of me.

This dialogue slows down the action and helps readers picture the event.

"You Korean?" she asked. She had narrowed eyes as brown as mine, shaped 7 like mine, like mock-orange leaves pinched up at the corners.

Thinking she could be my sister, another part-Korean, part-Caucasian *hapa* 8 girl, I nodded and welcomed her kinship with a smile.

"I thought so," she said, sneering. Her lips scrunched upward, almost fold- 9 ing over her nostrils. "You smell like one."

I held my smile, frozen, as she flitted away from me. She had punched me 10 in the stomach with her words. Days later, having replayed this confrontation endlessly in my mind (in one fantasy version, this girl mutated into a hairy Neanderthal that I karate-chopped into submission), I thought of the perfect comeback: "Oh yeah? Well, you smell like a chimpanzee." At the very least, I should have said *something* that day. Anything—a curse, a joke, a grunt—anything at all would have been better than a smile.

Keller gives examples of how the encounter with her classmate affected her.

I smiled. And I sniffed. I smiled and sniffed as I walked to the locker room 11 and dressed for P.E. I smiled and sniffed as I jogged around the field, trying to avoid the hall and other girls wielding field hockey sticks. I smiled and sniffed as I showered and followed my schedule of classes.

I became obsessed with sniffing. When no one was looking, I lifted my arms 12 and, quick, sniffed. I held my palm up to my face and exhaled. Perhaps, every now and then, I would catch the odor of garlic in sweat and breath. I couldn't tell: the smell of kim chee was too much a part of me.

I didn't want to smell like a Korean. I wanted to be an American, which 13 meant having no smell. Americans, I learned from TV and magazines, erased the scent of their bodies with cologne and deodorant, breath mints and mouthwash.

So I erased my stink by eliminating kim chee. Though I liked the sharp taste 14 of garlic and pepper biting my tongue, I stopped eating my mother's food.

I became shamed by the kim chee that peeked out from between the loaf of white bread and the carton of milk, by the odor that, I grew to realize, permeated the entire house. When friends pointed at the kim-chee jars lined up on the refrigerator shelves and squealed, "Gross! What's that?" I would mumble, "I don't know, something my mom eats." 15

Keller feels shame over and rejects her culture because of peer pressure.

I also stopped eating the only three dishes my mother could cook: *kalbi ribs*, *bi bim kooksoo*, and Spam fried with eggs. (The first "American" food my mother ever ate was a Spam and egg sandwich; even now she considers it one of her favorite foods and never tires of eating it.) 16

I told my mother I was a vegetarian. One of my sisters ate only McDonald's Happy Meal cheeseburgers (no pickle); the other survived for two years on a diet of processed-cheese sandwiches on white bread (no crust), Hostess DingDongs, and rice dunked in ketchup. 17

Keller gives examples of American food that her sisters ate.

"How can you do this to me?" my mother wailed at her American-born children. "You are wasting away! Eat, eat!" She plopped heaps of kim chee and *kalbi* onto mounds of steaming rice. My sisters and I would grimace, poke at the food, and announce: "Too fattening." 18

My mother had always encouraged us to behave like proper Korean girls: quiet, respectful, hardworking. She said we gave her "heartaches" the way we fought as children. "Worse than boys," she'd say. "Why do you want to do things like soccer, scuba, swimming? How about piano?" 19

This dialogue helps readers understand Keller's mother.

But worse than our tomboy activities were our various adolescent diets. My mother grieved over the food rejected. "I don't understand you," she'd say. "When I was growing up, my family was so poor, we could only dream of eating this kind of food. Now I can give my children meat every night and you don't want it." "Yeah, yeah," we said, as we pushed away the kim chee, the Koreanness. 20

As I grew up, I eventually returned to eating kim chee, but only sporadically. I could go for months without it, then be hit with a craving so strong I would run to Sack-n-Save for a generic, watery brand that only hinted at the taste of home. Kim chee, I realized, was my comfort food. 21

When I became pregnant, the craving for my own mother accentuated my craving for kim chee. During the nights of my final trimester, my body foreign and heavy, restless with longing, I hungered for the food I had eaten in the womb, my first mother-memory. 22

The baby I carried in my own womb, in turn, does not look like me. Except for the slight tilt of her eyes, she does not look Korean. As a mother totally in love with her daughter, I do not care what she looks like; she is perfect as herself. Yet I worry that—partially because of what she looks like—she will not be able to identify with the Korean in me, and in herself. I recognize that identifying herself as Korean will be a choice for her—in a way it wasn't for someone like me, who looks pure Asian. It hit me then, what my own mother must have felt looking at each of her own mixed-race daughters; how strongly I do identify as a Korean American woman, how strongly I want my child to identify with me. 23

When my daughter was fifteen months old, she took her first bite of kim chee. I had taken a small bite into my own mouth, sucking the hot juice from its leaves, giving it "mothertaste" as my own mother had done for me. Still, my 24

This description of her daughter eating kim chee echoes the description at the beginning of the essay.

daughter's eyes watered. "Hot, hot," she said to her grandmother and me. But the taste must have been in some way familiar; instead of spitting up and crying for water, she pushed my hand to the open jar for another bite.

"She likes it!" my mother said proudly. "She is Korean!"   25

I realized that for my mother, too, the food we ate growing up had always 26 been an indication of how Korean her children were—or weren't. I remember how intently she watched us eat, as if to catch a glimpse of herself as we chewed.

Now my mother watches the next generation. When she visits, my daughter 27 clings to her, follows her from room to room. They run off together to play the games that only the two of them know how to play. I can hear them in my daughter's room, chattering and laughing. Sneaking to the doorway, I see them "cooking" in the Playskool kitchen.

"Look," my mother says, offering her grandchild a plate of plastic spaghetti, 28 "noodles is *kooksoo*." She picks up a steak. "This *kalbi*." My mother is teaching her Korean, presenting words my daughter knows the taste of.

My girl picks up a head of cabbage. "Let's make kim chee, *Halmoni*," she 29 says, using the Korean word for *grandmother* like a name.

"Okay," my mother answers. "First, salt." My daughter shakes invisible salt 30 over the cabbage.

"Then mix garlic and red-pepper sauce." My mother stirs a pot over the 31 stove and passes the mixture to my daughter, who pours it on the cabbage.

My daughter brings her fingers to her mouth. "Hot!" she says. Then she 32 holds the cabbage to my mother's lips, and gives her *halmoni* a taste.

"Mmmmm!" My mother grins as she chews the air. "Delicious! This is the 33 best kim chee I ever ate." My mother sees me peeking around the door.

"Come join us!" she calls out to me and tells my daughter, who's gnawing 34 at the fake food. "Let your mommy have a bite."

By using Korean words in this dialogue, Keller shows the close connection between food and culture.

This process analysis is similar to the process analysis earlier in the essay, which gives the end of the essay a sense of closure.

READING ACTIVITY 1 Build Your Vocabulary

Determine the meanings of the following words from the context of Nora Okja Keller's essay. Then check their meanings by looking up the words in a dictionary: *slather* (2), *nestling* (4), *extract* (5), *flitted* (10), *Neanderthal* (10), *wielding* (11), *permeated* (15), *sporadically* (21), *accentuated* (22).

GROUP ACTIVITY 1 Discuss the Reading

Discuss the following questions about "My Mother's Food" with your classmates.

1. What did kim chee symbolize for Keller when she was a child? Why did she stop eating it?

2. How did Keller's mother react when her children refused to eat Korean food? What does her reaction suggest about what the dishes symbolized in her mind?

3. How did the meaning of kim chee change for the author after she had a child?

4. Why do you think the author wants her daughter to think of herself as Korean?

5. How does Keller use examples and process explanation to explain what kim chee is and what it means to her?

> **WRITING ACTIVITY 1 Share Your Ideas**

In her essay, Keller describes how important kim chee has been in her life because it reminds her of her culture and her childhood. She describes kim chee as a type of "comfort food" that she craves, or has a strong desire to consume. Write a paragraph or two about the "comfort food" in your life or in your culture. Why do you want to eat it? What memories does it bring back about your life and your culture? Share your writing with your classmates.

A Cultural Symbol

JHUMPA LAHIRI
Rice

Born in London, raised in the United States, and currently living in Italy, Jhumpa Lahiri has published two collections of short stories—*Interpreter of Maladies* (1999) and *Unaccustomed Earth* (2008)—and two novels, *The Namesake* (2003) and *The Lowland* (2013). She has won many awards for her writing, including the Pulitzer Prize. Much of Lahiri's writing concerns the immigrant experience in the United States, in particular the attempt to maintain the "old" culture while gaining the "new" American culture. The following essay, "Rice," first appeared in the *New Yorker* in 2009.

1   My father, seventy-eight, is a methodical man. For thirty-nine years, he has had the same job, cataloguing books for a university library. He drinks two glasses of water first thing in the morning, walks for an hour every day, and devotes almost as much time, before bed, to flossing his teeth. "Winging it" is not a term that comes to mind in describing my father. When he's driving to new places, he does not enjoy getting lost.

2   In the kitchen, too, he walks a deliberate line, counting out the raisins that go into his oatmeal (fifteen) and never boiling even a drop more water than required for tea. It is my father who knows how many cups of rice are necessary to feed four, or forty, or a hundred and forty people. He has a reputation for *andaj*—the Bengali word for "estimate"—accurately gauging quantities that tend to baffle other cooks. An oracle of rice, if you will.

3   But there is another rice that my father is more famous for. This is not the white rice, boiled like pasta and then drained in a colander, that most Bengalis eat for dinner. This other rice is pulao, a baked, buttery, sophisticated indulgence, Persian in origin, served at festive occasions. I have often watched him make it. It involves sautéing grains of basmati in butter, along with cinnamon sticks, cloves,

bay leaves, and cardamom pods. In go halved cashews and raisins (unlike the oatmeal raisins, these must be golden, not black). Ginger, pulverized into a paste, is incorporated, along with salt and sugar, nutmeg and mace, saffron threads if they're available, ground turmeric if not. A certain amount of water is added, and the rice simmers until most of the water evaporates. Then it is spread out in a baking tray. (My father prefers disposable aluminum ones, which he recycled long before recycling laws were passed.) More water is flicked on top with his fingers, in the ritual and cryptic manner of Catholic priests. Then the tray, covered with foil, goes into the oven, until the rice is cooked through and not a single grain sticks to another.

Despite having a superficial knowledge of the ingredients and the tech- 4 nique, I have no idea how to make my father's pulao, nor would I ever dare attempt it. The recipe is his own, and has never been recorded. There has never been an unsuccessful batch, yet no batch is ever identical to any other. It is a dish that has become an extension of himself, that he has perfected, and to which he has earned the copyright. A dish that will die with him when he dies.

In 1968, when I was seven months old, my father made pulao for the first 5 time. We lived in London, in Finsbury Park, where my parents shared the kitchen, up a steep set of stairs in the attic of the house, with another Bengali couple. The occasion was my *annaprasan*, a rite of passage in which Bengali children are given solid food for the first time; it is known colloquially as a *bhath*, which happens to be the Bengali word for "cooked rice." In the oven of a stove no more than twenty inches wide, my father baked pulao for about thirty-five people. Since then, he has made pulao for the *annaprasans* of his friends' children, for birthday parties and anniversaries, for bridal and baby showers, for wedding receptions, and for my sister's Ph.D. party. For a few decades, after we moved to the United States, his pulao fed crowds of up to four hundred people, at events organized by Prabasi, a Bengali cultural institution in New England, and he found himself at institutional venues—schools and churches and community centers—working with industrial ovens and stoves. This has never unnerved him. He could probably rig up a system to make pulao out of a hot-dog cart, were someone to ask.

There are times when certain ingredients are missing, when he must use 6 almonds instead of cashews, when the raisins in a friend's cupboard are the wrong color. He makes it anyway, with exacting standards but a sanguine hand.

When my son and daughter were infants, and we celebrated their *anna-* 7 *prasans*, we hired a caterer, but my father made the pulao, preparing it at home in Rhode Island and transporting it in the trunk of his car to Brooklyn. The occasion, both times, was held at the Society for Ethical Culture, in Park Slope. In 2002, for my son's first taste of rice, my father warmed the trays on the premises, in the giant oven in the basement. But by 2005, when it was my daughter's turn, the representative on duty would not permit my father to use the oven, telling him that he was not a licensed cook. My father transferred the pulao from his aluminum trays into glass baking dishes, and microwaved, batch by batch, rice that fed almost a hundred people. When I asked my father to describe that experience, he expressed no frustration. "It was fine," he said. "It was a big microwave."

READING ACTIVITY 2 Build Your Vocabulary

Determine the meanings of the following words from the context of Jhumpa Lahiri's essay. Then check their meanings by looking up the words in a dictionary: *methodical* (1), *oracle* (2), *pulverized* (3), *cryptic* (3), *sanguine* (6).

GROUP ACTIVITY 2 Discuss the Reading

Discuss the following questions about "Rice" with your classmates.

1. What are five words or phrases that describe Lahiri's father?
2. Why does Lahiri's father make pulao on so many different occasions?
3. What does pulao seem to symbolize to Lahiri's father? To Lahiri herself?
4. Examine the process explanation given in paragraph 3 about how Lahiri's father makes pulao. What details make this process clear to readers?

WRITING ACTIVITY 2 Share Your Ideas

Foods are frequently associated with cultural events, such as the rite of passage that Lahiri describes for which her father made rice. Write a paragraph or two about a type of food associated with a cultural event such as a Thanksgiving or Juneteenth celebration. Describe how the food is usually cooked and what kind of role it plays in your culture.

A Cultural Tradition

LIZETTE ALVAREZ
Latinas Make Sweet 16-ish Their Own

Lizette Alvarez, a reporter for the *New York Times*, writes on topics ranging from war to politics to yoga. She received a master's degree in journalism from Northwestern University in 1987 and has received several journalism awards since. In "Latinas Make Sweet 16-ish Their Own," published in 2009, Alvarez describes the impact that U.S. culture has had on the traditional Latin American coming-of-age tradition for girls.

Cathy Zuluaga rearranged her strapless pink froufrou gown, lightly touched   1
her updo and, to the recorded strains of a waltz, strode into the ballroom at Riccardo's catering hall in Astoria, Queens. As the applause from the crowd of Colombians, Puerto Ricans and Dominicans swelled, Cathy, 16, released her father's arm, twirled, curtsied and smiled. She glided past her court of honor, eight girls in long silver dresses and eight boys in Nehru tuxes, and positioned herself on the white swing festooned with tulle, ribbons and flowers. Then, in keeping with tradition, her father knelt and slid off Cathy's demure ballerina slippers, trading them for a

pair of womanly high-heeled cha-cha sandals. Her mother gently placed a tiara on her head.

"She's putting the crown on her beautiful princess," announced the evening's M.C. In a flash, Cathy, her boyfriend and the rest of the court, some with braces on their teeth, tentatively began the traditional waltz that is one mainstay of many Latin quinceañera parties: step-step-close, step-step-close. At that moment, Cathy crossed the threshold from girlhood to womanhood. 2

"It was a special moment," Cathy recalled a week later, referring to her party. "It all looked dead cute." Plus, she added, "I got gifts, money and a Lexus." 3

Some say it is the boom in the Hispanic population, while others point to today's party-mad, status-driven culture and the success of the MTV show "My Super Sweet 16." But there is no doubt that the Hispanic coming-of-age quinceañera is more popular, more lavish and, in subtle ways, more American than ever. Picture a souped-up debutante ball without the high-society trappings or a bat mitzvah with an extra dose of razzle-dazzle, and a portrait emerges of many modern-day quinceañeras, a term that derives from the word quince (pronounced KEEN-say), which means 15 in Spanish. "Quinceañeras have really taken off," said Will Cain, publisher of the new glossy, ad-filled magazine *Quince Girl*, a takeoff on bridal magazines. "Quinceañeras are something unique, something that ties Hispanics together." 4

Today a number of girls are shaking off a few time-honored quinceañera traditions, like the Catholic Mass that typically precedes the party, and adding new ones, like arriving as Belle from "Beauty and the Beast" or choreographing dance moves to hip-hop. Some teenagers, like Cathy, a 10th-grader at Sewanhaka High School on Long Island, are choosing to wait an extra year so they can ditch the old-fashioned "quinceañera" label for the hipper, more acculturated "Sweet 16" tag. 5

The quince-style coming-of-age parties have even managed to influence the coming-of-age celebrations of other groups, including West Indians, African-Americans and Asians, who have grown infatuated with the party's choreographed nature and family tributes. This trend is particularly evident in multicultural New York, where the tradition of trading slippers for heels, lighting 16 candles and surrounding the birthday girl with a weddinglike "court" of friends is winning over non-Hispanic girls. "I am amazed at how many nationalities come in and want these Sweet 16's—Indians, Filipinas, Chinese," said Angela Baker-Brown, who runs Tatiana's Bridal in Queens, which sells quinceañera dresses and props, like the scepter the birthday girl carries. "It is a Hispanic tradition, but these other groups are going to these parties and wanting one as well." 6

The quinceañera party, long venerated for its wallet-busting tendencies, even among families with modest incomes, is pricier and more flamboyant than ever, according to dress manufacturers and event planners. The trend has also spread to states like Georgia and North Carolina, where Hispanics now make up a larger percentage of the population. 7

Business owners have noticed the emerging market. In addition to *Quince Girl* magazine, which is in Spanish and English, a number of bridal gown manufacturers like David's Bridal and the House of Wu now offer quinceañera lines. 8

Event planners and choreographers are proliferating, carving out specialties in the quince party. And teenagers can frequent quinceañera expos, giant show-cases for dresses, props and ideas, in Miami, Houston, Dallas and Los Angeles.

Girls celebrate their quinces at Disneyland, where Prince Charming will greet   9 them as they step out of Cinderella's coach. They go on cruises with friends and hold their parties aboard the ship, or book quince trips to Europe. If they choose to stay at home, many girls are sure to step out of a Humvee stretch limo, change their dresses midparty, present videos of their journey from infancy to woman-hood and indulge in multilayered cakes.

Traditions vary depending on the culture. Cubans in Miami may not neces-   10 sarily do the slipper-to-shoe exchange, while Mexicans in Texas emphasize the Catholic Mass, during which the girls sometimes carry a doll (to be given up that night) and receive their tiara. Other traditions, though, are being tweaked, a nod to today's teenage consumerism and to teenage girls' sometimes exacting demands. The waltz, a holdover from European colonialism, is still popular at many parties, but some girls are choosing to dance it alone, with their partner or father, rather than with their entire court of friends, a project that requires a lot of rehearsal and coordination. Persuading today's teenagers to waltz to "The Blue Danube," or something close to it, is not easy, so Latin music is creeping into the ritual.

The most dramatic departure has been in places like Miami, where the par-   11 ties have turned into extravaganzas. With price tags of $10,000 to $80,000, quinceañeras now rival weddings in cost and, in some respects, outpace them. "We have seen a lot more of the bigger productions," said Isabel Albuerne, who goes by the name Event Lady and whose company, Florida Weddings and Special Events, is based in Naples, Fla. "The Hispanic community treats it this way: I have one or two daughters. She may get married several times but a '15' happens only once. It's once in a lifetime. And there is no other half giving an opinion. It is the mom, the dad and the girl. You spend $40,000 on a wedding and in a year you are divorced."

Many families who can't really afford the party have them anyway. Tradition-   12 ally, quinceañera parties have cut across class lines. "They save for this for years," Ms. Albuerne said. Mexican-Americans often share the cost with the extended family, naming several godparents specifically to participate in the process. Cuban families open special savings accounts. "I know some Hispanics who have placed second mortgages on their home for this," she said. "It's important."

In Miami, home to moneyed Latin Americans and wealthy Cuban-Americans,   13 quinces are fancier than ever, with some parties now veering into Broadway-esque stagecraft. It is not uncommon for a young girl in belly-dancing attire to be carried aloft on a bejeweled "Arabian Nights" bed by four young men or to step out of a custom-built Cinderella castle. Birthday girls saunter across sandy floors as mermaids, à la "Under the Sea," or dance in Victorian regalia, or put on hip-hop routines. Masquerade parties are popular, and costume changes, as in stage productions, are au courant. Even when the party involves just the traditional waltz, a choreographer is a must. "Some wear short dresses underneath their big dresses and during the disco, they rip off the big dress," said Ana Ricolt, owner of Fantastic Fiestas in Miami, whose clientele is 80 percent Cuban-American. In September, Ms. Ricolt is putting together a Cinderella party and the girl "is coming in a Cinderella carriage mounted on the stage," she said. "It's a production. It can take us from 8 to 12 weeks to get everything done."

By Miami standards, Natasha Poupariña's celebration last October was 14 notable. Hewing to the "Phantom of the Opera" theme, Natasha arrived on stage astride a white horse. Her escort was the Phantom. Natasha and her partner, a young man dressed like a prince, danced with their court, in masks and long ball gowns, to the "Phantom" theme song. All the details of the party, down to the cake's décor, revolved around the theme.

Some parents do still hold their parties in a church hall, cook their own food 15 and make their daughters' dresses. But that has quickly become a rare occurrence, particularly among girls who have grown up in America. At Tatiana's Bridal, the average cost of a dress is about $400. Choreographers charge at least $2,000 and photographers more than $3,000.

Milady Chaverra, Cathy's mother, who was born in New York and is half- 16 Puerto Rican, half-Colombian, said Cathy's party took more than a year of preparation, including finding dance halls for the waltz rehearsals. "It's a lot of planning and a lot of money," said Mrs. Chaverra, who owns Flushing Express Car Service with her husband, Adolfo. "It's a tradition. I didn't have one and Cathy really wanted one. It's worth it. I get the memories."

READING ACTIVITY 3 Build Your Vocabulary

Determine the meanings of the following words from the context of Lizette Alvarez's essay. Then check their meanings by looking up the words in a dictionary: *froufrou* (1), *demure* (1), *mainstay* (2), *infatuated* (6), *venerated* (7), *proliferating* (8), *saunter* (13).

GROUP ACTIVITY 3 Discuss the Reading

Discuss the following questions about "Latinas Make Sweet 16-ish Their Own" with your classmates.

1. What sentence or sentences best express the main idea of this essay?
2. Why do some girls wait until age 16 to celebrate their *quinceañeras*?
3. How have U.S.-style *quinceañeras* influenced coming-of-age traditions of other cultures?
4. Where is process explanation best used in this essay?

WRITING ACTIVITY 3 Share Your Ideas

Write a paragraph or two about a coming-of-age tradition that you are familiar with. In U.S. culture, for example, getting a driver's license or being able to drink legally for the first time can be considered coming-of-age traditions. Share what you have written with your classmates.

A Cultural Hero

JEFFREY ZASLOW

What We Can Learn from Sully's Journey

Jeffrey Zaslow was an author and journalist who specialized in writing about the lives of extraordinary people. He graduated from Carnegie Mellon University in 1980 and was a columnist for the *Wall Street Journal*. In addition to writing his regular column, he authored or coauthored three best-selling books, including *Highest Duty: My Search for What Really Matters* (2009), the memoir of Captain Chesley "Sully" Sullenberger. The following piece about Captain Sullenberger first appeared in the *Wall Street Journal* in 2009.

1   US Airways Capt. Chesley "Sully" Sullenberger has flown thousands of flights in the last 42 years. "But now," he says, "my entire career is being judged by how I performed on one of them." That flight, of course, came last Jan. 15, when his Airbus A320 suffered a bird strike en route from New York to Charlotte, N.C., and lost both engines. Sully and First Officer Jeff Skiles executed an emergency landing later dubbed "The Miracle on the Hudson," but that description never felt right to Sully.

2   He is a precise, methodical, cerebral man who carefully chooses his words. In recent months, while working on his new book, *Highest Duty: My Search for What Really Matters*, Sully spent a great deal of time reviewing his life and career. He has tried to understand what experiences from his past prepared him for Flight 1549.

3   As Sully's co-author, I clearly saw that it wasn't only his skills as a veteran pilot that carried him in those tense moments over Manhattan. It was also his upbringing, his family bonds, his sense of integrity—and his own losses. Flight 1549 wasn't just a five-minute journey from LaGuardia Airport to the Hudson. Sully's entire life led him safely to that river.

4   He was born in Denison, Texas, the son of a dentist and a teacher who had high expectations. "I grew up in a home where each of us had our own hammer," says Sully. That was because his dad kept enlarging the family home with the help of three not-always-willing assistants: Sully, his sister and his mom. "The goal was to do everything ourselves, to learn what we didn't know and then have at it," Sully says. The house wasn't perfect, but Sully knew where every nail was. "Sometimes I'd brood, wishing we lived in a professionally built house like everyone else," he says. "But each time the house grew, I felt a sense of accomplishment."

5   As a boy, Sully was a classic introvert who felt things deeply. In 1964, for instance, he saw news reports about a New York woman named Kitty Genovese. Her neighbors heard her screams as she was being stabbed to death by a stranger outside her apartment. Allegedly, they did nothing to help. "I made a pledge to

myself, right then at age 13," Sully recalls, "that if I was ever in a situation where someone such as Kitty Genovese needed my help, I would choose to act. No one in danger would be abandoned. As they'd say in the Navy: 'Not on my watch.'"

People tell Sully that his success on Jan. 15 showed a high regard for life. 6 Their words led him to reflection. "Quite frankly," he says, "one of the reasons I think I've placed such a high value on life is that my father took his." Suffering from depression, Sully's father killed himself in 1995. "His death had an effect on how I view the world," he says. "I am willing to work hard to protect people's lives, to not be a bystander, in part because I couldn't save my father."

There are other moments in Sully's personal life that he feels helped prepare 7 him for Flight 1549. Sully and his wife struggled with infertility, then endured the arduous journey of trying to become adoptive parents. "The challenges Lorrie and I faced made me better able to accept the cards I've been dealt," Sully says, "and to play them with all the resources at my disposal." The couple eventually adopted two daughters, now ages 16 and 14.

He first yearned to fly at age five. At 16, in 1967, he began taking lessons 8 from a no-nonsense crop-dusting pilot named L. T. Cook Jr. Sully was an earnest, hard-working student who paid close attention. One day he noticed a crumpled Piper Tri-Pacer at the end of Mr. Cook's grass airstrip. A friend of Mr. Cook's had tried to land the plane and didn't realize that power lines stretched across a nearby highway. The plane slammed into the ground nose first. The pilot died instantly.

Sully peered into the blood-splattered cockpit. "I figured his head must have 9 hit the control panel with great violence," he says. "I tried to visualize how it happened—his effort to avoid the power lines, his loss of speed, the awful impact. I forced myself to look into the cockpit, to study it. It would have been easier to look away, but I didn't." That sobering moment taught Sully to be vigilant and alert. For a pilot, one simple mistake could mean death.

He went on to the U.S. Air Force Academy, then a military career, and con- 10 tinued to study accidents. Twelve fellow military pilots died on training runs. "I grieved for my lost comrades," he says, "but I tried to learn all I could about each of their accidents." As an airline pilot, he helped develop an air-safety course and served as an investigator at crash sites. He'd page through transcripts from cockpit voice recorders, with the last exchanges of pilots who didn't survive.

Since childhood, Sully has been fascinated by Charles Lindbergh. In *We*, 11 Lindbergh's 1927 book, he explained that his success was due almost entirely to preparation, not luck. "Prepared Lindy" wouldn't have had the same magic as his nickname "Lucky Lindy," but his views resonated with Sully. One aspect of preparing well is having the right mind-set, he says. "In so many areas of life, you need to be a long-term optimist but a short-term realist. That's especially true given the inherent dangers in aviation. You can't be a wishful thinker. You have to know what you know and don't know, and what your airplane can and can't do in every situation."

Sully has always kept in mind the air-crew ejection study he learned about in 12 his military days. Many pilots waited too long before ejecting from planes that were about to crash. They either ejected at too low an altitude, hitting the ground before their parachutes could open, or they went down with their planes. Why did these pilots spend extra seconds trying to fix the unfixable? The answer is that many feared retribution if they lost million-dollar jets. And so they remained determined to try to save their airplanes.

Sully says he has never shaken his memories of fellow Air Force pilots who 13 didn't survive such attempts. Having those details in the recesses of his brain was helpful as he made quick decisions on Flight 1549. "As soon as the birds struck," he says, "I could have tried to return to LaGuardia so as not to ruin a US Airways aircraft. I could have worried that my decision to ditch the plane would be questioned by superiors or investigators. But I chose not to."

Sully values the concept of "goal sacrificing." When it's no longer possible 14 to complete all your goals, you sacrifice lower-priority goals. He instinctively knew that goal sacrificing was paramount on Flight 1549. "By attempting a water landing," he says, "I would sacrifice the 'airplane goal'—trying not to destroy an aircraft valued at $60 million—for the goal of saving lives."

Able to compartmentalize his thinking, even in those dire moments over the 15 Hudson, Sully says his family did not come into his head. "That was for the best. It was vital that I be focused; that I allow myself no distractions. My consciousness existed solely to control the flight path."

Since saving 155 lives that day, Sully has received thousands of emails and 16 now has 635,000 Facebook fans. His actions touched people so deeply that they felt compelled to reach out and share their own seminal experiences with him. "I am now the public face of an unexpectedly uplifting moment," Sully says, and he accepts that. Still, he's not comfortable with the "hero" mantle. A hero runs into a burning building, he says. "Flight 1549 was different because it was thrust upon me and my crew. We turned to our training, we made good decisions, we didn't give up, we valued every life on that plane—and we had a good outcome. I don't know that 'heroic' describes that. It's more that we had a philosophy of life, and we applied it to the things we did that day."

Sully has heard from people who say preparation and diligence are not the 17 same as heroism. He agrees. One letter that was particularly touching to Sully came from Paul Kellen of Medford, Mass. "I see a hero as electing to enter a dangerous situation for a higher purpose," he wrote, "and you were not given a choice. That is not to say you are not a man of virtue, but I see your virtue arising from your choices at other times. It's clear that many choices in your life prepared you for that moment when your engines failed. There are people among us who are ethical, responsible and diligent. I hope your story encourages those who toil in obscurity to know that their reward is simple—they will be ready if the test comes. I hope your story encourages others to imitation."

Sully now sees lessons for the rest of us. "We need to try to do the right 18 thing every time, to perform at our best," he says, "because we never know what moment in our lives we'll be judged on." He always had a sense of this. Now he knows it for sure.

READING ACTIVITY 4 **Build Your Vocabulary**

Determine the meanings of the following words from the context of "What We Can Learn from Sully's Journey." Then check their meanings by looking up the words in a dictionary: *cerebral* (2), *introvert* (5), *arduous* (7), *inherent* (11), *ejection* (12), *retribution* (12).

GROUP ACTIVITY 4 **Read to Improve Your Writing**

Discuss the following questions about "What We Can Learn from Sully's Journey" with your classmates.

1. What sentence or sentences in this piece best summarize the main point?
2. List three experiences from Captain Sullenberger's life that you think best prepared him for Flight 1549.
3. What is the concept of "goal sacrificing"? What goal did Captain Sullenberger sacrifice when he decided to land the plane on water?
4. Captain Sullenberger says that he is not a hero. Do you agree? Why or why not?

WRITING ACTIVITY 4 **Share Your Ideas**

Write a paragraph or two about your definition of a hero. In your writing, explain the characteristics and experiences that lead to heroic behavior. Who are some cultural heroes that fit your definition?

Writing Your Essay A Step-by-Step Guide

Now that you've read some essays explaining a cultural symbol, tradition, or hero, it's time to write your own essay. First, read the writing assignment below. Then, use the step-by-step advice that follows to discover ideas, develop them as you draft, and polish your writing into a finished essay that readers will find both interesting and informative:

Writing Assignment

What cultures do you belong to? Consider your ethnic heritage, religion, age group, schools, workplaces, interests, social activities, and pastimes.

Have you ever noticed that people who are unfamiliar with one of these cultures don't always understand it? No matter what your background is, your experience has given you specialized knowledge and a unique perspective. For this chapter's assignment, your goal is to teach readers something about a culture you know well. You (or your instructor) may decide to approach this assignment in one of several ways:

- Write about a cultural symbol you are familiar with.
- Write about a tradition that has special meaning for you.
- Write about a person who is a hero to members of a particular group.

(Step 1 **Explore Your Choices**

After a little thought, you should be able to identify several different cultures that have influenced who you are and how you look at the world. Your family heritage and the region where you grew up, for example, probably hold special meaning for you. You might belong to a club or a sports team, identify with fans of a particular kind of music, or participate in an online community. In addition to having multiple cultures to consider, you will explore three topic possibilities—a cultural symbol, a cultural tradition, and a cultural hero—before you choose one topic to develop.

As you begin to search for essay ideas, think about who might read your essay and what they may already know (or not know) about a culture you belong to. For now, you should keep your options open by working with all three of the topics suggested in the assignment. Once you have tried out these possibilities, you will have a better idea of what topic—or topics—will be most productive.

Analyzing Your Audience and Purpose

In addition to your instructor and classmates, your audience may consist of family members, friends, and even complete strangers. Because your readers may come from different cultures, you need to figure out how much they might already know about your topic and what their attitude toward it might be. You will also need to provide plenty of context and detail so that a person who is unfamiliar with your culture will be able to understand what you have to say about it.

For more on audience and purpose, see pp. 6–8.

Consider, also, what you want to accomplish with your essay. Remember that the assignment is to teach readers something about a culture they might not fully understand. Although you may also be interested in expressing your feelings or persuading your readers to do something or think a certain way, always keep in mind that your goal is informative—to give them new information.

Examine your online audience

If you are considering submitting your essay to a blog or website, find out as much as you can about the audience. Examine the comments readers have posted on the site in response to articles, photos, and so on. What do these comments reveal about the audience's interests and viewpoints? Use this information to make your essay appealing to your readers.

WRITING ACTIVITY 5 Analyze Your Audience and Purpose

Consider the audience that will be reading your essay. It can consist of your instructor, classmates, friends, and family. It can also consist of people you have never met if you decide to post your finished essay on a blog or another site on the Internet. Your responses to the following questions will help you decide how to approach your topic.

1. Does this assignment call for primarily expressive, informative, or persuasive writing?

2. What is the average age of your readers?

3. What percentage of your readers are likely to be female? Male?

4. What parts of the country or world could they be from?

5. What might your readers already know about your topic? If you asked them to list five words about your topic, which five might they list?

6. What do your readers need to know about your topic? What terms and concepts will you need to define? What objects or events would you need to describe in detail?

7. How might your readers feel about your topic? Will they find it interesting, or will you have to work to get their attention?

Gathering Ideas

For more on gathering ideas, see pp. 11–14.

Before you begin writing, it's always a good idea to explore a few topics by using different techniques. Trying out several possibilities often leads to unexpected ideas, and you might be surprised to discover which topic you have the most to say about. In the previous chapter, you gathered ideas by brainstorming, relating aloud, and clustering. In this chapter, you will again use clustering, but you will also add two more tools for gathering ideas about a cultural symbol, tradition, and hero—questioning and freewriting. Although the activities prompt you to use one technique for each topic possibility, don't hesitate to use additional approaches that work for you.

Clustering about a Cultural Symbol

For more on clustering, see p. 12.

A *symbol* is something that stands for or represents something else. For example, the American flag symbolizes the United States and also stands for freedom and democracy. The Star of David stands for Judaism, and a pink triangle symbolizes gay pride.

Some symbols are formal and permanent representations, such as the flag of the United States or the Statue of Liberty. As you discovered reading "My Mother's Food," however, symbols can be quite ordinary and represent any number of things for different people. Cultural symbols can take almost any form and often tell us what the people of the culture consider important.

To gather ideas about a cultural symbol that you might want to write about, try *clustering*, a technique that works especially well for visual topics. As you learned in the previous chapter, you start a cluster by putting a word or phrase in the center of a blank page and drawing a small circle around it. Write down other words or phrases that your topic brings to mind, draw small circles around them, and use lines to connect related ideas. If you need a starting point or if you get stuck, the following questions can help jump-start your thinking:

- How would you describe the object to someone who has not seen it before?
- When was the last time you encountered or used the object?
- What ideas, events, or other objects do you associate with the object?
- How does the object symbolize the culture's lifestyle or beliefs?

Here's how one student, Clara, used some of these questions to create a cluster about a cultural symbol that interested her—an artificial Christmas tree:

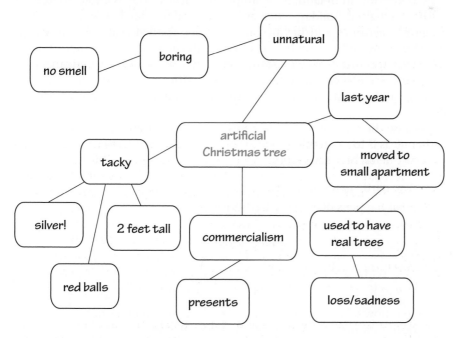

Figure 6.1 Clara's Clustering

> **WRITING ACTIVITY 6** Cluster about a Cultural Symbol

Select an object or image that symbolizes contemporary American culture or another culture that has influenced you. You could choose the food you wrote about after reading "My Mother's Food" (p. 135) or "Rice" (p. 139). Then create a cluster that connects the words and phrases you associate with this symbol. You may use the questions above to get started, but don't limit yourself to them.

Asking Questions about a Cultural Tradition

A *tradition* is an event or activity repeatedly performed in the same way, usually to celebrate a culture's heritage and to bring people closer together. Many families develop traditions, such as annual reunions, that bring them together. A *cultural tradition*, however, extends beyond a family's rituals because it reflects the values of an entire culture. In "Latinas Make Sweet 16-ish Their Own," for instance, Lizette Alvarez shows how a rite of passage for teenage girls is often celebrated in Latin American cultures.

To gather ideas about a cultural tradition you may want to write about, a good strategy is questioning to investigate what makes it interesting or unique. Thanksgiving and the Fourth of July are cultural traditions unique to the United States; you could ask when they developed as American holidays. Some American cultural traditions have been adapted from other parts of the world and changed to suit American lifestyles and values; you could ask questions about what values are displayed by celebrating other countries' traditions. In Ireland, for example, St. Patrick's Day is a solemn Roman Catholic religious holiday, whereas in America, the day has lost most of its religious overtones and has become a public festival that celebrates Irish heritage. New cultural traditions develop all the time; you could ask why. Kwanzaa, for instance, was started in 1966 by African Americans who adapted the customs and beliefs of several African tribes to celebrate their heritage and to foster a sense of community among Americans of African descent.

Because there can be many features to a cultural tradition, a good way to gather ideas is to use the six questions reporters often ask to ensure that they get every detail of a news story:

- *Who* participates in this tradition?
- *What* happens during the tradition?
- *Where* is this tradition practiced?
- *When* does this tradition take place?
- *How* is this tradition celebrated?
- *Why* is this tradition important to the participants?

Here is how one student, Sandra, answered the reporter's questions about a Mexican tradition, the holiday El Grito de Dolores:

Who? This tradition is celebrated by people in Mexico. The governor of
    each city pretends to be Miguel Hidalgo. The people of the city attend
    a parade.

What? This tradition has people reenact the time when Miguel Hidalgo
    persuaded the people of Dolores to fight for freedom from Spain.

Where? This tradition is celebrated in every town and city in Mexico.

When? El Grito de Dolores takes place on the evening of September 15 and
    the morning of September 16.

How? Fireworks are set off, a parade is held, and some people dress in tra-
    ditional costumes.

Why? The Mexican people use this tradition to celebrate their freedom from
    Spain.

> **WRITING ACTIVITY 7 Ask Questions about a Cultural
> Tradition**

Select a tradition that you know well. You could choose the tradition you wrote
about after reading "Latinas Make Sweet 16-ish Their Own" (p. 141). Then use the
journalist's questions—*Who? What? Where? When? How? Why?*—to generate
ideas for an essay that could explain the tradition to readers who aren't familiar
with it.

Freewriting about a Cultural Hero

We all have personal heroes—family members, friends, teachers, or
coaches—whom we admire because of their courage, dedication, or hard
work and who serve as role models. *Cultural heroes* are known by many
people within a culture and inspire an entire culture. Some cultural heroes
are part of a group's heritage, others come from contemporary life, and still
others are fictional characters. Sacagawea, the Dalai Lama, Mother Teresa,
Martin Luther King Jr., Nelson Mandela, César Chávez, and Maya Angelou
are just a few examples of real-life cultural heroes, while Luke Skywalker and
Wonder Woman are examples of fictional heroes. In "What We Can Learn
from Sully's Journey" (p. 145), you read about a cultural hero widely admired
in the United States and around the world for saving hundreds of people's
lives when he safely landed a disabled airplane.

Who are some of your heroes? Although you may be able to list several
people who have inspired you, you may not be certain that they are cultural
heroes or that you know enough about them to fill a whole essay. You can
find out if a person is a good subject for an essay by freewriting.

To freewrite, write without stopping for a certain period of time or until
you reach a given page limit. Don't pause, go back, or make corrections, and
don't try to put your thoughts in order; above all, don't worry about whether

your ideas are good or not. Just keep writing and see what you have to say. You can start by answering these questions:

- What facts do you know about this person (age, accomplishments, and so on)?
- Which five words best describe this person?
- What do you most admire about this person?
- What makes this person a cultural hero?

Here's how one student, Autumn, gathered ideas about cultural heroes Martin Luther King Jr. and Aung San Suu Kyi by freewriting:

> Aung San Suu Kyi and Martin Luther King Jr. are two of the greatest political leaders. What I most admire about them is that they were willing to fight against things that would get them punished. When I think of both of these heroes, the words that come to my mind are "brave," "religious," and "strong." Aung San Suu Kyi lives in Burma where there is a military dictatorship. Suu Kyi has been unable to leave her house for many years because she has led opposition to the dictatorship. She believes in Buddhism and says that violence is contrary to Buddhism. King was a Christian who thought that violence went against the teaching of Jesus. Both King and Suu Kyi won the Nobel Peace Prize. They both suffered for causes that they believed in.

GROUP ACTIVITY 5   Freewrite about a Cultural Hero

On your own or with a group of classmates, brainstorm a list of cultural heroes. Consider musicians, athletes, public officials, religious leaders, actors, entrepreneurs, celebrities, and ordinary people who are widely known because of their extraordinary talent, dedication, or achievements. Then select a hero who interests you and freewrite about that person for at least ten minutes. If you like, you can write more about the hero you may have written about after reading "What We Can Learn from Sully's Journey" (p. 145).

Step 2 Write Your Discovery Draft

Now that you have experimented with at least three different topics that you might want to explore in an essay, you should be ready to begin a discovery draft. Remember that nobody creates a perfect essay in one try. Writing a discovery draft is a lot like the freewriting you did earlier in this chapter: experiment, let yourself wander, and feel free to make mistakes. You can focus on the details later when you revise and edit.

Choosing a Topic

You have gathered ideas on three aspects of culture—a symbol, a tradition, and a hero—and now have a rich source of material for writing. But you need to decide how to proceed.

Start by looking over the materials you wrote during your clustering, questioning, and freewriting. Which topic generated the most useful ideas? Which topic (or topics) are you most interested in pursuing? Which one will your readers want to learn about?

As you consider options for your discovery draft, you may stick with one of the three topics listed in the assignment (a cultural symbol, tradition, or hero), or you could decide to combine related topics. For instance, you could describe how turkey and pumpkin pie have become symbols of the cultural tradition of Thanksgiving. Whatever you decide, the topic you choose should be one that interests you and that you are already fairly well informed about.

> ### WRITING ACTIVITY 8 Choose Your Topic
>
> Review your clustering, questioning, and freewriting, and identify or create a topic that you will enjoy writing about and that your audience will enjoy reading. If you wish, you may do more clustering, questioning, and freewriting (or whatever prewriting techniques work best for you) to gather additional ideas on one or more topics before you move forward.

Sharing Your Ideas

Once you have settled on a topic, write a preliminary thesis statement to help focus your thoughts. As you draft and new ideas emerge, you can revise your thesis as many times as you need to.

For more on thesis statements, see p. 18.

If necessary, you might want to collect some basic information—such as dates and names—to get started. Most of the material for your discovery draft, however, should come from your own knowledge and experience. Keep your audience and purpose in mind as you decide what to include. Above all, remember that your main goal right now is to get your ideas down on paper. You'll have time later on to expand, fine-tune, and edit your draft.

A Student's Discovery Draft

Student writer Autumn Harrison used freewriting to gather ideas about cultural heroes Aun San Suu Kyi and Martin Luther King Jr. (p. 154). She then wrote the following discovery draft, using a research source to add information. Her preliminary thesis statement is highlighted. After reading the draft, discuss with your classmates what Autumn might do to revise it. (Note that the example includes the types of errors that typically appear in a discovery draft.)

Autumn's preliminary
thesis statement

Martin Luther King Jr. and Aung San Suu Kyi are two of my cultural heroes. They both believed in civil disobedience and both were religious. King was Christian and Suu Kyi is a Buddhist. King was from the U.S. and Suu Kyi is from Burma. They both used civil disobedience to protest against injustice.

In 1963 King wrote "Letter from a Birmingham Jail" in which he expressed his philosophy about civil disobedience. King had received a message from Christian and Jewish leaders who thought these methods of civil disobedience were too radical. But he thought he was called by God to lead the protests. He wrote in the letter, "I say it as a minister of the gospel, who loves the church; who was nurtured in its bosom; who has been sustained by its spiritual blessings and who will remain true to it as long as the cord of life shall lengthen" (p. 213). King knew that change would come.

Sui Kyi also knew that nonviolent protests would bring democracy to her country of Burma. In "In Quest of Democracy" she wrote about the Buddhist belief in "The Ten Duties of Kings." These duties included non-violence and democracy. She tried to bring democracy to her country but she was placed on house arrest for many years.

These two leaders sacrificed their freedom, and in the case of Dr. King his life, to make the world a better place for everyone. They were two voices with one idea.

Works Cited

King, Martin Luther. "Letter From Birmingham Jail." *Reading the World: Ideas That Matter.* 2nd Edition. Ed. Michael Austin. New York: W.W. Norton & Company, 2010. 202-217. Print.

WRITING ACTIVITY 9 Write Your Discovery Draft

Prepare a preliminary thesis statement and build on the ideas you gathered during Step 1 to write a discovery draft. Remember that your purpose is to teach your audience something about a cultural symbol, tradition, or hero important to you. For now, focus simply on getting your ideas in writing. If you have any trouble, consider writing drafts on one or more topics before you decide which one to continue working on.

Step 3 Revise Your Draft

When you revise a discovery draft, you concentrate on clarifying and supporting your ideas. Resist the urge to correct errors when revising; you will do that during the editing stage.

The revision skills you learned in the previous chapter will also help you improve your essay about a cultural symbol, tradition, or hero. Check that your thesis statement identifies your topic and expresses your main idea, that each paragraph has a topic sentence, and that your essay is well focused. In the rest of this chapter, you will learn how to use examples and process explanation to develop your ideas. You will also learn strategies for writing an effective introduction and conclusion, and you will practice connecting ideas with keywords and transitions.

Developing Your Ideas

An essay must be well developed to be convincing. In other words, you need to support your points with information. Detailed information helps readers understand your subject and makes your essay more interesting. Two methods of development—examples and process explanation—are especially appropriate for an essay on a cultural symbol, tradition, or hero.

Examples

Examples provide specific details that make a main point vivid and concrete. The most common types of examples are facts, or statements that can be verified to be true. Examples may also be specific instances or events that illustrate your main point, relevant personal experiences, or other people's opinions.

For more on using examples, see pp. 75–77.

In her essay "Rice," Jhumpa Lahiri uses examples to support her point that her father always follows a certain routine. Notice that she starts her paragraph with a topic sentence (highlighted) and then provides several examples of the routines he follows:

> My father, seventy-eight, is a methodical man. For thirty-nine years, he has had the same job, cataloguing books for a university library. He drinks two glasses of water first thing in the morning, walks for an hour every day, and devotes almost as much time, before bed, to flossing his teeth. "Winging it" is not a term that comes to mind in describing my father. When he's driving to new places, he does not enjoy getting lost.

Like Lahiri's, a paragraph that provides examples should include a topic sentence that explains what point the examples are meant to illustrate. It

HOW TO Use Examples

- Express a main idea in a topic sentence.
- Support the main idea with facts, specific instances or events, personal experiences, or expert opinions.
- Be sure that every example is clear, believable, and interesting.
- Check that you have provided enough examples to help readers understand your main point.
- Add details that develop your examples.

should provide enough examples and details to help your readers understand your main point. In addition, the examples should be clear, believable, and interesting for your audience.

> ◖ **WRITING ACTIVITY 10** Use Examples to Develop Your Ideas ◗
>
> Review your discovery draft, looking for ideas that could be made clearer with examples. Add examples to at least one paragraph by expressing your point in the topic sentence and supporting that point with several facts, instances or events, experiences, or opinions. Be sure that your examples are clear, believable, and interesting, and that you provide enough examples to support your idea. Include details that help your readers understand your point.

Process Explanation

For more on using process explanation, see p. 77.

Writers use a technique called *process explanation* to show readers the series of steps needed to do something or to make something work. You may have read a recipe that explains how to cook something, a newspaper article that explains how wastewater is recycled or how a new law is passed, or a magazine article that describes how to repair a motorcycle or organize your desk. Each of these is an example of using a process explanation to develop a main idea.

Consider, for example, how Nora Okja Keller uses process explanation in "My Mother's Food" to explain how her mother made kim chee:

> Propping me in a baby carrier next to the sink, my mother would rinse the cabbage she had soaked in salted water the night before. After patting the leaves dry, she would slather on the thick red-pepper sauce, rubbing the cloves of garlic and green onion into the underarms of the cabbage, bathing it as she would one of her own children. Then, grabbing them by their dangling leafy legs, she would push the wilting heads into five-gallon jars. She had to rise up on tiptoe, submerging her arm up to the elbow, to punch the kim chee to the bottom of the jar, squishing them into their own juices.

> ⏻ **Use a numbered list**
>
> To help clarify the steps in the process you're writing about, use the number function on your word-processing program. Number the steps and review them to make sure they're in the right order. Be sure to omit the numbers when you revise your essay.

After reviewing her discovery draft, student writer Autumn Harrison decided that she could use process explanation to give her readers a better sense of the process of civil disobedience. For her second paragraph, she added this information about Dr. King.

He followed the process of civil disobedience by leading hundreds of people in boycotting businesses. Protesters sat at lunch counters that would not serve Blacks and refused to move. For the final step, hundreds of schoolchildren marching in the streets to integrate the city. The police then turned attack dogs and fire hoses on them and had them arrested.

HOW TO Use Process Explanation

- Introduce the process you will describe.
- Provide the steps in the process in the order that they occur.
- Include details so that your readers can follow the process easily.
- Use keywords and transitions to move your readers from step to step.

WRITING ACTIVITY 11 Develop Ideas with Process Explanation

Exchange discovery drafts with a classmate. Read your partner's draft and circle any sections that suggest a possibility for process explanation. (For example, in a draft about a cultural tradition, one paragraph might tell what participants do.) In the margins, say what you don't understand about a process and ask for more information. Your classmate should do the same for your draft. Using your partner's comments, add process explanation to your draft where it will make your topic easier to understand.

 Use the Comment feature when peer reviewing

The Comment feature of a word-processing program can help you give detailed suggestions for revision. Exchange electronic copies of drafts with your classmates and use Comment to insert notes, questions, and suggestions. Before you print a draft, you can keep, hide, or remove the comments.

Building Your Essay

Now that you have added details to your essay, you'll want to make sure that readers understand how those details work together to explain a cultural symbol, tradition, or hero. As you learned in Chapter 3, a strong thesis statement, clear topic sentences, and unified paragraphs will help you communicate your thoughts clearly. Readers also expect an essay to have an interesting introduction and a forceful conclusion, and keywords and transitions can help readers connect your points throughout an essay. Let's look first at introductions.

Write an Effective Introduction

The *introduction* to an essay serves three purposes: it gets your readers' attention, it narrows the topic, and it provides your thesis statement. By using the opening sentences of your essay to hook your readers' interest, you persuade them to continue reading. By narrowing your topic and presenting your thesis statement up front, you give your readers a road map of sorts. Although introductions are often only one paragraph with the thesis statement coming at the end, in longer essays, introductions may be two, three, or more paragraphs.

As you learned in Chapter 3, several techniques can help you hook your readers' attention, narrow your topic, and lead to your thesis statement. For an essay about a cultural symbol, tradition, or hero, consider opening with description, interesting or surprising facts, a brief story or anecdote, or a question—as the authors of the readings in this chapter do.

Give a Description   An introduction that contains vivid *description* sets the scene and draws readers into your essay. Lizette Alvarez, in "Latinas Make Sweet 16-ish Their Own," uses this technique to help readers picture the dancing at a quinceañera:

> Cathy Zuluaga rearranged her strapless pink froufrou gown, lightly touched her updo and, to the recorded strains of a waltz, strode into the ballroom at Riccardo's catering hall in Astoria, Queens. As the applause from the crowd of Colombians, Puerto Ricans and Dominicans swelled, Cathy, 16, released her father's arm, twirled, curtsied and smiled. She glided past her court of honor, eight girls in long silver dresses and eight boys in Nehru tuxes, and positioned herself on the white swing festooned with tulle, ribbons and flowers. Then, in keeping with tradition, her father knelt and slid off Cathy's demure ballerina slippers, trading them for a pair of womanly high-heeled cha-cha sandals. Her mother gently placed a tiara on her head.

Relate Facts   Introducing a topic with *facts*—statements that can be verified as true—has two important effects on readers: It signals to them that you know your topic well enough to teach them something, and it encourages them to read further to see what you have to say. Farther along in the introduction to "Latinas Make Sweet 16-ish Their Own," Lizette Alvarez adds facts to emphasize how the traditional ceremony of the quinceañera is changing:

> Today a number of girls are shaking off a few time-honored quinceañera traditions, like the Catholic Mass that typically precedes the party, and adding new ones, like arriving as Belle from "Beauty and the Beast" or choreographing dance moves to hip-hop. Some teenagers, like Cathy, a 10th-grader at Sewanhaka High School on Long Island, are choosing to wait an extra year so they can ditch the old-fashioned "quinceañera" label for the hipper, more acculturated "Sweet 16" tag.

Tell a Brief Story or Anecdote   Beginning with a brief *story* or *anecdote* can help draw readers into your essay because most readers like to read about other people's lives. Nora Okja Keller, for example, opens her essay about the cultural symbolism of kim chee with a personal anecdote about her love for the spicy pickled cabbage:

> I was weaned on kim chee. A good baby, I was "able to eat anything," my mother told me. But what I especially loved was the fermenting, garlicky Chinese cabbage my mother pickled in our kitchen. Not waiting for her to lick the red peppers off the won bok, I would grab and gobble the bits of leaves as soon as she tore them into baby-size pieces. She said that even if my eyes watered, I would still ask for more.

Jeffrey Zaslow, in "What We Can Learn from Sully's Journey," gets his readers' attention by referring to the event that made Captain Sullenberger famous:

> US Airways Capt. Chesley "Sully" Sullenberger has flown thousands of flights in the last 42 years. "But now," he says, "my entire career is being judged by how I performed on one of them." That flight, of course, came last Jan. 15, when his Airbus A320 suffered a bird strike en route from New York to Charlotte, N.C., and lost both engines. Sully and First Officer Jeff Skiles executed an emergency landing later dubbed "The Miracle on the Hudson," but that description never felt right to Sully.

Zaslow then forecasts the story that he will tell about Capt. Sullenberger and gives the thesis of the essay in the third and final paragraph of the introduction:

> As Sully's co-author, I clearly saw that it wasn't only his skills as a veteran pilot that carried him in those tense moments over Manhattan. It was also his upbringing, his family bonds, his sense of integrity—and his own losses. Flight 1549 wasn't just a five-minute journey from LaGuardia Airport to the Hudson. Sully's entire life led him safely to that river.

Ask a Question   Posing one or more questions early in an essay can rouse readers' curiosity about your topic and encourage them to keep reading to find the answers to those questions. To improve her discovery draft (p. 156), for example, student writer Autumn Harrison started her revised draft (p. 167) with a question:

> Have you ever seen marches, food strikes, boycotts, and other events where people are protesting?

In the next several sentences, Autumn explains the meaning of civil disobedience and uses the rest of her essay to explain how two great leaders' practice of civil disobedience made them cultural heroes.

HOW TO Write an Effective Introduction

- Grab your readers' attention—perhaps with description, a surprising fact, a brief story or anecdote, or a question.
- Narrow your topic.
- Conclude with a thesis statement.

WRITING ACTIVITY 12 Revise Your Introduction

Reread the introductory paragraph of your essay. Then rate your introduction on a scale of 1 to 4, according to the following list:

1. Effective (forceful, attention-getting hook; clearly stated thesis statement)
2. Adequate (satisfactory hook; clearly stated thesis statement)
3. So-so (uninteresting hook; vague thesis statement)
4. Ineffective (no hook; no thesis statement)

Discuss your rating with your classmates. Then revise the introduction to your essay using one of the techniques discussed in this chapter. Also, look at your thesis statement to see how you can make it more effective. It should announce your topic clearly and reveal its significance.

Write a Powerful Conclusion

The *conclusion* serves two major functions in an essay: It makes clear that you have made the point you introduced at the start of the essay, and it draws the essay to a satisfactory close. Thus, in the conclusion, you do not include new material or end abruptly; instead, you wrap up what you have already said. Try to leave your readers with a lasting impression about your topic and its significance. For most short essays, the most effective way to conclude is to reinforce your thesis and broaden your focus.

Reinforce the Thesis By *reinforcing the thesis*, you use different wording in your conclusion to remind readers of the significance of your topic and to emphasize your main point or idea. For example, Jeffrey Zaslow provides versions of his thesis statement in both the introduction and the conclusion to "What We Can Learn from Sully's Journey":

STATEMENT OF THESIS IN INTRODUCTION	Flight 1549 wasn't just a five-minute journey from LaGuardia Airport to the Hudson. Sully's entire life led him safely to that river.
REINFORCEMENT OF THESIS IN CONCLUSION	Sully now sees lessons for the rest of us. "We need to try to do the right thing everytime, to perform at our best," he says, "because we never know what moment in our lives we'll be judged on." He always had a sense of this. Now he knows it for sure.

Broaden the Focus   By *broadening the focus* of an essay in the conclusion, you connect your topic to something larger to show readers why it is important to them. A good way to broaden the focus of a personal essay about a cultural symbol, tradition, or hero is to conclude with a suggestion that your readers do something or that they continue thinking about how the topic affects them. You can also link the topic of the essay to a more general theme. In her revised draft of "Two Voices, One Idea," Autumn Harrison repeats the title of the essay as she connects civil disobedience to the theme of sacrifice:

> They sacrificed their freedom—and in the case of Dr. King, his life—to make the world a better place for everyone. They were two voices with one idea.

WRITING ACTIVITY 13 Revise Your Conclusion

Rate the concluding paragraph of your draft on a scale of 1 to 4, according to the following list:

1. Powerful (memorable closure; main point reinforced)
2. Adequate (interesting closure; main point reinforced)
3. So-so (uninteresting closure; main point reinforced)
4. Ineffective (no sense of closure; main point not reinforced)

Ask classmates to suggest how you could make your concluding paragraph more interesting and forceful. Use their suggestions and your own ideas to revise your conclusion, making sure that you reinforce your thesis and broaden your focus.

Connect Ideas

In addition to improving your introduction and conclusion when you revise your essay, be sure to show how your main idea and your supporting points are connected. You can do this by strengthening your thesis statement, by including topic sentences for each paragraph, and by using keywords and transitions.

Use Keywords   One way to connect your ideas is to repeat *keywords*—words that relate to the topic being discussed. By repeating a keyword, you keep your readers focused on the topic. In the following paragraph from "Rice," notice how the repetition of the keyword "rice" (highlighted) contributes to the flow of ideas and reminds readers of the topic:

> But there is another rice that my father is more famous for. This is not the white rice, boiled like pasta and then drained in a colander, that most Bengalis eat for dinner. This other rice is pulao, a baked, buttery, sophisticated indulgence.

In addition to repetition of the same keyword, you can use pronouns and synonyms as keywords. A *pronoun*, such as *it* or *them*, takes the place of the

> ⏻ **Improve the flow of ideas**
>
> Use **bold** to highlight the keywords in each paragraph. Check that the keywords pertain directly to the topic of the paragraph. (The Find-and-Replace tool can help you locate these keywords.) Add, delete, or revise keywords as needed. Then use *italic* to highlight the transitions in each paragraph. Add transitions where the flow of thought seems disconnected or where there are no transitions in a long section. (Remember to remove the highlighting of keywords and transitions before printing your essay.)

original word; a *synonym* is another word or phrase that refers to the same thing as the original keyword. In the following paragraph, notice how Nora Okja Keller's use of synonyms (highlighted) for the keyword *kim chee* helps connect her ideas:

> We went crazy for the smell of kim chee—a perfume that lured us to the kitchen table. When my mother hefted the jar of kim chee out of the refrigerator and opened the lid to extract the almost fluorescent strips of cabbage, she didn't have to call out to us, although she always did. "Girls, come join me," she would sing; even if we weren't hungry we couldn't resist. We all lingered over snacks that lasted two or three hours.

Add Transitions Another way to connect your ideas is to use *transitions*. Transitions show your readers how one idea relates to the next, making your writing easy to follow.

Most commonly, transitions are words or phrases that connect sentences within a paragraph. Here is a list of the relationships expressed by some of the most common transitions:

to add information	additionally, and, also, as well, furthermore, in addition, too
to show differences	but, in contrast, on the other hand, whereas
to show similarities	as, in comparison, in the same way, similarly
to show time	after, at that time, before, by then, during, meanwhile, now, since, sometimes, soon, then, until then, when, while
to show cause and effect	as a result, because, consequently, hence, thereby, therefore, thus
to contradict or contrast	although, but, however, in contrast, nevertheless, or, instead, still
to add emphasis	actually, furthermore, indeed, in fact, in truth, moreover, most important
to give an example	for example, for instance, specifically, such as
to show sequence	finally, first, last, next

When you use a transition, be sure it expresses the correct relationship between ideas. Notice how effectively Nora Okja Keller uses transitions (highlighted) to connect ideas about her daughter's reaction to her first taste of kim chee:

> When my daughter was fifteen months old, she took her first bite of kim chee. I had taken a small bite into my own mouth, sucking the hot juice from its leaves, giving it "mothertaste" as my own mother had done for me. Still, my daughter's eyes watered. "Hot, hot," she said to her grandmother and me. But the taste must have been in some way familiar; instead of spitting up and crying for water, she pushed my hand to the open jar for another bite.

In longer essays, writers sometimes use *transitional paragraphs* to make ideas flow smoothly. A transitional paragraph connects the main idea in one section of an essay to the main idea of a section that follows it. This type of paragraph is usually from one to three sentences in length and, unlike most paragraphs, does not need a topic sentence.

Nora Okja Keller, for instance, uses a transitional paragraph in "My Mother's Food":

> So I erased my stink by eliminating kim chee. Though I liked the sharp taste of garlic and pepper biting my tongue, I stopped eating my mother's food.

In this transitional paragraph, the author connects her feelings about being Korean with how those feelings affected her relationship with her mother.

HOW TO Use Keywords and Transitions

Keywords and transitions provide a road map that can help readers connect your ideas.

- To help readers follow your main idea, repeat keywords, and use pronouns and synonyms.
- To move your readers to a new idea, use transitional words and phrases.
- To move your readers from one major part of your essay to another, write a brief transitional paragraph.

GROUP ACTIVITY 6 Add Keywords and Transitions

In the following paragraphs from *And the Beat Goes On: A Survey of Pop Music in America* by Charles Boeckman, keywords and transitions have been deleted. Work with your classmates to make the paragraphs more coherent by adding keywords and transitions.

In the 1950s, a revolution began in America. There was nothing quiet about it. It had happened before most people woke up to what was going on. It has been one of the most curious things in our history. The young people banded together, splintered off into a compartment totally their own. They formed their own culture, economy and morals. A generation of young people was totally immersed in its own music. It symbolized, reflected, dictated the very nature of its revolution.

The stage was set. Out of the wings stepped a young Memphis truck driver with a ducktail hair style and a sullen, brooding expression — Elvis Presley with his rock 'n' roll guitar. In 1954, a black group, the Chords, had played the rock 'n' roll style. In 1955, Bill Haley and a white group, the Comets, recorded the hit "Rock around the Clock." They lacked Elvis's charisma. They lacked his sex appeal. Elvis did more than sing. He went through a whole series of gyrations filled with sexual implications. It was just the thing for the mood of the hour. His voice trembled and cried out. His guitar thundered. His torso did bumps and grinds and shimmies. A whole generation of young people blew its cool.

> **GROUP ACTIVITY 7** **Add Keywords and Transitions to Your Essay**

Working in a group of three or four students, distribute copies of each group member's draft, and evaluate how well ideas are connected. On each draft, circle the keywords, synonyms, and pronouns, and underline the transitions. Your peers should do the same for your draft. Discuss with your classmates how each of you can improve the use of transitions. Then revise your draft, using your group's suggestions to add keywords and transitions.

A Student's Revised Draft

Throughout this chapter, you have been following Autumn Harrison as she gathered ideas and drafted an essay about Dr. Martin Luther King Jr. and Aung San Suu Kyi, two cultural heroes she thought others would be interested in learning more about. Before you read Autumn's revised draft, review her discovery draft on page 156. Notice how Autumn revised by adding examples and process explanation to help her readers better understand her ideas. She inserted transitions to make her ideas flow more smoothly, and she added information about these cultural heroes that her readers may be unfamiliar with. (You may notice some errors in her revised draft; Autumn will correct these errors when she edits her essay.)

Two Voices, One Idea

Have you ever seen marches, food strikes, boycotts, and other events where people are protesting? If so, you have seen examples of civil disobedience. According to Henry David Thoreau, civil disobedience is passive and nonviolence resistance to injustice. In 1849 he published "Civil Disobedience" in which he wrote that any time a government enacted laws or acted in a manner that was unjust, the people had the right and duty to challenge this injustice through civil disobedience Like Thoreau, Dr. Martin Luther King Jr. and Aung San Suu Kyi were activists who felt that civil disobedience could be used to bring about change. Dr. King and Suu Kyi can be seen as examples of great people who practiced civil disobedience in order to overcome the injustice that their people experienced.

Dr. King expressed his philosophy about civil disobedience in "Letter From Birmingham Jail," which he wrote in 1963. Protesting segregation in Birmingham, Alabama. He followed the process of civil disobedience by leading hundreds of people in boycotting businesses. Protesters sat at lunch counters that would not serve Blacks. For the final step, hundreds of schoolchildren marched in the streets to integrate the city. The police then turned attack dogs and fire hoses on them and had them arrested (MLK Research). King had received a message from Christian and Jewish leaders who thought that these methods of civil disobedience were too radical. He felt that leading the protests was his duty. He wrote in the letter, "I say it as a minister of the gospel, who loves the church; who was nurtured in its bosom; who has been sustained by its spiritual blessings and who will remain true to it as long as the cord of life shall lengthen" (p. 213). Though these leaders felt King's preaching would cause chaos and confusion. He knew that true change would come.

Suu Kyi also knew that the most effective way to bring democracy to her culture was through nonviolent protests. In 1962, her country, Burma, was taken over by a dictatorship. They changed the name of the country from Burma to Myanmar.

1 Autumn poses a question to help capture readers' attention.

Autumn introduces the keyword *civil disobedience*.

Autumn clarifies her thesis to forecast the explanation to come.

Autumn repeats the keyword *civil disobedience*.

2

Autumn adds process explanation.

The transition *for the final step* makes the organization of the essay clear.

Autumn adds examples.

3

Autumn adds background facts.

Autumn adds background information.

A transition helps readers follow along.

Autumn adds a transition to highlight a comparison.

Suu Kyi wanted the Burmese people to use the Buddhist scripture and apply it to democracy. In "In Quest of Democracy" she wrote about the Buddhist belief in "The Ten Duties of Kings." These duties included non-violence and democracy. She wrote that these duties "could be applied just as well to the modern government as to the first monarch of the world" (p. 223). Like King, Suu Kyi's efforts to bring about change were met with strong resistance from the military junta. She was declared ineligible as an opposition leader. Accused of trying to split the government and start war, and eventually placed on house arrest for fifteen years.

The government was against Suu Kyi and her protest through civil disobedience. She knew the Burmese people were behind her because they wanted fairness. In "In Quest of Democracy" she wrote that "it was natural that people who have suffered much from the consequences of bad government should be preoccupied with theories of good government" (p. 221). She could not leave her house for fifteen years. She did not lose her faith. Similarly, Dr. King did not lose his faith even though the white religious leaders criticized him for coming to Birmingham as an outsider. He wrote, "I am compelled to carry the gospel of freedom beyond my particular hometown" (204). King knew that by continuing to disobey unjust laws he would have to face some consequences; he knew, however, that he was doing the right thing. Later in his life he was assassinated due to his non-violent protests against unjust laws. Like King, Suu Kyi also wanted her country to have a better way of living. Unfortunately she also paid a high price. Because of the efforts of the military junta to deny her freedom.

4

These two leaders were similar in many respects Dr. King and Suu Kyi challenged the status quo that both countries had been living by. They gave the people hope and fought for everyone to be treated equally. Their strong religious beliefs made them unable to let this inequality go on. They sacrificed their freedom, and in the case of Dr. King his life, to make the world a better place for everyone. They were two voices with one idea.

5

Works Cited

King, Martin Luther. "Letter From Birmingham Jail." *Reading the World: Ideas That Matter*. 2nd Edition. Ed. Michael Austin. New York: W.W. Norton & Company, 2010. 202-217. Print.

MLK Freedom and Education Institute. "Birmingham Campaign." Stanford University, n.d. Web. 26 Oct. 2014.

Suu Kyi, Aung San. "In Quest of Democracy." *Reading the World: Ideas That Matter*. 2nd Edition. Ed. Michael Austin. New York: W.W. Norton & Company, 2010. 219-225. Print.

The Works Cited list lets readers know where Autumn found her information.

parent   inventory

GROUP ACTIVITY 8 Analyze Autumn's Revised Draft

Use the following questions to discuss with your classmates how Autumn improved her draft.

1. Is the purpose of Autumn's revised draft clear? What is her purpose?
2. What is Autumn's thesis statement? Could it be improved?
3. Does Autumn give her readers enough information about the cultural heroes? Explain.
4. How effective is Autumn's introduction? Conclusion?
5. Are the paragraphs in Autumn's revised draft better developed than those in her discovery draft? Do the ideas flow together better? Explain, and give examples.
6. How could Autumn's revised draft benefit from further revision?

Peer Review for an Essay That Explains

Form a group with two or three other students and exchange copies of your drafts. Read your draft aloud while your classmates follow along. Take notes on your classmates' responses to the following questions about your draft.

1. What did you like best about my essay?
2. How interesting is my introduction? Did you want to continue reading the essay? Why or why not?
3. What is my thesis statement? Do I need to make my essay's thesis clearer?
4. Where in the essay could I add examples and process explanation to help deliver my message?
5. How can I use keywords and transitions to make my ideas flow better?
6. Where can I combine sentences to improve the writing?
7. Where in the draft did my writing confuse you? How can I clarify my thoughts?
8. How effective is my conclusion? Do I end in a way that lets you know it's the end?

WRITING ACTIVITY 14 Revise Your Draft

Finish revising your discovery draft by using the work you completed for the activities in this chapter as well as your classmates' suggestions for revision. Make your introduction and conclusion as strong as they can be. In addition, develop your ideas with examples and process explanation, and use keywords and transitions to connect ideas. If you have time, look for irrelevant or unnecessary material that can be omitted, and experiment with moving sections of your draft to achieve the best organization.

Step 4 Edit Your Sentences

So far in revising your paper, you have focused on improving your introduction and conclusion and on helping your ideas flow by using keywords and transitions. Now you're ready to make your sentences more readable and to edit your finished essay for correctness. Remember, errors distract your readers from what you have to say. In this section, you will learn how to combine sentences with conjunctive adverbs and how to identify and correct sentence fragments.

Combining Sentences Using Conjunctive Adverbs

By combining short, closely related sentences, you can clarify the relationship between ideas and make them easier to understand. Sentence combining also eliminates unnecessary words and keeps readers' interest by varying the types of sentences in an essay.

For more on sentence combining, see Chapter 18.

If your draft has short, complete sentences that are closely related, consider combining some of them with *conjunctive adverbs*—words and phrases that help readers understand how two ideas are related to each other. The following conjunctive adverbs are often used to combine sentences. Remember, a complete sentence has a subject and a verb.

Conjunctive Adverbs

also	meanwhile	specifically
besides	moreover	subsequently
consequently	nevertheless	then
finally	next	therefore
furthermore	otherwise	thus
however	similarly	

To combine sentences with a conjunctive adverb, place a semicolon before the adverb and a comma after it. Notice how the sentences in the following examples make more sense when they are combined this way.

DISCONNECTED	My neighbor brings me flan whenever she makes a batch for her children. My pants are getting tight.
COMBINED	My neighbor brings me flan whenever she makes a batch for her children; consequently, my pants are getting tight.
DISCONNECTED	Hurricane Katrina devastated New Orleans. The first Mardi Gras after the disaster was a success.
COMBINED	Hurricane Katrina devastated New Orleans; nevertheless, the first Mardi Gras after the disaster was a success.

The conjunctive adverb can also appear in the middle of the second sentence, as in this example from Autumn Harrison's edited draft:

DISCONNECTED   King knew that by continuing to disobey unjust laws
he would have to face some consequences. He knew he
was doing the right thing.

COMBINED   King knew that by continuing to disobey unjust laws
he would have to face some consequences; he knew,
however, that he was doing the right thing.

As you can see from this example, commas are placed both before and after
the conjunctive adverb when it is in the middle of the sentence.

HOW TO Combine Sentences Using Conjunctive Adverbs

- Check that each of the two sentences you plan to combine has a subject and a verb and expresses a complete thought.
- Select a conjunctive adverb that shows how the sentences are related.
- Combine the two sentences with a semicolon, the conjunctive adverb, and a comma.
- If a conjunctive adverb appears in the middle of the second sentence, put commas before and after it.

EDITING ACTIVITY 1 Combine Sentences Using Conjunctive Adverbs

Combine the following pairs of sentences with conjunctive adverbs. Be sure you punctuate the combined sentences correctly.

EXAMPLE In the United States, we play "soccer." The rest of the world calls the sport "football."
[handwritten edit: "soccer"; however, the]

1. Sports competitions are some of the most important cultural traditions throughout the world. International sports competitions increase national pride.

2. In many countries, soccer is the most popular sport. The World Cup tournament draws huge crowds of fans.

3. Many fans watch the games with friends at neighborhood bars. Celebrations often spill into the streets.

4. Some fans drink too much. Others take the competition very seriously.

5. Violent behavior and riots have caused problems at past tournaments. Most countries vie for the honor of hosting the World Cup.

Examine your revised draft for short, closely related sentences. Where it makes sense to do so, combine them with conjunctive adverbs.

Correcting Sentence Fragments

A *sentence fragment* is an incomplete sentence: it looks like a sentence, but something is missing.

For more on sentence fragments, see pp. 452–56.

A *complete sentence* contains a subject and a verb and expresses a complete thought. The subject tells who or what is doing the action. The verb explains the action or links the subject to the rest of the sentence.

The following are complete sentences. In each, the subject is italicized, and the verb is underlined.

Sentences

My *sister* <u>attended</u> graduation.

Jerry <u>enjoys</u> holidays.

I <u>left</u> class early.

He <u>is</u> my closest friend.

Unlike a sentence, a *sentence fragment* does not express a complete thought. A sentence fragment may be a *phrase*—a group of words that lacks a subject or a verb.

Phrases

Attended graduation. (missing subject)

Cinco de Mayo. Jerry's favorite holiday. (missing verb)

Left class early. (missing subject)

My closest friend. (missing subject and verb)

To correct a sentence fragment that is a phrase, add the missing subject, verb, or both.

Sentences

My *drill sergeant* attended graduation.

Cinco de Mayo *is* Jerry's favorite holiday.

Abrian left class early.

Liza is my closest friend.

A sentence fragment may also be a *dependent clause*—a group of words that contains a subject and a verb but doesn't express a complete thought.

Dependent Clauses

When my drill sergeant attended graduation.

Because it is Jerry's favorite holiday.

After Abrian left class early.

Since Liza is my closest friend.

There are three ways to correct a sentence fragment that is a dependent clause:

- ■ Combine it with another sentence.
- ■ Add information to make it a complete thought.
- ■ Delete the conjunction or pronoun that starts it.

Sentences

I was proud when my drill sergeant attended graduation. (added information)

We went out for Cinco de Mayo because it is Jerry's favorite holiday. (combined with another sentence)

Abrian left class early. (deleted conjunction)

Liza is my closest friend. (deleted conjunction)

HOW TO Correct Sentence Fragments

To identify a sentence fragment, ask yourself the following questions about each sentence in your essay:

- Does the sentence have a subject?
- Does the sentence have a verb?
- Does the sentence express a complete thought?

If you answer No to any of these questions, you have a sentence fragment. To correct the sentence fragment, do one of the following:

- Add the missing subject or verb or both.
- Combine the fragment with the sentence before or after it.
- Add information to make it a complete thought.
- Delete any words (such as conjunctions or pronouns) that make the clause dependent.

EDITING ACTIVITY 2 Correct Sentence Fragments

Correct each of the following sentence fragments by adding a missing subject or verb, by connecting a fragment to the sentence before or after it, or by adding information to form a complete thought.

1. My favorite custom is hiding Easter eggs. Because it's fun for everyone.

2. Since I left home. My mother calls me every other day.

3. Approaching my home.

4. Never a dull moment.

5. Forgot to celebrate my birthday!

WRITING ACTIVITY 16 **Edit Your Sentences**

Read your essay word for word, looking for errors in sentence structure, grammar, spelling, and punctuation. Focus on finding and correcting sentence fragments. Also ask a friend or classmate to help you spot errors you might have overlooked. Then correct the errors you find, using a dictionary and the Handbook in Part Four of this book to help you.

A Student's Edited Essay

You probably noticed that Autumn's revised draft contained errors in sentence structure and punctuation. Autumn corrected these errors in her edited essay. Her corrections are noted in the margin.

Autumn correctly changes a noun into an adjective.

Autumn corrects a sentence fragment by combining sentences.

Another sentence fragment is corrected by combining sentences.

Harrison 1

Autumn Harrison
Dr. Unger
English 100
Oct. 30, 2014

Two Voices, One Idea

Have you ever seen marches, food strikes, boycotts, and other events where people are protesting? If so, you have seen examples of civil disobedience. According to Henry David Thoreau, civil disobedience is passive and nonviolent resistance to injustice. In 1849 he published "Civil Disobedience," in which he wrote that any time a government enacted laws or acted in a manner that was unjust, the people had the right and duty to challenge this injustice through civil disobedience. Like Thoreau, Dr. Martin Luther King Jr. and Aung San Suu Kyi were activists who felt that civil disobedience could be used to bring about change. Dr. King and Suu Kyi can be seen as examples of great people who practiced civil disobedience in order to overcome the injustice that their people experienced.

Dr. King expressed his philosophy about civil disobedience in "Letter From Birmingham Jail," which he wrote in 1963 when he was protesting segregation in Birmingham, Alabama. He followed the process of civil disobedience by leading hundreds of people in boycotting businesses. Protesters sat at lunch counters that would not serve Blacks. For the final step, hundreds of schoolchildren marched in the streets to integrate the city. The police then turned attack dogs and fire hoses on them and had them arrested (MLK Research). King had received a message from Christian and Jewish leaders who thought that these methods of civil disobedience were too radical. He felt that leading the protests was his duty. He wrote in the letter, "I say it as a minister of the gospel, who loves the church; who was nurtured in its bosom; who has been sustained by its spiritual blessings and who will remain true to it as long as the cord of life shall lengthen" (King 213). Though these leaders felt King's preaching would cause chaos and confusion, he knew that true change would come.

1

2

Harrison 2

Suu Kyi also knew that the most effective way to bring democracy to her culture was through nonviolent protests. In 1962, her country, Burma, was taken over by a dictatorship that later changed the name of the country from Burma to Myanmar. Suu Kyi wanted the Burmese people to use the Buddhist scripture and apply it to democracy. In "In Quest of Democracy" she wrote about the Buddhist belief in "The Ten Duties of Kings." These duties included non-violence and democracy. She wrote that these duties "could be applied just as well to the modern government as to the first monarch of the world" (Suu Kyi 223). Like King, Suu Kyi's efforts to bring about change were met with strong resistance from the military junta. She was declared ineligible as an opposition leader, accused of trying to split the government and start war, and eventually placed on house arrest for fifteen years.

3

Sentences are combined.

In-text citations are edited to follow MLA format.

Sentence fragment is corrected.

The government was against Suu Kyi and her protest through civil disobedience. She knew the Burmese people were behind her because they wanted fairness. In "In Quest of Democracy," she wrote that "it was natural that people who have suffered much from the consequences of bad government should be preoccupied with theories of good government" (p. 221). Even though she could not leave her house for fifteen years, she did not lose her faith. Similarly, Dr. King did not lose his faith even though the white religious leaders criticized him for coming to Birmingham as an outsider. He wrote, "I am compelled to carry the gospel of freedom beyond my particular hometown" (204). King knew that by continuing to disobey unjust laws he would have to face some consequences; he knew, however, that he was doing the right thing. Later in his life he was assassinated due to his non-violent protests against unjust laws. Like King, Suu Kyi also wanted her country to have a better way of living. Unfortunately she also paid a high price because of the efforts of the military junta to deny her freedom.

4

Transition is added and sentences are combined.

Sentences are combined and transition is added.

Sentence fragment is corrected by combining sentences.

These two leaders were similar in many respects. Dr. King and Suu Kyi challenged the status quo that both countries had been

5

Run-on sentence is corrected.

Harrison 3

living by. They gave the people hope and fought for everyone to be treated equally. Their strong religious beliefs made them unable to let this inequality go on. They sacrificed their freedom, and in the case of Dr. King, his life, to make the world a better place for everyone. They were two voices with one idea.

Harrison 4

Works Cited

King, Martin Luther, Jr. "Letter from Birmingham Jail." *Reading the World: Ideas That Matter*. 2nd Edition. Ed. Michael Austin. New York: W.W. Norton & Company, 2010. 202-217. Print.

MLK Freedom and Education Institute. "Birmingham Campaign." Stanford University, n.d. Web. 26 Oct. 2014.

Suu Kyi, Aung San. "In Quest of Democracy." *Reading the World: Ideas That Matter*. 2nd Edition. Ed. Michael Austin. New York: W.W. Norton & Company, 2010. 219-225. Print.

Step 5 Share Your Essay

In addition to sharing your final essay with your instructor and class-mates, you can show it to other readers who might be interested in learning about a cultural symbol, tradition, or hero. You can easily get friends and family members to read it by attaching the document to your Facebook page. Another way to broaden your audience—and even to get people around the world interested in your subject—is to create a blog about your essay topic. A blog is different from a website because it is usually organized by date and category, with the most recent entry listed first. Blogs also allow for comments and feedback by readers. While you can "self host" a blog by creating your own domain name and paying for a web host (iPage is the most common service), you can also create a blog for free on a site such as blogger.com or WordPress.com. These free sites also connect people to communities of other bloggers who are interested in similar subjects. The more people who read your essay, the more likely it is that it will help someone become more knowledgeable, considerate, or accepting of someone else's culture—a change in attitude that you will have helped make happen.

CHAPTER CHECKLIST

- ❏ I read essays about culture to explore and learn about this chapter's theme.
- ❏ I gathered ideas on a cultural symbol, tradition, or hero by clustering, asking questions, and freewriting.
- ❏ I developed the ideas in my paragraphs with examples and process explanation.
- ❏ I strengthened my introduction by hooking readers, narrowing my focus, and providing a thesis statement.
- ❏ I wrote a strong conclusion that reinforces my thesis and broadens the topic.
- ❏ I made my ideas easier to understand by connecting them with keywords and transitions.
- ❏ I combined closely related sentences by using conjunctive adverbs.
- ❏ I eliminated sentence fragments.
- ❏ I shared my finished essay with my instructor and classmates.

REFLECTING ON YOUR WRITING

To help you continue to improve as a writer, answer the following questions:

1. Did you enjoy writing about an aspect of your culture? Why or why not?

2. Which topic did you choose—a cultural symbol, tradition, or hero? Why?

3. What types of changes did you make to your essay when you revised?

4. If you had more time, what further revisions would you make to improve your essay? Why?

After answering these questions, freewrite about what you learned in this chapter.

Visit **LaunchPad Solo for Readers and Writers > Writing Process** for more tutorials, videos, and practice developing your essay with each step.

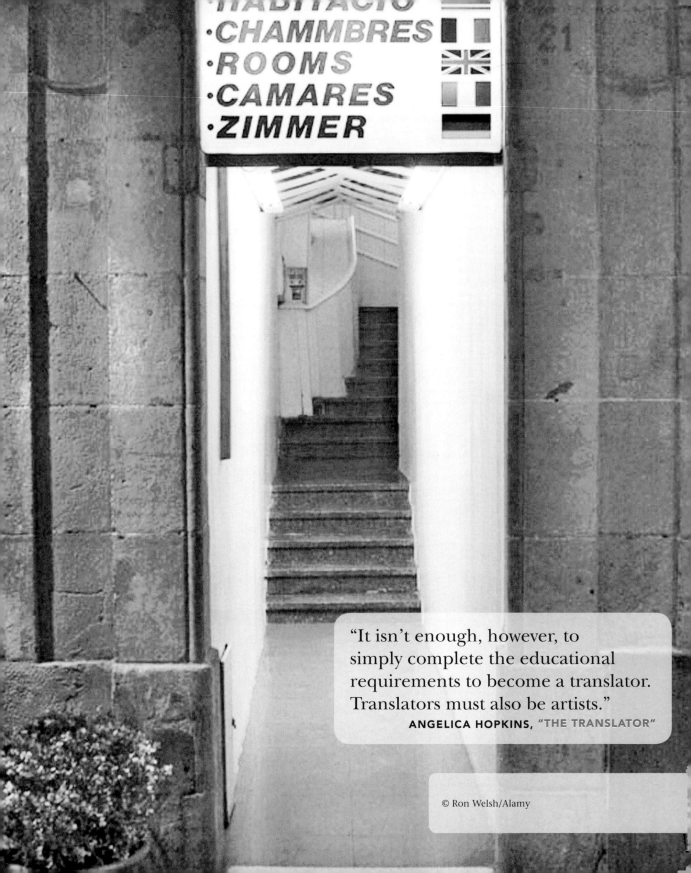

"It isn't enough, however, to simply complete the educational requirements to become a translator. Translators must also be artists."

ANGELICA HOPKINS, "THE TRANSLATOR"

© Ron Welsh/Alamy

Analyzing
Career Paths, Workplace Communication, and Job-Related Problems

When you analyze a topic, you define it, research it, and investigate how the parts come together to make up a whole. The goal of analysis is to study your topic or subject, revealing new information that will give you a deeper understanding of that subject. You can then share what you have learned with your readers, so they will be better informed about your subject. In this chapter, you will use this type of informative writing to investigate career paths and the workplace.

One of the first questions most of us ask when we meet someone new is, "What do you do?" This question shows the importance that we place on work. Most of us want our careers to be satisfying and rewarding. After all, at some point in our lives, we are likely to spend at least forty hours a week in the workplace. Finding the right career path is not an easy task, however. Most of us carefully plan our college education, choosing a major that prepares us for a career that interests us; once we graduate, we may work in that field or hold many different jobs and change career fields a few times during our lives. Look at the résumés of just a few of America's presidents, for instance: Harry S. Truman

In this chapter, you will write about a career path that interests you, a style of workplace communication, or a job-related problem. As you follow the steps of the writing process, you will

- Explore the chapter topic by reading essays about a work issue.
- Gather ideas by freewriting, brainstorming, and consulting with others.
- Develop your ideas using **classification** and **definition**.
- Practice using research material in your writing.
- Combine sentences with subordinating conjunctions.
- Learn how to correct pronoun reference and agreement.
- Submit your essay to a school, volunteer, or work-related newsletter.

owned a clothing store, Jimmy Carter farmed peanuts, George W. Bush drilled for oil, and Barack Obama worked to improve living conditions in poor Chicago neighborhoods. You might already have job experience yourself, and if you're like most students, you're probably preparing for a better future.

When you consider a particular career path, you'll need to determine how well the path you have chosen matches your interests and abilities. To succeed, you'll also need to understand the culture of a profession—how people think, dress, behave, and communicate. Finally, it helps to learn how people in a profession analyze the problems they encounter in the workplace.

In this chapter, you'll have the chance to write about your choice of a career path, to examine the communication styles in a given profession, or to look for ways to analyze a problem you may have encountered in the workplace. You will also follow a student, Angelica Hopkins, as she writes about her chosen career as a translator. Because your investigations will uncover information that will be helpful to your peers, you will share what you learn with other students who have similar career interests. ■

 GETTING STARTED Think about Workplaces

Examine the chapter opening photograph on page 182. Why do you think the sign above the door is in five languages? Imagine if you worked in an environment where multiple languages were used. With your classmates, brainstorm careers or workplaces that engage multiple languages. What are the benefits or drawbacks to these environments and career options?

Read to Write   Reading Essays That Analyze a Work Issue

One good way to learn more about career paths and workplace issues is to read about them. You can find information about a particular field in reference books and on websites, for example, as well as in personal essays and memoirs that describe people's experiences in college and the workplace.

Successful businesspeople and professionals often publish books and magazine articles filled with advice for overcoming problems and achieving their career goals. To get a feel for this kind of writing, read the following short essays that describe career paths, examine communication in the workplace, or analyze problems on the job. As you read, pay attention to how the writers use classification and definition to explain their ideas. Notice, too, how the writers support their ideas with information from outside sources and expand on their topic through analyzing the ideas they present.

A Career Path: An Annotated Reading

HEATHER ROBINSON
I Am Not a Babysitter

Being a schoolteacher can be a very rewarding occupation, but teachers often struggle to earn respect. In the following essay, "I Am Not a Babysitter," Heather Robinson, a seventh-grade science teacher, describes what people who are not in the profession sometimes think, compared to what it's really like to be a teacher. This article is from *Newsweek*, a news source that publishes a variety of news stories internationally, as well as personal essays from its readers.

As a teacher, I face many stereotypes about my job. But I wouldn't trade my career for any other. It is said that teaching is the profession that creates all other professions. That's a beautiful compliment for a job that often does not receive the respect one would predict given all of the platitudes bestowed upon teachers. "God bless you!" "What a noble profession" and "I couldn't do it, but thank goodness there are people like you out there" are a few that I've received.

1 The opening thesis statement immediately lets readers know what the essay is about.

A general definition of teaching is provided.

Like many of my colleagues, I didn't attend college intending to become a teacher. I worked in a related profession in youth services, helping high-school dropouts find social and vocational outlets other than the streets and dead-end jobs. Though the work was often rewarding, I realized I could be more influential working with young people before they became a statistic. Thus began my career in education.

2 Background information explains why Robinson became a teacher.

Some family and friends seemed to think the change was only temporary. Several asked, "How long do you think you'll teach?" Some inquired whether I had administrative aspirations. When one year became two, then three, etc., some friends actually questioned my sanity. Surely I wouldn't remain a lowly classroom teacher, they would insinuate, as if teaching is a stop-gap job. Unfortunately, too many people view teaching as a fallback, insurance, something stable to get them from their last corporate layoff to the next higher-paying job.

3 Robinson begins to classify stereotypes about teaching. The first one: teaching is a stop-gap job. For each stereotype, she provides her own view of teaching.

If those types of comments aren't bewildering enough, I still hear chiding responses about my "cream-puff" schedule. This always reminds me of a remark a salty veteran teacher once made to me: "If a teacher tells you she is done with her work any time before 7 p.m., she is lying or she isn't doing her job." What is sad about that statement is that it is not only true, it's sometimes an understatement. Eight or nine o'clock can be more like it, after a day that began at five or six a.m.

4 The second stereotype: teaching is a "cream-puff" job. Quoting a veteran teacher gives credibility to her statement about teaching loads.

Summers off? Think again. Teachers who truly aspire to make their mark and contribute only their very best to our nation's future enroll in summer training courses and continue their education in a constant pursuit to perfect their craft. We are a profession of lifelong learners. In a continually changing world, it's not only advised but imperative that we never cease to improve and devour each new piece of research that reveals to us some small piece of the education puzzle.

5 The third stereotype: teachers have summers off.

The fourth stereotype: teaching is a boring job.

"Don't you get bored doing the same thing each day?" is another question 6
I get a lot. It's a teacher's windfall if any two given class periods are identical and flow according to the lesson plan, let alone an entire day or more. What many people don't understand is that we teachers are working with wiggling, chatting children with varied needs. They are not robots who perform exactly as we direct without exception. Teachers are not on autopilot—we make thousands of decisions each day while working hard to produce a quality product that provides each student with what she needs and deserves. Teaching isn't simply perching at a lectern and pontificating to hungry minds; it's being an educator, a mentor, a parent, a nurse, a social worker, a friend, a diplomat and an expert on the curriculum. In short, we are professionals.

In these two sentences, Robinson provides a more comprehensive definition of teaching.

After all of the long hours, grueling days, mountains of paperwork, emo- 7
tional exhaustion and misperceptions about the profession that I dearly love and would trade for no other, we continue to pour ourselves into the work because it's too important not to. How can we not give all of ourselves, our intellect and our talents to this work? After all, it is our current students whom we will be voting for in a future presidential election, who will care for us when we're ill and who will educate our grandchildren.

Robinson explains why, in spite of all of the stereotypes, she remains a teacher.

The conclusion includes a call for action, asking readers to "respect" teachers.

Notice I've said nothing about increasing teachers' pay, improving benefits 8
or strong-arming uninvolved parents. Though those are all valid topics, they are not any more important than the need to increase an emergency medical technician's near minimum-wage compensation. What can easily be increased in education is the value placed upon the service that teachers provide to society. So the next time it's tempting to quiz a teacher about why she's not doing something more lucrative or supposedly more challenging with her talents, rib her about what is perceived to be a workday designed for the golf course or—worst of all—liken her job to a teenage babysitter's, offer up something utterly free: respect. A little of it goes a long way.

READING ACTIVITY 1 Build Your Vocabulary

Determine the meanings of the following words from the context of the essay. Then check their meanings by looking up the words in a dictionary: *platitudes* (1), *aspirations* (3), *insinuate* (3), *salty* (4), *imperative* (5), *pontificating* (6), *lucrative* (8).

GROUP ACTIVITY 1 Discuss the Reading

Discuss the following questions about "I Am Not a Babysitter" with your classmates.

1. In your own words, list the skills that, according to Robinson, a teacher needs to be successful in the classroom.

2. This essay classifies the different stereotypes that people have about teachers. How does this organizational pattern help readers understand what others think about teaching? Do you agree with any of these stereotypes? Why or why not?

3. In paragraphs 6 and 7, Robinson defines what teachers actually do and why they do it. Does this definition of teaching change your mind about the profession? Why or why not?

4. Based on this essay, do you have the characteristics and skills to be a teacher? Explain your answer.

WRITING ACTIVITY 1 Share Your Ideas

Write a paragraph or two about an occupation that interests you. First, define the occupation. Then, describe some of the stereotypes or perceptions that people have about this profession. Share what you have written with your classmates.

A Career Path

MIKE ROSE
Should Everyone Go to College?

What's the first thing that comes to mind when you think of a college education? Many people think of it as a pathway to a career, but there is much more to be gained from a college education. In the following essay, "Should Everyone Go to College?," Mike Rose describes how the skills he learned in college not only helped him get a better job but also helped him develop new talents and interests. Mike Rose, an educator and author, is on the faculty of the UCLA Graduate School of Education and Information Studies. His most recent book is *Back to School: Why Everyone Deserves a Second Chance at Education* (2012).

College changed my life, so when I think about the question of who should go to college, I can't help but consider it through my own experience. And what I've learned from teaching over the past 40 years leads me to think that my experience is not all that unusual.   1

I was an average student through elementary school, good at reading (which saved me), horrible at math and flat-out hopeless at tasks such as diagramming sentences. I drifted through high school, never in big trouble, but not going anywhere either. Then in my senior year, a young, charismatic English teacher gave us a crash course in Western literature, Homer through Emily Dickinson with a few modern writers thrown in. And we wrote and wrote, and he read every word—and he hooked me.   2

My overall academic record was dreary, but that teacher got me into a local small college on probation, where I stumbled my first year, luckily encountered some new mentors and eventually found my way.   3

According to data from the National Center for Educational Statistics, people with a college degree, on average, will earn significantly more over a lifetime than people without a degree. And the benefit increases with education beyond the baccalaureate. This relation of higher education and economic advancement   4 has been part of our cultural wisdom for generations and has contributed mightily to the nation's increase in college attendance. But this wisdom is being challenged as tuition skyrockets, as certain white-collar occupations have become prey to computerization and outsourcing, and as the Great Recession has made so many kinds of employment vulnerable. We all know the stories of young people who are saddled with college debt and are working part time at jobs that do not require a college degree.

There are good jobs available in midlevel technical fields, in the trades and in 5 certain services that do require training but not a four-year or even a two-year degree. The work of electricians, chefs and medical technicians cannot be outsourced. Why direct all our youth into a degree path that they might not complete (about 50%-60% of those who begin college graduate), that keeps them out of the labor market and that saddles them with debt?

Still, granted the above, the college degree on average and over time yields 6 labor market benefits. And certain majors—for example, in technical fields, financial services, health sciences—have a strong pathway to employment. So just using an economic calculus alone, it seems that college is advisable, realizing that other good career options are open that do not require a bachelor's degree. Researching those options would be the first order of business for students and parents looking for viable alternatives to college.

A limitation of a strictly economic focus on the college question is that it 7 doesn't take into account the simple but profound fact of human variability. Some young people are just not drawn to the kinds of activities that make up the typical academic course of study, no matter how well-executed. In a community college fashion program I've been studying, I see students with average to poor high school records deeply involved in their work, learning techniques and design principles, solving problems, building a knowledge base. Yet they resist, often with strong emotion, anything smacking of the traditional classroom, including the very structure of the classroom itself. So making the decision about college will have to blend both economics and personal interest. What does a young person want to do with his or her life?

That last sentence takes us to another aspect of the college question. While 8 some young people are pretty clear about what they want to do with their lives, many are not. So they go to a two- or four-year college in search of a career. And some succeed. I've talked to so many students over the years who find their calling through a course taken to fulfill a general-education requirement: astronomy to theater. And others have their eyes opened by a job they get on campus. A young man I know in a welding program was employed in his community college's tutoring center, and it transformed him. He's planning to transfer to a four-year school to become a teacher. His is not an unusual story.

Discussing interests and meaningful work takes us to another big question: 9 What is the purpose of education? It's understandable, given our time, that the focus of discussion is on economics and employment. But historically, we've also demanded of our schools and colleges the fostering of intellectual, social, ethical and civic development. I come from a poor family, and college made my economic mobility possible, but I also learned how to read and write more carefully and critically, how to research new topics systematically and how to think cooperatively with other people. And whole new worlds of history, philosophy and psychology were opened up to me. What is interesting is that many people entering straightforward occupational programs—seemingly with quite different motives than those informing my liberal arts degree—also express a wide range of goals: They want to improve their reading, writing and math; they want to be able to help their kids in school better; they want to learn new skills and bodies of knowledge. Some of them talk about changing their lives.

A traditional two- or four-year college degree might not be right for every-   10
one. But I do believe in the individual and social benefit of all people having the opportunity to experience what college—broadly defined—can provide: the chance to focus on learning, to spread one's intellectual wings and test one's limits. We certainly can learn new things in the workplace, but both the bucolic college on a hill and the urban occupational program operate without the production pressure of a job and with systematic feedback on performance—which increases the possibility of discovering new areas of talent and interest.

And that's what education, at its best, is all about.   11

READING ACTIVITY 2 Build Your Vocabulary

Determine the meanings of the following words from the context of Mike Rose's essay. Then check their meanings by looking up the words in a dictionary: *charismatic* (2), *viable* (6), *bucolic* (10).

GROUP ACTIVITY 2 Discuss the Reading

Discuss the following questions about "Should Everyone Go to College?" with your classmates.

1. What does Rose say about the relationship between higher education and economic advancement? Which college skills does Rose mention as transferring to the workplace? Can you think of other workplace skills that might transfer?

2. It is generally believed that people who attend college have better career opportunities. Why do you suppose this is a common assumption? Does Rose agree? Do you? Explain your answer.

3. What does Rose mean when he says that college also provides "the chance to focus on learning, to spread one's intellectual wings and test one's limits"?

4. How does Rose use examples from his own life to support his points? In your view, are these effective or ineffective examples? Explain your answer.

WRITING ACTIVITY 2 Share Your Ideas

Write a paragraph or two describing your own reason for going to college. Explain why these skills are important to your chosen career path and as a way to spread your wings and test your limits.

Workplace Communication

PERRI KLASS
She's Your Basic L.O.L. in N.A.D.

Often a doctor's work is hard for people to understand because it involves technical skills and terms. Because she's both a pediatrician and a writer, Perri Klass has helped her readers better understand her profession. In "She's Your Basic L.O.L. in N.A.D.," Klass explains her introduction to the language of medicine, what it means, and why doctors use it.

"Mrs. Tolstoy is your basic L.O.L. in N.A.D., admitted for a soft rule-out M.I.," the intern announces. I scribble that on my patient list. In other words Mrs. Tolstoy is a Little Old Lady in No Apparent Distress who is in the hospital to make sure she hasn't had a heart attack (rule out a myocardial infarction). And we think it's unlikely that she has had a heart attack (a *soft* rule-out). 1

If I learned nothing else during my first three months of working in the hospital as a medical student, I learned endless jargon and abbreviations. I started out in a state of primeval innocence, in which I didn't even know that "s̄ C.P., S.O.B., N/V" meant "without chest pain, shortness of breath, or nausea and vomiting." By the end I took the abbreviations so for granted that I would complain to my mother the English professor, "And can you believe I had to put down *three* NG tubes last night?" 2

"You'll have to tell me what an NG tube is if you want me to sympathize properly," my mother said. NG, nasogastric—isn't it obvious? 3

I picked up not only the specific expressions but also the patterns of speech and the grammatical conventions; for example, you never say that a patient's blood pressure fell or that his cardiac enzymes rose. Instead, the patient is always the subject of the verb: "He dropped his pressure." "He bumped his enzymes." This sort of construction probably reflects that profound irritation of the intern when the nurses come in the middle of the night to say that Mr. Dickinson has disturbingly low blood pressure. "Oh, he's gonna hurt me bad tonight," the intern may say, inevitably angry at Mr. Dickinson for dropping his pressure and creating a problem. 4

When chemotherapy fails to cure Mrs. Bacon's cancer, what we say is, "Mrs. Bacon failed chemotherapy." 5

"Well, we've already had one hit today, and we're up next, but at least we've got mostly stable players on our team." This means that our team (group of doctors and medical students) has already gotten one new admission today, and it is our turn again, so we'll get whoever is next admitted in emergency, but at least most of the patients we already have are fairly stable—that is, unlikely to drop their pressures or in any other way get suddenly sicker and hurt us bad. Baseball metaphor is pervasive: a no-hitter is a night without any new admissions. A player is always a patient—a nitrate player is a patient on nitrates, a unit player is a patient in the intensive-care unit and so on, until you reach the terminal player. 6

It is interesting to consider what it means to be winning, or doing well, in this ⁷ perennial baseball game. When the intern hangs up the phone and announces, "I got a hit," that is not cause for congratulations. The team is not scoring points; rather, it is getting hit, being bombarded with new patients. The object of the game from the point of view of the doctors, considering the players for whom they are already responsible, is to get as few new hits as possible.

These special languages contribute to a sense of closeness and professional ⁸ spirit among people who are under a great deal of stress. As a medical student, it was exciting for me to discover that I'd finally cracked the code, that I could understand what doctors said and wrote and could use the same formulations myself. Some people seem to become enamored of the jargon for its own sake, perhaps because they are so deeply thrilled with the idea of medicine, with the idea of themselves as doctors.

I knew a medical student who was referred to by the interns on the team as ⁹ Mr. Eponym because he was so infatuated with eponymous terminology, the more obscure the better. He never said "capillary pulsation" if he could say "Quincke's pulses." He would lovingly tell over the multinamed syndromes— Wolff-Parkinson-White, Lown-Ganong-Levine, Henoch-Schonlein—until the temptation to suggest Schleswig-Holstein or Stevenson-Kefauver or Baskin-Robbins became irresistible to his less reverent colleagues.

And there is the jargon that you don't ever want to hear yourself using. You ¹⁰ know that your training is changing you, but there are certain changes you think would be going a little too far.

The resident was describing a man with devastating terminal pancreatic can- ¹¹ cer. "Basically he's C.T.D.," the resident concluded. I reminded myself that I had resolved not to be shy about asking when I didn't understand things. "C.T.D.?" I asked timidly.

The resident smirked at me. "Circling the Drain."   ¹²

The images are vivid and terrible. "What happened to Mrs. Melville?"   ¹³

"Oh, she boxed last night." To box is to die, of course.   ¹⁴

Then there are the more pompous locutions that can make the beginning ¹⁵ medical student nervous about the effects of medical training. A friend of mine was told by his resident, "A pregnant woman with sickle-cell represents a failure of genetic counseling."

Mr. Eponym, who tried hard to talk like the doctors, once explained to me, ¹⁶ "An infant is basically a brainstem preparation." A brainstem preparation, as used in neurological research, is an animal whose higher brain functions have been destroyed so that only the most primitive reflexes remain, like the sucking reflex, the startle reflex, and the rooting reflex.

The more extreme forms aside, one most important function of medical ¹⁷ jargon is to help doctors maintain some distance from their patients. By reformulating a patient's pain and problems into a language that the patient doesn't even speak, I suppose we are in some sense taking those pains and problems under our jurisdiction and also reducing their emotional impact. This linguistic separation between doctors and patients allows conversations to go on at the bedside that are unintelligible to the patient. "Naturally, we're worried about adeno-C.A.," the intern can say to the medical student, and lung cancer need never be mentioned.

I learned a new language this past summer. At times it thrills me to hear 18 myself using it. It enables me to understand my colleagues, to communicate effectively in the hospital. Yet I am uncomfortably aware that I will never again notice the peculiarities and even atrocities of medical language as keenly as I did this summer. There may be specific expressions I manage to avoid, but even as I remark them, promising myself I will never use them, I find that this language is becoming my professional speech. It no longer sounds strange in my ears—or coming from my mouth. And I am afraid that as with any new language, to use it properly you must absorb not only the vocabulary but also the structure, the logic, the attitudes. At first you may notice these new alien assumptions every time you put together a sentence, but with time and increased fluency you stop being aware of them at all. And as you lose that awareness, for better or for worse, you move closer and closer to being a doctor instead of just talking like one.

READING ACTIVITY 3 Build Your Vocabulary

Determine the meanings of the following words from the context of Perri Klass's essay. Then check their meanings by looking up the words in a dictionary: *jargon* (2), *primeval* (2), *inevitably* (4), *metaphor* (6), *perennial* (7), *enamored* (8), *eponymous* (9), *locutions* (15), *jurisdiction* (17), *atrocities* (18).

GROUP ACTIVITY 3 Discuss the Reading

Discuss the following questions about "She's Your Basic L.O.L. in N.A.D." with your classmates.

1. According to Klass, what are some examples of the jargon that health professionals use?

2. Why do medical practitioners use jargon in the workplace? For example, why do the interns say "He dropped his [blood] pressure" instead of "His [blood] pressure dropped"?

3. Explain the significance of the last sentence of the essay: "And as you lose that awareness, for better or for worse, you move closer and closer to being a doctor instead of just talking like one."

4. Have you ever heard medical professionals use terminology you couldn't understand? If so, describe what this experience was like.

WRITING ACTIVITY 3 Share Your Ideas

Write a paragraph or two on jargon that you use or have used on the job, at school, or in your community. How has using this jargon helped you adapt to the culture of your workplace or organization? Share a few of these words with your classmates.

A Job-Related Problem

ELLEN GOODMAN

The Company Man

Ellen Goodman is a Pulitzer Prize–winning newspaper columnist. Her column in the *Boston Globe* was syndicated to more than 450 newspapers. With common sense and humor, Goodman writes about topics close to home. She focuses on families, women in the workplace, and the poor. In the essay that follows, Goodman provides a vivid definition of "the company man."

He worked himself to death, finally and precisely, at 3:00 a.m. Sunday morning. 1

The obituary didn't say that, of course. It said that he died of a coronary 2 thrombosis—I think that was it—but everyone among his friends and acquaintances knew it instantly. He was a perfect Type A, a workaholic, a classic, they said to each other and shook their heads—and thought for five or ten minutes about the way they lived.

This man who worked himself to death finally and precisely at 3:00 a.m. Sun- 3 day morning—on his day off—was fifty-one years old and a vice-president. He was, however, one of six vice-presidents, and one of three who might conceivably—if the president died or retired soon enough—have moved to the top spot. Phil knew that.

He worked six days a week, five of them until eight or nine at night, during 4 a time when his own company had begun the four-day week for everyone but the executives. He worked like the Important People. He had no outside "extra-curricular interests," unless, of course, you think about a monthly golf game that way. To Phil, it was work. He always ate egg salad sandwiches at his desk. He was, of course, overweight, by twenty or twenty-five pounds. He thought it was okay, though, because he didn't smoke.

On Saturdays, Phil wore a sports jacket to the office instead of a suit, because 5 it was the weekend.

He had a lot of people working for him, maybe sixty, and most of them liked 6 him most of the time. Three of them will be seriously considered for his job. The obituary didn't mention that.

But it did list his "survivors" quite accurately. He is survived by his wife, 7 Helen, forty-eight years old, a good woman of no particular marketable skills, who worked in an office before marrying and mothering. She had, according to their daughter, given up trying to compete with his work years ago, when the children were small. A company friend said, "I know how much you will miss him." And she answered, "I already have."

"Missing him all these years," she must have given up part of herself which 8 had cared too much for the man. She would be "well taken care of."

His "dearly beloved" eldest of the "dearly beloved" children is a hard- 9 working executive in a manufacturing firm down South. In the day and a half before the funeral, he went around the neighborhood researching his father, asking the neighbors what he was like. They were embarrassed.

His second child is a girl, who is twenty-four and newly married. She lives 10 near her mother and they are close, but whenever she was alone with her father, in a car driving somewhere, they had nothing to say to each other.

The youngest is twenty, a boy, a high-school graduate who has spent the last 11 couple of years, like a lot of his friends, doing enough odd jobs to stay in grass and food. He was the one who tried to grab at his father, and tried to mean enough to him to keep the man at home. He was his father's favorite. Over the last two years, Phil stayed up nights worrying about the boy.

The boy once said, "My father and I only board here."   12

At the funeral, the sixty-year-old company president told the forty-eight- 13 year-old widow that the fifty-one-year-old deceased had meant much to the company and would be missed and would be hard to replace. The widow didn't look him in the eye. She was afraid he would read her bitterness and, after all, she would need him to straighten out the finances—the stock options and all that.

Phil was overweight and nervous and worked too hard. If he wasn't at the 14 office, he was worried about it. Phil was a Type A, a heart-attack natural. You could have picked him out in a minute from a lineup.

So when he finally worked himself to death, at precisely 3:00 a.m. Sunday 15 morning, no one was really surprised.

By 5:00 p.m. the afternoon of the funeral, the company president had 16 begun, discreetly of course, with care and taste, to make inquiries about his replacement. One of three men. He asked around: "Who's been working the hardest?"

READING ACTIVITY 4 Build Your Vocabulary

Determine the meanings of the following words from the context of Ellen Goodman's essay. Then check their meanings by looking up the words in a dictionary: *obituary* (2), *extracurricular* (4), *board* (12), *deceased* (13), *discreetly* (16).

GROUP ACTIVITY 4 Discuss the Reading

Discuss the following questions about "The Company Man" with your classmates.

1. What details about Phil make him the definition of "the company man"?

2. What point is Goodman trying to make by ending her piece with the line: "He [the president] asked around: 'Who's been working the hardest?' "

3. What about her style helps Goodman convince readers that Phil was a true "company man"?

4. In your view, does this essay accurately depict the modern workplace? Why or why not?

WRITING ACTIVITY 4 Share Your Ideas

Write a paragraph or two describing your workplace or college experience. Is the work you are doing causing you stress and affecting your health? Why or why not? Compare your experiences with those of your fellow students.

Writing Your Essay A Step-by-Step Guide

Now that you've read some essays analyzing career paths, workplace communication, and a job-related problem, it's time to write your own essay. First, read the writing assignment that follows. Then, use the step-by-step advice that follows to discover ideas, develop them as you draft, and polish your writing into a finished essay that readers will find both interesting and informative:

Step 1   Explore Your Choices 195
Step 2   Write Your Discovery Draft 200
Step 3   Revise Your Draft 202
Step 4   Edit Your Sentences 214
Step 5   Share Your Essay 223

Writing Assignment

Whether you are a full- or part-time student, have worked in just one or many jobs, or have no work experience, you will probably be thinking about a job or working toward a specific career goal while in college. So it's a good idea to think about potential careers and investigate your options. For this assignment, you'll help yourself and other students plan for the future by writing about a career field that interests you or with which you have experience. You (or your instructor) may decide to approach this assignment in one of several ways:

■ Examine a career path that interests you.

■ Analyze the ways people communicate in a place where you work now or have worked in the past, or analyze the communication styles in an organization to which you belong.

■ Analyze a job-related problem.

Step 1 Explore Your Choices

Are you thinking about what career path you would like to have? You may have a specific career in mind already, or maybe you haven't decided yet. Perhaps learning more about how people communicate at their jobs will help you think about possible careers. Analyzing a workplace problem might also give you valuable information about a particular type of work. This chapter's writing assignment will help you think about the workplace, possibilities for career paths, and ways to achieve your goals. Before you choose a profession, communication issue, or job-related problem to write about, you will think about who your readers are and what you want them to learn. Then you will experiment with three techniques for gathering ideas as you apply one to each of the assignment's topic choices. Gathering ideas before you start to write will give you a wealth of material from which to work.

Analyzing Your Audience and Purpose

For more on audience and purpose, see pp. 6–8.

Before you begin gathering ideas for your topic, think about who will read your essay and what they might expect.

You are writing an essay that investigates the workplace for people who are interested in the same kind of work that appeals to you. Your readers, then, might be students in your major, members of a club or volunteer group that you belong to, or coworkers at your current place of employment. Before you begin writing for this audience, give some thought to their experiences and hopes, and ask yourself what will interest them. What can you tell them that they don't already know? How will they benefit from reading your essay?

Consider, also, what you want to accomplish by writing about the workplace. This chapter assignment asks you to *inform* your readers about a career path, a style of workplace communication, or a job-related problem. You can include some expressive writing, but you don't need to persuade your readers to take action on what you say. Your purpose is primarily informative. Knowing your purpose before you begin writing will make it easier for you to write an essay that both you and your readers will value.

> ◖ **WRITING ACTIVITY 5** Analyze Your Audience and Purpose ◗
>
> Your responses to the following questions will help you decide how to approach this chapter's writing assignment. Be sure to come back to these questions after you have chosen a topic.

1. This assignment calls for primarily informative writing, but you could also include some expressive writing. What personal experience related to this topic could you share?

2. Who will read your essay? Will you share it with students in your major, members of a club or volunteer group, coworkers, or someone else?

3. Are your readers in college or a specialized program to prepare for a particular career?

4. What types of jobs do your readers want to have?

5. How do your job interests resemble or differ from those of your readers?

6. How can you interest your readers in an essay that deals with the workplace?

Gathering Ideas

As you learned in Chapter 1, several techniques can help you find good ideas. For this chapter's assignment, you will practice using three of these methods—freewriting, brainstorming, and consulting with others—as you explore your thoughts about workplace topics.

For more on gathering ideas, see pp. 11–14.

Feel free, however, to gather additional ideas using any other methods that work for you. Your goal at this stage is to collect as many ideas and details as you can to help you determine what you want to write about.

Freewriting about a Career Path

Many of us choose a major and decide to pursue a particular career path without thinking it through. For instance, being an actor appears to be glamorous until you realize that most actors are unemployed in their chosen profession. Or you might daydream of flying until you learn that pilots are away from their families for days at a time. Some people, such as the author of "I Am Not a Babysitter" (p. 185), change career paths to find one better suited to their personalities. When thinking about a particular career, you need to consider whether the job matches your interests, needs, and personality.

One useful way to investigate a profession that appeals to you is to freewrite about it. To freewrite, you write for a set period of time without worrying about what you have to say or how you say it. You simply put all of your thoughts down as they come to you. If your mind wanders, let it. The point of freewriting is to discover ideas you didn't know you had. You could continue to write about the profession you wrote about after reading "I Am Not a Babysitter," or you could freewrite about a different profession that also interests you.

If you either don't know where to start or get stuck, the following questions can help stimulate your thoughts:

- When did you first become interested in pursuing this career path?
- If you're already in this profession, in what way do you want to change (such as to obtain a higher position or go into another specialty)?
- List three things that interest you about this profession.
- What aspects of your personality do you think will make you successful in this profession?
- What don't you like about this profession?
- List at least two things you want to learn about this career path.

One student, Angelica, freewrote about her desire to become a translator.

I've wanted to become a translator since I read the Harry Potter series and learned that the seven books have been translated into over 60 languages. As

I researched the process for translation, I better understood what it is to be a translator of books. First you have to go through years of school. I guess I could handle that, but I'm not sure I have the patience and dedication required to do a good job of translating important texts.

WRITING ACTIVITY 6 Freewrite about a Career Path

Gather ideas about a career path you're interested in pursuing by freewriting about it for ten minutes. Follow your ideas without pausing, and do not stop, go back, or try to correct your writing. Just write.

Brainstorming about Workplace Communication

Coworkers in every workplace develop their own way of communicating with one another, often by using specialized language known only to their peers. For instance, police officers use special terminology when referring to crimes, telemarketers label incoming and outgoing calls according to numerical codes, and attorneys write contracts that are difficult for non-specialists to understand. One of the first things a person entering a profession needs to learn is its jargon.

Whether on the job or at a student or community organization, you probably speak more jargon than you realize. To gather ideas for an essay that explains this language to others, try brainstorming a list of terms used in your field. You might continue to add to the list of words you used when writing about workplace jargon after reading "She's Your Basic L.O.L. in N.A.D." (p. 190). Write your general topic at the top of a page, and then list all of the words and phrases that come into your head. Jot down a brief definition for each term. Don't worry about whether your examples are good ones or not; just write down everything you think of.

One student, Omari, brainstormed about the jargon used by the teachers in the elementary school where he was a teacher's aide:

> TAAS test — the standardized test that the students have to take every year
> ADD — attention deficit disorder
> Hyper — a child with ADD
> SW — the "student of the week" award, also known as the "sweetheart" award
> Sub — substitute teacher
> Meeting with the Pal — a meeting with the principal
> Sight words — common words, like "dog" or "the," that students should know
> Portfolio — a collection of student work
> In-service training — educational sessions to update experienced teachers
> Eager Beaver — a new teacher who thinks he or she knows everything

WRITING ACTIVITY 7 Brainstorm about Communication at Work

Pick a job you're familiar with. It can be a job you've had or a job held by a friend or family member. Brainstorm about the jargon that you've encountered by listing words and their definitions. Alternatively, you may list examples of another aspect of communication that interests you, such as levels of formality, uses of humor, spoken versus written communication, or body language.

Consulting Others about a Job-Related Problem

No matter how much you like your job, you're always going to encounter difficulties. Perhaps your boss is hard to talk to, or one of your coworkers likes to gossip too much. Your hours might be long, or you might object to a recent change in policy. To be successful, you need to be able to find solutions to problems such as these.

An excellent way to analyze problems is to ask other people what they think about your situation and what solutions they suggest. You might ask people at the workplace or college you described after reading Ellen Goodman's "The Company Man" (p. 193). You might also consult with an expert or two, ask those who have had similar experiences, or simply choose to share your problem out loud and get reactions from people who can offer you a fresh perspective.

Student writer Alfredo was interested in writing about a problem he had been having at his job in a restaurant. He decided to describe the issue out loud to his classmates and ask for their suggestions. Here is what he told them:

> "Whenever I'm on the night shift at the restaurant where I work, I see other workers steal food. We're allowed to eat one meal after a shift, but what these people are doing goes way beyond that. They carry out bags of food! The owner is never there when we close up so I don't think she knows what's happening. If I tell on the workers they might hate me, but if I keep quiet my conscience bugs me. What should I do?"

Alfredo's classmates had these suggestions:

BRENDA: I think you should tell the owner. Who cares what the workers think? What they're doing is wrong.

JOE: But what if the other workers deny it? What if the owner doesn't believe Alfredo?

BRENDA: It's a chance Alfredo will have to take. It's the right thing to do.

ALFREDO: I make good tips at this job. I really don't want to lose it.

JOE: Maybe you could talk to the people who are stealing? Tell them they should knock it off.

RUDY: Can you change shifts? That way you won't see it being done.

> **KIM:**   But it will still be happening. Do you know why they're stealing food? Maybe they don't think they're paid enough. Or would it be thrown out if they didn't take it home?

Alfredo used his classmate's comments to gather more ideas about his topic. Kim's questions, for example, made him realize that his coworkers might not think they were doing anything wrong. He decided to investigate how other area restaurants handled the problem of employee theft before talking to his boss.

GROUP ACTIVITY 5 Consult with Others about Your Topic

Identify a problem or an issue related to a job—it could be your job or someone else's. For instance, you might have a problem with a work schedule, the attitudes of coworkers, or difficult customers. Describe the problem to your classmates, and ask them for suggestions. Or you might choose to interview an expert on the subject and ask how he or she would address the problem. Take notes on the responses. As you write your informative essay, you may want to include some of the proposed solutions to your problem, but remember that your main goal is to inform your readers of the possibilities, not to try to persuade them to accept a particular solution.

Step 2 Write Your Discovery Draft

For more on drafting, see pp. 15–19.

You have now gathered ideas about a career path, workplace communication, and a job-related problem. The next step is to write a discovery draft that explains something you have learned about working.

It's okay if your ideas and your writing are rough at this stage. The discovery draft is just your first try at putting your thoughts in essay form. You'll have plenty of time later to develop your ideas, add supporting information, and fix any mistakes.

Choosing a Topic

You have collected rich materials for writing, but you need to decide how to proceed. Keeping in mind that you are writing to share something you know with others who may be interested in a particular occupational field, you need to pick a topic for your essay. Look over the ideas you have gathered and try to identify a topic that will enable you to give your readers useful information.

Remember that you have three general choices to work with: examining a specific career path, analyzing workplace communication, or analyzing a job-related problem. You may select one of the topics you have already explored, gather ideas on a new topic, or even combine related topics. For example, while freewriting about a career path, you may have discovered that you have some concerns about it. Rather than decide the path is not good for you, you could consult with some people and write about ways to address your concerns. Whatever you do, be sure to select a topic that matters to you, that you have considered carefully, and that your readers will want to learn about.

> ◖ **WRITING ACTIVITY 8 Choose Your Topic** ▷
>
> Review your freewriting, brainstorming, and consultation notes, and choose or create a topic that will be interesting for you and your readers. If you're not confident that you have something to say about your topic, you may go back and freewrite, brainstorm, or consult more on the topic of your choice.

Sharing Your Ideas

When you sit down to write your discovery draft, first write a preliminary thesis statement that says what your topic is and what you think your main point will be. You can always revise your thesis statement if your writing takes you in an unexpected direction, but having a general plan in mind will help get you started.

Keep your audience and purpose in mind as you draft, but remember that your main goal at this stage is to find out what you have to say. Focus on writing and don't worry about every supporting detail or how you express yourself. You'll have a chance later on to expand, revise, and edit your discovery draft.

A Student's Discovery Draft

Here's a discovery draft written by Angelica Hopkins, the student whose freewriting about her desire to be a translator you read earlier in this chapter. Notice that her preliminary thesis statement (highlighted) expresses her main idea and maps out a few of the reasons she is interested in pursuing a career as a translator. Angelica will also add more sources as she continues to research her topic. (Like most discovery drafts, this one includes errors; Angelica will fix them later.)

> Many of us have read or heard of books that have been translated such as the New York Times bestsellers "The Girl with the Dragon Tattoo," "The Alchemist," and "Anne Franks Diary," to name a few. These books have become known nationally. But you may ask yourself how does the whole world know about this book? Don't we all speak different languages? These are some of the questions that may come to mind while reading a nationally known best seller book. We as the reader need to take into mind that most of these books have been translated. There are people called translators who have studied, read the book, and defined what the book will need in order to translate it.

Angelica's preliminary thesis statement

While translating a certain piece of work the translator needs to take into mind that the language needs to be precise. Precision is important while writing in any language especially when translating a work of any kind. The reader will be bored if the language is repetitive. Another factor that the writer needs to keep in mind while translating is making sure that the piece makes sense. Other languages when translated can sound wordy or repetitive but it is up to the translator whether they will keep the same words or the same meaning which are two distinct factors.

Also while translating one needs to take into mind what words are being used and why. There is much research to be done when translating a certain word. Not only does research have to be done but the translator needs to think of what he or she intended in the first place. There could be a metaphor that in that certain language or culture can be defined but if translated it will not make any sense to the reader. A lot of translation has to do with the cultural region and language that is being used. Once that research has been done it makes it easier for the translator to translate.

Once a book has been translated and published it is up to the reader what they will understand and get from it. Readers need to also do research before reading a translated book.

WRITING ACTIVITY 9 Write Your Discovery Draft

Write at least three to five paragraphs that state why you are interested in a particular career path, that analyze workplace communication, or that discuss a job-related problem. Prepare a preliminary thesis statement and use your prewriting materials to get started, but feel free to write anything that occurs to you while you're drafting. If you're not sure what to write about, that's fine. You may write drafts on several topics to see which one will be most productive for you.

Step 3 Revise Your Draft

For more on thesis statements, see p. 18.

Now that you have completed your discovery draft, it's time to make it better. Start by looking for anything you can improve by using the skills you have learned in other chapters of this book. For example, you can probably clarify and support your main ideas by improving your thesis statement and topic sentences (Chapter 5), making your ideas flow more smoothly by adding transitions (Chapter 6), organizing your paragraphs (Chapter 3), and strengthening your introduction and conclusion (Chapter 6).

As you revise your essay about the workplace, you will learn how to develop your ideas using classification and definition, and you will practice adding support with information from books, articles, and the web. Keep your audience and purpose in mind as you revise by reviewing the analysis you completed in Writing Activity 5 (p. 196). What information do your readers need to know to understand your topic? How can you keep them interested as they read your essay?

Developing Your Ideas

Because you are writing to teach your readers something about career paths and the workplace, it's important that you explain your points clearly. Two methods of development—classification and definition—are especially useful when you want to help people unfamiliar with a topic understand what you have to tell them.

Classification

Classification shows the relationship between different people, things, or ideas by organizing them into logical categories. A single *principle*, or *theme*, links those categories together as a group. For instance, college students can be classified according to the principle of demographics: age, place of birth, marital status, income. Or they can be classified by participation in groups: fraternities or sororities, athletic teams, clubs. Because classification breaks a large concept into parts, it makes a topic easier to understand.

For more on classification, see p. 78.

Classification is used in all four of the essays that open this chapter. In "I Am Not a Babysitter," Heather Robinson classifies stereotypes about teachers. Mike Rose, in "Should Everyone Go to College?," classifies the reasons for going to college: economic, personal interest, and benefit to society. Perri Klass, in "She's Your Basic L.O.L. in N.A.D.," classifies medical jargon according to how it helps health care professionals communicate. In "The Company Man," Ellen Goodman classifies perceptions other people, such as employees, neighbors, and survivors, had of the company man. By using classification, these authors order their ideas logically and clearly.

When you classify, be sure to explain your principle of classification and to discuss each category separately. Although you might occasionally write one paragraph to classify the parts of your topic, you will usually need a full paragraph to identify and explain each category in an academic essay. (You

---

HOW TO Use Classification

- Decide on what basis you'll classify the topic. For example, the topic of "workplace stress" can be classified into "causes of workplace stress."
- Break the topic down into parts. For example, "causes of workplace stress" can be grouped into "stress from coworkers," "stress from supervisors," and "stress from customers."
- Discuss one category at a time.
- Give examples to support the classification.

may need to write two or three paragraphs to explain the most important category.)

Student writer Angelica Hopkins reviewed her discovery draft and noticed that she had described a translator as someone who must write precisely, do research, and take the time to understand an author's intended meaning. She decided to use classification to explain these and other characteristics in more detail.

 GROUP ACTIVITY 6 Use Classification to Develop Your Ideas

With several classmates, brainstorm ways you could use classification to make your essay easier to understand. For instance, if you wrote a discovery draft about dealing with a difficult supervisor, you might classify difficult supervisors into categories (those who yell, those who expect too much, those who give confusing instructions, and so on). If appropriate, use your classmates' suggestions to organize your topic into categories for your revision.

Definition

For more on definition, see p. 79.

To *define* something is to explain what it means. *Definition* is a helpful strategy to use when developing your essay because it can help you clarify important points. When you define a term, first place it in a general category. Then explain how it fits within that category according to what sets it apart—its distinguishing features. For example, in the introduction of her discovery draft, Angelica Hopkins defines *translator* by placing it in a general category—writers. She then explains the characteristics of this type of writer (someone who communicates what others have written in another language), which highlights the profession's distinguishing features.

Although a simple one-sentence definition is always useful, writers often use more than one sentence to define complex terms or concepts. In "I Am Not a Babysitter," for example, the author first defines teaching in very general terms as "the profession that creates all other professions" and then later uses several sentences to describe what teachers do. In some cases, you may devote entire paragraphs to describing each distinguishing feature of the term.

HOW TO Use Definition

- Introduce the word, phrase, or concept to be defined.
- Place the word, phrase, or concept in a general category and explain what sets it apart from others in that category.
- Provide details (such as description, narration, examples, process explanation, or comparison and contrast) to explain your term.
- Organize the details so that readers will easily understand your definition.

GROUP ACTIVITY 7 Use Definition to Develop Your Ideas

Exchange your discovery draft with a classmate. Underline any words, phrases, or concepts in your partner's draft that you don't understand or that could be made clearer with a sentence or paragraph of definition. Your classmate should do the same for your paper. Use your partner's suggestions to add definitions to your own draft as necessary.

Building Your Essay

In addition to developing your own ideas fully, you need to make sure that you have provided enough information to keep your audience interested and informed. Because you may be writing about a topic that is new to you or unfamiliar to your readers, consider doing a little research to gather additional information that will help you explain something about the workplace. Used carefully, a handful of facts and opinions from reliable sources can make your ideas more convincing.

Find Information to Strengthen Your Support

To learn more about any aspect of a career path, workplace communication, or a job-related problem, start by consulting a general reference—such as an encyclopedia, a dictionary, or a handbook—for basic facts. For instance, if you wrote your discovery draft about a profession that interests you, you can look it up in the *Occupational Outlook Handbook*, updated every other year by the U.S. Department of Labor and available online at www.bls.gov/oco. The *Handbook* contains detailed information—such as job descriptions, educational requirements, and average salaries—about a wide variety of occupations. Some other useful resources are listed on pages 366–71 of this book; your college librarian will be happy to suggest additional resources if you ask.

Also helpful are newspaper, magazine, and web articles written by people with related experience in the workplace. Consider Mike Rose's essay "Should Everyone Go to College?," which you read earlier in this chapter. Even though Rose is highly respected by educators, he includes data from the National Center for Educational Statistics to support his claim that there are advantages to having a college degree. Like Rose, you can include the opinion of another writer to make one of your own points more convincing.

To find additional information for your draft, search a library database or the web for information about your topic. Use *keywords*, or words that pertain to your topic, to find useful articles. Keep in mind that you won't be able

For more on library databases and keywords, see pp. 368–69.

 Research jobs online

Research your career path at online sites such as LinkedIn, Monster, or CareerBuilder to learn the professional qualifications and to get a sense of job requirements.

to use every source you find. As you read, look for facts, ideas, or opinions that can help you back up one of your points or explain one of your ideas.

WRITING ACTIVITY 10 **Locate Additional Information for Your Essay**

Reread your discovery draft and look for any ideas that could be better explained or made more convincing. Look for information to support these ideas by checking a reference work and reading some articles on your topic. Photocopy or print out any useful material that you find; you will refer to it in the next stage of revising your draft.

Outline Your Plan

Once you find facts, ideas, and opinions that can help you explain your topic to your readers, pay special attention to where you will include this information in your essay.

Review your discovery draft and your research notes, and make a rough outline of your major points. Indicate where you could add information from a book, an article, or a web site to make your points clearer. Your outline should include the ideas you've already drafted and any additional support from your research that you plan to provide in each paragraph. Follow the outline format that works best for you. If you're unsure of how to make an outline, just create a simple list.

Student writer Angelica Hopkins, for example, found some good information about translators in the online version of the *Occupational Outlook Handbook*. Here is the rough outline she put together to plan her revised draft. (Note that *P* in this outline stands for *paragraph*. The research information Angelica plans to add is underlined.)

P1: Introduce topic. Define *translator*. Thesis: There are writers called translators who have studied, read the book, and defined what the book will need in order to share it with readers of other languages. The job is challenging and artistic.

P2: Describe the job of a translator and the training required to become one as defined in the *Occupational Outlook Handbook*.

P3: Translators must also be artists. Use translation of Lorca's *Poet in New York* as an example.

P4: Translators must research what the writer intended. Use translator Marcel Smith and the *Occupational Outlook Handbook* for examples.

P5: Translators must try to be precise and to write clearly. Use Lorca's poem, "1910."

P6: Translators face many challenges. Mention that the reader must also be willing to do some research. The translator just helps bridge the gap.

P7: Conclusion. Go back to thesis. It's the job for me.

Remember that your outline, like Angelica's, is *tentative*—in other words, it is subject to change. As you revise, you might think of new ideas or a better way to order your points. Don't hesitate to rework your plan as needed.

 Use the outline view

To help you organize your outline, use the Outline View function found in many word-processing programs. This function will give you the option of outlining your ideas for the whole essay or for individual paragraphs. The Help function of your program will lead you through the appropriate steps.

 WRITING ACTIVITY 11 Outline Your Revision Plan

Outline your ideas for your revised draft. Use the format in Angelica's outline or a format of your own. List the major ideas that you will keep from your discovery draft and note where you'll add new ideas and information from your research.

Correctly Use Research Material

As you revise your draft, remember that you are writing to express your own ideas about career paths and the workplace and not to give a report on what other people have said. Although it can be tempting to include several long chunks of research in your essay, select only the most pertinent ideas to support your points. Do not let the research take over your essay. As a rule of thumb, limit information from outside sources (articles, books, websites) to no more than 10 to 20 percent of your essay.

Keep the following three principles in mind when you add information from research to your own writing.

Put Information in Your Own Words Summarize or paraphrase—don't quote—facts or statistics from an article about your topic. You can select the key ideas that will support your point without having to repeat the whole of your source.

A *summary* is a short version of a piece of text that is written in your own words. To summarize, you explain the most important idea from a source while omitting the details. Suppose, for example, that you were writing an essay about your desire to be a teacher. To address any stereotypes that your family and friends may have, you could summarize information from the essay "I Am Not a Babysitter," which you read earlier in this chapter:

> As the author of "I Am Not a Babysitter" explains, there are a number of stereotypes about teaching, including that it is an easy, boring job that people do only until they can find something better. In reality, though, teaching is a challenging but rewarding profession that makes a real difference in students' lives.

For more information on quoting, paraphrasing, and summarizing information, see pp. 384–87.

When you *paraphrase*, you also put information from a source into your own words, but you use about the same number of words as the original source uses, as Angelica does in this example:

ORIGINAL   Although interpreters and translators typically need at least a bachelor's degree, the most important requirement is to have native-level fluency in English and at least one other language. Many complete job-specific training programs. (*Occupational Outlook Handbook*, 2014–15 ed.)

PARAPHRASE   Translators usually have a bachelor's degree and professional training in translation, but always have fluency in at least two languages. (*Occupational Outlook Handbook*)

Quote Sparingly   A well-placed quotation can help you express an idea in a distinct way, but you should use another writer's exact words only to emphasize or explain an important point. One or two quotations are sufficient for a three-page essay.

When you do include a direct quotation, weave it smoothly into your sentences. Use an introductory phrase and put quotation marks around your source's words, as Angelica does in her revised draft:

There are plenty of opportunities for employment in this field because of "increasing globalization and . . . large increases in the number of non-English-speaking people in the United States" (Bureau of Labor Statistics).

> (**!**) **Use color for research material**
>
> Use the color feature in your word-processing program to highlight quotations in your draft. Use another color to highlight paraphrased and summarized material. This technique will help you monitor how much research material you have in your draft and how often you vary your strategy for incorporating information from sources. For instance, if more than 10 to 20 percent of the draft is in color, you know that the research is taking over your own ideas.

For more on documenting sources, see pp. 388–92.

Document Your Sources   Whether you summarize, paraphrase, or quote material from a source, you must always inform your readers that the ideas or words are not your own. Indicate where you obtained information by citing the source in the text of your essay and in a list of works cited at the end:

- In most cases, introduce a summary, paraphrase, or quotation by identifying the author or title of the book, article, or website in which you found the information.

- At the end of a summary, paraphrase, or quotation, provide the author's last name and the page number where you found the information in parentheses. (Exclude the author's name if you gave it when you introduced the material.)
- At the end of the essay, include a Works Cited list that gives publication information for each source you used.

HOW TO Use Research Material in an Essay

- Limit the amount of research material to no more than 10 to 20 percent of your essay.
- Use brief quotations only to emphasize or explain an important point.
- Summarize or paraphrase—put into your own words—information such as facts or statistics.
- Introduce most source material with a phrase such as *According to* or *In the words of*.
- Indicate where you obtained any quoted, summarized, or paraphrased information in the text of the essay and at the end of the essay.

For the most up-to-date information on documenting sources in MLA, check the official *MLA Style Manual* or the Handbook in Part Four of this book. Most college libraries also keep updated information in a research guide.

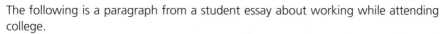

GROUP ACTIVITY 8   Quote, Paraphrase, and Document Information

The following is a paragraph from a student essay about working while attending college.

> Working your way through college has many advantages. Unlike students who depend on large checks from their parents, working students learn to be self-reliant and independent. Because they pay their own bills every month, they realize the value of a college education in getting a well-paid job. They learn how to manage time well, an important skill in the working world. They also gain excellent work experience for their résumés after they graduate. While they might be tempted to grumble about lack of free time or the old car they drive, working students have many advantages over students who don't work.

Quoting, paraphrasing, and documenting information are essential. Otherwise, you can be accused of plagiarism. For more help, see pp. 378–79.

Here's a quotation from a magazine article on the same topic:

> I believe the fact that my husband and I are happy and financially stable is a direct result of our learning how to manage time and money in college.
>
> —*"Pay Your Own Way! (Then Thank Mom),"* by Audrey Rock-Richardson, *page 12 in* Newsweek *on Sept. 11, 2000.*

Working in groups of two or three students, first rewrite the paragraph by inserting the quotation into it. Be sure to introduce the quotation and correctly document the source in parentheses.

Then rewrite the paragraph again. Rather than inserting the quotation into the paragraph, paraphrase the information by putting it into your own words. Don't forget to document the source in the paragraph.

> **WRITING ACTIVITY 12 Add Researched Information to Your Draft**

Using the outline you prepared for Writing Activity 11 as a guide, add two or three summaries, paraphrases, or quotations to your draft. Be careful that you use this researched information to support your own points: Don't expect it to speak for you. Also, make sure you correctly cite your sources in the body of your essay and in a Works Cited list.

A Student's Revised Draft

After writing a discovery draft about her desire to become a translator, student writer Angelica Hopkins realized she needed more details to describe why she wanted to be a translator, so she did a little research to get more information. Before you read her revised draft, reread her discovery draft (p. 201). Notice how she has used classification to organize her ideas and added information from the Bureau of Labor Statistics' *Occupational Outlook Handbook* and two translated books to support her points. (You will also notice some errors in the revised draft; these will be corrected when Angelica edits her essay later.)

The Translator

Many books have been translated, such as the *New York Times* bestsellers *The Girl with the Dragon Tattoo*, *The Alchemist*, and *Anne Franks Diary*, to name a few. These books have become known internationally. But how does the whole world know about these books? Don't we all speak different languages? Writers called translators study the author and topic, read the book, and define what it needs in order to share it with readers of other languages. I think that it's a job that I would enjoy. I enjoy reading and sharing my love of reading with others.

The primary job of the translator is to "convert information from one language into another" (Bureau of Labor Statistics). Not to be confused with interpreters, translators use written language, whereas interpreters use spoken words. Translators usually have a bachelor's degree and

Angelica clarifies the thesis statement.

1

2

professional training in translation, but always have fluency in at least two languages. There are plenty of opportunities for employment in this field because of "increasing globalization and . . . large increases in the number of non-English-speaking people in the United States" (Bureau of Labor Statistics).

It isn't enough, however, to simply complete the educational requirements to become a translator. Translators must also be artists. Each language has a different grammatical structure, and this can impact the way words are expressed, so research is a crucial element of the translator's job. Before translating any form of literary work, the translator first needs to research the author and the text to be translated. For example, in Poet in New York, a literary translation of Federico Garcia Lorca's Spanish poems, translators Pablo Medina and Mark Statman describe their work this way: "It was only when we started translating Lorca's Poet in New York that our sense of the work of a translator took on a dramatic change, or shift in perspective, because suddenly the goal became how to take the language Lorca wrote in — which looks remarkably like Spanish but is really a language called Lorca — and render that into a language that looks remarkable like English but remains, again, a language called Lorca" (Introduction xix).

Not only does background research on the author have to be done, but the translator needs to think of what he or she intended to communicate in the first place. There are often words that in a certain language or culture can be defined, but if translated will no longer make sense to the reader. For example, the translator Marcel Smith who translated poems by Ana Enriqueta Terán, says that "a Spanish toro is not an English bull." In other words, you have to live in Spain to fully appreciate the meaning of the word toro. A translation can never be a duplicate of the original, only an imitation (20). A lot of translation has to do with the cultural region and language that is being used, so the "translator must properly transmit any cultural references, including slang, and other expressions that do not translate literally" (Bureau of Labor Statistics).

Translating a certain piece of work is precise work. The translator must remember that the language needs to be precise. Precision is important while writing in any language, but especially when translating a work of any kind. The reader will become bored if the language is

3 A new paragraph summarizes the Bureau of Labor Statistics definition of a translator.

Angelica adds a transitional sentence to help readers move from one idea to the next.

Another new paragraph helps classify the job of a translator.

A direct quote with source information clarifies and supports the point.

4

Angelica provides another example from an outside source.

5

repetitive. Another factor that the translator needs to keep in mind is making sure that the piece is clearly written. Other languages when translated can sound wordy, but it is up to the translator to decide whether to keep the same words or keep the same meaning, which are two distinct things. Medina and Statman give examples from the poem "1910" by Lorca. This is Lorca's line: "Aquellos ojos míos de mil novecientos diez." The translated version is "My eyes in 1910" (6). In the Spanish version, the line is longer because the year is spelled out, but there is also a more sensual feel to the line in Spanish than in English. Lorca's work to bring sensuality to the poem is diminished when it is translated literally into English.

Angelica adds a short summary of the source's view of the importance of precision to support her point.

Translating is a tough job and once a work is translated and published, the reader must be willing to take over the process. I once read a book of short stories written by Etgar Keret, an Israeli writer. All his books have been translated in over ten languages. I didn't know this before I read the book, so I didn't understand what was being said. After reading the back page of the book about the author, I realized that I had been reading a translated book, and it then made sense to me why I couldn't understand some of the terminology. I realized then that I wanted to become a translator because I wanted to be the person who helps readers make sense of great literary works written in other languages.   6

Once a book has been translated and published, it is like an agreement between translator and reader. Although it is a challenging job to be a translator, it would be satisfying to be the one to read and research authors' works and span the divide between them and their readers.   7

A new conclusion brings the essay full circle.

Works Cited

The Works Cited list is added.

García Lorca, Federico. *Poet in New York = Poeta En Nueva York*. Trans. Pablo Medina and Mark Statman. New York: Grove, 2008. Print.

Bureau of Labor Statistics, U.S. Department of Labor. "Interpreters and Translators," *Occupational Outlook Handbook*, 2014-15 Edition. Bureau of Labor Statistics. U.S. Bureau of Labor Statistics, 9 Jan. 2014. Web. 19 Oct. 2014.

Terán, Enriqueta Ana. *The Poetess Counts to 100 and Bows Out: Selected Poems*. Trans. Marcel Smith. Princeton: Princeton UP, 2003. Print.

GROUP ACTIVITY 9 Analyze Angelica's Revised Draft

Use the following questions to discuss with your classmates how Angelica revised her draft.

1. How well has Angelica hooked her readers, given background information, and stated her thesis in her introduction?

2. What is Angelica's thesis statement? How much better is it than the thesis in her discovery draft? How can it be improved even more?

3. How has Angelica used classification and definition to develop her points? Are these revisions effective? Explain.

4. What kind of research did Angelica conduct on her topic?

5. How well has Angelica used research in her essay? Is the research connected to the ideas before and after it? Are quotations introduced? Is the research documented in her essay and in her Works Cited list?

6. In your view, what point or points are best supported with facts, examples, and statistics? Is there any idea that needs more support?

7. How could Angelica's draft benefit from more revision?

Peer Review for an Essay That Analyzes

Form a group with two or three other students and exchange copies of your current drafts. Read your draft aloud while your classmates follow along. Take notes on your classmates' responses to the following questions about your draft.

1. What did you like best about my essay?

2. How interesting is my introduction? Did you want to continue reading the essay? Why or why not?

3. What is my thesis statement? Do I need to make the essay's thesis clearer?

4. How well have I supported my points? Do I need to add facts, examples, or statistics to extend what I say?

5. How can classification or definition improve my supporting points?

6. How well have I used summaries, paraphrases, and quotations from my research? Have I given the correct information about my sources in the text of my essay and in the Works Cited list?

7. Where in the essay did my writing confuse you? How can I clarify my thoughts?

8. How effective is my ending? Do I end in such a way that you know it's the end?

> **WRITING ACTIVITY 13** Revise Your Draft

Using the plan you outlined in Writing Activity 11 and the research you added in Writing Activity 12 as a starting point, take your classmates' peer review suggestions into consideration and revise your essay. Use researched information only to support your most important points, and summarize, paraphrase, and quote properly. Finally, document your sources—both in the text of your essay and in a Works Cited list at the end.

Step 4 Edit Your Sentences

At this point, you have worked hard to investigate a career path, analyze workplace communication, or analyze a workplace problem. Now that you have finished developing and supporting your ideas, you're ready to focus on your words and sentences. Remember that the fewer errors you make, the more your readers will pay attention to what you have to say. In this section, you'll concentrate on two editing tasks—combining sentences using subordinating conjunctions and correcting pronoun reference and agreement.

Combining Sentences Using Subordinating Conjunctions

For more on subordination, see pp. 441–45.

By combining short, closely related sentences in your draft, you can eliminate unnecessary words, clarify connections between your sentences, and improve sentence variety. For now, you'll focus on combining sentences using subordinating conjunctions.

Often, one sentence in a paragraph is *subordinate* to—less important than—another, closely related sentence. Combining sentences with a subordinating conjunction tells readers that one idea is less important than another. Here are some of the most frequently used subordinating conjunctions:

Subordinating Conjunctions

after	if	unless	where
although	since	until	wherever
because	that	when	whether
before	though	whenever	while

The subordinating conjunction comes at the beginning of the less important sentence, which is called a *subordinate clause*.

Student writer Angelica Hopkins's revised draft has short, closely related sentences that can be combined with subordinating conjunctions. In the following examples, the less important sentence, or subordinate clause, is italicized:

ORIGINAL I think that it's a job that I would enjoy. *I enjoy reading and sharing my love of reading with others.*

REVISED I think that it's a job that I would enjoy because *I enjoy reading and sharing my love of reading with others.*

ORIGINAL   *Translating a certain piece of work is precise work*. The translator must remember that the language needs to be precise.

REVISED   *While translating a certain piece of work*, the translator must also remember that the language needs to be precise.

As these examples illustrate, the subordinate clause can appear at the beginning or end of the sentence. When the subordinate clause comes at the beginning of the sentence, a comma divides it from the rest of the sentence. When the subordinate clause comes at the end of the sentence, no comma is used.

HOW TO Combine Sentences Using Subordinating Conjunctions

- Combine sentences that are short and closely related in meaning.
- Decide which sentence is subordinate to, or less important than, the other.
- Turn the less important sentence into a subordinate clause by beginning it with an appropriate subordinating conjunction.
- When the subordinate clause begins the sentence, use a comma to divide it from the main clause.
- Don't use a comma when the subordinate clause is at the end of the sentence.

EDITING ACTIVITY 1 Use Subordinating Conjunctions

Combine the following pairs of sentences. First, decide which sentence is less important in conveying the message; this sentence will become the subordinate clause. Then, select an appropriate subordinating conjunction to begin the subordinate clause. Finally, combine the two sentences. You may need to eliminate unnecessary words or move some words around.

EXAMPLE For many people, it's hard to decide on a career. *because there* ~~There~~ are so many careers to choose from.

1. I'm studying to become a photojournalist. I like both photography and journalism.

2. I've always wanted to be a photojournalist. I remember wanting to be a photojournalist when I was a child.

3. A photojournalist takes photographs of current events. These photographs are published in print and online magazines and newspapers.

4. Often people read a magazine just for the photographs. This is why photojournalists are important to magazine editors.

5. Photojournalists have exciting jobs. They get to travel and take pictures of important people.

> **WRITING ACTIVITY 14** Combine Your Sentences

Examine your revised draft for short, closely related sentences. Where it makes sense to do so, combine them with subordinating conjunctions.

Correcting Pronoun Reference and Agreement

A *pronoun* usually refers to or takes the place of a specific noun in a sentence. If a pronoun does not clearly refer to a specific noun or agree in number with the noun it replaces, your readers will be confused.

Here are some of the most common English pronouns:

I, me, mine, we, us, our, ours
you, your, yours
he, him, his, she, her, hers
it, its
they, them, their, theirs
this, these, that, those
who, whom, whose, which, that, what
any, anyone, anybody, each, everybody, everyone, everything
someone, something

Pronoun Reference

For more on pronoun reference, see pp. 432–33.

When you use a pronoun to refer to a noun, make sure the reference is clear, not vague. Here are two ways to correct vague pronoun reference:

- Replace the pronoun with the noun it refers to.
- Rewrite the sentence so that the pronoun is no longer needed.

VAGUE	In the article "Dealing with a Difficult Boss," *it* said that good communication between boss and employee is essential. [What does *it* refer to?]
CLEAR	In the article "Dealing with a Difficult Boss," *the author* said that good communication between boss and employee is essential.
VAGUE	Ms. Ortiz told Rachel *she* was going to be late. [Does *she* refer to Ms. Ortiz or to Rachel?]
CLEAR	Ms. Ortiz said, "I'm going to be late."

VAGUE	In the art world, *they're* used to unusual clothing. [Whom does *they* refer to?]
CLEAR	People in the art world are used to unusual clothing.
VAGUE	Raymond loved traveling with his band and recording a CD. *It* made him decide to make music a career. [Does *it* refer to traveling with the band, recording a CD, or both?]
CLEAR	Because Raymond loved traveling with his band and recording a CD, *he* decided to make music a career.

Pronoun Agreement

Every pronoun must agree in number with the noun it takes the place of. That is, use a singular pronoun to replace a singular noun and a plural pronoun to replace a plural noun. Indefinite pronouns—such as *any, anybody, anyone, each, everybody, everyone, everything, someone,* and *something*—are singular. Here are two ways to correct pronoun agreement:

For more on pronoun agreement, see pp. 433–34.

■ Make the pronoun and noun agree in number.

■ Rewrite the sentence to eliminate the problem.

INCORRECT	A successful job applicant will prepare for *their* job interview.
REVISED	A successful job applicant will prepare for *his or her* job interview.
REVISED	Successful job applicants will prepare for *their* job interviews.
INCORRECT	To get a good job, *everyone* should try to get the best education *they* can afford.
REVISED	To get a good job, *everyone* should try to get the best education *he or she* can afford.
REVISED	To get a good job, *young people* should try to get the best education *they* can afford.

As these examples illustrate, you may wish to use a plural noun (such as *young people*) to avoid saying *he or she* or *his or her* throughout an essay.

HOW TO Correct Pronoun Reference and Agreement

- Identify the pronouns in each sentence of your draft.
- Identify the noun that each pronoun replaces. Make sure the noun is easy to identify and is close to the pronoun.
- Check to see that the noun and pronoun agree in number.
- Remember that indefinite pronouns (*any, anybody, anyone, each, everybody, everyone, everything, someone,* and *something*) are singular. Use singular nouns with them.

EDITING ACTIVITY 2 **Correct Pronoun Reference and Agreement**

Correct the problems with pronoun reference and agreement in the following paragraph.

Whenever I tell anyone my college major is food science, they get a puzzled look on their face. Most people haven't heard of it. I first read about food science in a magazine article about the invention of different varieties of corn for undeveloped countries. They said that scientists spend years in the laboratory and in greenhouses trying to get plants to grow in extreme climates or different types of soils. They take years to develop. Last semester in my Introduction to Food Science course, they had us experiment with making a type of yogurt that doesn't need refrigeration. It isn't available to consumers in poor countries. It didn't taste very good, but it was interesting to make. My ultimate goal is to contribute to the elimination of starvation throughout the world.

 WRITING ACTIVITY 15 **Edit Your Sentences**

Read your essay word for word, looking for errors in spelling, punctuation, and grammar. Also ask a friend or classmate to help you spot errors you might have overlooked. Pay particular attention to vague pronoun reference and faulty pronoun agreement. Use a dictionary and the Handbook in Part Four of this book to help you correct the errors you find.

A Student's Edited Essay

This essay shows how to give information about your sources in the body of the essay and in the Works Cited list. You can find another sample essay on pp. 394–99.

You may have noticed that Angelica's revised draft contained some choppy sentences as well as errors in spelling, punctuation, and grammar. Angelica fixed these problems in her edited essay. Her corrections are noted in the margin.

Hopkins 1

Angelica Hopkins ——————————————————————————————— Angelica uses correct MLA
                                                                                  format.
Professor Baca

English 3101

2 Mar. 2015

The Translator

    Many books have been translated, such as the *New York Times*   1

bestsellers *The Girl with the Dragon Tattoo*, *The Alchemist*, and

Anne Frank's *The Diary of a Young Girl*, to name a few. These books ——— Apostrophe is added and
                                                                                  book title is corrected.
have become known internationally. But how does the whole world

know about these books? Don't we all speak different languages?

Writers called translators study the author and topic, read the ——————————— Thesis statement is clearer.

book, and define what it needs in order to share it with readers of

other languages. I think that it's a job that I would enjoy because ——— Two short sentences
                                                                                  are combined with a
I enjoy reading and sharing my love of reading with others.   subordinating conjunction.

    The primary job of the translator is to "convert information   2

from one language into another" (Bureau of Labor Statistics). Not

to be confused with interpreters, translators use written language,

whereas interpreters use spoken words. Translators usually have a

bachelor's degree and professional training in translation, but

always have fluency in at least two languages. There are plenty of

opportunities for employment in this field because of "increasing

globalization and . . . large increases in the number of non-English-

speaking people in the United States" (Bureau of Labor Statistics).

    It isn't enough, however, to simply complete the educational   3

requirements to become a translator. Translators must also be

artists. Each language has a different grammatical structure, and

this can impact the way words are expressed, so research is a

crucial element of the translator's job. Before translating any form

of literary work, the translator first needs to research the author

and the text to be translated. For example, in *Poet in New York*,

a literary translation of Federico García Lorca's Spanish poems,

translators Pablo Medina and Mark Statman describe their work

this way: "It was only when we started translating Lorca's *Poet*

in New York that our sense of the work of a translator took on a

Hopkins 2

Spelling is corrected.

dramatic change, or shift in perspective, because suddenly the goal became how to take the language Lorca wrote in — which looks remarkably like Spanish but is really a language called Lorca — and render that into a language that looks remarkably like English but remains, again, a language called Lorca" (Introduction xix).

Pronoun reference is clearer.

Not only does background research on the author have to be done, but the translator needs to think of what the writer intended to communicate in the first place. There are often words that in a certain language or culture can be defined, but if translated will no longer make sense to the reader. For example, the translator Marcel Smith, who translated poems by Ana Enriqueta Terán, says that "a Spanish toro is not an English bull." In other words, you have to live in Spain to fully appreciate the meaning of the word *toro*. A translation can never be a duplicate of the original, only an imitation (20). A lot of translation has to do with the cultural region and language that is being used, so the "translator must properly transmit any cultural references, including slang, and other expressions that do not translate literally" (Bureau of Labor Statistics).

4

Two short sentences are combined with a subordinating conjunction.

While translating a certain piece of work, the translator must also remember that the language needs to be precise. Precision is important while writing in any language, but especially when translating a work of any kind. The reader will become bored if the language is repetitive. Another factor that the translator needs to keep in mind is making sure that the piece is clearly written. Other languages when translated can sound wordy, but it is up to the translator to decide whether to keep the same words or keep the same meaning, which are two distinct things. Medina and Statman give examples from the poem "1910" by Lorca. This is Lorca's line: "Aquellos ojos míos de mil novecientos diez." The translated version is "My eyes in 1910" (6). In the Spanish version, the line is longer because the year is spelled out, but there is also a more sensual feel to the line in Spanish than in English. Lorca's work to bring sensuality to the poem is diminished when it is translated literally into English.

5

Hopkins 3

Translating is a tough job, and once a work is translated and
published, the reader must be willing to take over the process. I
once read a book of short stories written by Etgar Keret, an Israeli
writer. All his books have been translated in over ten languages.
I didn't know this before I read the book, so I didn't understand
what was being said. After reading the back page of the book
about the author, I realized that I had been reading a translated
book, and it then made sense to me why I couldn't understand
some of the terminology. I realized then that I wanted to become
a translator because I wanted to be the person who helps readers
make sense of great literary works written in other languages.

6

Once a book has been translated and published, it is like
an agreement between translator and reader. Although it is a
challenging job to be a translator, it would be satisfying to be
the one to read and research authors' works and span the divide
between them and their readers.

7

Works Cited

Bureau of Labor Statistics, U.S. Department of Labor. "Interpreters
and Translators," *Occupational Outlook Handbook*, 2014-15
Edition. Bureau of Labor Statistics. U.S. Bureau of Labor
Statistics, 9 Jan. 2014. Web. 19 Oct. 2014.

García Lorca, Federico. *Poet in New York = Poeta En Nueva York*.
Trans. Pablo Medina and Mark Statman. New York: Grove,
2008. Print.

Terán, Enriqueta Ana. *The Poetess Counts to 100 and Bows Out:
Selected Poems*. Trans. Marcel Smith. Princeton: Princeton UP,
2003. Print.

Step 5 Share Your Essay

You've worked hard to write an essay that will be useful to people who share your interest in a particular career path, workplace communication, or a job-related problem, so give them a chance to read it. Many organizations distribute periodic newsletters that include articles of interest to their members. For example, your school might e-mail news and career ideas to students every term, your volunteer group might have a quarterly newsletter, or your employer might share monthly updates on staff activities. Whether these newsletters are printed, posted to the web, or e-mailed, the people who distribute them are almost always looking for reader submissions. Find out who edits one of the newsletters you receive and send your essay to him or her.

CHAPTER CHECKLIST

❏ I read essays about career paths and work-related issues to learn about this chapter's theme.

❏ I gathered ideas on a career path, workplace communication, and a job-related problem by freewriting, brainstorming, and consulting with others.

❏ I developed ideas using classification and definition.

❏ I located sources on my topic to help support my ideas.

❏ I wrote an outline before I revised.

❏ I correctly used summaries, paraphrases, and quotations in my draft.

❏ I documented source materials in the body paragraphs and at the end of my essay in a Works Cited list.

❏ I combined short, closely related sentences using subordinating conjunctions.

❏ I corrected errors in pronoun reference and agreement.

❏ I submitted my essay to a newsletter.

REFLECTING ON YOUR WRITING

To help you reflect on the writing you did in this chapter, answer the following questions:

1. What did you learn from writing on your topic?

2. If you used research in your essay, what part of the research process was hardest? What was easiest?

3. Compare and contrast writing this essay with writing previous essays.

4. If you had more time, what further revisions would you make to improve your essay? Why would you make these revisions?

After answering these questions, freewrite about what you learned in this chapter.

Visit **LaunchPad Solo for Readers and Writers > Writing Process** for more tutorials, videos, and practice developing your essay with each step.

"This is an effective and diverse display that is emotionally moving and often disturbing."

PAUL LAPRADE, *THE DISAPPEARED*

Antonio Frasconi, *The Disappeared*, woodcut prints, 1988 as installed at Stanlee and Gerald Rubin Center for the Visual Arts, The University of Texas at El Paso, 2009, in the exhibition *The Disappeared*, curated by Laurel Reuter and organized by North Dakota Museum of Art.

8

Evaluating
Products, Performances, and Places

Evaluation is something you do every day, often without even thinking about it. In the morning, you may decide that a new brand of breakfast cereal tastes better than your old brand. During the school day, you may realize that this semester's chemistry instructor explains experiments more carefully than a previous instructor did. In the evening, you may channel surf to find a television show that is worth watching.

When you *evaluate* something, you judge its value, worthiness, or merit. An evaluation is based on *standards*, or criteria: a breakfast cereal should taste good and be good for you, a chemistry instructor should know his subject and communicate it clearly, and a television show should entertain or inform you. When you evaluate, you apply standards like these to your subject. You taste the cereal and examine the nutritional label on the box. You listen to determine how well your chemistry instructor explains an experiment. You examine television shows for amusing plots or interesting settings.

Everyday evaluations are usually simple, but you can apply standards to make decisions about less routine subjects—such as whether to buy a new computer game, see a movie that looks interesting, or eat at a particular restaurant. When you have limited personal knowledge of a subject, you probably seek out other people's opinions and

In this chapter, you will use evaluation to share your opinion of a product, performance, or place. As you follow the steps of the writing process, you will

- Explore the chapter topic by reading essays about a product, performance, or place.
- Gather ideas by brainstorming, asking questions, and freewriting.
- Develop your ideas using **comparison and contrast**.
- Practice expressing a judgment, giving criteria, providing evidence, and keeping a balanced perspective.
- Combine sentences with relative clauses.
- Learn how to correct comma splices.
- Consider posting your evaluation to a blog for consumers.

experiences to help form a judgment about it. You might ask friends or family members what they think, look for expert reviews in newspapers and magazines, or search the web for comments and reviews.

Just as you seek out people's evaluations when you need to make a choice, other people may be interested in knowing your opinions. In this chapter, you will learn how to write an essay that evaluates a product, performance, or place. You will begin by reading essays by professional writers who make evaluations. You will also follow a student, Paul LaPrade, as he writes about an art exhibit in his essay "The Disappeared." As you work through the readings and activities in this chapter, you will practice developing and supporting your opinions, which will help you write a convincing essay that shares your point of view with others and helps them make up their own minds. ■

[📷] **GETTING STARTED** **Think about Subjects**

The photo on page 224 shows an art exhibit called *The Disappeared* that focuses on the disappearances of hundreds of Latin American people who protested their oppressive governments. Student writer Paul LaPrade chose to write about this exhibit for an Introduction to Art course. How would you describe the art in this photo? How might the technique or presentation of the art fit the topic of the exhibit? Compare your opinions with those of your classmates, then discuss some other products, performances, or places that you would like to evaluate.

Read to Write   Reading Essays That Evaluate a Product, Performance, or Place

Evaluation essays, often called *reviews*, are popular with both readers and writers. Readers like them because they offer practical information; if you're planning a trip, for instance, you can read what other travelers have written about their experiences. Writers also like reviews because they provide an opportunity to influence what other people think and do. Because they're so popular, formal reviews are a regular feature of newspapers, magazines, radio and television broadcasts, apps, blogs, and websites. Although reviewers might not agree with one another and readers might have their own opinions, disagreement is part of the fun—and learning to disagree thoughtfully and reasonably builds your critical thinking and writing skills.

Before you decide on a subject to evaluate, read the following professional reviews of two products (the iPad and a trail bike), a performance (the children's TV show *Sesame Street*), and a place (the Rock and Roll Hall of Fame and Museum). As you read them, try to identify some of the methods, such as comparison and contrast, that these writers use to explain their evaluations and to persuade their readers to agree with them. Notice, too, how the writers explain the criteria, or basis, for their evaluations, provide evidence to support their judgments, and try to show that they have balanced perspectives. Finally, pay attention to how you respond to the writers' arguments. Do they surprise you? Make you angry? Raise more questions? Jot down your reactions as they occur to you.

Evaluation of a Product: An Annotated Reading

NICHOLAS CARR
The PC Officially Died Today

Nicholas Carr writes on the effects of technology in our lives. In one of his best-known essays, "Is Google Making Us Stupid?," he argues that the Internet is making people less able to concentrate on ideas or contemplate spiritual matters. In addition to publishing articles, Carr is the author of four books. His latest, *The Glass Cage: Automation and Us* (2014), explores the benefits and costs of relying on machinery and technology to do the hard work that humans used to do. Carr's previous book, *The Shallows: What the Internet Is Doing to Our Brains* (2010), expands on his idea that the Internet is changing (mostly for the worse) the way people think. The following review of the iPad was originally published in the *New Republic* in January 2010. Steve Jobs, the founder of Apple, passed away on October 5, 2011, but his inspiring legacy lives on.

1   The PC era ended this morning at ten o'clock Pacific time, when Steve Jobs stepped onto a San Francisco stage to unveil the iPad, Apple's version of a tablet computer. Tablets have been kicking around for a decade, but consumers have always shunned them. And for good reason: They've been nerdy-looking smudge-magnets, limited by their cumbersome shape and their lack of a keyboard. Tablets were a solution to a problem no one had.

This opening statement grabs readers' attention.

2   The rapturous reaction to Apple's tablet—the buildup to Jobs's announcement blurred the line between media feeding-frenzy and orgiastic pagan ritual—shows that our attitude to the tablet form has finally changed. Tablets suddenly look attractive. Why? Because the nature of personal computing has changed.

Carr's judgment about the iPad is expressed here: it is a device that is suitable for the way people use computers today.

3   Until recently, we mainly used our computers to run software programs (Microsoft Word, Quicken) installed on our hard drives. Now, we use them mainly to connect to the vast databases of the Internet—to "the cloud," as the geeks say. And as the Internet has absorbed the traditional products of media—songs, TV shows, movies, games, the printed word—we've begun to look to our computers to act as multifunctional media players. The computer business and the media business are now the same business.

With these examples of traditional media, such as songs and TV shows, Carr is providing evidence to support his judgment.

4   The transformation in the nature of computing has turned the old-style PC into a dinosaur. A bulky screen attached to a bulky keyboard no longer fits with the kinds of things we want to do with our computers. The obsolescence of the

By comparing the iPad to a PC, Carr strengthens his point that the iPad is the right answer to how people communicate electronically.

PC has spurred demand for a new kind of device—portable, flexible, always connected—that takes computing into the cloud era.

Suddenly, in other words, the tablet is a solution to a problem everyone has. 5 Or at least it's one possible solution. The computing market is now filled with all sorts of networked devices, each seeking to fill a lucrative niche. There are dozens of netbooks, the diminutive cousins to traditional laptops, from manufacturers like Acer and Asus. There are e-readers like Amazon's Kindle and Barnes & Noble's Nook. There are smartphones like Apple's iPhone and Google's Nexus One. There are gaming consoles like Nintendo's Wii and Microsoft's Xbox. In some ways, personal computing has returned to the ferment of its earliest days, when the market was fragmented among lots of contending companies, operating systems, and technical standards.

With the iPad, Apple is hoping to bridge all the niches. It wants to deliver the 6 killer device for the cloud era, a machine that will define computing's new age in the way that the Windows PC defined the old age. The iPad is, as Jobs said today, "something in the middle," a multipurpose gadget aimed at the sweet spot between the tiny smartphone and the traditional laptop. If it succeeds, we'll all be using iPads to play iTunes, read iBooks, watch iShows, and engage in iChats. It will be an iWorld.

But will it succeed? The iPad is by no means a sure bet. It still, after all, is a 7 tablet—fairly big and fairly heavy. Unlike an iPod or an iPhone, you can't stick an iPad in your pocket or pocketbook. It also looks to be a cumbersome device. The iPad would be ideal for a three-handed person—two hands to hold it and another to manipulate its touchscreen—but most humans, alas, have only a pair of hands. And with a price that starts at $500 and rises to more than $800, the iPad is considerably more expensive than the Kindles and netbooks it will compete with.

But whether it finds mainstream success or not, there's no going back; we've 8 entered a new era of computing, in which media and software have merged in the Internet cloud. It's hardly a surprise that Apple—more than Microsoft, IBM, or even Google—is defining the terms of this new era. Thanks to Steve Jobs, a bohemian geek with the instincts of an impresario, Apple has always been as much about show biz as about data processing. It sees its products as performances and its customers as both audience members and would-be artists.

Apple endured its darkest days during the early 1990s, when the PC had lost 9 its original magic and turned into a drab, utilitarian tool. Buyers flocked to Dell's cheap, beige boxes. Computing back then was all about the programs. Now, computing is all about the programming—the words and sounds and pictures and conversations that pour out of the Internet's cloud and onto our screens. Computing, in other words, has moved back closer to the ideal that Steve Jobs had when he founded Apple. Today, Jobs's ambitions are grander than ever. His overriding goal is to establish his company as the major conduit, and toll collector, between the media cloud and the networked computer.

Jobs doesn't just want to produce glamorous gizmos. He wants to be the 10 impresario of all media.

Margin notes:

Carr states his first criterion: this device must take computing into the cloud era.

Carr lists many examples of networked devices to support his point that too many devices with separate functions are available on the market.

This is Carr's second criterion for his judgment: this device should be able to satisfy the consumers' need for an all-in-one device.

In this paragraph, Carr gives a balanced perspective to his evaluation by discussing the drawbacks to the iPad.

Carr's description of Jobs reinforces his third criterion: the iPad is exciting and attractive.

The use of the word *glamorous* emphasizes once more Carr's point about the iPad being a new, and exciting, device.

READING ACTIVITY 1 Build Your Vocabulary

Determine the meanings of the following words from the context of "The PC Officially Died Today." Then check their meanings by looking up the words in a dictionary: *cumbersome* (1), *rapturous* (2), *multifunctional* (3), *obsolescence* (4), *lucrative* (5), *ferment* (5), *impresario* (8), *utilitarian* (9), *conduit* (9).

GROUP ACTIVITY 1 Discuss the Reading

Discuss the following questions about "The PC Officially Died Today" with your classmates.

1. Why does Carr think that the iPad is superior to the personal computer (PC)?

2. Why does Carr compare the iPad with the PC? Do you agree with his description of the PC?

3. What does Carr mean in paragraph 3 when he writes that "The computer business and the media business are now the same business"?

4. What do you think is Carr's strongest point in support of his evaluation of the iPad? What do you think is his weakest point? Explain your answers.

5. Based on this review, would you suggest that a friend buy an iPad or tablet, or would you recommend another electronic device? Why?

WRITING ACTIVITY 1 Share Your Ideas

In a paragraph or two, evaluate an electronic device that you use, such as a smartphone, a computer, or a video game console. Express your opinion about the quality of the device and explain why you have that opinion. Share what you have written with your classmates.

Evaluation of a Product

AARON GULLEY
Trail Tested: Salsa Bucksaw

Aaron Gulley says that he was destined for a lifetime of travel and writing. He lived in Nigeria as a child, and his writing career has taken him to the United States, West Africa, Switzerland, Laos, and the Moroccan Sahara, among other places. After graduating from the University of Denver in 1996, he worked at a variety of magazines. Currently, he is the deputy editor of *Outside's GO,* a travel and style magazine. The following review of the Salsa Bucksaw trail bike was published in *Outside* in 2014.

When a bike company rep tells me, "This bike will change everything," I 1
generally dismiss the claim faster than I can roll my eyes. If I had a dollar for every
"ground-breaking" cycling development I've been pitched in the last decade, I'd
probably have enough for a set of Zipp Firecrest 404s.

While I love fatties, which have transformed my winter riding experience, 2
when I heard about the Bucksaw last spring from Salsa brand ambassador Brian
Hanson I was dubious of both the application and performance. With four inches
of front and rear travel and hydraulic disc brakes and dropper post, the Bucksaw
is intended for use on roads and trails—not snow. And while I had my doubts
about the idea alone, I also imagined that even if the concept was right, the sheer
heft of a four-inch fatty would make it as sprightly as a Honda Goldwing.

I was wrong. In six weeks of testing, I had more fun aboard the Bucksaw 3
than I've had on any single bicycle in years.

There was virtually nothing we couldn't ride on this bike, especially uphill. 4
That might sound counterintuitive given just how meaty the Bucksaw is, but the
combination of four inches of suspension and 3.8-inch tires makes for traction
that rivals a rally car.

On my first ride out, I took it up the stoutest climb we have in Santa Fe, a 5
45-minute ascent called Atalaya that packs lots of sustained loose steeps as well
as a handful or two of techy steps, roots, and tricky moves. I've never cleaned the
entire ascent, and I'm 50-50 on a few of the obstacles, which I've worked repeatedly. Aboard the Bucksaw, I rode over those few tough spots with such ease that
I almost wondered if I had missed them. I cleared every single bit of the climb but
one, an extremely tight corner that I think would only go with trials skills. I was
flabbergasted how casual the Bucksaw made everything.

The ease comes partly from traction, with tires run at 10 psi and the suspen- 6
sion working to keep the bike in contact with the ground over any surface. The
extra width in the tires also allows for extremely slow-speed riding because the
bike can nearly balance on its own.

Surprisingly, it took more effort to adjust to the bike's descending manners. 7
Unlike on a standard XC bike, where you can fudge five or 10 psi in the shock or
tires and still be fine, finding the right pressures on the Bucksaw was critical. Too
much air in either tires or shock, and the bike felt jouncy, almost like riding on
one of those children's air castles. Too little, and it felt wallowing and sluggish.

Once we nailed the pressure, however, the Bucksaw delivered a ride that 8
reminded us of skiing powder. You could literally float from obstacle to obstacle,
kicking the rear end off berms, launching off kickers, and never worrying about
a bad landing as the huge surface area of the tires delivered a 747-like touch-
down. Technical terrain was a cinch, too, as the tires plowed through chunder,
smoothed out rock gardens like they were little more than gravel, and afforded
confidence on steep rolls and drops thanks to the extra grip. And though the
dropper post initially seemed like overkill, in the end it made the riding that much
more fun.

The Bucksaw isn't perfect, of course. The new Bluto fork from Rockshox, 9
while very good, is a bit underpowered for such hefty wheels. We'd rather see at
least a 34mm stanchion, as well as the internals of the company's beefier Pike

model. And it's definitely a lot of bike to push around. Our size medium, top spec Bucksaw 1 weighed in at smack on 32 pounds, though halfway through testing I dropped a little over a pound by switching wheels to the new Whisky/45 North carbon tubeless setup. Still, in places with steep ups and downs, like Santa Fe, you have to be fit to manhandle this machine, even with the smartly spec'd 28-tooth ring on the 1x11 drivetrain setup.

Still, as a premier iteration of the first-ever full-suspension fat bike, the Buck-   10
saw is impressive. It is the mountain bike equivalent of fat, shaped skis because it similarly transforms the way you ride. The confidence and leniency delivered by the extra tire girth very literally made us feel—and ride—like better mountain bikers.

The Bucksaw is not for everyone. It's probably a niche machine that only   11
devotees will ride, at least for now. But it proves that big tires aren't the ponderous impediment that everyone has long made them out to be, and certainly future iterations of the bike will be lighter and quicker, especially now that Salsa has delved into carbon.

More importantly, we feel that once people experience the benefits of fat   12
tires, with their added traction and suspension qualities, most won't go back. The trend is already toward bigger diameters and meatier contact patches, even on the road. The Bucksaw is ahead of its time in that way, but we're optimistic that it will help usher in an era of bigger, lighter rubber. We're not talking fat tires all around—just a move toward more big tires, 2.4-inches and up, for nearly every discipline of riding. Manufacturers take note: Bikes ride better with chunkier tires, so it's time for development of some lighter, fatter, more durable treads.

In the meantime, I'll be giggling my way down techy trails on the Bucksaw,   13
looking—and riding—like a better mountain biker than my skills should really allow.

READING ACTIVITY 2 Build Your Vocabulary

Determine the meanings of the following words from the context of "Trail Tested: Salsa Bucksaw." Then check the meanings by looking up the words in a dictionary: *heft* (2), *ascent* (5), *flabbergasted* (5), *traction* (6), *sluggish* (7), *iteration* (10), *girth* (10), *niche* (11).

GROUP ACTIVITY 2 Discuss the Reading

Discuss the following questions about "Trail Tested: Salsa Bucksaw" with your classmates.

1. What is Gulley's opinion about the Bucksaw trail bike? What are his criteria (or standards) for evaluating the bike?

2. Why does Gulley compare the Bucksaw to other trail bikes? How do these comparisons help support his evaluation?

3. At times in the review Gulley uses technical terms such as psi (pounds per square inch) and refers to other trail bikes. Considering that this review was

published in *Outside*, do you think that these terms and references fit the audience?

4. Throughout the review Gulley uses description and examples when he writes about riding the Bucksaw. Why does he do this?

5. Based on this review, would you be interested in trying out the Bucksaw bike? Why or why not?

◀ **WRITING ACTIVITY 2** **Share Your Ideas** ▶

In a paragraph or two, evaluate a product that you use in your daily life, such as a backpack or food product, or in a special context, such as a pair of cleats or a travel app. Express your opinion about the quality of the product and explain why you have that opinion. Share what you have written with your classmates.

Evaluation of a Performance

DIANE HEIMAN AND PHYLLIS BOOKSPAN
Sesame Street: Brought to You by the Letters M-A-L-E

Diane Heiman, a former attorney and public policy consultant, is a senior editor at *Moment Magazine* and a children's book co-author, and Phyllis Bookspan, former law professor at Widener University School of Law in Wilmington, Delaware, is a family lawyer with her own practice. Both Heiman and Bookspan are mothers, and when they wrote this article for the *Seattle Times* in 1994, their children were very young. In this evaluation of *Sesame Street*, Heiman and Bookspan explain how the popular children's television show could be more girl-friendly.

1   A recent report released by the American Association of University Women, "How Schools Shortchange Women," finds that teachers, textbooks, and tests are, whether intentionally or unintentionally, giving preferential treatment to elementary-school boys. As a result, girls who enter school with equal or better academic potential than their male counterparts lose confidence and do not perform as well.

2   An earlier study about law students, published in the *Journal of Legal Education*, found a similar disparity. "Gender Bias in the Classroom" found that male law students are called upon in class more frequently than females, speak for longer periods of time, and are given more positive feedback by law professors.

3   The article raised some disturbing questions about whether women and men receive truly equal education in American law schools.

4   Unfortunately, this insidious gender bias appears long before our children enter school and pervades even the television show *Sesame Street*. Yes, *Sesame*

Street is sexist! But, just as in the story of the emperor and his new clothes, many of us do not notice the obvious.

The puppet stars of the show, Bert and Ernie, and all the other major *Sesame Street* animal characters—Big Bird, Cookie Monster, Grover, Oscar the Grouch, Kermit the Frog, and Mr. Snuffleupagus—are male. Among the secondary characters, including Elmo, Herry Monster, Count VonCount, Telemonster, Prairie Dawn, and Betty Lou, only a very few are girls.   5

The female Muppets always play children, while the males play adult parts in various scenes. In a recently aired skit "Squeal of Fortune," this disparity is evident when the host of the show introduces the two contestants. Of Count VonCount of Transylvania the host asks, "What do you do for a living?" to which the count responds authoritatively, "I count!" Of Prairie Dawn, he inquires, "And how do you spend your day?" Sure, it would be silly to ask a schoolgirl what she does for a living. But none of the female Muppets on *Sesame Street* are even old enough to earn a living.   6

Further, almost all the baby puppet characters on *Sesame Street* are girls. For example, Snuffie's sibling is Baby Alice; in books, Grover's baby cousin is a girl, and when Herry Monster's mother brings home the new baby—it's a girl. Since babies are totally dependent and fairly passive, the older (male) relatives take care of them and provide leadership.   7

Also, the female Muppets almost never interact with each other. In sharp contrast, consequential and caring friendships have been fully developed between male Muppets: Ernie and Bert; Big Bird and Snuffie; even Oscar the Grouch and his (male) worm, Squirmy.   8

Any parent of toddlers or preschoolers can testify that the "girls" on *Sesame Street* are not very popular. Children ask their parents for Bert and Ernie dolls, not Baby Alice. Is this just because the girls are not marketed via books, tapes, place-mats and toy dolls the same way the boys are? Or is it that the *Sesame Street* writers simply have not developed the girls into the same types of lovable, adorable personalities that belong to the main characters?   9

Interestingly and peculiarly, the minor "girls" look more human than most of the well-loved animal roles. They are not physically cuddly, colorful or bizarre, as are the more important male characters. Prairie Dawn has ordinary blonde hair and brown eyes—nothing even remotely similar to Big Bird's soft yellow feathers or Cookie Monster's wild, bright blue, mane.   10

Yes, we believe that *Sesame Street* is one of the best shows on television for small children. Our children—boys and girls—are regular viewers. In addition to its educational value, lack of violence and emphasis on cooperation, the adult characters on the show are admirably balanced in terms of avoiding sexual stereotypes.   11

But even the best of the bunch has room for improvement. Just as elementary through professional school educators must learn to be more sensitive to subtle and unintentional gender bias, so too should the folks at Children's Television Network. We can stop sexism from seeping into our children's first "formal" educational experience.   12

The message was brought to you by the letter F: fairness for females.   13

READING ACTIVITY 3 Build Your Vocabulary

Determine the meanings of the following words from the context of Diane Heiman and Phyllis Bookspan's essay. Then check their meanings by looking up the words in a dictionary: *disparity* (2), *insidious* (4), *authoritatively* (6), *inquires* (6), *consequential* (8), *peculiarly* (10).

GROUP ACTIVITY 3 Discuss the Reading

Discuss the following questions about "*Sesame Street:* Brought to You by the Letters M-A-L-E" with your classmates.

1. What is the authors' opinion of *Sesame Street*? Do they express this opinion in a single sentence? If so, indicate what sentence this is.

2. Why do the authors begin their essay describing reports about preferential treatment given to male students?

3. What elements of a children's television program are important to Heiman and Bookspan? How well does *Sesame Street* meet their expectations of a good children's show?

4. Throughout the essay, the authors compare and contrast male and female characters on *Sesame Street*. How does this help them support their opinion of the show?

5. How do Heiman and Bookspan support their argument that *Sesame Street* is sexist? Is their evidence convincing? Why or why not?

WRITING ACTIVITY 3 Share Your Ideas

People may be stereotyped based on their ethnicity, body type, occupation, and so on. For instance, a common stereotype is the "dumb jock." Write a paragraph or two in which you evaluate a certain television show or movie according to how well or how poorly it avoids stereotyping people. Share your responses with your classmates.

Evaluation of a Place

NICHOLAS JENNINGS
A Palace of Rock

Nicholas Jennings lives and works in Toronto, Canada, where he writes about music and pop culture. His books include *Before the Gold Rush: Flashbacks to the Dawn of the Canadian Sound* (1998) and *Fifty Years of Music: The Story of EMI Music Canada* (2000). He has also written and produced several TV documentaries about contemporary music. In "A Palace of Rock," written soon after the Rock and Roll Hall of Fame and Museum opened in 1995 in Cleveland, Ohio, Jennings evaluates the museum's exhibits about rock and roll from its birth in the 1950s to the present.

As museum pieces, they are the most humble of artifacts: a few report cards, a black leather jacket, a pair of government-issue eye glasses. Yet for many, the three objects are priceless. Once the property of John Lennon, those treasures are now on display at the recently opened Rock and Roll Hall of Fame and Museum in Cleveland, Ohio, where they are already among its most popular exhibits. Looking at the articles, it is easy to see why: each of them brings the viewer closer to the real Lennon. His elementary school report card reveals that one of his teachers found rock's future genius "hopeless," while the well-worn, sloppy jacket somehow perfectly captures the musician's irreverent charm. And Lennon's wire-rimmed spectacles trigger a flood of emotions because they are so evocative of the artist, who was fatally shot by a crazed fan in December, 1980. "Rock music has a power that makes you want to be a part of it," says museum director Dennis Barrie. "Hopefully, we represent some of that." 1

Judging by the scores of fans who flooded into the facility during its Labor Day weekend opening—an estimated 8,000 on the first day—Barrie need not worry: despite a once-shaky history, the Rock and Roll Hall of Fame and Museum is now a resounding success. Visitors can feast on more than 3,500 items, ranging from posters, album jackets and handwritten lyric sheets to movies and interactive exhibits that play requested songs and videos. Among the most memorable displays: a replica of the old Sun Studios in Memphis, Tenn., where Elvis Presley made his first records; a piece of Otis Redding's private airplane, which crashed in 1967; and the 1945 Magnavox tape recorder that pioneering musicologist Alan Lomax used to record blues legends such as Lead Belly and Muddy Waters. And Hall of Fame inductees Neil Young and The Band are reminders that rock has also thrived in Canada. 2

Meanwhile, hundreds of photographs, instruments and costumes—including Michael Jackson's famed sequinned glove and Madonna's gold bustier—are also housed in the museum's impressive, seven-level structure, a $123-million geometric shrine designed by New York City–based architect I. M. Pei, whose other accomplishments include the additions to the National Gallery of Art in Washington and the Louvre in Paris. From the air, the lakefront building resembles a record player with turntable, tonearm and a stack of 45s. But from the ground level, the elaborate structure is a cheeky mix of pyramid-like facades, rectangular towers and trapezoidal extensions that boldly jut out over Lake Erie. 3

The contents of the museum, like the all-star concert that launched it on Sept. 2—the roster of performers included Chuck Berry, James Brown, The Kinks, Creedence Clearwater Revival, Robbie Robertson and Bruce Springsteen—reflect rock in all of its ragged glory. For some, the very idea of chronicling the history of rock 'n' roll in a serious, curated institution is offensive. They argue that, like caging a wild beast, it runs counter to the laws of nature, as though rock music should always be allowed to roam free of commerce and academia. "Absolute nonsense," scoffs Rob Bowman, a professor of rock at Toronto's York University. "Rock has been institutionalized for at least the last 40 years, by record 4 companies, radio stations and other media. Anyone who doesn't understand that is a hopeless romantic." Still, it is difficult to ignore some of the contradictions raised by the museum. Thirty years ago, The Who's Pete Townshend was smashing his guitar in a display of anarchic frenzy, yet the museum has one of his instruments respectfully encased in a glass cabinet. The irony is not lost on Ron House of the Columbus, Ohio–based band Thomas Jefferson Slave Apartments. The musician has written a punk protest song called "RnR Hall of Fame" that angrily tackles the subject. "I don't want to see Eric Clapton's stuffed baby / I don't want to see the shotgun of Kurt Cobain," sings House. "I don't want to see the liver of David Crosby / Blow it up before Johnny Rotten gets in."

Although Rotten's Sex Pistols have yet to be inducted by the Hall of Fame 5 Foundation (artists become eligible 25 years after their first recording), the British punk band is part of the museum's "Blank Generation" exhibit, which examines punk's birth in London and New York City between 1975 and 1980. Included is an 11-inch Sid Vicious doll, complete with chains, ripped T-shirt and swastika, that was used as a prop in the 1980 documentary *The Great Rock 'n' Roll Swindle*, made a year after his death from a heroin overdose.

In fact, the museum strives mightily to keep up to date with rock's more 6 recent developments, charting the rise of rap music and Seattle's grunge scene. According to chief curator James Henke, a former editor at *Rolling Stone*, the museum's collection will be in constant flux. That is partly due to the fact that most display items are on loan, partly due to the nature of its subject matter. Says Henke: "Like the music, it'll always be evolving."

However, the collection is shamelessly skewed to the past. Above the 7 entrance to the main exhibition area is a neon sign quoting Chuck Berry: "Roll Over Beethoven." Berry and other such pioneers as Little Richard and Presley are well represented in a noisy, arcade-like space that includes small cinemas, record booths and computer screens. Amateur musicologists can trace the 500 songs that the museum has deemed to have shaped the history of rock 'n' roll. Among the oldest entries: Woody Guthrie's 1956 folk anthem "This Land Is Your Land" and Louis Jordan's jump-blues classic "Caldonia," written in 1945. But the most revealing exhibit is The Beat Goes On, which traces musical family trees. Touch-screen computers allow museum-goers to click on images of musicians and discover their influences through video clips and songs. In some cases, the technology bridges generations. Lucy Schlopy, an 82-year-old visitor from Bradford, Pa., found that her favorite artist, Roy Orbison, had in turn influenced one of her great-niece's musical heroes, Bruce Springsteen. "I'm learning all kinds of things," said Schlopy.

Responses like that, says director Barrie, who previously worked at the 8 Smithsonian Institution in Washington and Cincinnati's Contemporary Arts Center, prove that the museum is a success. "People are actually reading, taking in the content of the exhibits," he beamed. "They're not just looking at the glittery costumes, which is very gratifying." At the same time, the costumed mannequins throughout the museum are proving to be among the biggest draws. Especially popular are Presley's leather stage outfit from his 1968 comeback TV special, Lennon's lime-green Sgt. Pepper's uniform and the "butterfly dresses" of Motown's

The Supremes. For the kids, rock's schlock meister Alice Cooper, standing next to a guillotine and a bloody, severed head, is an awesome, cartoonish highlight.

By contrast, the actual Hall of Fame, housed on the top floor, is a model of 9 decorum. To get there, visitors climb a long, spiral staircase to reach a darkened room honoring the inductees (123 so far). Images of such legends as Buddy Holly and Bob Marley dissolve on tiny video screens like ghosts, while their signatures, etched on backlit glass plaques, seem to float in the ether. After the musical cacophony and video chaos downstairs, the Hall of Fame is a welcome sanctuary.

For the Hall of Fame's creators, the museum was a pipe dream that almost 10 never materialized. Founders Jann Wenner, editor of *Rolling Stone*, and Ahmet Ertegun, president of Atlantic Records, steered the project through three directors and one site change before the groundbreaking two years ago. Cleveland was chosen over Memphis and New York after residents collected 600,000 signatures and local businesses raised $87 million. But the city had already earned a place in rock history: Alan Freed, its famous deejay, popularized the term rock 'n' roll in the 1950s.

At the museum's ribbon-cutting ceremony, Jimi Hendrix's version of "The 11 Star Spangled Banner" played over the loudspeakers. The guitarist's rendition, conceived as an anti-Vietnam statement at Woodstock in 1969, is full of feedback and guitar distortions designed to simulate war sounds. But suddenly, Hendrix's tortured notes were punctuated by the real-life sounds of two Marine Corps Harrier jets flying overhead. The irony was not lost on some in the crowd, including Wenner, who later addressed the issue of how rock has now joined the establishment. The hall, said Wenner, standing next to Lennon's widow Yoko Ono, was built to remind people of the "power of innocence, rebellion and youth," but also the value of "maturity and growth and perspective." Rock 'n' roll, once scruffy and rebellious, is all grown up. Although it will strike some as contradictory, a hall of fame and museum is simply a natural step in its evolution.

READING ACTIVITY 4 Build Your Vocabulary

Determine the meanings of the following words from the context of Nicholas Jennings's essay. Then check their meanings by looking up the words in a dictionary: *artifacts* (1), *irreverent* (1), *replica* (2), *roster* (4), *contradictions* (4), *anarchic* (4), *inducted* (5), *skewed* (7), *sanctuary* (9), *scruffy* (11).

GROUP ACTIVITY 4 Discuss the Reading

Discuss the following questions about "A Palace of Rock" with your classmates.

1. What is the author's evaluation of the Rock and Roll Hall of Fame and Museum? Where in the essay is this evaluation expressed?

2. What are the reasons that Jennings gives to support his evaluation?

3. Why does Jennings describe in some detail the exhibits in the museum?

4. Explain in your own words what Jennings means when he writes in paragraph 4 that "it is difficult to ignore some of the contradictions raised by the museum." What are these contradictions? Give an example.

5. Rock and roll artists can be inducted into the museum twenty-five years after their first recording. In your opinion, what current rock and roll groups or performers will be inducted into the Hall of Fame when they become eligible?

WRITING ACTIVITY 4 Share Your Ideas

Write a paragraph or two in which you evaluate a museum, gallery, monument, or similar place. Decide on suitable criteria, such as the quality of the exhibits, the accessibility of the site, and the attractiveness of the structure or layout. Exchange your writing with several classmates and discuss the evaluations that each of you wrote.

Writing Your Essay A Step-by-Step Guide

Now that you've read some essays evaluating a product, performance, or place, it's time to write your own essay. First, read the following writing assignment. Then, use the step-by-step advice that follows to discover ideas, develop them as you draft, and polish your writing into a finished essay that readers will find both interesting and persuasive.

Writing Assignment

You make judgments and share your opinions all the time. For example, you may have complained to a friend that your expensive new athletic shoes don't provide enough arch support, argued with a coworker about the results of *Top Chef*, or tried to persuade your family that Disney World would be a good vacation spot. Your task in this chapter is to share your opinion with a wider audience by writing an essay that evaluates something you feel strongly about. You (or your instructor) may decide to approach this assignment in one of several ways:

- Evaluate a product you are familiar with.

- Evaluate a performance you have seen.

- Evaluate a place you have been to.

☾ Step 1 **Explore Your Choices**

You can write an evaluation essay about almost anything that you have an opinion about, from topics as narrow as the latest smartphone or whole-grain snack to those as broad as the full run of a television series or the bus system in your city. So how should you begin? The first two things to consider are who might read your essay and why you're writing it for them. Even more so than other kinds of writing, reviews are written to inform and persuade people who are curious about a particular subject. As you gather ideas for possible topics, choose something that you have personal experience with, that you have a strong opinion about, and that others are interested in.

Analyzing Your Audience and Purpose

Your audience will include people who have sought opinions about the product, performance, or place you'll be writing about because they are directly affected by it. Your readers might include consumers deciding whether they should purchase a product or employees of the company that makes the product. They might include people who are considering a play, movie, or television show as well as those who have already seen it. Or they might include people interested in visiting a restaurant, shopping mall, museum, or tourist attraction and possibly some of the managers or tour guides who are responsible for that site. Whatever your topic, your readers probably know something about it, but they are seeking other people's opinions to help themselves form a judgment or make improvements.

For more on audience and purpose, see pp. 6–8.

Knowing who your audience is will help you identify your purpose. What do you want your readers to do as a result of reading your essay? Do you want to encourage or discourage them from purchasing, watching, or visiting something? If your readers are in some way responsible for your subject, do you want to persuade them to change something about it?

▨ WRITING ACTIVITY 5 Analyze Your Audience and Purpose ▨

Your responses to the following questions will help you select possible topics for your evaluation. Be sure to come back to these questions after you have chosen a topic to write about.

1. Does this assignment call for primarily expressive, informative, or persuasive writing?

2. Are you writing for an audience of consumers or for the people who make or manage something?

3. Have you recently purchased any consumer products that your audience might be interested in reading about?

4. What movies, television shows, music groups, or books might your readers be curious about?

5. What places—restaurants, shopping malls, museums, amusement parks—have you visited recently? Why would readers be interested in them?

6. How interested will your readers be in an essay that evaluates a product, performance, or place? How can you make sure you keep your readers' interest as they read your essay?

Gathering Ideas

For more on gathering ideas, see pp. 11–14.

Before you settle on a product, performance, or place to evaluate, explore your choices by gathering ideas for at least one subject in each of these three categories. Even if you already have a specific subject in mind for your essay, you may be surprised by where your explorations lead you.

To gather ideas for your evaluation, you may use any of the techniques you learned in Chapter 1 and applied in previous assignments. The student writers in this chapter will use brainstorming, asking questions, and freewriting.

Brainstorming about a Product

As a consumer, you evaluate products before purchasing them. If the product is inexpensive, such as a can of soup, your preliminary evaluation might be as simple as reading the label. If the product is a major purchase, such as an electronic device or a car, you might consult friends, check the reviews on an app or website, read a magazine such as *Consumer Reports*, and comparison shop. Even after you purchase the product, you probably continue to evaluate it to confirm that you made a good choice.

To identify a product worth evaluating in your essay, try brainstorming a list of items you use every day or have recently purchased. Include the products you wrote about after reading "The PC Officially Died Today" and "Trail Tested: Salsa Bucksaw." Don't worry yet about whether any of these items would make a good essay topic. Just write down as many products as you can think of.

Student writer Ellie, for example, brainstormed the following list of products by looking around her apartment:

ramen noodles	foam pillow
Sephora hand-smoothing system	iPhone
coffeemaker	running shoes
school newspaper	fake butter spray
scanner/printer	Red Bull
new laptop	digital e-reader
dead laptop	tennis racquet

Once you have a list of products in hand, check off the items you have strong feelings about. Think of your audience as people who are interested in purchasing the product. Your evaluation will affect their decision to purchase (or not to purchase) the item. Select one product and brainstorm a list of what you like and don't like about it. If you wish, you can select one of the products you wrote about after reading "The PC Officially Died Today" or "Trail Tested: Salsa Bucksaw." Student writer Ellie, for example, reviewed her list and realized that she had been telling friends how much she loved her new coffeemaker, which she received as a gift. Here is her brainstorming on the Cuisinart Automatic Grind and Brew:

> I love this thing!
> wanted it for ages
> expensive: $99
> couldn't bring myself to spend the money on it
> has the coffee grinder built right in
> and a timer
> fresh ground coffee tastes so much better
> grinder makes a lot of noise
> scares the cat every time
> wakes me up better than my alarm clock
> automatic shut-off
> can't figure out how to measure the beans for less than a full pot
> a lot of parts
> have to dismantle the pieces and wash them by hand every day
> sometimes the parts jam from the wet coffee grounds
> if you don't close the basket right, coffee pours all over the counter
> more maintenance than my old coffeemaker
> it's worth it
> a luxury, but I don't think I could do without it now

WRITING ACTIVITY 6 Brainstorm about a Product

Brainstorm a list of products that you use every day or have recently obtained. Select one item from your list and brainstorm again, this time writing down what you like and don't like about the product. You may brainstorm about as many products as you like, but focus on one at a time.

Asking Questions about a Performance

As you probably know, newspapers, magazines, websites, and apps carry reviews of all sorts of performances, including movies, concerts, art shows, dance performances, television programs, and sporting events. Readers often rely on these reviews to help them decide whether a performance is worth seeing or not. Before investing your hard-earned money in a movie ticket, for example, you may decide to read a few reviews at rottentomatoes.com or the Internet Movie Database (imdb.com). If the reviews are positive, you're more likely to see the film.

Because many professional critics are trained as reporters, they often use the journalist's questions as a starting point to gather ideas for their reviews:

- *Who* is (or was) involved in this performance? Include relevant producers, directors, and talent (such as actors, singers, dancers, and announcers).

- *What* is the show about?

- *Where* is (or was) the performance held or broadcast?

- *When* is (or was) the show performed or broadcast?

- *How* effective is (or was) the show?

- *Why* is (or was) this performance worth seeing or not worth seeing?

By using these questions as prompts, critics can be sure that their essays cover the basics that readers expect to find in a review. The questions also help writers gather details to explain what they liked or didn't like about a performance.

Here's how one student, Rob, used the journalist's questions to gather ideas about the cable television program *Mythbusters*. Here's a sample:

Who is involved?	Peter Rees, producer (Australian documentary filmmaker)
	Adam Savage, cohost (artist and model builder)
	Jamie Hyneman, cohost (Hollywood special-effects expert with a degree in Russian literature)
	Buster, subject of experiments (crash test dummy)
What is it about?	Cast members conduct science experiments to see if urban legends are true.
Where is it?	Discovery Channel
When is it?	Wednesdays at 9:00 p.m.
How effective is it?	I like that they use real science to bust the myths. The tests are really involved and over the top. Lots of surprises: sometimes the urban legends are actually true! The experiments are creative and always very thorough, but sometimes they get carried away with themselves and forget the point. They'll redo an experiment if viewers write in and question their methods.
Why is it worth seeing?	Generally very informative, always entertaining. They manage to make science cool.

WRITING ACTIVITY 7 Ask Questions about a Performance

Select a performance that you might want to evaluate. The performance may be live (such as a concert, comedy show, sporting event, dance performance, or play) or recorded (such as a movie or television show). You may choose a past performance that you remember well or select a current performance and attend it in person. You could select the show or movie that you wrote about after reading "*Sesame Street: Brought to You by the Letters M-A-L-E*" if this topic still interests you. Answer each of the reporter's questions—*who, what, where, when, how, why*—about the performance to gather ideas for an evaluation essay.

Freewriting about a Place

A new shopping mall opens near your town, and you spend an afternoon visiting the stores, examining the layout, and sampling products from the food court. Afterward, you decide that you like the mall but wish it had a parking garage: You have just evaluated a place.

Other places you might evaluate include a museum, park, college or office building, classroom, theater, store, library, restaurant, or city. Almost any place you've been to and that other people might want to visit can be a good candidate for an evaluation essay.

Although a quick judgment of a place can be useful, a formal evaluation needs plenty of details to be convincing and useful for readers. To gather information to support a full essay that evaluates a place, consider freewriting (the practice of writing nonstop about a topic without trying to decide if your ideas are any good). Tell yourself that you will write for a certain amount of time or a certain number of pages, and keep writing. Don't pause to think, don't make corrections, and don't try to organize your thoughts. If you get stuck, write something like "I don't have anything to say" or "stuck! stuck! stuck!" until a new thought comes to you. Just keep writing, and see what you have to say.

Student writer Paul decided to write about an art exhibit he had visited for his Introduction to Art class. Here is part of his freewriting:

> Right at the entrance is a huge collection of portraits. The faces are blurred—I wonder what this means. "The Disappeared." I guess it means people who disappeared in Latin America because they were murdered by their governments. This series includes some interesting interrogation scenes. Huddled detainees. Surprising this happened so recently, and in Latin America. I didn't know what had happened. Hard to understand what some of these photos mean. There's no explanation. These family pictures seem so real. They make you see how awful it was. Why isn't there a fuller explanation of what these governments did somewhere?

WRITING ACTIVITY 8 Freewrite about a Place

Choose a place that is important to you and that others might want to know about, such as a new restaurant close to campus or an entertainment park that recently opened. You can also continue to write about the museum or other place you wrote about after reading "A Palace of Rock." Freewrite about this place for at least ten minutes. Follow your ideas without pausing and do not stop, go back, or try to correct your writing. Just write.

(Step 2 Write Your Discovery Draft

For more on drafting, see pp. 15–19.

At this point, you have explored at least three possible topics for your evaluation essay. It's time to choose a topic and prepare a rough draft.

Don't be concerned if you're not sure how you're going to evaluate a product, performance, or place. The purpose of writing a discovery draft is to discover what you have to say. For now, you'll focus on organizing what you already know and try to put it into words. As you draft, keep in mind that anything you write at this stage can (and should) be revised later.

Choosing a Topic

When you choose a topic for an evaluation essay, it's crucial to remember your audience and your purpose. Gather your notes from brainstorming, asking questions, and freewriting and look again at your responses to the writing activities earlier in this chapter. Review as well the writing you completed after reading the four professional essays that start this chapter. Of the topics you have considered for your essay, which one do you feel most strongly about? Even more important, which one would be most interesting and informative for your readers? After all, you don't want to put a lot of effort into evaluating something that nobody else cares about.

Because you will write a persuasive essay in which you make an evaluation, be sure to select a subject you feel confident about judging. As you contemplate your choices, remember that you may combine closely related topics and gather additional ideas on any topic that interests you. For example, in reviewing your paragraphs about the show or movie you wrote about after the *Sesame Street* review, you might realize that you had a strong positive reaction to the new stadium-style seating at the local multiplex. If you decide to evaluate the theater rather than the movie, you could use brainstorming, asking questions, or freewriting (or any other methods that work for you) to explore your thoughts.

WRITING ACTIVITY 9 Choose Your Topic

Review your responses to Writing Activities 6 to 8 and decide which of the topics you explored (a product, performance, or place) would be most useful to your readers. Be careful to select a topic you can judge. If you're not confident that you can turn any of your working ideas into a well-supported evaluation, use your favorite techniques to gather ideas on additional topic possibilities until you find one that will interest both you and your readers.

Sharing Your Ideas

Before you begin writing your discovery draft, narrow your topic and write a preliminary thesis statement that identifies your subject and expresses your judgment of it. You can always change your thesis later, but starting with a judgment in mind will help you focus and stay on track.

For more on narrowing your topic, see pp. 16–17.

As you write your draft, keep in mind that most readers expect an evaluation essay to address the following questions:

- What experiences have you had with the product, performance, or place you are writing about?
- What is your overall opinion of this product, performance, or place?
- Why do you have this opinion?
- What is good about your subject?
- What is bad about your subject?
- Compare your subject with other similar subjects: How is it better? How is it worse?

 Use online rating systems

To get others' thoughts on your subject, refer to social media and sites with user-generated content, such as Facebook, Yelp, Amazon, or TripAdvisor, where people can post ratings. Several of these sites offer their own criteria. For example, TripAdvisor allows reviewers to rate hotels based on standards such as "sleep quality" and "cleanliness."

Answering each of these questions in order is one way to create your draft, but don't hesitate to follow your train of thought as you write—even if it means revising your thesis statement later on. Keep your audience and purpose in mind and remember that your main goal at the drafting stage is to get your ideas down on paper. You'll have time later to revise and edit your discovery draft.

A Student's Discovery Draft

Here's the discovery draft written by student writer Paul LaPrade, whose freewriting you read earlier. In this draft, Paul evaluates an art exhibit at his university. After reading the draft, discuss with your classmates what Paul might do to revise it. (Note that the example includes the types of errors that typically appear in a first draft.)

Paul's preliminary thesis
statement.

The Rubin Art Gallery's current exhibit *The Disappeared* depicts the tragedy that occurred in Latin America in the last decades of the twentieth century, when military dictators in countries such as Argentina, Chile, and Guatemala kidnapped and killed thousands of people who resisted their dictatorships. The different types of art are prints, photos, video installations, and three-dimensional installations. The methods of expression here range from realistic documentation to symbolism, there are several works that fit into each of these categories. This display offers various artists' interesting interpretations of these tragic events.

The first collection, "In Memoriam," by Antonio Frasconi, consists of forty-eight prints that personalize the tragic situation. These prints show victims of violence, their faces surrounded by dark colors as if they are vanishing in front of our eyes. "The Disappeared," also by Frasconi, consists of woodblock prints. The woodblock prints show people with bags over their heads, huddled as if they were in concentration camps.

Marcelo Brodsky's "Good Memory" is a large display of forty-three photographs and two videos. It includes a grade school portrait that shows his class with personal notes written beside the children. A video installation shows a school reunion in which ninety-eight missing class members are remembered in roll call.

The most moving and effective part of this exhibit is a series of photographs by Marcelo Brodsky. These photographs deal with his personal and family history. Pictures of Marcelo with his younger brother Fernando show happy family scenes. The two boys having fun on a boat or playing with bows and arrows and falling down and playing dead. Then photos of Fernando are shown in which he looks skinny and worn down. A caption says that Fernando was killed in a concentration camp.

On the whole, this exhibit very effectively represents the killings that have occured in South America over decades. Artists express this reality in various styles and mediums, including prints, sculpture, and photography. Its hard to forget what happened to these people.

WRITING ACTIVITY 10 Write Your Discovery Draft

Using your preliminary thesis statement and the questions on page 245 as a guide, write a discovery draft that evaluates a product, performance, or place. For now, focus on getting your ideas in writing; you'll have a chance to clarify and support your ideas when you revise. If you're not sure that the topic you've selected is a good one, remember that you may write separate drafts on two or three other topics to see which one gives you the best results.

◖Step 3 Revise Your Draft

Most writers find that the discovery draft of an evaluation needs additional information to make it interesting and informative. Because reviews attempt to persuade readers, you'll also need to make sure that your ideas are clearly stated and well supported—from your audience's point of view.

For more on revising, see pp. 20–21.

How will you develop your ideas so that you communicate effectively with your readers? Start by applying the skills you acquired in earlier chapters: organize your paragraphs (Chapter 3), strengthen your focus (Chapter 5), outline your ideas (Chapter 7), and write an effective introduction and conclusion (Chapter 6). As you build your essay, you will learn how to use comparison and contrast to help your readers understand your points. You will then focus on expressing your judgment clearly while explaining your criteria, providing convincing evidence, and keeping a balanced perspective.

Developing Your Ideas with Comparison and Contrast

One good way to support an evaluation is to compare and contrast your subject with other subjects. Your audience may not know very much about the product, performance, or place that you are reviewing, but they probably have some knowledge of similar products, performances, or places. By relating what your readers know to what they don't know, you can support your judgment while helping your readers better understand your subject.

For more on comparison and contrast, see p. 80.

When you compare two things, you point out similarities; when you contrast two things, you focus on differences. Comparison and contrast can be combined, as in this example from "A Palace of Rock":

> Once the property of John Lennon, those treasures are now on display at the recently opened Rock and Roll Hall of Fame and Museum in Cleveland, Ohio, where they are already among its most popular exhibits. Looking at the articles, it is easy to see why: each of them brings the viewer closer to the real Lennon. His elementary school report card reveals that one of his teachers found rock's future genius "hopeless," while the well-worn, sloppy jacket somehow perfectly captures the musician's irreverent charm.

In this example, the report card and jacket are similar because they make the viewer feel close to Lennon, yet they are different because they reveal different aspects of his personality.

You can also focus more on just similarities or just differences. Notice how the differences between the female and male characters are described in the review of *Sesame Street*:

Interestingly and peculiarly, the minor "girls" look more human than most of the well-loved animal roles. They are not physically cuddly, colorful or bizarre, as are the more important male characters. Prairie Dawn has ordinary blonde hair and brown eyes—nothing even remotely similar to Big Bird's soft yellow feathers or Cookie Monster's wild, bright blue, mane.

When making comparisons, be sure that you focus on similar subjects and that you explain the basis of your comparison. In his review of the Rock and Roll Hall of Fame and Museum, Nicholas Jennings notes that the architect of the building has designed additions to other museums. If you were evaluating the new campus recreation center, you would not compare it to the college library (unless you are comparing the architecture of the buildings). Instead, you might contrast the new center with the old center to highlight the improvements that have been made. Once you have established the points of your comparison, provide several detailed examples to support each of those points.

HOW TO Use Comparison and Contrast

- Use comparison to explain similarities and use contrast to explain differences.
- Decide on what basis you will compare and contrast. For instance, you can compare and contrast energy drinks on the basis of ingredients, flavor, and effectiveness.
- Support the comparison and contrast with examples.

WRITING ACTIVITY 11 Draft Comparisons for Your Essay

For your topic, list several similar subjects. (If you're evaluating a product, list similar products; if your topic is a performance, list similar performances; if your essay is about a place, list similar places.) Choose one of these subjects and write one or two paragraphs that compare or contrast it with the subject of your essay. Remember that the point of using comparison and contrast is to support your judgment and to help your readers understand your subject better.

Building Your Essay

When you revise an evaluation essay, you need to make sure that you have stated your opinion clearly and have provided enough information to persuade your readers that your opinion is reasonable. To do this, you'll first revise your thesis statement to ensure that it expresses a judgment. Next, make sure that readers understand the reasons for your opinion and double-check that you have included enough evidence to support your points. Finally, reexamine your evaluation from your readers' perspective to ensure that your audience will accept your judgment as fair and carefully considered—even if they don't agree with it.

Express Your Judgment

As you may recall, the thesis statement does three things—announces the topic of your essay; shows, explains, or argues a particular point about the topic; and gives readers a sense of what the essay will be about. For an evaluation essay, the thesis statement argues a particular point. Specifically, it expresses your judgment of the product, performance, or place you are reviewing. Let's look in more detail at how to write an effective thesis statement for an evaluation.

For more on thesis statements, see p. 18.

State an Opinion   A judgment is an opinion about the value or merit of something. It's not a fact. Notice the difference between fact and judgment in these statements:

FACT   The Ford Mustang was among the most popular cars of the 1960s.

JUDGMENT   The Ford Mustang was one of the best cars made in the 1960s.

The first statement is factual because it can be verified by statistics about the best-selling cars in the 1960s. The second statement expresses an evaluation based on the worthiness of the car. Some but not all people will agree with this statement.

Focus on the Subject   A judgment focuses on the subject being evaluated, not on the writer.

FOCUS ON THE WRITER   I really like the new thirty-minute circuit program at the local health club.

FOCUS ON THE SUBJECT   The new thirty-minute circuit program at the local health club is surprisingly effective.

In the first example, the first-person *I* emphasizes the writer. In the second example, the reference to the writer has been removed, shifting readers' focus to the product being evaluated—the new thirty-minute circuit program.

Be Moderate, Not Extreme   A good thesis statement for an evaluation essay gives a sensible opinion about the subject. A sensible opinion is moderate rather than extreme:

EXTREME   Central College's library is the best library in the state.

MODERATE   Central College's library has the most useful collection of business journals in Essex County.

The extreme statement cannot be proven without visiting every library in the state, whereas the moderate version is much easier to support.

Be Clear and Specific   A good thesis statement for an evaluation essay expresses a judgment that is immediately understandable. If your readers can't understand your thesis statement, they won't understand the rest of your evaluation either. To make your thesis statement clear, use standard written English, and tell readers why you have reached your judgment:

UNCLEAR   The new Student Union is gross.

CLEAR   The design of the new Student Union is disappointing because of its plain exterior and cold, gray cinderblock interior.

The nonstandard (in this context) *gross* has been replaced with *disappointing*, which is a more precise word. Details that explain the judgment have also been added to help readers understand the writer's opinion about the topic.

HOW TO Write a Thesis Statement for an Evaluation Essay

- State an opinion about the value or merit of something.
- Focus on the subject, not yourself.
- Use a moderate rather than an extreme tone.
- Be clear and specific.

GROUP ACTIVITY 5 Express Judgments

Review the characteristics of a good thesis statement for an evaluation essay. Then, working with your peer response group, determine the problem in each of the following thesis statements. Revise the thesis statements to eliminate the problems.

1. The worst jeans ever made are manufactured by Salisbury, Inc.
2. Brad Pitt is an OK actor.
3. The Super Bowl is seen by millions of people around the world.
4. The National Air and Space Museum is my favorite museum.
5. The Bradley running shoe is one of the newest shoes on the market.

WRITING ACTIVITY 12 Express Your Judgment

Revise the thesis statement for your essay so that it meets the requirements for an evaluation essay. It needs to state an opinion about the value or merit of your subject, focus on the subject, be moderate and not extreme, and be clear and specific.

Give Criteria

To support your thesis statement in an evaluation essay, you must inform your readers of the *criteria*, or standards, on which you based your judgment.

For example, in "A Palace of Rock," Nicholas Jennings uses the authenticity of the exhibits as one criterion. According to Jennings, one reason the museum is successful is because it contains so many exhibits of real-life objects. Remember, you should include enough criteria to inform your readers, your criteria should suit the topic, and if your criteria are not obvious, you should explain them.

Include Enough Criteria   An effective evaluation is based on having enough criteria. In most cases, a good evaluation essay will discuss three to five criteria. Judging a subject on the basis of only one or two criteria will usually not be enough to persuade your readers to accept your judgment. Imagine, for instance, if Aaron Gulley had evaluated the Bucksaw trail bike only on how well it went uphill. As readers, we would have been left with unanswered questions about other aspects of the bike, such as how well it went downhill and handled difficult terrain.

Use Suitable Criteria   The criteria on which your judgment is based should be suitable for your subject. Nicholas Carr, in "The PC Officially Died Today," does not claim that the iPad is good technology because he likes the colorful covers he can buy for it. Rather, the criteria that Carr uses—ease of use, attractiveness, and suitability for the new computer era—are appropriate because most potential buyers are interested in these features.

Suppose, however, that Carr was writing his review for an audience of elementary school teachers. In this case, the quality of educational apps designed for the iPad would be a suitable criterion. In other words, the criteria that are "suitable" depend on the characteristics or interests of your intended readers.

HOW TO Select and Explain Criteria

- Fill in the blanks: "I think that _____ is good/bad because _____."
- Identify three to five reasons for your opinion.
- Review your reasons to make sure they're suitable for the topic and your audience.
- Will your readers automatically see why your criteria are suitable to your subject? If not, you need to explain the criteria.
- For readers familiar with your subject, include a brief explanation of the criteria (such as, "Jeans need to be comfortable because they're worn frequently").
- For readers unfamiliar with your subject, include a detailed explanation of the criteria (such as, "All the seats in a sports arena should give spectators good visibility. They shouldn't have to sit behind a post that partially obstructs their view").

Explain Your Criteria   If your readers might not understand your criteria, you'll need to explain them. For example, in an evaluation of a smartphone, you would probably need to explain the importance of a replaceable battery, an expandable storage capacity, and a unified in-box. Similarly, in evaluating a fashion show, you would need to explain why music is essential to the show's success.

Not all criteria require explanation. In evaluating the Bucksaw trail bike, Aaron Gulley does not explain why the ability to handle difficult terrain is an important criterion for a trail bike. Only when you think readers may have questions about a particular criterion should you explain it.

GROUP ACTIVITY 6 Determine Criteria

Following is a list of subjects and audiences. Working with your classmates, determine the criteria to use for an evaluation essay for each subject and audience. Make sure that you provide enough criteria to evaluate the subject and that the criteria are appropriate for the audience.

EXAMPLE Subject: sports car

Audience: readers of *Consumer Reports*

Criteria: _____ handling, horsepower, style, price _____

1. Subject: grocery store chain

   Audience: readers of *Real Simple*

   Criteria: _____

2. Subject: apartment

   Audience: readers of the classified ads in your local newspaper

   Criteria: _____

3. Subject: amusement park

   Audience: readers of *Parents* magazine

   Criteria: _____

4. Subject: the new Student Union at your college

   Audience: readers of the alumni magazine

   Criteria: _____

5. Subject: a television situation comedy

   Audience: potential advertisers

   Criteria: _____

WRITING ACTIVITY 13 Revise the Criteria in Your Essay

Examine the criteria in your discovery draft. Keeping your audience in mind, determine if you have enough criteria and whether your criteria are suitable. Then identify any criteria that need to be explained for your readers. Make any necessary changes and add any necessary explanations.

Provide Evidence

An evaluation essay consists largely of evidence that supports a judgment. By presenting *evidence*—including examples, facts, and expert testimony—writers explain how a subject measures up to their criteria.

Examples   Using *examples* to support your judgment makes your essay more interesting to readers as well as more convincing. In "The PC Officially Died Today," Nicholas Carr gives examples of types of networked devices to support his point that the iPad fills an important gap in the computer marketplace:

> There are dozens of netbooks, the diminutive cousins to traditional laptops, from manufacturers like Acer and Asus. There are e-readers like Amazon's Kindle and Barnes & Noble's Nook. There are smartphones like Apple's iPhone and Google's Nexus One. There are gaming consoles like Nintendo's Wii and Microsoft's Xbox. In some ways, personal computing has returned to the ferment of its earliest days, when the market was fragmented among lots of contending companies, operating systems, and technical standards.

⏻ Write on two screens

If you need to gather more evidence to support your judgment, consider creating a new blank document where you can brainstorm ideas. This new screen will give you a fresh space to brainstorm ideas without worrying about how they will fit into your essay draft. After you have your ideas down, you can review them and decide which pieces of evidence will be effective in supporting your judgment.

Facts   *Facts* are a highly persuasive kind of evidence, primarily because they can be verified by readers. And because facts demonstrate your knowledge of the topic, including them makes readers more likely to trust your judgment. In "A Palace of Rock," Nicholas Jennings shows that he is an expert on the topic by demonstrating his knowledge of the history of rock and roll:

> Among the most memorable displays: a replica of the old Sun Studios in Memphis, Tenn., where Elvis Presley made his first records; a piece of Otis Redding's private airplane, which crashed in 1967; and the 1945 Magnavox tape recorder that pioneering musicologist Alan Lomax used to record blues legends such as Lead Belly and Muddy Waters.

Expert Testimony   *Expert testimony*—the opinion of people knowledgeable about a subject—can be used as evidence to confirm the significance of a topic or to support a writer's own judgment. In "The PC Officially Died Today," Nicholas Carr uses expert testimony when he describes Steve Jobs, the creator of Apple computers, unveiling the iPad to an audience of reporters and consumers. Because Jobs was such a significant figure in the development of digital technology, his presence lends importance to the topic of the iPad. Nicholas Jennings, in his review of the Rock and Roll Hall of Fame and Museum, uses expert testimony when he refers to the opinions of established musicians. Diane Heiman and Phyllis Bookspan, in their review of *Sesame Street*, use expert testimony from a respected association for a specific purpose—to show the effects of gender bias on students:

> A recent report released by the American Association of University Women, "How Schools Shortchange Women," finds that teachers, textbooks, and tests are, whether intentionally or unintentionally, giving preferential treatment to elementary-school boys. As a result, girls who enter school with equal or better academic potential than their male counterparts lose confidence and do not perform well.

As you revise your evaluation essay, consider looking for expert testimony that can help back up your judgment of a subject. In evaluating a product, you might refer to *Consumer Reports'* rating of the product. In evaluating a performance or a place, you could check a magazine or newspaper to see whether your subject has been evaluated by others. Awards can be considered a form of expert testimony because they're given by experts in a particular field. If a movie wins an Academy Award for best director, for example, it means that a team of successful movie directors thought highly of the film's director.

Be sure that your evidence is closely connected to your criteria. To help visualize this connection, create a chart with two columns. In the left column, list the criteria that you will use to make your judgment. In the right column, list the evidence that supports each criterion. Before revising your essay, review your chart to make sure you have enough evidence to support your judgment.

HOW TO Generate Evidence

- List examples that support your criteria.
- Identify facts that support your criteria by observing the subject carefully.
- Refer to expert testimony. Look in a library database and on the Internet for articles on the subject you're evaluating.

WRITING ACTIVITY 14 Provide Evidence for Your Judgment

Examine the evidence you used in your discovery draft. Is your judgment supported by sufficient examples, facts, and expert testimony? Where can you include additional evidence to support your criteria and make your points more convincing? Add evidence where needed.

Keep a Balanced Perspective

Readers know that few subjects are all good or all bad. Acknowledging both the negative and the positive aspects of your subject shows readers that your judgment is fair, reasonable, and believable.

You may recall from the evaluation of the iPad that Nicholas Carr describes these drawbacks to the iPad:

> The iPad is by no means a sure bet. It still, after all, is a tablet—fairly big and fairly heavy. Unlike an iPod or an iPhone, you can't stick an iPad in your pocket or pocketbook. It also looks to be a cumbersome device. The iPad would be ideal for a three-handed person—two hands to hold it and another to manipulate its touchscreen—but most humans, alas, have only a pair of hands. And with a price that starts at $500 and rises to more than $800, the iPad is considerably more expensive than the Kindles and netbooks it will compete with.

By sharing this information with readers, Carr maintains a balanced perspective and thereby strengthens the believability of his positive evaluation of the iPad.

You don't have to give equal space in an evaluation essay to the strengths and weaknesses of your subject. If your judgment about the subject is positive, briefly describe the negative aspects, as Carr does in his piece. If your judgment about the subject is negative, briefly describe the positive aspects.

Student writer Paul LaPrade, for example, decided to add a paragraph about what he didn't like about *The Disappeared* exhibit to balance his praise:

> While this exhibit is shocking and moving, it is also confusing because there is so little information given about the political situation in Latin America. This political situation led to these mass murders. Most people haven't kept track of all of the dictators that were in charge of Latin American countries in the 1970s and 1980s. This lack of information distracted me from the exhibits and kept me from totally appreciating them.

WRITING ACTIVITY 15 Chart Aspects of Your Subject

Gather ideas about the positive and negative aspects of your subject in a two-column chart. Label the columns "Positive Aspects" and "Negative Aspects." Then list the positive and negative features of your subject. Number the items in each column in the order that you plan to use them in your essay. As you revise your draft, use this chart to maintain a balanced perspective in your evaluation essay.

A Student's Revised Draft

After charting his criteria and evidence, student writer Paul LaPrade decided that he needed to give more details to help his readers understand why *The Disappeared* was such a moving exhibit. Before you read Paul's revised draft, reread his discovery draft (pp. 245–46). Notice, in particular, how Paul has expressed his judgment more explicitly, explained his criteria, and added evidence and comparison to improve his evaluation. (You will also notice some errors in the revised draft; these will be corrected when Paul edits his essay.)

The Disappeared

1   Most people, when they think of art, picture beautiful paintings of landscapes or portraits of important people. However, art can also be a way for people to record tragic events. Such is the case for the current exhibit at the Rubin Art Gallery, *The Disappeared*. This exhibit depicts the tragedy that occurred in Latin America in the last decades of the twentieth century, when military dictators in countries such as Argentina, Chile, and Guatemala kidnapped and killed thousands of people who resisted their dictatorships. The different types of art are prints, photos, video installations, and three-dimensional installations. The methods of expression here range from realistic documentation to symbolism, there are several works that fit into each of these categories. On the whole, this is an effective and diverse display that is emotionally moving and often disturbing.

2   An exhibit such as *The Disappeared* should contain skillfully made art, educate people about the political situation, and make people feel compassion for what happened. *The Disappeared* does all of these things. The first collection, "In Memoriam," by Antonio Frasconi, consists of forty-eight prints that personalize the tragic situation. These prints show victims of violence, their faces surrounded by dark colors as if they are vanishing in front of our eyes. "The Disappeared," also by Frasconi, consists of woodblock prints. The woodblock prints show people with bags over their heads, huddled as if they were in concentration camps. In one case, a skull seems to glow eerily through it's bag. The images that I found particularly powerful among Frasconi's prints are the dark nighttime shots of buildings. Drab cells are shown in red and grays, with

Paul's introduction contrasts this exhibit with other kinds of art.

The thesis statement gives a judgment about the quality of the exhibit.

Paul adds criteria.

Facts and examples support Paul's point.

the sky a twilight blue. These prints are similar to impressionist artwork with their use of colors and inexact drawings of real-life subjects, however, most impressionist works I have seen deal with more cheerful events or landscapes, not with tragic events, as in this exhibit.

Paul adds more comparison.

Photography plays an important role in this exhibit. Marcelo Brodsky's "Good Memory" is a large display of forty-three photographs and two videos. It includes a grade school portrait that shows his class with personal notes written beside the children. Some are among the disappeared, others reunite in photographic portraits in which they, as adults, blend into the class photo. Perhaps as images of the lost potential of those who were killed. A video installation shows a school reunion in which ninety-eight missing class members are remembered in roll call.

3 An added topic sentence expresses the paragraph's main idea.

Paul adds more facts.

The most moving and effective part of this exhibit is a series of photographs by Marcelo Brodsky. The photographs deal with his personal and family history. Pictures of Marcelo with his younger brother Fernando show happy family scenes, such as the two boys having fun on a boat or playing with bows and arrows and falling down and playing dead. Then photos of Fernando are shown in which he looks skinny and worn down. A caption says that Fernando was killed in a concentration camp. This ties their young innocence to the horrors of mass murder. This is much more effective than just reading about tragic historical events in a textbook.

4

Paul explains the significance of the exhibit better.

While this exhibit is shocking and moving, it is also confusing because there is so little information given about the political situation in Latin America. This political situation led to these mass murders. Most people haven't kept track of all of the dictators that were in charge of Latin American countries in the 1970s and 1980s. This lack of information distracted me from the exhibits and kept me from totally appreciating them.

5 In this paragraph, Paul explains the limitations of the exhibit.

On the whole, this exhibit very effectively represents the killings that have occured in South America over decades. Artists express this reality in various styles and mediums, including prints, sculpture, and photography. This exhibit makes viewers understand the effects that oppressive governments can have on individuals and their families. Its hard to forget what happened to these people.

6

The last sentence emphasizes the emotional impact the exhibit had on the writer.

GROUP ACTIVITY 7 Analyze Paul's Revised Draft

Use the following questions to discuss with your classmates how Paul has improved his discovery draft.

1. How has Paul improved his introduction?

2. Why is his thesis more effective now?

3. What criteria does Paul use to evaluate *The Disappeared*? Does he use enough suitable criteria? Are they obvious, or do they need explanation?

4. How well does Paul support his judgment with examples, facts, and expert testimony?

5. Does the comparison of the style of the "In Memoriam" prints with impressionism further support Paul's judgment? Why or why not?

6. How well does Paul maintain a balanced perspective? Explain.

7. How could Paul's revised draft benefit from further revision?

Peer Review for an Essay That Evaluates

Form a group with two or three other students and exchange copies of your revised drafts. Read your draft aloud while your classmates follow along. Then take notes on your classmates' responses to the following questions about your draft.

1. What did you like best about this essay?

2. How interesting is my introduction? Do you want to continue reading the essay? Why or why not?

3. What is my thesis statement? Is it effective? Does it express a judgment about the value or merit of my subject? Is it focused on the subject? Is it moderate rather than extreme? Is it clear and specific?

4. What are my criteria? Are there enough of them, and are they suitable? Are they obvious, or do I need to explain them?

5. How well do I support my judgment with examples, facts, and expert testimony?

6. Do I maintain a balanced perspective? Why or why not?

7. Do I make effective comparisons? Explain.

8. How effective is my ending? Do I conclude in such a way that you know it's the end?

WRITING ACTIVITY 16 Revise Your Draft

Building on the work you completed for Writing Activities 9 to 15, refer to your class-mates' peer review suggestions as you finish revising your discovery draft. Focus on improving your thesis statement, criteria, and evidence. Add comparisons where they might be helpful, and ensure that your essay maintains a balanced perspective. You may also decide to omit unnecessary material or to rearrange parts of your essay more effectively.

> (⏻) **Comment on your draft**
>
> Use the Comment function of your word-processing program to insert your own ideas for revising your draft. This function highlights the suggestions for revision (or comments) in your text, similar to your instructor's or classmates' handwritten comments.

◖Step 4 Edit Your Sentences

At this point, you have worked hard to write a convincing evaluation of a product, performance, or place. But before you can share your essay with your audience, you must edit it for readability and correctness. Remember, an important part of the writing process is to revise your words and sentences to be clearer, more interesting, and free of distracting errors.

As always, consult a dictionary and the Handbook in Part Four of this book to check that your words are the right ones and that your sentences are structured correctly. As you edit your evaluation, you will practice combining sentences with relative clauses. You will also learn how to correct comma splices.

Combining Sentences Using Relative Clauses

Although short sentences can be powerful, using too many of them in a row can force you to repeat yourself. To eliminate unnecessary repetition and help your readers know which of your ideas are most important, consider using *relative clauses* to combine sentences.

You can turn a short sentence into a relative clause by beginning it with a relative pronoun (*who, whose, which*, or *that*). A relative clause contains a subject and a verb but cannot stand alone as a sentence.

Here's how student writer Paul LaPrade combined two pairs of sentences in his revised draft by using relative clauses:

ORIGINAL "The Disappeared," also by Frasconi, consists of woodblock prints. The woodblock prints show people with bags over their heads, huddled as if they were in concentration camps.

REVISED "The Disappeared," also by Frasconi, consists of woodblock prints that show people with bags over their heads, huddled as if they were in concentration camps.

ORIGINAL The most moving and effective part of this exhibit is a series of photographs by Marcelo Brodsky. The photographs deal with his personal and family history.

REVISED The most moving and effective part of this exhibit is a series of photographs by Marcelo Brodsky that deals with his personal and family history.

For more on combining sentences, see Chapter 15.

Notice that a relative clause can appear either in the middle or at the end of a combined sentence and that the revised sentence may or may not include commas. How do you know when to use commas?

- Use commas when the relative clause gives information that's *not* essential to understanding the sentence, as in the following example:

    The book, *which is on the table,* is by one of my favorite authors.

    Commas are used in this example because the relative clause—*which is on the table*—is simply adding information. The sentence makes sense without it: *The book is by one of my favorite authors.*

- Don't use commas when a relative clause identifies who or what it is referring to, as in the following example:

    The book *that is on the table* belongs to Wilbur.

    No commas are used before or after the relative clause because it's a necessary part of the sentence: it tells which book—the one on the table—is the one that belongs to Wilbur.

HOW TO Combine Sentences Using Relative Clauses

- Turn the less important sentence into a relative clause by starting it with a relative pronoun: *who, whose, which,* or *that.*
- Check that the relative clause contains a subject and verb and cannot stand on its own.
- Add the relative clause to the middle or end of a complete sentence.
- Use a comma or commas when the relative clause adds information not necessary to the meaning of the sentence.
- Don't use commas when a relative clause identifies the word that it's referring to.
- Don't use commas when the relative clause begins with *that.*

EDITING ACTIVITY 1 Combining Sentences Using
Relative Clauses

Combine the following pairs of sentences using relative clauses. You may need to eliminate unnecessary words or move words around. Use a comma or commas when the relative clause is unnecessary for the sentence to be understood.

EXAMPLE *North by Northwest* is one of my favorite movies. ~~It was directed by~~ ~~Alfred Hitchcock. It was made in 1959.~~

, which Alfred Hitchcock directed in 1959,

1. Cary Grant plays an advertising executive. His name is Roger Thornhill.

2. Cary Grant is framed for killing a UN diplomat. He is mistaken for a man named George Kaplan.

3. James Mason plays a foreign spy. The spy's name is Phillip Vandamm. James Mason was a British actor.

4. Eva Marie Saint plays a beautiful blonde woman. The woman's name is Eve Kendall. Eve Kendall is actually Phillip Vandamm's lover.

5. *North by Northwest* is typical of many Hitchcock movies. It has mistaken identities, a cool blonde woman, and a man. The man is chased by people he doesn't know.

WRITING ACTIVITY 17 Combine Your Sentences

Search your revised draft for short, closely related sentences that cause unnecessary repetition. Where it makes sense to do so, combine them with relative clauses. Once you have done so, review your draft again to make sure you have not used commas that separate essential information from the sentence.

Correcting Comma Splices

A *comma splice* is a common error that occurs when two complete sentences are combined *only* with a comma. (Remember that a complete sentence contains both a subject and a verb and expresses a complete thought.)

For more on comma splices, see pp. 459–62.

COMMA SPLICE   The plot was full of twists, the ending of the movie was predictable.

There are three ways to correct a comma splice.

■ Replace the comma with a period to make two sentences:

The plot was full of twists. The ending of the movie was predictable.

■ Add a coordinating conjunction after the comma:

The plot was full of twists, *but* the ending of the movie was predictable.

■ Replace the comma with a semicolon:

The plot was full of twists; the ending of the movie was predictable.

When using a semicolon, many writers include a conjunctive adverb, such as *in addition, although, nevertheless, however, moreover, in fact,* or *for example.* The conjunctive adverb will tell your readers how the two parts of the sentence connect together. The conjunctive adverb comes after the semicolon and is followed by a comma:

The plot was full of twists; nevertheless, the ending of the movie was predictable.

Here is an example of a comma splice from Paul LaPrade's draft, followed by three different ways he could correct it:

COMMA SPLICE	The methods of expression here range from realistic documentation to symbolism, there are several works that fit into each of these categories.
CORRECT	The methods of expression here range from realistic documentation to symbolism. There are several works that fit into each of these categories.
CORRECT	The methods of expression here range from realistic documentation to symbolism, and there are several works that fit into each of these categories.
CORRECT	The methods of expression here range from realistic documentation to symbolism; there are several works that fit into each of these categories.

HOW TO Correct Comma Splices

- Break the comma splice up into two sentences.
- OR use a comma and a coordinating conjunction (*for, and, nor, but, or, yet, so*).
- OR use a semicolon instead of a comma. If you wish, you may follow the semicolon with a conjunctive adverb and a comma.

Correct each of the following comma splices.

EXAMPLE My next-door neighbor is a great singer, she's always entertaining

my kids.

1. The chocolates are crunchy on the outside, they are soft on the inside.

2. Mexico City was polluted, it was also expensive.

3. Some people think hybrid cars are sluggish, they're actually pretty quick.

4. When I was in Rome, I saw the pope say Mass, it was inspiring.

5. Some people find the movie *Grandma's Boy* offensive, I think it's funny.

Using the Handbook in Part Four of this book as a guide, edit your revised essay for errors in grammar, spelling, and punctuation. In particular, look for comma splices and correct them using any of the three techniques listed on page 262. Your class-mates can help you locate and correct errors you might have overlooked. Add the errors you find and their corrections to your editing log.

A Student's Edited Essay

You might have noticed that Paul's revised draft contained some wordy sentences and a few errors in grammar, spelling, and punctuation. Paul fixed these problems in his edited essay. His corrections are noted in the margin.

LaPrade 1

Paul LaPrade
Professor Hall
English 0311
21 Mar. 2015

The Disappeared

Most people, when they think of art, picture beautiful
paintings of landscapes or portraits of important people. However,
art can also be a way for people to record tragic events. Such is
the case for the current exhibit at the Rubin Art Gallery, *The
Disappeared*. This exhibit depicts the tragedy that occurred in
Latin America in the last decades of the twentieth century, when
military dictators in countries such as Argentina, Chile, and
Guatemala kidnapped and killed thousands of people who resisted
their dictatorships. The different types of art are prints, photos,
video installations, and three-dimensional installations. The
methods of expression here range from realistic documentation
to symbolism; there are several works that fit into each of these
categories. On the whole, this is an effective and diverse display
that is emotionally moving and often disturbing.

An exhibit such as *The Disappeared* should contain skillfully
made art, educate people about the political situation, and make
people feel compassion for what happened. *The Disappeared* does
all of these things. The first collection, "In Memoriam," by Antonio
Frasconi, consists of forty-eight prints that personalize the tragic
situation. These prints show victims of violence, their faces
surrounded by dark colors as if they are vanishing in front of
our eyes. "The Disappeared," also by Frasconi, consists of
woodblock prints that show people with bags over their heads,
huddled as if they were in concentration camps. In one case, a
skull seems to glow eerily through its bag. The images that I
found particularly powerful among Frasconi's prints are the dark
nighttime shots of buildings. Drab cells are shown in red and
grays, with the sky a twilight blue. These prints are similar to
impressionist artwork with their use of colors and inexact drawings

The correct MLA
format is used.

Comma splice is corrected.

Sentences are combined
with a relative clause.

Apostrophe mistake
is corrected.

1

2

LaPrade 2

of real-life subjects; however, most impressionist works I have
seen deal with more cheerful events or landscapes, not with tragic
events, as in this exhibit.

Comma splice is corrected.

3

Photography plays an important role in this exhibit. Marcelo
Brodsky's "Good Memory" is a large display of forty-three
photographs and two videos. It includes a grade school portrait
that shows his class with personal notes written beside the
children. Some are among the disappeared, but others reunite in
photographic portraits in which they, as adults, blend into the
class photo, perhaps as images of the lost potential of those who
were killed. A video installation shows a school reunion in which
ninety-eight missing class members are remembered in roll call.

Coordinating conjunction is added.

4

The most moving and effective part of this exhibit is a series
of photographs by Marcelo Brodsky that deals with his personal
and family history. Pictures of Marcelo with his younger brother
Fernando show happy family scenes, such as the two boys having
fun on a boat or playing with bows and arrows and falling down
and playing dead. Then photos of Fernando are shown in which he
looks skinny and worn down. A caption says that Fernando was
killed in a concentration camp, tying their young innocence to
the horrors of mass murder. This is much more effective than just
reading about tragic historical events in a textbook.

Sentences are combined with a relative clause.

Sentences are combined.

5

While this exhibit is shocking and moving, it is also confusing
because there is so little information given about the political
situation in Latin America that led to these mass murders. Most
people haven't kept track of all of the dictators that were in
charge of Latin American countries in the 1970s and 1980s. This
lack of information distracted me from the exhibits and kept me
from totally appreciating them.

Sentences are combined with a relative clause.

6

On the whole, this exhibit very effectively represents the
killings that have occurred in South America over decades.
Artists express this reality in various styles and mediums,
including prints, sculpture, and photography. This exhibit makes
viewers understand the effects that oppressive governments can
have on individuals and their families. It's hard to forget what
happened to these people.

Spelling error is corrected.

Apostrophe error is corrected.

(Step 5 Share Your Essay

You're ready to share your evaluation with your audience—your instructor, your classmates, and others interested in your topic. For instance, if you evaluated a product, people who are deciding whether to purchase that product will want to know your opinion of it. If you evaluated a movie, other moviegoers will be curious to read your review, whether they've already seen the film or are trying to decide what to see over the weekend. If you evaluated a place, you could share your essay with someone who is interested in going to that place.

An excellent way to share your evaluation with people interested in your subject is to post your review online. As you probably know, many websites provide a forum for consumer reviews of products, performances, and places. Sites such as Epinions and TripAdvisor consist entirely of user comments. Others, such as the Internet Movie Database and Amazon, encourage visitors to add their own reviews to the site's professional content. Before uploading your review, you most likely will need to shorten it to a paragraph or two because of space limitations on the site. You also might need to include a ranking, such as one to five stars. Be sure to check back for comments from other site visitors about how useful your review was for them.

CHAPTER CHECKLIST

- ❏ I read essays to learn more about evaluating a product, performance, and place.
- ❏ I gathered ideas for evaluating a product, performance, and place.
- ❏ I compared my subject with other similar subjects to support a judgment.
- ❏ I revised my thesis statement to express an opinion or a judgment about the value or merit of the subject, to focus on the subject and not the writer, to be moderate and not extreme, and to be clear and specific.
- ❏ I gave the criteria on which the judgment is based, used enough suitable criteria, and explained those criteria that weren't obvious.
- ❏ I provided evidence—examples, facts, and expert testimony—to support each criterion.
- ❏ I gave both the positive and negative aspects of my subject to maintain a balanced perspective.
- ❏ I combined short, closely related sentences with relative clauses.
- ❏ I edited to eliminate comma splices and other errors in grammar, punctuation, and spelling.

REFLECTING ON YOUR WRITING

To help you reflect on the writing you did in this chapter, answer the following questions:

1. Compare your experience writing an evaluation with writing an expressive or informative essay. What did you find easiest and most difficult about these assignments?

2. What did you learn from writing this essay?

3. How will your audience benefit from reading your essay?

4. If you had more time, what more would you do to improve your essay before sharing it with readers?

Visit **LaunchPad Solo for Readers and Writers** > **Writing Process** for more tutorials, videos, and practice developing your essay with each step.

After you anwer these questions, freewrite about what you learned in this chapter.

"Despite women making up half of the video game culture, the representation and treatment of women in games contribute to sexism and negative stereotyping."

SUSANNAH GOYA-PACK,
"GIRLS JUST WANT TO PLAY GAMES: SEXISM IN VIDEO GAMING"

9

Arguing a Position
Media, Censorship, and Stereotypes

People have always tried to change other people's minds. The topic might be serious—land disputes that could lead to war—or minor—couples debating about where to go to dinner. Countless songs have been written about arguments between lovers, from George and Ira Gershwin's "Let's Call the Whole Thing Off" to Taylor Swift's "We Are Never Ever Getting Back Together." In addition to songs, arguments can be expressed in speeches, essays, works of art, even refrigerator magnets—however people choose to express themselves and take a position. These arguments can also appear in a variety of media, including newspapers, books, magazines, radio, television, and the Internet.

Media options have expanded to include texting, e-mail, social websites, online shopping, blogs, tweets, videos, chat groups, photo apps, and podcasts. This interactive technology—often called *new media*—allows us to alter what we watch, listen to, or read to suit our own tastes or to communicate with others. Instead of being vulnerable to the trickery of commercials, for instance, we can skip through them. We can create our own song playlists, shows, and videos and send them to people we've never met.

In this chapter, you will write an essay that argues your position on media, censorship, and stereotypes. As you follow the steps of the writing process, you will

- Explore the chapter topic by reading essays that argue a position.
- Gather ideas by consulting with others, freewriting, and brainstorming.
- Develop your ideas using **cause-and-effect** analysis.
- Practice making an argument claim, generating pro and con points to support your ideas, and ordering your points effectively.
- Learn to avoid logical fallacies.
- Combine sentences using introductory phrases.
- Practice correcting problems with subject-verb agreement.
- Consider submitting your finished essay to a campus or local newspaper.

But do we really control the media, or do the media control us? Critics and consumers argue about many aspects of the media, such as whether there is too much or too little government regulation, the ways that people are portrayed, and the media's effect on people's lives. How are viewers and performers affected when the media portray people in particular ways? Are our society's ever-changing forms of communication helpful or harmful to the people who use them?

In this chapter, you'll read and analyze argument essays on these issues. You will also follow a student, Susannah Goya-Pack, as she writes an argument about the portrayal of women in video games. Then you'll join the debate by writing an argument on a media-related topic. Once you have completed your argument, you can share it with friends and classmates, or you can expand your audience by sending it to a campus or local newspaper. By writing this essay, you have the opportunity to affect the way people think about a topic you care about.   ■

[O] GETTING STARTED Think about the Media

The photograph on page 268 shows young men and women playing video games. Do the identities and body language of the players strike you as typical? Why or why not? Discuss the stereotypes of gaming culture with your classmates. What are some other cultural identities or practices that are often stereotyped?

Read to Write   Reading Essays That Argue a Position about Media, Censorship, and Stereotypes

Debates about media have become intense, as the following four readings show. The authors of these essays each take a position on a current or controversial issue associated with media, censorship, and stereotypes. As you read, notice how they use cause-and-effect analysis to develop their points. Also note how these authors try to persuade their audience. What arguments do they make to support their points? How do they try to win over readers who disagree with them? How do they order their ideas? How logical are their arguments? Consider, too, how you react to their arguments. To what degree do these authors change your mind on these topics? You can use what you learn from reading these arguments to get started writing your own argument.

A Media Issue: An Annotated Reading

TARA PARKER-POPE
An Ugly Toll of Technology: Impatience and Forgetfulness

Tara Parker-Pope writes a consumer health column and blog for the *New York Times*, where this article was published. Previously she wrote for the *Wall Street Journal*, where she won several awards for her writing on women's health. Parker-Pope's book *For Better: The Science of a Good Marriage* gives advice based on scientific research for how to have a successful marriage. In "An Ugly Toll of Technology: Impatience and Forgetfulness," Parker-Pope reminds us of the dangers of too much dependence on technology.

1　Are your Facebook friends more interesting than those you have in real life? Has high-speed Internet made you impatient with slow-speed children? Do you sometimes think about reaching for the fast-forward button, only to realize that life does not come with a remote control? If you answered yes to any of those questions, exposure to technology may be slowly reshaping your personality. Some experts believe excessive use of the Internet, cell phones and other technologies can cause us to become more impatient, impulsive, forgetful and even more narcissistic.

Parker-Pope uses a series of questions to engage her readers.

Parker-Pope's thesis statement provides a preview of the essay and shows that the primary method of development will be cause and effect.

2　"More and more, life is resembling the chat room," says Dr. Elias Aboujaoude, director of the Impulse Control Disorders Clinic at Stanford. "We're paying a price in terms of our cognitive life because of this virtual lifestyle." We do spend a lot of time with our devices, and some studies have suggested that excessive dependence on cell phones and the Internet is akin to an addiction. Websites like NetAddiction.com offer self-assessment tests to determine if technology has become a drug. Among the questions used to identify those at risk: Do you neglect housework to spend more time online? Are you frequently checking your e-mail? Do you often lose sleep because you log in late at night? If you answered "often" or "always," technology may be taking a toll on you.

Parker-Pope's first point quotes an expert, which lends credibility to her argument.

Answering these questions helps readers relate to this topic on a personal level.

3　In a study to be published in the journal *Cyberpsychology, Behavior and Social Networking*, researchers from the University of Melbourne in Australia subjected 173 college students to tests measuring risk for problematic Internet and gambling behaviors. About 5 percent of the students showed signs of gambling problems, but 10 percent of the students posted scores high enough to put them in the at-risk category for Internet "addiction." Technology use was clearly interfering with the students' daily lives, but it may be going too far to call it an addiction, says Nicki Dowling, a clinical psychologist who led the study. Ms. Dowling prefers to call it "Internet dependence."

The use of facts and statistics in the second point makes the argument more convincing.

Another expert gives a name to the cause.

4　Typically, the concern about our dependence on technology is that it detracts from our time with family and friends in the real world. But psychologists have become intrigued by a more subtle and insidious effect of our online interactions.

Parker-Pope moves to some of the effects of technology dependence.

It may be that the immediacy of the Internet, the efficiency of the iPhone and the anonymity of the chat room change the core of who we are, issues that Dr. Aboujaoude explores in a book, *Virtually You: The Internet and the Fracturing of the Self*, to be released next year.

Dr. Aboujaoude also asks whether the vast storage available in e-mail and on   5 the Internet is preventing many of us from letting go, causing us to retain many old and unnecessary memories at the expense of making new ones. Everything is saved these days, he notes, from the meaningless e-mail sent after a work lunch to the angry online exchange with a spouse. "If you can't forget because all this stuff is staring at you, what does that do to your ability to lay down new memories and remember things that you should be remembering?" Dr. Aboujaoude said. "When you have 500 pictures from your vacation in your Flickr account, as opposed to five pictures that are really meaningful, does that change your ability to recall the moments that you really want to recall?"

There is also no easy way to conquer a dependence on technology. Nicholas   6 Carr, author of the new book *The Shallows: What the Internet Is Doing to Our Brains*, says that social and family responsibilities, work and other pressures influence our use of technology. "The deeper a technology is woven into the patterns of everyday life, the less choice we have about whether and how we use that technology," Mr. Carr wrote in a recent blog post on the topic. Some experts suggest simply trying to curtail the amount of time you spend online. Set limits for how often you check e-mail or force yourself to leave your cell phone at home occasionally. The problem is similar to an eating disorder, says Dr. Kimberly Young, a professor at St. Bonaventure University in New York who has led research on the addictive nature of online technology. Technology, like food, is an essential part of daily life, and those suffering from disordered online behavior cannot give it up entirely and instead have to learn moderation and controlled use. She suggests therapy to determine the underlying issues that set off a person's need to use the Internet "as a way of escape."

The International Center for Media and the Public Agenda at the University   7 of Maryland asked 200 students to refrain from using electronic media for a day. The reports from students after the study suggest that giving up technology cold turkey not only makes life logistically difficult, but also changes our ability to connect with others. "Texting and I.M.'ing my friends gives me a constant feeling of comfort," wrote one student. "When I did not have those two luxuries, I felt quite alone and secluded from my life. Although I go to a school with thousands of students, the fact that I was not able to communicate with anyone via technology was almost unbearable."

Another expert provides hypothetical examples of the effect of technology dependence.

Parker-Pope implies an opposing point and offers a rebuttal—that it's not easy to avoid technology, but it can be done.

Parker-Pope continues to rely heavily on expert opinion. This expert explains how to cut back on technology use.

Quotes from students help readers relate to the problem because they show the effect of technology in every walk of life.

READING ACTIVITY 1 Build Your Vocabulary

Determine the meanings of the following words from the context of "An Ugly Toll of Technology: Impatience and Forgetfulness." Then check their meanings by looking up the words in a dictionary: *narcissistic* (1), *cognitive* (2), *insidious* (4), *anonymity* (4), *curtail* (6), *logistically* (7).

Discuss the following questions about "An Ugly Toll of Technology: Impatience and Forgetfulness."

1. How does Parker-Pope attempt to attract readers' attention at the beginning of her piece?

2. What is Parker-Pope's thesis, or claim, about technology, and where does it appear in the essay?

3. In supporting her claim, Parker-Pope relies on information from recent scientific studies. In your view, what is her most persuasive point and why is it persuasive?

4. Evaluate Parker-Pope's conclusion. How effective is it? Does it give you a sense of closure, or does it leave you hanging? Explain your answer.

Write a paragraph or two in which you express your views about the effect that cell phones, the Internet, and other technologies have had on your life. Are your experiences similar to Parker-Pope's analysis, or are they different? Explain your ideas and compare them with the ideas of your classmates.

A Media Issue

JESSICA WINTER
Selfie-Loathing

Jessica Winter is a senior editor for *Slate* and is best known for writing on business, technology, and culture. Her writing has also appeared in *Time*, *O*, the *Boston Globe*, and the *Los Angeles Times*. She holds a bachelor's degree from Yale and a master's degree from University College London. "Selfie-Loathing," which appeared online at *Slate*, describes how looking at photos on Instagram can be even more harmful to self-esteem than reading Facebook posts.

It's a truism that Facebook is the many-headed frenemy, the great underminer. We know this because science tells us so. The Human–Computer Institute at Carnegie Mellon has found that your "passive consumption" of your friends' feeds and your own "broadcasts to wider audiences" on Facebook correlate with feelings of loneliness and even depression. Earlier this year, two German universities showed that "passive following" on Facebook triggers states of envy and resentment in many users, with vacation photos standing out as a prime trigger. Yet another study, this one of 425 undergrads in Utah, carried the self-explanatory title "'They Are Happier and Having Better Lives Than I Am': The Impact of Using 1

Facebook on Perceptions of Others' Lives." Even the positive effects of Facebook can be double-edged: Viewing your profile can increase your self-esteem, but it also lowers your ability to ace a serial subtraction task.

All of these studies are careful to point out that it's not Facebook per se that   2
inspires states of disconnection, jealousy, and poor mathematical performance—rather, it's specific *uses* of Facebook. If you primarily use Facebook to share interesting news articles with colleagues, exchange messages with new acquaintances, and play Candy Crush Saga, chances are the green-eyed monster won't ask to friend you. But if the hours you log on Facebook are largely about creeping through other people's posts—especially their photos, and *especially*-especially their vacation snaps—with an occasional pause to update your own status and slap on a grudging "like" here or there, then science confirms that you have entered into a semi-consensual sadomasochistic relationship with Facebook and need to break the cycle.

A closer look at Facebook studies also supports an untested but tantalizing   3
hypothesis: that, despite all the evidence, Facebook is actually not the greatest underminer at the social-media cocktail party (that you probably weren't invited to, but you saw the pictures and it looked *incredible*). Facebook is not the frenemy with the most heads. That title, in fact, goes to Instagram. Here's why.

Instagram distills the most crazy-making aspects of the Facebook experience.

So far, academic studies of Instagram's effects on our emotional states are   4
scarce. But it's tempting to extrapolate those effects from the Facebook studies, because out of the many activities Facebook offers, the three things that correlate most strongly with a self-loathing screen hangover are basically the three things that Instagram is currently for: loitering around others' photos, perfunctory likeing, and "broadcasting" to a relatively amorphous group. "I would venture to say that photographs, likes, and comments are the aspects of the Facebook experience that are most important in driving the self-esteem effects, and that photos are maybe the biggest driver of those effects," says Catalina Toma of the Department of Communication Arts at the University of Wisconsin–Madison. "You could say that Instagram purifies this one aspect of Facebook."

Instagram is exclusively image-driven, and images will crack your mirror.

"You get more explicit and implicit cues of people being happy, rich, and   5
successful from a photo than from a status update," says Hanna Krasnova of Humboldt University Berlin, co-author of the study on Facebook and envy. "A photo can very powerfully provoke immediate social comparison, and that can trigger feelings of inferiority. You don't envy a news story."

Krasnova's research has led her to define what she calls an "envy spiral"   6
peculiar to social media. "If you see beautiful photos of your friend on Instagram," she says, "one way to compensate is to self-present with even better photos, and then your friend sees your photos and posts *even better* photos, and so on. Self-

promotion triggers more self-promotion, and the world on social media gets further and further from reality." Granted, an envy spiral can unspool just as easily on Facebook or Twitter. But for a truly gladiatorial battle of the selfies, Instagram is the only rightful Colosseum.

Instagram messes more with your sense of time.

"You spend so much time creating flattering, idealized images of yourself, sorting through hundreds of images for that one perfect picture, but you don't necessarily grasp that everybody else is spending a lot of time doing the same thing," Toma says. Then, after spending lots of time carefully curating and filtering your images, you spend even more time staring at other people's carefully curated and filtered images that you assume they didn't spend much time on. And the more you do that, Toma says, "the more distorted your perception is that their lives are happier and more meaningful than yours." Again, this happens all the time on Facebook, but because Instagram is image-based, it creates a purer reality-distortion field.   7

Instagram ups your chances of violating "the gray line of stalkerism."

"If you don't know someone, and Facebook is telling you that you have interests in common," says Nicole Ellison of the University of Michigan School of Information, "you can see their profile as a list of icebreakers." But that same profile is also a potential list of icemakers. If you meet a vague acquaintance at a party and strike up a conversation about a science article he posted to his Facebook wall, that probably seems normal. If you meet a vague acquaintance at a party and strike up a conversation about the eco-lodge he chose for his honeymoon in the Maldives, he will likely back away from you slowly. "And then," Ellison says, "you've violated the gray line of stalkerism." Instagram's image-driven format gives you the eco-lodge but not the science article.   8

And arguably, you've violated the gray line of stalkerism simply by looking at those photos in the first place, even if you don't reveal yourself in public as the sad lurker that you are. Each time you swipe through more images of people's meals and soirees and renovation projects and holiday sunsets, you are potentially blurring the boundary between stranger-you-haven't-met and sleazy voyeur skulking around the cabana with an iPhone. To be sure, daily acts of stalkerism are all but part of the social contract at this point. But stalkerism heavily diluted with links to articles, one-on-one messaging, Dr. Oz ads, and second cousins who still play FarmVille will always seem more palatable than the uncut version.   9

▌ READING ACTIVITY 2 Build Your Vocabulary ▌

Determine the meanings of the following words from the context of Jessica Winter's article. Then check their meanings by looking up the words in a dictionary: *truism* (1), *frenemy* (1), *sadomasochistic* (2), *extrapolate* (4), *perfunctory* (4), *amorphous* (4), *palatable* (9).

For more on claims, see
pages 291–93 later in this
chapter.

For more on evaluation,
see Chapter 8. For more
on characteristics of an
argument, see pp. 291–99
in this chapter.

GROUP ACTIVITY 2 Discuss the Reading

Discuss the following questions about "Selfie-Loathing" with your classmates.

1. What is Winter's argumentative claim, or thesis, and where does she express this claim in her article?
2. Why does Winter begin her piece by citing studies that criticize Facebook?
3. What points does Winter make to support her argumentative claim? In other words, what are her "pro points"?
4. Why, according to Winter, is Instagram even more harmful than Facebook?
5. Evaluate Winter's main points, and rank them from 1 (poor) to 5 (effective). Explain your ranking.

WRITING ACTIVITY 2 Share Your Ideas

Write a paragraph or two about the advantages and disadvantages of posting to social media sites such as Facebook and Instagram. Have you ever felt <u>envious</u> of others as a result of reading their postings? Do you think that you, your family, and friends should post to social media sites? Why or why not?

羨慕

A Censorship Issue

1) About control & rules

MCKENZIE MAXSON
What You Aren't Seeing on Social Media

McKenzie Maxson studied journalism and history at Northwestern University and is a blogger for the *Huffington Post*'s Millennial Outreach. In the following essay, published online at the *Huffington Post*, she argues that we all spend too much time self-censoring our posts on social media sites.

make a posting on social media

As an inhabitant of the social media world, it's easy to forget that there's still 1
a lot going on outside the realm of the screen or the smartphone. Beyond the
Facebook statuses we comment on and the profile pictures we "like," there are
real people out there who are carefully choosing what to post, and more importantly, what not to.

Before posting online, we all take a minute to consider it from the views of 2
our social network and how it will shape their opinion of us. Thinking before
speaking, or typing or <u>tweeting</u>, is not a bad thing. But in the world of social
media, thoughtfulness can easily turn to self-censorship as our profiles allow us
to actively create an online version of ourselves.

According to a study on Facebook self-censorship, over a 17-day period, 71 3
percent of all users censored their own content at least once, and of those users,
51 percent censored their own posts—4.52 posts on average. The study also

notes that "older users seemed to censor substantially fewer posts than younger users."

Millennials, who are supposed to be the most engaged online, are increas- 4 ingly self-censoring. This isn't so different than what we do in real life, but social media provides a whole new level of control with the power to post, delete and repost our edited thoughts and feelings.

When I open Facebook every day, the status box politely asks me, "What's 5 on your mind?" But the true answer to that question is almost never what I would post. Maybe I'd want to truthfully type: "I'm having a really stressful day. Life kind of sucks right now." But instead, I'll probably craft a line about my fun-filled weekend, a standard post about hating Mondays or nothing at all. Sure, I'll post when I receive exciting news, when I pass an important milestone, when I take some cute #selfies with a friend or read a good article. But not when I have an off day, experience a setback or feel like a failure.

Scroll down my Facebook profile, and you will see that I enjoy spending time 6 with friends and family, am planning on travelling this fall, that I go to a good school and have a good job. My Facebook exclaims, "I am happy! I am living the life!" And maybe I am. Or maybe underneath all of that, I'm struggling with a personal problem, an illness, trouble at home or in relationships, lack of success at work or unhappiness.

This focus on achievement on social media, epitomized in picture perfect, 7 filtered Instagram snapshots, eclipses all of the tiny imperfections that make us who we are, the shared struggles that make connecting with another person feel so meaningful. After all, a person is defined by their struggles and weaknesses and how they handle them, not by their successes. No, I'm not suggesting that we all begin oversharing online more than we already do, but that this habit of self-censorship has tangible effects IRL.

Generation Y is characterized by its ability to be driven to extremes. We 8 operate in a more competitive job market, fight for spots in top universities with constantly shrinking acceptance rates and rising tuitions, trade personal time for higher grades or salaries. And we ignore the reality of the resulting mental and emotional problems, pushing them aside in pursuit of the unattainable Facebook-perfect life that we present online.

I find it more than consequential that Millennials, the most plugged-in and 9 connected generation, suffer from the highest levels of stress, according to *USA Today*. Higher percentages of Millennials also report being diagnosed with depression or anxiety, and dealing with these problems through sedentary behaviors, like listening to music, eating and, of course, surfing the Internet.

In a paper on stigma and mental health care, Patrick Corrigan of the University 10 of Chicago points out: "Less than 30 percent of people with psychiatric disorders seek treatment." On college campuses especially, the effects of ignoring stigmatized mental health concerns are very real and devastatingly dangerous. My fellow Northwestern students and I have felt them, as have those at other universities.

Living lives so heavily based on social media gives us a false sense of control, 11 one we cannot have in the real world. And it can reinforce the stigma associated with mental illness. It's perfectly normal for me to share an accomplishment online, but never a failure. Even if I overcame my own personal fear of judgment, what if it was seen by a professor? A potential employer? And it makes it possible for me to scroll through my news feed, marveling at my friends' wonderful lives in comparison to my own, or, even worse, to miss a very real problem by communicating with my friends in a public forum rather than face to face.

con argument

Social media itself is not the problem, but it can sometimes help to enforce 12 it. According to Pew Research's Internet Project, Facebook is often a positive tool used to maintain social connections. It affords many opportunities for users to band together, to create groups focused on shared struggles and to reach out to others who may be far away but are dealing with similar issues. It can foster community and healing, but it also allows us the chance to ignore the reality of our problems, or to overlook our friends', and rely on the smiling face in their profile picture as reality.

So leave your happy profile pictures, your excited statuses and your pictur- 13 esque Instagrams. But next time you connect with someone in real life, not on LinkedIn, take a second to think about everything you don't know about them from social media, and talk about that instead.

READING ACTIVITY 3 Build Your Vocabulary

Determine the meanings of the following words from McKenzie Maxson's essay. Then check their meanings by looking up the words in a dictionary: *Millennials* (4), *epitomized* (7), *IRL* (7), *Generation Y* (8), *stigmatized* (10).

GROUP ACTIVITY 3 Discuss the Reading

Discuss the following questions about "What You Aren't Seeing on Social Media" with your classmates.

1. What is Maxson's thesis? State this in your own words.
2. What are Maxson's pro points, or the points that support her main claim? *repost* *good*
3. What are the arguments against the author's thesis (the con points)? How does she refute these? *bad*
4. Explain this sentence in Maxson's essay: "No, I'm not suggesting that we all begin oversharing online more than we already do, but that this habit of self-censorship has tangible effects IRL." Give an example of the effects of your self-censorship of posts and other writing. Also give an example of how you've chosen not to add friends or have blocked or unfollowed others on social media sites. How is this a form of censorship?

WRITING ACTIVITY 3 Share Your Ideas

Write a paragraph or two about the advantages and disadvantages of self-censoring posts and photos on sites such as Facebook and Instagram. Do you think that self-censoring is beneficial or harmful? Does it depend on the situation? Explain your answer.

A Stereotyping Issue

SAMUEL L. JACKSON

In Character

Actor Samuel L. Jackson is a graduate of Morehouse College and has appeared in more than one hundred films, including *Do the Right Thing* (1989), *Jungle Fever* (1991), *Pulp Fiction* (1994), *Star Wars* (Episodes I–III; 1999, 2002, 2005), *Snakes on a Plane* (2006), and *The Avengers* (2012). He often works with directors Spike Lee and Quentin Tarantino. In the following essay, Jackson considers the issue of racism in Hollywood and argues that although roles for minority actors have improved over the last few decades, there's more work to be done.

I think it's significant for the growth of the [movie] business that a black   1
actor like me is being cast in race-neutral parts when 20 years ago I wouldn't
have been. It's significant for young actors who have aspirations to be things
other than criminals and drug dealers and victims and whatever rap artist they
have to be to get into a film. The things I've done and Morgan's done and Denzel's done, that Fish has done, that Wesley's* done, everybody's done, have
allowed us to achieve a level of success as other kinds of people. We've been
successful in roles as doctors, lawyers, teachers, policemen, detectives, spies,
monsters—anything that we have been able to portray on-screen in a very realistic way that made audiences say, I believe that, and that brought them into the
theaters to see us do it. This has allowed young black actors the opportunity to
become different kinds of characters in the cinematic milieu we're a part of.

Before, I used to pick up scripts and I was criminal number two and I looked   2
to see what page I died on. We've now demonstrated a level of expertise, in
terms of the care we give to our characters and in terms of our professionalism—
showing up to work on time, knowing our lines, and bringing something to the
job beyond the lines and basic characterizations. Through our accomplishments
and the expertise we have shown, studios know there is a talent pool out there
that wants to be like us, and hopefully, these young actors will take care to do
the things we did.

As the fabric of our society changes in certain ways, the fabric of the cine-   3
matic world changes in the same ways. For a very long time, the people that were
in power were white men. They tended to hire other white men, and when they
saw a story, the people in those stories were white men or specific kinds of white
women. As we get younger producers and younger people in the studios, we
have a generation, or several generations, of people who have lived in a society
where they have black friends. They have Asian friends. They have Hispanic friends
who do a wide variety of jobs, who went into a wide variety of vocations. When
the studio heads look at a script now, they can see their friend Juan or they can

---

*Jackson is referring to African American actors Morgan Freeman, Denzel Washington,
Laurence Fishburne, and Wesley Snipes.

see their friend Kwong or they can see their friend Rashan. So all of a sudden you see a different look in the movies, as they reflect the way this younger generation of producers and studio executives live their lives. And consequently, through the worldwide network of cinema, you meet other top-quality actors from other cultures. The world of cinema brings us all together. And we've started to cast films in a whole other way that reflects the way we live and the pattern of our society. Outside of *Spider-Man*, all the big action heroes now seem to be ethnic. The new Arnold Schwarzenegger is The Rock, and the new Bruce Willis is about to be Vin Diesel. So we're doing something right. But it's difficult to do a film that's of a serious nature and that does not have guns, sex, and explosions in it if it's ethnic.

There are many ways to answer the question whether Hollywood is racist. 4 The direct and honest answer, I guess, is yes, only because Hollywood is anti anything that's not green. If something doesn't make money, they don't want to be bothered with it. Therefore, it's still difficult to get a movie about Hispanics made; it's difficult to get a movie about blacks made that doesn't have to do with hip-hop, drugs, and sex. You can get a black comedy made. Eddie Murphy's funny, Will Smith is funny, Martin Lawrence is funny. We have huge black comics. But getting a film like *Eve's Bayou* made is practically impossible. For five years, nobody knew what that movie was. Like, what is it? It's a family drama. Yeah, but how do we market that? Nobody wanted to be bothered with it. Or *Caveman's Valentine*. What is it? It's a mystery, a murder mystery. But it's a black murder mystery. No, there's white people in it; it just happens that a black person is the lead. So Hollywood is racist in its ideas about what can make money and what won't make money. They'll make Asian movies about people who jump across buildings and use swords and swing in trees, like *Crouching Tiger*, but we can't sell an Asian family drama. What do we do with that? Or if we're going to have Asian people in the film, they've got to be like the tong, or they're selling drugs and they got some guns and it's young gang members. It's got to be that. And Hollywood is sexist in its ideals about which women are appealing and which women aren't. It's a young woman's game. Women have got to be either real old or real young to be successful. If they're in the middle, it's like, what do we do with her? Put her in kids' movies, you know, with some kids.

Hollywood can be perceived as racist and sexist, because that's what audi- 5 ences have said to them they will pay their money to come see. It's difficult to break that cycle, because it's a moneymaking business and it costs money to make films. Hollywood tends to copy things that make lots of money. The first thing they want to know is how many car chases are there and what's blowing up. They're over the how-many-people-die thing, because of 9/11. Now it's like, how many people can we kill and get away with it? We can't blow up anything right now unless it's in the right context. We can blow something up over there, and the bad guy can be a guy with a turban. So there's all kinds of things that go into what people say about Hollywood being racist. There have been times I had to go in a room and convince people I'm the right person for their script and the fact that I'm black will not impact on the script in a negative way. I've had to explain that my being black won't change the dynamics of the interaction; it won't change the dynamics of the story in terms of my character's interaction with the other characters. I'll just happen to be a black guy who's in that story doing those things.

We [African Americans] need to produce our own films. We need to own our own theaters in addition to producing our own films. The more theaters we own, the sooner we can have our own distribution chain. It's a matter of us having that kind of network [as major Hollywood studios do], so when we do make small films that we want to distribute to a specific group of people or to a wider audience, we're able to do it.   6

I want to be able to produce films for friends of mine who haven't had the opportunity to be seen in the way I've been seen. They're good at what they do, and they deserve an opportunity to be seen by a greater public.   7

READING ACTIVITY 4 Build Your Vocabulary

Determine the meanings of the following words from the context of Samuel L. Jackson's essay. Then check their meanings by looking up the words in a dictionary: *cinematic* (1), *milieu* (1), *vocations* (3), *tong* (4), *dynamics* (5).

GROUP ACTIVITY 4 Discuss the Reading

Discuss the following questions about "In Character" with your classmates.

1. According to Jackson, is Hollywood racist?
2. Name at least three reasons that Jackson gives to support his opinion.
3. In Jackson's view, how does the desire to make money affect the way movies portray minority characters?
4. Why is the situation in Hollywood about the representation of minorities improving, according to Jackson?

WRITING ACTIVITY 4 Share Your Ideas

Write a paragraph or two in which you agree or disagree with Jackson's claim about racism in Hollywood. In your view, are minorities and women fairly or unfairly represented? Are things changing? Give examples to support your points. Compare your viewpoint with those of several of your classmates.

Writing Your Essay A Step-by-Step Guide

Now that you've read some essays arguing a position on media, censorship, and stereotypes, it's time to write your own essay. First, read the following writing assignment. Then, use the step-by-step advice that follows to discover ideas, develop them as you draft, and polish your writing into a finished essay that readers will find both interesting and persuasive:

Writing Assignment

Types of media are all around you. Even this textbook is a medium of communication. While you read this book, you might have a television on or music playing. Periodically, you take a break by texting a friend or checking your Twitter feed.

These technologies can have a strong influence on us. In this chapter, you'll write a persuasive essay that takes a position on a controversial aspect of the media that interests you. You (or your instructor) may approach this assignment in one of several ways:

- Argue about how a dependence on a particular communication medium has changed our lives for good or bad.
- Argue for or against some type of media censorship.
- Argue a point about how a group of people is represented or stereotyped in the media.

(Step 1 Explore Your Choices

Because the media encompass everything from "old" one-way media (newspapers, magazines, television, and radio) to "new" interactive media (such as blogs, wikis, social media sites, and texting), you have many possible topics to choose from for your essay. Remember that most writers do their best work when they really care about the topic. At the same time, the topic that you select needs to keep your readers engaged and willing to listen to what you have to say. Before you think about possible topics, take some time to think about who your readers are and what they care about. Consider also what you want them to believe or do after they read your essay.

Analyzing Your Audience and Purpose

For more on audience and purpose, see pp. 6–8.

Keep your readers in mind from the very beginning. For this assignment, you might want to submit your finished essay to your campus or local newspaper. The readers of your campus newspaper will be mostly students, while the readers of your local newspaper will be of various ages and have many kinds of occupations. The type of newspaper you select will affect the way you write your essay.

Also, consider your purpose for writing this essay. You may need to inform your readers about something they know little about, and you may want to express your feelings about the topic, but the primary purpose of an essay that argues a position is persuasive. Are you trying to persuade your readers to change their minds about some aspect of the media or to do something about it? What do you want them to think? To do? Knowing your purpose will help you stay focused and make it more likely that your essay will succeed.

WRITING ACTIVITY 5 Analyze Your Audience and Purpose

Your responses to the following questions will help you decide how to approach this chapter's writing assignment. Be sure to come back to these questions after you have chosen a topic.

1. Consider the readers of your campus or local newspaper. How old do they tend to be? What topics relating to the media, censorship, or stereotyping might they be most interested in?

2. What types of media do the readers of your campus newspaper typically use? Are these types of media the same or different from the kinds that the readers of your local newspaper might use?

3. What, if anything, do you know about your readers' political views? Would most readers have conservative, moderate, or liberal views? Give examples.

4. How interested would your readers be in an essay on the media? Explain your answer.

Gathering Ideas

To make sure you choose a topic that you care about and wish to argue, take the time to gather ideas on each of the three possible topics for this essay—media, censorship, and stereotypes. Even if you already have an idea for a topic, it's good to experiment with other ideas so that you don't miss an even better one. The activities and examples in this chapter will focus on consulting with others, freewriting, and brainstorming, but you may use any additional techniques for gathering ideas that work for you.

For more on gathering ideas, see pp. 11–14.

Consulting with Others about Media

As new media forms emerge and become popular, they change how we live, from childhood to adulthood. Children text and upload photos and videos onto their phones or other electronic devices. In online classes, college students chat online and tweet with their instructors and classmates without ever having any face-to-face interactions. Online dating profiles allow people to search databases for possible partners with specific character traits—and to reject undesirable dates without ever speaking to them. Social networking sites allow people to screen out groups of people who disagree with them, which can limit their exposure to diverse ideas.

To what extent are such media interactions beneficial? To what extent are they damaging? You may already have explored this point when you wrote in response to "An Ugly Toll of Technology: Impatience and Forgetfulness" (p. 271) or "Selfie-Loathing" (p. 273). However, it may be helpful to look beyond your own experiences to make a decision. To understand how such changes have affected other people, it makes sense to ask them some questions.

To consult with others, first decide what you want to know more about. For instance, if you're interested in knowing how much time college students spend texting one another, you might survey your classmates, perhaps on your class website or using an online polling site. If you're curious about the effect that advertising in schools has on children, you could interview an elementary school teacher. Prepare a few questions before you talk to this person, and keep careful notes of the discussion.

Student writer Marshall was concerned that using television to keep small children occupied might stunt their intellectual growth. To gather ideas on this topic, Marshall consulted with a friend, Miguel, who was studying for a master's degree in child development. In an e-mail message, Marshall asked Miguel what experts thought about children who watch a lot of television. Here is Miguel's response:

> Most child development experts think that many children are being exposed to too much media. Some researchers have shown that more and more children have TV sets and video games in their bedrooms, and 53 percent of children ages 8 to 18 report that their parents don't restrict their TV watching. Children whose parents don't limit TV viewing report that they read less than children whose parents restrict their viewing. They're also more likely to be overweight, and they have fewer friends. In general, in households with parents who monitor children's TV viewing, the children are better off.

⏻ **Connect with others online to discuss your topic**

Consider going online to ask others about your topic using social media posts, blog comments, online discussion forums, or chat sessions. One advantage to online communication is that you have a written record of the interaction that you can refer to later.

◄ **WRITING ACTIVITY 6** Consult with Others about Media ►

After choosing a topic that interests you, consult with at least two people who are knowledgeable about the issue. Ask your consultants to give their opinions and describe their experiences with the topic.

Freewriting about Censorship

Even though the U.S. Constitution guarantees freedom of expression, restrictions on the media have always existed. For example, the Federal Communications Commission (FCC) has always regulated the content of radio, film, and television. It applied a morality code to movies in the 1930s and recently fined television stations for indecency. School boards often remove controversial books (including *Huckleberry Finn* and *The Catcher in the Rye*) from library shelves and reading lists, and some religious institutions discourage their members from reading or watching certain books or movies. Most Internet providers offer to block sites (often of a sexual or violent nature) that might upset their customers, parents can prevent their children from viewing materials they find inappropriate, and users of social media sites can block other users' posts or be selective about their own posts.

What is your opinion about these kinds of restrictions? You may have strong feelings about censorship, or you may not be sure what you think. Freewriting can be a productive way to explore your thoughts and get a better sense of where you stand on the issue. As you know, to freewrite, you simply write for five or ten minutes without trying to make sense of your thoughts. By letting your mind wander on the page, you can discover ideas you didn't know you had.

If you've had a personal experience with some kind of censorship, try writing about that for a few minutes and see where it leads you. You can also refer to the writing you completed after reading "What You Aren't Seeing on Social Media" (p. 276). If you're stuck for ideas, you might explore your reactions to any of the following questions:

- Should there be more or less censorship of the media? Explain your answer.

- In what ways has technology changed the way that news is delivered to us? Is the news more or less censored as a result of these changes?

- How effective is the rating system used for movies? What about the warning labels on television shows and video games? What changes, if any, would you suggest?

- Do you believe that people spend too much time worrying about what others are posting online or about what they themselves are posting? Explain your position.

⏻ Tips for freewriting

When you freewrite, avoid being distracted by the appearance of potential errors in your document. Consider turning off your word-processing program's spell-check and grammar-check features, or use a word-processing program with no proofing tools, such as Notepad, TextEdit, or Pages. You can also log on to a site such as 750words.com, which was created for people who want to freewrite every day.

One student, Reginald, was interested in a controversy that erupted over an unpopular ad that ran in his college newspaper. Here is his freewriting on the issue:

> A school newspaper ad states that blacks should not receive reparations (a method of making up for past injustices) for slavery. There were ten reasons given for why blacks aren't entitled to damages for the effects of slavery. As you can imagine, a lot of people were really worked up about this ad and wanted the paper to apologize. But the editor of the paper said that he wouldn't, stating freedom of speech as his reason. Well, I don't agree with the ad, either, but I agree with the editor that the paper doesn't have to apologize.

WRITING ACTIVITY 7 Freewrite about Censorship

Select a recent controversy about media censorship that interests you and freewrite about it for at least ten minutes. If nothing comes to mind, you may use one or more of the questions on page 285 to stimulate your thinking.

Brainstorming about Stereotypes

Mass entertainment—music, gossip magazines, radio programs, movies, television shows, video games, and the like—has always represented people in ways that at least some audience members have considered unfair or unrealistic. In the early days of television, for example, the typical American family was a white mother, father, and children who lived in a large house in a safe suburb. Today, television families are depicted in a variety of ways. For another example, consider shows and movies that feature young working professionals. Typically, the characters are portrayed as if they had no money problems and enough spare time to regularly sit around and talk. In fact, many young professionals have limited incomes, are raising children, and have little spare time. What effect do inaccurate portrayals, such as this one, have on viewers? How are other groups of people portrayed by different kinds of media? As a starting point, think about the following questions:

- Do you believe that song lyrics that are hostile to women or LGBTQ people affect the way these people are treated in the real world?
- Do you agree with Samuel L. Jackson that today's movies portray minorities more realistically than earlier movies did?
- How do video games typically represent people? Can gamers develop a distorted view of the world as a result of how characters are depicted?
- What do you think of the ways that contestants are represented on reality television shows?

To explore ideas about media representations, pick one type of media and consider how it portrays different people. Then brainstorm a list of thoughts and questions that occur to you. If you pick film, you might want to further develop the ideas from your writing in response to Samuel L. Jackson's "In Character." For example, one student, Susannah, was concerned about the ways that women are depicted in video games. She brainstormed the following:

- As video games become more popular, more people are playing them, including more women. But gaming is often seen as a male hobby, so women can be ignored.
- Women are occasionally strong but often sexualized (Lara Croft), are damsels in distress (Princess Zelda), or are feminine versions of male characters (Ms. Pac-man).
- Anita Sarkeesian is a perfect example. Just by wanting to study the ways that women are portrayed she received a horrifying backlash from the male side of the gaming community.
- Stereotyping of women in games can lead to stereotyping in real life.
- Male representations in video games are also often skewed, but there is still a much wider range of representation.
- "It's just a game": it is not just a game, it is yet another reinforcement of gender stereotypes prevalent across most media.

WRITING ACTIVITY 8 Brainstorm about Stereotypes

Pick a form of media you enjoy (such as a particular TV show, movie, or website) and think about how people are represented in it. Brainstorm your thoughts about how stereotyping might be evident in your chosen medium.

Step 2 Write Your Discovery Draft

At this point, you've gathered ideas for three possible topics for your persuasive essay: media, censorship, and stereotypes. You'll now choose one of these topics and write a discovery draft.

For more on drafting, see pp. 15–19.

Choosing a Topic

You have explored three different topics, but which one should you pick for your discovery draft? When deciding on a topic to write about, keep these three points in mind:

- Choose a topic that you're interested in and that you know something about. Your knowledge can come from your personal experiences, the experiences of others, your reflections and observations, and your reading on the topic.

- Choose a topic that is controversial and about which you have a strong opinion. Keep in mind that your primary purpose is to persuade your readers.
- Choose a topic that you think would interest your audience, which might include readers of your campus or local newspaper.

Consider the writing you completed for Writing Activities 1–8. If the topic of one of these writing exercises meets all three of the criteria listed above, you're in a good position to start drafting. But if you're not completely happy with any of your ideas, consider gathering some more ideas, trying a new topic, or combining related topics for your essay.

For more on thesis statements and narrowing your topic, see pp. 16–18.

Your topic should be narrow enough to be well developed in a short essay. For instance, if you want to write about how types of media have affected our lives, you couldn't cover all the ways that all media have affected us. Instead, select just one type of media and one change.

> ◖ **WRITING ACTIVITY 9** Choose Your Topic ◗

Review the writing you have completed for this chapter so far, as well as the three criteria for a good topic listed above. Then choose or create a topic for your essay and narrow it as necessary. If you wish, you may gather additional ideas before you start drafting.

Sharing Your Ideas

Before writing your discovery draft, write a preliminary thesis statement that identifies the issue you are writing about and expresses your position on it.

As you write, follow your train of thought, even if it means you'll need to revise your thesis statement later on. Keep your audience and purpose in mind, but remember that your main goal at the drafting stage is to get your ideas down on paper. You'll have time later on to revise and edit your draft.

A Student's Discovery Draft

Here's a preliminary thesis statement and discovery draft written by a student, Susannah Goya-Pack, on the issue of the portrayal of women in video games. After reading the draft, discuss with your classmates what Susannah might do to revise it. (Note that the example includes the types of errors that typically appear in a first draft.)

Susannah's preliminary thesis statement.

Picture a video gamer. Although women make up about half of all video gamers, the lack of representative female characters in and about video games is disturbing. Anita Sarkeesian knows about this first-hand. She is a feminist pop culture critic who didn't get a whole lot of attention. When she started a crowdfunding campaign to fund a YouTube series about the portrayal of women in video games, she received a lot of different responses. While many women backed her up, she also had comments from threatened male gamers threatening to kill her or rape her.

So, what is a woman in a video game normally like? In many games, the only way to play the game is as a male. There are a few reoccurring types that female characters in games fall into. You have Princess Peach or Princess Zelda, from the popular Mario and Legend of Zelda games, who are damsels in distress that the male character has to save. On the other hand, you have Lara Croft from Tomb Raider or the host of scantily-clad women in the Mortal Kombat series, who are very sexy and not very realistic.

Male characters in video games are not always true to life, either. Video game men are often very macho and muscular in appearance, and they are aggressive and not very different from each other. Still, a young boy playing a video game can always play as a character he can relate to on that basic level, whereas even some popular games still don't have playable female characters. Even Pokémon, a game often associated with female gamers, didn't add a way to play as a girl until its seventh version. And there are more varied representations of men than women.

Video games are not just hobbies. They are an increasingly important part of our culture. Unless we begin to address the ways women are represented in games, the cycle will continue. Dismissing video games as unimportant is dangerous when more people are growing up with them, and young boys and girls will take what they see in games and internalize it into their view of how men and women behave and appear.

That is how institutional sexism works. It is not as obvious as someone saying "women can't be heroes" or "women need to dress in sexy clothes." It is much more subtle. It is the undercurrent every time a girl picks up a game and realizes that she is the object to be rescued instead of the person saving the world. It is another space where women are expected to look and dress a certain way, in this case in a sexualized way that young girls can't relate to and older women don't want to deal with.

Shigeru Miyamoto, a main Nintendo designer, is at the forefront of a changing video game environment. Nintendo has a few playable female characters in recent games, although their games are often dismissed as softer games and the female characters are somewhat of an afterthought. When New York Times writer Chris Sullentrop asked Miyamoto about why his women need saving, Miyamoto was quoted as saying: "Maybe it's just because I'm a male, I haven't given it a lot of deep thought over the years."

Yes, Mr. Miyamoto. It is because you are a male, and you have not had to think about it. But the fifty percent of gamers who are female have given it a lot of thought, because it is never just a game. It is their lives, being played out in a game and in the world.

> **WRITING ACTIVITY 10 Write Your Discovery Draft**

Using your preliminary thesis statement and the ideas you've gathered on your topic, write a discovery draft. Keep in mind that your purpose is to express and support your opinion. If you're unsure about your topic, consider writing two or three discovery drafts on different topics to see which one will work best for you.

Step 3 Revise Your Draft

For more on revising, see pp. 20–21.

When you revise your draft, use the skills you acquired in the preceding chapters: organize your paragraphs (Chapter 3), strengthen your focus (Chapter 5), outline your plan (Chapter 7), and write an effective introduction and conclusion (Chapter 6). Also, consider conducting primary or secondary research to gather more information about your topic (Chapter 7).

In this chapter, you'll focus on writing a persuasive argument. You'll learn how to develop your ideas with cause-and-effect analysis, make a claim, develop support for that claim, respond to opposing arguments, and organize your points.

Developing Your Ideas with Cause-and-Effect Analysis

For more on cause and effect, see p. 81.

When you use cause-and-effect analysis, you explain the reason that something happened (the cause) or the result of something that happened (the effect). You use cause-and-effect analysis often in your daily life. You might notice that when your tires aren't correctly inflated (cause), your car gets worse gas mileage (effect). After starting to drink high-calorie smoothies every day for breakfast (cause), you discover you've gained a few pounds (effect). With cause-and-effect analysis, you show your readers a logical connection between two or more events.

The writers of the four essays at the beginning of this chapter all use cause-and-effect analysis to develop their arguments. In "An Ugly Toll of Technology: Impatience and Forgetfulness," Tara Parker-Pope uses scientific research to argue how certain types of media can have a negative effect on the way people think. In "Selfie-Loathing," Jessica Winter describes the effects of constantly viewing positive social media posts and photographs. In "What You Aren't Seeing on Social Media," McKenzie Maxson explains the effects that self-censorship has on the lives of people who use social media. Samuel L. Jackson, in "In Character," develops his views about the causes of racism in

Hollywood movies. When you use cause-and-effect analysis to develop your argument, remember that there is a difference between cause and coincidence. To prove that there is a true relationship between events, give evidence—in the form of examples, statistics, or facts—to show how they are related. Draw on your personal experiences and knowledge, and on the experiences and knowledge of people you know. You might also want to include expert testimony to support your points. Consider, for example, how Tara Parker-Pope uses expert testimony to support her point in this paragraph from her essay:

> The problem is similar to an eating disorder, says Dr. Kimberly Young, a professor at St. Bonaventure University in New York who has led research on the addictive nature of online technology. Technology, like food, is an essential part of daily life, and those suffering from disordered online behavior cannot give it up entirely and instead have to learn moderation and controlled use. She suggests therapy to determine the underlying issues that set off a person's need to use the Internet "as a way of escape."

This expert testimony, which compares excessive Internet use with an eating disorder, helps support Parker-Pope's claim that technology is having a negative effect on people's ability to think and function.

HOW TO Use Cause-and-Effect Analysis

- Use cause and effect to show why something happened or what the result was when something happened.
- Show a logical connection between the cause and the effect.
- Use examples, statistics, facts, and expert testimony to support your analysis.

WRITING ACTIVITY 11 Draft Cause-and-Effect Sentences

Write several sentences that contain cause-and-effect analysis for your essay. Refer to these sentences when you revise your draft.

Building Your Essay

To be persuasive, your essay must be well developed. In other words, it must contain supporting details that convince your readers that your position is valid. First, though, you need to make an effective claim.

Make a Claim

A *claim* is a statement asserting that something is true. In persuasive writing, a claim is a type of thesis statement. As you may recall from Chapter 1, the *thesis statement* announces the topic of your essay; shows, explains, or argues a particular point about the topic; and gives readers a sense of what you will discuss in your essay. For an argumentative essay, you announce your topic and the point you will argue. Let's look at each of the qualities of an effective claim in more detail.

Express an Opinion   An effective claim expresses an opinion, not a fact. An *opinion* is an idea that some but not all people share. In contrast, a *fact* is something that can be verified as true by an objective observer.

> FACT   There is a great deal of spam on the Internet.
> OPINION   Because spam wastes people's time and money, it should be better regulated by the government.

The first statement can be verified by turning on a computer. There's no need to prove that it's true. The second statement, however, is a claim because some people will disagree with it. Notice that the claim includes the word *should*. Similar words used in claims include *needs to*, *ought*, and *must*.

Relate to Your Readers   An effective claim also seeks to persuade readers by pointing out how the topic relates to their lives. A claim that conveys only your personal interests, tastes, or experiences is not likely to persuade or interest readers. Rather, connect the claim to some aspect of your readers' lives.

> PERSONAL   Drivers should be able to use cell phones when they drive because I've never been in danger when this has happened.
> PERSUASIVE   Drivers should be able to use cell phones when they drive because researchers have shown that this practice is no more dangerous than any other distraction, such as changing the channel on the radio.

The first statement focuses on the writer. But the second statement relates the topic—drivers' use of cell phones—to a concept relevant to readers' lives.

Narrow the Focus   An effective claim focuses the topic so that it can be fully developed and supported. If your claim isn't sufficiently focused, you won't be able to discuss it in detail in your essay.

> UNFOCUSED   There's too much violence on television.
> FOCUSED   The graphic violence on the television show *The Walking Dead* glamorizes a grisly use of force.

To support the claim made in the first example, you would have to cover all types of violence on all types of television shows—a large topic that would be better suited for a book than an essay. The second claim requires only that you focus on one type of violence (graphic violence) on one television show (*The Walking Dead*). Because it's narrowly focused, this claim could be fully supported in an essay.

In addition, a focused claim does not leave readers with unanswered questions.

UNFOCUSED	Pornography should be banned.
FOCUSED	To prevent the sexual abuse of children, Congress should pass a law banning child pornography on the Internet.

In the first example, readers might ask: What type of pornography? Why should it be banned? How should it be banned? In the second, readers are told the type of pornography, why it should be banned, and how it could be banned (through federal legislation).

HOW TO Make a Claim

- Express an opinion.
- Be persuasive by relating the claim to readers' lives.
- Keep the claim narrowly focused.

WRITING ACTIVITY 12 Revise Your Claim

Revise the claim for your essay so that it expresses an opinion, relates to your readers' lives, and is sufficiently focused.

Provide Pro Points

Once you have an effective claim, you need to concentrate on developing support for that claim—your reasons, or pro points (*pro* means "in favor of"). *Pro points* tell readers why you believe your claim is true or valid. Keep in mind that pro points should always be supported with details (such as examples, facts, and statistics) and that the best supporting material is up-to-date, relevant, and easily understood by readers. A brief argumentative essay will usually need between three and five pro points. You can generate and develop pro points from your experiences, observations, and research.

Pro and con points are usually stated in topic sentences. For more on topic sentences, see pp. 50–53.

Experience   When trying to persuade others, we often look first to our own experiences with the topic. This is what Samuel L. Jackson does when he describes the types of acting roles he was offered early in his career. Suppose, for example, you're writing about a topic that you love—rock music. You've heard all of the criticism of rock music's loud sound, hard beats, rebel poses, and obscene lyrics, but you don't agree and decide to write an essay on why you believe rock lyrics are harmless because listeners tend to focus on the music, not the words. Thus, you have one pro point:

> Because most listeners focus on the music and not the words, obscene lyrics in rock music don't harm listeners.

How would you support this pro point? You could detail your own experiences with rock music. For instance, you could point out that even though you know the lyrics to your favorite song, you don't dwell on them because you are more interested in the music and the overall message of the lyrics.

Observation Personal experiences alone are not enough to support an argument convincingly. In "What You Aren't Seeing on Social Media," McKenzie Maxson begins by describing her own experiences with social media, but she doesn't stop there. She goes on to describe what she has observed about her fellow Northwestern University students as they build their online identities. Your observations of how the issue has affected others can also lead to pro points. Imagine, for instance, that you're arguing against censoring literature in high schools. Books weren't censored in your high school, but your cousin attended a school that banned several classics, including John Steinbeck's *Of Mice and Men* and George Orwell's *1984*. Because your cousin was unable to study these books in school, she was poorly prepared for her college entrance exams. From observing your cousin's experiences, you generate this pro point:

> Censoring important works of literature can limit students' opportunities in higher education.

You can support this point by describing your cousin's experience with censorship. However, what happened to your cousin might not happen to everyone, and unless your cousin is still in high school, her example might not be up to date. Thus, to strengthen your case, you could interview other students about their experiences with censorship or conduct research to collect facts and statistics that support your position.

For more on conducting research and evaluating sources, see Chapters 11 and 12.

Research As we have seen, you will usually want to conduct some research on your topic to strengthen points gathered from your own experiences and observations. To convince readers of the harmful effects of too much access to media, Tara Parker-Pope presented recent scientific research that supported her points. Perhaps you're arguing that cable television companies should fund public-access television because it provides a necessary forum for groups that are misrepresented or ignored by the mainstream media. You could interview producers, question viewers, or look for information about the kinds of programming that are available only on public-access TV. From your research, you might generate the following pro point:

Because commercial television news programs present few positive portrayals of immigrant neighborhoods, cable TV providers should use some of their profits to give community groups access to production equipment and free air time.

To support this pro point, you could provide information about the cable company's budget or describe a public-access show that focuses on a community rarely seen in network news.

HOW TO Support Pro Points

- **Use recent material.** Because you're probably writing about a current issue, be sure to use supporting material that is up to date. By using recent material, you show your readers you're knowledgeable about your topic.
- **Use relevant material.** If your information isn't directly related to your topic, your readers will dismiss or ignore it. For example, if your topic is the portrayal of disabled people in recent movies, don't use examples from 1990s television shows as support.
- **Use understandable material.** You probably know more about your topic than your readers do. You may need to explain the plot of a book, the meaning of a term, or the lyrics of a song to readers who are not familiar with the subject.

GROUP ACTIVITY 5 Evaluate Supporting Material

Working in a group, examine the following claim. Determine whether the supporting material given for it is up to date, relevant, and easily understandable.

CLAIM The current rating system for movies needs to be improved.

1. More and more television shows are showing scenes of graphic violence.
2. Owners of movie theaters are reluctant to enforce the current rating system.
3. In 2001, half of all profitable movies contained sexually oriented material.
4. The profit margin for R-rated movies is almost 21 percent of all movies when aggregated.
5. When I sold movie tickets, I almost never checked people's IDs.
6. Movie producers avoid the R rating by making two versions of the same movie: a mild version for movie theaters and an explicit version for DVD or electronic sales and rental.

> **WRITING ACTIVITY 13** List and Support Your Pro Points

Review the pro points in your discovery draft. Are they sufficient? Are they effectively developed? Draw on your experiences, observations, and research to add additional pro points if you need them, and make sure that each point is supported by recent, relevant, and understandable information.

Respond to Con Points

An argument essay is most persuasive when you anticipate readers' objections and argue against them. Therefore, in addition to presenting pro points, you need to argue against the *con points* (*con* means "against"). To do this, put yourself in the place of the readers who might not agree with your pro points. Con points tell readers why someone might object to your claim, how these objections might be stated, and how you would respond to them.

List Con Points First, you need to identify the most important con points against your claim. To do this, imagine that you disagree with your claim, and then think of reasons you might disagree with it. Suppose this is your claim:

> Companies that send unwanted spam e-mails and pop-up advertisements should be heavily taxed and regulated so that they'll go out of business.

Now imagine that you disagree with this claim—that you think the government should leave these companies alone. Here are two reasons:

> Although these companies are annoying, they still have a right to exist.

> If the government starts regulating these companies, it can start regulating other companies as well, which isn't right in a free-market economy.

These are your con points—the points that someone might make against the claim you are making. List just the most important con points. Depending on your topic, you might end up with two or three con points.

Refute Con Points Examine your list of con points and consider how you would respond to readers' objections. You want to *refute*, or argue against, the con points so that you can persuade readers to accept your claim. First, acknowledge what, if anything, is true about the con point; then, explain what you think is not true about it.

Let's continue the example about spam and pop-up advertisements on the Internet. Here's your first con point:

> Although these companies are annoying, they aren't really harming anyone.

Here's what you can say to *refute*, or argue against, this point:

> At times, annoyances can't be avoided. This is not one of those times. Because the spam and pop-ups are so numerous, individuals and companies have to spend a lot of money and time to get rid of them, which hurts productivity and the economy.

Here's your second con point:

> If the government starts regulating these companies, it can start regulating other companies as well, which isn't right in a free-market economy.

Here's one way to refute this con point:

> Even a free-market economy needs some regulation to protect consumers. By taxing and regulating spam and pop-ups, we can protect consumers, just as we already protect consumers by outlawing false advertisements and regulating drugs.

As these examples show, when you refute your con points, you're actually arguing in support of your pro points.

GROUP ACTIVITY 6 List and Refute Your Con Points

Read your claim aloud to the students in your group. Ask them to disagree with your claim and to explain their reasons. List their responses and use them as the con points for your claim. Refute each con point in writing (you will use them when you revise your draft).

Organize Pro and Con Points

Now that you've developed the ideas in your draft, you're ready to begin organizing those ideas. If you order your pro and con points in a logical way, your readers will become more convinced of your claim as they read your essay.

Order Pro Points   Some of your pro points will be more persuasive than others. Save your most convincing pro point for last so that you leave readers thinking about it. You might begin a paper with the least convincing pro point and build up to the most convincing one. Or you might begin with the second most convincing point, place the less convincing points in the middle, and end with the most convincing one.

Arrange Con Points   Where should you put the con points? You have several options. You may put con points at different spots in an essay, particularly when certain con points are closely connected to certain pro points. This pattern can help make the pro and con points flow smoothly in an essay. You may also begin an essay with the con points. After refuting them, give your pro points. Finally, you may save your con points until the end of the essay, but only do so when you can refute those points well. You don't want readers to finish your essay agreeing with the opposition.

HOW TO Organize Pro and Con Points

Pro points
- Save your most convincing pro point for last.
- OR, begin your essay with the least convincing pro point, and build up to the most convincing point.
- OR, begin with a fairly strong point, put the weaker points in the middle, and end with the strongest point.

Con points
- Connect each con point to its related pro point.
- OR, begin with con points, and then refute them and give pro points.
- OR, save con points for near the end of the essay, and refute them all at one time.

GROUP ACTIVITY 7 Order Pro and Con Points

Review Susannah's discovery draft on pages 288–90. Working in a group, list her pro points, and then create several con points. Put these pro and con points in the order you think is the most effective. Finally, compare your group's ordering of the pro and con points with the order that Susannah uses in her revised draft (pp. 300–302). Notice how Susannah improved her pro and con points in the revised draft.

WRITING ACTIVITY 14 Order Your Pro and Con Points

Think about the pro and con points you can use to develop your discovery draft. List your pro points in the order in which they should appear in your revised draft. Then decide where you can include your con points, and insert them in your list.

Avoid Faulty Logic

Even if your argument is well supported and organized, it won't be persuasive unless it logically makes sense. Your readers will find your ideas worthwhile if you base your points on logical reasoning rather than faulty logic. Let's look at three common forms of faulty logic.

Hasty Generalization   A *hasty generalization* is a conclusion drawn from too little evidence. Suppose, for example, that you discovered a factual error in your local newspaper. Based on that single experience, you conclude your local newspaper is always inaccurate. Your conclusion, based on insufficient evidence (this single occasion), would be a hasty generalization. Just because you discovered one inaccuracy doesn't mean that all of the articles are inaccurate. One instance can't prove a point.

Here's another example: you argue that advertising in public schools has no harmful effects because it didn't harm you as a child. Your conclusion is based on insufficient evidence (only one example). More convincing evidence would include studies conducted to determine the effects of advertising on schoolchildren or surveys of children and teachers.

Either-Or Reasoning   *Either-or reasoning* proposes only two possible alternatives even though more than two options actually exist. For instance, you would use faulty either-or reasoning if you said, "Either I lose ten pounds, or I won't get a date." The reasoning is faulty because more than these two alternatives exist. You might get a date without losing any weight. Or you might lose ten pounds and still not get a date. Or you could lose five pounds and get several dates.

Likewise, a writer who argues "Either we regulate cigarette advertisements, or more and more people will die from lung cancer" is using faulty logic because other alternatives also exist, such as efforts to decrease smoking through public-service announcements and educational programs. Because of these efforts, fewer people might get lung cancer, whether or not cigarette advertising is regulated.

Faulty Cause-and-Effect Reasoning   *Faulty cause-and-effect reasoning* attributes an event to an unrelated cause. Superstitions are based on faulty cause-and-effect reasoning, such as when we blame a bad day on the black cat that crossed our path, the salt we spilled, or the mirror we broke. Logically, these events couldn't have caused the bad day because they were unrelated to what we experienced. Thus, we cannot assume that one event was caused by another event simply because one took place before the other.

Political candidates often use faulty cause-and-effect reasoning: "Since my opponent has been in the Senate, your taxes have increased." However, just because taxes went up after the senator was elected doesn't mean the senator raised the taxes. Perhaps they were increased by the previous Congress. Similarly, an essay writer who argues "Ever since certain types of music have become popular, teenage suicide rates have risen" fails to acknowledge other possible causes for the rise in teenage suicides. Unless the writer provides evidence to support this point, the argument is based on faulty cause-and-effect reasoning.

◖ WRITING ACTIVITY 15 Eliminate Faulty Logic in Your Draft ◗

Exchange your draft with a partner. Ask your partner to point out any hasty generalizations, either-or reasoning, faulty cause-and-effect reasoning, or other logical errors in your draft. Do the same for your partner. Correct any errors in logic that your partner identifies.

A Student's Revised Draft

Student writer Susannah Goya-Pack was relatively happy with her discovery draft about the portrayal of women in video games, but her classmates weren't as persuaded by her argument as she thought they'd be. With their help, she added support for her pro points and identified additional con points that she needed to address. Before you read Susannah's revised draft, reread her discovery draft (pp. 288–90). Notice how her argument is stronger in the revision. (You will also notice some errors in the revised draft; these will be corrected when Susannah edits her essay later on.)

Girls Just Want to Play Games:

Sexism in Video Gaming

Susannah makes her introduction more interesting with this image of a stereotype.

Facts and statistics make Susannah seem knowledgeable.

Susannah makes the claim more specific.

Picture a video gamer. The image you likely create is a boy living with his parents. Yet, according to the 2014 version of the Entertainment Software Association's annual report, women make up 48% of video game players and 50% of purchasers (2–3). Why does the myth of the male gamer persist? Despite women making up half of the video game culture, the representation and treatment of women in games contributes to sexism and negative stereotyping.   1

A strong pro point about the repercussions of challenging the status quo comes first.

Anita Sarkeesian knows about this firsthand. She is a feminist pop culture critic who didn't get a whole lot of attention. When she started a crowdfunding campaign to fund a YouTube series, *Tropes Vs. Women In Video Games*, she received polarized responses. She found some support, but also a staggering number of rape and death threats from male gamers. Angry gamers tried to locate her home, and a video game was created where a player could "beat up" an image of Sarkeesian (Lewis). All she wanted to do was to take a look at women in games.   2

Susannah supports a second pro point with facts, observations, and classification.

There are a few common types of video game women, Princess Peach or Princess Zelda, from the popular *Mario* and *Legend of Zelda* games, are often fit into the "damsel in distress" role, to be saved by a male, though Princess Peach does have a playable role in the *Smash Bros.* games. Lara Croft from *Tomb Raider* or the scantily-clad women in *Mortal Kombat* series are strong but not very realistic. Outliers do exist, like the female Samus from the *Metroid* series, whose gender was not revealed until the end, but even her outfits have gotten progressively more revealing over the years.   3

Some might argue that male characters in video games are not always accurately portrayed, either. Video game men are often macho and muscular in appearance, and they are frequently aggressive and non-emotional. Still, a young boy playing any video game can relate to a character at least on the basis of being male, whereas some popular games still don't have playable female characters. Even *Pokémon*, a game often associated with female gamers, didn't add a way to play as a girl until its seventh version. Also, male characters more often have both functional and stylish appearance options, while female characters are usually stuck with standard issue costumes, like armor that looks sexy but wouldn't save them.

This lack of female characters may be due to the incorrect assumption that women are not a main demographic. Video game creators maintain that their audience is primarily male and that they need to generate profits. In recent years, gamers of all genders have taken to questioning the leaders of the industry about hypersexualized characters, especially in otherwise highly customizable games like Blizzard's popular *World of Warcraft* series. One Blizzard executive, Dustin Browder, issued a thoughtful response regarding criticism about the representation of women in his games: "It takes work to make compelling characters, but it's important to take a step back to ensure that we're not alienating our players." This response is a great indicator of positive change in an industry that is only gaining in popularity. Video games are not just hobbies or a fringe interest. They are an increasingly important part of our culture. Unless we begin to address the ways women are represented in games, the cycle will continue. Dismissing video games as unimportant is dangerous when more people are growing up with them, and young boys and girls will take what they see in games and internalize it into their view of how men and women behave and appear. That is how institutional sexism works. It is not as obvious as someone saying "Women can't be heroes," or "Women need to dress in sexy clothes." It is much more subtle. It is the undercurrent every time a girl picks up a game and realizes that she is the object to be rescued instead of the person saving the world. It is another space where women are expected to look and dress a certain way, in this case in a sexualized way that young girls can't relate to and older women don't want to deal with.

4 A con point comes next.

Susannah refutes the con point.

5

Susannah introduces another con point.

Susannah uses cause and effect.

Susannah refutes the con point with expert testimony that suggests that there has been a shift in attitudes.

Susannah introduces another pro point.

The final pro point drives home the point.

Shigeru Miyamoto, a main Nintendo designer, is at the forefront of this changing environment, and Nintendo now has a few playable female characters in games. When a *New York Times* writer asked Miyamoto about why his women so often need saving, Miyamoto replied: "Maybe it's just because I'm a male, I haven't given it a lot of deep thought over the years" (Sullentrop). Although the industry is changing, Miryamoto's statement shows that men may still need to give more thought to how women are portrayed in videogames.

6

Susannah's conclusion restates the claim and issues a call for action.

The fifty percent of gamers who are female have given it a lot of thought, because it is never just a game. It is their lives, being played not in a series of platforms on a console, but in the real world, because the problems that women face in the virtual world are similar to those faced in day to day life: unfair expectations about appearance, being pigeonholed into certain kinds of work, or having trouble with their voices being heard. Games have more options than ever, but there is still much work to be done, and what has been accomplished is due to much pressure and persuasion. If game executives like Dustin Browder and players like Anita Sarkeesian work towards a better gaming culture, hopefully that can better our real culture, and we can address unfair expectations for men and women on-screen and off.

7

Works Cited

Browder, Dustin. "On Character Design." *Battle.net*. Blizzard
    Entertainment, Inc., 23 Nov. 2013. Web. 02 Oct. 2014.

Entertainment Software Association. *2014 Essential Facts About
    the Computer and Video Game Industry* . . . /AppData/Local
    /Microsoft/Windows/Temporary Internet Files/Content
    .Outlook/GW6OEEG4/ESA Entertainment Software Association,
    Apr. 2014.

Lewis, Helen. "Game Theory: Making Room for the Women."
    ArtsBeat Game Theory Making Room for the Women Comments.
    New York Times. New York Times, 25 Dec. 2012. Web. 02 Oct.
    2014.

Sullentrop, Chris. "In the Footsteps of Lara Croft." *New York Times*
    163 56351 (2013): 9. *Academic Search Complete*. Web. 06 Nov.
    2014.

GROUP ACTIVITY 8 Analyze Susannah's Revised Draft

Use the following questions to discuss with your classmates how Susannah has improved her draft.

1. Is Susannah's claim more effective now? Why or why not?
2. How has Susannah improved her pro points?
3. How well has she refuted her con points?
4. In your view, how well does she organize her pro and con points?
5. How well did she avoid faulty logic?
6. How could Susannah's draft benefit from further revision?

Peer Review for an Essay That Argues a Position

Form a group with two or three other students and exchange copies of your drafts. Read your draft aloud while your classmates follow along. Take notes on your classmates' responses to the following questions about your draft.

1. What do you like best about my essay?
2. How interesting is my introduction? Do you want to continue reading the essay? Why or why not?
3. How effective is my claim? Suggest an improvement.
4. Do I provide enough pro points to support my thesis? How well do I support my pro points? Is my supporting material recent, relevant, and easily understood?
5. Do I bring up con points? How well do I refute them?
6. Are my pro and con points effectively organized? Can you suggest a better way to order them?
7. Did I avoid faulty logic?
8. Where in the draft does my writing confuse you? How can I clarify my thoughts?
9. How clear is the purpose of my essay?

WRITING ACTIVITY 16 Revise Your Draft

Taking your classmates' suggestions for revision into consideration, revise your essay. Focus on using cause-and-effect analysis, making your claim more specific, supporting your pro points, refuting your con points, organizing these points, and avoiding faulty logic.

Step 4 Edit Your Sentences

At this point, you have worked hard to improve your essay's claim, development, and organization. Now you need to edit it to polish the language and eliminate distracting errors. In this section, you'll focus on combining sentences with introductory phrases and on correcting subject-verb agreement errors.

Combining Sentences Using Introductory Phrases

For more on combining sentences, see Chapter 15 in the Handbook.

As you know from the other Part Two chapters, sentence combining is a good way to connect closely related, short sentences. Sentence combining can make your writing clearer and more interesting.

One way to combine short, closely related sentences is to turn the sentence with the least important information into an introductory phrase for the other. A *phrase* is a group of words that lacks a subject, a verb, or both. It cannot stand alone as a sentence. When you combine sentences with an introductory phrase, begin with the phrase and follow the phrase with a comma.

In Susannah's discovery draft, for example, she wrote two sentences to describe one woman's efforts to address the portrayal of women in video games.

> Anita Sarkeesian knows about this first hand. She is a feminist pop culture critic who didn't get a whole lot of attention.

In her revised draft, she combined these two sentences by using an introductory phrase and eliminating unnecessary words to create a stronger sentence.

> A feminist pop culture critic, Anita Sarkeesian knows about this firsthand.

HOW TO Combine Sentences Using Introductory Phrases

- Combine two short, closely related sentences by turning the sentence with the least important information into a phrase (a group of words that lacks a subject, verb, or both).
- Place the phrase at the beginning of the remaining sentence.
- Use a comma after the introductory phrase.

EDITING ACTIVITY 1 Use Introductory Phrases

Use an introductory phrase to combine the following pairs or groups of sentences. You may need to eliminate unnecessary words, change words, or move words around.

EXAMPLE *Founded in 2001,* Wikipedia is an online, interactive encyclopedia. ~~It was founded in 2001~~.

1. Its founder was Jimmy Wales. He wanted to create an encyclopedia that everyone on the planet could access for free.

2. Anyone can create an entry or edit an entry that already exists. Wikipedia uses software called wiki.

3. Hundreds of thousands of people contribute to Wikipedia. These contributors come from a variety of backgrounds.

4. Some people prefer to correct or change information that is already posted to the site. They don't actually add information.

5. Some researchers have studied the entries in Wikipedia. They have found that it contains more errors than do traditional encyclopedias, such as *Britannica*. Some of these errors are major.

EDITING ACTIVITY 2 Combine Your Sentences

Examine your revised draft for short, closely related sentences. Where it makes sense to do so, combine them with introductory phrases. You may also use any of the other sentence-combining techniques you have learned (coordinating conjunctions, conjunctive adverbs, subordinating conjunctions, or relative clauses) if you wish.

Correcting Subject-Verb Agreement Errors

You may recall that a complete sentence contains a subject and a verb. The subject tells who or what is doing the action, and the verb tells the action or links the subject to the rest of the sentence. The subject and the verb must *agree* in number. In other words, a *singular subject* must have a *singular verb*, and a *plural subject* must have a *plural verb*.

To make sure that your subjects and verbs agree in number, you need to identify the subject of your sentence and know whether it is singular or plural. Problems in subject-verb agreement often happen when the subject and verb of the sentence are not obvious.

For more on subject-verb agreement, see pp. 416–23 in the handbook.

> **INCORRECT** *Harry don't* care for my podcasts.
> **CORRECT** *Harry doesn't* care for my podcasts.

INCORRECT	Talk-show *hosts* on the radio *is* meaner than they were a decade ago.
CORRECT	Talk-show *hosts* on the radio *are* meaner than they were a decade ago.

The following pronouns are all singular. When using any of them as the subject of a sentence, use a singular verb.

anybody	everyone	nothing
anyone	everything	somebody
anything	nobody	someone
everybody	no one	something

INCORRECT	*Anybody write* better than I do.
CORRECT	*Anybody writes* better than I do.

INCORRECT	*Someone need* to take care of this.
CORRECT	*Someone needs* to take care of this.

EDITING ACTIVITY 3 Correct Subject-Verb Agreement

Circle the correct form of the verb in the following sentences.

EXAMPLE Everybody (needs) need) to be considerate of others in public places.

1. The movies I wanted to download (was, were) unavailable.

2. Nobody (feel, feels) the way I do about WiFi hotspots.

3. Of all the bands I listen to, my favorite one (is, are) Red House Painters.

4. Everyone I talk to (agrees, agree) with me on this.

5. The Chicago Bears (doesn't, don't) excite me.

A Student's Edited Essay

You may have noticed that Susannah's revised draft contained a few errors in grammar, spelling, and punctuation. Susannah corrected these errors in her edited essay. Her corrections are noted in the margin.

Goya-Pack 1

Susannah Goya-Pack
Professor Heller
English 1301
2 Mar. 2015

Girls Just Want to Play Games:

Sexism in Video Gaming and How We Can Fix It

Picture a video gamer. The image you likely create is a boy
living with his parents. Yet, according to the 2014 version of
the Entertainment Software Association's annual report, women
make up 48% of video game players and 50% of purchasers
(Entertainment Software Association 2–3). Why does the myth
of the male gamer persist? Despite women making up half of the
video game culture, the representation and treatment of women
in games contribute to sexism and negative stereotyping.

A feminist pop culture critic, Anita Sarkeesian knows about
this firsthand. When she started a crowdfunding campaign to
fund a YouTube series, *Tropes Vs. Women In Video Games*, she
received polarized responses. She found some support, but also
a staggering number of rape and death threats from male gamers.
Angry gamers tried to locate her home, and a video game was
created where a player could "beat up" an image of Sarkeesian
(Lewis). All she wanted was to take a look at women in games.

There are a few common types of video game women: Princess
Peach or Princess Zelda, from the popular *Mario Bros.* and the
Legend of Zelda games, are often fit into the "damsel in distress"
role, to be saved by a male, though Princess Peach does have a
playable role in the *Super Smash Bros.* games. Lara Croft from *Tomb
Raider* or the scantily-clad women in the *Mortal Kombat* series are
strong but not very realistic. Outliers do exist, like the female
Samus from the *Metroid* series, whose gender was not revealed
until the end, but even her outfits have gotten progressively more
revealing over the years.

Some might argue that male characters in video games are
not always accurately portrayed, either. Video game men are
often macho and muscular in appearance, and they are frequently
aggressive and non-emotional. Still, a young boy playing any video

1

2

3

4

The correct MLA format
is used.

A subject-verb agreement
problem is corrected.

Short sentences are
combined using an
introductory phrase.

A comma splice is corrected.

Goya-Pack 2

game can relate to a character at least on the basis of being male, whereas some popular games still don't have playable female characters. Even *Pokémon*, a game often associated with female gamers, didn't add a way to play as a girl until its seventh version. Also, male characters more often have both functional and stylish appearance options, while female characters are usually stuck with standard issue costumes, like armor that looks sexy but wouldn't save them.

This lack of female characters may be due to the incorrect assumption that women are not a main demographic. Video game creators maintained that their audience is primarily male and that they need to generate profits. In recent years, gamers of all genders have taken to questioning the leaders of the industry about hypersexualized characters, especially in otherwise highly customizable games like Blizzard's popular *World of Warcraft* series. One Blizzard executive, Dustin Browder, issued a thoughtful response regarding criticism about the representation of women in his games that called for immediate action: "It takes work to make compelling characters, but it's important to take a step back to ensure that we're not alienating our players." This response is a great indicator of positive change in an industry that is only gaining in popularity.

5

Video games are not just hobbies or a fringe interest; they are an increasingly important part of our culture. Unless we begin to address the ways women are represented in games, the cycle will continue. Dismissing video games as unimportant is dangerous when more people are growing up with them, and young boys and girls will take what they see in games and internalize it into their view of how men and women behave and appear. That is how institutional sexism works. It is not as obvious as someone saying "Women can't be heroes," or "Women need to dress in sexy clothes." It is much more subtle. It is the undercurrent every time a girl picks up a game and realizes that she is the object to be rescued instead of the person saving the world. It is another space where women are expected to look and dress a certain way, in this case in a sexualized way.

6

Two short sentences are combined with a semi-colon, and a new paragraph indicates a transition to a new point.

Hasty generalization about young girls and older women is removed.

Goya-Pack 3

Shigeru Miyamoto, a main Nintendo designer, is at the   7
forefront of this changing environment, and Nintendo even has a
few playable female characters in recent games. Even so, when a
New York Times writer asked Miyamoto about why his women so
often need saving, Miyamoto replied: "Maybe it's just because I'm
a male, I haven't given it a lot of deep thought over the years"
(Sullentrop).

The fifty percent of gamers who are female have given it a lot   8
of thought, because it is never just a game. It is their lives, being
played not in a series of platforms on a console, but in the real
world, because the problems that women face in the virtual world
are similar to those faced in day to day life: unfair expectations
about appearance, being pigeonholed into certain kinds of work,
or having trouble with their voices being heard. Games have
more options than ever, but there is still much work to be done,
and what has been accomplished is due to much pressure and
persuasion. If game executives like Dustin Browder and players like
Anita Sarkeesian work towards a better gaming culture, hopefully
that can better our real culture, and we can address unfair
expectations for men and women on-screen and off.

Works Cited

Browder, Dustin. "On Character Design." *Battle.net*. Blizzard
    Entertainment, Inc., 23 Nov. 2013. Web. 02 Oct. 2014.

Entertainment Software Association. *2014 Essential Facts About
    the Computer and Video Game Industry*. /AppData/Local
    /Microsoft/Windows/Temporary Internet Files/Content.
    Outlook/GW6OEEG4/ESA Entertainment Software Association,
    Apr. 2014. PDF file.

Lewis, Helen. "Game Theory: Making Room for the Women."
    ArtsBeat Game Theory Making Room for the Women
    Comments. *New York Times*. New York Times, 25 Dec. 2012.
    Web. 02 Oct. 2014.

Sullentrop, Chris. "In the Footsteps of Lara Croft." *New York Times*
    163 56351 (2013): 9. *Academic Search Complete*. Web. 06 Nov.
    2014.

Step 5 Share Your Essay

Now that you have gathered ideas on your topic and drafted, revised, and edited your essay, you're ready to share your essay. Interested readers might include friends and family members, but to reach a broader audience, consider submitting your essay to your campus or local newspaper. If your essay is about something that most college students are interested in, such as censoring campus speakers or privacy issues with social media sites, your campus newspaper might be most appropriate. If your topic is about something with a broader appeal, such as controversial websites or the effects of too much technology on the brain, your local newspaper might be best. By submitting your essay for publication, you can reach a wide audience and influence more people.

To submit your essay to a newspaper, first find out the newspaper's policy about submissions from the public. Most newspapers explain this policy somewhere on their editorial or opinion pages, where opinion pieces from the public are usually published. Typically an e-mail address is provided so that you can submit your essay electronically.

As an alternative to trying to get your entire essay published in a newspaper, you can shorten it to a paragraph or two and submit it as a letter to the editor. Most newspapers publish several letters from the public every day, so the chances of getting published are typically good. If you choose this method of sharing, limit your essay to your claim and several of your pro points. You can usually find directions for submitting a letter to the editor on the same pages that these letters are published.

By reaching out to a wider audience, such as the readers of a campus or local newspaper, you will be able to influence more people—which is what writing is all about.

 Respond to a post

Many local newspapers and television stations have Facebook and Twitter sites on which people can post responses and ideas. If one of your local news organizations has a story on your topic, consider sending an online response. These sites allow only brief comments, so you'll be limited to stating a main idea. However, this is another way to share your viewpoint with a broad audience.

CHAPTER CHECKLIST

❏ I read essays that argued about the media, censorship, and stereotypes to explore and learn about this chapter's theme.

❏ I used cause-and-effect analysis, as well as other methods of development, to support my ideas.

❏ I wrote an effective claim that expresses an opinion, relates to my readers' lives, and is focused.

❏ I used pro points—which came from experiences, observations, and research—to support my claim.

❏ I supported pro points with material that is recent, relevant, and easily understood.

❏ I argued against con points, or objections, to my claim.

❏ I arranged pro and con points so that readers become more convinced of my claim as they read through my essay.

❏ I avoided faulty logic when arguing my points.

❏ I combined short, closely related sentences using introductory phrases or other techniques to improve my flow of ideas.

❏ I edited my draft to correct errors, including problems with subject-verb agreement.

❏ I submitted my essay to my campus or local newspaper—or to another print or online publication.

REFLECTING ON YOUR WRITING

To help you reflect on the writing you did in this chapter, answer the following questions:

1. How did you decide on your topic for this essay?

2. Which pro point do you think is your strongest?

3. How persuasive do you think your essay would be to someone who strongly disagrees with your claim?

4. How did you feel submitting your essay to your campus or local newspaper?

5. If you had more time, what more would you do to improve your essay before sharing it with readers?

Visit **LaunchPad Solo for Readers and Writers** > **Writing Process** for more tutorials, videos, and practice developing your essay with each step.

After you answer these questions, freewrite about what you learned in this chapter.

"If you make the choice to go vegan, you can take a big step toward improving the environment."

ANDREA BENITEZ, "WHY GO VEGAN?"

10

Proposing a Solution
Health, Education, and Environment

At the center of any argument is an *issue*—a question or topic on which people disagree. Because some issues—such as those involving health, education, or the environment—affect many people, we often read or hear about them in the media. What is the best way to promote a healthy lifestyle for college students? How can eating disorders be prevented? How can college be made more affordable? Is online learning as effective as face-to-face learning? What steps should be taken to deal with climate change? Politicians, columnists, and talk-show hosts argue with one another and their audiences every day about problems and how to solve them.

People often argue about important issues because they want to make a difference. Writing is an especially effective way to accomplish this goal. You can help solve a problem by writing an essay that states your position on an issue, provides evidence that a problem exists, and proposes a solution. This chapter will show you how to write an argument that can convince your readers to take action on something that is important to you.

You will begin by reading essays by professional writers that propose solutions to problems of importance to them. You will also follow a student, Andrea Benitez, as she

In this chapter, you will identify a health, education, or environmental problem that is important to you and propose a solution for it. As you follow the steps of the writing process, you will

- Explore the chapter topic by reading essays that propose a solution.
- Gather ideas by relating aloud, consulting with others, and researching your topic.
- Practice adding outside sources to your essay.
- Develop your ideas using **argumentative** techniques.
- Use appeals and a reasonable tone to help persuade your readers.
- Combine sentences using appositives.
- Practice correcting shifts in person.
- Send your essay to someone with the authority to act on your proposal.

writes about veganism and its impact on the environment. You will then write about an issue of importance to you and send your essay to someone in authority who can act on your proposal. ■

📷 **GETTING STARTED** Think about Problems and Solutions

As you can see, the woman in the photograph on page 312 appears to be happy while she holds up a bag of fruits and vegetables. Are healthy eaters happier than people who don't eat healthily? What are some stereotypes of healthy eaters, such as their age, socioeconomic class, and appearance? In your view, how accurate are these stereotypes? Think of some other topics related to health, education, and our environment and compare your ideas with your classmates'.

Read to Write   Reading Essays That Propose a Solution to a Problem

Writing an argument that identifies an issue and proposes a solution requires all of your writing skills. You must identify a problem, use evidence to illustrate the problem, investigate what has worked and not worked to solve the problem, propose a solution, and then convince your readers that your proposal will work.

As you read the following four argument essays, jot down the evidence that the authors present to convince you that the problems exist. Do these authors convince you that these problems are real and that their solutions are workable? Can you think of other possible solutions to these problems?

Notice how the authors use their own ideas but also use outside sources to provide additional information and strengthen their arguments. An outside source is an expert on a particular topic. You may have the opportunity to personally interview an outside source, but you usually learn by reading what the source has to say in a book, magazine, newspaper, print or online journal, or website.

A Health Problem: An Annotated Reading

LOUISE ARONSON
The Future of Robot Caregivers

Louise Aronson is both a doctor and a writer. She received her medical degree from Harvard Medical School, is an associate professor of geriatrics at the University of California, San Francisco, and works at San Francisco General Hospital. She focuses on training health professionals to care for older adults. Her fiction has appeared in both medical and literary journals. Her book, *A History of the Present Illness*, published in 2014, takes readers into the nursing homes, hospitals, and neighborhoods of San Francisco. The selection included here was originally published in the *New York Times*.

Each time I make a house call, I stay much longer than I should. I can't leave because my patient is holding my hand, or because she's telling me, not for the first time, about when Aunt Mabel cut off all her hair and they called her a boy at school, or how her daddy lost his job and the lights went out and her mother lit pine cones and danced and made everyone laugh. Sometimes I can't leave because she just has to show me one thing, but getting to that thing requires that she rise unsteadily from her chair, negotiate her walker through the narrow hallway, and find whatever it is in the dim light of her bedroom.

I can, and do, write prescriptions for her many medical problems, but I have little to offer for the two conditions that dominate her days: loneliness and disability. She has a well-meaning, troubled daughter in a faraway state, a caregiver who comes twice a week, a friend who checks in on her periodically, and she gets regular calls from volunteers with the Friendship Line.

It's not enough. Like most older adults, she doesn't want to be "locked up in one of those homes." What she needs is someone who is always there, who can help with everyday tasks, who will listen and smile.

What she needs is a robot caregiver.

That may sound like an oxymoron. In an ideal world, it would be: Each of us would have at least one kind and fully capable human caregiver to meet our physical and emotional needs as we age. But most of us do not live in an ideal world, and a reliable robot may be better than an unreliable or abusive person, or than no one at all.

Caregiving is hard work. More often than not, it is tedious, awkwardly intimate and physically and emotionally exhausting. Sometimes it is dangerous or disgusting. Almost always it is 24/7 and unpaid or low wage, and has profound adverse health consequences for those who do it. It is women's work and immigrants' work, and it is work that many people either can't or simply won't do.

Many countries have acknowledged this reality by investing in robot development. Last year in Japan, where robots are considered "iyashi," or healing, the health ministry began a program designed to meet work-force shortages and help prevent injuries by promoting nursing-care robots that assist with lifting and moving patients. A consortium of European companies, universities and research institutions collaborated on Mobiserv, a project that developed a touch-screen-toting, humanoid-looking "social companion" robot that offers reminders about appointments and medications and encourages social activity, healthy eating and exercise. In Sweden, researchers have developed GiraffPlus, a robot that looks like a standing mirror cum vacuum cleaner, monitors health metrics like blood pressure and has a screen for virtual doctor and family visits.

Researchers in the United States are developing robot-caregiver prototypes as well, but we have been slower to move in this direction. Already, we have robots to assist in surgery and very basic "walking" robots that deliver medications and

1   Aronson captures readers' attention and appeals to readers' sympathy in the opening of her essay by telling the story of one of her homebound patients.

2   Aronson shows that she is a concerned doctor, which makes her essay more persuasive.

     Aronson summarizes the problem: there are not enough caregivers to provide proper medical care to older adults.

3

4   Aronson provides her solution to the problem.

5

     Aronson expects her readers to be surprised by her solution, so she repeats it.

6   Here, Aronson explains why there are not enough caregivers.

7

     In this paragraph, Aronson shows that she is knowledgeable about her solution: other countries have successfully used robots to help patients.

8   Aronson explains that the medical community has been slow to use robots. She acknowledges that many people will disagree with her.

other supplies in hospitals. Robots are increasingly used in rehabilitation after debilitating events like strokes. But a robot that cleans out your arteries or carries linens isn't the same as a robot meant to be your friend and caregiver. Even within the medical community, this idea that machines could help fulfill more than just physical needs meets largely with skepticism, and occasionally with outrage.

As Jerald Winakur, a San Antonio internist and geriatrician, put it, "Just because we digitally savvy parents toss an iPad at our kids to keep them busy and out of our hair, is this the example we want to set when we, ourselves, need care and kindness?" 9

And yet, search YouTube and you can watch developmentally delayed children doing therapy with a cute blue-and-yellow CosmoBot that also collects information about their performance. Or you can see older Japanese people with dementia smiling and chatting happily with a robot named Paro that looks like a baby seal and responds to human speech. Sherry Turkle, an M.I.T. professor and technology skeptic, questions such artificial emotional relationships in her book *Alone Together: Why We Expect More from Technology and Less from Each Other*. Yet after watching a 72-year-old woman named Miriam interact with Paro, she noted that the woman "found comfort when she confided in her Paro. Paro took care of Miriam's desire to tell her a story" (9). 10

One proof of the social and emotional potential of robot caregivers is probably right in front of you. If you have walked down any street recently, or sat in a restaurant, or entered a workplace, you've probably seen numerous people oblivious to the humans with or around them, while fully engaged with the machines in their hands or on their desks. Admittedly, such people are often interacting with other humans via their machines, but the fact remains that the primary interaction is between person and machine, and despite compelling protests that such interactions do not constitute meaningful, empathic relationships, they seem to provide stimulation and satisfaction to millions, if not billions, of us. Maybe you are one of those people, reading this article on a device. 11

But the biggest argument for robot caregivers is that we need them. We do not have anywhere near enough human caregivers for the growing number of older Americans. Robots could help solve this work-force crisis by strategically supplementing human care. Equally important, robots could decrease high rates of neglect and abuse of older adults by assisting overwhelmed human caregivers and replacing those who are guilty of intentional negligence or mistreatment. 12

In the next decade, robot caregiver prototypes will become much more sophisticated. According to Jim Osborn, the executive director of the Quality of Life Technology Center at Carnegie Mellon, the current limitation is not the technology, but finding a viable business model to make it affordable. He said, "I really expect there will be a robot helping me out when I retire. I just hope I don't have to use all my retirement savings to pay for it." 13

In that new world, my lonely, disabled patient's life would be improved by a robot caregiver. 14

Imagine this: Since the robot caregiver wouldn't require sleep, it would always be alert and available in case of crisis. While my patient slept, the robot could do laundry and other household tasks. When she woke, the robot could greet her 15

Margin notes:

Aronson quotes an expert who points out that people can be comforted by a robot.

In this paragraph, Aronson acknowledges that people using electronic devices are interacting with other people. She argues against this opposing point by saying that the primary interaction is still between people and their machines.

Aronson gives two more arguments in favor of robot caregivers: they supplement human care and help prevent abuse.

Aronson refers to another expert to support her point with evidence.

Aronson appeals to the readers' emotions by referring back to the story of the frail woman from the beginning of the essay.

with a kind, humanlike voice, help her get out of bed safely and make sure she was clean after she used the toilet. It—she? he?—would ensure that my patient took the right medications in the right doses. At breakfast, the robot could chat with her about the weather or news.

And then, because my patient loves to read but her eyesight is failing, the 16 caregiver robot would offer to read to her. Or maybe it would provide her with a large-print electronic display of a book, the lighting just right for her weakened eyes. After a while the robot would say, "I wonder whether we should take a break from reading now and get you dressed. Your daughter's coming to visit today."

Are there ethical issues we will need to address? Of course. But I can also 17 imagine my patient's smile when the robot says these words, and I suspect she doesn't smile much in her current situation, when she's home alone, hour after hour and day after day.

Aronson admits that her solution is not perfect, but she then reinforces her point that robots can help people.

Works Cited

Osborn, Jim. Personal Interview. 19 July 2014.

Turkle, Sherry. *Alone Together: Why We Expect More from Technology and Less from Each Other.* New York: Basic Books, 2011. Print.

Winakur, Jerald. Personal Interview. 19 July 2014.

READING ACTIVITY 1 Build Your Vocabulary

Determine the meanings of the following words from the context of Louise Aronson's essay. Then check their meanings by looking up the words in a dictionary: *oxymoron* (5), *tedious* (6), *adverse* (6), *prototypes* (8), *debilitating* (8), *geriatrician* (9), *oblivious* (11), *viable* (13).

GROUP ACTIVITY 1 Discuss the Reading

Discuss the following questions about "The Future of Robot Caregivers" with your classmates.

1. According to Aronson, why will robots help solve the problem of the lack of good caregivers for older adults?

2. Why are some people skeptical of this idea? How does Aronson respond to their skepticism?

3. Why does Aronson compare interacting with robots to interacting with electronic devices? How effective is this comparison?

4. Do you find Aronson's solution achievable? Why or why not?

WRITING ACTIVITY 1 Share Your Ideas

Write a paragraph or two about a health problem that interests you. First, describe the problem, provide evidence that the problem exists, and then propose a solution. Where might you find outside sources to support your position? Share what you have written with your classmates.

A Health Problem

SALLY SATEL
How E-cigarettes Could Save Lives

Psychiatrist and author Sally Satel is a lecturer at the Yale University School of Medicine and a resident scholar at the American Enterprise Institute. She focuses on mental health policy and political trends in medicine. She has published a number of articles in prominent newspapers, magazines, and journals. Her 2013 book, *Brainwashed: The Seductive Appeal of Mindless Neuroscience*, co-authored with Scott Lilienfeld, was a finalist for the *Los Angeles Times* Book Prize in Science. "How E-cigarettes Could Save Lives" was published in the *Washington Post* in 2014.

1   Should electronic cigarettes be regulated like tobacco products, emblazoned with warnings and subject to tight marketing restrictions? Those are among the questions before the Food and Drug Administration as it decides in the coming weeks how to handle the battery-powered cigarette mimics that have become a $1.5 billion business in the United States.

2   Groups promoting intensive regulation include the American Lung Association and the Campaign for Tobacco-Free Kids. They worry that the health risks haven't been fully established and that e-cigarettes will make smoking commonplace again, especially among teens. They are quick to push back in response to anything that might make e-cigarettes more attractive, such as the NJOY King ad that aired during the Super Bowl or when actors Leonardo DiCaprio and Julia Louis-Dreyfus were shown "vaping" at the Golden Globes.

3   A surgeon general's report released last month, on the 50th anniversary of the office's first warning about the dangers of smoking, had little to say about e-cigarettes. Its suggestions for further reducing tobacco use were familiar, including: increase taxes on cigarettes, prohibit indoor smoking, launch media campaigns and reduce the nicotine content of cigarettes (Lushniak).

4   E-cigarettes, however, could be what we need to knock the U.S. smoking rate from a stubborn 18 percent to the government's goal of 12 percent by 2020. We should not only tolerate them but encourage their use.

5   Although critics stress the need for more research, we can say with high confidence that e-cigarettes are far safer than smoking. No tobacco leaves are combusted, so they don't release the tars and gases that lead to cancer and other smoking-related diseases. Instead, a heating element converts a liquid solution into an aerosol that users exhale as a white plume.

6   The solution comes in varying concentrations of nicotine—from high (36 mg per milliliter of liquid) to zero ("Choosing")—to help people wean themselves off cigarettes, as well as e-cigarettes, and the addictive stimulant in them. But even if people continue using electronic cigarettes with some nicotine, regular exposure has generally benign effects in healthy people, and the FDA has approved the extended use of nicotine gums, patches and lozenges.

The other main ingredients in e-cigarettes are propylene glycol and glycerin. 7
These are generally regarded as harmless—they're found in toothpaste, hand
sanitizer, asthma inhalers, and many other FDA-approved foods, cosmetics and
pharmaceuticals. There are also traces of nitrosamines, known carcinogens, but
they are present at levels comparable to the patch and at far lower concentrations than in regular cigarettes—500- to 1,400-fold lower. Cadmium, lead and
nickel may be there, too, but in amounts and forms considered nontoxic.

"Few, if any, chemicals at levels detected in electronic cigarettes raise serious 8
health concerns," a 2011 study in the *Journal of Health Policy* determined. "A
preponderance of the available evidence shows [e-cigarettes] to be much safer
than tobacco cigarettes and comparable in toxicity to conventional nicotine
replacement products" (Cahn and Siegal 18).

The potential for e-cigarettes to help people quit smoking is encouraging. 9
Yet so far there has been little research on their effectiveness. A study published
in the *Lancet* in November concluded that e-cigarettes, with or without nicotine,
were as effective as nicotine patches for helping smokers quit (Bullen et al.).
Granted, patches have had a disappointing record in helping people stay off cigarettes for more than a few months. But there are reasons to think that e-cigarettes
would be even more effective outside the laboratory.

Participants in the *Lancet* study were randomly assigned to nicotine 10
e-cigarettes, patches or placebo e-cigarettes. In the real world, of course, people
get to choose. And e-cigarettes have several advantages over patches and gums.
For one, they provide a quicker fix, because the pulmonary route is the fastest
practical way to deliver nicotine to the brain. They also offer visual, tactile and
gestural similarities to traditional cigarettes.

Reporter Megan McArdle tested the comparison for a *Bloomberg Business-* 11
week article this month: "After I'd put it together, I had something surprisingly
close to one of the cigarettes I used to smoke. The mentholated tobacco flavor
rolled sinuously over my tongue, hit the back of my throat in an unctuously familiar cloud, and rushed through my capillaries, buzzing along my dormant nicotine
receptors. The only thing missing was the unpleasant clawing feeling in my chest
as my lungs begged me not to pollute them with tar and soot."

This is where anti-smoking advocates get worried about e-cigarettes being 12
too attractive and encouraging people—especially young people—to become
addicted to nicotine and, in some cases, to progress to smoking. The Centers for
Disease Control and Prevention stoked concerns with data released in September
showing that 1.78 million middle and high school students had tried e-cigarettes
and that one in five middle school students who reported trying them said they
hadn't tried traditional cigarettes. "This raises concern that there may be young
people for whom e-cigarettes could be an entry point to use of conventional
tobacco products, including cigarettes," the CDC concluded ("E-cigarette Use").

According to that same CDC study, however, an extremely small percentage 13
of teenagers use e-cigarettes regularly—only 2.8 percent of high school students
reported using one in the previous 30 days in 2012. And while that number is
rising—it was 1.5 percent in 2011—teenage cigarette smoking rates are at
record lows ("E-cigarette Use"). That might suggest that increased exposure to

e-cigarettes isn't encouraging more people to smoke. But the numbers are so small that it's too early to make definitive claims about the relationship between teen vaping and smoking.

Yes, we still need research on the long-term health and behavioral impacts of 14 e-cigarettes. Brad Rodu, a pathologist at the University of Louisville, offers an apt analogy between electronic cigarettes and cellphones. When cellphones became popular in the late '90s, there were no data on their long-term safety. As it turns out, the risk of a brain tumor with prolonged cellphone use is not zero, but it is very small and of uncertain health significance.

In the case of e-cigarettes, Rodu says that "at least a decade of continued 15 use by thousands of users would need to transpire before confident assessments could be conducted." Were the FDA to ban e-cigarette marketing until then, the promise of vaping would be put on hold. Meanwhile, millions of smokers who might otherwise switch would keep buying tobacco products. "We can't say that decades of e-cigarette use will be perfectly safe," Rodu told me, "but for cigarette users, we are sure that smoke is thousands of times worse."

The FDA should call for reliable, informative labeling and safe manufactur- 16 ing standards for e-cigarettes. It should also allay concerns about potential gateway use and youth addiction to nicotine by banning the marketing and sale of e-cigarettes to minors. It should not be heavy handed in restricting marketing and sales to adults.

Instead, promoting electronic cigarettes to smokers should be a public health 17 priority. Given that the direct medical costs of smoking are estimated to be more than $130 billion per year, along with $150 billion annually in productivity losses from premature deaths, getting more smokers to switch would result in significant cost savings—as well as almost half a million lives saved each year.

We should make e-cigarettes accessible to smokers by eschewing hefty taxes, 18 if we tax them at all, and offering free samples and starter kits. Those kits, which contain a battery, a charger and nicotine-liquid cartridges, typically run between $30 and $90. To reduce the hurdle to initiation, any payer of smoking-related costs—health insurers, Veterans Affairs medical centers, companies that offer smoking-cessation programs for their employees, Medicare, Medicaid—should make the starter kits available gratis. Users should have to pay for their own replacement cartridges, but those are much cheaper than cigarette packs.

Also, we should allow and welcome public vaping in adult environments 19 such as bars, restaurants and workplaces. Vapers would serve as visual prompts for smokers to ask about vaping and, ideally, ditch traditional cigarettes and take up electronic ones instead.

It may be hard for anti-smoking activists to feel at ease with e-cigarettes in 20 light of their view that traditional cigarette makers have long downplayed the health dangers of their product. This perception has generated distrust of anything remotely resembling the act of smoking. It doesn't help that major tobacco companies are now investing in e-cigarettes.

But if we embrace electronic cigarettes as a way for smokers to either kick 21 their nicotine addictions or, at least, obtain nicotine in a safer way, they could help instigate the wave of smoking cessation that anti-smoking activists—and all of us—are hoping for.

Works Cited

Bullen, Christopher, et al. "Electronic Cigarettes for Smoking Cessation: A Randomised Controlled Trial." *The Lancet,* 16 Nov. 2013: 1629–37. Web. 14 Feb. 2014.

Cahn, Zachary, and Michael Siegal. "Electronic Cigarettes as a Harm Reduction Strategy for Tobacco Control: A Step Forward or a Repeat of Past Mistakes?" *Journal of Public Health Policy* 32.1 (2011): 16–31. Print.

"Choosing Nicotine Strength." Vapor4Life. n.d. Web. 14 Feb. 2014.

"E-cigarette Use More Than Doubles Among U.S. Middle and High School Students from 2011–2012." CDC Newsroom Press Release. Centers for Disease Control and Prevention, 5 Sept. 2013. Web. 14 Feb. 2014.

Lushniak, Boris D. *The Health Consequences of Smoking—50 Years of Progress: A Report of the Surgeon General.* Atlanta, GA: U.S. Department of Health and Human Services, Office on Smoking and Health, 2014. Web. 14 Feb. 2014.

McArdle, Megan. "E-cigarettes: A $1.5 Billion Industry Braces for FDA Regulation." *Bloomberg Businessweek*, 6 Feb. 2014, n. pag. Web. 14 Feb. 2014.

Rodu, Brad. Personal Interview. 14 Feb. 2014.

READING ACTIVITY 2 Build Your Vocabulary

Determine the meanings of the following words from the context of "How E-cigarettes Could Save Lives." Then check their meanings by looking up the words in a dictionary: *mimics* (1), *combusted* (5), *carcinogens* (7), *placebo* (10), *tactile* (10), *gestural* (10), *transpire* (15), *allay* (16), *eschewing* (18), *gratis* (18).

GROUP ACTIVITY 2 Discuss the Reading

Discuss the following questions about "How E-cigarettes Could Save Lives" with your classmates.

1. According to Satel, how can e-cigarettes save lives?

2. Some experts are against promoting e-cigarettes. What are their objections to e-cigarettes, and how well does Satel respond to their objections?

3. Throughout her essay, Satel refers to research studies on e-cigarettes. Which studies do you think were most persuasive, and which were least persuasive? Why?

4. This essay was published in the *Washington Post.* If it appeared in your school newspaper, how persuasive would it be? How could it be revised to make it more appealing to an audience of college students?

> **WRITING ACTIVITY 2** Share Your Ideas

Write a paragraph or two about an unhealthy habit, such as smoking, relying too much on energy drinks, eating or drinking too much, or sleeping too little. First, describe the problem created by this unhealthy habit and then propose a solution. Where might you find outside sources to support your position? Share what you have written with your classmates.

An Education Problem

MARY SHERRY
In Praise of the F Word

Mary Sherry graduated from Dominican University with a degree in English and has published a number of articles on a range of topics. She worked for over twenty years teaching creative and remedial writing to adults. In the following essay, "In Praise of the F Word," first published in *Newsweek*, she identifies the problem of high school graduates who are poorly prepared for work or higher education. She suggests that the threat of failure can be a valuable way to teach students that they must take responsibility for their own learning.

Tens of thousands of 18-year-olds will graduate this year and be handed meaningless diplomas. These diplomas won't look any different from those awarded their luckier classmates. Their validity will be questioned only when their employers discover that these graduates are semiliterate. 1

Eventually a fortunate few will find their way into educational-repair shops — adult-literacy programs, such as the one where I teach basic grammar and writing. There, high-school graduates and high-school dropouts pursuing graduate-equivalency certificates will learn the skills they should have learned in school. They will also discover they have been cheated by our educational system. 2

As I teach, I learn a lot about our schools. Early in each session I ask my students to write about an unpleasant experience they had in school. No writers' block here! "I wish someone would have made me stop doing drugs and made me study." "I liked to party and no one seemed to care." "I was a good kid and didn't cause any trouble, so they just passed me along even though I didn't read well and couldn't write." And so on. 3

I am your basic do-gooder, and prior to teaching this class I blamed the poor academic skills our kids have today on drugs, divorce, and other impediments to concentration necessary for doing well in school. But, as I rediscover each time I walk into the classroom, before a teacher can expect students to concentrate, he has to get their attention, no matter what distractions may be at hand. There are many ways to do this, and they have much to do with teaching style. However, if style alone won't do it, there is another way to show who holds the winning hand in the classroom. That is to reveal the trump card of failure. 4

I will never forget a teacher who played that card to get the attention of one   5
of my children. Our youngest, a world-class charmer, did little to develop his intellectual talents but always got by. Until Mrs. Stifter.

Our son was a high-school senior when he had her for English. "He sits in   6
the back of the room talking to his friends," she told me. "Why don't you move
him to the front row?" I urged, believing the embarrassment would get him to
settle down. Mrs. Stifter looked at me steely-eyed over her glasses. "I don't move
seniors," she said. "I flunk them." I was flustered. Our son's academic life flashed
before my eyes. No teacher had ever threatened him with that before. I regained
my composure and managed to say that I thought she was right. By the time I
got home I was feeling pretty good about this. It was a radical approach for these
times, but, well, why not? "She's going to flunk you," I told my son. I did not
discuss it any further. Suddenly English became a priority in his life. He finished
out the semester with an A.

I know one example doesn't make a case, but at night I see a parade of   7
students who are angry and resentful for having been passed along until they
could no longer even pretend to keep up. Of average intelligence or better, they
eventually quit school, concluding they were too dumb to finish. "I should have
been held back" is a comment I hear frequently. Even sadder are those students
who are high-school graduates who say to me after a few weeks of class, "I don't
know how I ever got a high-school diploma."

Passing students who have not mastered the work cheats them and the   8
employers who expect graduates to have basic skills. We excuse this dishonest
behavior by saying kids can't learn if they come from terrible environments. No
one seems to stop to think that—no matter what environments they come
from—most kids don't put school first on their list unless they perceive something is at stake. They'd rather be sailing.

Many students I see at night could give expert testimony on unemployment,   9
chemical dependency, abusive relationships. In spite of these difficulties, they
have decided to make education a priority. They are motivated by the desire for
a better job or the need to hang on to the one they've got. They have a healthy
fear of failure.

People of all ages can rise above their problems, but they need to have a   10
reason to do so. Young people generally don't have the maturity to value education in the same way my adult students value it. But fear of failure, whether
economic or academic, can motivate both.

Flunking as a regular policy has just as much merit today as it did two gen-   11
erations ago. We must review the threat of flunking and see it as it really is—a
positive teaching tool. It is an expression of confidence by both teachers and
parents that the students have the ability to learn the material presented to them.
However, making it work again would take a dedicated, caring conspiracy between
teachers and parents. It would mean facing the tough reality that passing kids
who haven't learned the material—while it might save them grief for the short
term—dooms them to long-term illiteracy. It would mean that teachers would
have to follow through on their threats, and parents would have to stand behind

them, knowing their children's best interests are indeed at stake. This means no more doing Scott's assignments for him because he might fail. No more passing Jodi because she's such a nice kid.

This is a policy that worked in the past and can work today. A wise teacher, 12 with the support of his parents, gave our son the opportunity to succeed—or fail. It's time we return this choice to all students.

READING ACTIVITY 3 Build Your Vocabulary

Determine the meanings of the following words from the context of Mary Sherry's essay. Then check their meanings by looking up the words in a dictionary: *validity* (1), *semiliterate* (1), *impediments* (4), *trump card* (4), *flustered* (6), *composure* (6), *illiteracy* (11).

GROUP ACTIVITY 3 Discuss the Reading

Discuss the following questions about "In Praise of the F Word" with your classmates.

1. What problem does Sherry identify, and what is her solution?
2. What evidence of the problem does the author provide? Is this sufficient? Why or why not?
3. The author refers to her own experience as a teacher and a parent. Why does she do this, and does it make her essay stronger or weaker? Why?
4. Unlike the other essays in this chapter, this piece does not include any outside research. What kind of researched information might make this essay stronger?

WRITING ACTIVITY 3 Share Your Ideas

Write a paragraph or two on an education problem. Has this problem affected you personally? Why or why not? Share your proposed solution to this problem with your classmates. What research can you do to support your position that this solution is workable?

An Environmental Problem

TARA HAELLE
Childhood Obesity Is a Product of Environment

Tara Haelle is a journalist who specializes in health and science reporting. Her articles have appeared in *Slate*, the *Washington Post*, *HealthDay*, and *Wired*, among other publications. In addition to being a journalist, she is a photographer, blogger, and journalism professor. "Childhood Obesity Is a Product of Environment" was published in 2013 in *Scientific American*.

New evidence is confirming that the environment kids live in has a greater   1
impact than factors such as genetics, insufficient physical activity or other elements in efforts to control child obesity. Three new studies, published in the April
8 *Pediatrics*, land on the import of the "nurture" side of the equation and focus
on specific circumstances in children's or teen's lives that potentially contribute to
unhealthy bulk.

In three decades child and adolescent obesity has tripled in the U.S., and   2
estimates from 2010 classify more than a third of children and teens as overweight or obese. Obesity puts these kids at higher risk for type 2 diabetes, car-
diovascular disease, sleep apnea, and bone or joint problems ("Childhood Obesity
Facts"). The variables responsible are thought to range from too little exercise to
too many soft drinks. Now it seems that blaming Pepsi or too little PE might
neglect the bigger picture.

"We are raising our children in a world that is vastly different than it was 40   3
or 50 years ago," says Yoni Freedhoff, an obesity doctor and assistant professor
of medicine at the University of Ottawa. "Childhood obesity is a disease of the
environment. It's a natural consequence of normal kids with normal genes being
raised in unhealthy, abnormal environments." The environmental factors in these
studies range from the seemingly minor, such as kids' plate sizes, to bigger challenges, such as school schedules that may keep teens from getting sufficient
sleep. But they are part of an even longer list: the ubiquity of fast food, changes
in technology, fewer home-cooked meals, more food advertising, an explosion of
low-cost processed foods and increasing sugary drink serving sizes as well as easy
access to unhealthy snacks in vending machines, at sports games and in nearly
every setting children inhabit—these are just a handful of environmental factors
research has linked to increasing obesity, and researchers are starting to pick
apart which among them play bigger or lesser roles in making kids supersized.

Size matters in "obesogenic environments."

In one of the three new studies dishware size made a big difference.   4
Researchers studied 42 second-graders in which the children alternately used
child-size 18.4-centimeter (7.25-inch) diameter plates with 237-milliliter (8-ounce)
bowls or adult-size 26-centimeter (10.25-inch) diameter plates with 473-milliliter
(16-ounce) bowls. Doubling the size of the dishware, the researchers found,
increased the amount of food kids served themselves in a buffet-style lunch line
by an average of 90 calories. They ate about 43 percent of those extra calories,
on average (DiSantis et al.).

Although kids can typically adjust their energy intake by regulating their   5
food, Temple University public health professor Jennifer Fisher says, their surroundings and options may change that equation for kids in the same way that it does
in adults. "This notion that children are immune to the environment is somewhat
misguided," says Fisher, who headed up the study. "To promote self-regulation,

you have to constrain the environment in a way that makes the healthy choice the easy choice."

Fisher says much recent research in nutrition has focused on the "obeso- 6 genic" environments of today's society: a dietary environment offering widespread access to highly palatable foods in large portion sizes. "If we look at adult studies on dieting and weight loss, we know that the prospect of maintaining self-control in this environment is fairly grim," Fisher says. "I think most scientists believe our bodies have evolved to pretty staunchly defend hunger and prevent weight loss, and maybe are not so sensitive in preventing overconsumption."

Link between obesity and screen time.

Overconsumption might be a key component in the link between obesity 7 and screen time, too, according to another of the new studies. Although past research already had linked increased TV time to widening waistlines, this study dug deeper. Ninety-one 13- to 15-year-olds filled out diaries for TV, video games and computer use during a one-week period. About four to seven times a day the teens were paged to record what they were paying the most attention to at that particular moment, followed by activities receiving their second- and third-most attention (Bickham et al.). "Kids live in a multitasking world," says Harvard Medical School pediatrics professor David Bickham, lead author of the screen-time study. "We're trying to assess their technology use when they're using different forms of technology at once."

Bickham says three theories have been floated for the link between screen 8 time and obesity: food advertising, unconscious eating and displacement—that is, the idea that the media use replaces physical activity. His team's findings lent more support to the first two variables and less to the third. They found video games and computer use had no impact on BMI (body mass index). Television did, but only if it was the main event. Background TV, for example, didn't matter.

"We're saying the level of attention may make a difference," Bickham says. 9 "You have to pay attention to advertising for it to have the impact, and [food] advertising is much less common in computers and video games. In terms of unconscious eating, when you're watching TV, your hands are free and you're stimulating your senses with the TV, so concurrent eating is more likely to happen." Previous research has found support for both these theories, such as a study earlier this year showing that neighborhoods with more food and soft drink outdoor advertising had higher rates of obesity (Harris, Bargh, and Brownell). Freedhoff adds that even viewing commercials for fruits and vegetables has been shown to increase consumption of unhealthy foods. "Our hunger hormones have been honed after millions of years of dietary insecurity, so when we want to eat, we tend not to crave green leafy salads," he says.

Less physical activity is not the problem.

The screen-time study did find that kids engaged in more physical activity 10 had lower BMIs, but that does not mean that more exercise is keeping those teens lighter, Freedhoff says. "What we've seen for so many years is research looking at physical activity as the preventative or the curative solution for childhood obesity, but the data on physical activity as a means to set children's weight is abysmal," he says. "What this study confirmed is that screen time increases obesity consequent to calorie intake, not to a lack of physical activity. That's a crucial message that people don't understand—obesity is not a disease of inactivity."

The third new study, looking at the link between sleep duration and obe- 11 sity in teens, further blunts the idea that physical activity accounts for much of the increase in kids' weight. Researchers tracked nearly 1,400 teenagers from ninth through 12th grade and found, like past studies, that less sleep translates to higher BMIs. By analyzing BMI distribution rather than using cutoff points, University of Pennsylvania postdoctoral fellow Jonathan Mitchell says his team detected much stronger sleep effects among already obese teens. The effect of each additional hour of sleep among teens in the 90th BMI percentile was twice as big as among those in the 10th percentile. Increasing sleep from 7.5 to 10 hours a day among 18-year-olds could shave four percentage points off the proportion of teens with a BMI over 25, the researchers predicted (Mitchell et al.).

They also looked at the teens' physical activity levels. "If you're sleeping less, 12 you're fatigued during the day and less likely to be active," Mitchell says. "But the link we observed was not fully explained by lower levels of physical activity." Another possibility is that being awake longer means more opportunities to eat, but Mitchell's team did not look at dietary intake. Past research has also found that sleep deprivation might alter the body's regulation of hormones leptin and ghrelin, which control satiety and hunger (Knutson). Or, the problem may not be the total caloric intake but the timing of eating, Mitchell says. He noted mice studies where the nocturnal critters became obese if they ate during day and night but remained a normal weight if they only ate at night.

Regardless of the mechanism, these findings also support the notion that 13 the entirety of kids' 21st-century environment—not their self-control or reduced physical activity—is the key culprit in the rise in obesity. "People like to make obesity a disease of blame, but the last 40 years has not seen an epidemic of our children losing willpower," Freedhoff says. "There are dozens and dozens of these environmental factors. Unless we reengineer our children's environments, we are not likely to see any changes in children's weights."

Freedhoff points to cities such as Philadelphia and New York, where modify- 14 ing children's environments, especially in schools, may be responsible for recent reductions in obesity. Philadelphia removed sugary drinks from vending machines in 2004, then reduced snack food serving sizes, removed deep fryers from school cafeterias and replaced whole milk options with 1 percent and skim. Outside of school, more than 600 corner stores participate in the Food Trust initiative to stock their shelves with healthier snacks (Tavernise). New York has instituted new nutrition standards in schools and daycare centers, as well as screen-time limits in day cares. The two metropolises also have some of the most comprehensive menu labeling laws in the country ("Declining").

"This is a lot more complicated than 'eat less, exercise more,'" Freedhoff 15 says. "If weight management or childhood obesity prevention and treatment were intuitive, we'd have a lot of skinny kids running around." Freedhoff himself is developing a program for families that focuses on "redrafting" kids' and families' environments, starting with more home cooking. "Every parent would die for their child, but most won't cook for their children on a consistent basis with whole ingredients," he says.

But Freedhoff also says the problem of increasing childhood obesity cannot 16 be tackled by parents alone. He suggests starting with changes within school boards, sports teams, PTAs and others who already care about kids. "What I'm amazed by is the constant use of fast food to pacify children and reward children — there is no event too small for candy or fast food." There are many places communities could start: making school lunches healthier, ditching vending machines and access to fast food inside schools, not celebrating sports wins at fast food joints, and ending the use of candy or fast food as rewards, such as "pizza days" and other unhealthy food-themed school events, to name a few. "People don't appreciate that parents are around children a minority of their days," he says, so it really will take a village to turn back the clock in terms of kids' environments. "If we had a time machine, it would be the world's best weight-loss program," Freedhoff says. "It's the world that has changed, not people."

Works Cited

Bickham, David. S. Personal Interview. 9 Apr. 2013.

Bickham, David S., et al. "Characteristics of Screen Media Use Associated with Higher BMI in Young Adolescents." *Pediatrics* 131.5 (2013), n. pag. Abstract. Web. 9 Apr. 2013.

"Childhood Obesity Facts." *Nutrition, Physical Activity, & Obesity.* Centers for Disease Control and Prevention, Apr. 2013, n. pag. Web. 9 Apr. 2013.

"Declining Childhood Obesity Rates: Where Are We Seeing the Most Progress?" *Health Policy Snapshot.* Robert Wood Johnson Foundation, Sept. 2012, n. pag. Web. 8 Apr. 2013.

DiSantis, Katie Isselman, et al. "Plate Size and Children's Appetite: Effects of Larger Dishware on Self-Served Portions and Intake." *Pediatrics* 131.5 (2013), n. pag. Abstract. Web. 9 Apr. 2013.

Fisher, Jennifer. Personal Interview. 9 Apr. 2013.

Freedhoff, Yoni. Personal Interview. 7 Apr. 2013.

Harris, Jennifer L., John A. Bargh, and Kelly D. Brownell. "Priming Effects of Television Food Advertising on Eating Behavior." *Health Psychology* 28.4 (2009): 404–13. Print.

Knutson, Kristen L. "Does Inadequate Sleep Play a Role in Vulnerability to Obesity?" *American Journal of Human Biology* 20.4 (2012): 361–71. Web. 8 Apr. 2013.

Mitchell, Jonathon A. Personal Interview. 9 Apr. 2013.

Mitchell, Jonathon A., et al. "Sleep Duration and Adolescent Obesity." *Pediatrics* 131.5 (2013), n. pag. Abstract. Web. 9 Apr. 2013.

Tavernise, Sabrina. "Obesity in Young Is Seen as Falling in Several Cities." *New York Times.* New York Times, 10 Dec. 2012. Web. 9 Apr. 2013.

READING ACTIVITY 4 Build Your Vocabulary

Determine the meanings of the following words from the context of Tara Haelle's essay. Then check their meanings by looking up the words in a dictionary: *genetics* (1), *obese* (2), *overconsumption* (6), *honed* (9), *abysmal* (10), *deprivation* (12), *satiety* (12), *pacify* (16).

GROUP ACTIVITY 4 Discuss the Reading

Discuss the following questions about "Childhood Obesity Is a Product of Environment" with your classmates.

1. According to Haelle, what are some things that do *not* cause children to be obese?

2. According to the research that she describes, what are several environmental causes for childhood obesity? Do you find this research and evidence reliable and convincing?

3. What solutions does Haelle recommend for improving children's environments? How practical are these solutions?

4. If you were to recommend to Haelle how she might improve her essay, what would you say?

WRITING ACTIVITY 4 Share Your Ideas

Write a paragraph or two on an environmental problem you have identified. What research might you do to find evidence that this is a problem? What solution would you propose? Share your writing with your classmates.

Writing Your Essay A Step-by-Step Guide

Now that you've read some essays proposing a solution to a health, education, or environmental problem, it's time to write your own essay. First, read the following writing assignment. Then, use the step-by-step advice that follows to discover ideas, develop them as you draft, and polish your writing into a finished essay that readers will find both interesting and persuasive:

Step 1   Explore Your Choices 330
Step 2   Write Your Discovery Draft 336
Step 3   Revise Your Draft 339
Step 4   Edit Your Sentences 348
Step 5   Share Your Essay 355

Writing Assignment

Think about the issues of health, education, and the environment. Is there a problem you often complain about or feel strongly about? Now is your chance to do something about it. By writing about a problem and suggesting a possible solution, you are both getting involved in important issues and honing your argument skills. In this chapter, you will select a problem, give your position on it, provide evidence that the problem exists, and propose a workable solution. You (or your instructor) may decide to do this assignment in one of several ways:

- Write about a health problem of particular importance to you.
- Write about an education problem that affects you or a person or group you care about.
- Write about an environmental problem that you both know and care about.

Step 1 Explore Your Choices

The radical civil rights activist Eldridge Cleaver once said, "You're either part of the solution, or you're part of the problem." You can, in fact, be part of the solution by writing a persuasive essay about an issue that is important to you.

To do this, start by identifying a problem and gathering evidence that supports a workable solution. If you want your essay to make a difference, you must be careful to choose a position that you can argue with some authority, both by drawing on your own knowledge and by doing some research to learn more about it. But if you think you don't know enough about any problems to write an effective essay, don't worry. You will evaluate your audience, your purpose, and at least three potential topics before you settle on a problem and a solution to write about.

Analyzing Your Audience and Purpose

For more on audience and purpose, see pp. 6–8.

If you take the time to write about an important problem, you want someone to read your essay and do something about it. For example, if you choose a health problem, such as the need for a student health center on your campus, your audience might include a dean or the school's president. Similarly, for an education problem, such as the federal government's proposed cuts in financial-aid benefits to students, your audience could include your congressional representative and possibly even the president of the United States. For an environmental problem, such as the need to stop a local factory from polluting the air, your audience might include the factory owner, local government officials, or the state governor.

Because you're trying to convince at least one of your readers to act on your suggestions, your purpose is primarily persuasive. You'll want to appear well informed, respectful, and fairly formal. You'll also need to consider how readers might disagree with you and what information you should gather to help convince them to change their minds.

 WRITING ACTIVITY 5 **Analyze Your Audience and Purpose**

Your responses to the following questions will help you decide how to approach this chapter's assignment. Be sure to come back to these questions after you have chosen a topic.

1. Why does this assignment call for primarily persuasive writing?

2. What is the average age of your audience?

3. What is your audience's average educational level? Economic level? Political orientation: conservative, moderate, or liberal? What other characteristics of your audience might be appropriate to consider?

4. How might your responses to the previous three questions affect how you write your essay?

Gathering Ideas

Before you decide which issue you want to write about, explore your choices by gathering ideas for at least one subject in three categories: health, education, and the environment. Even if you think you already know which problem you would like to write about, it's always a good idea to explore a few topics to be sure you have chosen the best one. To gather possible topics, you may use any of the techniques you learned in Chapter 1. The student writers in this chapter gather ideas by relating aloud, consulting with others, and researching.

For more on gathering ideas, see pp. 11–15.

Relating Aloud about a Health Problem

Relating aloud means discussing your subject with others who might be able to give you additional insights into the problem or provide alternative solutions for you to consider. As you talk with others about your subject, you'll discover new ideas and gather additional evidence. Based on their responses, you'll also be able to determine if others are interested in this problem and if they think your solution is workable.

Here's how one student, Bruce, related his ideas about a health problem to his peer response group:

My biggest concern is how the health-care system seems to ignore unwed mothers. Did you know that in this state if a teenage girl becomes pregnant, she can't receive health care for her baby unless she moves out of her parents' home? Because of this law, teenage girls from poor families are forced to leave home and try to make it on their own. They not only have a rough time making it alone, but they also lose the emotional support of their family when they need it most. I would like to see this law changed.

Bruce's topic idea prompted several reactions from his classmates. One student, for example, said she had never heard of this law and couldn't believe it was true. Another student argued that free health care is available from private charities and asked why taxpayers should have to pay for it. A third student wondered if the law was intended to discourage teenage girls from becoming pregnant. In response to his group members' questions about his topic, Bruce admitted that he didn't know the answers and needed to do some additional research on his issue:

> I don't think we want to encourage teenagers to have babies, but if they do, I think they should be able to remain with their families and still receive health benefits. I'll need to find more about why the health-care system is set up this way and how it could be changed without costing taxpayers more money. I'm sure the idea is to save money, but I'm not sure how this works. I think I'll go to the government health-care website for more information. Then I'll rethink my position.

 Create a video

Ask someone to record you relating aloud about a health problem (or other issue). Upload the video to an online space and ask your group members to respond. Use their questions and comments to add details to your essay.

 GROUP ACTIVITY 5 **Relate Aloud about a Health Problem**

Relate your ideas about a health problem aloud to the members of your peer response group. You could talk about a health problem you wrote about in response to "The Future of Robot Caregivers" or "How E-cigarettes Could Save Lives," or you could choose another topic. You or another classmate should take notes on (or audio-record) group members' responses to your description of the problem and your proposed solution. Respond to questions about your topic as best you can. Then use the group's suggestions to gather additional ideas about your topic.

Consulting with Others about an Education Problem

Think about some of the problems affecting students on your campus or in your community. What could be done to improve education or campus life? Perhaps you would like to see more courses offered in photography or more school spirit among students. Maybe you want the state to fund a new medical research lab at your college or the federal government to increase financial aid benefits.

Even if you have a problem in mind, you may not yet be sure what kinds of solutions are possible. To unearth ideas you may not even know you have, try consulting with others. As you know from Chapter 1, *consulting with others* involves talking with people who can provide you with valuable insights into your topic. Consulting with others is a way of researching your topic and then using the information you gather to help you develop your essay. In the area of education, for example, there may be fellow students who are experiencing the problem or experts who have researched the problem and its possible solutions. If you find yourself staring at a blank page without any idea of how to begin, consult with others to stimulate your thinking. For example, if you are writing on the need for more federal financial aid, you might interview the director of financial aid on your campus to find out more about the problem and to explore possible solutions. Before you conduct an interview, though, be sure that you have answered the following questions for yourself:

1. What is the problem I am interested in?
2. What do I already know about it?
3. What more do I need to know about the problem?
4. What do I think should be done?
5. Who has the power to act on my proposed solution?

Li, a student writer concerned about the computer lab on his campus, answered these questions before interviewing the vice president of academic affairs. Here's what Li wrote:

> I am concerned about the computer lab on campus. It does not serve the needs of students. Even though we pay a $150 user fee each semester, we don't get good service. I spend most of my spare time at the lab. I don't own a computer and must use the lab to complete assignments. I really hate the computer lab it's so frustrating. The hardware is outdated. The software selection is inadequate. It's so dark in there. And it's always crowded. Long lines of people waiting for their turn. And there are definitely not enough computers! The students who work there are not very helpful. They ignore you and spend all their time on their own homework. Nice job if you can get it! I wonder if other students are as annoyed as I am.

Li decided to ask the vice president of academic affairs the following questions:

1. Why hasn't the college administration made any attempt to improve the computer lab?
2. How expensive would new computer equipment be?
3. Shouldn't part of the computer fee students pay each semester be used to update the computer lab on a regular basis?

4. What does the fee now pay for?

5. Why hasn't the university done anything about the old equipment?

6. Do you agree that it's a problem?

7. Do you agree that it's important to solve the problem?

8. What is the solution?

⟨ **WRITING ACTIVITY 6** Consult about an Education Problem ⟩

For more on conducting an interview, see pp. 364–65.

Choose an education problem that concerns and interests you. It might be a problem specific to your school, an issue that affects college students all over the country, or perhaps a problem that involves grade school children or high school students. Or you could choose the problem you wrote about in response to "In Praise of the F Word." Set aside ten or fifteen minutes to write your ideas on your topic. You may use the preceding questions as a starting point. Then generate a list of questions you might use to interview someone about the problem and its possible solutions.

Researching an Environmental Problem

Blogs, websites, magazines, newspapers, and television all include pieces on environmental issues, such as recycling programs, low-emission vehicles, and the destruction of the rain forests. You have probably noticed more local problems as well. Perhaps your neighbors insist on burning their leaves every fall. Maybe a local factory's wastewater leaks into the river, or nearby cities are taking water needed to irrigate farms in your county.

Sometimes writers think they know the solution to an environmental problem but can't provide evidence that the problem exists or that a solution is workable. Researching the issue can provide a lot of valuable information for an essay. Be sure to check your sources for reliability and relevance. For example, a respected newspaper is likely to be more reliable than a Twitter post by a celebrity. For more information about conducting research, refer to Chapters 11 and 12.

For help evaluating online sources, see Chapter 12, pp. 376–77.

Reliable Sources A reliable source should present accurate information. Library reference materials are screened for accuracy, so they are usually reliable. Most students today, however, look for outside sources on the web. Anyone can post information to the web, so be sure that what you read was posted by an author you trust, in a well-known source, such as a national magazine, a newspaper, an educational institution, or a government agency. You can follow the links provided on the site to learn more about the author and the organization sponsoring the information.

The authors of the readings at the beginning of this chapter used reliable sources, such as magazines (*Bloomberg Businessweek*), journals (*Pediatrics*, the *Lancet*), and reputable websites sponsored by the Centers for Disease Control and Prevention, the Food and Drug Administration, and the Surgeon General. They also used information provided by professors and researchers at colleges and universities.

Relevant Sources   A relevant source should provide current information on your specific topic. To find relevant sources, use a keyword search to be sure the books and articles you find will be useful to you. Then look to see when the information was posted. It is usually best to avoid sources that are more than five years old, and you should resist the temptation to include material just because it was easy to find or interesting to read. To be relevant, it must relate to your specific topic for this essay.

For more information on how to conduct a keyword search, see p. 368.

For more information about finding and evaluating sources, see Chapters 11 and 12.

If you look at the Works Cited of the readings at the beginning of this chapter, you'll see that the authors used recent newspaper and journal articles, mostly from the year in which they published their own article.

Use the following questions to evaluate the sources you find:

1. Do most of the sources support or oppose your solution to the problem?

2. Are these articles from reliable sources?

3. Is the information relevant to your specific topic?

4. Is the information current?

5. What supporting details do the authors use to convince readers that they are knowledgeable about the topic?

6. Can you add additional details to these arguments?

7. Do the authors propose any worthwhile solutions?

Andrea, a student interested in writing about veganism, hoped to persuade fellow students to share her view that going vegan could help protect the environment. To learn more about the issue, Andrea researched her topic by first visiting her campus library to discuss her topic with a reference librarian. The librarian gave her suggestions for reliable print and web sources she might use. Her statement of her topic and her answers to the preceding questions follow:

Preliminary thesis statement: By becoming a vegan and not eating or wearing animal products, you can really help the environment.

1. There are plenty of websites that explain how to go vegan. Most of the online articles I've read support the idea that veganism not only helps improve your health, but it also improves the environment.

2. I have to be careful because some of these websites really promote veganism, so they might not be completely objective. I'll go to their home pages to read more about the organization, and I'll pay attention to the tone of the website to be sure that they are providing reliable information.

3. It's pretty easy to find information on how veganism helps the environment; what will be difficult is to decide which information to include in my essay.

4. I'm going to limit myself to articles posted within the last five years, except that I will use *The Vegan Sourcebook* published in 1998 because it has some excellent basic definitions of veganism. I feel certain that I'm getting the latest information on veganism.

5. Most authors use statistics to support the view that veganism is helping the environment. Readers always respond well to facts and statistics, so I'll be sure to include some of these in my essay.

6. I can cite several specific examples of how veganism helps the environment.

7. One solution to the problem of how to protect the environment is to go vegan.

 WRITING ACTIVITY 7 Research an Environmental Problem

For more on conducting research, see Chapter 11.

Identify an environmental problem that you might want to write about. If you like, you can expand on what you wrote about an environmental problem in response to "Childhood Obesity Is a Product of Environment." Or you can choose another topic. Locate at least three sources on your topic and read them carefully for ideas and supporting evidence. Use the questions on page 335 to evaluate the sources.

Step 2 Write Your Discovery Draft

For more on drafting, see pp. 15–19.

You have explored at least three possible topics for your argument essay. It's time now to choose one health, education, or environmental issue and prepare a discovery draft that explains a problem and proposes your solution. The purpose of this draft is to discover what you have to say, so focus on organizing what you already know by trying to put it on paper. Remember that you will have the opportunity to revise later.

Choosing a Topic

As you get ready to write your discovery draft, choose a topic that concerns you, that you know something about, and that your readers can take action on if you convince them to accept your position. Start by reviewing your materials from the gathering-ideas step. Which topic—health, education, or the environment—generated the most ideas for you? If you find that you feel strongly about one of the topics, it's probably a good pick for your discovery draft. On the other hand, if you're not excited about any of the topics you've explored so far, go back and use your favorite idea-gathering technique to try out some other possibilities.

Once you have a topic that interests you, make sure it is narrow enough to handle in a short essay. You would not be able to address world hunger, the cost of a college education, or climate change thoroughly in one essay, but you could focus on one specific aspect of any of those problems. To write about the cost of college, for example, you could narrow the topic to a proposed tuition hike at your school and explain why and how the administration might avoid the increase.

▰ WRITING ACTIVITY 8 Choose Your Topic

Review your responses to Writing Activities 1 through 7, and decide which of the issues you explored (health, education, or the environment) is most important to you and would be most interesting to your readers. Be careful to select a problem for which you can propose a solution and for which you'll be able to do some research. If necessary, narrow your topic to something that can be fully addressed in the assigned length of your essay.

Sharing Your Ideas

Before you begin drafting, write a preliminary thesis statement that identifies a problem and proposes a solution. A working thesis statement will help keep you focused as you draft, but remember that you might change your mind about your topic as you write about it. You can always revise your thesis statement later on.

For more on thesis statements, see p. 18.

Feel free to use material you've already gathered as part of your discovery draft. If you related your issue aloud to your classmates, for example, you might want to refer to your notes as you write. If you consulted with others, be sure to include some of what you learned. Using a few direct quotes from the people you interviewed will make your essay more interesting to read. Similarly, if you conducted other research on your topic during the gathering-ideas step, you might want to include these outside sources in your draft.

As you draft, remember to incorporate your outside sources into your essay by quoting directly, paraphrasing, or summarizing what you heard or read. Notice how the authors of the readings at the beginning of the chapter integrate their outside materials. In her article, Tara Haelle *quotes* an obesity doctor by putting the doctor's exact words in quotation marks.

> "We are raising our children in a world that is vastly different than it was 40 or 50 years ago," says Yoni Freedhoff, an obesity doctor and assistant professor of medicine at the University of Ottawa.

Later in her article Haelle *paraphrases* from another research article when she proposes some solutions to childhood obesity. Notice how a paraphrase doesn't include quotation marks because the author is not quoting exactly what another person said but rephrasing the idea in different words.

> Outside of school, more than 600 corner stores participate in the Food Trust initiative to stock their shelves with healthier snacks (Tavernise).

Sally Satel, in her article on e-cigarettes, *summarizes* research on how helpful e-cigarettes are in helping people to stop smoking:

The potential for e-cigarettes to help people quit smoking is encouraging. Yet so far there has been little research on their effectiveness. A study published in the *Lancet* in November concluded that e-cigarettes, with or without nicotine, were as effective as nicotine patches for helping smokers quit (Bullen et al.).

As these authors do, be sure to give credit to your sources both in your essay and in a Works Cited page at the end. If you use someone else's ideas without giving them credit, you have committed *plagiarism*, even if it wasn't your intention.

By citing your sources, you let your readers know which ideas you learned from your research and which are original. You'll notice that the authors of the readings at the beginning of the chapter cite a lot of sources to strengthen their arguments. They know that these outside sources make their writing more interesting and convincing.

Although you may be incorporating sources at this stage, you may also choose to focus more on using sources to support your argument when you revise your draft. While writing your discovery draft, your main goal is to get your ideas down on paper while also keeping your audience and purpose in mind.

Quoting, paraphrasing, and documenting information is essential. Otherwise, you could be accused of plagiarism. For more help, see pp. 384–90.

To learn how to cite your sources in an essay and in a Works Cited page, see pp. 390–93.

A Student's Discovery Draft

Here's a discovery draft written by Andrea Benitez, the student whose writing about veganism you read earlier. You will notice that Andrea used some outside sources in her discovery draft. She will add more when she revises her essay. (Note, too, that Andrea's writing includes the types of errors that typically appear in a first draft.)

Most of us are not born vegan, so why should you go vegan? People often become vegans because they are concerned about the way society treats animals. Others don't want to eat meat or dairy products for health reasons. But the biggest reason to go vegan and not eat or wear animal products is to help our environment. According to Dr. Pamela Wood, professor in our university's Department of Public Health Science, "If you make the choice to go vegan, you can take a big step toward improving the environment. You do this by not consuming animal products such as meat, fish, dairy, or eggs, and not wearing animal products such as fur or leather." What really makes me angry, though, is that many people think veganism is a big joke. What gives with this attitude?

Not only does eating meat use many resources, but it also uses them very inefficiently. Livestock animals do not produce as many calories as they consume, making them a very inefficient way to get food. To produce an equivalent amount of vegetables and meat, the meat takes ten times as much

Andrea's preliminary thesis statement

land as the vegetables (Bittman). Its not just livestock on land—fishermen must throw away on average a third of what they catch.

Many assume it is very difficult to take on a vegan lifestyle because everything contains some kind of animal product. But then some crazy people think that any diet that doesn't include hamburgers is difficult! It can be difficult when you are just starting the transition to veganism because of the lack of available health information, like any new diet it is important to do research and make wise decisions about what you are consuming and how it will affect your body and health.

Works Cited

Bittman, Mark. "Rethinking the Meat Guzzler." *New York Times*. New York
    Times, 27 Jan. 2008. Web. 25 Feb. 2015.

Wood, Pamela. Personal Interview. 15 Mar. 2015.

◖ **WRITING ACTIVITY 9** Write Your Discovery Draft ▶

Using your notes from the gathering-ideas step, write a preliminary thesis statement and a discovery draft to identify a problem and propose a solution on a health, education, or environmental issue of your choosing. If you included outside sources in your notes, you may want to practice putting these sources into your discovery draft. Most important is to focus on putting your ideas into words and try not to worry about the details. If you wish, you may write drafts on two or three topics to see which one you prefer to continue working on.

◖ Step 3 Revise Your Draft

Because convincing others to act on your proposed solution to a problem can be a challenge, you must ensure that your essay provides evidence of the problem and offers a workable solution. Refer to the audience analysis you completed in Writing Activity 5. What does your audience need to know to understand the problem? How can you propose your solution so that your readers will act on it? As you review your discovery draft, use the skills you acquired in earlier chapters of this book. In the pages that follow, you will learn how to further strengthen your draft by using argumentation, incorporating additional outside sources into your essay, appealing to your readers, and improving your tone.

For more on revising, see pp. 20–21.

Developing Your Ideas with Argumentative Techniques

Now that you have recorded some of your ideas in a discovery draft, you have probably noticed that you need to further develop what you have to say.

For example, you may need to present evidence that illustrates the seriousness of the problem, and you may need to investigate any solutions that have already been tried. You may also need to explain how your solution will resolve the problem.

To develop your argument, use the *logical appeal*, which means that you will rely on logic, claims, and evidence to persuade your audience. First, revise your thesis statement to be sure that it states a problem and your position on it. Next, check that you have provided evidence that the problem exists and that you have proposed a workable solution. Be sure that you have included outside sources to help strengthen your argument. If necessary, return to the gathering-ideas stage of the writing process to do additional research on your topic. Let's see how these techniques of argumentation are put into action.

State the Problem

As you may recall from Chapter 1, the thesis statement announces your topic; shows, explains, or argues a particular point about the topic; and gives readers a sense of what the essay will be about. An effective thesis statement for a problem-and-solution essay also

- describes a specific problem or issue.
- conveys your position on the issue.

Here are some examples of vague and specific thesis statements:

VAGUE	Something should be done about students' health.
SPECIFIC	Our college should develop a wellness program to encourage students to take care of their health.
VAGUE	Students need financial aid.
SPECIFIC	Thousands of college students rely on the Stafford Loan to finance their education, so Congress should reject proposed cuts to the loan program.
VAGUE	Cement factories pollute the water.
SPECIFIC	The local cement factory should be shut down because it is polluting Jacob's Creek.

▌GROUP ACTIVITY 6 Analyze Thesis Statements ▐

Working in small groups, rewrite each of the following thesis statements to define the specific problem or issue at hand and to state a clear position on the issue.

1. Students shouldn't have to pay for vaccinations.
2. The cost of health care for illegal immigrants is an important issue.
3. The spotted owls in our area need protection.
4. Cigarette taxes should be raised.
5. Standardized testing is a bad idea.

WRITING ACTIVITY 10 Revise Your Thesis Statement

Evaluate the preliminary thesis statement you wrote for your discovery draft about a health, education, or environmental issue. Does it identify a specific problem and clearly state your position? Revise your thesis statement accordingly.

Provide Evidence

When writing a persuasive essay, simply stating the problem isn't enough. You need to convince readers that the problem is serious enough to require a solution. Evidence—such as examples, facts, and expert testimony—can help you do this. You may also include a brief history of the problem, its causes, and the consequences of leaving it unsolved. If necessary, you can always do additional research to get more evidence to support your position.

Let's look at an overview of Tara Haelle's essay, "Childhood Obesity Is a Product of Environment," to see how she uses evidence to develop her argument that the environment in which children live contributes to childhood obesity.

Problem
The environment in which children live can lead to obesity, which is harmful to their health.

Why We Haven't Addressed the Problem
We focus too much on genetics and physical activity as the sole causes.

Reliable and Relevant Evidence
- Food plates are too big. A study showed that when children are given large food plates, they consume more calories.
- Food commercials on TV increase children's appetites. A study showed that watching food commercials led to more eating than similar commercials on video games and computers.
- Less sleep can make children gain weight. A study found that children who slept less than other children had a higher body mass index.

Solution
We can help reduce obesity in children by paying more attention to their environment. In particular, we should give children smaller plates to eat on, ensure that they watch less TV, and make them sleep between 7.5 to 10 hours a day (for teenagers).

GROUP ACTIVITY 7 Examine Your Evidence

Share discovery drafts with two or three other students in your class and examine the types of evidence each draft uses to support its problem statement. Does each draft provide enough supporting details to convince readers that the problem is serious and in need of a solution? Are the outside sources of information reliable and relevant? Ask your group members to suggest how you can revise to make your evidence more persuasive, and do the same for them.

Propose a Solution

After you state the problem and provide evidence of it, you're ready to propose a solution. A good *solution* recommends specific and workable actions for correcting the problem or addressing the issue. If you are proposing a solution that you discovered while conducting research, be sure to give credit to the person who first proposed it.

Let's look again at the solutions proposed in this chapter's readings. Notice that in each case, the writer identifies a specific and workable resolution to the problem:

ARONSON'S PROBLEM	We do not have enough caregivers for the growing number of older Americans.
ARONSON'S SOLUTION	In many situations, robot caregivers can take the place of human caregivers.
SATEL'S PROBLEM	Too many Americans still smoke.
SATEL'S SOLUTION	E-cigarettes are safer than tobacco and can help people kick the smoking habit.
SHERRY'S PROBLEM	Too many high school graduates are not prepared for work or higher education.
SHERRY'S SOLUTION	Fail high school students who have not mastered the academic work.
HAELLE'S PROBLEM	Too many children are obese.
HAELLE'S SOLUTION	Give children smaller dishware, reduce the amount of television, and make sure they get sufficient sleep.

HOW TO Propose a Solution

- Identify a problem.
- Provide evidence of the problem.
- Provide a specific solution.
- Make sure the solution is workable.

GROUP ACTIVITY 8 Revise Your Solution

Working with your peer response group, use the following questions to discuss the solution you proposed in your discovery draft about a health, education, or environmental problem.

1. Is the proposed solution to the problem specific? Why or why not?

2. Is the proposed solution workable? Why or why not?

3. How would you implement your solution? Are there outside sources that support your idea for how to implement a solution? Use your classmates' feedback to revise your solution accordingly.

Building Your Essay

When you revise an argument essay, it's important to consider whether you have done all you can to persuade your readers. Earlier in this chapter, you learned to use the logical appeal by relying on logic, claims, and evidence. In addition, your argument will be more convincing if you appeal to your readers' emotions and trust. Finally, using a reasonable tone will further strengthen your position.

Persuade Your Readers

In identifying a problem or an issue and proposing a solution, you want your readers to understand the problem, accept your proposed solution, and perhaps take action on the issue. In addition to making a logical argument, two other types of appeals—emotional and ethical—can help you be persuasive.

Emotional Appeals   Sometimes even the tightest logic is not enough to spur readers to action. In this case, an *emotional appeal* may be more effective; it aims to make readers feel strongly about a problem or an issue— compassionate, proud, sad, angry, or intolerant, for example. But be careful when using an appeal to emotion. Readers dismiss appeals that are overly emotional because they assume that the writer is too close to the problem to propose an objective solution. Remember, too, that emotional appeals should be made in addition to a logical argument. You must always include logical evidence to support your thesis statement.

Louise Aronson, for example, uses several emotional appeals in "The Future of Robot Caregivers." She begins her essay by describing a patient who is lonely and disabled. This arouses readers' sympathy, which makes readers more open to the idea that more caregivers are needed for the elderly. At the end of her essay she returns to her lonely, disabled patient and describes how a robot caregiver could improve her life. This conclusion makes readers feel relieved that the patient can receive the help she needs.

Ethical Appeals   With an *ethical appeal*, you aim to demonstrate that you are a trustworthy authority on the topic. To do this, you show your genuine concern about the problem or issue, your commitment to the truth, and your respect for others' differing opinions. You acknowledge that reasonable people might disagree with your proposal. Finally, you support your position with verifiable evidence (such as examples of facts, statistics, and expert testimony you discovered while researching your topic), and you ask readers to make a fair judgment based on that evidence.

Earlier in the chapter, you saw how several writers use ethical appeals in this way. In "The Future of Robot Caregivers," Louise Aronson shows concern for her elderly patient. In "In Praise of the F Word," Mary Sherry demonstrates her commitment to student success by explaining that she is both a teacher and a parent. These writers also provide verifiable evidence to demonstrate their commitment to the truth and show respect for their readers' opinions. In return, they ask us, as open-minded readers, to evaluate their arguments fairly.

HOW TO Use Logical, Emotional, and Ethical Appeals

- Use logical appeals to provide believable evidence for your position.
- Use emotional appeals to help readers feel strongly about your problem.
- Use ethical appeals to demonstrate your respect for your readers and your genuine concern about the problem.
- Use all three appeals to keep a balanced perspective.

WRITING ACTIVITY 11 Strengthen Your Appeals

Evaluate your draft to determine where an appeal to emotion or an appeal to ethics would make your logical argument more persuasive. Where in your essay might you appeal to your readers' compassion, pride, anger, or some other emotion to spur them to action? Do you demonstrate genuine concern about the issue, your commitment to the truth, and your respect for others' opinions? Add or revise your appeals as appropriate and eliminate any details that are exaggerated or not factual.

Use a Reasonable Tone

Writers create *tone* through their choice of words and the structure of their sentences. You'll always want to strive for a reasonable tone, especially if you're proposing a solution. Readers rarely respond well to anger, sarcasm, accusation, hostility, or negativity. Calm, rational, and respectful language is always more effective.

Earlier you saw several examples of an angry and snide tone in Andrea Benitez's discovery draft:

> **ANGRY TONE** What really makes me angry, though, is that many people think veganism is a big joke. What gives with this attitude?

> **SNIDE TONE** But then some crazy people think that any diet that doesn't include hamburgers is difficult!

Venting your anger in writing has the same effect as raising your voice, stomping your feet, or slamming the door in an argument. Remember, your goal is to persuade your readers to acknowledge the problem and to accept your solution. A harsh, negative tone won't accomplish this because it makes the writer look immature and puts readers on the defensive. To be persuasive, you must show respect for your readers' opinions by maintaining a reasonable tone.

WRITING ACTIVITY 12 Improve Your Tone

Reread your draft, looking for remarks that come across as angry or that show a lack of respect for others' opinions. Revise as needed to create a reasonable tone.

A Student's Revised Draft

After considering the appeals she used and the tone of her essay, student Andrea Benitez decided that she could strengthen her appeals and moderate her tone. Before you read Andrea's revised draft, reread her discovery draft (pp. 338–39). Notice how she researched her topic, added more outside evidence, and improved the tone in the revision. (You will still notice some errors in the revised draft; these will be corrected when Andrea edits her essay later on.)

Why Go Vegan?

It's no surprise that we are abusing our environment. We use too many natural resources that we can't replace, we polute our air and water, and we do very little to stop the effects of climate change. While there are lots of things you can do to treat the environment better, few people look at the food choices they make every day as a solution. The fact that animal products harm the environment is not heard all that often. According to Dr. Pamela Wood, professor in our university's Department of Public Health Science, "If you make the choice to go vegan, you can take a big step toward improving the environment. You do this by not consuming animal products such as meat, fish, dairy, or eggs, and not wearing animal products such as fur or leather."

Most of us are not born vegan, so why should you go vegan? People often become vegans because they are concerned about the way society treats animals. Others don't want to eat meat or dairy products for health reasons. But the biggest reason to go vegan is to help our environment. Modern animal agriculture uses vast amounts of natural resources, is an inefficient way to transfer those resources into calories, and is a major source of both polutants and greenhouse gases. By going vegan, you can personally reduce your own negative impact on the environment.

1   Andrea adjusts the tone of her introduction so that her readers will focus on the problem rather than on her feelings about it.

Andrea gives credit to the professor she interviewed about her topic.

2

Andrea clarifies the focus of her essay: veganism can help the environment.

One major problem with our environment is that we are using too many resources without the ability to replace them quickly. This includes clean water, food, and land, and also sources of energy like oil and natural gas. According to a recent article in the *New York Times*, a full 30% of the land on earth not covered by ice is currently being used in some way in livestock production (Bittman). Livestock is also the largest source of water usage: all other uses of water in the United States combined are equivalent to the amount of water used in animal agriculture. Cattle ranching has caused a vast disappearance of rain forests in Central America. The United States imports millions of pounds of beef from Costa Rica, causing a loss of 83% of its forests (Stepaniak 250). Going vegan means not supporting this overuse of resources. If you do not consume or use animal products, you do not contribute to the demand for land, water, oil, and the earth's dwindling rain forests.

Not only does eating meat use many resources, but it also uses them very inefficiently. Livestock animals do not produce as many calories as they consume, making them a very inefficient way to get food. To produce an equivalent amount of vegetables and meat, the meat takes ten times as much land as the vegetables (Bittman). Its not just livestock on land—fishermen must throw away on average a third of what they catch, as it dies or becomes contaminated in the process. A plant-based diet allows a direct line between the land and energy and your plate. Instead of having to feed an animal to produce a food that you then eat, as a vegan you simply eat what is grown, which is a far more efficient use of resources.

Finally, animal agriculture is responsible for vast amounts of polution. According to the website vegansociety.com, one person going vegan could reduce carbon dioxide emissions by one and a half tons per year. In addition, runoff from concentrated feedlots polutes waterways. Cows are among the world's greatest producers of methane, which is the second most significant greenhouse gas in the world (Take Part). If you—and others—choose to become vegan, fewer of these animals would need to be raised, so both polution and greenhouse gas emissions could be reduced.

Side notes:

In this paragraph, Andrea adds evidence, using facts and statistics she found in outside sources. These strengthen her appeals.

Andrea continues to add evidence to support her position.

Andrea summarizes information she found on reliable websites.

Paragraph markers: 3   4   5

Many assume it is very difficult to take on a vegan lifestyle because, after all, everything contains some kind of animal product. It can be difficult when you are just starting the transition to veganism because of the lack of available health information, like any new diet it is important to do research and make wise decisions about what you are consuming and how it will affect your body and health. There are many resources available for a person who decides to become vegan, including cookbooks and several organizations, both local and national or international. Why go vegan? Each of us must follow our own conscience and live life as we see fit, but if you want to help protect the environment, you will continue to learn more about being vegan and join me in spreading the word about this valuable lifestyle.

6   Andrea develops her conclusion by explaining how you can go vegan. She uses a moderate tone to strengthen both her logical argument and her ethical appeal.

Works Cited

Bittman, Mark. "Rethinking the Meat Guzzler." *New York Times*. New York Times, 27 Jan. 2008. Web. 25 Feb. 2011.

Stepaniak, Joanne. *The Vegan Sourcebook*. Los Angeles, CA: Lowell House, 1998. Print.

Take Part. *ClimateCrisis*. Participant Media, 2011. Web. 25 Feb. 2011.

The Vegan Society. The Vegan Society. 2011. Web. 25 Feb. 2011.

Wood, Pamela. Personal Interview. 15 Mar. 2011.

Andrea further develops her Works Cited list.

GROUP ACTIVITY 9 Analyze Andrea's Revised Draft

Use the following questions to discuss with your classmates how Andrea improved her draft.

1. What is Andrea's thesis statement? Is it effective?
2. What kinds of evidence does Andrea provide to show that a problem exists?
3. Does her solution seem workable?
4. How does Andrea appeal to her readers logically, emotionally, and ethically?
5. How has Andrea adjusted her tone to make it more reasonable than it was in her discovery draft?
6. How could Andrea's revised draft benefit from further revision?

Peer Review for an Essay That Proposes a Solution

Read your draft aloud to the members of your peer response group. Take notes on your classmates' responses to the following questions about your draft.

1. What do you like best about this essay?
2. How effective is my thesis statement? Do I clearly state the problem?
3. Do I provide adequate evidence of the problem? Do I need to add more outside sources to strengthen my argument?
4. Do I propose a workable solution to the problem?
5. How could I improve my logical, emotional, and ethical appeals?
6. Where in my essay do I need to adjust my tone?
7. How clear is the purpose of my essay?

WRITING ACTIVITY 13   Revise Your Draft

Using the work you have completed for Writing Activities 10 to 12 and Group Activities 7 and 8, and taking your classmates' suggestions for revision into consideration, finish revising your discovery draft. Focus on improving your thesis, evidence, and solution. Also evaluate your use of emotional and ethical appeals, and adjust your tone as needed. Finally, make sure you have supported your argument with outside sources that are reliable and relevant.

Step 4 Edit Your Sentences

For more on editing, see pp. 23–25.

At this point, you have worked hard to communicate your position on a health, education, or environmental issue. Now that you're satisfied with the content of your revised draft, you're ready to edit it for correctness.

Editing is important because it removes errors that distract readers from focusing on the writer's ideas. Errors create the impression that a careless writer is untrustworthy. A clean, error-free essay, in contrast, suggests that a writer is careful and probably genuinely concerned about the topic. Therefore, edit your essay carefully before sharing it with your readers.

Combining Sentences Using Appositives

For more on combining sentences, see Chapter 15.

As you have learned, combining sentences can turn short, weak sentences into longer, stronger ones. Thus far, you have used several techniques for combining sentences. Another way to combine sentences is by using appositives. An *appositive* is a word or group of words that is set off by commas and that defines or renames a person or thing in the sentence.

Here's how Andrea used appositives to combine sentences when she edited her draft:

ORIGINAL   One major problem with our environment is that we are using too many resources without the ability to replace them quickly. This includes clean water, food, and land, and also sources of energy like oil and natural gas.

REVISED   One major problem with our environment is that we are using too many resources, including water, food, land, oil, and natural gas, without the ability to replace them quickly.

HOW TO Combine Sentences Using Appositives

- Eliminate the subject and verb in one sentence.
- Add the remaining phrase that describes the noun to the other sentence.
- Set off the phrase with commas.

EDITING ACTIVITY 1 Combine Sentences Using Appositives

Combine the following pairs of sentences by using appositives.

EXAMPLE Jane ~~is my sister. She~~ has type 2 diabetes.
, my sister,

1. The new campus plan is an improvement. It is called Student Access.

2. My biology book isn't difficult to understand. The title is *Life Science for Dummies*.

3. This holiday is important for the environment. It's called Arbor Day.

4. Jerry asked that the campus cafeteria serve more fresh vegetables. He is short and heavyset.

5. Don't even ask my girlfriend to go with you to the student council session. Luisa isn't interested in the college's problems.

WRITING ACTIVITY 14 Combine Your Sentences

Reread your discovery draft, looking for short, closely related sentences. Where it makes sense to do so, combine them using appositives.

Correcting Shifts in Person

Authors write in one of three persons: first (*I, we*), second (*you*), or third (*he, she, they*). Here is a complete list of singular and plural pronouns in first, second, and third person:

SINGULAR

First Person	Second Person	Third Person
I	you	he, she, it, one
me	you	him, her, it
my, mine	your, yours	his, her, hers, its, one's

PLURAL

First Person	Second Person	Third Person
we	you	they
us	you	them
our, ours	your, yours	their, theirs

As a general rule, avoid shifting from one pronoun to another, because it confuses the readers:

CONFUSING *I* never wanted to complain about the food served at the campus cafeteria. *You* know that it can be unhealthy. *I* finally wrote to the school newspaper to express *our* views. *We* believed something needed to be done about this situation, and so *I* took action.

REVISED *I* never wanted to complain about the food served at the campus cafeteria even though *I* know that it can be unhealthy. *I* finally wrote to the school newspaper to express *my* views. *I* believed something needed to be done about this situation, and so *I* took action.

EDITING ACTIVITY 2 Correct Shifts in Person

Revise the following paragraph to correct unnecessary shifts in person.

My favorite pastime is writing letters to the editor. I always have something to say about what's going on in our city. And there is plenty for you to write about: poor water quality, smog, and trash everywhere. They are always saying how much we need to improve the environment. You should never take a beautiful city for granted. I know I will continue to let people know how we feel about changing things around here.

WRITING ACTIVITY 15 Edit Your Essay

Edit your revised draft, looking for errors in grammar, spelling, and punctuation. Focus on finding and correcting any unnecessary shifts in person. If you know you often make a particular type of error, read the essay one time while you look only for that error. Ask a friend, family member, or classmate to help you spot errors you may have overlooked. Then use a dictionary and the Handbook in Part Four of this book to help you correct the errors you find.

A Student's Edited Essay

You probably noticed that Andrea's revised draft contained some errors in grammar, spelling, and punctuation. Andrea corrected these errors in her edited essay. Her corrections are noted in the margin.

Andrea uses correct
MLA format.

Misspelled word is
corrected.

Misspelled word is
corrected.

Sentences are combined.

Benitez 1

Andrea Benitez

Professor Posey

English 1311

7 Apr. 2011

Why Go Vegan?

1 It's no surprise that we are abusing our environment. We use too many natural resources that we can't replace, we pollute our air and water, and we do very little to stop the effects of climate change. While there are lots of things you can do to treat the environment better, few people look at the food choices they make every day as a solution. The fact that animal products harm the environment is not heard all that often. If you make the choice to go vegan, you can take a big step toward improving the environment. According to Dr. Pamela Wood, professor in our university's Department of Public Health Science, "You do this by not consuming animal products such as meat, fish, dairy, or eggs, and not wearing animal products such as fur or leather."

2 Most of us are not born vegan, so why should you go vegan? People often become vegans because they are concerned about the way society treats animals. Others don't want to eat meat or dairy products for health reasons. But the biggest reason to go vegan is to help our environment. Modern animal agriculture uses vast amounts of natural resources, is an inefficient way to transfer those resources into calories, and is a major source of both pollutants and greenhouse gases. By going vegan, you can personally reduce your own negative impact on the environment.

3 One major problem with our environment is that we are using too many resources, including water, food, land, oil, and natural gas, without the ability to replace them quickly. According to a recent article in the *New York Times*, a full 30% of the land on earth not covered by ice is currently being used in some way in livestock production (Bittman). Livestock is also the largest source of water usage: all other uses of water in the United States combined are equivalent to the amount of water used in animal

Benitez 2

agriculture. Cattle ranching has caused a vast disappearance of rain forests in Central America. The United States imports millions of pounds of beef from Costa Rica, causing a loss of 83% of its forests (Stepaniak 250). Going vegan means not supporting this overuse of resources. If you do not consume or use animal products, you do not contribute to the demand for land, water, oil, and the earth's dwindling rain forests.

Not only does eating meat use many resources, but it also uses them very inefficiently. Livestock animals do not produce as many calories as they consume, making them a very inefficient way to get food. To produce an equivalent amount of vegetables and meat, the meat takes ten times as much land as the vegetables. It's not just livestock on land — fishermen must throw away on average a third of what they catch, as it dies or becomes contaminated in the process. A plant-based diet allows a direct line between the land and energy and your plate. Instead of having to feed an animal to produce a food that you then eat, as a vegan you simply eat what is grown, which is a far more efficient use of resources.

Punctuation is added to create a contraction.

4

Finally, animal agriculture is responsible for vast amounts of pollution. According to the website vegansociety.com, one person going vegan could reduce carbon dioxide emissions by one and a half tons per year. In addition, runoff from concentrated feedlots pollutes waterways. Cows are among the world's greatest producers of methane, which is the second most significant greenhouse gas in the world (Take Part). If you — and others — choose to become vegan, fewer of these animals would need to be raised, so both pollution and greenhouse gas emissions could be reduced.

Misspelled words are corrected.

5

Many assume it is very difficult to take on a vegan lifestyle because, after all, everything contains some kind of animal product. It can be difficult when you are just starting the transition to veganism because of the lack of available health information; like any new diet, it is important to do research and make wise decisions about what you are consuming and how it will affect

Run-on sentence is corrected.

6

Benitez 3

your body and health. There are many resources available for a person who decides to become vegan, including cookbooks and several organizations, both local and national or international. Why go vegan? Each of us must follow our own conscience and live life as we see fit, but if you want to help protect the environment, you will continue to learn more about being vegan and join me in spreading the word about this valuable lifestyle.

Works Cited

Bittman, Mark. "Rethinking the Meat Guzzler." *New York Times*. New York Times, 27 Jan. 2008. Web. 25 Feb. 2011.

Stepaniak, Joanne. *The Vegan Sourcebook*. Los Angeles, CA: Lowell House, 1998. Print.

Take Part. *ClimateCrisis*, Participant Media, 2011. Web. 25 Feb. 2011.

The Vegan Society. The Vegan Society, 2011. Web. 25 Feb. 2011.

Wood, Pamela. Personal Interview. 15 Mar. 2011.

(Step 5 Share Your Essay

You're ready to share your solution to a health, education, or environmental problem with your audience. In addition to submitting your essay to your instructor and sharing it with your classmates, mail a copy of it to someone with the authority to act on your proposal.

According to an ancient Chinese proverb, "A journey of a thousand miles begins with a single step." Perhaps your essay will be the first step in bringing about a needed change in the areas of health, education, or the environment.

You may be surprised by the power of your writing. If you receive a reply, share it with your instructor and classmates. Student writer Andrea Benitez sent her essay to her campus newspaper. As a result, she was asked to start a vegan group on campus.

(¹) Submit your essay online

Look for an online form or e-mail address where you might submit your essay to the person in authority who might act on your recommendations. Check for any special requirements for submitting the information online. You might also think about how to revise your essay to turn it into a letter to the editor to submit to your local or campus newspaper.

CHAPTER CHECKLIST

❏ I read essays about problems and proposed solutions to explore and learn about this chapter's theme.

❏ I analyzed my audience and purpose.

❏ I gathered ideas by relating aloud, consulting with others, and researching to find outside sources.

❏ I stated a specific problem and position in a thesis statement.

❏ I researched to find evidence to persuade my readers that the problem exists and merits their attention.

❏ I proposed a workable solution to the problem.

❏ I used logical, emotional, and ethical appeals to persuade my readers to accept my position on the issue.

❏ I used a reasonable tone.

❏ I combined short sentences by using appositives.

❏ I corrected shifts in person.

❏ I edited to eliminate errors in grammar, punctuation, and spelling.

REFLECTING ON YOUR WRITING

To help you reflect on the writing you did in this chapter, answer the following questions:

1. Why did you choose the issue you did?
2. How did you determine the audience for your essay?
3. Which supporting details in your essay do you think provide the strongest evidence for your position? Why?
4. Which type of appeal—logical, emotional, or ethical—do you think you use most effectively in your essay? Why?
5. If you had more time, what would you do to improve your essay before sharing it with readers?

After you answer these questions, freewrite about what you learned in this chapter.

Visit **LaunchPad Solo for Readers and Writers > Writing Process** for more tutorials, videos, and practice developing your essay with each step.

Writing with Sources

Whether exploring a topic of personal interest or writing for class or for the workplace, you will find that basic research skills and strategies are essential. In addition to traditional print sources, you can now turn to websites, blogs, and wikis, and online journals, periodicals, and newspapers. Because of the volume of information available, you face the challenge of not only finding sources, but evaluating the quality of those sources. In Part Three, you'll learn valuable research skills and practice some strategies for writing with sources as you work through a successful research project toward the end goal of a researched essay.

An entire chapter on conducting research (Chapter 11) is included here to show how to respond to a writing assignment by choosing your topic and asking questions to guide your inquiry as you find information on your topic. The chapter on evaluating and using sources (Chapter 12) responds to the same writing assignment, showing you how to determine if a source is reliable and useful and how to incorporate it into your project. Throughout Chapters 11 and 12, you will follow a student, Aileen Ly, as she writes about the relationship between stereotypes and mental illness among Asian Americans.

Conducting Research

magine that you have received the following writing assignments in your college courses:

- Describe the life cycle of the diamondback rattlesnake.
- Analyze César Chávez's leadership of migrant farmworkers.
- Explain the origin of the Internet in the late 1970s.

How do you find information on these topics? Of course, you start looking online or head to the library. But then what? If you had looked for this information in a library thirty years ago, you would have consulted the card catalog to find the name of a book on your topic and to see where it was located. You also might have examined a reference book that listed magazine articles on your subject.

Today, however, most information is available electronically. Because of computer technology, libraries can now access information from around the world in seconds. But how do you know where to look? How do you sort through this information to decide what is most useful and valid? What if you want to conduct surveys or interviews as part of your research—in person or electronically?

This chapter will give you strategies for effectively conducting research for a researched essay. The first step in any research project is effective planning: you will start by narrowing your topic and writing questions that you want to answer as you look for sources. This chapter will introduce you to conducting your own research through interviews,

> **In this chapter, you will research a topic to find sources for a brief researched essay in Chapter 12. As you begin working on your essay, you will**
>
> - Prepare to conduct research on a topic.
> - Make observations, survey others, and conduct interviews.
> - Familiarize yourself with your campus library resources.
> - Locate sources of information in person and online.

surveys, and observations, but it will also teach you about the research you'll conduct most often in your academic career: secondary research. You'll become familiar with the resources your library offers as you investigate what others have said about your topic. You will also follow student writer Aileen Ly as she searches for appropriate, relevant, and reliable sources for her researched essay, which appears at the end of the next chapter. ■

Writing Assignment: Part One

Your campus's Student Affairs division is holding a public meeting to help enhance and share students' cultural experiences, and your psychology instructor has volunteered your class to participate in this forum. To prepare for the forum, your instructor has asked each student to write an essay that explores a cultural experience or expectation.

For Part One of the assignment, you will narrow your topic and gather sources for your essay.

◖ Preparing to Conduct Research

To conduct research, you first need to know what information you're seeking. Otherwise, you might spend a great deal of time finding information that doesn't pertain to your topic.

Narrow Your Topic

For more on brainstorming, see p. 11. For more on choosing and narrowing your topic, see pp. 16–17.

Before beginning your research, narrow your topic so that your ideas can be well developed. If you choose a topic that is too broad, you will have difficulty communicating your ideas, supporting your points, and creating a clearly written, well-structured essay. For the Student Affairs forum, you could explain aspects of another culture that are important for students to understand. You could also discuss and dispel a cultural stereotype or introduce and describe a particular cultural tradition or lifestyle. Another choice would be to focus on the pressures of a particular culture—societal, familial, and personal. Narrowing your topic to just one of these ideas will allow you to focus on an aspect of your topic, go into more detail in your essay, and make the research process easier. It will also help you know exactly what information you need to find to support your points.

On the other hand, if your topic is *too* narrow, you will have difficulty finding a variety of reliable sources to support your points. Keep in mind that research is exploratory, too: by conducting research and reading about how others have approached the topic, you might discover an interesting approach and a narrowed topic that will focus your essay.

Student writer Aileen Ly wanted to share her own experiences of her Asian American culture with participants in the Student Affairs forum. She thought about writing an essay on a variety of stereotypes about Asian Americans, but she knew the topic was too broad. After brainstorming, she narrowed her topic to a stereotype about Asian Americans being high achievers and its effect on Asian American mental health.

Write Research Questions

After you narrow your topic, think of questions that you might have about this topic. These *research questions* will guide you in conducting your research. For instance, you might ask these questions:

- What is the definition of your topic? How did that definition come about, or how has it evolved?
- Who participates in or experiences your topic?
- What are the emotional, physical, or social effects of your topic?
- How can your topic be improved or prevented?

As you research your topic, refer to your research questions to help you stay focused on the information you need.

Student writer Aileen Ly was interested in how the Model Minority Stereotype (the misperception that the members of a certain racial or ethnic group do nothing but study and are always gifted in areas such as math and science) affected Asian Americans. Here are the questions she asked about the topic:

- What is the origin of the Model Minority Stereotype?
- Who is affected by this stereotype and in what ways?
- What are the emotional and physical effects of being subjected to such a stereotype?
- How can stereotyping like this be prevented, and how can the effects be treated?

HOW TO Plan a Research Project

- Choose a topic that interests you.
- Review your purpose and audience.
- Narrow your topic.
- State the following questions: *Who? What? When? Where? Why? How?*
- Select a few of these questions to explore.
- Establish a timeline for conducting research to answer these questions and for completing the project. Allow plenty of time to work on each part of the project.

Primary Research

Research that you do on your own, rather than read about, is called *primary research*. Thus, when you conduct an experiment in science, you're doing primary research. When you ask friends to suggest a good movie, you're essentially taking a survey, another form of primary research.

Three common types of primary research involve making observations, surveying others, and conducting interviews. These types of primary research are used for different purposes:

- When you want to explain how something works or how something is done, consider making observations.
- When you want to explain your topic's importance in people's lives, consider surveying others.
- When you require specialized information or information known only to experts, consider conducting interviews.

Making Observations

To *observe* something is to watch it closely. Observations enable you to explain your points clearly to your readers. For example, if you're explaining cell mitosis, you could observe cell division under a microscope. In your essay, you could describe what you saw to make the process come alive for your readers. Similarly, in an essay about the Internet, you might describe your observations of some online conversations and include a quotation that illustrates a key point. For an essay that explains an aspect of another culture, if you wanted to observe by participating, you might attend a concert or festival featuring particular cultural music or activities and record your impressions of the occasion.

HOW TO Make Observations

- Obtain permission (if necessary) to observe an event relevant to your topic.
- Remain visible, but do not participate in the event, if your presence will change the behavior of the participants.
- OR, observe the event by participating in the event or activity, if you think participating is necessary to fully understand the proceedings.
- Decide what to focus on when you observe.
- Take detailed notes as you observe the event.
- Ask participants questions about what you observe but may not understand. You may need to ask more questions later.

Surveying Others

A *survey* contains information collected from many people about a certain topic. Newspapers often conduct surveys to find out how citizens plan to vote in an upcoming election. Manufacturers hire market-research companies to survey users of their products and thereby learn how to improve them. In writing, a survey can help you gather people's opinions or knowledge about an issue and use these data in your essay. For example, if your topic for the Student Affairs forum is cultural stereotyping and its effects, you could survey people to determine how many of them have been subject to a cultural stereotype. Your research findings might support the point that many people experience cultural stereotyping but few know how it can be overcome.

HOW TO Conduct Surveys

- Decide how you will conduct the survey—with an *oral survey* or a *written survey*. In an oral survey, respondents reply immediately but do not have much time to think about the questions. A written survey generates detailed responses, but many people may not have the time to fill out a questionnaire.

- Decide where you will conduct the survey. You want to find a place where many people come and go, such as the entrance of the college library or student union. You might also want to create an online survey and distribute it through e-mail or social media.

- Create five to ten survey questions. Make them brief and easy to understand. Also use various types of questions—that is, questions that can be answered with yes or no mixed with questions that require short answers. Test questions on classmates for suggestions for improvement.

- Decide whom you will survey. For instance, do you want to survey both men and women from various age groups? Or do you want to narrow your survey to a specific group? Avoid surveying only people you know.

- Decide how many people you will survey. The more people you include in a survey, the more reliable your results will be. But you need to consider your time limitations as well.

- If you conduct an oral survey, write out your questions ahead of time, and either take careful notes or record the conversation (with the permission of the person you are recording).

> ⏻ **Conduct an online survey**
> A survey can be sent to people to fill in electronically via e-mail or via online services such as SurveyMonkey or Google Forms. One of the benefits of an online survey is that the site will total the results for you. Consider sharing the results of the survey with those who participated in it.

Conducting Interviews

Interviewing others is a great way to gather information. For a review of how to consult with others, see pp. 13–14.

In addition to making observations and surveying others, you can conduct *interviews* to learn more about a research topic. By interviewing a knowledgeable person, you can collect information and gain an expert's perspective. If you're writing an essay on water quality in your region, for example, you could interview an environmental engineer who has studied this subject. For the topic of cultural experience or expectation, you could interview students who have studied abroad or international students who can describe first-hand what it's like to experience culture shock.

Here's one more tip: if you're reluctant to contact a stranger for an interview, remember that most people enjoy talking about what they know and sharing their knowledge with interested students.

HOW TO Conduct Interviews

- Choose a knowledgeable person to interview. To determine whether someone is an expert on your topic, check his or her credentials (such as academic degrees, professional activities, and published works). In some situations, a person's personal experience with your topic is more relevant than formal credentials.
- Contact the person in advance to set up an appointment.
- Prepare your interview questions.
- If you conduct the interview in person, dress appropriately and arrive on time.
- Keep the conversation focused on your questions. Be considerate of your interviewee's limited time.
- Listen carefully, and take good notes. Put quotation marks around the person's actual words. You may digitally record the conversation only if you obtain the interviewee's permission beforehand.
- Ask the interviewee to clarify anything you do not understand.
- Send a thank-you note to the person soon after the interview.

Conduct an online interview

To conduct an interview with a person in a different location, consider conducting a face-to-face interview using Skype or Google+ Hangouts, or a text interview using e-mail or chat. Be sure to keep a copy of the video or a transcript of the conversation to view or read later.

GROUP ACTIVITY 1 Conduct Primary Research

Discuss your writing topic with other students in your class. Determine the type of primary research that will best suit your topic. Then use the appropriate set of questions to discuss how you and your classmates can go about making observations, surveying others, or conducting interviews.

Questions about Making Observations

1. What information do you need to obtain from your observations?
2. Where will you make the observations?
3. Do you need permission to observe? If so, from whom?
4. What questions do you have about the event you want to observe?

Questions about Surveying Others

1. What information do you want the survey to provide?
2. Do you want your respondents to answer orally or in writing? Why?
3. Who will your respondents be, and how many people will you survey?
4. Where will you conduct the survey?
5. What questions will you ask in the survey?

Questions about Conducting Interviews

1. What information do you hope to obtain from the interview?
2. Who could give you this information?
3. What questions will you ask?

Secondary Research

Secondary research involves reading what others have written about your topic and is the kind of research that you will use most often in your college courses. To conduct secondary research, you need to know where and how to locate relevant sources of information first. (The other important elements of research include how to evaluate sources; how to avoid plagiarism; how to take notes; how to quote, paraphrase, and summarize sources of information; and how to document the sources you cite in your research paper. These elements are covered in Chapter 12, beginning on page 375.)

Locating Sources of Information

Use a Search Engine

When you are asked to do research, your first impulse might be to look up your subject on Wikipedia or conduct a Google search. While most professors will not consider this to be scholarly research, these sources may provide a helpful starting point. Keep in mind that "wiki" websites such as Wikipedia can be edited by anyone and so may contain inaccurate information. However, Wikipedia articles offer additional reference lists and links to external websites that may be helpful. Similarly, Google can be helpful when used properly. A Google search will yield a variety of commercial websites that may not provide the most reliable information. However, you can use a search filter to focus your results or an Advanced Search to limit your search to .edu, .gov, and .org sites, which are generally more reliable and credible sources of information. Google Scholar limits your search to scholarly articles, and Google Books allows you to read the full text of many books for free.

Following are two examples from Aileen Ly's research through the popular search engine Google. Figure 11.1 shows the results Aileen got from a

Figure 11.1 Basic Google search for "Asian American mental illness"

simple Google search. Figure 11.2 shows the results she got when she searched the same keywords on Google Scholar. What differences do you notice between each of the search results?

Visit Your Campus Library

Sources of information in libraries can be found in both print and electronic formats, including books, periodicals (newspapers, magazines, and journals), and media (online videos and podcasts, CDs, DVDs). Periodicals are any written sources that are published on a regular schedule and may be published by week or month, issue or volume. Unlike newspapers and magazines, which are typically written by journalists for a general audience, journals contain articles by experts for a more specialized audience; therefore, journals are often valuable sources of information for academic writing. Many books and periodicals can be found in print, media, and electronic formats. Electronic formats are increasingly popular and are becoming more accessible, and many materials that once appeared only in print now also appear in electronic form; in fact, some resources are only available in digital formats. To do secondary research, therefore, you need to know how to access both print and electronic resources.

Figure 11.2 Google Scholar search for "Asian American mental illness"

Consult a Reference Librarian

To find scholarly sources, you can talk to a reference librarian, either in person or online. Librarians are invaluable sources of information and are willing to help all researchers, from first-year students to professors. They have specialized knowledge about all that the library contains, including its special and digital collections. They also create and cultivate the library's research guides, which can help you find resources and information by subject or course. For example, the librarian might direct you to your library's online course research guide for English 101, or to a subject research guide devoted to psychology.

Librarians can help you find the content you need, but they can also show you how to use the resources available in the library. To speak with a librarian to help you research your project, you can go to your library's reference desk and ask for assistance. If you're working off campus, you can also log on to your library's website. Many library websites now have an Ask a Librarian chat feature, where you can instant-message or text-message a librarian to ask your questions; if chat is offline, an e-mail address is usually provided. You may also choose to e-mail directly a subject librarian who specializes in your topic.

Search Your Library's Resources Online

The most reliable place to find resources online is through your campus library. Many library home pages feature a search bar that serves a Search All or One Search function. Entering keyword search terms in this space will locate resources in the library catalog, in databases for which the library has subscriptions, in the library's digital collections, and more. Other library

---

HOW TO Use Keywords to Search

- Narrow your search by connecting keywords with the word *AND*, as in "cultural experience AND education."
- You can also narrow your search by using the word *NOT*, as in "cultural experience NOT immigration."
- If your keywords don't result in enough items for you to examine, broaden your search by using the word *OR*, as in "cultural experience OR cultural studies."
- Use synonyms to help your search. For example, instead of "cultural stereotype," try "cultural perception" or "cultural assumption."
- If you still can't find the right keywords, ask a reference librarian. He or she can then check the subject headings in the database for you.

home pages feature a search bar that leads directly to the catalog, which searches only the library holdings. Catalog searches may offer options to search just for books, for articles and databases, for e-journals, or other types of resources. This catalog will indicate which resources are available. The online catalog allows you to search by title, author, subject, keyword, call number, or ISSN/ISBN, and in some cases allows you to link directly to an abstract (a summary of an article) or a full article. It's important to familiarize yourself with your library's online search options to make your research project easier.

Consult an Encyclopedia

If you have little experience doing research, or you don't know much about your topic or subject, you might want to start with a general resource such as an encyclopedia. Encyclopedias give broad descriptions, definitions, and background information about all kinds of topics. The library likely has print as well as electronic encyclopedias, such as the *Encyclopaedia Britannica*. There are also discipline-specific or specialized encyclopedias in many subject areas. Specialized encyclopedias are a better source of in-depth information because they cover specific fields. Some specialized encyclopedias are the *Encyclopedia of Computer Science and Technology*, *Encyclopedia of Psychology*, *Encyclopedia of the Biological Sciences*, and *Harvard Guide to American History*. To locate specialized encyclopedias, start by checking the library catalog or consult with a reference librarian. Print encyclopedias are usually for use in the library only and may not be checked out.

Find a Print Source

If you've located the title of a useful book or article but it is not available in full text online, you can look for a hard copy via your college's library catalog (for a periodical, you should use a journal title search, not an article title search). Then, using a call number—the number the library assigns to each book, journal, or other item in its collection—you will need to physically locate the resource. Every item in the library will have a unique call number, arranged in alphabetical and numerical order. Books your library houses can also be searched for by topic, author, or subject in your college library's online catalog, and the books will also have call numbers to help you locate them on the shelves.

If the library doesn't have access to the periodical or book you need, you may request it through interlibrary loan. It can take anywhere from a few days to a couple of weeks to receive an item, so submit your request well in advance of when you need the source.

Find an Electronic Source

In addition to the print resources, many books, encyclopedias, magazines, journals, and newspapers are available online—in fact, more online versions of these types of resources are available than print versions. Databases may contain full articles or only the titles and abstracts of articles from thousands of magazines, journals, and newspapers. Some databases, such as *Periodical Abstracts* and *Readers' Guide Abstracts*, list magazine and journal articles, whereas others, such as *InfoTrac Newspapers*, include only newspaper articles. A reference librarian is usually available to help you choose the databases that are most useful for your topic. Compared with print sources, electronic databases and indexes are generally more current because they are updated more frequently. You may also access your library's computer databases from your home or another campus computer.

Consult a Database Your librarian might direct you to an academic journal archive, like *JSTOR*, or an online research database, like *EBSCOhost*. These sites offer bibliographical information, abstracts, and links to the full texts of thousands of scholarly articles. In addition to journals, databases also offer access to indexes, which list magazine, journal, or newspaper articles by title, subject, or author. The library subscribes to many resources that will provide this sort of information. Some of them provide not only citations and abstracts but full articles as well.

When consulting a database, use *keywords*, or words that pertain to your topic, to locate articles. The wrong keywords can give you either too many or too few items from the database. For her essay on Asian American mental illness that you will read in Chapter 12, Aileen Ly visited *EBSCOhost* through her library's website and clicked on the link marked "Choose Databases." Some databases allow you to browse journals specific to your major or discipline. Aileen decided to choose *Academic Search Premier* because she wanted a database that would offer results across various disciplines and fields of study. Using the keywords "Asian American Mental Illness," she received a list of 257 articles (Figure 11.3 on page 371).

A database often gives you an abstract, or a brief summary, of each article it contains. This abstract will help you determine whether the article is likely to answer one of your research questions. Aileen skimmed through a few

HOW TO Find Electronic Resources

- Identify a database, such as *LexisNexis* or *Academic Search Premier* (*EBSCOhost*), in which to search for information. A list of databases is available at your campus library.
- Enter keywords on your topic to access information.
- Read the abstract or summary to determine whether an article sounds useful.
- If the article seems useful, print or take notes on the information.
- Record the publication information for your Works Cited page.

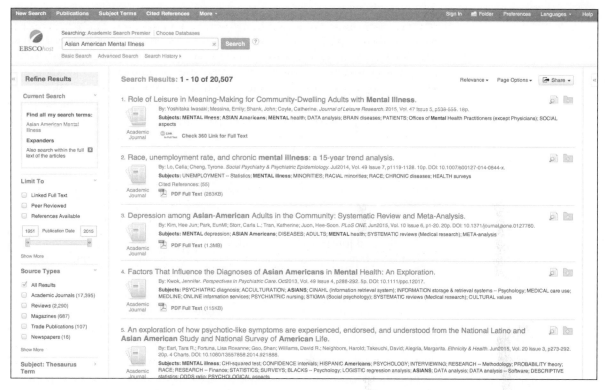

Figure 11.3 Aileen's *Academic Search Premier* Search Results

abstracts and then found one that seemed related to her topic, "Working with Culture: Culturally Appropriate Mental Health Care for Asian Americans." Based on the abstract, she decided she might be able to use it in her essay on Asian American mental illness. She was in luck. A link to the full article was included in the database, saving her the time of retrieving it from the periodical section of the library. Figure 11.3, above, shows Aileen's search results. After reading the article, she e-mailed a copy to herself and printed it out, so she could take notes on it at a later time.

Use Other Sources of Information

Secondary research need not be limited to written sources found in the library or on the web. Check television listings for relevant documentaries or news shows. *All Things Considered*, broadcast daily on National Public Radio and digitally archived in podcasts on NPR.org, is another excellent source of current news and cultural topics.

GROUP ACTIVITY 2 Conduct Library Research

Team up with a classmate to do some library research on your topic. First, explain to your partner the type of information you need to find. Then, visit the campus library and, working together, locate websites and specialized journals, magazine and newspaper articles, and books on each of your topics. Don't hesitate to ask a librarian for assistance if you can't find the sources you need. Finally, record the titles and authors of the various sources you find on your topic so you can find them later and cite them properly if you decide to use them (see Chapter 12 for more on proper citation).

1. **Website article** Give the author or compiler of the work, title of the work, title of the website, version or edition used, publisher or sponsor of the site, date of publication, medium of publication, and date you accessed this material.

2. **Specialized journal** Give the author's name, the title of the article, the title of the journal, the volume and issue numbers, the year of publication, the page numbers, and the medium of publication.

3. **Magazine article** Give the author's name, title of the article, title of the magazine, date of publication—day, month, and year for a weekly magazine, or month and year for a monthly magazine—page number[s] of the article, and medium of publication.

4. **Newspaper article** Give the author's name, title of the article, name of the newspaper, city of publication unless it is a national paper, date it was published—day, month, and year—page number[s] of the article, and medium of publication.

5. **Book** Give the author's name, title of the book, city of publication, publisher, date of publication, and medium of publication.

CHAPTER CHECKLIST

❑ Narrow your topic before beginning research.

❑ Write research questions to help keep the research process focused.

❑ Conduct primary research by observing, surveying, and interviewing.

❑ Conduct secondary research by locating sources of information in the library and on the Internet.

REFLECTING ON YOUR RESEARCH

To help you continue to improve as a writer, answer the following questions about the writing assignment for this chapter.

1. Was it difficult to decide on a topic to research and write about? Why or why not?

2. How easy or hard was it to write a good research question? What revisions did you make to your question and why?

3. What were the easiest and hardest parts of doing research?

4. Which types of primary research do you find most useful and why? Which types of secondary sources do you find most useful and why?

5. If you could do the research for your essay over again, what would you do differently?

Once you answer these questions, freewrite about what you learned in this chapter about conducting research and what you would still like to learn.

Visit **LaunchPad Solo for Readers and Writers** > **Research** for more tutorials, videos, and practice searching for and working with sources.

12

Evaluating and Using Sources

In Chapter 11, you narrowed your topic and formulated research questions to help you identify research sources. You also learned how to conduct primary research—interviews, observations, and surveys—and where to find secondary sources—books, database articles, and more. Chapter 12 asks you to continue your research project, using the same writing assignment. In this chapter, you will evaluate the sources you find to determine if they're reliable and if they're a good fit for your essay—that is, you'll determine if the resources you find will develop and support your thesis and main points. To do so, you'll need to learn the criteria for useful resources, strategies for taking notes, and how to incorporate your research into your essay without plagiarizing. At the end of the chapter, you'll find a guide to citing resources in MLA format as well as student writer Aileen Ly's final researched essay, which includes resources she found in the previous chapter.

When conducting research, as you did in Chapter 11, it's important to realize that not all of the relevant sources you find are reliable, credible sources. With so much information available to you within an instant on the Internet, it is important to understand where the information is coming from and how reliable it is before you use the information in your essay. Pay attention to whether the source has a particular bias—meaning a strong, usually unfair opinion—or an agenda that would prevent the authors of the source from presenting a full and factual picture of your topic. As you read, ask yourself

In this chapter, you will evaluate and use your research to write a brief researched essay. As you complete your essay, you will

- Evaluate sources of information.
- Learn what plagiarism is and how to avoid it.
- Learn note-taking strategies.
- Quote, paraphrase, and summarize information.
- Document sources correctly.

whether all sides of an issue have been considered and are being presented, whether the personal opinion of the author is apparent and perhaps even forceful, and whether key information seems to be missing. Considering these elements of a source can help you determine whether the source is fair, accurate, and unbiased.

Of course, for those sources you choose for your essay, be sure to use the information from them properly. When using the copy and paste functions of any word-processing program, it is easy to inadvertently insert another writer's words into your own work, without even realizing it. Therefore, it is important to be sure you accurately quote, paraphrase, and summarize all sources, and to properly cite each source in your essay. This chapter will guide you in evaluating sources for your research and in responsibly using the information from those sources in your own essays. ■

Writing Assignment: Part Two

Your campus's student affairs administration is holding a public meeting to help enhance and share students' cultural experiences, and your psychology instructor has volunteered your class to participate in this forum. To prepare for the forum, your instructor has asked each student to write an essay that explores a cultural experience or expectation.

For Part Two of the assignment, you will evaluate your research, take notes on your sources, and responsibly incorporate your research into your essay to support your ideas.

❰ Evaluating Sources of Information

The credibility of the sources you consult is an important concern. A report isn't necessarily objective simply because it appears in print or on television. Many magazines have a political bias. The *National Review*, for instance, has a conservative slant, whereas the *Nation* is considered liberal. Recent sources (that is, those published within the last five years) are more up-to-date than older ones. Journal articles are often peer reviewed before being published—meaning they are evaluated by experts in that field—which makes them an excellent source of information. If you gather information from television sources, be especially skeptical about what you watch. Many television news discussion programs have a political bias, and some news-entertainment shows may exaggerate facts to make their stories more interesting to their audience. Avoid using material from a talk show unless you are certain it's not hearsay or gossip.

HOW TO Evaluate Web Resources

- Determine who put the information on the website. Does this person have credentials, such as college degrees or university affiliations? If no author is named or if the author's credentials aren't given, find another source of information.

- Is the website trying to sell you something? If so, it might not contain objective information.

- Be cautious when accessing websites with *com* in their addresses, as in **apple.com**. *Com* is an abbreviation for "commercial"; most of these websites are connected to commercial companies that are trying to sell you something.

- Websites with *edu* in their addresses, as in **lib.iastate.edu**, are usually maintained by colleges or universities; websites with *gov* in their addresses, as in **loc.gov**, are sponsored by governmental agencies; and websites with *org*, such as **votesmart.org**, are sponsored by nonprofit organizations. Information provided on such sites is likely to be reliable, although you still need to determine the author of the site and its purpose.

Evaluating sources you find online is especially important. For the most part, no independent person or agency screens material before it is put online. Therefore, *you* need to screen the material. If you were searching for information on culture shock, for instance, you might find websites advertising a therapist's treatment for culture shock, a site dedicated to a rock band named Culture Shock, and a high school student's research paper on this topic.

GROUP ACTIVITY 1 Evaluate Websites

With a few of your classmates, evaluate several websites that deal in some way with a cultural experience. (To access these websites, use a search engine and type in the keywords "cultural experience," "cultural perceptions," "cultural traditions," or a similar keyword combination.) Which sites would be appropriate for an essay on this topic? How did you determine their appropriateness and relevance?

⏻ Use favorites and bookmarks

Use the Bookmark feature in your browser to help you quickly access websites you plan to examine more than once. A bookmark allows you to link directly to a site rather than having to type in the entire URL address. You can return to the site by choosing it from your list of favorites or bookmarks.

Avoiding Plagiarism

A very serious offense, *plagiarism* is using another writer's ideas or words without giving credit to that writer as the source. Handing in someone else's work with your name on it is an obvious act of plagiarism. But using another writer's words or ideas in your paper without indicating where they came from, even if you do so unintentionally, is also an act of plagiarism.

Therefore, you must be careful to avoid plagiarism. Always identify your sources when you borrow ideas, information, or quotations so that your readers can clearly distinguish between what has been borrowed and what is your own.

HOW TO Avoid Plagiarism

- When you reproduce a writer's exact words, use quotation marks to enclose the quote. Be sure to name your source.
- When you restate an author's words in your own words, omit the quotation marks but still name your source.
- List all of the sources named in your paper in the Works Cited list.

The following sections on taking notes and on quoting, paraphrasing, summarizing, and documenting sources will also help you avoid plagiarism.

GROUP ACTIVITY 2 Talk about Plagiarism

Plagiarism can come in many forms. Discuss the following situations with your class-mates.

1. Because of her busy work schedule, Anne puts off writing a research paper until the night before the deadline. As a result, she doesn't take the time to identify the sources of borrowed words and ideas in her paper. A week later, her instructor calls her into his office and tells her that she has plagiarized.
   - Why is this plagiarism?
   - How might Anne revise to avoid plagiarism?

2. Karita is on the web doing research for her paper, and she finds an essay there on her topic. She copies several paragraphs from the essay, word for word, without indicating where they came from. Later, Karita's instructor asks her why part of her paper sounds as if someone else wrote it.
   - Why is this plagiarism?
   - How might Karita revise to avoid plagiarism?

3. Coworkers Sam and Eloise are asked by their supervisor to write a report on the company's recent sales figures. Eloise volunteers to draft the report, and

Sam agrees to revise, edit, and submit it to the supervisor. The report that Sam submits, however, has only his name on it.

- Why is this plagiarism?

- How might Sam revise to avoid plagiarism?

4. Kwan and Joe are roommates. Kwan is enrolled in the same history course that Joe took last semester. Kwan comes across one of Joe's old notebooks, and in it is the history paper that Joe wrote for last semester's course. Kwan reformats the paper and submits it as his own.

- Why is this plagiarism?

- How might Kwan revise to avoid plagiarism? How might Kwan's experience influence his behavior in the future?

- What advice would you give Kwan if you could?

Taking Notes

Once you locate a book, an article, or another source on your topic, skim it to see if it answers any of your research questions. To *skim* a source, simply read the introduction, the headings and subheadings, and the conclusion. If the source answers any of your research questions, take notes. You can also photocopy the relevant pages and highlight the important ideas. However, highlighting shouldn't replace taking careful notes. Note taking forces you to evaluate the reliability and relevance of a source, to select only what is useful from a source, to restate the information in your own words, and to reflect on its meaning.

Consider taking notes using a word-processing program. You can create a folder for your research project and save notes on each resource as an individual file. Or, you can use one file for all of your research notes but just use the Insert Page Break feature to start notes on each resource on a new page. At the top of the page, record all of the information you will need for your Works Cited page. Then, using bullet points or multiple paragraphs, write your notes about the source, including your reactions to the author's points, suggestions for how to use the source to support one of your main points, and any information you'll want to reference in your essay. For each note, be sure to include the page or paragraph number from the source so you can correctly cite it. For an example, see student writer Aileen Ly's notes on page 381.

Another option for taking notes is by hand on paper or by using index cards—or a digital program that resembles them. Index cards help you focus on the information you need because space is limited. Also, you can arrange the cards in various ways, which can be helpful in organizing your ideas during revision. Take notes for only one source per note card.

Whichever note-taking method you use, for each source, be sure to record the author's name, the title, and the publication information you will need for your Works Cited page at the end of your essay. This information varies depending on the type of source you consult. For magazine, journal, and newspaper articles, encyclopedia entries, books, and websites, you must record the following information for each source you use.

MAGAZINE OR NEWSPAPER ARTICLE	ENCYCLOPEDIA ARTICLE OR ENTRY
■ Author (if given) ■ Title of article ■ Name of magazine or newspaper ■ Date of publication ■ Page numbers of the whole article or printout ■ Medium of publication If you accessed the article on a database from your library, also record the following: ■ Name of the database (such as *ProQuest*) ■ Medium of publication ■ Date that you accessed the article	■ Author (if given, it usually appears at the end of the entry) ■ Title ■ Name of the encyclopedia (and edition) ■ Year of publication ■ Medium of publication
	BOOK
	■ Author ■ Title ■ City and name of publisher ■ Year of publication ■ Medium of publication
JOURNAL ARTICLE	**WEBSITE**
■ Author ■ Title of article ■ Name of journal ■ Number of volume and issue ■ Date of publication (year) ■ Page numbers of the whole article or printout ■ Medium of publication If you accessed the article on a database from your library, also record the following: ■ Name of the database ■ Medium of publication ■ Date that you accessed the article	■ Author ■ Title ■ Name of any institution or organization associated with the site ■ Date of publication or last update ■ Medium of publication ■ Date of access

Following is an example of a note file Aileen Ly created in a word-processing program on her computer. The note is based on Mijung Park et al.'s article "Working with Culture: Culturally Appropriate Mental Health Care for Asian Americans" (the fifth result in Figure 11.3 on page 371). This journal article helped Aileen answer her research question, "How can stereotyping like this be prevented, and how can the effects be treated?"

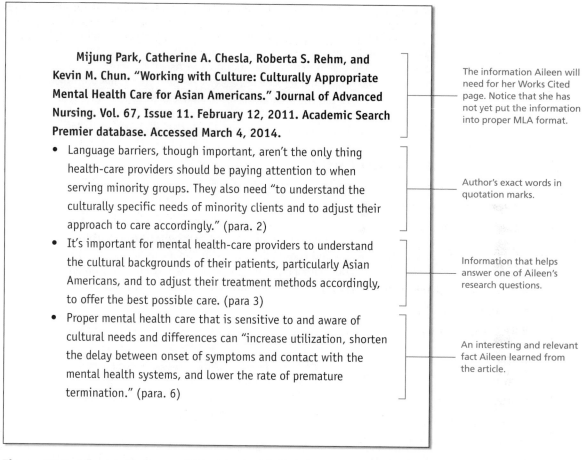

Mijung Park, Catherine A. Chesla, Roberta S. Rehm, and Kevin M. Chun. "Working with Culture: Culturally Appropriate Mental Health Care for Asian Americans." Journal of Advanced Nursing. Vol. 67, Issue 11. February 12, 2011. Academic Search Premier database. Accessed March 4, 2014.

The information Aileen will need for her Works Cited page. Notice that she has not yet put the information into proper MLA format.

- Language barriers, though important, aren't the only thing health-care providers should be paying attention to when serving minority groups. They also need "to understand the culturally specific needs of minority clients and to adjust their approach to care accordingly." (para. 2)

Author's exact words in quotation marks.

- It's important for mental health-care providers to understand the cultural backgrounds of their patients, particularly Asian Americans, and to adjust their treatment methods accordingly, to offer the best possible care. (para 3)

Information that helps answer one of Aileen's research questions.

- Proper mental health care that is sensitive to and aware of cultural needs and differences can "increase utilization, shorten the delay between onset of symptoms and contact with the mental health systems, and lower the rate of premature termination." (para. 6)

An interesting and relevant fact Aileen learned from the article.

Figure 12.1 Aileen's Notes on "Working with Culture: Culturally Appropriate Mental Health Care for Asian Americans"

HOW TO Take Notes

- Refer frequently to your research questions to keep you focused on your topic.
- Don't just copy information from sources; add your own thoughts. You might note, for instance, where you could use the information in your essay.
- Use quotation marks to indicate where you record an author's exact words. Write the rest of your notes completely in your own words.
- When you change a source's words and sentence structure into your own words, you are *paraphrasing* the source. Most of your notes should be paraphrased.

> ◀ **GROUP ACTIVITY 3** Practice Taking Notes ▶
>
> Imagine that you, like Aileen, are writing an essay on the issue of depression in Asian Americans and that one of your research questions is "What can be done to reduce the rate of depression and suicidal thoughts in Asian Americans?" To answer this question, take notes on the following essay. Compare your notes with several classmates' note cards. Did you answer the research question without giving unnecessary information? Did you put quotation marks around the authors' exact words? Did you record the necessary publication information for the source?

MIMI KO CRUZ
Desperate Measures

The following article was written by Mimi Ko Cruz, a staff writer for Public Affairs at California State University, Fullerton. She highlights the research of Eliza Noh, associate professor and coordinator of Asian American Studies. Noh joined the CSU faculty in 2003 with a Ph.D. in ethnic studies and a B.A. in women's studies. Her many research and teaching interests include Asian American and ethnic studies, Asian American women and psychology, and race and gender. Noh offers this advice for students: "Trust your passions; great things will come from them, even if you don't see a place for them yet."

1   Eliza Noh remembers her older sister being depressed from the time she started high school until the day she killed herself as a 20-year-old college student in 1990.

2   "She had problems with depression and I've found that my sister's experience is not unique," said Noh, associate professor and coordinator of Asian American studies.

3   Noh was a Columbia University undergrad two years after her sister's death when she began researching suicide among Asians. Today, she continues her research in her quest to raise awareness about the problem and find effective interventions.

4   "It just became my expertise," said Noh, who is of Korean and Vietnamese descent.

5   Noh's research has produced the following findings:

- Suicide is the second leading cause of death among Asian American women, ages 15-24.
- Asian American women, ages 15-24 and over 65, have the highest female suicide rates across all racial/ethnic groups.
- Asian American adolescent girls (grades 5-12) demonstrate the highest rates of depression across both race/ethnicity and gender.
- "Model minority" expectations and family pressures often are cited as factors of suicide.

6   "Recent data on the alarming suicide rates among Asian American women are directing increasing public attention to this important mental health issue," Noh said. "While raising consciousness about these data is crucial, very little is

known about Asian American women's suicides due to the scarcity of empirical studies on the subject, particularly from the perspectives of Asian American women themselves."

The "model minority" pressure—socially produced pressure internalized by 7 families of some Asian-American children to be high achievers at school and professionally—is a big part of the problem, Noh said.

She has been studying Asian-American women who attempted or contem- 8 plated suicide and finds the majority cite the "model minority" pressure as the main culprit for their behavior.

Girls are more affected by family pressure than boys, she said. They are 9 expected to be the "perfect mother, daughter, wife and get only As in school and choose the right type of job."

Besides family pressure, there are other factors that contribute to the high 10 suicide rate of Asian American women, including social alienation, sexism, and racism, Noh said.

The stereotype that Asians are smart and always do well at work, at home, 11 and at school also can lead to depression, she said.

Noh said her sister thought she was ugly and got plastic surgery to make her 12 eyes and nose appear more like the white women she grew up around in Houston in the 1970s and '80s.

Some of the suicidal women Noh has studied reported that their mothers 13 also were suicidal.

While the causes of depression are varied, so are the ways to cope, the 14 researcher said.

"Asian American women suicide survivors employ diverse healing strate- 15 gies from traditional therapies to alternative practices, such as cultural decolonization through writing and art, spirituality, social activism and Asian medicine, such as acupuncture," Noh said. "This seems to suggest that healing models must be flexible enough to accommodate therapeutic as well as extra-therapeutic interventions."

Because Asian American women tend to stay away from mental health 16 services, "I think more radical approaches are necessary, especially when it comes to matters of life and death as in suicide intervention," she added. "Ultimately, it may be that achieving mental well-being cannot be found simply through psychotherapy, but by making necessary changes in the sociopolitical environment and creating new, empowering forms of subjectivity that draw from the unique experiences of Asian American women."

Based on her research, Noh is writing a book on Asian American women's 17 suicides and depression.

❰ Integrating Your Research

Once you've found information from your sources that will help support your thesis and main ideas, you'll need to determine how to responsibly integrate it into your essay. "Integrating" a source's ideas means weaving

For more information on avoiding plagiarism, refer to p. 378.

them into your essay. Instead of listing quotes from sources or piecing together summaries, you introduce the sources' ideas and explain how the information supports your main ideas. Every time you refer to an idea from your research, you'll need to properly cite it to avoid plagiarism. The three ways to integrate research are quoting, paraphrasing, and summarizing.

Quoting Information

As a general rule, use quotations sparingly. But when an author uses an especially memorable phrase, you might want to quote it directly in your paper. You also might use quoted material to emphasize a point or sum up an idea. These should be brief quotations of one or two sentences.

You should include an introductory phrase to tell your readers the source of each quotation. After the quoted information, put the page number of the source (if it's a print source) in parentheses. If it is an online source, and therefore no page numbers are given, put the last name of the author of the source in parentheses. Here are some examples:

> According to professor and researcher Eliza Noh, "Recent data on the alarming suicide rates among Asian American women are directing increasing public attention to this important mental health issue" (Cruz).

> Professor and researcher Eliza Noh's research has found that "recent data on the alarming suicide rates among Asian American women are directing increasing public attention to this important mental health issue" (Cruz).

> "Recent data on the alarming suicide rates among Asian American women are directing increasing public attention to this important mental health issue," says professor and researcher Eliza Noh (Cruz).

Also notice in the examples how the quotations are punctuated.

Refer to pp. 503–506 for guidelines about punctuating quotations.

When you use a quotation, you can't just drop it into a paragraph. You need to explain its relevance to your topic or point. In the following paragraph from Aileen Ly's essay on the connection between a stereotype and depression in Asian Americans, the writer quotes a phrase from the Cruz essay about Eliza Noh's research findings and then explains its relevance to her point:

> One of the key contributors to depression in Asian Americans is the Model Minority Stereotype. According to professor and researcher Eliza Noh, "The 'model minority' pressure — socially produced pressure internalized by families of some Asian American children to be high achievers at school and professionally — is a big part of the problem" (Cruz). Therefore, it is important to be aware that this stereotype exists in society and to understand the negative impact it can have on Asian Americans. Dissolving this stereotype would be an important step in reducing the rate of depression in Asian Americans.

Note, too, as this paragraph demonstrates, that the topic-illustration-explanation (TIE) order of organization is often used in paragraphs containing quotations.

For more information about using the TIE order of paragraph organization, refer to pp. 55–56.

> ## HOW TO Quote Information
>
> - Use quoted information to repeat memorable phrases, to emphasize a point, or to sum up.
> - Include a phrase that provides the source of the information.
> - Add quotation marks at the beginning and end of the quoted material.
> - Explain why the quotation is relevant to your topic.

GROUP ACTIVITY 4 Quote Sources

Working with several other students, write a paragraph about one of the main ideas in "Desperate Measures." Use a quotation from the essay to help you develop the paragraph. Then create an introductory phrase for the quotation and consider using the topic-illustration-explanation order of paragraph organization. Compare your group's paragraph with those written by the other groups in the class.

Paraphrasing Information

To *paraphrase* is to restate a source in your own words. By paraphrasing information, you simplify complicated information and use your own writing style.

A paraphrase should be about the same length as the original passage and express the same ideas. Although when paraphrasing you might be tempted to simply substitute keywords with synonyms (words that have the same meaning), this can lead to plagiarism. Use your own writing style instead. This might mean changing the sentence structure or word order. Here's an example of an original passage, a poor paraphrase, and a good paraphrase. In the poor paraphrase, words from the original are highlighted:

ORIGINAL	"The 'model minority' pressure—socially produced pressure internalized by families of some Asian American children to be high achievers at school and professionally—is a big part of the problem, Noh said" (Cruz).
POOR PARAPHRASE	Professor and researcher Eliza Noh said that the "model minority" pressure, a socially produced concept that says Asian Americans are high achievers at school and at work, is part of the problem (Cruz).

GOOD PARAPHRASE   According to professor and researcher Eliza Noh, the stereotype of the "model minority"—the idea that Asian Americans need to excel in everything they do—is largely to blame (Cruz).

When paraphrasing, you don't need to use quotation marks because the words are your own. You must, however, indicate the source of the idea or information.

Here is the same student paragraph from Aileen Ly you saw on page 384, except here the quotation is replaced with a good paraphrase (highlighted):

> One of the key contributors to depression in Asian Americans is the Model Minority Stereotype. According to professor and researcher Eliza Noh, the stereotype of the "model minority"—the idea that Asian Americans need to excel in everything they do—is largely to blame (Cruz). Therefore, it is important to be aware that this stereotype exists in society and to understand the negative impact it can have on Asian Americans. Dissolving this stereotype would be an important step in reducing the rate of depression in Asian Americans.

Notice, too, that the TIE (topic-illustration-explanation) order of paragraph organization is used with the paraphrased information.

HOW TO Paraphrase Information

- Read the material you want to paraphrase, then put it away. Write down the information or idea on a note card, using your own words and writing style.
- After the paraphrase, write the name of the author whose ideas you have borrowed (if you haven't already given the author's name) and the page number of the source.
- Reread the original passage to make sure you have accurately captured the author's information or ideas without plagiarizing.

GROUP ACTIVITY 5 Paraphrase Sources

Working with a group of students, paraphrase one or two paragraphs from "Desperate Measures." Compare your group's paraphrases with those of the other groups in your class.

Summarizing Information

For more on summarizing, see pp. 39–41.

A *summary* is a condensed version of a piece of text that contains that text's key ideas. A summary is always much shorter than the original because it omits most details. Summary writing is one of the most common types of writing used in college and the workplace. On the job, you might write a summary of sales over the past six months. In college courses, you might be asked to write summaries of lectures, lab experiments, or journal articles. In an essay, information summarized from primary or secondary research can provide good supporting examples, observations, definitions, facts, statistics, and expert testimony.

Depending on your purpose for writing, a summary may be as short as a sentence or as long as a paragraph. Here's a one-sentence summary of "Desperate Measures."

> In "Desperate Measures," Mimi Ko Cruz reports on professor Eliza Noh's experience with Asian American mental illness and on Noh's research findings on the high rates of depression and suicidal thoughts among this group.

Here's a longer summary of the same article:

> In "Desperate Measures," Mimi Ko Cruz reports on professor Eliza Noh's experience with Asian American depression and suicide and on Noh's research findings related to this topic. Noh has discovered high rates of depression and suicidal thoughts in Asian Americans, particularly in women. She cites several reasons for these mental health issues, including societal and familial pressures to excel in all aspects of life and reluctance to seek help from mental health professionals. Noh also offers the opinion that perhaps more than psychotherapy is needed to help Asian American women, in particular, who struggle with depression and suicidal thoughts, suggesting that more holistic and well-rounded healing options should be explored.

When you summarize information in your essay, remember that your ideas come first. Summarized information should be used only to support your own points.

HOW TO Summarize Information

- Reread the source and write down the main ideas. These ideas are usually expressed in the thesis statement, the topic sentences, and, at times, the conclusion. If the source has headings and subheadings, they may express main ideas as well.
- Focus on the main points only and omit the details.
- At the beginning of your summary, give the title and author of the source.
- Write the summary in your own words. Use a quotation only to emphasize an important point that cannot be conveyed as powerfully in your own words.

◀ **GROUP ACTIVITY 6** Analyze Summaries ▶

Read the following two summaries of "Desperate Measures." With your group, discuss how these summaries could be improved.

1. In "Desperate Measures," Mimi Ko Cruz shares professor Eliza Noh's research on depression and suicidal thoughts in Asian Americans, particularly women. Noh is of Korean and Vietnamese descent and had a sister who had problems with depression, which is what led her to do her research. Noh has found that "model minority" expectations and family pressures are often the main reasons for high suicide rates among Asian American women.

2. According to Eliza Noh's research, explained in Mimi Ko Cruz's "Desperate Measures," many Asian American girls and women experience depression and suicidal thoughts, but not many seek help from mental health services. Instead they tend to employ many different healing strategies from traditional therapies to alternative treatments.

◖ Documenting Sources

Documentation of sources is an important aspect of the research paper. To *document* is to refer your reader to your primary and secondary research sources. Proper documentation allows readers to locate and verify your sources for their own future research. It also keeps you from inadvertently plagiarizing others' words or ideas. You document sources both in the essay itself (where you identify the author and page number for quotations, paraphrases, and summaries) and in a list of sources at the end of the paper (called a Works Cited page).

In-Text Documentation

You need to document whenever you quote, paraphrase, or summarize a research source in the text of the paper itself. For each source you refer to, you will write a citation. Follow these guidelines for writing citations:

- Identify the author in an introductory phrase and give the page number in parentheses.

  > In her book *Asian Americans: Vulnerable Populations, Model Interventions, and Clarifying Agendas*, Lin Zhan states, "Asian Americans suffer a disproportionate burden of mental illnesses, such as high rates of suicide and posttraumatic stress disorder. However, they under-utilize mental health services" (11).

- If you don't give the author's name in an introductory phrase, include the author's last name along with the page number (if it is a print source) in parentheses. (The second example that follows is a paraphrase from an online source with no page numbers.)

Because many later-generation Asian American students come from immigrant families who place high value on their children's education, "Some students spoke of the responsibility and guilt they felt for their parents' sacrifices" (Lee 66).

Often in Asian cultures, the emphasis is on the family unit, unlike Western philosophy, which places importance on the individual. This discourages those being affected by mental illness from speaking out, in fear that it will harm the image of the family line (Nikolchev).

- If the source has two or three authors, include all of the last names in the citation.

According to Ritter and Lampkin, "Despite the progress in understanding the causes of mental illness and tremendous advances in finding effective mental health treatments, far less is known about the mental health of African Americans, American Indians and Alaska Natives, Asian American and Pacific Islanders, and Hispanic Americans" (93).

Experts in the field of community mental health tell us that "Despite the progress in understanding the causes of mental illness and tremendous advances in finding effective mental health treatments, far less is known about the mental health of African Americans, American Indians and Alaska Natives, Asian American and Pacific Islanders, and Hispanic Americans" (Ritter and Lampkin 93).

- If the source has four or more authors, either give the names of all the authors, or give the name of the first author followed by *et al.*, which is an abbreviation for "and others."

Park et al. make the excellent point that "until healthcare providers understand how to adapt practice to deal successfully with the issues of culture and health, their ability to deliver patient centered, culturally sensitive care will be hampered" (2374).

Experts point out that "until healthcare providers understand how to adapt practice to deal successfully with the issues of culture and health, their ability to deliver patient centered, culturally sensitive care will be hampered" (Park, Chesla, Rehm, and Chun 2374).

- If no author is given for a source, give the title in an introductory phrase or a shortened version of the title in parentheses.

The Counseling Center at University of Illinois Urbana-Champaign describes this stereotype on their website in an article titled "Model Minority Stereotype," stating, "This stereotype suggests that Asian Americans as a racial/ethnic group are achieving a higher level of success than the population average." The Model Minority Stereotype "suggests that Asian Americans as a racial/ethnic group are achieving a higher level of success than the population average" ("Model Minority").

■ Remember that you need to include in-text documentation for paraphrased or summarized information, in addition to quoted information.

> For example, the Asian Pacific Family Center in Rosemead, California, is a nonprofit organization that provides help for Asians with mental illness, particularly in a community that doesn't know much about mental illness, or perhaps doesn't know of its existence in the community at all (Ni).

■ Use transitions or keywords to connect the documented material to the point being made. Some keywords and transitions used in the previous examples are "For example," and "in fact."

■ Finally, study the format of the previous examples. Notice that only the number of the page is given (don't use *page* or *p.*). Also, put the period after the parentheses.

Works Cited Page

The *Works Cited page* is a list of sources that appears at the end of your paper. Every source you mention in your essay should be included in the Works Cited. Be sure to include *only* those sources you actually cited in the paper and not any additional resources that you may have researched but didn't use. Different fields of study use different formats and titles for the Works Cited list. The following discussion and sample entries are based on the format established by the Modern Language Association (MLA).

HOW TO Use MLA Format

- Put the Works Cited list on a separate page at the end of your paper.
- Arrange the source entries alphabetically by the authors' last names or by title if the author is not named.
- Double-space the entries.
- The first line of each entry should line up with the left-hand margin. The other lines of each entry should be indented one-half inch.
- Italicize the titles of books, journals, magazines, and newspapers.
- Put the titles of magazine and newspaper articles in quotation marks.

⏻ **Get assistance from citation links**

Although it is essential to learn to use a manual or handbook to learn documentation styles for your Works Cited page, many websites and online sources now include a "citation" or "cite this" link that shows you the citation in the appropriate style. However, always double-check with the most up-to-date guidelines in the official style manual.

MLA format also requires that you present the information about your sources in a specific way. Books, magazines, journals, and newspapers require different formats. Encyclopedias are different still, and there is a particular way to list an interview. Also, the form varies slightly when a source has more than one author. Here are some sample MLA-style entries.

BOOK WITH ONE AUTHOR

Lee, Stacey J. *Unraveling the "Model Minority" Stereotype: Listening to Asian American Youth*. 2nd ed. New York: Teachers College Press, 2009. Print.

BOOK WITH MORE THAN ONE AUTHOR

Ritter, Lois, and Shirley Lampkin. *Community Mental Health*. Sudbury: Jones & Bartlett, 2012. Print.

CHAPTER OR ARTICLE FROM AN EDITED BOOK

Kurasaki, Karen S., and Alan K. Koike. "Assessing Psychiatric Prevalance Rates Among Asian Americans." *Asian American Mental Health: Assessment Theories and Methods*. Ed. Karen S. Kurasaki, Sumie Okazaki, and Stanley Sue. New York: Springer Science and Business Media, 2002. Print.

MAGAZINE ARTICLE

Peng, Tina. "Mental Illness May Go Untreated in Asian Americans." *Newsweek*. Newsweek, 11 Aug. 2008. Web. 2 Mar. 2015.

JOURNAL ARTICLE

After the author and title of the article, follow with the journal title, volume and issue numbers (if given), and the date.

Narikiyo, Trudy A., and Velma A. Kameoka. "Attributions of Mental Illness and Judgments about Help Seeking Among Japanese-American and White American Students." *Journal of Counseling Psychology* 39.3 (1992): 363–69. Print.

In this example, "39.3" refers to volume 39, issue 3.

NEWSPAPER ARTICLE

Watters, Ethan. "The Americanization of Mental Illness." *New York Times*. New York Times, 8 Jan. 2010. Web. 2 Mar. 2015.

If the article appears in print on more than one page, and the pages are not consecutive, add a plus sign after the number of the first page: *C4+*.

ENCYCLOPEDIA ARTICLE

"Minority." *Encyclopædia Britannica. Encyclopædia Britannica Online.* Encyclopædia
Britannica Inc., 2014. Web. 2 Mar. 2015.

PERSONAL INTERVIEW

Wucinich, Sophia. Personal interview. 10 Jan. 2015.

If the interview is conducted by telephone or the Internet, simply change
"personal interview" to "telephone interview" or "e-mail interview."

ARTICLE FROM AN ONLINE DATABASE

To cite a source you obtained from an online database, give the same
information you would give if you had used a print format. Additionally,
give the name of the database, italicized; the medium (*Web*); and the date of
access.

Park, Mijung, et al. "Working with Culture: Culturally Appropriate Mental Health Care for
Asian Americans." *Journal of Advanced Nursing* (2011). *Academic Search Premier.*
Web. 4 Mar. 2015.

WORK FROM A WEBSITE

If you used information from a website, give the author's name (if
included), the title of the document, and the title of the site (italicized); follow with the name of any institution or organization sponsoring the site (use
n.p., if none is given), the date of publication (use *n.d.*, if no date is given),
the medium (*Web*), and the date you accessed the site.

"Model Minority Stereotype." *U of Illinois at Urbana-Champaign Counseling Center.* U of
Illinois, n.d. Web. 5 Mar. 2015.

For more information on how to document sources, consult the *MLA Handbook for Writers of Research Papers*, Seventh Edition (2009), or the *MLA Style
Manual and Guide to Scholarly Publishing*, Third Edition (2008). Both are available in the reference section of your library. These resources also give many
more examples of documentation models, showing how to document
e-mails, audio or video interviews, letters, reviews, blogs, paintings, films,
and much more.

> **GROUP ACTIVITY 7 Create a Works Cited Page**

With several classmates, create a Works Cited page in MLA format for the following
five sources. All necessary information is given (as well as unnecessary information
you won't need to use).

1. *What Do International Students Think and Feel? Adapting to U.S. College Life
and Culture* by Jerry G. Gebhard. Page 23. 2010. University of Michigan Press,
located in Ann Arbor, Michigan.

_____

_____

2. Interview by telephone with Helen Mar, who is Chinese American, about her experiences as a college student student. Boise, Idaho. June 30, 2014.

_____

_____

3. "Asians in America: What's Holding Back the 'Model Minority'?" by Sylvia Ann Hewlett. Published in _Forbes_ magazine on July 28, 2011. Accessed online November 12, 2014.

_____

_____

4. Erica Goode's article, called "Disparities Seen in Mental Care for Minorities," which was published on the online version of the _New York Times_ on August 27, 2001. Accessed November 29, 2014.

_____

_____

5. "Asian American Mental Health: A Call to Action" by Stanley Sue, Janice Ka Yan Cheng, Carmel S. Saad, and Joyce P. Chu. Published in a journal called _American Psychologist_, volume 67, issue 7, in October 2012 on pp. 532–44. Accessed online in the database _Academic Search Premier_ on December 15, 2014.

_____

_____

Sample Researched Essay

The following essay was written by student writer Aileen Ly for the International Students Forum on her campus. She used the writing process—exploring choices, drafting, revising, and editing—before presenting this essay to the audience at the forum. In order to have space to annotate her essay, we have reproduced it on these pages in a narrower and longer format than you will have on a standard 8½ × 11-inch sheet of paper.

Aileen Ly

Professor Hall

Psychology 101

8 May 2014

An Illness of the Mind

I can picture her thrashing back and forth on her plaid blue
bed sheets, restless. It has been a few years since my mother was
diagnosed with depression, but I recall those moments as if they
had just occurred. She would have no appetite, only forcing herself
to eat so that her stomach wasn't empty. Simple tasks like
showering and putting on clothes seemed like a laborious chore.
According to results from the 2012 National Survey on Drug Use
and Health, 9.6 million adults were diagnosed that year with a
serious mental illness. Of the millions of Americans diagnosed with
mental illness each year, "Asian Americans and Pacific Islanders
show higher levels of depressive symptoms than whites" (NAMI).
In fact, as Dr. Eliza Noh's research reveals, both young and elderly
Asian American women have one of the highest suicide rates when
compared to other racial and ethnic groups — a pressing problem
that should be recognized and addressed (qtd. in Cruz).
Stereotypes, cultural characteristics, and difficulties in getting
help are some of the factors to blame for the high rate of mental
illness among Asian American populations.

Preconceived notions have often limited, altered, and broken
the thoughts and ideas of certain groups, as is the case with Asian
Americans. Often the Model Minority Stereotype is used to define
this ethnic group. The Counseling Center at University of Illinois
Urbana-Champaign describes this stereotype in an article titled
"Model Minority Stereotype" on their website: "This stereotype
suggests that Asian Americans as a racial/ethnic group are
achieving a higher level of success than the population average."
It is with no help from Amy Chua, who seems to advocate for strict
"Chinese mother" parenting in her memoir *The Battle Hymn of the
Tiger Mother*, that this stereotype has not yet been dismantled.

Aileen formats the heading properly.

The introduction attracts readers with a personal element.

Double-spacing is used throughout.

This citation is for Dr. Eliza Noh's research findings, which are quoted in the Cruz article listed on Aileen's Works Cited page.

Thesis is clear.

The author and online article are named in the introductory phrase, so no information needs to be given in a parenthetical citation.

1

2

Ly 2

The standards set by such stereotypes have continued to fuel the ongoing mental illness crisis. Take, for example, the alarming statistics provided by the American Psychological Association examining rates of mental illness in Asian Americans (see Fig. 1). The expectation to maintain such an impossible standard has only strengthened the stereotype's grip on Asian American individuals. In a recent interview, journalist Ryan Macasero of Northern California spoke of how the pressures of the Model Minority Myth affected the mental states of his classmates: "They would be so pressured that they were getting good grades, but they had no fun. I didn't see them going out and, you know, having a good time with their friends or anything like that because of the

Aileen incorporates a figure, in the form of a graph, into her essay.

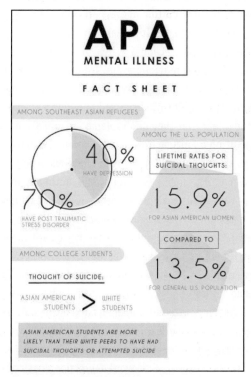

Fig. 1 American Psychological Association Mental Illness Fact Sheet

Ly 3

Aileen cites the name of the person interviewed, not the interviewer.

pressure" (Macasero). Time to relax and have fun, especially as a youth, is essential to good mental health, but finding that downtime can be impossible for some Asian Americans who feel pressured by the Model Minority Myth. In addition to the infliction of such adverse social constructs, other factors also amplified the rate of mental illness among Asian Americans.

Aileen explains the meaning and significance of the source material she cited and connects it to her main point.

Cultural traits, for instance, have played a significant role in the prominence of depression among Asians. Often in Asian cultures, the emphasis is on the family unit, unlike Western philosophy, which places importance on the individual. This discourages those being affected by mental illness from speaking out, in fear that it will harm the image of the family line (Nikolchev). Sharline Chiang, for example, decided against telling her parents of her postpartum depression (PPD) in order to avoid tarnishing her family name. In her article "Sharline Chiang Goes Beyond the Baby Blues," Chiang writes, "For many reasons, largely cultural (they're Chinese immigrants), I didn't want them to know because I didn't want them to worry. . . . The reason why I still haven't told them? PPD isn't discussed enough in any society or culture, and I fear that they might blame me or make me feel like I'm exaggerating about my experience." Chiang's experience exemplifies a situation that many Asian families experience. This shame and fear of exposure is also how my mother approached her illness. Not only did it take her longer to recover, as a result, but her silence also made the process more difficult because her pride prevented her from coming forward when her condition was less severe and therefore more easily treated. In addition to the embedded cultural fear of damaging the family's reputation by admitting to mental illness, the concept of mental illness itself is one that is not integrated into many Asian cultures. According to a Fact Sheet on Asian American and Pacific Islander (AA/PI) Community and Mental Health, published by the National Alliance on Mental Illness (NAMI), "The word *depression* does not exist in certain Asian languages." The overall understanding of mental

A source is paraphrased and cited.

Aileen uses a quotation to support the point that Asian culture and family dynamics play a part in the prevalence of mental illness.

3

Ly 4

illness in Asian cultures is small, which also contributes to the
absence of external aid in such issues.

   A final important factor contributing to the high rate of
mental illness among the Asian American population is difficulty
in getting proper help. Although Asian Americans as a group hold
a higher rate of mental illness than people think, they have a very
low rate of seeking professional care. In her book *Asian Americans:
Vulnerable Populations, Model Interventions, and Clarifying Agendas*,
Lin Zhan states, "Asian Americans suffer a disproportionate burden
of mental illnesses, such as high rates of suicide and posttraumatic
stress disorder. However, they under-utilize mental health services"
(11). In fact, a little less than 30 percent of Asian American
women seek help (Nikolchev). That's an alarmingly low percentage,
one that is certainly cause for concern. In 2014, the American
Psychiatric Association published a fact sheet on mental health
disparities in Asian Americans. In this publication, the Association
states a number of reasons, based on a multitude of research, for a
low percentage overall of Asian Americans seeking help for mental
illness. Some of the reasons cited in the publication include "lack
of awareness about mental health issues and services," "language
and cultural barriers," and "stigma associated with mental illness"
(American Psychiatric Association). In America, we take mental
illness seriously and make a large effort to help those who suffer
from mental illness. In many Asian countries, however, this is not
the case. As mentioned earlier, a family's reputation and honor are
of utmost importance in many Asian societies, and mental illness
is viewed as shameful and burdensome (American Psychiatric
Association). We can, however, certainly do more in our mental
healthcare efforts in America, particularly in effectively helping
and treating Asian Americans. Mijung Park et al. published their
research on this topic in the *Journal of Advanced Nursing* (JAN) in
2011. In their paper "Working with Culture: Culturally Appropriate
Mental Health Care for Asian Americans," Park et al. make the
excellent point that "until healthcare providers understand how to

4

Page number follows
quotation.

Source is paraphrased and
cited.

Aileen balances the
information from her
research with her own ideas.

No page number is given
because the information
was retrieved from a
website.

Quote is introduced.

Ly 5

adapt practice to deal successfully with the issues of culture and health, their ability to deliver patient centered, culturally sensitive care will be hampered" (2374). That is to say that it's important for mental health care providers to understand the cultural backgrounds of their patients, particularly Asian Americans, and to adjust their treatment methods accordingly, to offer the best possible care. All of these factors have contributed to the high percentage of Asian Americans with mental illness who go without help and treatment.

The high rate of mental illness among Asian Americans is attributed to the externally inflicted stereotypes, cultural expectations, and an unwillingness or inability to seek proper help. This is a pressing crisis in the country, and there should be a stronger effort to abolish it. The first step in doing so would be to destigmatize mental illness — to familiarize people with an accurate understanding of what mental illness is and to do away with negative connotations. This could be accomplished in much the same way that homosexuality has been largely destigmatized — through its growing presence in popular culture, which has led to the public's increasing understanding of it and the slow but steady removal of negative stereotyping. Educational programs, such as the effective anti-smoking campaigns, could also prove highly beneficial in raising awareness of mental health. Additionally, establishing health centers as a safe place for individuals with mental health issues to come and receive help would also combat the high mental illness rates among Asian Americans. For example, the Asian Pacific Family Center in Rosemead, California, is a nonprofit organization that provides help for Asians with mental illness, particularly in a community that doesn't know much about mental illness, or perhaps doesn't know of its existence in the community at all (Ni). Mental illness is a pressing crisis that must be addressed immediately — for all ethnic groups — and these are just a few ways to begin to address the problem.

5

These are Aileen's own words—her understanding of the quotation and its relevance to her point—so no citation is needed.

These ideas are Aileen's, so no citations are needed.

This is an important example to support her point, so Aileen paraphrases and cites Ni.

Ly 6

Works Cited

American Psychiatric Association, Division of Diversity and Health

Equity. "Mental Health Disparities: Asian Americans: Fact

Sheet." *Psychiatry.org*. American Psychiatric Association,

2014. PDF file.

Chiang, Sharline. "Sharline Chiang Goes Beyond the Baby Blues."

Mutha Magazine. Mutha Magazine, 16 Oct. 2013. Web. 05 Mar.

2014.

Cruz, Mimi Ko. "Desperate Measures: Push to Excel Linked to

Suicide in Asian-American Women." *Spotlight*. CSU, Fullerton,

18 Oct. 2010. Web. 05 Mar. 2014.

Macasero, Ryan. "Depression, Stigma and the Model Minority Myth

in the Asian American Community." Interview by Jenee

Darden. *Peers Envisioning and Engaging in Recovery Services*

(PEERS). 25 Mar. 2013. Radio.

"Model Minority Stereotype." *U of Illinois at Urbana-Champaign

Counseling Center*. U of Illinois, n.d. Web. 05 Mar. 2014

NAMI Multicultural & International Outreach Center. "Asian

American and Pacific Islander (AA/PI) Community and Mental

Health: Fact Sheet." *NAMI.org*. The National Alliance on

Mental Illness, June 2003. Web. 04 Mar. 2014.

Ni, Ching-Ching. "Center Helps Asian Americans Combat Mental

Illness." *Los Angeles Times*. Los Angeles Times, 23 Nov. 2009.

Web. 06 Mar. 2014.

Nikolchev, Alexandra. "Among Asian-American Women, a Little

Known Battle with Depression." *PBS*. Creative News Group,

12 Oct. 2010. Web. 05 Mar. 2014.

Zhan, Lin. *Asian Americans: Vulnerable Populations, Model

Interventions, and Clarifying Agendas*. Sudbury: Jones and

Bartlett, 2003. Print.

Aileen begins the Works Cited list on a new page and uses double-spacing throughout.

Website sources are properly formatted.

Source from an interview is properly formatted.

CHAPTER CHECKLIST

❏ Evaluate sources of information in the library and on the Internet.

❏ Avoid plagiarism by documenting sources.

❏ Use note taking as an effective research tool.

❏ Use quotation marks to indicate an author's exact words.

❏ Use your own words to paraphrase an author's ideas.

❏ Summarize an author's main ideas to condense lengthy passages.

❏ Document sources properly by identifying them in the essay and listing them on a Works Cited page at the end of the essay.

❏ Include a Works Cited entry with full publication information for every source cited in your essay. Format these entries correctly.

REFLECTING ON YOUR WRITING

To help you continue to improve as a writer, answer the following questions about the writing assignment for this chapter.

1. What were the easiest and hardest parts about evaluating and incorporating research in your essay?

2. What did you learn about plagiarism?

3. Compare writing a researched essay with writing an essay that doesn't contain research.

4. What information about your topic did you learn from conducting research?

5. If you had more time, what would you do to improve your essay before sharing it with readers?

Visit **LaunchPad Solo for Readers and Writers > Research** for more tutorials, videos, and practice searching for and working with sources.

After you answer these questions, freewrite about what you learned in this chapter about evaluating and using sources and writing a researched essay and what you still hope to learn.

PART FOUR

Handbook with Exercises

When we write, we want to communicate our ideas clearly to demonstrate our knowledge of our topic and to ensure that our readers understand what we mean. In this Handbook, you'll find opportunities to practice and improve your writing. For example, you'll learn to improve your sentences and to combine short sentences into longer, more interesting ones. You'll learn how to vary your word choice and to eliminate errors. If you are a multilingual writer, you'll find an entire section devoted to helping you write more effectively.

Plan to use this Handbook in several ways. Use it as a reference guide when you have a question about sentence structure, grammar, spelling, or punctuation. Complete practice exercises to help you target specific errors that occur in your writing. Consult it during the editing stage. And, most important, use it as a resource to help you become the best writer you can be.

Handbook Contents

13

Writing Sentences

Every sentence must have a subject and a verb and express a complete thought. Sentences can be simple, with an easily identifiable subject and verb, or they can be complex, with multiple subjects, verbs, and phrases built with other parts of speech like prepositions. It is important to be able to identify and use the parts of a sentence to avoid common errors like sentence fragments and to ensure that your writing conveys your ideas clearly.

> **In this chapter, you will review and practice using**
> A. Subjects
> B. Verbs
> C. Subject-Verb Agreement

A. Subjects

The **subject** tells *who* or *what* is doing something or being something. Usually, the subject is a **noun**—a person, place, or thing. But a subject can also be a **pronoun**—a word that takes the place of a noun:

Anita laughs.

She is in a good mood.

> Visit **LaunchPad Solo for Readers and Writers** > **Grammar: Basic Sentences** for tutorials and additional practice with sentences.

Compound Subjects

Sometimes a sentence has more than one subject. A subject with more than one part is called a **compound subject**:

John and Emily planned the party.

The dog and the cat ran across the street.

ACTIVITY 1 Add Subjects

Complete each of the following sentences by adding a subject.

EXAMPLE The ____puppy____ chases his tail all day long.

1. My ____uncle____ served in the marines for twenty-five years.

2. The ____customers____ complained about the slow service.

3. ____Mom____ and ____Dad____ lived together after college.

4. Every ____student____ deserves a quality education.

5. ____Sherry____ attended the concert last weekend.

> Visit **LaunchPad Solo for Readers and Writers** > **Grammar: Parts of Speech** for tutorials and additional practice with parts of speech.

13 A

6. The dark _____ made the room feel small.

7. The _____ is very hot and spicy at that restaurant.

8. Lola's _____ is due tomorrow morning.

9. _____ and _____ want to visit the Grand Canyon.

10. The _____ is often crowded in the afternoon.

Subject Pretenders

Sometimes the subject of a sentence is hard to identify because the sentence contains other words that may look like the subject—called a **subject pretender**. The most common type of subject pretender is a prepositional phrase, which begins with a preposition.

Visit **LaunchPad Solo for Readers and Writers > Grammar: Parts of Speech > Prepositions and Conjunctions** for tutorials and additional practice with prepositions.

Prepositions

A **preposition** is a word that expresses how other words are related in time, space, or direction.

Common Prepositions

about	below	for	off	until
above	beneath	from	on	up
after	beside	in	out	upon
against	between	inside	over	with
among	by	into	past	within
as	despite	like	since	without
at	down	near	to	
before	during	next to	toward	
behind	except	of	under	

ACTIVITY 2 Identify Prepositions

Underline the prepositions in the following paragraph.

EXAMPLE Nick and José drove to the library.

They had many questions for the reference librarian because they had a research project due in their history class the following week. Nick left the assignment directions in his car, but José had brought an extra copy with him in his backpack. The librarian found several history reference books on the shelves behind her desk. She helped Nick and José find newspaper and magazine articles by using the library databases and looking under the most useful subject headings. The students sent copies of the best articles to their e-mail accounts. Then they copied entries _from_ the reference books using the photocopier next to the library stairs. Driving home from the library, Nick suggested they stop _for_ a snack before going back _to_ their dorm.

HOW TO Choose the Correct Preposition to Show Time

Prepositions that show time—such as _for_, _during_, and _since_—may have differences in meaning.

- _For_ usually refers to an exact period of time that something lasts— one that has a beginning and an end:

    We have been waiting _for_ thirty minutes.

- _During_ usually refers to an indefinite period of time in which something happens:

    It rained _during_ the night, but I don't know exactly when.

- _Since_ usually refers to a period of time that has passed between an earlier time and the present:

    Since losing weight, I've been more confident.

ACTIVITY 3 Add Prepositions

Complete each of the following sentences by writing a preposition in the space provided.

EXAMPLE I never travel ____without____ my cell phone charger.

1. The swimmer dove ____in____ the pool.

2. The Harry Potter books were written ____by____ J. K. Rowling.

3. Kendra has several tattoos ____on____ her back.

4. Evan found a pen pal ____on____ the Internet.

5. ____In____ her last class, Berta checks her e-mail.

6. Zach never goes to sleep ____at____ midnight.

7. Hiding your house key ____under____ the doormat is a bad idea.

8. Jessica had Dr. Millhauser ____as____ her biology professor.

9. Jo suspected that everyone had been talking ____with____ her.

10. I walk _____ the playground every morning on my way to work.

Prepositional Phrases

13 A

A **prepositional phrase** consists of a preposition and its object. The object is a noun or pronoun, together with any words that describe or refer to the object. Here are some examples.

Preposition	+ Object	= Prepositional Phrase
into	the classroom	into the classroom
before	you	before you
on	a bright summer day	on a bright summer day

ACTIVITY 4 Write Prepositional Phrases

Complete each of the following sentences by adding a prepositional phrase.

EXAMPLE The babysitter took the children ___*for a walk*___.

1. Isaac bought his iPad _____.

2. My economics study group meets ___*in the meeting room*___.

3. Movies _____ are very popular.

4. I ate the pasta that I found ___*in the kitchen*___.

5. When Sal called, I was ___*on the bed*___.

6. _____, Lucy practiced her violin.

7. _____, the plumber fixed the leak.

8. Zaini caught the train _____.

9. The seagulls flew _____.

10. Jesse and Sarah walked home ___*on a bright summer day*___.

A prepositional phrase cannot be the subject of a sentence.

The children *in the bus* need to be brought inside.

In the sentence above, *in the bus* is a prepositional phrase. The subject of the sentence is *children*.

The dog *from across the street* chased my cat.

From across the street is a prepositional phrase. The subject of the sentence is *dog*.

Because you know that the subject of a sentence is never part of a prepositional phrase, you can find the subject easily. First, cross out all the prepositional phrases. Then decide which of the other words is doing or being something.

13 A

The man ~~in the photograph~~ resembles my grandfather.

The subject of the sentence is *man*.

The door ~~at the end of the hall~~ is locked.

The subject of the sentence is *door*.

HOW TO Find the Subject of a Sentence

- Cross out all prepositional phrases.
- Decide which of the remaining words is doing or being something.

ACTIVITY 5 Find Prepositional Phrases and Sentence Subjects

In each of the following sentences, cross out the prepositional phrases and circle the subject.

EXAMPLE The (box) ~~on the table~~ was open.

1. The (neighbors) ~~down the hall~~ are very loud.
2. (Darryl) bought a laptop ~~for five hundred dollars.~~
3. The (pumpkins) ~~in that garden~~ need to be picked.
4. ~~After the midterm,~~ the (sociology) class became more difficult.
5. ~~Inside those drawers,~~ (you) will find my old sweaters.
6. The (guests) ~~at the wedding~~ loved the food.
7. ~~Without his friends,~~ (Nicky) felt somewhat shy.
8. The (information) ~~in that article~~ is not very reliable.
9. The (questions) ~~on the test~~ covered the whole semester.
10. Two ~~of~~ (Kristina's brothers) joined the military.

ACTIVITY 6 Identify Subject Pretenders

In the following paragraph, cross out the prepositional phrases and circle the subject of each sentence.

EXAMPLE (I) entered the photographs ~~on that wall in the art show.~~

(Everybody) who participated in the student art show benefited ~~from the expe-~~ rience. My friend (Jill) won a prize ~~for one of her paintings.~~ Consequently, (three) ~~of her~~ (pieces) are now on display ~~in the student center.~~ Although (I) did not win anything, I received lots of compliments on my photographs. A person who asked for my telephone number has purchased a photo from me. Around the campus green where the show took place were temporary walls made of plywood. Graffiti artists painted the walls with their best efforts. These walls were the most popular work of art at the show. They have been moved next to the art building and will remain on display.

◖ B. Verbs

Visit **LaunchPad Solo for Readers and Writers > Grammar: Basic Sentences > Verbs** for tutorials and additional practice with verbs.

The **verb** in a sentence expresses action or links the subject to the rest of the sentence.

Action and Linking Verbs

Action Verbs

In the following sentences, the verb expresses action:

My grandmother *knits* quilts for family members.
The dog *ate* my homework.
That band always *plays* my favorite songs.

Linking Verbs

The most common linking verbs are forms of the verb *to be*: *am, are, is, was, were, be, been, being*. In the following sentences, the verb links the subject to the rest of the sentence:

I *am* short.
The children *were* grumpy.
Miriam *is* ready to perform.

Helping Verbs

Helping verbs include *am, are, is, was, were, be, have, has, had, do, does, did, may, might, must, can, could, shall, should, will, would*. A helping verb is used with another verb form, called the **main verb**, to form a phrase that acts as the verb of the sentence:

Moira *was helping* her brother with the meal.
Ramón *had studied* all morning.
You *must reply* this afternoon.

Compound Verbs

Sometimes a sentence has more than one verb. A verb with more than one part is called a **compound verb**:

Edgar Allan Poe *frightened* and *thrilled* readers.

The children *sat* and *waited* for their parents to get them.

I *can use* your help and *would be* grateful for it.

ACTIVITY 7 Find Subjects and Verbs in Sentences

In each of the following sentences, circle the subject and underline the verb.

EXAMPLE ⌐I⌐enjoy performing in front of people.

1. My friends and I started a band a few years ago.

2. Currently, we are writing new songs.

3. We have enjoyed playing music together.

4. A neighbor helped us record our first demo on my computer.

5. She was happy to offer us advice.

6. We have played shows at a small club downtown.

7. The club owner has asked us to come more often.

8. Our bass player and our drummer are brothers.

9. They have written some of our best songs.

10. We have dreamed of stardom since we were kids.

ACTIVITY 8 Add Verbs

Complete each of the following sentences by adding a verb.

EXAMPLE A typical student ____*desires*____ many electronic devices, such as a cell phone, a laptop, and an e-reader.

1. An anonymous donor _____ a million dollars to the scholarship fund.

2. Lisa _____ student body president.

3. A flock of seagulls _____ overhead.

4. The children _____ free swimming lessons.

5. Armando _____ a rabbit hide behind the fence.

6. Our biology class _____ DNA last week.

7. Frederick _____ at a friend's house last night.

8. The soccer team _____ on the football field.

9. Police officers _____ the hillside for clues.

10. Many champion gymnasts _____ their training at a very young age.

Verb Pretenders

Verb pretenders (also called *verbals*) look like verbs but do not act as verbs in sentences. The most common verb pretenders are verb + *-ing* and *to* + verb combinations.

cooking	to cook
working	to work
studying	to study

Verb + *-ing*

When an *-ing* verb appears in a sentence without a helping verb, it does not act as the verb of the sentence. Instead, it modifies, or describes, other words in the sentence. These words are called **modifiers**.

I took a picture of the boy *swimming* in the fountain. [*Swimming* describes the boy.]

Working hard, we completed the job in a day. [*Working* describes the subject of the sentence, *we*.]

The *laughing* partygoers kept me awake at night. [*Laughing* describes the partygoers.]

ACTIVITY 9 Identify *-ing* Verbs

In the space provided, indicate whether the *-ing* verb in each of the following sentences acts as a modifier or as part of a verb.

EXAMPLE The panting dog needed to drink some water. _____ modifier _____

1. Claudia is hiking the Appalachian Trail. _____

2. Joanne sent her father a singing telegram for his birthday. _____

3. That diving board is too high. _____

4. I was weeding the garden when I scraped my knee. _____

5. The cookie recipe requires a teaspoon of baking powder. _____

6. Stomping on the floor, William showed his displeasure. _____

7. Susan is moving to Las Vegas the day after tomorrow. _____

8. Nina went to the mall for a new pair of knitting needles. _____

9. Because of her back problems, Kata was sleeping on the floor. _____

10. Jumping up and down, the children showed their excitement. _____

ACTIVITY 10 Use Verbs and Verb Pretenders

For each of the following -ing verbs, write two sentences. In the first sentence, use the word as a verb. (You'll need a helping verb, too.) In the second sentence, use the word as a modifier to describe another word.

EXAMPLE drinking

Verb: _____ *I was drinking cranberry juice when you called.*

Modifier: _____ *Clean drinking water is harder and harder to find.*

1. viewing

Verb: _____

Modifier: _____

2. planting

Verb: _____

Modifier: _____

3. sleeping

Verb: _____

Modifier: _____

4. playing

Verb: _____

Modifier: _____

5. searching

Verb: _____

Modifier: _____

To + Verb

The *to* + verb combination also looks like a verb but does not act as a verb in a sentence. Instead, it acts as either a noun or a modifier that describes something:

I can't wait to open my gifts. [Because *to* comes in front of *open, open* does not act as a verb. Instead, *to open* modifies *wait*.]

I always open my gifts before my birthday. [Here *open* acts as a verb.]

Stephanie had a plan to buy apples. [Because *to* comes in front of *buy, buy* does not act as a verb. Instead, *to buy* modifies *plan*.]

13 B

Stephanie buys apples from the farm. [Here *buys* acts as a verb.]

My goal is to study medicine. [Because *to* comes in front of *study*, *study* does not act as a verb. Instead, *to study* acts as a noun.]

Many Americans study medicine overseas. [Here *study* acts as a verb.]

HOW TO Find the Verb in a Sentence

- Locate the word or words that express the action or link the subject to the rest of the sentence.
- Check that the word is not a verb pretender.
- When a verb + *-ing* combination appears in a sentence without a helping verb, it's a verb pretender.
- When a *to* + verb combination appears, it's a verb pretender.

ACTIVITY 11   Use *to* + Verb Combinations

Complete each of the following sentences with a *to* + verb combination.

EXAMPLE Mauricio used a hammer _____*to crack the coconut*_____.

1. Rebecca waited _____.

2. _____ was the children's favorite thing to do.

3. Sunay promises _____.

4. Half the apartments in this building do not seem _____.

5. Before sitting down to breakfast, Erica's parents needed _____.

6. _____ is Kyle's only chore this morning.

7. Bryan likes _____.

8. After a day of skiing, Richard and Elizabeth want _____

   _____.

9. Connie's old job was _____.

10. _____ may be Lon's greatest talent.

ACTIVITY 12   Find Subjects and Verbs

In each of the following sentences, circle the subject and underline the verb. Do not confuse verbs and verb pretenders.

EXAMPLE The smiling (woman) accepted the award.

1. Kim agreed to have the meeting at her house.

2. While taping the playoffs, Hugo watched a documentary.

3. Stepping carefully, Nizar tried to avoid the wet paint.

4. The hikers reached their campground by sunset.

5. Mosquitoes were annoying the hikers.

6. Adam washed his hands before kneading the bread dough.

7. The people on the street hoped to glimpse the famous actress.

8. Opening the newspaper, Maya began to read the arts section.

9. After work, Tim and Linda lack the energy to cook dinner.

10. Slipping the diamond ring on Leticia's finger, Nahum asked her to marry him.

ACTIVITY 13 Identify Subjects and Verbs

In the following paragraph, circle the subjects and underline the verbs.

EXAMPLE (Ivor) decided to major in music.

Ivor needed to interview a local drummer for a term project. Before con-
tacting the musician, he read about her career. Feeling nervous, he wrote her
an e-mail to request an appointment. To his surprise, the drummer invited
him to watch a rehearsal. Her band was playing a new song. Ivor took many
notes while listening to them. He wanted to describe his first impressions
completely. After the rehearsal, the band kept asking him questions about
his assignment. Answering the musicians politely, he wondered how to
change the subject. Finally, the drummer told the band to let Ivor begin his
interview.

Verb Tense

The **tense** of a verb shows the time that the action or condition takes
place. The three basic tenses in English are *present, past,* and *future.*

The **present tense** shows an action or condition taking place at the time
the writer is writing. The present tense can also show an action that happens
more than once:

Anthony *has* a big kitchen.

He *cooks* every evening.

13 B

The **past tense** shows something that began and ended in the past. To form the past tense of most verbs, use the *-ed* form of the verb:

Last week, Anthony *cooked* for his friends and family.

The **future tense** shows something that will take place or will probably take place. To form the future tense, use *will*, *is going to*, or *are going to* and the present tense of the verb:

I *will learn* my lines by next week.

This extra credit assignment *is going to make* a difference in my grade.

As a general rule, stay with the tense you begin with at the start of a paragraph unless the time you are talking about changes. Avoid shifting from one tense to another for no reason because these shifts may confuse your readers.

ACTIVITY 14 Correct Awkward Shifts in Verb Tense

Edit the following paragraph to correct unnecessary shifts in verb tense. The first sentence in the paragraph is correct.

EXAMPLE   My stepson angered me, but I ~~try~~ to understand.
                                                      tried

> For a long time, my stepson, Jonathan, was unhappy to have me as part of his family. I try to get to know him better, but he will complain that I invade his privacy. As a newcomer, I understood that our relationship will require effort from both of us. It was not enough that I was friendly. Jonathan also has to want us to be friends. I am not happy with the two of us being strangers, but I can wait for him to feel more comfortable around me.

Regular Verbs

Regular verbs are verbs whose past tense and past participle end in *-ed*. Past participles are forms of a verb that are used with *has*, *have*, or *had*, as in the following examples:

I *have studied* Portuguese for three years.

Niko *had purchased* all of the champagne.

COMMON REGULAR VERBS

Verb	Past Tense	Past Participle
cook	cooked	cooked
measure	measured	measured
study	studied	studied
walk	walked	walked

Irregular Verbs

Irregular verbs are verbs whose past tense and past participle do not end in *-ed* but are formed in a variety of ways. As a result, they are often misused or misspelled. Review the forms of irregular verbs so you won't make errors.

COMMON IRREGULAR VERBS

Verb	Past Tense	Past Participle
be	was, were	been
begin	began	begun
catch	caught	caught
choose	chose	chosen
come	came	come
do	did	done
drink	drank	drunk
eat	ate	eaten
feel	felt	felt
fly	flew	flown
get	got	got, gotten
go	went	gone
leave	left	left
ride	rode	ridden
see	saw	seen

ACTIVITY 15 Identify Regular and Irregular Verbs

In each of the following sentences, underline the verb and identify it as a regular or an irregular verb.

EXAMPLE The letter carrier knocked on the door. _____regular_____

1. Kate placed the grapes in the bowl. _____

2. Nathan knew Robin and Simon already. _____

3. Somebody stole my purse! _____

4. Dwayne read comic books at night. _____

5. Chen baked a cake for his family. _____

6. The moths flew around the lamp. _____

7. Alice drank a bottle of water. _____

8. Zafir caught a cold on the airplane. _____

9. The mechanic looked under the hood. _____

10. The cell phone rang at midnight. _____

ACTIVITY 16 Use Regular and Irregular Verbs

In each of the following sentences, write the correct form of the verb in the space provided. If necessary, consult your dictionary for the correct form.

EXAMPLE Richard _____lost_____ his train ticket last night. (*lose*)

1. When she was young, Jayne _____ her money under her bed. (*hide*)

2. Isabel has _____ with a gospel choir for five years. (*sing*)

3. Last semester, Meg _____ about her grades. (*worry*)

4. Yesterday morning, the actors _____ very convincing in their costumes. (*look*)

5. Patrick and Hugh have _____ music at every school in town. (*teach*)

6. Experts say that the ocean liner *Titanic* _____ because it was too big. (*sink*)

7. My grandmother _____ that picture when she was ten years old. (*draw*)

8. Who has _____ my car without my permission? (*drive*)

9. The cousins _____ for hours at the family reunion last July. (*talk*)

10. Sigrid has _____ Naomi for her dance partner. (*choose*)

C. Subject-Verb Agreement

Visit **LaunchPad Solo for Readers and Writers >** Grammar: Basic Sentences > Subject-Verb Agreement for tutorials and additional practice with verbs.

A complete sentence contains a subject and a verb. The subject tells who or what is doing or being something, and the verb either expresses the action or links the subject to the rest of the sentence. To maintain **subject-verb agreement**, a singular subject must have a singular verb form, and a plural subject must have a plural verb form.

Singular and Plural Forms

A singular subject consists of one thing:

the student

A singular verb form in the present tense usually ends in -*s:*

The student studies for the test.

A plural subject consists of more than one thing:

the students

A plural verb form in the present tense generally does not end in *-s*:

The students study for the test.

To check for subject-verb agreement, you must first identify the subject of the sentence. Remember that prepositions and other words sometimes occur between the subject and the verb. Once you identify the subject, you can add the correct verb form.

INCORRECT	Elaine go to the recycling center. [singular subject, plural verb form]
CORRECT	Elaine goes to the recycling center. [singular subject, singular verb form]
INCORRECT	The cars swerves to avoid hitting the dog. [plural subject, singular verb form]
CORRECT	The cars swerve to avoid hitting the dog. [plural subject, plural verb form]

ACTIVITY 17 Identify Subject-Verb Agreement

In each of the following sentences, underline the correct verb form.

EXAMPLE I (naps, <u>nap</u>) every afternoon.

1. This book (costs, cost) less online than at the store.

2. The swimmers (competes, compete) against one another every year.

3. The windows (sticks, stick) in humid weather.

4. The airlines (offers, offer) advice for children traveling alone.

5. Liam (works, work) as a computer help desk technician.

6. Strawberries (remains, remain) fresh for only a few days.

7. Dr. Perry (sees, see) new patients.

8. Phoebe (drives, drive) a vintage Ford truck.

9. Kathy and Lauren (attends, attend) an accelerated Spanish program.

10. Dancing (is, are) a form of art, a form of exercise, and a form of recreation.

ACTIVITY 18 Add Verbs That Agree

Add a singular or plural verb form to each of the following sentences as needed to maintain subject-verb agreement.

EXAMPLE My mother-in-law _____*bakes*_____ the best vegan cookies.

13 C

1. At dusk, the city's skyline _____ especially beautiful.

2. I _____ your good grades.

3. Pandora online radio _____ personalized music.

4. Those magazines _____ the best information on fly-fishing.

5. Katie _____ French and Spanish fluently.

6. Empanadas _____ best when served fresh from the oven.

7. Professor Lopez _____ his students to write two research papers.

8. Bruce _____ at a gym several times a week.

9. Tracy and Lincoln _____ together at the soup kitchen.

10. Listening to soothing music _____ an effective way to relax.

Read about subject pretenders on p. 404.

To determine correct subject-verb agreement, be sure that you have correctly identified the subject. Watch out for subject pretenders such as prepositional phrases.

INCORRECT   The cup of pencils *are* on the table. [The prepositional phrase *of pencils* is a subject pretender.]

CORRECT   The cup of pencils *is* on the table. [*Cup* is the subject of the sentence.]

ACTIVITY 19 Use Correct Verbs

In each of the following sentences, underline the correct verb form.

EXAMPLE The books on those shelves (belongs, belong) to my roommate.

1. To do one hundred sit-ups a day (is, are) my goal.

2. The pieces of gum (sticks, stick) to the roof of my mouth.

3. The keys lost in the backyard (needs, need) to be found.

4. The Halloween masks in the store (looks, look) scary.

5. The books that I like best (is, are) mysteries and thrillers.

6. One of the professors (has, have) a bad cold.

7. To beat my brother in checkers (is, are) my greatest wish in the world.

8. The royal baby's milestones (is, are) always in the news.

9. Movies of popular books often (becomes, become) very successful.

10. My pet ferrets, whose names are George and Laura, (eats, eat) more food than I do.

ACTIVITY 20 Maintain Subject-Verb Agreement

Add a singular or plural verb form to each of the following sentences as needed to maintain subject-verb agreement.

EXAMPLE The clothes in that box _____*belong*_____ to Michael.

1. That cable channel always _____ reruns.

2. The vase of tulips _____ on the kitchen counter.

3. The applicants did not _____ a good first impression.

4. Those mushrooms around that tree _____ poisonous.

5. Our basement, filled with broken furniture and old toys, _____ to be cleaned out.

6. Professor Wu, joined by many of her students, _____ for animal rights.

7. The apples on that tree _____ ripe.

8. The nurses in the children's hospital _____ excellent care.

9. Poppy's collection of amusement park souvenirs _____ valuable.

10. A jar full of coins _____ in the back of my closet.

ACTIVITY 21 Insert Correct Verbs

In the following paragraph, underline the correct verb forms.

EXAMPLE Many people (is, are) interested in football, but few people (is, are) as obsessed as my husband.

Paul, who (has been, have been) my husband for three years, (is, are) in love with only one sport. Being married to a football fanatic (has, have) its drawbacks. During the football season, each and every Sunday (is, are) dedicated to the sport. Paul and his friends (gather, gathers) at our house before noon to begin watching the games. Fortunately, his friend Rico, who is one of the best cooks I've ever met, (bring, brings) the snacks and drinks. All day, I (hear, hears) cheers and boos coming from the living room. Paul and his friends (take, takes) the game so seriously they get depressed when their teams lose. Personally, I'd rather have a hobby that is less stressful.

See p. 403 for the definition of a pronoun.

13 C

Indefinite Pronouns

Sometimes the subject of a sentence is an **indefinite pronoun**, a pronoun that refers to one or more unspecified beings, objects, or places. Here are some singular indefinite pronouns, which take singular verb forms:

anybody	everyone	somebody
anyone	everything	someone
anything	nobody	something
each	no one	
everybody	nothing	

INCORRECT Each of us *need* to pay twenty dollars. [*Each* is singular and requires a singular verb form.]

CORRECT Each of us *needs* to pay twenty dollars.

INCORRECT Anyone *know* the answer. [singular pronoun, plural verb form]

CORRECT Anyone *knows* the answer. [singular pronoun, singular verb form]

INCORRECT Everybody *go* to the movies on Friday night. [singular pronoun, plural verb form]

CORRECT Everybody *goes* to the movies on Friday night. [singular pronoun, singular verb form]

HOW TO Check for Subject-Verb Agreement

- Remember that singular subjects take singular verb forms and that plural subjects take plural verb forms.
- Be sure that you have correctly identified the subject.
- Watch out for subject pretenders, such as prepositional phrases.
- Most indefinite pronouns—such as *everyone, anyone, something,* and *no one*—are singular and take singular verb forms.

ACTIVITY 22 Identify Subject-Verb Agreement

In each of the following sentences, underline the correct verb form.

EXAMPLE Something about that story (makes, make) me uneasy.

1. Nothing about that movie (is, are) worthwhile.

2. Everybody with a special permit (parks, park) in the same lot.

3. Somebody living on my street (plays, play) bongos in the middle of the night.

4. No one in that laboratory (has, have) a degree in science.

5. Something inside the car (makes, make) a strange clunking noise.

6. Everyone in Carmela's family (speaks, speak) English and Italian.

7. Everything remaining on the floor (does, do) not belong there.

8. Nobody with a new computer (uses, use) that outdated software.

9. Someone wearing strong perfume (leaves, leave) a trail of scent behind her.

10. Anything made of wood that is exposed to rain (requires, require) a water-proof finish.

ACTIVITY 23 Add Singular Verbs

Add a singular verb form to each of the following sentences to maintain subject-verb agreement.

EXAMPLE No one in the room _____wants_____ to stand up.

1. Everyone on the roller coaster _____ a little queasy.

2. Someone in this class _____ the answers to the test.

3. Anything in that store _____ a dollar or less.

4. Somebody _____ to clean the dishes in the sink.

5. Nobody _____ Suraj to pass his driving test.

6. Something in this room _____ like oranges.

7. Nothing _____ wrong with your plan.

8. Everything in the storage unit _____ to Lorraine and Howie.

9. No one in my class _____ group projects.

10. Everybody _____ to return next year.

ACTIVITY 24 Write Using Correct Subject-Verb Agreement

Complete each of the following sentences, making sure that the verb you add agrees with the subject that is provided.

EXAMPLE Everybody _____*goes to the movies*_____ after work on Friday.

1. These young couples _____.

2. This website _____.

3. Everyone on this list _____.

4. We _____.

5. I _____.

13 C

6. None of the telemarketers _____.

7. The little boy who forgot his permission slip _____.

8. The director of the church choir _____.

9. The presidents of both classes _____.

10. Nobody _____.

⬛ **ACTIVITY 25** **Select Subjects and Verbs That Agree**

In the following paragraph, underline the correct verb forms.

EXAMPLE Guo (feel, <u>feels</u>) proud of his Chinese heritage.

Guo (belongs, belong) to a troupe of lion dancers. Beginning in October, Guo meets once a week with the other lion dancers and (begins, begin) rehearsing for Chinese New Year. After being in the troupe for three years, Guo now (dances, dance) as the lion's head. He (shakes, shake) the mane and (pretends, pretend) to roar. Being the lion's head (is, are) a great honor as well as hard work. After Christmas, as Chinese New Year approaches, the troupe members, who all attend the same university, (rehearses, rehearse) every night. Everyone (looks, look) forward to the festivities. In addition to dancing in the Chinese New Year parade, the group of dancers (visits, visit) city schools to teach children about Chinese culture. The children sitting closest to the lion (screams, scream) when it approaches them. The dancing creature, with his comical but threatening gestures, (delights, delight) and (frightens, frighten) young spectators.

⬛ **ACTIVITY 26** **Correct Subject-Verb Agreement**

Revise the following paragraph as needed to correct errors in subject-verb agreement.

EXAMPLE Tanya's job of managing a plumbing supply business <u>satisfy</u> her.
satisfies

Tanya manage her father's plumbing supply business. The first thing every morning, with the telephone already ringing, she turns on the computer and take the first orders of the day. The orders early in the morning is usually for emergency jobs and generates repeat business. Tanya's father, who has a good reputation among local plumbers, ask her to give these orders priority. No one, especially someone with clogged pipes, want to wait longer than necessary for repairs. Filling emergency orders are not Tanya's only job. She maintains the company budget and decide which bills to pay each day. Surrounded by boxes of hardware, Tanya admit that she had expected to work somewhere more glamorous after receiving her business degree. However, everybody who remembers the company before her improvements admire her work. Her decision to streamline office procedures have made the company more efficient and more profitable.

14

Expanding Sentences

In addition to containing subjects and verbs, sentences can be expanded to include phrases, clauses, pronouns, adjectives, and adverbs. Using expanded sentences gives you the opportunity to express yourself effectively for a variety of audiences.

See pp. 403–408 and 408–16 for more information about subjects and verbs.

A. Phrases

If a group of words lacks a subject or a verb or both, it's called a **phrase**. A phrase is not a complete sentence. Notice the difference between phrases and sentences in these examples:

PHRASE	To get to class on time.
SENTENCE	To get to class on time, I need to leave my apartment at 8:30.
PHRASE	To come up with the right answer.
SENTENCE	Mel was unable to come up with the right answer.
PHRASE	Making her a good dinner.
SENTENCE	I want to please my girlfriend by making her a good dinner.
PHRASE	Such as a new backpack, a Barbie, a walkie-talkie, a stuffed lizard, and even a cell phone.
SENTENCE	My nine-year-old daughter wants a lot of things for her birthday, such as a new backpack, a Barbie, a walkie-talkie, a stuffed lizard, and even a cell phone.
PHRASE	On the shelf.
SENTENCE	I can't reach the box on the shelf.

ACTIVITY 1 Identify Phrases and Sentences

For each of the following items, write *S* next to the word groups that are sentences and *P* next to the word groups that are phrases.

EXAMPLE Within the last fifteen years. ___P___

1. To drive over the bridge at night. _____

2. Before sending the e-mail, she carefully reviewed it. _____

3. To find a new job, Frida updated her résumé. _____

4. On Friday my singing lesson. _____

5. The blog posting turned out to be a joke. _____

6. For example, a pencil, a notebook, and a flash drive. _____

7. Over there on the floor. _____

8. He used his keys to open the door. _____

9. To study for Spanish, English, algebra, biology, and economics. _____

10. The fire in the national forest was caused by a careless smoker. _____

14 A

ACTIVITY 2 Turn Phrases into Sentences

Expand each of the following phrases into a complete sentence.

EXAMPLE after the fire

After the fire, there was nothing left of the house. _____ .

1. talking with their parents

   _____

2. before the start of the semester

   _____

3. presented his oral report

   _____

4. due to the increase in gas prices

   _____

5. to maintain a good relationship

   _____

6. avoiding his old friends from high school

   _____

7. a flight of creaky stairs

   _____

8. the park in my family's neighborhood

   _____

9. an unusual but attractive hairstyle

_____

10. saving her wages from her after-school job

_____

▸ **ACTIVITY 3** **Connect Phrases to Sentences** ◂

Revise the following paragraph to connect the phrases to the sentences that come before or after them.

EXAMPLE Families need to be flexible. ~~In~~ order to deal with hard times.
$_{in}$

Ever since my early teen years. My parents have had an untraditional marriage. My mother held a full-time job while my father stayed at home. Taking care of us kids. Until I was thirteen, both my parents worked full time. Then my dad lost his job. Mom earned enough to support the family as a buyer. For a large department store. She frequently had to travel. The whole family enjoyed her stories about the exciting places she visited. Including New York City, Paris, Hong Kong, and Milan. It was comforting having Dad there. Caring for us when we were sick and congratulating us when we did well at school. Because of this unconventional arrangement. We kids learned that people sometimes have to be flexible to succeed.

◗ B. Clauses

Visit **LaunchPad Solo for Readers and Writers** > **Grammar: Basic Sentences** > **Sentence Variety** for tutorials and additional practice with clauses.

A **clause** can be a whole sentence or a part of a sentence. There are two kinds of clauses: independent and dependent.

Independent or Main Clauses

An **independent clause**, also called a *main clause*, is a group of words with a subject and a verb that can stand alone as a complete sentence. All sentences contain at least one independent clause, and some contain more than one:

Femi enjoyed her first piano lesson. [This sentence is an independent clause because it contains a subject and a verb and can stand alone as a sentence.]

She learned how to hold her hands, and she learned how to sit. [This sentence consists of two independent clauses.]

She decided to sign up for more lessons through the summer. [This sentence consists of one independent clause.]

| **ACTIVITY 4** Write Independent Clauses |

Expand each of the following word groups into a sentence so that it contains an independent clause.

EXAMPLE After I broke up with my girlfriend, _____*I felt determined not to make*_____

*the same mistake again.*_____.

1. The day it happened, _____.

2. Although my girlfriend and I were not getting along, _____

   _____.

3. Because I really liked her, _____.

4. _____ even though we tried so hard

   to stay together.

5. Because we had no friends in common, _____.

6. When we saw each other for the last time, _____.

7. _____ because the bad memories are

   fading.

8. A year after the breakup, _____.

9. Although I haven't found someone else, _____.

10. Because I don't want to make the same mistake again, _____

   _____.

Dependent or Subordinate Clauses

Although a **dependent clause** contains a subject and a verb, it cannot stand alone as a sentence. To be part of a complete sentence, it needs to be attached to or part of an independent clause. Dependent clauses are also called **subordinate clauses** because they often begin with one of these words, called **subordinating conjunctions**:

after	if	until
although	since	when
as	that	where
because	though	while
before	unless	

Because my car broke down, I had to reschedule my dentist appointment. [The subordinate clause at the beginning of the sentence contains a subject and a verb, but it cannot stand alone as a sentence.]

Before my uncle retired, he was a welder. [This sentence also starts with a subordinate clause.]

I didn't fly in a plane *until I was seventeen years old*. [This subordinate clause comes at the end of the sentence.]

As these examples show, you use a comma after a subordinate clause that begins a sentence. You generally do not use a comma before a subordinate clause that ends a sentence.

14 B

ACTIVITY 5 Identify Subordinate Clauses

In each of the following sentences, underline the subordinate clause. One sentence contains two subordinate clauses.

EXAMPLE Though I had a bad cold, I still played in the championship game.

1. When the supervisor entered the office, Dean stopped watching YouTube videos.

2. On my street, the garbage is always collected before I wake up.

3. We toasted marshmallows and told ghost stories until the fire died.

4. If nobody has any questions, Ms. Skov will distribute the free samples.

5. Antonio wants to become a social worker because a social worker helped him through his long stay in the hospital.

6. While the turkey roasted in the oven, the family played touch football.

7. Unless you pay your parking fines, you will not be allowed to register for classes when the next semester begins.

8. Since Jazlynn began jogging, she has been having pain in her knees.

9. After he graduates, Achmed wants to tour Mexico.

10. I have hidden your birthday present where you will never find it.

ACTIVITY 6 Identify Subordinate Clauses

In the following paragraph, underline the subordinate clauses.

EXAMPLE Before he moved into his own apartment, Brendan lived with his parents.

This year Brendan moved into his own apartment. After he moved in, he began to clean house regularly. In fact, he enjoys doing housework. If he cleans a little every day, his place always looks presentable. Solutions to his problems pop into his head while he is scrubbing something. When he was cleaning his bathtub, he thought of a better way to budget his paycheck.

Although Brendan is not a perfectionist, he takes pride in his apartment because it represents a new stage in his adult life.

Relative Clauses

A subordinate clause may also begin with one of these words, called **relative pronouns**:

that	who
what	whoever
whatever	whom
which	whomever
whichever	whose

A subordinate clause that begins with a relative pronoun is often called a **relative clause**:

Whoever passes the obstacle course will be allowed to leave. [This relative clause is the subject of the sentence.]

Any soldier *who passes the obstacle course* will be allowed to leave. [This relative clause describes the subject and is essential to the meaning of the sentence.]

Private Mejia, *who passed the obstacle course*, was allowed to leave. [Here the relative clause also describes the subject but is not essential to the meaning of the sentence.]

As the last example shows, sometimes commas are used to set off relative clauses from the rest of the sentence. If the relative clause interrupts the flow of the sentence and could be removed without changing the basic meaning of the sentence, use a comma before it, and use another comma after it unless it is at the end of the sentence. Do not use a comma before or after a relative clause that is essential to the meaning of the sentence, as in the first two examples above.

ACTIVITY 7 Identify Relative Clauses

In each of the following sentences, underline the relative clause.

EXAMPLE I will support whomever you nominate for club president.

1. Alethea is the only student who talked to the professor on the first day of class.

2. Tom is one of those people who work at night and sleep all day.

3. I worry about students whose extracurricular activities interfere with their studies.

4. Whoever ate Asher's sandwich should fix him another one.

5. I recommend you buy the vehicle that has the least impact on the environment.

14 B

6. Jolene is the one student whose research paper received an A.

7. Whoever comes home last needs to let the cat out.

8. Frankie is the only boyfriend who ever gave me a bouquet of roses.

9. Miss Sweden was the contestant who played the accordion in the talent competition.

10. I feel sorry for the people whose jobs were eliminated last year.

ACTIVITY 8 Turn Relative Clauses into Sentences

Add information to each of the following relative clauses to make it a complete sentence.

EXAMPLE who can sing, dance, and act

The play requires performers who can sing, dance, and act.

1. that tasted the best

   _____

2. who do not smoke

   _____

3. whoever sits at the head of the table

   _____

4. whom Elena admires

   _____

5. who just left for vacation

   _____

6. that leaves at 11:15 tonight

   _____

7. who does not mind a little hard work

   _____

8. that does not require batteries

   _____

9. whose smile could light up a room

   _____

10. that the dog ate

   _____

ACTIVITY 9 **Expand Sentences with Subordinate Clauses**

Expand each of the following sentences by adding a subordinate clause.

EXAMPLE Andrew is studying geology.

Andrew is studying geology because he likes exploring caves.

1. Carmen wanted a new job.

   _____

2. The day-care center is having a bake sale.

   _____

3. Derek rode a bicycle to work.

   _____

4. The drugstore downtown is closed.

   _____

5. The coffee will not taste any better.

   _____

6. Demetria collects old magazines.

   _____

7. The roads have been undergoing repairs.

   _____

8. The Blumenfelds hired a gardener.

   _____

9. Monique wanted a tablet.

   _____

10. You will not improve your physical condition.

   _____

C. Pronouns

When you expand sentences, you'll be making grammatical choices about how you express your thoughts. One of these choices will concern the use of pronouns. A **pronoun** is a word that grammatically takes the place of a noun or another pronoun. Usually, it refers to a specific noun that appears earlier in the sentence or in a previous sentence. The following are common pronouns:

Visit **LaunchPad Solo for Readers and Writers** > **Grammar: Parts of Speech** > **Pronouns** for tutorials and additional practice with pronouns.

14 C

I, me, mine, we, our, ours

you, your, yours

he, him, his, she, her, hers

it, its

they, them, their, theirs

this, these, that, those

who, whom, whose, which, that, what

all, any, another, both, each, either, everyone

few, many, most, nobody, several, some, such

myself, yourself, himself, herself, itself

ourselves, themselves, yourselves

Pronoun Reference

For more information about pronoun reference, see pp. 216–18.

When you use a pronoun that refers to a noun, make sure that it's clear what the noun is. Don't use a pronoun that refers to a vague idea or that could refer to more than one noun.

VAGUE	In my history class, *they* claimed that the Vietnam War protesters were unpatriotic. [Who are *they*?]
CLEAR	In my history class, *a group of students* claimed that the Vietnam War protesters were unpatriotic.

UNCLEAR	John told Martin *he* needed to study. [Who needed to study?]
CLEAR	John told Martin, "I need to study."
CLEAR	John told Martin, "You need to study."
CLEAR	John needed to study, as he told Martin.
CLEAR	John thought Martin needed to study and told him so.

ACTIVITY 10 Correct Vague Pronoun Reference

In each of the following sentences, correct vague pronoun reference.

EXAMPLE On that television show, ~~they~~ are always saying the dumbest things.
the characters

1. At that office, they require both male and female employees to wear suits.

2. The musicians played a waltz and a traditional ballad. It was beautiful.

3. Fabiola confessed to Leah that she left her class notes at the restaurant.

4. At my health club, they recommend that we warm up before we do aerobics.

5. Seth told Andrew that he needed to drink less on the weekends.

6. There are too many scenes of violence and brutality. It should not have been on network television.

7. In the documentary, it claimed that the mayor is corrupt.

8. While on vacation, I learned how to water ski and how to play croquet. It is not as easy as it looks.

9. In San Francisco, they have many landmarks of interest to tourists.

10. If Alicia tries to explain logarithms to Samia, she will become confused.

14 C

Pronoun Agreement

A pronoun should agree in number with the noun it refers to. To maintain pronoun agreement, use a singular pronoun to refer to a singular noun and a plural pronoun to refer to a plural noun. Remember that a singular noun also requires a singular verb form, and a plural noun requires a plural verb form.

Learn more about pronoun agreement on pp. 217–18.

INCORRECT PRONOUN AGREEMENT	My *friend* is bringing *their* own food to the picnic. [*Friend* is singular, but *their* is plural.]
CORRECT PRONOUN AGREEMENT	My *friend* is bringing *her* own food to the picnic.
CORRECT PRONOUN AGREEMENT	My *friends* are bringing *their* own food to the picnic.

Remember also to use a singular pronoun to refer to a singular indefinite pronoun. Singular indefinite pronouns include *anybody, anyone, anything, everybody, everyone, everything, nobody, somebody, someone,* and *something.*

INCORRECT PRONOUN AGREEMENT	My professor told *everyone* to take *their* laptop off the counter. [*Everyone* is singular, but *their* is plural.]
CORRECT PRONOUN AGREEMENT	My professor told the *students* to take *their* laptops off the counter.
CORRECT PRONOUN AGREEMENT	My professor told *everyone* to take *his or her* laptop off the counter.

ACTIVITY 11 Correct Errors in Pronoun Agreement

In each of the following sentences, correct the errors in pronoun agreement.

EXAMPLE   Plumbers
A plumber will have to charge you more if they find cracks in the pipes.

1. A student will find more errors in an essay if they wait a few hours after writing it before proofreading it.

2. I need to talk to someone who has put snow chains on their tires.

3. Everybody brought their donation to the main office.

4. The player shouts "Bingo!" as soon as they have a winning card.

5. A psychiatrist must not betray their patients' confidentiality.

6. A movie star saves their biggest smiles for the camera.

7. Nobody admitted that they had committed the vandalism.

8. Someone allows their dog to bark all day long.

9. Let me know when everyone has completed their questionnaires.

10. Every parent wants their children to be happy and successful.

14 C

HOW TO Correct Errors in Pronoun Agreement

- Check that singular pronouns (such as *I*, *he*, *she*, *his or her*, or *it*) refer either to singular nouns or to singular indefinite pronouns (such as *anyone*, *everyone*, *everybody*, *somebody*, and *someone*).
- Check that plural pronouns (such as *we*, *us*, *them*, and *their*) refer to plural nouns.
- Correct errors in pronoun agreement by making pronouns and nouns agree.

ACTIVITY 12 Correct Pronoun Agreement

In the following paragraph, correct the errors in pronoun agreement.

EXAMPLE As long as we focus on the task at hand, each person in my study group
his or her
can get ~~their~~ needs met.

The last meeting of my statistics study group was disastrous. We met at the studio apartment of one of the group members, and they did not have enough chairs. Everyone who came was worried about their grade, but not everyone had completed their section of the homework problems. One person had loaned their calculator to a friend and had to share mine. Someone else only wanted us to do their work for them. A third person had to have every little thing explained to them. Finally, one person got angry and left, saying they would save time by doing all the work themselves. This experience taught me something. The success of a study group requires every member to contribute as much as they can. Though each person must still understand the basic concepts for themselves, the group can help the individual refine what they already know.

D. Adjectives

One of the best ways to expand sentences is to use adjectives, which can add interest to your writing. **Adjectives** modify nouns or pronouns by describing or adding information about them:

My *beautiful* mother never goes outside without makeup.

The *green* meadow is always restful on the eyes.

Adjectives may also show comparisons between things. When comparing two things, add *-er* to adjectives with one syllable or adjectives with two syllables ending in *-er*, *-le*, *-ow*, or *-y*. Use the word *more* before all other adjectives with two, three, or more syllables.

This car is *smaller* than the one I owned before.

The seats are also *narrower*.

This car is *more unusual* than my other one.

When comparing three or more things, add *-est* to adjectives with one syllable or adjectives with two syllables ending in *-er*, *-le*, *-ow*, or *-y*. Use the word *most* before all other adjectives with two, three, or more syllables.

This car is the *smallest* one I have ever owned.

This car has the *narrowest* seats of any car I have ever owned.

This car is the *most unusual* one on campus.

Visit **LaunchPad Solo for Readers and Writers** > **Grammar: Parts of Speech** > **Adjectives and Adverbs** for tutorials and additional practice with adjectives.

ACTIVITY 13 Identify Adjectives

In each of the following sentences, underline the adjectives. Some sentences have more than one adjective.

EXAMPLE Senator Johnson is a <u>powerful</u> person.

1. Professor Gupta teaches a worthwhile class.

2. The overdue book is a biography.

3. Andrea likes to eat dark chocolate with a glass of cold milk.

4. Jerome is the tallest person in his family.

5. The cold student pulled her wool hat over her ears while she waited for the next train.

6. Rene wears a waterproof jacket in rainy weather.

7. Among the three friends, Carlita is the best dancer.

8. Jamie owns a dented blue car.

9. I returned by the fastest route.

10. The defeated team ran off the muddy field.

14 E

> **ACTIVITY 14 Add Adjectives**

Complete each of the following sentences by adding an adjective.

EXAMPLE The _____green_____ coat fits you well.

1. The _____ cat sits in the window.

2. These cherries taste _____.

3. Alfredo took his _____ friend to the party.

4. Soraya has _____ brothers and sisters.

5. On _____ days, we wear _____ clothing.

6. I think that the _____ carpet looks pretty with the _____ wallpaper.

7. His family needs to move to a _____ house.

8. That hospital serves _____ meals to its patients.

9. That _____ child never seems to get what he deserves.

10. Arzella is one of the _____ workers but one of the best students.

E. Adverbs

Visit **LaunchPad Solo for Readers and Writers** > **Grammar: Parts of Speech** > **Adjectives and Adverbs** for tutorials and additional practice with adverbs.

Adverbs are another useful way to expand sentences. **Adverbs** modify verbs, adjectives, or other adverbs by describing or adding information about them. Adverbs usually answer the questions *how?*, *when?*, *where?*, *why?*, or *how often?* Many adverbs end in *-ly*, such as *slowly*, *noisily*, and *loudly*:

> My favorite episode is *never* broadcast in syndication. [The adverb answers the question *How often is the episode broadcast?*]

> The children played *nearby*. [The adverb answers the question *Where did the children play?*]

> My wife *often* ate the dinner I made. [The adverb answers the question *When did the wife eat the dinner?*]

> **ACTIVITY 15 Identify Adverbs**

In each of the following sentences, underline the adverbs.

EXAMPLE Doro <u>forcefully</u> threw the ball at the hitter.

1. The fans waited eagerly for concert tickets.

2. Is it true that crime never pays?

3. Traffic moved slowly on Van Ness Avenue.

4. The bored, complaining student soon dropped the class.

5. The pupils entered the school reluctantly.

6. My aunts and uncles secretly planned a surprise party for my grandfather.

7. The instructor of my Introduction to Ceramics class is very interesting.

8. My study group often remains in the library until it closes.

9. The candidate campaigned well in the urban neighborhoods.

10. Klaus speaks persuasively in front of large groups.

ACTIVITY 16 Add Adverbs

Complete each of the following sentences by adding an adverb.

EXAMPLE Guy practiced the saxophone _____*daily*_____.

1. The customers _____ drank their iced tea.

2. You have _____ gotten to work on time.

3. Melina _____ eats at fast-food restaurants.

4. The punishment for plagiarism is _____ severe.

5. Darryl worked _____ on his English essay.

6. Winnie was talking _____ before she was interrupted.

7. My classmates _____ do their weekend homework on Sunday nights.

8. The football team _____ won the game.

9. Chong is _____ reliable.

10. Yolanda _____ sneaked up behind her boyfriend.

14 E

15

Combining Sentences

Visit **LaunchPad Solo for Readers and Writers** > **Grammar: Basic Sentences** > **Coordination and Subordination** for tutorials and additional practice with coordination.

To express different kinds of ideas, you need to know how to write different kinds of sentences. One way to create different kinds of sentences is to combine them. Learning the various ways to join sentences will help you add style and variety to your writing.

◖ A. Coordination

When you have two or more short, closely related sentences in a row that are equally important, your ideas can seem choppy and unconnected. To avoid this problem, combine the sentences, making them *coordinate*, or equal. To join two equally important sentences, use a coordinating conjunction and a comma or a conjunctive adverb and a semicolon.

Coordinating Conjunctions and Commas

One way to combine equally important sentences is to use one of the **coordinating conjunctions**, which are *for, and, nor, but, or, yet,* and *so*. To remember these conjunctions, imagine the word *FANBOYS*. Each letter in this word is the first letter of one of the coordinating conjunctions.

COORDINATING CONJUNCTIONS

Conjunction	Definition
F—for	because
A—and	in addition, also
N—nor	not, neither
B—but	however, unless
O—or	as another possibility
Y—yet	however, unless
S—so	as a result

438

When you use a coordinating conjunction to combine short, closely related sentences, put a comma before the conjunction. Be sure to select a conjunction that logically connects the sentences.

CHOPPY SENTENCES	The traffic jam delayed us. We arrived on time for the party.
SENTENCES COMBINED WITH *BUT*	The traffic jam delayed us, *but* we arrived on time for the party.
CHOPPY SENTENCES	I braided my niece's hair. I ironed her dress.
SENTENCES COMBINED WITH *AND*	I braided my niece's hair, *and* I ironed her dress.
CHOPPY SENTENCES	Adam was hungry. He microwaved a slice of pizza.
SENTENCES COMBINED WITH *SO*	Adam was hungry, *so* he microwaved a slice of pizza.

15 A

ACTIVITY 1 Combine Sentences Using Coordinating Conjunctions

Combine each of the following pairs of sentences using a coordinating conjunction and a comma.

EXAMPLE Jorge has a law degree. He has never practiced law.
(, but he)

1. Leigh was upset when she opened her cell phone bill. She owed more than four hundred dollars.

2. Rosa insisted on buying strawberry ice cream. I would have preferred chocolate chip.

3. I fell asleep in class. I missed next week's reading assignment.

4. Elizabeth carefully read the contract for the loan. She still couldn't understand it.

5. I went grocery shopping this morning. I did the laundry this afternoon.

6. Michael set his alarm clock for 7:30. He had an early class in the morning.

7. Hetty forgot to return the library book. She received a fine.

8. Malik worked really hard on his résumé. He got the job he wanted.

9. You can buy the racy red sports car. You can buy the practical brown sedan.

10. Adrianna spent hours looking over travel brochures. She ended up going to the same beach she had visited for the past three years.

Conjunctive Adverbs and Semicolons

Another way to join equally important sentences is to use a **conjunctive adverb** and a *semicolon*. The conjunctive adverb (often called a *transition*) shows how the two sentences fit together. A semicolon is used before the conjunctive adverb, and a comma is used after it.

15 A

Conjunctive Adverbs

Add an idea: *also, furthermore, in addition, moreover*

Show a different point: *however, instead, nevertheless, on the other hand, otherwise*

Show a similar point: *likewise, similarly*

Stress a key idea: *certainly, indeed, in fact, undoubtedly*

Show a consequence or result: *as a result, consequently, so, therefore, thus*

Point out a sequence: *first, second, next, finally*

CHOPPY SENTENCES	My daughter majored in psychology in college. She really wanted to be a writer.
SENTENCES COMBINED WITH *HOWEVER*	My daughter majored in psychology in college; *however*, she really wanted to be a writer.
CHOPPY SENTENCES	I am traveling to Argentina next summer. I want to learn Spanish.
SENTENCES COMBINED WITH *THEREFORE*	I am traveling to Argentina next summer; *therefore*, I want to learn Spanish.
CHOPPY SENTENCES	The neighborhood grocery store is small. It's very expensive.
SENTENCES COMBINED WITH *MOREOVER*	The neighborhood grocery store is small; *moreover*, it's very expensive.

ACTIVITY 2 Combine Sentences Using Conjunctive Adverbs

Combine each of the following pairs of sentences using a semicolon and a conjunctive adverb. Be sure to include a comma after the conjunctive adverb.

EXAMPLE My hours at work have been increased*; therefore,* I have more money to save.

1. Akio disliked the political ads during the last election. He decided to register as an Independent.

2. The children gathered roses, violets, and irises from their grandmother's garden. They ironed the flowers in waxed paper and labeled them with black ink.

3. Owners of small specialty stores find it hard to compete with large department stores. They need to advertise their products well using social media.

4. Corinne was hired as a salesclerk. She got a better job the following week and quit.

5. Einstein had a reputation as an absentminded scientist. He could be very forgetful.

6. Landscape artists are more than just gardeners. They are both scientists and artists.

7. I stepped out into the foggy morning unable to see a thing. I heard something crunch beneath my feet.

8. This semester I'm working the graveyard shift at the food mart. I can barely stay awake in my 8:00 a.m. class.

9. Pacifists often demonstrate against warfare. They have been conscientious objectors during various wars.

10. Steve Jobs changed our lives with electronic devices such as the Apple computer and the iPhone. Some people call him this century's Thomas Edison.

15 B

B. Subordination

Use **sentence subordination** to combine two sentences that aren't equally important. Subordinating conjunctions and relative pronouns help you express the logical connection between the sentences.

Visit **LaunchPad Solo for Readers and Writers > Grammar: Basic Sentences > Coordination and Subordination** for tutorials and additional practice with subordination.

Subordinating Conjunctions

One way to combine two sentences using subordination is to use an appropriate **subordinating conjunction**.

Subordinating Conjunctions

after	before	though	when	wherever
although	if	unless	whenever	whether
because	since	until	where	while

The subordinating conjunction begins the part of the combined sentence that's less important to expressing the message.

CHOPPY SENTENCES	Internet memes are popular today. I wonder what the next social media experiment will be.
SENTENCES COMBINED WITH *ALTHOUGH*	*Although* Internet memes are popular today, I wonder what the next social media experiment will be.

CHOPPY SENTENCES	Greg made sure to save several thousand dollars. He did this before he quit his job.
SENTENCES COMBINED WITH *BEFORE*	Greg made sure to save several thousand dollars *before* he quit his job.
CHOPPY SENTENCES	You'll never understand the experience of being homeless. The only way to understand it is to live through it.
SENTENCES COMBINED WITH *UNLESS*	You'll never understand the experience of being homeless *unless* you live through it.

Sometimes you can just put the conjunction before the less important sentence of the original two, as in the first example. But often you'll also need to delete part of that sentence or change it in other ways, as in the second and third examples. Sometimes the conjunction you need will already be in the less important sentence, like *before* in the second example.

The word group that begins with a subordinating conjunction is called a **subordinate clause** or a **dependent clause**. Put a comma after a subordinate clause when it begins a sentence. In general, don't use a comma before a subordinate clause that ends a sentence.

COMMA	*After the children sat down*, the family began Thanksgiving dinner.
NO COMMA	The family began Thanksgiving dinner *after the children sat down*.

HOW TO Combine Sentences Using Subordinating Conjunctions

- Decide which sentence is less important.
- Choose an appropriate subordinating conjunction to express the way the ideas in the two sentences are connected.
- Combine the sentences by putting the subordinating conjunction before the less important part of the new sentence and then deleting or changing any other words as necessary.
- Use a comma after the subordinate clause when it begins the combined sentence.
- In general, don't use a comma before the subordinate clause when it ends the sentence.

ACTIVITY 3 Combine Sentences Using Subordinating Conjunctions

Combine each of the following pairs of sentences using a subordinating conjunction. Add or delete words as necessary.

EXAMPLE I aced my art history exam ͵ because I studied for three hours last night.

1. The number of arrests for drunk driving has increased. This has happened because there are stricter DUI laws.

2. The newspaper arrived late. I wasn't able to read about the big earthquake in Alaska.

3. I couldn't find the book at the library. Finally, I asked one of the librarians for help.

4. I saw my friends in the restaurant. They were gossiping about their coworkers.

5. I have a hard time recycling my garbage. The recycling center is too far from my house.

6. You have to create a secure password. Then, you can access your account again.

7. I kept the music low. My roommate left.

8. The politician finished her speech. Her followers cheered.

9. I would have stayed in class. The professor did not show up.

10. I didn't rent the apartment. The building didn't have a laundry room.

15 B

Relative Pronouns

Another way to combine choppy sentences is to use a **relative pronoun** to subordinate the information in the less important sentence.

Relative Pronouns

that	who
what	whoever
whatever	whom
which	whomever
whichever	whose

As with a subordinating conjunction, the relative pronoun goes before the part of the combined sentence that is less important to the meaning. The word group that begins with a relative pronoun is called a **relative clause**.

CHOPPY SENTENCES	Athletes will stay in shape. They'll stay in shape if they work out regularly.
SENTENCES COMBINED WITH *WHO*	Athletes *who* work out regularly will stay in shape.
CHOPPY SENTENCES	Ayana baked the cupcakes. They were moist and delicious.
SENTENCES COMBINED WITH *WHICH*	Ayana baked the cupcakes, *which* were moist and delicious.

CHOPPY SENTENCES	One of my favorite songs is "Big Yellow Taxi." I mean the version that the Counting Crows recorded.
SENTENCES COMBINED WITH *THAT*	One of my favorite songs is the version of "Big Yellow Taxi" *that* the Counting Crows recorded.

Don't use commas before or after a relative clause that is necessary to identify what it refers to, as in the following example:

The letter to the editor *that Anita wrote* was published on the local newspaper's website.

No commas are used before or after the relative clause because it's a necessary part of the sentence. It tells which letter to the editor—the one that Anita wrote—was published on the website.

In contrast, use commas when the relative clause gives information that's not essential to the sentence:

The letter, *which is on the topic of school funding*, is somewhere in my backpack.

Commas are used in this example because the relative clause—*which is on the topic of school funding*—simply adds information about a letter that's already been mentioned. The meaning of the sentence is still clear without it: *The letter is still in my backpack*.

Don't use commas with relative clauses that begin with *that*:

The letter *that I wrote* was not published.

HOW TO Combine Sentences Using Relative Pronouns

- Decide which sentence is less important.
- Choose an appropriate relative pronoun to connect the information in the less important sentence to that in the other sentence.
- Use commas when the relative clause can be deleted and the sentence still includes all necessary information.
- Don't use commas when the relative clause is a necessary part of the sentence.

ACTIVITY 4 Combine Sentences Using Relative Pronouns

Combine each of the following pairs of sentences using a relative pronoun. Add or delete words as necessary.

EXAMPLE Jeans ^, which are pants made out of denim, were often worn by cowboys because they were so sturdy. ~~Jeans are pants made out of denim.~~

1. Jeans have changed a great deal over the years. Jeans are still very popular.

2. Jeans were invented by Levi Strauss. They were first worn by miners in the 1850s.

3. The jeans never tore or fell apart. The jeans were worn by the miners.

4. In the 1950s, jeans became popular with teenagers. The teenagers thought that they were cool.

5. Jeans were a big part of the 1960s. Hippies started wearing them.

6. One popular style was bell-bottom jeans. This style was often decorated with flowers and peace signs.

7. I have a picture of my mother wearing jeans. The jeans have frayed hems and many holes.

8. Now just about everyone wears jeans. These jeans come in many styles.

9. Skinny jeans have very straight and tight legs. Skinny jeans are the most fashionable style today.

10. People wear jeans. These people live all over the world.

C. Sentence-Combining Strategies

The following sentence-combining exercises will give you practice using sentence coordination and subordination.

Visit **LaunchPad Solo for Readers and Writers** > **Grammar: Basic Sentences** > **Sentence Variety** for tutorials and additional practice with combining sentences.

Specific Methods of Combining Sentences

Use the methods identified in the directions for combining sentences in the following activities.

ACTIVITY 5 Combine Sentences Using Coordination

Combine each of the following pairs of sentences using either a comma and a coordinating conjunction or a semicolon, a conjunctive adverb, and a comma. Add or delete words as necessary.

EXAMPLE The station wagon used to be one of America's most popular vehicles. The *; however, the* SUV (sports utility vehicle) replaced the station wagon in popularity.

1. In the 1990s, SUVs became popular with many American consumers. They helped automobile companies make big profits.

2. At first, they were built for people to drive in extreme conditions and on dirt roads. Now, they are mostly used for city driving.

3. They are bought by parents who like the large size of the vehicles. They can fit their growing families into them with ease.

4. Some buyers imagine themselves driving off-road in a rugged, beautiful area of the country. They would never actually do that.

5. Increases in gas prices have influenced the size of SUVs. Many SUVs are now smaller and more energy efficient.

6. Americans prefer large cars. Europeans buy much smaller cars.

7. Gas in Europe is much more expensive than in the United States. European consumers have good reason to use as little as possible.

8. At one time, Japanese-made SUVs were more popular with American consumers. The profits of American car companies declined.

9. In general, American-made vehicles have become more popular. Their resale rates are higher than they used to be.

10. Many Americans still love their SUVs. It will be interesting to see if this love affair continues when gas prices rise.

ACTIVITY 6 Combine Sentences Using Subordination

Combine each of the following pairs of sentences using a subordinating conjunction. Add or delete words as necessary.

EXAMPLE Scientists often use placebos in experiments. ~~They~~ *because they* want to test the effectiveness of a new treatment.

1. A placebo is a fake treatment for an illness. Sometimes a placebo works as well as real medicine.

2. Scientists use placebos when they test the effectiveness of a new medicine. They do this to make sure the new medicine will really help patients get well.

3. In an experiment, one group of patients receives the medicine being tested. Another group of patients receives the placebo.

4. Both the medicine being tested and the placebo can be given in the form of a pill. The placebo pill might be made up entirely of sugar or some other harmless substance.

5. The patients who receive the new medicine are called the *experimental group*. The patients who receive the placebo are called the *control group*.

6. The patients don't know which group they're in. This process is called a "blind" experiment.

7. The new medicine must be very successful in treating the patients in the experimental group. The power of suggestion is so strong.

8. Sometimes the patients who receive placebos improve a great deal. The patients who receive the actual medicine improve less.

9. Scientists speculate that placebos work for some people. These people strongly believe that the placebo will make them get better.

10. The placebo effect can be very powerful. Scientists are beginning to study it seriously.

15 C

ACTIVITY 7 Combine Sentences Using Subordination

Combine each of the following pairs of sentences using a relative pronoun. Add or delete words when necessary.

EXAMPLE Rocky Mountain National Park , which is located in one of the most beautiful areas in the country. It contains remote areas where you can find solitude.

1. Rocky Mountain National Park is in Colorado. It is one of America's favorite vacation spots.

2. This park is also one of America's most popular national parks. It is visited by over 3 million people a year.

3. Several trails in the park are not well known. These trails are in remote locations.

4. The Tonahutu Creek trail follows the Continental Divide. The trail is 21 miles long.

5. The Never Summer Loop trail is well named. This trail has mountains that are almost 13,000 feet high.

6. Sometimes the snow never melts on this trail. The snow can be very deep.

7. Casual hikers don't use the very steep Lost Lake Trail very much. Casual hikers may not have the stamina for difficult climbs.

8. The Lost Lake trail leads to Lost Lake. This lake is surrounded by breathtaking mountain scenery.

9. These three trails are great for backpacking. Not many people use these trails.

10. If you go backpacking, you can experience nature without crowds. Backpacking is strenuous and fun.

Various Methods of Combining Sentences

You have practiced combining sentences using just one or two methods at a time. Now you will be able to choose the method to use:

1. **a coordinating conjunction with a comma:**

   for, and, nor, but, or, yet, so

2. **a semicolon and a conjunctive adverb:**

   to add an idea: also, furthermore, in addition, moreover

   to show a different point: however, instead, nevertheless, on the other hand, otherwise

   to show a similar point: likewise, similarly

   to stress a key idea: certainly, indeed, in fact, undoubtedly

   to show a consequence or result: as a result, consequently, so, therefore, thus

   to point out a sequence: first, second, next, finally

3. **a subordinating conjunction:**

   after, although, because, before, even though, if, once, since, that, though, unless, until, when, whenever, where, whether, while, whomever

4. **a relative pronoun:**

   that, what, whatever, which, whichever, who, whoever, whom, whomever, whose

ACTIVITY 8 Combine Sentences Using Different Methods

Combine each of the following pairs of sentences using an appropriate method from the preceding list. Add or delete words as necessary.

EXAMPLE The recent economic downturn ,which has changed the entire U.S. economy. The downturn has affected college students a great deal.

1. To cover their operating expenses, colleges and universities rely on money from the state and federal governments. State and federal government budgets have been cut because of the bad economy.

2. Most colleges and universities have had to raise tuition and fees. This increase in tuition and fees has made college much more expensive.

15 C

3. More and more students are applying for student loans. When they graduate, they owe more money than previous students owed.

4. The job market is also more challenging than it used to be. This is because of the high unemployment rate in many parts of the country.

5. College degrees are still very important for economic success. The degrees can be in any major.

6. People earn about 38% more over the course of their careers than do people with only a high school diploma. These are people who graduate from college.

7. People who go to college also tend to be healthier than those who don't go to college. They are healthier both physically and mentally.

8. College graduates also advance higher in the workplace than do those without college diplomas. They are more likely to become CEOs and other leaders.

9. Getting a college degree is more expensive than it has been in the past. This is because of the recent economic downturn.

10. In the long run, a college degree is worthwhile. A college degree now costs more.

15 C

ACTIVITY 9 Combine Sentences Using Different Methods

Combine each of the following sets of sentences using an appropriate method from the list on page 448. Add or delete words as necessary.

EXAMPLE Television shows about spring break have been popular for years. ~~These~~ *, which often show college students partying on a beach,*

~~episodes often show college students partying on a beach.~~

1. To many people, spring break is a time when college students go wild. Spring break is a weeklong break in March or April.

2. Spring break is notorious for misbehavior. Some college students drink excessively at this time.

3. Not all college students party over spring break. Many college students don't have time to party.

4. Last spring break, I worked overtime to save up money. I needed the money to go to summer school.

15 C

5. This spring break, I'll probably catch up on my studies. I'm taking six courses. In three of these courses, I have to write research papers.

6. My friend Mike spent spring break taking care of his children. Mike is a single father. He has sole custody of the kids.

7. Some people think college students just goof off. Those people don't know what we go through.

8. Most college students have to work their way through college. They might have children to raise. They might have parents to support.

9. Nationwide, only a small percentage of college students are supported by their parents. Most college students pay their own way.

10. I wish spring break were a real break. It's really just a chance to do more work.

 ACTIVITY 10 Combine Sentences Using Different Methods

Combine each of the following sets of sentences using an appropriate method from the list on page 448. Add or delete words as necessary.

EXAMPLE Blindness can lead to lifestyle restrictions. ~~These restrictions will occur~~ unless help is available.

1. Dan Shaw's life was changed. His doctor diagnosed him with retinitis pigmentosa. This is an incurable eye disease. This happened when Dan Shaw was seventeen.

2. Slowly he lost his sight. His life became very limited.

3. He wanted to be more involved with the world. He checked out his options.

4. He didn't want a seeing-eye dog. He had owned a dog. The dog died.

5. He heard about a program run by Janet and Don Burleson. They were training miniature horses as guides for the visually impaired.

6. Dan was interested in having a guide horse. Miniature horses have a life span of thirty to forty years. He would likely not have to endure the death of the horse.

7. His guide horse leads him everywhere. His guide horse is named Cuddles.

8. Cuddles responds to more than twenty-five voice commands. She is housebroken. She can see in the dark.

9. People are often curious. This happens when they see Dan being guided by Cuddles. They ask Dan questions about Cuddles.

10. Dan is happy to talk about Cuddles. He wants others to know about guide horses.

ACTIVITY 11 Combine Sentences Using Different Methods

Combine each of the following sets of sentences using an appropriate method from the list on page 448. Add or delete words as necessary.

EXAMPLE *If people*
People have a healthy lifestyle. *, their* Their chances of getting diabetes will be reduced.

15 C

1. About 29.1 million children and adults in the United States are believed to have diabetes. Nearly 8.1 million of these people don't know they have diabetes.

2. Diabetes has no cure. It can be controlled.

3. Diabetes can cause heart disease, blindness, kidney failure, and amputations. It is a very serious disease.

4. Most diabetes is type 2. It is associated with obesity. It is also associated with poor lifestyle habits.

5. Children today are fatter. Children exercise less. They eat unhealthy food.

6. Obese children will develop serious health problems. This will happen if they don't lose weight.

7. Children are our future. We need to help children be healthier. We need to help them live long lives.

8. Many schools are teaching children about diabetes. They have many other subjects to teach.

9. Parents should be good role models. They are very busy. Parents should eat well and exercise regularly.

10. Diabetes is a major health problem. It will continue to get worse. We need to stop the spread of this disease.

16

Improving Sentences

To improve sentences, you'll need to eliminate sentence fragments, run-on sentences, and comma splices. Also, you should correct misplaced and dangling modifiers, try to use the active voice as much as possible, and use parallel sentence structure for groups of words that are part of a pair or series.

A. Sentence Fragments

A **sentence fragment** is an incomplete sentence that is presented as if it were a complete sentence. Some sentence fragments are **phrases**: they lack a subject or a verb or both.

The grocery store next to the bank.

Built a playhouse in the backyard.

At the bus station.

Other sentence fragments are **subordinate clauses**, or **dependent clauses**: they have a subject and a verb, but they begin with a subordinating conjunction or a relative pronoun.

Subordinating Conjunctions

after	since	where
although	that	wherever
because	though	whether
before	unless	while
even though	until	whomever
if	when	
once	whenever	

Here are three sentence fragments that begin with subordinating conjunctions:

After the party is over.

Because it was raining outside.

When I come back from vacation.

In this chapter, you will review and practice correcting

A. Sentence Fragments
B. Run-on Sentences
C. Comma Splices
D. Misplaced Modifiers
E. Dangling Modifiers
F. Active and Passive Voice
G. Parallelism

Visit **LaunchPad Solo for Readers and Writers > Grammar: Basic Sentences > Fragments** for tutorials and additional practice with correcting fragments.

For more about subordinate clauses, turn to pp. 427–29.

Relative Pronouns

that	who
what	whoever
whatever	whom
which	whomever
whichever	whose

Here are three fragments that begin with relative pronouns:

That they ate at the bakery.

Who left the rambling message.

Which caused him to cry.

ACTIVITY 1 Identify Sentence Fragments

16 A

In the space provided, indicate whether each of the following word groups is a sentence fragment or a complete sentence.

EXAMPLE Since it will be rainy tomorrow. _____*fragment*_____

1. My son plays soccer and basketball. _____

2. In Mimi's old backpack. _____

3. Which was the first house constructed of recycled materials. _____

4. May I charge that to your credit card? _____

5. Because these french fries are too salty. _____

6. The shoe salesman earned a large commission. _____

7. Speaking as softly as she could. _____

8. A perfect score on the pop quiz. _____

9. This vacuum cleaner is effective on both deep carpets and bare floors.

_____

10. Vandalized mailboxes throughout the neighborhood. _____

How do you correct a sentence fragment? One way is to connect it to the sentence that comes before or after it.

FRAGMENT *Although he had to get up early in the morning.* Kotoyo didn't get home until midnight.

SENTENCE Although he had to get up early in the morning, Kotoyo didn't get home until midnight.

FRAGMENT Her favorite gift was the silk scarf. *That her grandmother had given her.*

SENTENCE Her favorite gift was the silk scarf that her grandmother had given her.

Another way to correct a sentence fragment is to turn it into a complete sentence. If the fragment is a phrase, add any missing subject or verb. If the fragment begins with a subordinating conjunction, delete the conjunction. If the fragment begins with a relative pronoun, change the pronoun to a noun.

FRAGMENT Running down the hall.
SENTENCE Matthew was running down the hall.

FRAGMENT *Because* the plane was late getting into Austin.
SENTENCE The plane was late getting into Austin.

FRAGMENT *Which* violated the drug laws in Michigan.
SENTENCE The prescription violated the drug laws in Michigan.

16 A

ACTIVITY 2 Correct Sentence Fragments

Make each of the following fragments a complete sentence.

EXAMPLE ~~Polluting~~ Trash from campers is polluting our beautiful national parks.

1. After taking a monthlong tour of Malaysia.

2. Because the batteries were low.

3. The load of sheets in the dryer.

4. The laptop next to the photocopier.

5. Who looked frightened enough to faint.

6. The car with the small scratch.

7. Although fried food is not very healthy.

8. While Victor was learning how to type.

9. If I knew these people better.

10. Surprised by the unexpected news.

ACTIVITY 3 Correct Sentence Fragments

Each of the following word groups contains one or more sentence fragments. Make each word group into a single complete sentence, either by connecting each fragment to a complete sentence or by rewriting each fragment as a complete sentence.

EXAMPLE Magda jogged every morning. ~~Because~~ *because* she was preparing to run a

   marathon.

1. The concert that begins at 8:30 tonight.

2. Whomever Ryan picks as his wife. I'm prepared to like her.

3. That gave the children more freedom.

4. Alonzo cares for his sister's children on Wednesday and Thursday nights.
   Because he's free on those nights.

5. Let's try to go to the concert. If the tickets aren't too expensive and my car is
   working.

6. I'm jealous of Pilar. Who received an A on her report. Even though she didn't
   spend much time writing it.

7. I could clean my whole house. While the website loads.

8. His mother didn't like Jason's dyed blue hair. Said it was an embarrassment to
   the family.

9. I really liked my blind date. Until he lit up a cigarette.

10. Trying to keep my balance while standing on one foot, bending at the waist,
    and holding my arms in a graceful arc above my head.

16 A

ACTIVITY 4 Correct Sentence Fragments in a Paragraph

Edit the following paragraph to eliminate sentence fragments.

EXAMPLE ~~Studying~~ *I am studying* to become an elementary school teacher.

   Because I want to teach my students to take care of themselves I have a

special interest in physical education. During my student teaching I remem-

bered my childhood experiences playing team sports like softball. Alone in left

field. My classmates laughing at my mistakes. I should have been taught how

to catch a fly ball. Without fear of being hit in the face. I never learned games

like soccer and basketball. Which keep every player constantly involved in the

game. I want P.E. to be better for my students. All children can learn to enjoy

using their bodies. Though not everybody can become a professional athlete.

I want my future students to enjoy a lifetime of fitness.

B. Run-on Sentences

Visit **LaunchPad Solo for Readers and Writers** > **Grammar: Basic Sentences** > **Run-ons and Comma Splices** for tutorials and additional practice with correcting run-ons.

A **run-on sentence** occurs when two sentences (or sometimes more) are incorrectly presented as a single sentence, without any punctuation between them.

RUN-ON   The party was over it was time to go home.
CORRECT   The party was over. It was time to go home.

RUN-ON   I went to the store I forgot to get the flour.
CORRECT   I went to the store, but I forgot to get the flour.

ACTIVITY 5 Identify Run-on Sentences

In the space provided, indicate whether each of the following word groups is a run-on sentence or a correct sentence.

EXAMPLE Boyz II Men was a famous R&B group from the 1990s it was based in
Philadelphia. _____run-on_____

1. David is friendlier than he appears he only frowns to hide his nervousness.

   _____

2. With her fingers poised over the piano keys, Carmel waited for the conductor's baton to drop. _____

3. That yogurt is too high in carbohydrates for my diabetic diet I need to have the low-fat cottage cheese. _____

4. Hard hats are required in this area the roof is being replaced.

   _____

5. No one volunteered to supervise the dance until the principal offered to buy the chaperones dinner. _____

6. My wife likes pizza my son likes hamburgers I prefer sushi.

   _____

7. Ray and Serena put a green decal on their black suitcase so that they could recognize it more easily at the airport. _____

8. Delia ran out the door in such a hurry that she left her coat draped over the sofa. _____

9. Kazuko welcomed the visitor into her office she asked her assistant to bring them both coffee. _____

16 B

10. Nigel was astonished when he received first prize he never thought that he

would win an award. _____

One way to correct a run-on sentence is to turn it into two sentences, adding a period at the end of the first sentence and capitalizing the first word of the second sentence.

RUN-ON The concert was supposed to begin at 8:00 it actually began at 9:30.

CORRECT The concert was supposed to begin at 8:00. It actually began at 9:30.

RUN-ON The digital camera is too expensive it costs more than three hundred dollars.

CORRECT The digital camera is too expensive. It costs more than three hundred dollars.

A run-on sentence can also be corrected by putting a comma and a coordinating conjunction (*for*, *and*, *nor*, *but*, *or*, *yet*, or *so*) between the two sentences.

RUN-ON The apartment is dirty the kitchen appliances are broken.
CORRECT The apartment is dirty, and the kitchen appliances are broken.

RUN-ON I registered for classes late I still got a good schedule.
CORRECT I registered for classes late, but I still got a good schedule.

A third way to correct a run-on sentence is to put a semicolon between the two sentences. Often, you can also use a conjunctive adverb—such as *however*, *therefore*, *also*, *instead*, or *as a result*—after the semicolon. If you use a conjunctive adverb, put a comma after it.

RUN-ON I've been working out I still haven't lost any weight.
CORRECT I've been working out; however, I still haven't lost any weight.

RUN-ON Computer technology is improving computers are getting cheaper.
CORRECT Computer technology is improving; computers are getting cheaper.

16 B

See Chapter 15 to find out more about these methods of combining sentences.

━━ **ACTIVITY 6 Correct Run-on Sentences** ━━━━

Correct each of the following run-on sentences using a period and a capital letter; a comma and a coordinating conjunction; or a semicolon, a conjunctive adverb, and a comma.

EXAMPLE While Fred was watching the news, the electricity went out *, and* it was two

hours before it came back on again.

1. Solange posed for the picture, the feather on her antique hat framing her face she found the waist and collar of the dress a little confining.

2. Before Benjamin applied for a job at Datacorp, he researched the company at the library he wanted to be well prepared for the interview.

3. Waiting for the tour bus, the family shivered on the windy corner they had expected warmer weather on their summer vacation.

4. Leland's motorcycle is his prized possession he had to sell it to pay his college tuition.

5. Because Olivia had never been surfing, she took lessons she felt ready to tackle the waves.

6. Paolo has thinning hair, glasses, and stooped shoulders everyone thinks he is a librarian he is a meteorologist at an Antarctic research station.

7. Toni gives her son a generous allowance and does not expect any help around the house from him Toni's brother expects his children to do chores if they want spending money.

8. Dark clouds gather overhead while trees toss in the wind rain does not fall.

9. Tai wanted to prove her trustworthiness to her parents she made it her responsibility to take her younger brother and sister to school.

10. Using a sharp jerk of his wrist, Simón flipped the pancake in the skillet his uncle taught him this trick when Simón was a child.

16 B

ACTIVITY 7 Correct Run-on Sentences in a Paragraph

Edit the following paragraph to correct the run-on sentences.

EXAMPLE Watching the natural world is soothing$\overset{\text{; in fact,}}{\wedge}$it is as good for the soul as meditating.

The sun burns bright and hot the world is shady and cool under the pine tree. Nestled within a deep hole in the thick needles underfoot, a turtle dozes. I look up a bird feeder is in my hand. The feeder weighs over four pounds I search for a strong, low branch. Two startled doves take flight their wings whistle as if to express their alarm. Three grackles hop from limb to limb, black and almost as big as crows. More grackles join the flock they scream their long, thick beaks gape menacingly. A tiny hummingbird darts between the large, black birds its bright patch of throat feathers flashes red in the flickering light. Several sparrows wait on a nearby telephone wire. Far from the trunk, I find a good branch and attach the feeder with sturdy twine. After I step back, a sparrow flies to the feeder another sparrow joins its companion. The grackles become quiet the doves return. I watch the birds gather on the branches around the feeder it is like a doorway to a world where I do not belong.

C. Comma Splices

A **comma splice** consists of two sentences incorrectly joined with only a comma.

16 C

Visit **LaunchPad Solo for Readers and Writers** > **Grammar: Basic Sentences** > **Run-ons and Comma Splices** for tutorials and additional practice with correcting comma splices.

COMMA SPLICE	Karima liked the aroma of coffee, she never liked the taste.
CORRECT	Karima liked the aroma of coffee, but she never liked the taste.
COMMA SPLICE	My daughter is stationed in Afghanistan, she'll be home for the holidays.
CORRECT	My daughter is stationed in Afghanistan. She'll be home for the holidays.
COMMA SPLICE	The domestic cat is a great pet, it's a ferocious hunter.
CORRECT	The domestic cat is a great pet; furthermore, it's a ferocious hunter.

One way to correct a comma splice is to make the comma splice into two separate sentences by changing the comma to a period and capitalizing the first word of the second sentence.

COMMA SPLICE	The Department of Homeland Security was created in 2002, it is responsible for the protection of the United States within its own borders.
CORRECT	The Department of Homeland Security was created in 2002. It is responsible for the protection of the United States within its own borders.

Another way to correct a comma splice is to add a coordinating conjunction (*for, and, nor, but, or, yet,* or *so*) after the comma.

Turn to pp. 438–39 for more information about these ways of combining sentences.

COMMA SPLICE	Our car trip across the country was exhausting, it was also exciting and educational.
CORRECT	Our car trip across the country was exhausting, but it was also exciting and educational.

A third way to correct a comma splice is to change the comma to a semi-colon. You can also add a conjunctive adverb (such as *however, therefore, also, instead,* or *as a result*) after the semicolon. If you use a conjunctive adverb, put a comma after it.

COMMA SPLICE	Antibiotics have been widely used, they aren't as effective as they used to be.
CORRECT	Antibiotics have been widely used; as a result, they aren't as effective as they used to be.

ACTIVITY 8 Correct Comma Splices

Correct each of the following comma splices by making two separate sentences, adding a coordinating conjunction after the comma, or changing the comma to a semicolon and adding a conjunctive adverb and a comma.

EXAMPLE Graduating from college in four years is always good, but don't worry if you can't do it.

1. There were never two people more different than Arnulfo and Hadley, they have been best friends since the second grade.

2. The audience members jumped to their feet and would not stop applauding, I was very proud that I had started the Drama Club.

3. Frank set the tray of ice cream cones on the passenger seat to his right, the children would be delighted with his surprise.

4. Jessica gave the old dog a pat on the head, he thumped his tail in greeting without opening his eyes.

5. When we returned home, all the clocks were blinking, the power had gone off and come back on while we were away.

6. Adalena balanced her baby brother on her hip, almost three, he was becoming too big for her to carry.

7. Ceci inhaled the rich perfume of the cactus flower, the glowing white blossom would last less than a day.

8. Todd knew that there was a spare key hidden in the rock garden, he could not remember which rock concealed the key.

9. Ajamil bought several folk paintings while sailing around the Caribbean islands, his friends appreciated these colorful souvenirs.

16 C

10. Waiting for class to begin, Lei read her essay one last time, she found a few remaining errors.

ACTIVITY 9 Correct Comma Splices

Correct each of the following comma splices by making two separate sentences, adding a coordinating conjunction after the comma, or changing the comma to a semicolon and adding a conjunctive adverb and a comma.

EXAMPLE The number of young people who vote is declining*; however,* the number of elderly people who vote is increasing.

1. Akio immersed the spinach in a basin of water, he separated the leaves from the stems.

2. Our sixth-grade class collected starfish, sea urchins, and periwinkles on our field trip to the tide pools, we kept the animals alive in a saltwater aquarium.

3. When Noel was in high school, his aunt gave him five hundred dollars to invest in the stock market, six months later, he had doubled his money.

4. After Corinne became a salesclerk, she realized that she had not always been a very nice customer, she resolved to be more patient when she went shopping.

5. I got my first paycheck, the government deducted a lot in taxes.

6. The war disrupted Neil and Joanna's wedding plans, they decided to marry at the courthouse and have a reception after Neil returned home.

7. I heard a sickening crunch, I realized I had stepped on another snail.

8. Tim appreciated the rich, nutty aroma of fresh coffee, he did not like its taste nearly as much.

9. The firefighters shook their heads in disgust, another pedestrian had tossed a lit cigarette onto a restaurant awning.

10. Reaching the top of the steep, narrow trail, Bronwen admired the view, the beauty of the green river valley made her forget her fear of heights.

ACTIVITY 10 Correct Comma Splices in a Paragraph

Eliminate the comma splices from the following paragraph.

EXAMPLE Single people always envy married people*, and* married people always envy single people.

After Rachel became engaged, the first person she told was her sister, Bonnie. Rachel was hesitant to tell her parents because they wanted her to wait until after she graduated from college to get married, Bonnie would understand because she had married Kurt when she was Rachel's age. Rachel didn't want her parents to overhear her on the telephone, she went to her sister and brother-in-law's apartment to talk. Rachel did not mind helping her sister carry dirty clothes down to the laundry room, she did not mind giving Bonnie change for the machines, ever since she got married, Bonnie never seemed to have any money. Although the laundry room was hot and stuffy, Bonnie said it was a good place for them to talk. Kurt was studying for a midterm, the apartment was so small that Rachel and Bonnie's conversation would have disturbed him. Bonnie admired her sister's new diamond ring, she was even more interested in the ski trip that the engaged couple had planned. Bonnie and Kurt used to take weekend trips together when they each lived with their parents. Folding Kurt's worn jeans, Bonnie said that she envied Rachel, being engaged, according to Bonnie, is much more romantic than being married.

Visit **LaunchPad Solo for Readers and Writers > Grammar: Basic Sentences > Modifier Placement** for tutorials and additional practice with modifiers.

◖ D. Misplaced Modifiers

A **modifier** is a word or group of words that describes or adds information about another word. A modifier should appear as close as possible to the word it modifies:

Binh spent *almost* fifty dollars on her haircut. [The modifier appears next to the word it modifies, *fifty*.]

Spinach contains lutein, a vitamin *that strengthens the eyes*. [The modifier appears next to *vitamin*, which is the word it modifies.]

A modifier is *misplaced* when it appears in the wrong place in the sentence. Either it seems to modify a word other than the one the writer intended, or there's more than one word it could modify and the reader can't tell which one.

MISPLACED The carpentry student nailed the plank to the floor *with red hair*. [Did the floor have red hair?]

CLEAR The carpentry student *with red hair* nailed the plank to the floor.

MISPLACED	The restaurant *only* serves lunch on Sundays. [Is lunch the only meal served on Sundays, or are Sundays the only days that lunch is served?]
CLEAR	The restaurant serves *only* lunch on Sundays.
CLEAR	The restaurant serves lunch on Sundays *only*.
MISPLACED	Leo walked outside to smell the flowering rosemary plant *wearing his bathing suit*. [Is the plant wearing his bathing suit?]
CLEAR	*Wearing his bathing suit*, Leo walked outside to smell the flowering rosemary plant.

ACTIVITY 11 Identify Misplaced Modifiers

Underline the misplaced modifier in each of the following sentences.

EXAMPLE My supervisor said I needed to improve my attitude <u>in her office</u>.

1. The beer can almost hit my grandmother thrown out of the car window.
2. The new standards for graduation only required a low-level statistics class.
3. Boris found a pink and squirming nest of baby mice.
4. Aamir borrowed a shirt from his brother with long sleeves.
5. The waiter brought a steak to the man covered with mushrooms.

16 D

To correct a misplaced modifier, place the modifier closer to the word it describes.

MISPLACED	The Italian visitors drove a rental car *leaving on vacation*. [It appears the rental car is leaving on vacation.]
CLEAR	*Leaving on vacation*, the Italian visitors drove a rental car. [The modifier is placed closer to the word it describes, *visitors*.]

ACTIVITY 12 Correct Misplaced Modifiers

Edit each of the following sentences to eliminate misplaced modifiers.

EXAMPLE *Wearing his expensive new suit,* Parker told the noisy employees to shape up ~~in his expensive new suit~~.

1. My boyfriend and I volunteered at the food bank with the best of intentions.
2. The volunteers put out the hillside fire from the next county.
3. The kids I was babysitting from next door played video games for hours.
4. Liam greeted the unexpected guests in his old pajamas.
5. My learning group always arranged to meet in the Student Union at my previous college.

6. Rosie almost spent two weeks in Las Vegas and went on to Reno for another week.

7. Dean took the rabbit to the veterinarian that had the sore paw.

8. Taka polished the antique cabinet standing on a stepladder.

9. Annick only told her coach what the doctor had said, but the coach told her parents.

10. The faucet dripped water all day that I need to replace.

E. Dangling Modifiers

A modifier is *dangling* when there's no word in the sentence that it can logically modify. Most dangling modifiers occur at the beginning of sentences.

DANGLING	*Smiling broadly*, the award fulfilled Renee's dreams. [It appears that the award is smiling.]
CLEAR	*Smiling broadly*, Renee accepted the award that fulfilled her dreams.
DANGLING	*In running for the taxi*, my foot tripped on the crack in the sidewalk. [Is the foot running for the taxi?]
CLEAR	*As I was running for the taxi*, my foot tripped on the crack in the sidewalk.

ACTIVITY 13 Identify Dangling Modifiers

Underline the dangling modifiers in each of the following sentences.

EXAMPLE <u>Deciding to join the team</u>, the coach enthusiastically shook Jennica's hand.

1. After finishing all of the basic classes, college became easier.

2. Staring into the distance, dark skies approach.

3. No one realized the problem with the proposal, pleased by the low cost.

4. To control your anger, a psychologist may be necessary.

5. Tired from the long flight, the crowds in the parking lot were depressing.

To correct a dangling modifier, rewrite the sentence so the reader knows what is being modified. You can add this information either to the modifier or to the rest of the sentence.

DANGLING	*Waiting in line*, the wind began to blow. [The reader can't tell who is waiting in line.]
CLEAR	*While I was waiting in line*, the wind began to blow.
CLEAR	Waiting in line, *I* felt the wind begin to blow.

ACTIVITY 14 Correct Dangling Modifiers

Edit each of the following sentences to eliminate dangling modifiers.

EXAMPLE ~~Gusting~~ to forty-five miles an hour, the tree limb hit the tin roof loudly.
The wind, gusting ... *caused* ... *to*

1. Shaking the principal's hand, Clarence's goal of earning a high school diploma became a reality.

2. Fed by hot winds and dry grass, the firefighters faced a difficult challenge.

3. Mom's jigsaw puzzle was complete, snapping the last piece into place.

4. Searching for a new way to treat diabetes, medical advances were made.

5. Seeing her nephew win a prize at the science fair, her heart was overwhelmed with pride.

6. Removing her foot from the accelerator, Diana's car rolled to a stop.

7. Having saved for years to buy a house, it was exciting that the Kangs' dream was coming true.

8. While window shopping at the mall, a sports watch caught my eye.

9. Deliriously happy, the newlyweds' limousine slowly drove to their hotel.

10. Water leaked into my boat while rowing as fast as possible.

16 F

F. Active and Passive Voice

In a sentence written in **active voice**, the subject performs the action; it does something. In a sentence written in **passive voice**, the subject receives the action; something is done to it. Readers prefer the active voice in most sentences because they normally expect the subject to be performing the action, so a sentence in which the subject doesn't perform the action takes longer to understand. The active voice is also less wordy than the passive voice.

| PASSIVE VOICE | The tail of the kite *was caught by* the boy. |
| ACTIVE VOICE | The boy *caught* the kite by the tail. |

| PASSIVE VOICE | The newspaper *is read by* my mother each morning. |
| ACTIVE VOICE | My mother *reads* the newspaper each morning. |

Visit **LaunchPad Solo for Readers and Writers > Grammar: Basic Sentences > Active and Passive Voice** for tutorials and additional practice with voice.

ACTIVITY 15 Use the Active Voice

Edit each of the following sentences to eliminate passive voice.

EXAMPLE The golfer ~~was given~~ the green jacket ~~by the tournament's sponsor~~.
The tournament's sponsor gave

1. The runners were encouraged by the spectators.

2. The memos had been signed by the manager.

3. A doctoral degree in physics was earned by Professor Patel.

4. An educational play about AIDS was performed by the juniors.

5. The baby was taken to the park by his older brother.

6. The party was planned by Milo, but all the work was done by his family.

7. The assignment was given at the beginning of class by the teaching assistant.

8. A swimming pool was installed by the previous owners of the house.

9. The movie was made by the Coen brothers, and the villain was played by John Goodman.

10. Our pets were fed by a neighbor.

16 G

(ACTIVITY 16 Correct Passive Voice in a Paragraph)

Edit the following paragraph so that all sentences are in the active voice.

EXAMPLE Because of the poor economy, my college money ~~was used~~ *I used* for rent and gas.

A university education must be paid for. School and work are balanced differently by my friends and me. Monica had both a full-time and a part-time job for two years following high school. Now a job isn't needed during college. She earns high grades because she doesn't have to divide her energies between work and school. A full-time night job was chosen by Bill, and only nine credits are taken by him. He does data entry for the business office of a department store. An administrative position in the same office will be taken by him after graduation. Bill earns enough money working at night to make payments on a new car. I don't need a car. However, money for college is needed. I chose to take out student loans to pay for my education. My friends and I live very different lives.

(G. Parallelism

Visit **LaunchPad Solo for Readers and Writers** > Grammar: Basic Sentences > **Parallelism** for tutorials and additional practice with using parallel structure.

When two or more groups of words in a sentence are parts of a pair or series, these word groups should be **parallel**, or similar in their grammatical structure. The following sentences are written using parallel structure:

Today, we *drove to Philadelphia, visited the Liberty Bell,* and *ate at our favorite restaurants.*

The italic word groups in this sentence are parallel because they each follow the same grammatical structure: past-tense verb followed by words that modify the verb or complete its meaning.

My girlfriend is *smart in school, friendly to everyone,* and *fun to be with.*

The italic word groups in this sentence are parallel because they follow the same grammatical structure: adjective followed by words that modify the adjective.

Here are examples of sentences that do not have parallel structure, each followed by a revised sentence that has parallel structure. Notice that the revised sentences are easier to read and understand.

NOT PARALLEL	I love going to the movies, reading, and to walk.
PARALLEL	I love going to the movies, reading, and walking.
NOT PARALLEL	He drove dangerously fast, missed the curve, and wrecks his car.
PARALLEL	He drove dangerously fast, missed the curve, and wrecked his car.
NOT PARALLEL	I don't like to fill out financial aid forms that are difficult, long, and have too many words.
PARALLEL	I don't like to fill out financial aid forms that are difficult, long, and wordy.

16 G

HOW TO Write Using Parallel Structure

- Reread each sentence, looking for pairs or series of word groups in a sentence.
- Check that each of the groups of words in the pair or series has a similar grammatical structure.
- Rewrite any parts of the pair or series that are not parallel in structure.

ACTIVITY 17 Use Parallelism

Edit each of the following sentences for correct parallel structure.

EXAMPLE My favorite activities include horseback riding, hiking, and ~~to play~~ ^playing^ soccer.

1. My mother was a hairdresser, a taxi driver, and being a secretary.

2. In my University Studies class, I have learned how to study more effectively and preparing for an exam.

3. The bookstore has my favorite books: books about cooking, biographies, and novels.

4. I found the concert to be loud, expensive, and was not very entertaining.

5. Going to the dentist is worse than to go to the hospital.

6. The buffet included undercooked shrimp, limp lettuce, and the muffins were stale.

7. Haruko was filled with fear, anticipation, excited.

8. The squirrel peeked out, stole the nut, and then back to his home.

9. The Ferris wheel is my favorite carnival ride, but my sister prefers the haunted house and to ride the merry-go-round.

10. She likes to play basketball, but he prefers skiing.

16 G

ACTIVITY 18 Correct Faulty Parallelism in a Paragraph

Edit the paragraph so that all sentences are parallel.

EXAMPLE We need a visionary leader in each of our groups, but ~~we're knowing~~ this isn't likely. *we know*

A visionary leader is someone who is not afraid to lead and of taking the group to a place it would not otherwise be. A visionary leader isn't necessarily the most dynamic person in the group but who is willing to listen to others. Such a leader works hard to improve conditions for every member of the group, seeks to put the needs of the group members first, and a desire to see the group succeed as a whole. The visionary leader is not always the group member with the most imaginative ideas but is the member who has the skills and energy to put these ideas into action. We could use more visionary leaders: they touch, inspire, and are changing the world we live in.

17

Improving Vocabulary and Word Choice

Speaking and writing are key ways to communicate your thoughts and feelings to others, and different situations require different word choices. Just as you wouldn't go to a job interview in a wedding dress or to a football game in a bathing suit, you wouldn't write to your boss in the same way that you write to a friend or daughter. You choose the best words for the person and the occasion. But how do you improve your word choice? Following are several strategies for expanding and improving the words you choose when you write.

> **In this chapter, you will review and practice improving or avoiding**
>
> A. Vocabulary
> B. Unnecessary Repetition
> C. Wordiness

☾ A. Vocabulary

One way to expand your word choice and to better understand what you read is to develop a broad vocabulary. A **vocabulary** is a set of words you are familiar with and can use in your speech and writing. If you have difficulty finding the words to express what you want to say or write in class, or if you find yourself skipping a lot of words in newspapers, magazines, or your college textbooks because you don't know what they mean, you'll want to work to improve your vocabulary.

> Visit **LaunchPad Solo for Readers and Writers** > **Reading** > **Vocabulary** for tutorials and practice with vocabulary.

Strategies for Improving Vocabulary

Relate to what you already know. Research on how people learn has demonstrated that we come to understand new information by connecting it to what we already know. Rather than memorizing lists of words, focus on linking new words to what you already have in your brain: ideas, actions, experiences, and knowledge.

Pay attention to when the word is used. Another way to remember a new word is to list terms and phrases that often accompany it. To do so, pay attention to the use of the new word. You might be surprised at how frequently you spot this word in your everyday life. Make a point of using the word yourself by mentioning it in a conversation (when appropriate) or using it when you write.

Make the most of online resources. Online dictionaries, thesauruses, and translators can be useful tools for vocabulary building.

Online dictionaries are easy to access; you can even download dictionary apps. In addition to including word definitions, these online dictionaries give the origins of the words, list synonyms (words with similar meanings), show words that are trending, and demonstrate how to pronounce words. Use a dictionary website to register for its word-of-the-day e-mail, take quizzes that test your vocabulary, and play word games. You can also find bilingual dictionaries, such as Chinese/English or Spanish/English, online.

A thesaurus contains lists of synonyms for particular words. If, for instance, you're writing an essay and can't think of another word for *pretty*, a thesaurus will give you lists of similar words, such as *beautiful*, *cute*, and *gorgeous*.

A translator can translate passages of text from one language to another. You can download translator apps or access them online. Translators are most helpful in giving meanings for individual words rather than for passages because they cannot distinguish subtleties of meaning, tone, or structure.

Use images to help remember new words. If you're a visual learner, you can improve your vocabulary by linking a new word to a related image. Take a photo or draw an image related to the new word. Write or type the word over or next to the image. Just the process of linking words and images strengthens mental connections and retention.

17 A

Keep word lists. Another effective way to improve your vocabulary is to keep word lists that give the definition of each word and examples of how it is used. You can keep a word list the old-fashioned way on index cards, or you can download a Notecard app to your phone or tablet or even use the "sticky notes" function on your computer desktop.

Read, read, read. As you learned in Chapter 2, you can improve your vocabulary by reading, whether for information or for entertainment. A great deal of research has shown that the more people read, the greater their vocabularies.

ACTIVITY 1 Build Your Vocabulary

Skim a textbook, novel, or social media post and select several words that are new to you. Apply several of the strategies listed in this section for learning these new words. How effective were these strategies? Which ones would you recommend to others and why?

Meaning from Context

Reading is the most effective way to improve vocabulary. While reading, if you come across a word you don't know, see if you can determine the meaning of the word from the **context**—that is, from the other words in the sentence. For example, consider the following sentence:

Although Bree is often *morose*, she seems happy today.

What does *morose* mean? Because you know that the word *although* shows contrast and that Bree seems happy today, then *morose* must be the opposite of *happy*. Bree must often be sad.

ACTIVITY 2 Determine Meaning from Context

Read the following passage from an article about figure skating. Try to determine the meanings of the underlined words from the words around them. Write the meanings next to the words in the spaces provided.

There are many athletic and artistic <u>elements</u> in figure skating. <u>Initial</u> skills include the all-important basics—stroking forward, skating backward, and doing forward and backward crossovers. Jumps are so <u>predominant</u> in modern figure skating that we could say that this is the "jump era." In the six <u>preliminary</u> jumps, the skater <u>rotates</u> once in the air. Since their <u>inception</u> in the beginning of the twentieth century, these jumps have been doubled and now are commonly <u>trebled</u> by both men and women.

elements _____

initial _____

predominant _____

preliminary _____

rotates _____

inception _____

trebled _____

17 A

Learn Roots, Prefixes, and Suffixes

Many words in the English language consist of a word root with a prefix and/or suffix. A **word root** is the base of a word, a **prefix** is a group of letters that appears before the word root, and a **suffix** is a group of letters that comes after it. For instance, *bicycle* consists of the word root *cycle* and the prefix *bi*, while *comfortable* consists of the word root *comfort* and the suffix *able*.

ENGLISH WORD ROOTS

Root	Meaning	Examples
audi	to hear	audience, audio
bene	good, well	benefit, benevolence

Root	Meaning	Examples
geo	earth	geography, geometry
logo	word or thought	analogy, dialogue, logic
manu	hand	manufacture, manual
photo	light	photography, telephoto
tele	far away	telegraph, telepathy
vid, vis	to see	video, vision, visit

Because so many words in English have the same prefixes and suffixes, you can improve your vocabulary by learning the most common prefixes and suffixes.

ENGLISH PREFIXES

Prefix	Meaning	Examples
ante-	before	antebellum, antedate
anti-	against	antibody, antisocial
bi-	two	bilateral, bipolar
de-	from	declaw, desensitize
dis-	not, opposite	disbelief, disallow
hyper-	over, more	hypersensitive
mal-	bad	malpractice
mis-	wrongly	misguide, misdirect
pre-	before	prefix, prenatal
post-	after	postscript, postwar
trans-	across	transition, transport
uni-	one	unicycle, uniform

ENGLISH SUFFIXES

Suffix	Meaning	Examples
-able	can be done	doable, capable
-acy	state or quality	democracy, privacy
-dom	state of being	freedom, kingdom
-en	cause or become	blacken, cheapen
-ful	full of	careful, peaceful
-ish	having the quality of	clownish
-less	lack of, without	childless, humorless
-ology	the study of	biology, psychology
-ment	condition of	employment, payment
-sion, -tion	state of being	confusion, transition

17 A

ACTIVITY 3 Learn Roots, Prefixes, and Suffixes

Create a vocabulary list for each root, prefix, and suffix listed on pages 471–72. Write the root, prefix, or suffix in the first column. Write the meaning and an example in the second column. Review these regularly until you have memorized them. Alternatively, you can use "sticky notes" or another note-taking application on your computer, phone, or tablet.

B. Unnecessary Repetition

Repetition results from repeating the same idea in different words. Although repetition can help you emphasize and connect ideas as you write, too much repetition may cause you to lose your readers' attention. At times, you may not even realize that you're repeating words or using words that mean the same thing. Notice the unnecessary words in the following sentences:

REPETITION	There are several positive benefits to eating a healthy breakfast.
REVISED	There are several benefits to eating a healthy breakfast.
REPETITION	We tried to forget the sad events of that day and put them out of our minds.
REVISED	We tried to forget the sad events of that day.
REPETITION	When leaving the train, remember to take your personal belongings.
REVISED	When leaving the train, remember to take your belongings.

HOW TO Avoid Unnecessary Repetition

To avoid unnecessary repetition, check that each word in a sentence

- Adds interest.
- Is specific.
- Does not restate what you have already said.

ACTIVITY 4 Avoid Unnecessary Repetition

Revise each of the following sentences to avoid unnecessary repetition.

EXAMPLE I will never ~~ever~~ do anything like that again ~~in the future~~.

1. My very favorite song I like the most is "I Can't Make You Love Me."

2. Jerry wanted to get caught up and be up-to-date on what was going on in class.

3. Don't confuse me with the facts and data!

4. We never knew or realized how important this event would be.

5. Let's just wait and pass the time until she returns.

(C. Wordiness

Visit **LaunchPad Solo for Readers and Writers** > **Basic Sentences** > **Wordiness** for more practice with wordiness.

Eliminating wordiness is similar to avoiding unnecessary repetition. **Wordiness** results from using too many words to say something or using "filler" phrases that don't contribute to the meaning of a sentence. Notice the wordiness in the following sentences:

WORDY   I would really very much like to go to that game.
REVISED   I would really like to go to that game.

WORDY   I get to make the choice of where I go.
REVISED   I get to choose where I go.

WORDY   I feel that we have a greater amount of freedom to choose these days.
REVISED   We have more freedom to choose today.

17 C

(ACTIVITY 5 Eliminate Wordiness

Revise the following sentences to eliminate wordiness.

EXAMPLE I̶ ̶b̶e̶l̶i̶e̶v̶e̶ ̶t̶h̶a̶t̶ ̶y̶o̶u̶ are wrong.   *You*

1. I would like to say that I agree with you.

2. I am of the opinion that anyone who writes on this topic as a subject for an essay is not thinking straight.

3. A large number of students in the near future will agree with us.

4. At an earlier point in time, this wouldn't have happened, or it would have been postponed until a later time.

5. I believe that this is true for the reason that students feel differently today than they did at an earlier point in time.

18

Improving Spelling

As you edit your writing, you'll want to be sure to check your spelling. Misspelled words will cause your readers to focus on your lack of spelling skills rather than on the meaning of what you have written. You can often tell if a word is misspelled just by looking at it, or you can use a computer spell-check to catch errors. Because the spell-check can't catch every error, though, it's useful to improve your spelling.

In this chapter you will review
A. Spelling Rules
B. Commonly Misspelled Words
C. Commonly Confused Words

A. Spelling Rules

Visit **LaunchPad Solo for Readers and Writers > Grammar: Style and Mechanics > Spelling** for more practice with spelling.

One way to improve your spelling is to learn spelling rules that can help you master the spelling of commonly misspelled words.

Rule 1 Use *i* before *e* except after *c* or when sounded like *ay* as in *neighbor* and *weigh*.

believe, niece, piece, fierce

receive, ceiling, conceive, deceive

eight, freight, sleigh, weight

Exceptions: either, neither, leisure, height, seize, weird, science, counterfeit

ACTIVITY 1 Use *i* before *e* except after *c*

In the space provided, correct each of the following misspelled words, or write "correct" if the word is spelled correctly.

EXAMPLE hieght _____*height*_____

1. conceited _____
2. recieve _____
3. neighbor _____
4. weigh _____
5. cieling _____

6. decieve _____
7. seize _____
8. beleive _____
9. niether _____
10. neice _____

◼ ACTIVITY 2 Correct *i* before *e* except after *c* Errors

Underline each of the misspelled words in the following sentences. Then write the correct spelling of these words in the space provided. If a sentence has no spelling errors, write "correct."

EXAMPLE Jerry has a <u>neice</u> and nephew. _____*niece*_____

1. Patrice asked Amando for a piece of paper. _____

2. It is important not to carry excess wieght when you are backpacking.

   _____

3. A good pair of shoes releived Kenia's backaches. _____

4. In his liesure time, Hal likes to go bow hunting. _____

5. Majel concieved of a way to pass the exam without reading the textbook.

   _____

6. Terrelle was so concieted that people tried to avoid him.

   _____

7. On Christmas, Grandfather treated us to an old-fashioned sleigh ride.

   _____

8. My favorite beige jacket always looks dirty. _____

9. Tim decieved his teacher by forging his father's signature on his report card.

   _____

10. When we recieve your order, we will notify you by e-mail.

    _____

18 A

Rule 2 When adding an ending that begins with a vowel (such as *-ed* or *-ing*) to a word that ends with a consonant, double the consonant if it (1) is preceded by a single vowel and (2) ends a one-syllable word or stressed syllable.

    bet, betting
    stop, stopped
    commit, committed
    occur, occurrence

Exception: Even if the consonant ends a stressed syllable, do not double it if the syllable is no longer stressed when the ending is added: *refer, reference.*

ACTIVITY 3 Double the Final Consonant

In the space provided, add the correct ending to each of the following words.

EXAMPLE get + ing _____*getting*_____

1. travel + ed _____
2. dig + ing _____
3. omit + ed _____
4. control + ing _____
5. prefer + ence _____

6. scan + er _____
7. nag + ing _____
8. persist + ence _____
9. defer + al _____
10. hop + ed _____

ACTIVITY 4 Correct Final Consonant Errors

Underline each of the misspelled words in the following sentences. Then write the correct spelling of these words in the space provided. If a sentence has no spelling errors, write "correct."

EXAMPLE The rabbit hoped to the side of the house. _____*hopped*_____

1. Mary stoped kicking the bottom of Bill's chair when he fell asleep. _____
2. They never succeeded at ridding their house of ants. _____
3. Felicia admited that she was sad when her friend moved away. _____
4. After tiping over his glass, Lewis apologized and left the room. _____
5. Ron and Leni held hands and planed their future. _____
6. Efren made a referrence to his former girlfriend. _____
7. Delphine repeatted her name three times before the clerk said it correctly.

   _____

8. The occurence of car theft in the parking lot has doubled in the last year.

   _____

9. Pegeen believed that Neville was betting on a losing team. _____
10. Stuart laborred over his statistics homework for six hours. _____

18 A

Rule 3 Drop a final silent *e* from a word when adding an ending that begins with a vowel. Keep the final *e* if the ending begins with a consonant.

   retire, retiring;   age, aging;   desire, desiring

   hate, hateful;   state, statement;   lone, lonely

Exceptions: courageous, manageable, ninth, truly, argument, judgment

ACTIVITY 5 Drop the Final Silent e

In the space provided, add the specified ending to each of the following words.

EXAMPLE perspire + ing ____perspiring____

1. bite + ing _____
2. encourage + ment _____
3. safe + ty _____
4. nine + th _____
5. care + ful _____

6. shine + ing _____
7. true + ly _____
8. fade + ing _____
9. use + able _____
10. state + ment _____

ACTIVITY 6 Correct Final Silent e Errors

Underline each of the misspelled words in the following sentences. Then write the correct spelling of these words in the space provided. If a sentence has no spelling errors, write "correct."

EXAMPLE He thought he was ageing too quickly. _____aging_____

1. Mira's greatest achievment was hiking the entire Appalachian Trail.

   _____

2. This coat has a removable lining. _____
3. The lavish meal left us desireing nothing more. _____
4. Stan remained quiet to avoid an arguement with his friends in public.

   _____

5. The shoppers were hopeing to find bargains. _____
6. The audience made hatful remarks as the senator tried to speak.

   _____

7. Clarence used good judgement in choosing a roommate. _____
8. The surest way to be fired from a job is to not show up. _____
9. Denise found her courses in managment more interesting than those in

   marketing. _____
10. Sheldon spent the rest of the afternoon writeing his résumé. _____

Rule 4 When adding an ending other than -*ing* to a word that ends in *y*, you sometimes need to change the *y* to *i*. If the *y* is preceded by a consonant, change it to *i*:

easy, easiest; duty, dutiful; marry, married

18 A

If you're adding -s, also add an e after the i:

  reply, replies;   dry, dries

If you're adding -ing or the y is preceded by a vowel, don't change it to i.

  apply, applying;   dry, drying;   play, played;   monkey, monkeys

ACTIVITY 7 Change y to i

In the space provided, add the specified ending to each of the following words, and write the new word.

EXAMPLE carry + ed _____ *carried* _____

  1. pay + ing _____   6. plenty + ful _____

  2. turkey + s _____   7. hurry + s _____

  3. say + ing _____   8. fly + ing _____

  4. fry + ed _____   9. happy + ness _____

  5. pretty + ily _____   10. play + ful _____

ACTIVITY 8 Correct y to i Errors

Underline each of the misspelled words in the following sentences. Then write the correct spelling of these words in the space provided. If a sentence has no spelling errors, write "correct."

EXAMPLE The couple's happyness left us inspired. _____ *happiness* _____

  1. To find employment, he read the classified ads. _____

  2. We were puzzled by the trickyness of the test question. _____

  3. Lester has been studiing all day. _____

  4. After several apologys, Wanda finally forgave her brother. _____

  5. Rainer easly jumped over the puddle. _____

  6. Yesterday's sunset was especially beautyful. _____

  7. In warm weather, the clothes dryed very quickly on the line. _____

  8. The sounds of the children playing in the street carryed into my sixth-floor apartment. _____

  9. The two attornies made an agreement to avoid going to court.

     _____

  10. After staying at campgrounds, I found the motel luxurious. _____

18 A

B. Commonly Misspelled Words

The following are one hundred commonly misspelled words. Create spelling lists or cards to practice spelling them correctly.

absence	hoarse	procedure
accommodate	holiday	pursue
all right	hygiene	receipt
analyze	icicles	receive
anoint	imagine	recommend
anonymous	indispensable	repetition
benefit	innocent	rhythm
boundary	irresistible	ridiculous
business	irritable	roommate
category	jealousy	schedule
committee	league	seize
conscience	leisure	separate
conscious	license	sergeant
corroborate	losing	sheriff
counterfeit	maneuver	sophomore
dealt	marriage	subtle
definitely	meant	succeed
despair	minute	supersede
dilemma	misspelled	surgeon
disappoint	necessary	tongue
ecstasy	ninth	tragedy
eighth	noticeable	truly
embarrass	occurrence	tyranny
exceed	often	undoubtedly
existence	optimistic	until
fascinate	pamphlet	vacuum
February	parallel	vengeance
forty	peculiar	vicious
fulfill	perseverance	warrant
government	persistent	weird
grammar	phenomenon	wholly
guarantee	principal	yacht
guard	principle	
height	privilege	

18 B

ACTIVITY 9 Correct Sentences for Spelling

Underline the misspelled words in each of the following sentences. Then write the correct spelling of these words in the space provided. (There may be more than one error in each sentence.)

EXAMPLE I always <u>recomended</u> <u>vacumming</u>, but I <u>definitly</u> see the <u>benafit</u> of it now.

recommended, vacuuming, definitely, benefit

1. When Rafa telephoned, Yoli was studing her chemistry, so he apologyzed for bothering her.

   _____

2. After beging for three weeks to be given a better work schedule, Steve stoped asking.

   _____

3. Gino had been liveing in his apartment for fifteen years when he recieved the eviction notice.

   _____

4. A counterfiet coin may wiegh less than a genuine one.

   _____

5. Shelley was carful when she tryed to remove the splinter from the child's finger.

   _____

6. You can easly waste your liesure time on activities you don't really enjoy.

   _____

7. A student writeing a persuasive essay needs to construct a very strong arguement supporting his or her opinions.

   _____

8. Rasa prefered ordering from a website to shoping at the mall.

   _____

9. Unfortunately, Vincent omited his social security number when he applyed for a scholarship.

   _____

10. The dutys of the store manager never stoped at five o'clock.

   _____

18 B

C. Commonly Confused Words

Commonly confused words are words that sound similar but have different spellings and meanings.

accept: to agree to	I *accept* your offer.
except: excluding	Everyone *except* Joan was invited.
adapt: to adjust	Kenji had to *adapt* to his new town.
adopt: to take on	He realized that he would have to *adopt* a new attitude.
advice: a suggestion	Please take my *advice*.
advise: to suggest	I *advise* you to slow down.
affect: to influence	Her partying did not *affect* her grades.
effect: a result	The *effect*, though, was that she was under stress.
all ready: prepared	We are *all ready* for the holidays.
already: previously	We have *already* bought all of the food we need.
cite: to refer to	Jerome is always careful to *cite* his sources.
sight: vision	The eye surgery improved her *sight*.
site: a location	The article was about the *site* of the new museum.
complement: to go well with something else	This tie does not *complement* your shirt.
compliment: to admire; an expression of admiration	I *compliment* you on your choice of pants.
conscience: moral principles	Josue's *conscience* wouldn't permit him to cheat.
conscious: aware	He was *conscious* of students cheating around him.
farther: a longer physical distance	My aunt lives *farther* away than my family can drive in one day.
further: additional; more	The committee agreed to *further* discussion of the issue.
loose: not tight or secure	Wasim's tooth was *loose*.
lose: to misplace	He didn't want to *lose* it if it fell out.
principal: head of a school; main or leading	The *principal* of my high school was one of the *principal* supporters of the new gym.
principle: a basic truth or belief	He believed in the *principle* of daily exercise.

to: toward	Aja ran *to* the lake.
too: excessively; also	Her brother, Ankur, was *too* slow to keep up and stopped along the way, *too*.
two: the number between one and three	The *two* of them arrived an hour apart.
weather: conditions such as sun, rain, and wind	The *weather* in Washington, D.C., was beautiful.
whether: a word indicating choice or possibility	I had to decide *whether* to leave or stay.

ACTIVITY 10 Correct a Paragraph for Spelling

Correct the misspelled words in the following paragraph by crossing them out and writing the correct spelling above each misspelled word.

EXAMPLE Ahmad wishes he knew more about this word-processing program
                    affects
        because it ~~effects~~ the way he writes.

Ahmad feels the campus computer labs need improveing. Before geting his own computer, he relyed heavily on the labs. Although they were convient, they were to noisey and crowded. Computers were often unavailable because the maintance was so bad. Even when he found a free computer, he was often distractted by the rowdyness of the other students. After recieving a laptop from his father, Ahmad lookked foreward to his life being easyer. Unffortunatly, he still had problems when continueing projects he had begun at home. Once, he accidently reformated his hard drive, loosing all his data. He often had difficultys printing at the lab, discoverring pages of wierd symbols weather he wanted two or not. The technicians said that his laptop software wasn't compattible with the software at the lab. Now he's more conscience of mistakes than ever before. Ahmad's father says that computers have all ready created new problems while solveing other ones.

18 C

19

Improving Punctuation

You use **punctuation** to make it easier for your readers to follow your meaning. Just as your car's taillights communicate that you are planning to stop, turn right, or turn left, punctuation communicates to your readers what to expect next. Readers depend on punctuation to guide them through your text. For example, what does the following sentence mean?

Don't let the snake eat Ryan.

Is the snake about to eat Ryan, or is Ryan supposed to prevent the snake from eating? Adding a comma to this sentence makes it clear.

Don't let the snake eat, Ryan.

The reader now understands that Ryan is supposed to prevent the snake from eating its food.

The following punctuation rules will help you make your meaning clear and communicate to your readers more effectively.

A. Commas

Visit **LaunchPad Solo for Readers and Writers > Grammar: Style and Mechanics > Commas** for more practice with commas.

The **comma (,)** is used to separate parts of a sentence to make the meaning clear.

Rule 1 Use a comma after an introductory word, phrase, or clause.

Actually, snakes like to eat rodents.

After feeding the snake, you can leave for the NASCAR race.

As Ryan explained, snakes eat a variety of foods.

ACTIVITY 1 Use Commas with Introductory Words

Add a comma after the introductory word, phrase, or clause in each of the following sentences.

EXAMPLE Although I usually like the opera‸I didn't like this one.

1. Smelling Janelle's perfume in the apartment Oscar knew that she had dressed up to go to the party.

2. First Corey fastened his seatbelt and put on his sunglasses.

3. Whether you agree or not I'm taking biology next semester.

4. In Wendy's opinion renting a large apartment is more convenient than owning a house.

5. While the children ate cake and played games their parents became better acquainted.

ACTIVITY 2 Write Using Commas with Introductory Words

In each of the following sentences, add an introductory word, phrase, or clause followed by a comma.

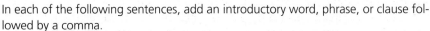

EXAMPLE Dan and Andrea would not stop talking.

1. I heard the drone of a small airplane overhead.

2. She put on more lipstick and mascara.

3. Your parents were watching you through the kitchen window.

4. We keep reams of paper and extra cartridges for the printer.

5. Philip admitted that he was wrong.

Rule 2   Use commas to separate three or more words, phrases, or clauses in a series. Do not use a comma before the first item in the series or after the last item.

Jane bought books, games, and DVDs at the bookstore.

Before leaving, she talked to her roommate, turned off her computer, and locked her desk.

Jane forgot to feed the dog, left her bed unmade, and didn't clean the bathroom.

ACTIVITY 3 Use Commas in a Series

Add commas as needed to each of the following sentences to separate words, phrases, or clauses used in a series.

EXAMPLE My favorite foods are salmon fried rice and chocolate cake.

1. All I had in the refrigerator was a pint of sour milk a block of moldy cheese and a jar of olives.

19 A

2. Eileen packed underwear jeans sweaters socks shoes and maps.

3. Vikram walked down the street past the supermarket and around the corner.

4. Jorge filled the sandbox Gunilla set up the swings Noah built the seesaws Calvin welded the slide and Mahela painted the benches.

5. Chewing gum pacing the floor and watching the clock were the only things to do in the waiting room.

ACTIVITY 4 Write Using Commas with a Series

For each of the following lists of items, write a complete sentence using the items in a series.

EXAMPLE hills, riverbeds, dusty trails

We hiked hills, river beds, and dusty trails.

1. pens, pencils, notebooks, folders, erasers

2. a pad of paper, a pair of scissors, a bottle of glue

3. on the dashboard, under the front seat, in the trunk

4. decorating the house, preparing a festive meal, spending time with family

5. sang songs, told funny stories, did magic tricks, made balloon animals

19 A

For more on subordinate, or dependent clauses, see pp. 427–29.

Rule 3 Use a comma to separate two independent clauses joined by a coordinating conjunction.

I wanted to go to the concert, and I wanted to study for my exam.

I knew my exam was important, but Taylor Swift is my favorite singer.

I studied all afternoon, so I was able to go to the concert after all.

ACTIVITY 5 Use Commas with Coordinating Conjunctions

Add a comma to each of the following sentences to separate the two independent clauses joined by a coordinating conjunction.

EXAMPLE I wanted to leave early, yet my husband wanted to leave at noon.

1. The wind howled and the snow fell more thickly.
2. Margarita stood on a stepladder but she could not reach the ceiling.
3. Julio drank a second bottle of water yet he was still thirsty.
4. Marcia couldn't sleep for the next day she was going to start a new job.
5. I wanted to call you on your birthday but you were out all night.

ACTIVITY 6 Join Sentences with Coordinating Conjunctions

Use a comma and a coordinating conjunction to join each of the following pairs of sentences into a single sentence.

EXAMPLE My mother loves to travel, but she's ~~. She's~~ a little afraid of flying.

1. Yusef sat in the driver's seat. His brothers pushed the car.
2. Aurelia found the strength to run even faster. She saw the banners at the finish line.
3. I realized that I had answered the essay question on my history midterm badly. I had only enough time to write a brief concluding paragraph.
4. The doctor gave Samia a pair of crutches. She could walk without further injuring her foot.
5. You could come to the dance with me. You could watch reruns on television.

19 A

Rule 4 Use commas before and after an appositive (a noun that renames the noun right before it) or a descriptive word, phrase, or clause if the appositive, word, phrase, or clause interrupts the flow of the sentence or could be removed from the sentence without changing its meaning. If the appositive, word, phrase, or clause is at the end of the sentence, use a comma before it.

For more on appositives, see pp. 348–49; for more on clauses, see pp. 426–31.

My high school reunion, sadly, was missing the person I most wanted to see.

Jessie, who was my high school sweetheart, doesn't live here anymore.

The reunion, held over the Thanksgiving weekend, wasn't nearly as much fun as the last one.

I would really like to see Jessie, my old flame.

ACTIVITY 7 Use Commas with Descriptive Words and Phrases

Add commas to each of the following sentences to set off the appositive or the descriptive word, phrase, or clause.

EXAMPLE Johnny, my closest friend, never has to study.

1. Mateo the youngest child is the first in his family to attend a university.

2. The driver of the car in front of us ignoring the stop sign sped through the intersection.

3. Ricky's new saxophone which had cost him his life savings enabled him to join his favorite jazz band.

4. My date a massage therapist named Yolanda asked me in to meet her parents.

5. Janine's former roommate surprisingly was happy to see her.

 ACTIVITY 8 Add Descriptive Words and Phrases with Commas

Rewrite each of the following sentences by inserting the appositive or descriptive word, phrase, or clause provided. Include the required commas.

EXAMPLE Corky flew from his perch to my shoulder. (*my parakeet*)

   Corky, my parakeet, flew from his perch to my shoulder.

1. Mr. Gardner ran unsuccessfully for state senator. (*my history teacher in middle school*)

   _____

   _____

2. Hector's grandchildren ran into the kitchen. (*smelling the cookies in the oven*)

   _____

   _____

3. The library book gathered dust at the back of my closet. (*which I had never read*)

   _____

   _____

19 A

4. Gavin's wife has just published a magazine article about their trip to Bhutan. (*an agricultural advisor*)

_____

_____

5. Sally could not afford a new truck. (*unfortunately*)

_____

_____

Rule 5   Use commas to set off transitional words and phrases from the rest of the sentence.

It wasn't until I visited the museum, however, that I realized how much I liked art.

For example, I discovered I really enjoyed Remington's sculptures.

My friend, on the other hand, preferred Monet's paintings.

For more on transitional words and phrases, see pp. 164–65.

ACTIVITY 9 Use Commas with Transitional Words and Phrases

Add commas as needed to each of the following sentences to set off the transitional words and phrases.

EXAMPLE Surely my car will be ready soon.

1. Subsequently the rest of the family came down with the flu.

2. Fritz likewise saved copies of his work in his digital cloud.

3. Furthermore the larger company has superior benefits.

4. The two-lane road alongside the freeway nevertheless is very scenic.

5. It wasn't until Belinda heard the applause however that she truly believed her speech was convincing.

ACTIVITY 10 Add Transitional Words and Phrases with Commas

Rewrite each of the following sentences by inserting the transitional word or phrase provided. Include the required commas.

EXAMPLE Sandy wants to try out for the marching band. (*nonetheless*)

Sandy, nonetheless, wants to try out for the marching band.

19 A

1. Consuelo is allergic to feathers and animal fur. (*however*)

   _____

   _____

2. Farak prefers snorkeling to scuba diving. (*on the other hand*)

   _____

   _____

3. The people who arrived late waited in the lobby for the first intermission. (*meanwhile*)

   _____

   _____

4. Some members of the city council want to increase the budget for public parks. (*in addition*)

   _____

   _____

5. The tenants are pooling their money to buy the apartment building from the bank. (*as a result*)

   _____

   _____

Rule 6   Use a comma to separate the day of the month from the year. If the year is in the middle of a sentence, also use a comma after it.

I will start graduate school on September 4, 2017.

I was born on July 4, 1979, and immediately became the center of my grandmother's attention.

My goal is to have my master's degree by the time I turn forty on July 4, 2019.

19 A

ACTIVITY 11   Use Commas in Dates

Add commas as needed to each of the following sentences.

EXAMPLE My birthday is December 8,1987.

1. My father was born on September 18 1956.

2. The automobile accident occurred on October 30 2011.

3. February 29 2005 is a date that never existed.

4. I first filed an income tax return on April 15 2008.

5. November 8 1990 was the day my aunt and uncle were married.

ACTIVITY 12 Write Sentences Using Commas in Dates

Complete each of the following sentences, giving the month, day, and year. Use commas as necessary.

EXAMPLE I received my degree on _____ May 5, 2015 _____.

1. Today's date is _____.

2. _____ is my date of birth.

3. The first day I attended class this semester was _____.

4. _____ is the date of the last holiday I celebrated.

5. Next Saturday's date is _____.

Rule 7 Use commas in addresses and place names to separate the various parts, such as the street, city, county, state or province, and country. If the address or place name ends in the middle of a sentence, also use a comma after it.

I have lived at 400 Elm Street, Chicago, Illinois, all of my life.

My closest friend now lives at 402 Oak Avenue, Bexar County, Texas.

ACTIVITY 13 Use Commas in Addresses and Place Names

Add commas as needed to each of the following sentences.

EXAMPLE Another friend lives at 632 Pecan Street, Toronto, Canada.

1. His office is located at 4100 Manchester Drive Albany New York.

2. I have some relatives who live in Atlanta Georgia and some who live in Tampa Florida.

3. There is a large medical center in Dane County Wisconsin.

4. Tamara celebrated New Year's Eve in Paris France.

5. I mailed the warranty card to 762 Wallingford Boulevard Fremont Virginia.

19 A

ACTIVITY 14 Write Using Commas in Addresses and Place Names

Complete each of the following sentences, providing the information indicated. Use commas as necessary.

EXAMPLE My favorite relative lives at 13 Main Street, Phoenix, Arizona _____.
(*street address • city • state*)

1. I know someone who lives at _____.
(*street address • city • state*)

2. I was born in _____.
   (*city* or *county* • *state* • *country*)

3. A place I have visited is _____.
   (*city* • *state*)

4. My dream vacation would be in _____.
   (*city* • *state*)

5. My address is _____.
   (*street address* • *city* • *state*)

Rule 8   Use commas to set off dialogue or a direct quotation from the rest of the sentence. Commas always go *before* quotation marks.

"Go ahead and start your engines," the announcer said.

According to my brother, "He didn't say it loud enough for all of the racers to hear."

"I said it loud enough," the announcer replied, "for all of the other racers to hear."

ACTIVITY 15 Use Commas with Dialogue and Direct Quotations

Add commas as needed to each of the following sentences.

EXAMPLE My father always says, "Don't judge a book by its cover."

1. "I think Douglas likes you" Charlene whispered to Amber.

2. Jon Stewart said "Insomnia is my greatest inspiration."

3. "Don't kill that spider" Alberto told his son.

4. "You don't need to insure your car" Yasmin joked "if you never drive it."

5. Professor Ambrosini reminds us "Even if it's not on the test, you still need to know it."

ACTIVITY 16 Write Using Commas with Dialogue and Direct Quotations

Complete each of the following sentences by providing a one-sentence piece of dialogue or quotation. Use commas as necessary.

EXAMPLE I heard a singer on the radio repeat , "I'm a creep; I'm a weirdo."

1. My friend always tells people _____

2. I like to say _____

19 A

3. My favorite movie character says _____

4. _____ according to someone in my family.

5. One memorable teacher often said _____

ACTIVITY 17 Use Commas Correctly in Sentences

Using all of the comma rules you have learned in this chapter, add commas as necessary to each of the following sentences.

EXAMPLE Since I had never been to that ski resort‸ he explained that it was in

Jackson Hole‸ Wyoming.

1. The oldest son Steven surprised his family by bringing home his new wife for they had not known that he had even been dating somebody special.

2. In high school Sofia amazingly decided to take a cooking class to learn how to read package labels how to select and store fresh vegetables and how to prepare quick meals from basic ingredients.

3. Because he knew that I was worried Alexei my oldest friend telephoned to announce "Jackie my new address is 1561 Kendall Avenue Minneapolis Minnesota."

4. Mastering new software therefore involves solving two important problems which are learning what the software can do and figuring out how to get the software to do it.

5. On July 20 1969 when Neil Armstrong stepped onto the surface of the moon he said "One small step for [a] man; one giant leap for mankind."

19 A

ACTIVITY 18 Use Commas Correctly in a Paragraph

Using all of the comma rules you have learned in this chapter, add commas as needed to the following paragraph.

EXAMPLE The day that John F. Kennedy died‸ November 22‸ 1963‸ remains

important to older Americans.

One of them remarked "On that day everything changed." Many people began working to end war racism sexism and poverty. Violence increased and two other leaders were shot and killed: Martin Luther King Jr. and Robert Kennedy the president's brother. Finally public figures lost their privacy. In a famous photograph President Kennedy's son salutes the funeral procession.

No situation should be more private than a boy saying good-bye to his father.

However a child had to share this moment with millions of strangers.

B. Semicolons

For more about independent clauses, see pp. 426–27.

Visit **LaunchPad Solo for Readers and Writers > Grammar: Style and Mechanics > Colons and Semicolons** for more practice with semicolons.

The **semicolon (;)** is used to join independent clauses and to make meaning clear.

Rule 1   Use a semicolon to join two related independent clauses that could each stand alone as a sentence. Semicolons work especially well if the two independent clauses are short and closely related.

I never liked science fiction; it just doesn't make sense to me.

Stephen King is my favorite writer; he knows how to grab his readers' attention.

I can't believe how many books King has written; *Carrie* is still my all-time favorite.

> **ACTIVITY 19** Write Using Semicolons to Join Independent Clauses

Add a semicolon and an independent clause to each of the following independent clauses.

EXAMPLE Candace is an accomplished figure skater ; she studied ballet to add
        grace to her routines.

1. For me, the morning is the most frustrating time of day _____

   _____

2. My cousin is an excellent athlete _____

   _____

3. They have a beautiful view from their window _____

   _____

4. Every day, I put up with someone with an annoying habit _____

   _____

5. Next semester, I will have an ideal schedule _____

   _____

19 B

Rule 2   Use a semicolon to link two clauses that are joined by a transitional word.

> Some people think Stephen King is too gory; nevertheless, they read every one of his books.

> I wanted to send a copy of *Misery* to my cousin; however, my father wouldn't let me.

> I will buy every book King publishes; for example, I just bought *Finders Keepers*.

Rule 3   Use a semicolon to separate items in a series that already includes commas.

> My favorite places to visit are Des Moines, Iowa; Orlando, Florida; and Denver, Colorado.

ACTIVITY 20 Use Semicolons Correctly

Use a semicolon to correctly punctuate each of the following sentences.

EXAMPLE   I always go to the movies on Friday night ; that's the night new movies open.

1. It would be difficult to work full time while taking five classes however, Noe accepted the job.

2. In the heat of the afternoon, the flowers began to droop a single bee stirred the roses.

3. Next summer, Nadine will see Madrid, Spain Paris, France Rome, Italy and Athens, Greece.

4. Patrick did not have enough time to finish cooking dinner consequently, the stew is very watery.

5. We had to wait two hours to pose for the family photograph by that time, unfortunately, the children were no longer clean and neat.

19 C

C. Colons

The **colon (:)** is also useful for making meaning clear.

Use a colon to introduce a list or an explanation. However, use the colon only when the words before it are a complete sentence that could stand alone. Do not use a colon after expressions like *such as* or *for example*.

Visit **LaunchPad Solo for Readers and Writers > Grammar: Style and Mechanics > Colons and Semicolons** for more practice with colons.

When you go to the movies, be sure to get the following snacks: popcorn, soda, and a candy bar.

There is only one way to please Brandon at the movies: buy the foods he loves.

His friends know this about Brandon: the food is more important to him than the film.

ACTIVITY 21 Use Colons Correctly

Add colons as needed in each of the following sentences to introduce a list, clause, or phrase that explains the independent clause. If the sentence is correct without a colon, write "correct" in the space provided.

EXAMPLE I went to the bookstore to buy supplies : a ruler, graph paper, and a

calculator. _____

1. To make your own salsa, you need tomatoes, onions, chiles, cilantro, and salt.

_____

2. I have to do many things to prepare for my guests clean the house, shop for

groceries, buy concert tickets, and repair the brakes on my car.

_____

3. Ian can play four different wind instruments flute, clarinet, oboe, and bassoon.

_____

4. This afternoon, two-year-old Ryan was impossible he poured maple syrup on

the floor, tore the pages out of a photo album, and flushed a doll down the

toilet. _____

5. Vanessa's mother taught her many old popular dances, such as the twist,

pony, swim, jerk, frug, and monkey. _____

ACTIVITY 22 Write Sentences Using Colons

To each of the following sentences, add a list, clause, or phrase of explanation. Introduce your list, clause, or phrase with a colon.

EXAMPLE Many courses fulfill your science requirement : *Crime and Chemistry,*

Urban Geography, and Celestial Myths. _____

1. Ava has autographs from her favorite actors _____

_____

2. There are many things we can do next Saturday _____

   _____

3. That couple broke up for some very good reasons _____

   _____

4. I have a lot of homework for tonight _____

   _____

5. In spite of its reasonable prices, that Italian restaurant has its bad points _____

   _____

◖ D. End Punctuation

The **period (.)**, the **question mark (?)**, and the **exclamation point (!)** are the three types of punctuation used to end sentences.

Rule 1 Use a period to end most sentences, including indirect questions and commands. An indirect question reports a question rather than asks one.

He never believed her lies.

He asked her where she had heard such things.

Never lie to me again.

Rule 2 Use a question mark to end a direct question.

Why didn't he realize that she was telling the truth?

How could she make herself any clearer?

Rule 3 Use an exclamation point to give emphasis or show emotion.

Don't ever doubt my word again!

I will always tell you the truth!

19 D

◗ **ACTIVITY 23 Add End Punctuation to Sentences**

Insert the correct end punctuation mark at the end of each of the following sentences.

EXAMPLE Would you like to go to the store?

1. Now that he is an adult, Rogelio relies on his parents' good advice more than ever

2. When Vera stepped into the cabin that had been in her family for years, she noticed its old, familiar smell

3. Caleb and Genevieve were happy to see that Mr. Siegel had not changed much over the years

4. What did people do with their evenings before the Internet

5. Shame on you for behaving that way with my friends

ACTIVITY 24 Revise for Correct End Punctuation

Revise each of the following sentences as needed for end punctuation. If the end punctuation does not need to be changed, write "correct" in the space provided.

EXAMPLE Jessie likes me. _____*correct*_____

1. Ah, this is the life! _____

2. Does anyone know where the nearest police station is? _____

3. I wondered what my boss had planned for me? _____

4. This coat appears to be in good condition! _____

5. Olga wanted to know whether a new director had already been chosen.

   _____

ACTIVITY 25 Add End Punctuation to a Paragraph

In the following paragraph, insert the correct end punctuation in the spaces provided.

EXAMPLE Because of my cousin, Martin, our family just had the best reunion ever __!__

After leaving the army, Martin decided to go to college _____ Did he study something normal, like history or psychology _____ You don't know Cousin Martin _____ He majored in recreation _____ We all used to ask ourselves if this was a real major _____ It is very real, for our reunion was his senior project _____ He organized everything: transportation, accommodations, catering, and even our matching T-shirts _____ Among the games he invented for us, my favorite was the scavenger hunt _____ The family has become so big that many of us had never met before, so instead of finding objects in our scavenger hunt, Martin made us become acquainted with our more distant relatives _____ For example, I had to find a rocket scientist, and to my surprise, Gwen Zawada, my second cousin, works for NASA _____ Even the newest family members were involved; I met the very young man who had just learned to stand up unassisted _____ Who was that _____ The answer is on the family reunion web page that Martin constructed as part of his project _____ What grade did he receive _____ The professor gave him an A, of course _____

E. Apostrophes

An **apostrophe (')** is used to show possession and to form contractions.

Visit **LaunchPad Solo for Readers and Writers > Grammar: Style and Mechanics > Apostrophes** for more practice with apostrophes.

Rule 1   Use an apostrophe to show that something belongs to someone. If the thing belongs to one person, use *'s* after the noun that refers to the person, even if the noun already ends in *-s*.

Jessica's nose ring is the topic of conversation in class.

Her friend's ear stud, however, does not generate much interest.

Classmates do not even know about Doris's belly-button ring.

Rule 2   If the thing belongs to more than one person and the noun that refers to these persons ends in *-s*, use only an apostrophe *after* the *-s*.

All of the students' conversations are about Jessica.

Her friends' body piercings never come up.

If the noun doesn't end in *-s*, use *'s* after it.

The men's faces were painted with white streaks.

The women's hair was braided with vines and flowers.

Rule 3   Do not use an apostrophe in the plural form of a name unless the word is also showing possession. In that case, use an apostrophe after the *-s* of the plural.

We always enjoyed seeing the Kennedys.

The Kennedys' house always seemed warm and welcoming.

Rule 4   Do not use an apostrophe in possessive forms of pronouns: *yours, his, hers, its, ours,* or *theirs.*

The car was missing one of its rear hubcaps.

Because our car was being repaired, our friends let us use theirs.

19 E

ACTIVITY 26 Use Apostrophes to Show Possession

In each of the following sentences, add any missing apostrophes. If the sentence is not missing any apostrophes, write "correct" in the space provided.

EXAMPLE The Smiths home is located in town. _____

1. Donalds clothes were always neatly pressed. _____

2. The three professors worksheets needed to be photocopied.

   _____

3. The womans umbrella refused to open, but the rain came down steadily.

   _____

4. This couch is ours. _____

5. Seth Wilsons motorcycle fell over while he was in the restaurant. _____

6. Javiers favorite movie is *Boyhood*. _____

7. The Smiths always spend holidays together. _____

8. The Georges favorite holiday is Labor Day. _____

9. Jennys wedding will be on Labor Day weekend. _____

10. The Varelas and Fraires will be at the wedding. _____

ACTIVITY 27 Write with Apostrophes That Show Possession

Each of the following words has an apostrophe that shows possession. Use each word correctly in a sentence of your own.

EXAMPLE driver's

   The driver's windshield was covered with dust and squished bugs.

1. Doctor Rice's

   _____

2. children's

   _____

3. man's

   _____

4. baseball players'

   _____

5. Melissa's

   _____

6. Today's

   _____

7. girls'

   _____

19 E

8. Brandon's

_____

9. Joneses'

_____

10. club's

_____

Rule 5   Use an apostrophe to form a contraction. A contraction is formed by combining two words into one and omitting one or more letters, with an apostrophe taking the place of the omitted letter or letters. Some college instructors prefer that you not use contractions in college writing.

> It's [it is] always fun to go hunting.
>
> I don't [do not] care if others think that my father and I shouldn't [should not] hunt.
>
> We've [we have] always enjoyed it and wouldn't [would not] stop for anything.

ACTIVITY 28 Use Apostrophes in Contractions

In each of the following sentences, correct any contractions that have missing apostrophes.

EXAMPLE I cant find my way home.

1. Perry doesnt think that its a good idea for his daughter to go swimming while shes getting over a cold.

2. When youre tired of shoveling snow, have some of the hot cocoa I just made.

3. Well arrive at Yellowstone National Park before sunset.

4. The Mitchells arent going to the restaurant tomorrow because they cant get a reservation for that night.

5. Because its breezy today, Ive decided to show you how to fly your new kite.

6. Dont even get me started on where theyre going.

7. Were never going to make it to the top of the hill.

8. Weve always wanted to try our hand at doubles racquetball, but we couldnt find anyone who wanted to play.

9. She isnt my favorite, but shes my brother's favorite singer.

10. Hell never come around to your way of thinking.

19 E

ACTIVITY 29 Identify Possible Contractions

In each of the following sentences, underline the words that can be made into common contractions. Then write the contractions in the space provided.

EXAMPLE It <u>does not</u> matter if <u>he is</u> ready to take the test. _____*doesn't, he's*_____

1. Although it is against the rules, we are going to allow you to photograph the science exhibit for your school newspaper. _____

2. Greg and Celine are not sure if the bridge is safe, because they cannot see very far ahead through the thick mist. _____

3. The Hendersons hope that they will stay with us. _____

4. After you are finished with the weight bench, please wipe it down with the towel. _____

5. Sidra and Darrell do not realize that it is easier to replace the toner in the copy machine before it warms up. _____

6. There is never enough bread in your house. _____

7. Who is going to the movies with me? _____

8. I would rather not have to take the dog's toy away. _____

9. You should not recommend that restaurant to someone if you would not eat there yourself. _____

10. It is hard to talk with Dylan because he does not seem to listen to what I say.

_____

19 E

ACTIVITY 30 Use Apostrophes Correctly

Each of the following sentences contains apostrophe errors. Add apostrophes where necessary to correct those errors.

EXAMPLE I went with the Joneses to their summer cabin. They̌re really lucky to
have such a place.

1. If I could earn my employers trust, Id be able to do more to improve her business.

2. If Isaac would accept that Jenny isnt interested in him, hed notice the other attractive women in his life.

3. After were finished with the days chores, we can go to the beach.

4. Because Colin still had Raquels car, she wasnt able to join us at the club.

5. Misty couldnt admit to the professor that she hadnt written the research paper herself.

> ### ACTIVITY 31 Use Apostrophes Correctly in a Paragraph

The following paragraph contains several apostrophe errors. Add apostrophes where necessary to correct those errors.

EXAMPLE It isn't always pleasant for me and my son, Donnie, to visit my mother on Sundays.

Donnie doesnt like dressing up, and Mom wont let him accompany her to church unless he wears slacks, a long-sleeved shirt, and a tie. Long before the ministers sermon, hes squirming in the pew and pulling at his collar. His grandmothers stern glances certainly dont help the situation. After church, she ignores her grandsons request to go out for hamburgers. My moms idea of a perfect Sunday lunch is a nice plate of liver and onions, which even I cant eat without a lot of ketchup. Mom believes that its childrens duty to obey their elders. As Donnies father, I believe that its an adults responsibility to make obedience fun and easy.

F. Quotation Marks

Quotation marks (" ") are used to enclose the exact words of a speaker or writer and the titles of essays, articles, poems, songs, and other short works.

Rule 1 Use quotation marks to set off a speaker's or writer's exact words.

"I can't believe I said that!" Joshua exclaimed.

"I don't know what you were thinking," I replied, "when you said that."

According to my textbook author, "We often say things we don't mean when we're stressed."

As these examples show, a period or a comma always goes before closing quotation marks. A question mark or an exclamation point, on the other hand, sometimes goes before the quotation marks and sometimes after them. It goes before the quotation marks if the quotation itself is a question or an exclama-

Visit **LaunchPad Solo for Readers and Writers > Grammar: Style and Mechanics > Quotation Marks** for more practice with question marks.

tion, as in the first example. It goes after the quotation marks if your sentence is a question or an exclamation but the quotation itself isn't, as in the following example:

When did people begin to say "Have a nice day"?

Do not use quotation marks around an **indirect quotation**—one that doesn't use the speaker's or writer's exact words. An indirect quotation is usually introduced with *that:*

Henry said that he had always wanted to study medicine.

ACTIVITY 32 Use Quotation Marks to Show Exact Words

In the following sentences, place quotation marks around each occurrence of a speaker's or writer's exact words.

EXAMPLE "That was my favorite dress," she said to her roommate.

1. How was the play? my professor asked the class.

2. You should get more exercise, the doctor said.

3. I'll take popcorn and a soda, I said to the clerk.

4. My aunt always says, A bird in the hand is worth two in the bush.

5. Guess what? she said. I'm pregnant.

6. Kim cried, You should have told me that the dog would bite!

7. Harold shouted, Let's play ball!

8. Even though I didn't want to go, my brother said, Give it a try; you'll have a great time.

9. The officer stated the obvious: Don't drink and drive.

10. How did you respond when he said, Forget about it?

19 F

Rule 2 Use quotation marks to enclose the titles of articles, essays, book chapters, speeches, poems, short stories, and songs.

I especially enjoy the newspaper column "Our Views."

My last essay was titled "Día de los Muertos."

Emily Dickinson wrote the poem "I Dwell in Possibility."

Sandra Cisneros wrote my favorite short story: "Woman Hollering Creek."

When we go caroling, we always sing "Deck the Halls."

Use italics or underlining, not quotation marks, for the titles of longer works, such as books, newspapers, and magazines.

ACTIVITY 33 Use Quotation Marks to Enclose Titles

In the following sentences, place quotation marks around the title of each short work. Some sentences do not require any quotation marks.

EXAMPLE Martin Luther King's "I Have a Dream" speech is often read aloud in history

classes.

1. Her essay, Women in the Military, was a hit with the ROTC cadets.

2. Vivek's favorite column on the website is Latest in Health News.

3. I'm currently reading the novel *The Goldfinch* by Donna Tartt.

4. I bought the *Wall Street Journal* to read the article Stocks You Can Bet On.

5. Edgar Allan Poe's poem The Raven is usually assigned in American literature

   courses.

6. Bruce read the chapter in his textbook titled Marketing Genius.

7. Shailendra never left home without reading her daily horoscope in *USA Today*.

8. Hugo wrote an essay titled Get the Most out of College While Jogging.

9. Adele's Someone Like You was an extremely popular song.

10. The short story Hills Like White Elephants is written almost entirely in dialogue.

ACTIVITY 34 Use Quotation Marks Correctly

In each of the following sentences, insert quotation marks as necessary.

EXAMPLE My favorite essay this term was "Giving It My All."

1. Dencil said, Ms. Levin will be sorry that she missed you.

2. Yes, Aunt Lydia agreed, the autumn leaves were prettier last year.

3. Why do you always wear purple clothing? asked Josh.

4. Angela recited Walt Whitman's poem A Noiseless Patient Spider at her eighth-

   grade graduation ceremony.

5. After we read the essay I Just Wanna Be Average by Mike Rose, our class had

   an interesting discussion.

19 F

ACTIVITY 35 Revise for Quotation Marks

In the following paragraph, insert quotation marks as necessary.

EXAMPLE I recited John Gould Fletcher's poem "The Groundswell" for the challenge of mastering the difficult pronunciation.

In my speech class last fall, we began the semester by reciting short creative works to practice using our voices well. Choose anything you like, Professor Keroes told us, but make it sound like natural speech. I enjoyed the variety presented by my classmates. Two students performed the husband and wife in the poem The Death of the Hired Man by Robert Frost. Three classmates took turns telling Shirley Jackson's short story The Lottery. Many students chose songs. Alan did a great job reciting One of the Boys by Katy Perry. Professor Keroes seemed pleased. I wish I had a copy of everything to read for fun, he said.

19 F

Improving Mechanics

20

Just as with punctuation, the correct use of the **mechanics** of writing—elements like capital letters, italics, abbreviations, and numbers—helps your readers understand your meaning. This chapter focuses on the correct use of these elements.

A. Capital Letters

In this chapter, you will review and practice using
A. Capital Letters
B. Italics
C. Abbreviations
D. Numbers

Rule 1 Capitalize **proper nouns**: nouns that refer to a specific person, place, event, or thing. Do not capitalize **common nouns**: nouns that refer to a general category of persons, places, events, or things.

Visit **LaunchPad Solo for Readers and Writers > Grammar: Style and Mechanics > Capitalization** for more practice using capital letters.

Proper Noun	Common Noun
Ball State University	a university
Costa Rica	a country
Thursday	a day
Dad (used as a name)	my dad
President Obama	a president
Professor Lee	a professor
God	a god
the North	north of the city
Bill of Rights	amendments
Political Science 102	a political science class

Rule 2 Capitalize names of organizations, institutions, and trademarks.

My father belongs to the Order of the Elks.

I always vote for the Independent Party candidate.

My next computer will be a MacBook Pro.

ACTIVITY 1 Correct Errors in Capitalization

Correct the errors in capitalization in each of the following sentences.

                  The Four Agreements
EXAMPLE Have you read the book ~~the four agreements~~?

1. Gabriel has wanted to be a green beret since he was a little boy.

2. Pearl dreams of owning a lexus.

3. Rita's family goes to extremes when they decorate their house for halloween.

4. Among the police officers who helped me after my backpack was stolen, officer franklin was the most sympathetic.

5. Michael's Uncle is a transit worker in new york city.

6. At one time, presidents' day was two separate holidays, lincoln's birthday and washington's birthday.

7. There are better things for you to do than sit around watching soap operas and eating doritos.

8. Alfredo's Mother wants us to join her at the opera.

9. I rode the elevator to the top of the empire state building, but I took the stairs back down.

10. Is Deanna from kansas city, kansas, or kansas city, missouri?

ACTIVITY 2 Use Correct Capitalization in a Paragraph

Correct the errors in capitalization in the following paragraph.

              Thursday   Thanksgiving
EXAMPLE On ~~thursday~~ night after our ~~thanksgiving~~ dinner, the family was sitting around.

20 A

    aunt edna, who teaches geography at middlefield junior high school, proposed a contest. The losers would have to clean up. We divided into teams to see who could name the most states of the united states. My team included my youngest cousins and uncle raymond, who always falls asleep after a meal, so we only had thirty-two states. The best team, which had both grandpa and aunt edna, named only forty-five, and all the teams together couldn't name every one. While little tracy insisted that mexico was a state, everyone forgot delaware. aunt edna said that we were all losers and distributed reese's pieces as a consolation prize. Then we all did the dishes together.

Rule 3 Capitalize all words in titles except articles (*a*, *an*, and *the*), coordinating conjunctions (such as *for, and, nor, but, or, yet,* and *so*), and prepositions (such as *of, on, in, at, with, for*) unless they are the first or last word in the title. Do not capitalize *the* before the names of newspapers.

For Whom the Bell Tolls

Law and Order

The Art of Possibility

the *Washington Post*

ACTIVITY 3 Capitalize Titles

Correct the errors in capitalization in each of the following sentences.

EXAMPLE Students from ~~westwood community college~~ *Westwood Community College* sold ~~Cookies~~ *cookies*, ~~Brownies~~ *brownies*, and ~~Cupcakes~~ *cupcakes* for a fundraiser.

1. Because we have pets, my children enjoyed the movie *Cats And Dogs*.
2. Henry was surprised to learn that *fight club* was a book before it was a film.
3. Because of the clever robotic toys she invented, Meredith was interviewed by a reporter from the *Christian science monitor*.
4. At my high school, a history teacher and an English teacher both discussed *a tale of two cities* during the same two weeks.
5. When I was a child, my favorite album was *Peter And The Wolf*.
6. My favorite teacher recommended that I read the *House of the seven Gables* by Nathaniel Hawthorne.
7. Naturally, the only holiday song that my grumpy sister likes is Elvis's "blue Christmas."
8. Harlan dreams of winning money and a record deal by appearing on the voice.
9. Chrissie always has the latest issue of *reader's digest* on her coffee table.
10. I had to reserve my niece's copy of *Harry Potter and the deathly hallows* before it arrived at the bookstore.

20 A

ACTIVITY 4 Capitalize Titles in a Paragraph

Correct the errors in capitalization in the following paragraph.

EXAMPLE During ~~study skills~~ 101, ~~professor~~ Weston used the materials we had
with us to demonstrate how readers use different techniques.

(Study Skills) *(Professor)*

He compared the *Campus sun* and the *New York times* to show that not even two newspapers should be read the same way. *Portrait Of The Artist As A Young Man* is a difficult book that should be read slowly because the sounds of the words help the meaning. The textbook *physics* also should be read slowly; its vocabulary is difficult, but the sounds of these words add little to their meaning. Both *Applications in electrical engineering* and *Western Architecture* have diagrams, but for different reasons. A student is not expected to construct a church from the floor plan in a textbook!

B. Italics

Visit **LaunchPad Solo for Readers and Writers** > **Grammar: Style and Mechanics** > **Italics and Hyphens** for more practice using italics.

Italicize (or underline in handwritten copy) the titles of books, magazines, movies, television shows, newspapers, journals, computer software, and longer musical works, such as CDs. Do not italicize (or capitalize) *the* before the title of a newspaper.

I read *The Scarlet Letter* in my American literature class.

People magazine is always interesting to read while you're waiting for the doctor.

Captain America: The First Avenger is exciting to watch.

My sister and I love to watch *The Big Bang Theory*.

A copy of the *New York Times* is delivered to my door daily.

I have seen copies of the journal *College English* in my instructor's office.

The latest version of *Windows* works well on Jerry's computer.

Acapulco Sunrise by Santana is a departure from his past music.

20 B

ACTIVITY 5 Use Italics Correctly

Use underlining to indicate where italics are needed in each of the following sentences.

EXAMPLE The Grand Budapest Hotel was a funny and visually engaging movie.

1. The first novel that I ever read was Treasure Island by Robert Louis Stevenson.

2. When Uriel and Shayna got married, they received a subscription to National Geographic magazine.

3. Every spring, the family gathers around the television to watch our favorite movie, The Wizard of Oz.

4. Brendan has every episode of the original Star Trek series.

5. Sarah reads the Wall Street Journal and the New York Times every day.

ACTIVITY 6 Use Italics Correctly in a Paragraph

In the following paragraph, underline to indicate where italics should be used.

EXAMPLE The reference librarians were happy to receive Professor David's complete Oxford English Dictionary.

When Professor David retired, he donated much of his large personal library to the university. For thirty years, he had subscribed to the Classical Journal. His copies filled a gap in the library's collection. He also donated extra copies of books that were important to his career, including the Iliad and the Odyssey, both translated by Richmond Lattimore. Friends of the professor say that his collection of vinyl jazz records is equally impressive. His copy of the album Kind of Blue, autographed by Miles Davis, is very valuable.

C. Abbreviations

An **abbreviation** is a shortened version of a word or phrase.

Rule 1 Use standard abbreviations for titles before or after proper names.

Dr. Charles Elerick
Ms. Nancy Chin
Peggy Sullivan, DDS
Josiah Washington Jr.

Rule 2 Use abbreviations for the names of organizations, corporations, and societies. The first time you use the name in a piece of writing, spell out the name and give the abbreviation in parentheses after it. If you mention the name again, you may use just the abbreviation.

20 C

National Broadcasting Company (NBC)

International Business Machines (IBM)

People for the Ethical Treatment of Animals (PETA)

Rule 3 Use abbreviations for specialized terms. If the term is unfamiliar to your readers, spell it out the first time you use it.

digital versatile disc (DVD)

random-access memory (RAM)

extrasensory perception (ESP)

ACTIVITY 7 Use Common Abbreviations

In each of the following sentences, underline the words that could be written as abbreviations. Write the abbreviation in the space provided.

EXAMPLE My favorite news station is <u>Cable News Network</u>. __CNN__

1. Doctor Koster is always very busy late in the afternoon. _____

2. The headquarters of the United Nations is in New York City. _____

3. The most common degree is a bachelor of arts degree in business. _____

4. Many people observe the birthday of Martin Luther King Junior by going to church. _____

5. Don't forget to set the digital video recorder before we leave for the game. _____

D. Numbers

When to spell out numbers and when to use numerals can be confusing. In general, spell out numbers from one through ninety-nine, numbers expressed in two words (two hundred, three thousand), or numbers that begin a sentence. Use numerals for all other numbers, including decimals, percentages, page numbers, years, and time of day.

20 D

Justin counted twenty-six people in his marketing class.

The football player weighed 280 pounds.

Three hundred people is a lot to invite to your wedding.

My GPA is now 3.25, but I hope to graduate with at least a 3.50.

Maya got 85 percent of the questions right on her psychology midterm.

His computer science professor asked the students to turn to page 48 in the text.

The yoga class was at 7:00 p.m.

▌ **ACTIVITY 8 Use Numbers Correctly**

Using the preceding guidelines, underline the correct form in each of the following sentences.

EXAMPLE Page (thirteen/13) contains all of the information you need.

1. (One hundred/100) winners were selected at random.

2. Students who are in the top (10 percent/ten percent) of their graduating class in high school are guaranteed a place at state universities.

3. (3 out of 4/Three out of four) people who take the motivational training say that they notice significant benefits.

4. Becky intends to have (6/six) children.

5. Coatl bought a bottle of (50/fifty) aspirin for his desk drawer at work.

▌ **ACTIVITY 9 Write Numbers Correctly**

Complete each of the following sentences, inserting a spelled-out number or a numeral as necessary.

EXAMPLE Bookings of international flights are down _____40_____ percent.

1. There are approximately _____ people in my smallest class.

2. When I was a child, _____ people lived with me.

3. I own _____ pairs of shoes.

4. Where I live, the sales tax is _____ percent.

5. I plan to graduate in _____ semesters.

20 D

21

Guide for Multilingual Writers

If you are multilingual—in other words, if you speak more than one language—you have several advantages over people who can speak only one language. Because of the global marketplace, you are better prepared to work with people who come from different parts of the world. You also have a better understanding of other people's cultures and values. According to linguist David Crystal in his book *How Language Works*, most people worldwide are multilingual, and most people who speak English learned it as a second or foreign language. If English is not your first language, you are far from alone.

The English language developed from a mixture of languages spoken centuries ago by people who lived in Great Britain, Scandinavia, Germany, France, and Italy. As a result, some aspects of the English language, such as spelling, can be difficult for native speakers and nonnative speakers alike. Other aspects of English might be particularly challenging for nonnative English speakers. This chapter will provide you with step-by-step guidelines to help both native speakers and multilingual writers with the unique challenges of the English language. After each section, activities will allow you to practice what you have learned. By focusing on these topics, you will be able to express yourself more clearly and confidently in English.

A. Omitted or Repeated Subjects

For more help with subjects, turn to pp. 403–408.

In English, every sentence has a subject and a verb. The **subject** tells who or what is doing the action; the **verb** expresses an action or a state of being.

Omitted Subjects

Visit **LaunchPad Solo for Readers and Writers** > **Grammar: Resources for Multilingual Writers** > **Sentence Structure** for more practice with subjects.

The subject of a sentence must be stated, even when the meaning of the sentence is clear without its being stated.

> **INCORRECT** Want to get my degree in mechanical engineering.
> **CORRECT** *I* want to get my degree in mechanical engineering.

514

INCORRECT	My sister loves to read. Goes to the library twice a week.
CORRECT	My sister loves to read. *She* goes to the library twice a week.

The subject of a subordinate clause must also be stated. A **subordinate clause**, or **dependent clause**, contains a subject and a verb but can't stand alone as a sentence because it begins with a subordinating conjunction (such as *because* or *although*) or a relative pronoun (such as *who, that,* or *which*).

To learn more about subordinate, or dependent, clauses, turn to pp. 427–29.

INCORRECT	I already knew that wanted to major in math.
CORRECT	I already knew that *I* wanted to major in math.

INCORRECT	I threw the package away because was empty.
CORRECT	I threw the package away because *it* was empty.

English sentences and dependent clauses often begin with the word *it* or *there* followed by a form of *be,* as in *it is, there is,* and *there were.* In such a sentence or clause, the *it* or *there* acts as a kind of subject and can't be omitted.

INCORRECT	Is too late to hand in the paper.
CORRECT	*It is* too late to hand in the paper.

INCORRECT	Are three bottles on the shelf.
CORRECT	*There are* three bottles on the shelf.

ACTIVITY 1 Add Missing Subjects to a Paragraph

Using the preceding guidelines, add a subject in each place where one is missing in the following paragraph.

EXAMPLE *There are* ~~Are~~ several different kinds of friends.

Every Friday evening, a group of us meet at a café. Enjoy the time we spend together. Formerly, we went to bars. Then my friend Cassie developed a problem with alcohol because was going to bars too often. We decided to stop drinking as a group. Is still fun sometimes to go to meet new people at the café, where many people gather for conversation and studying. Is an extensive menu of coffee drinks and delicious sandwiches that we enjoy trying.

Repeated Subjects

Be careful not to repeat a subject that has been stated earlier in the sentence.

INCORRECT	The lady in the store *she* was rude.
CORRECT	The lady in the store was rude. [The pronoun *she* repeats the subject *lady*.]

INCORRECT	Some people *they* like to go to parties.
CORRECT	Some people like to go to parties. [The pronoun *they* repeats the subject *people*.]

21 A

> **ACTIVITY 2 Identify Repeated Subjects**

Draw a line through the repeated subjects in the following paragraph.

EXAMPLE The people in the class ~~they~~ decided to postpone the test.

    The members of my fraternity we decided to give holiday presents to children in local hospitals. Cliff and Rodney, who suggested the project in the first place, they contacted businesses for contributions. Andre, whose family owns a discount store, he was able to purchase toys at wholesale prices. Several members with trucks and vans they delivered the gifts to hospitals. All of us who worked on this charitable project we enjoyed watching the children open their presents.

B. Word Order

In English, the basic word order of a sentence is *subject, verb, object*.

$$\overset{s}{\text{Jordan}} \overset{v}{\text{ironed}} \text{ the } \overset{o}{\text{dress}}.$$

Adjectives and adverbs are placed close to the words they modify.

$$\overset{s}{\text{Jordan}} \text{ quickly } \overset{v}{\text{ironed}} \text{ the blue } \overset{o}{\text{dress}}.$$

Adjective Placement

In English, adjectives almost always come before the noun they modify.

See pp. 435–36 for more information about adjectives.

An *important* thing to remember is to stop at stop signs.

George prepared to take the *difficult* test.

Ulie bought the *red* motorcycle.

In addition, different kinds of adjectives appear in a particular order. Though exceptions exist, this order is usually followed:

1. Articles and pronouns: *a, an, the, my, your*
2. Words that evaluate: *ugly, handsome, honest, appealing, flavorful*
3. Words about size: *big, small, large*
4. Words about length or shape: *round, square, wide, narrow*
5. Words about age: *old, young, new*
6. Words about color: *red, blue, yellow*
7. Words about nationality: *Irish, Mexican, Canadian, Chinese*
8. Words about religion: *Muslim, Buddhist, Protestant, Jewish*

21 B

9. Words about the material of the noun: *wooden, glass, brick, adobe, stucco*

10. Nouns used as adjectives: *bathroom* floor, *track* team

Finally, the noun goes last: *book, car, movie, church, bench, computer.*

The handsome old house sat at the top of the hill.

My German Catholic grandmother died last year.

The square wooden jewelry box sat on the table.

HOW TO Use Commas between Adjectives

To decide whether you need a comma between two or more adjectives, use this tip: If you can place *and* between the adjectives and the sentence still makes sense, then you need the comma.

Suppose you want to write this:

The tall fragile rosebush was blooming.

A comma is needed between *tall* and *fragile* because "the tall *and* fragile rosebush" makes sense.

The tall, fragile rosebush was blooming.

ACTIVITY 3 Revise Sentences to Use Adjectives Correctly

Revise each of the following sentences so that the adjectives are placed correctly and commas are used between them where necessary.

EXAMPLE Please hand me the brown ~~big~~ box.
                                       big ^

1. We bought the leather sofa most comfortable.

2. Curtis promised to throw out his plaid old pajamas.

3. The dark Belgian delicious chocolates were a gift.

4. A spotted big snake crawled under the house.

5. The car little red fit in the parking space.

6. After the movie, Marisol remembered her assignment boring and difficult.

7. I gave the cheerful friendly child a cookie.

8. His leather black beautiful jacket was ruined.

9. We admired the aluminum elegant animal sculptures.

10. My grandmother recited a Jewish short prayer over the candles.

21 B

ACTIVITY 4 Add Adjectives Correctly

In each of the following sentences, add the number of adjectives indicated in parentheses in the space provided. Use commas as necessary.

EXAMPLE A _____*curved stone*_____ path led to the house. (2)

1. I wanted a _____ car. (2)

2. Smoking is a _____ habit. (2)

3. The sight of the _____ tacos made my mouth water. (3)

4. Linda wanted to take one of the _____ puppies home. (2)

5. The _____ sweater fit Ivan perfectly. (2)

6. Whenever Kevin wanted to quit school, he remembered his _____ _____ parents back home. (2)

7. To be accepted into the program, I had to pass a _____ exam. (2)

8. Eunice refused to climb the _____ steps. (3)

9. Last year, I dated a _____ student. (2)

10. Our assignment was to read a chapter in our _____ textbook. (3)

Adverb Placement

For more information about adverbs, turn to pp. 436–37.

Adverbs that modify verbs can appear at the beginning or end of a sentence, before or after the verb, or between a helping verb and the main verb. Most often, the adverb appears as close as possible to the verb.

Hurriedly, we escaped out the back door.

The dog scratched *frantically* against the window.

Abner *eagerly* wrote the letter.

My brother has *often* stayed out after midnight.

Sarah has *never* been on an airplane.

Do not put an adverb between a verb and its direct object. A direct object receives the action of the verb.

INCORRECT   Li put *quickly* the package on the table.
CORRECT   Li *quickly* put the package on the table.

INCORRECT   The hairdresser cut *carefully* my hair.
CORRECT   The hairdresser *carefully* cut my hair.

21 B

ACTIVITY 5 Place Adverbs Correctly

Revise the following paragraph, adding at least one adverb to each sentence.

impatiently
EXAMPLE Many students wait in line to be advised during late registration.

Some students complain to the people around them about the lack of advisors. Other students, who had to bring their children, make sure the kids don't run around the building screaming. A few students laugh with their friends. Many students check their smartphones and wonder how long they can wait. Everyone wishes the lines were shorter. One student realizes she has an appointment and rushes out of the building.

C. Verbs

A **verb** expresses an action (*smile, work, hit*) or a state of being (*be, seem, become*). This section will help you correctly use verb tenses, helping verbs, and verbs followed by gerunds or infinitives.

To learn more about verbs, turn to pp. 408–16.

Visit **LaunchPad Solo for Readers and Writers > Grammar: Resources for Multilingual Writers > Verbs** for more practice with verbs.

Verb Tense

The **tense** of a verb indicates the time in which the action or condition that the verb expresses takes place or exists. All such actions or conditions are expressed as happening now, or in the **present**; at some point before the current time, or in the **past**; or at some point in time still to happen, or in the **future**.

Basic Tenses

The three basic tenses in English are *simple present*, *simple past*, and *simple future*. These tenses are often referred to as simply *present*, *past*, and *future*.

Present Tense   The **present tense** shows an action or a condition that is taking place at the time it is mentioned. The present tense can also show an action or a condition that occurs repeatedly or one that is scheduled to occur in the future. Except for *be* and *have*, the present tense uses the base form of the verb (*swim, work*), with an *-s* or *-es* added if the subject is a singular noun or *he, she*, or *it*.

Jamilla *seems* depressed recently.

Pierre *studies* at least five hours a day.

I *drive* my daughter to school every weekday morning.

The new store *opens* next week.

21 C

Past Tense   The **past tense** indicates an action or a condition that began and ended in the past. Except for irregular verbs like *go* or *teach*, the past tense consists of the base form of the verb with *-ed* added to the end.

Yesterday I *passed* my driver's test.

For a list of common irregular verbs and their past-tense forms, see p. 415.

When he *was* a student, he *walked* wherever he *had* to go. [The action of walking happened more than once in the past, but it's not happening now.]

Future Tense   The **future tense** shows an action or a condition that will take place or will probably take place. The future tense requires the use of *will* or *be going to* followed by the base form of the verb.

I *will spend* next summer in Kansas City.

These economic conditions *are going to continue* indefinitely.

Perfect Tenses

The perfect tenses show a completed action or condition. They are formed using the past participle of the verb and the appropriate form of *have*.

Present Perfect Tense   The **present perfect tense** shows an action or a condition that began in the past and that either is now finished or continues into the present. Unlike with the past tense, the specific time of the action or condition is not given. To form this tense, use *has* or *have*, followed by the past participle. Except for irregular verbs, the past participle consists of the base form of the verb with *-ed* added to the end.

For a list of common irregular verbs and their past participles, see p. 415.

Alex *has cooked* the dinner.

The lawyers *have argued* their case.

When the present perfect expresses an action or condition that began in the past and continues into the present, it is usually used with an expression of time beginning with *since* or *for*.

Susan *has played* the trumpet since she was a child.

(Susan has played in the past and continues to play in the present.)

They *have been* in Seattle for three years.

(They went to Seattle in the past, and they are still there.)

Past Perfect Tense   The **past perfect tense** indicates an action or a condition occurring in the past before another time in the past. To form this tense, use *had* and the past participle of the verb.

I *had learned* the formulas by the day of the test.

They *had smelled* smoke before they saw the fire.

21 C

Future Perfect Tense   The **future perfect tense** indicates a future action or condition that will end by or before a specific future time. To form this tense, use *will have* and the past participle of the verb.

By next Tuesday, I *will have finished* all my classes for the semester.

Heather *will have left* the office before you get there.

Progressive Tenses

The progressive tenses show a continuing action or condition. They are formed using the present participle (the *-ing* form of the verb) and the appropriate form of *be*.

Present Progressive Tense   The **present progressive tense** indicates an action that is happening at the time it is mentioned or an action that is scheduled to happen in the future. To form this tense, use *am*, *is*, or *are* and the *-ing* form of the verb.

Eduardo *is helping* us move the furniture.

We *are leaving* for the beach tomorrow.

Past Progressive Tense   The **past progressive tense** shows an action or a condition that continued for some time in the past and is now over. To form this tense, use *was* or *were* and the *-ing* form of the verb.

Over the summer, I *was spending* my money mostly on food.

Last night, the sick man's words *were becoming* very faint.

Future Progressive Tense   The **future progressive tense** indicates a continuing action or condition in the future. To form this tense, use *will be* and the *-ing* form of the verb.

The judge *will be hearing* your case soon.

By next week, you *will be feeling* better.

Perfect Progressive Tenses

The perfect progressive tenses show an action in the process of occurring before a specific event or time.

Present Perfect Progressive Tense   In the **present perfect progressive tense**, the action continues from the past until the present. Usually the length of time from the past to the present is included. To form this tense, use *has been* or *have been*, followed by the *-ing* form of the verb.

He *has been shopping* for three hours.

The students *have been studying* since midnight.

21 C

Past Perfect Progressive Tense In the **past perfect progressive tense**, the action takes place during a specified length of time and ends at a specific time in the past. This tense is formed with *had been* and the *-ing* form of the verb.

> My children *had been driving* for an hour when the bad weather started.

> Rajendra *had been cooking* all afternoon when his wife called to say she would not be home until after dinner.

Future Perfect Progressive Tense When the **future perfect progressive tense** is used, the length of the action already begun and the time in the future when the action will be completed are both indicated. To form this tense, use *will have been* and the *-ing* form of the verb.

> By the end of the semester, they *will have been preparing* the report for three months.

> By the time my children graduate high school, I *will have been serving* as a scout leader for ten years.

ACTIVITY 6 Identify Verb Tenses

Identify the verb tense in each of the following sentences.

EXAMPLE The cake *will be* ready tonight. _____*future*_____

1. Julian *has completed* all the prerequisites. _____

2. You *have wasted* the whole semester. _____

3. Before getting married, Bill and Jenny *had decided* to move to Colorado.

   _____

4. Last week, I *was recovering* from surgery. _____

5. The tomatoes *will be ripening* next week. _____

6. They *work* at City Hall. _____

7. *Will* Marcie *compete* in the next essay contest? _____

8. They *have taken* all morning to buy groceries. _____

9. Wayne *had been eating* for ten minutes before he noticed the bug in his salad. _____

10. Dolores *is talking* to her doctor. _____

21 C

> **ACTIVITY 7** Use Verb Tenses Correctly

For each of the following sentences, write the required verb tense of the verb in parentheses.

EXAMPLE You _____ *had been* _____ (be) doing very well in that class until now.

(*past perfect*)

1. I _____ (do) my best to make you happy. (*present progressive*)

2. Lillian _____ (whisper) her secret to Josie. (*past*)

3. The children _____ (play) for an hour. (*present perfect*)

4. Hans _____ (be) here tomorrow. (*future*)

5. We _____ (hire) a band for the party. (*future*)

6. Jonathan _____ (walk) for a half hour when it began to rain.

(*past perfect progressive*)

7. I _____ (work) at the ski resort over the winter. (*past progressive*)

8. Before the day of the show, the advertisements _____ (say) the

tickets would be thirty-five dollars apiece. (*past perfect*)

9. The politician _____ (decide) to run for reelection. (*present perfect*)

10. Fred _____ (take) the children to the circus. (*present pefect*)

Helping Verbs

A **helping verb** is a verb that is used with another verb, called the **main verb**, to create a phrase that acts as a verb in a sentence. Sometimes, such a phrase includes two or even three helping verbs in addition to the main verb. Helping verbs are used for a number of different purposes, including to form the future, the perfect, and the progressive tenses and the passive voice; to ask questions and make negative statements; and to show that something is possible or required.

See p. 408 for more information about helping verbs.

Micah has left the room. [*Has* is the helping verb; *left* is the main verb.]

You must wait for the train to leave the station. [*Must* is the helping verb; *wait* is the main verb.]

I have been sitting here for two hours. [*Have* and *been* are the helping verbs; *sitting* is the main verb.]

Modals

Some helping verbs, known as **modals**, are used only as helping verbs:

can	may	must	should	would
could	might	shall	will	

21 C

When using a modal in a sentence, use the base form of the main verb after it unless the modal is followed by another helping verb.

Luisa *might travel* to Cambodia.

My sister *would sing* if she *could read* music.

Rupert *can carry* the suitcase.

Carlos *could have been* a better candidate.

Our chorus *may be performing* in New York next year.

Unlike other helping verbs, a modal does not change form to agree in number with the subject, and neither does the main verb that follows it.

INCORRECT	He wills leave.
INCORRECT	He will leaves.
CORRECT	He will leave.

ACTIVITY 8 Identify Modals

Circle the modals in the following paragraph.

EXAMPLE Friends (should) help each other out.

Three of my best friends are leaving town next week. Frank is going to Los Angeles, where he will begin his career as a movie editor. He should be able to find a job quickly. Janice is moving to Chicago to attend medical school. She might be able to afford her own apartment, should she be able to find one. Finally, Leroy is going to New York. Because he has very little money saved up, he must find a job right away.

Do, Does, Did

Like modals, the helping verbs *do, does,* and *did* are followed by the base form of the verb. These verbs are used

- To ask a question:

  Do you want to dance?

  Did my brother pick up his suit?

- To make a negative statement (when used with *not*):

  I did not request this car.

  Sammy does not eat broccoli.

- To emphasize a main verb:

  Once again, I do appreciate the gift.

  She does look beautiful.

Unlike modals, the helping verbs *do* and *does* change in number to agree with the subject of the sentence.

> **INCORRECT** He do not enjoy watching football.
>
> **CORRECT**   He does not enjoy watching football.

Have, Has, Had

The helping verbs *have*, *has*, and *had* are used to indicate the perfect tenses. *Have* and *has* change form to agree in number with the subject.

> **INCORRECT** They has broken all the good plates.
>
> **CORRECT**   They have broken all the good plates.

Forms of *Be*

Forms of the verb *be*—*be, am, is, are, was, were, been*—are used as helping verbs for two purposes. Together with the present participle of the main verb, they are used to indicate the progressive tenses.

> I am taking calculus this year.
>
> The birds were singing in the tree near my window.

Together with the past participle of the main verb, forms of *be* are used to indicate the passive voice, in which the subject doesn't perform the action of the verb but receives the action. Here are some examples:

For more information about the passive voice, turn to pp. 465–66.

> Jonathan was hit by the flying glass.
>
> The book was written by Thomas Wolfe.
>
> Parts of the city have been closed by the chief of police.

ACTIVITY 9 Use Helping Verbs

In each of the following sentences, fill in the blank with an appropriate helping verb, followed by the correct form of the verb in parentheses.

EXAMPLE After our argument, my brother _____*did not speak*_____ (speak) to me for

two years.

1. Nobody _____ (see) Caroline for the past few weeks.

2. Barney _____ (paint) the kitchen before his in-laws arrived.

3. Until November, the weather _____ (be) pleasant.

4. With this excellent progress, you _____ (convince) me that

   you are motivated.

5. For three years, I _____ (accept) these strict rules.

6. Until she took organic chemistry, Aunt Lucy _____ (want) to

   be a doctor.

21 C

7. To my surprise, Angel _____ (win) a spelling contest when he was in the fifth grade.

8. Johnny Depp _____ (act) in many unusual roles.

9. To be independent in many rural areas, you _____ (own) a car.

10. Shawna _____ (work) at McDonald's while she takes college classes.

ACTIVITY 10 Use Helping Verbs in a Paragraph

In the following paragraph, fill in each of the blanks with an appropriate helping verb, followed by the correct form of the verb in parentheses.

EXAMPLE Elyse _____*should thank*_____ (thank) her family for their support.

Later today, at the graduation ceremony, Elyse _____ (receive) her diploma from the university. She began her studies at the age of forty, after she _____ (work) for many years. Since then, she _____ (struggle) to earn her degree. Many obstacles _____ (interrupt) her education, mostly health and financial difficulties. However, nothing _____ (stop) her from reaching her goal. Indeed, she _____ (graduate) with honors. Throughout these difficult and rewarding years, her family _____ (remain) her first priority. She _____ (celebrate) tonight among her loved ones.

Verbs Followed by Gerunds or Infinitives

A **gerund** is a form of a verb that ends in -*ing* and is used as a noun.

I enjoy *walking*.

Cooking is his favorite hobby.

In contrast, an *infinitive* is the base form of a verb with the word *to* in front of it.

I decided *to stop* my car.

I went home *to wash* my clothes.

The following verbs can be followed by either a gerund or an infinitive without changing the meaning of the sentence:

21 C

begin	love
continue	stand
hate	start
like	try

I started *to like* him right away.

I started *liking* him right away.

With other verbs, the meaning changes depending on whether they're followed by a gerund or an infinitive.

She stopped *smoking* cigarettes. [She gave up the habit of smoking.]

She stopped *to smoke* a cigarette. [She paused so she could light up a cigarette.]

George remembered *to buy* the gift. [George had planned to buy the gift and did so.]

George remembered *buying* the gift. [George recalled the act of purchasing the gift.]

The following verbs may be followed by a gerund but not by an infinitive:

admit	discuss	imagine	quit	suggest
appreciate	enjoy	miss	recall	tolerate
avoid	escape	practice	resist	
deny	finish	put off	risk	

Jonah denied *witnessing* the car accident.

My father missed *opening* the presents.

The following verbs may be followed by an infinitive but not by a gerund:

agree	expect	mean	pretend	want
ask	have	need	promise	wish
beg	hope	offer	wait	
decide	manage	plan		

She planned *to take* the 7 a.m. flight.

Fred asked *to leave* the room.

ACTIVITY 11 Use Verbs Plus Gerunds or Infinitives Correctly

Complete each of the following sentences with the gerund or infinitive form of the verb in parentheses, whichever is correct.

EXAMPLE Lucy enjoyed _____*seeing*_____ (see) her parents.

21 C

1. We decided _____ (take) the scenic road to the lake

   rather than the freeway.

2. Theodore can't stand _____ (wait) for an elevator, so he always takes the stairs.

3. April planned _____ (attend) the community college before transferring to a university.

4. Ward denied _____ (be) my secret admirer.

5. Nora practiced _____ (drive) in a parking lot before she went on the road.

6. Chester started _____ (collect) fossils when he was in high school.

7. The teens expected _____ (receive) a reward for returning the lost wallet.

8. Dorcas imagined _____ (win) the lottery.

9. Students resist _____ (use) the university library.

10. My little sister continues _____ (bother) me when my friends visit.

ACTIVITY 12 Use Verbs Plus Gerunds or Infinitives Correctly

Complete each of the following sentences with a gerund or an infinitive, as well as other words if necessary.

EXAMPLE Because of her age, my daughter avoided *taking the test* _____.

1. Tomorrow, Richie will finish _____.

2. Whenever possible, I avoid _____.

3. My children love _____.

4. You do not need to beg _____.

5. Sheila only pretended _____.

6. A busy student certainly appreciates _____.

7. I made a New Year's resolution to quit _____.

8. I never succeed when I try _____.

9. In one hour, Maurice will start _____.

10. My parents hope _____.

Two-Part Verbs

Many verbs in English consist of two words. Here are some of the most common ones:

ask out	get along	leave out	put together	For more on two-part verbs, see p. 540.
break down	give up	make up	shut up	
clean up	help out	pick up	wake up	
drop in	keep up	play around		

Be careful not to leave out the second word of such verbs.

> **INCORRECT** Susan picked aspirin at the drugstore.
> **CORRECT** Susan picked up aspirin at the drugstore.

> **INCORRECT** When buying gifts, James left his cousin.
> **CORRECT** When buying gifts, James left out his cousin.

ACTIVITY 13 Use Two-Part Verbs Correctly

For each of the following sentences, complete the two-part verb.

EXAMPLE Let me help you clean _____*up*_____ the kitchen.

1. Professor Zindell wants us to drop _____ for a visit whenever we wish.

2. Please pick _____ your dirty clothes before you go to sleep.

3. The cat and dog get _____ very well.

4. Whenever I make that fruit salad, I always leave _____ the bananas.

5. Children always want to help _____ in the kitchen when they are too young to be useful.

ACTIVITY 14 Add Two-Part Verbs

Use a two-part verb to complete each of the following sentences.

EXAMPLE Roland _____*picked up*_____ his girlfriend in his car to take her to dinner on their anniversary.

1. Mary Alice has _____ a professional wardrobe using a few basic garments.

2. I _____ my mess so well that nobody knew I had made one.

3. Yesterday, Jim _____ a story to amuse the neighbor's children.

4. The truck always _____ in hot weather.

5. If you do these assignments, you will be able to _____ your classmates.

21 C

Participles Used as Adjectives

The present and past participles of verbs that refer to feelings or senses are often used as adjectives. Such verbs include the following:

bore	disappoint	encourage	frighten
charm	disturb	excite	interest
confuse	embarrass	fascinate	tire

When the adjective refers to a person or an animal *having* the feeling, use the past participle form, the one that ends in *-ed*.

The *frightened* cat jumped on the shelf.

The student was *bored*.

The *confused* child began to cry.

When the adjective refers to a thing or person *causing* the feeling, use the present participle form, the one that ends in *-ing*.

The *frightening* movie scared the children.

The book was *boring*.

The *confusing* message was not conveyed.

> **INCORRECT** I was *interesting in* the show.
> **CORRECT** I was *interested in* the show.

> **INCORRECT** The story was *excited*.
> **CORRECT** The story was *exciting*.

ACTIVITY 15 Use Participles as Adjectives

Complete each of the following sentences with the correct participle of the verb in parentheses.

EXAMPLE I was ___encouraged___ (encourage) by the positive reviews of my show.

1. I was _____ (fascinate) by the butterfly collection.

2. The butterfly collection was _____ (fascinate).

3. Jane, who was _____ (embarrass) by all the attention, wanted to be left alone.

4. The children's play was _____ (charm).

5. I have never seen such a _____ (disturb) collection of artwork in my life.

6. The spectators enjoyed the _____ (excite) fireworks display.

7. Frankly, I found the speech rather _____ (tire).

8. The _____ (disappoint) viewers turned off the television.

9. I am _____ (charm) to meet you.

10. When will this _____ (embarrass) display of affection end?

◖ D. Active and Passive Voice

In English, **voice** refers to the way that the action in a sentence is expressed. In the **active voice**, the subject of the sentence is the person or thing performing the action, and the object is the person or thing receiving the action.

[subject doing the action] + [action verb] + [object receiving the action]

Joyce   lit   the candles.

[subject doing the action] [action verb] [object receiving the action]

Rajendra   cooked   the meal.

[subject doing the action] [action verb] [object receiving the action]

In the **passive voice**, the subject is the person or thing receiving the action; something is being done to it.

[subject receiving the action] + [be] + [past participle of the verb] + [thing or person doing the action]

The candles   were   lit   by Joyce.

[subject receiving the action] [be] [past participle] [person doing the action]

The meal   was   cooked   by Rajendra.

[subject receiving the action] [be] [past participle] [person doing the action]

Note that when you use the passive voice, you do not always include who or what is performing the action.

The car was driven by Samuel.

The car was driven.

In English, the active voice is more common than the passive voice. Readers normally expect the subject to be performing the action. Also, the active voice is more direct and not as wordy as the passive voice. At times, however, you need to use the passive voice.

Use the passive voice when you don't know who or what is performing the action.

I was shocked to discover that the truck had been stolen. [You don't know who stole the truck.]

All I know is that the floor was mopped. [You don't know who mopped the floor.]

21 D

Use the passive voice when you don't want to say who or what was performing the action.

A mistake was made. [You don't want to say who made the mistake.]

All I know is that the coat was lost. [You don't want to say who lost the coat.]

You can also use the passive voice when it does not matter who or what performed the action.

The candidate was elected. [You do not need to say that voters elected the candidate.]

The exam was taken. [You do not need to say that students took the exam.]

Keep in mind that the passive voice is commonly used in scientific or technical writing.

The calculation was performed.

The experiment was concluded.

> **ACTIVITY 16 Use the Active and Passive Voice**

Each of the following sentences is written in the active or passive voice. If the sentence is in the active voice, change it to the passive voice. If it is in the passive voice, change it to the active voice.

EXAMPLE ~~The health club was~~ visited daily ~~by my sister.~~
My sister ^ *the health club* ^ ^

1. The cat scratched the sofa.

2. The watermelon was eaten by my nephew.

3. Calista played the clarinet at the concert.

4. Facebook was created by Mark Zuckerberg.

5. The police chased the protesters out of the street.

6. The college raised tuition by 3 percent.

7. My grandmother's scrapbook was destroyed in the flood.

8. The apple trees were ruined by the bad weather.

9. The graduation ceremony was attended by over five hundred family members and friends.

10. Almost all politicians use social networking extensively to communicate their messages.

21 D

(E. Articles

English has three articles: *the*, *a*, and *an*. *The* is the definite article; *a* and *an* are indefinite articles. A **definite article** refers to one or more specific things (*the*, *these*, *that*, *those*). An **indefinite article** refers to things not specifically known (*a*, *an*).

Any one of these articles appears before the noun it refers to. If the noun is preceded by one or more adjectives, the article comes before the adjectives.

- *The* is used with nouns that refer to one or more specific things.

  I love *the* beautiful Victorian house. [Here *the* is referring to a specific house.]

  I love beautiful Victorian houses. [No house in particular is being referred to.]

  The roses bloom in May. [Particular roses are indicated.]

  Roses bloom in May. [Roses in general bloom in May.]

- In many cases, *the* refers to a noun that has been mentioned before.

  In buying a *car*, Chon focused mainly on appearance.

  The car he purchased looked sleek and sporty.

- *A* and *an* are used with nouns that refer to things not specifically known to the reader, perhaps because they haven't been mentioned before.

  A bird swooped out of the sky. [The reader has no prior knowledge of the bird.]

  A factory can create both jobs and pollution. [No factory in particular is being mentioned.]

  A day in the sun would do me good. [This article refers to some day in the sun but not to a specific day.]

- *A* and *an* are used only with singular count nouns. Count nouns name things that can be counted, such as *book* or *cat*. They have plural as well as singular forms: *books*, *cats*. *The* is used with both singular and plural count nouns as well as with noncount nouns. Noncount nouns name things that can't be counted, such as *information*, *homework*, or *advice*.

- *A* comes before words that begin with consonant sounds (such as *b*, *c*, *d*, *f*, and *g*). Notice that even though the letter *u* is a vowel, *a* is used before some words beginning with *u*, in which the *u* is pronounced with a *y* sound before it.

  a book   a cat   a movie   a speech   a unicycle

  My husband said he will never wear *a* tie again.

  I plan to buy *a* uniform at the store.

Visit **LaunchPad Solo for Readers and Writers** > **Grammar: Resources for Multilingual Writers** > **Articles and Nouns** for more practice with articles.

For more on count and noncount nouns, see p. 536.

21 E

■ *An* comes before words that begin with vowel sounds (*a, e, i, o,* and *u*) to make them easier to pronounce. Notice that even though the letter *h* is a consonant, *an* is used before some words beginning with *h*, in which the *h* is silent (not pronounced).

an effort   an honor   an illness   an opera   an umbrella

An elephant is *an* interesting animal to watch.

I wanted to give him *an* honest answer.

ACTIVITY 17 Add Missing Articles

In each of the following sentences, add the missing articles.

EXAMPLE ~~First~~ concert of the season is always held first week in September.
         The first   *the*

1. I found wallet and key chain; wallet was leather, and key chain was brass.

2. On plane flight to Bangkok, Petcharat met old friend.

3. Only way to succeed as writer is to write and learn from your mistakes.

4. When she tripped over rock, Penny tore jeans she had bought day before.

5. When you finish with stationary bicycle, please let Howard use it.

6. Please come to our party on first Saturday of April.

7. Spices in bottles on shelf are too old to use.

8. Campground near beach is best place for us to spend night.

9. After hour, Yesenia decided to leave house and go to movie.

10. Sandor bought T-shirt and decal for his car at only bookstore on campus.

ACTIVITY 18 Add Missing Articles in a Paragraph

Revise the following paragraph to include the missing articles.

EXAMPLE Cynthia completed her homework for last day of class.
                                              the

Beryl is specialist in textiles. She can tell difference between handmade and machine-made lace and knows names of different kinds of lace. Mostly she works with antique rugs, because purchase of rug is big investment. When investor wants to buy rug, he or she consults Beryl. Beryl will tell buyer if rug was made from natural or synthetic fibers. She can also tell whether dyes used in rug were natural or synthetic. These factors will determine true value of rug. Beryl has prevented many people from making big mistake.

21 E

- Do *not* use an article before a noun that is used in a general sense to include all examples of that type of person, place, or thing.

> INCORRECT   I'm trying to lose weight, but *the candy* is hard to resist. [No specific kind of candy is being referred to.]
>
> CORRECT   I'm trying to lose weight, but *candy* is hard to resist. [Candy in general is being referred to.]
>
> INCORRECT   *The horses* are my favorite animal. [No specific horses are mentioned.]
>
> CORRECT   *Horses* are my favorite animal. [Horses in general are mentioned.]

- Do *not* use an article before the names of people, towns, streets, cities, states, countries, churches, mountains, parks, or lakes. *Do* use an article before the names of seas, rivers, and oceans.

> INCORRECT   We traveled to *the Lake Erie.*
>
> CORRECT   We traveled to *Lake Erie.*

- Do *not* use an article before the days of the week or the months of the year.

> INCORRECT   My favorite day of the week is *the Saturday.*
>
> CORRECT   My favorite day of the week is *Saturday.*

- Do *not* use an article before the names of sports, languages, or academic subjects.

> INCORRECT   My sister is majoring in *the physics.*
>
> CORRECT   My sister is majoring in *physics.*

ACTIVITY 19 Use Articles Correctly

Correct each of the following sentences by adding missing articles and crossing out incorrectly used articles.

EXAMPLE Our neighbor used to live in ~~the~~ Spain.

1. My classmates and I had picnic at the Reid Park.

2. Eating in an restaurant is not always a pleasant experience.

3. The going through security in airports can take a long time.

4. Everyone needs the water to survive.

5. The driving can be dangerous on slippery streets.

6. Most popular sport in the world is soccer.

7. My goal while in college is to learn the Chinese.

8. The paying attention to the instructions is always important.

21 E

9. Jobless rate is high even though the inflation is low.

10. My daughter had a important meeting earlier today.

F. Count and Noncount Nouns

Visit **LaunchPad Solo for Readers and Writers** > **Grammar: Resources for Multilingual Writers** > **Articles and Nouns** for more practice with nouns.

As mentioned earlier, **count nouns** can be singular or plural: *computer* or *computers*. **Noncount** (or **mass**) **nouns** can usually only be singular, even though their meaning may be plural. Here are some noncount nouns:

advice	employment	homework	justice
anger	equipment	honesty	mail
courage	evidence	information	poverty
education	furniture	knowledge	vocabulary

- Do not use indefinite articles (*a* and *an*) with noncount nouns.

  INCORRECT Molly's mother gave Molly *an advice* about her boyfriend.
  CORRECT Molly's mother gave Molly *advice* about her boyfriend.

- Noncount nouns can't be made plural, so do not add *s* or *es* at the end.

  INCORRECT I need to buy *furnitures* for my apartment.
  CORRECT I need to buy *furniture* for my apartment.

- To express a quantity for a noncount noun, use **quantifiers**, or words that indicate the amount of something. Quantifiers used with non-count nouns include *some, any, more, less, a little, all, a lot of,* and *a great deal of.*

  CORRECT Molly's mother gave Molly *some* advice about her boyfriend.
  CORRECT I need to buy *more* furniture for my apartment.
  CORRECT I need *a great deal of* information to finish my assignment.
  CORRECT I saw *a lot of* poverty when I traveled around the world.

ACTIVITY 20 Use Count and Noncount Nouns Correctly

Revise each of the following sentences in which there is an error in the use of count and noncount nouns. If a sentence is correct, write "correct" in the space provided.

EXAMPLE Cynthia completed her homeworks a few minutes before class started.

_____

1. All four of my grandparents experienced poverties when they were young.

_____

2. Too much knowledges can be a dangerous thing. _____

3. My roommate showed more courage than I did by confronting the burglar in the kitchen. _____

4. I will buy furnitures after I move into my new apartment. _____

5. My mails arrived every weekday by 3:00. _____

6. I learned some vocabularies by keeping a list of words and their definitions.

_____

7. My professor lets me use an equipment in the lab. _____

8. You will need more evidence to prove your hypothesis. _____

9. I gained so much informations just by reading the book about economics.

_____

10. Martin Luther King Jr. fought for civil rights and a justice for African Americans.

_____

G. Prepositions

Prepositions always begin a **prepositional phrase**—that is, a phrase that includes a preposition and its object.

To learn more about prepositions, turn to pp. 404–408.

    at her dinner   in her office   on his folder

In English, the most common prepositions are *in*, *on*, and *at*.

Visit **LaunchPad Solo for Readers and Writers** > **Grammar: Resources for Multilingual Writers** > **Prepositions** for more practice with prepositions.

- *In* indicates an enclosed area; a geographical area such as a city, state, or country; or a period of time, such as a month, a year, a season, or part of a day.

in a box	in the car	in the fall
in Egypt	in the classroom	in 2016
in June	in the evening	in winter
in Chicago	in Texas	in the 1990s

He wanted to get the book that was in the math lab.

In Kathmandu, you can buy beautiful wool hats and scarves.

In 2018, I will graduate from college.

I hoped to take a short trip in June.

- *On* indicates the top of something, a street or road, a day of the week, or a specific date.

You'll find the envelope on the table.

I prefer to read articles on the magazine's website.

Harriet lives on Memorial Drive.

Let's go to a movie on Friday night.

I'll start my new job on September 18.

21 G

- *At* indicates a specific address or location or a specific time.

I live at 100 Main Street.

You'll find the snowshoes at the sporting goods store.

I'll meet you at your favorite restaurant.

I'll see you at 7:30 p.m.

At midnight, the townspeople set off fireworks.

ACTIVITY 21 Use *in*, *on*, and *at* in Sentences

Fill in the blanks in each of the following sentences, using *in*, *on*, and *at* correctly.

EXAMPLE I arrived _____*at*_____ the party a few minutes early.

1. Calvin is always ready to leave the house _____ 7:15 a.m.

2. Professor Chen's office is _____ the Physical Sciences building.

3. Please don't leave your shopping bags _____ the floor.

4. There is a telephone _____ the kitchen.

5. We live _____ an apartment but are looking for a house to buy.

6. Elliot is paid _____ the first and fifteenth of the month.

7. Your lunch break is _____ 1:00.

8. The ice cream bars are _____ the freezer _____ the top shelf.

9. Genevieve will leave for Taipei _____ June 5.

10. Like Easter, Passover is celebrated _____ the spring.

ACTIVITY 22 Use *in*, *on*, and *at* in a Paragraph

Fill in the blanks in the following paragraph, using *in*, *on*, and *at* correctly.

EXAMPLE I first met Mireille _____*at*_____ the university.

Last summer, I visited my friend Mireille, who lives _____ Québec City. She and I met _____ Toronto two years ago. I arrived _____ Jean Lesage International Airport _____ June 3 _____ 3:30 _____ the afternoon. That evening, she took me to dinner _____ a bistro _____ the Old City. The moonlight sparkled _____ the surface of the Saint Lawrence River. I stayed with Mireille for five days. While I was there, we made plans to see each other again _____ the fall. We plan to stay _____ a small hotel _____ Victoria.

Besides *in*, *on*, and *at*, the most common prepositions for showing time are *for*, *during*, and *since*.

- *For* usually refers to an exact period of time that something lasts, a period that has a beginning and an end.

  I was in the army for six years.

  It has been snowing for two hours.

  I've been jogging for a month.

- *During* usually refers to an indefinite period of time in which something happens.

  Several times during the hike, I stopped to catch my breath.

  I plan to climb Mount Everest sometime during the summer.

  It hailed during the night.

- *Since* usually refers to a period of time that has passed between an earlier time and the present.

  I've gained weight since the holidays.

  Since last spring, Nicola has been working at the zoo.

  Pete's been so happy since quitting smoking.

ACTIVITY 23 Use *for*, *during*, and *since* in Sentences

Fill in the blanks in each of the following sentences, using either *for*, *during*, or *since* correctly.

EXAMPLE I visited my mother _____*during*_____ spring break.

1. Madeline has been a vegetarian _____ thirteen years.

2. _____ he turned eighteen, Trent has been living on his own.

3. The telephone rang _____ dinner.

4. I haven't seen Benny _____ three weeks.

5. Advertisers make special commercials to show _____ the World Cup.

6. After taking the pills, you should not eat _____ two hours.

7. The air conditioner runs nonstop _____ the hottest weeks of summer.

8. Somebody in the audience started coughing _____ the performance.

9. Caronne has been feeling sick _____ last night.

10. Mr. Jensen will be out of town _____ five days.

21 G

> **ACTIVITY 24** Use *for*, *during*, and *since* in a Paragraph

Fill in the blanks in the following paragraph, using either *for*, *during*, or *since* correctly.

EXAMPLE Karate has been popular in the United States _____*for*_____ many years.

    Anthony has been practicing karate _____ seven years, _____ he was twelve years old. _____ the school year, he trains three days a week, and _____ vacations, he trains nearly every day. He intends to practice this martial art _____ the rest of his life.

    Certain verbs are often followed by prepositions. The preposition is actually part of the verb, creating what is sometimes called a **phrasal verb**. Here are some common verb/preposition combinations:

apply for	eat out	look into	set off
believe in	feel up to	look up	smile at
concentrate on	get around	make up	succeed in
consist of	hand in	pass out	worry about
depend on	insist on	run into	
draw out	kick out	search for	

Junius *smiled at* the cute baby.

Mavis *applied for* a summer job at an insurance company.

At the mall, I *ran into* my best friend from high school.

Some adjectives are also followed by prepositions:

angry at	frightened of	responsible for
anxious about	good at	sad about
capable of	happy about	similar to
curious about	known for	sorry about
dedicated to	late for	tired of
disappointed with	opposed to	typical of
experienced in	proud of	

These adjective + preposition combinations are typically followed by a noun or a **gerund**—a verb that ends in *–ing* and acts as a noun:

Peter was *late for* the exam.

The children were *happy about* going to the park.

We were all *tired of* waiting for the bus to come.

I was *angry at* my new boss when she didn't give me a raise.

21 G

Acknowledgments

INDEX

A QUICK REFERENCE TO EDITING SYMBOLS

adj	adjective error	14D
adv	adverb error	14E
awk	awkward wording	
cap	capital letter needed	20A
coord	correct coordination in sentence	15A
cs	comma splice	16C
dm	dangling modifier	16E
frag	sentence fragment	16A
jar	avoid jargon	
lc	use lowercase letter	20A
mm	misplaced modifier	16D
no cap	no capital	20A
pass	avoid passive voice	16F
prep	preposition error	13A
pr agr	pronoun agreement error	14C
ref	error in pronoun reference	14C
rep	repetitious	17B
r-o	run-on sentence	16B
-s	*s* needed at the end of word	
sp	spelling error	18A
sub	correct subordination in sentence	14B
s-v agr	error in subject-verb agreement	13C
trans	transition needed	p. 164
v or vb	verb error	13B, 21C
vt	shift in verb tense	13B
w	too wordy	17C
ww	wrong word	18C
¶	begin new paragraph	p. 49
?	meaning unclear	
√	good idea or expression	
x	error marked or crossed out	
^	insert	
ℓ	delete	